sixth edition

SOCIAL PSYCHOLOGY

ALFRED R. LINDESMITH

Indiana University at Bloomington

ANSELM L. STRAUSS

University of California at San Francisco

NORMAN K. DENZIN

University of Illinois at Urbana

Prentice Hall, Englewood Cliffs, New Jersey 07632

Library of Congress Cataloging-in-Publication Data

Lindesmith, Alfred Ray.
  Social psychology.

  Bibliography: p.
  Includes index.
  1. Social psychology. I. Strauss, Anselm L.
II. Denzin, Norman K. III. Title.
HM251.L477 1988   302   87-17533
ISBN 0-13-817990-5

Editorial/production supervision and
  interior design: *Marjorie Borden Shustak*
Cover design: *Lundgren Graphics, Ltd.*
Manufacturing buyer: *Ray Keating*
Photo research: *Page Poore*

Chapter opening photo credits:

1: *Rapho/Photo Researchers*
2: *David Hume Kennerly*
3, 13, 14, Epilogue: *Laimute E. Druskis*
4: *Official U.S. Navy Photograph*
5, 6, 7, 9: *Ken Karp*
8: *Charles Gatewood*
10: *U.S. Army Photograph*
11: *Hawaii Visitors Bureau Photo*
12: *Balloon Excellsior, Inc.*
15: *Eugene Gordon*

ISBN 0-13-817990-5   01

Prentice-Hall International (UK) Limited, *London*
Prentice-Hall of Australia Pty. Limited, *Sydney*
Prentice-Hall Canada Inc., *Toronto*
Prentice-Hall Hispanoamericana, S.A., *Mexico*
Prentice-Hall of India Private Limited, *New Delhi*
Prentice-Hall of Japan, Inc., *Tokyo*
Prentice-Hall of Southeast Asia Pte. Ltd., *Singapore*
Editora Prentice-Hall do Brasil, Ltda., *Rio de Janeiro*

Contents

PART II   SOCIAL STRUCTURE AND LANGUAGE

3   Language: Theoretical Perspectives   *50*

4   Language, Groups, and Social Structure   *69*

5   Emotions, the Naming Process, and the Internal Environment   *93*

Preface

The sixth edition of *Social Psychology* reflects an extensive revision and expansion of the previous edition. We have sought to clarify and amplify our symbolic interactionist point of view. We have compared it with more recent developments in semiotics, historical social psychology, ethnomethodology, identity–dramaturgical theories, and recent statements within cognitive psychology concerning artificial intelligence. The rise of sociobiology since the fifth edition has occasioned an extensive discussion of this point of view.

We have restructured this edition in order to make it more accessible to the reader. We have combined all of our previous discussions of language into two chapters. We have deleted outdated materials, and materials on which complex literatures now exist and to which we could not do justice (for example, mental retardation). We have added a new section about emotions, and also offer brief discussions on AIDS, Anorexia Nervosa, Alzheimer's Disease, cocaine use and abuse, alcoholism, and family violence. In discussing the origins of self, we briefly analyze Lac-

an's theories, we also offer extended discussions of gender differentiation and gender belief systems as they pertain to child development. In this context we have a long section on the socializing of emotionality in childhood, which was written by Martha Bauman Power.

We re-introduce a chapter on "Interaction and the Self" which was not in the fifth edition. In this chapter, we discuss the concept of mesostructure and relate it to the literature on collective behavior. In our treatment of illness, aging and death, we discuss dying children, the worlds of chronic illness and pain, life in nursing homes, medical technology, the treatment of chronic illness, and the social shaping of the emotion of grief.

The Epilogue, "Science as Symbolic Activity," presents each of our views of science, grounded theory, and interpretation. It is at the end of the book because the instructor may not want to directly enter this area of discourse. We also include a glossary of terms.

This edition is written in the spirit of C. W.

Mills's "Sociological Imagination." We ask how our social psychological imagination can speak to the current historical moment in which we and our readers find ourselves. The social psychology we present is at once historical, interactionist, and interpretive. As with the last edition, we hope that *Social Psychology* communicates the excitement and understanding that comes from the application of symbolic interactionism to the study of human group life. We have presented what we regard as the basic implications of this, the most sociological of all social psychologies.

At Prentice-Hall, we thank Bill Webber, Kathleen Dorman, and Marjorie Borden Shustak for their interest in this book and the enthusiasm they brought to it. We would also like to thank Margaret Quinn and Sheila Welch for their outstanding typing services, and Richard Louisell for preparing the Bibliography. Finally, this revision could not have been accomplished without the assistance of Martha Bauman Power.

CHAPTER ONE
Social Psychology: A Statement of Position and Method

In our opening chapter we have three major goals in mind. The first is to define the field of social psychology. The second is to make a statement concerning our position as social psychologists; we call our point of view *symbolic interactionism*. Our third aim is to compare this point of view with other theories of social psychology.

A DEFINITION OF THE FIELD

Social psychology studies how humans experience freedom and constraint in their daily lives. Humans create and define social experience, but the situations where experience occurs are often given beforehand by the institutions of society. Social, political, gender, economic, cultural, kinship, legal, and religious institutions structure the social situations which give rise to social experience and human consciousness. Social psychology, then, is the study of the interplay between lives and social structure, or biography and society (see Bertaux, 1981).

Social psychologists address two fundamental questions: How humans are created by social order, and in turn how humans create the social orders that shape and mold their behavior. These two questions produce four basic problems pertaining to (1) stability and change in human interaction; (2) the emergence of new forms and patterns of interaction in everyday life; (3) conformity, conventionality, deviance, and power; and (4) social order, constraint, and personal freedom.

Perhaps an example will serve to make our point. American society is a drug-taking society. Not only do Americans use and abuse prescription drugs at a high rate, but alcohol, cocaine, marijuana, and other "street drugs" are regularly consumed by over one-half of the adult American population. Twenty-two million Americans—one out of every ten—report having used cocaine at least once (Gold, 1984, p. 1). In fact, it has become middle-class America's drug of choice, for everyone from athletes and doctors to rock musicians and railroad employees.

Recently the major league baseball commissioner ruled that all professional baseball players must submit to regular drug tests to determine if they were free of illegal drugs, including cocaine. Drug testing for all federal employees also may be required. If it is, some say it will be an invasion of personal freedom.

As society reaches out through its laws and legal agencies into the workplace and home, it creates social situations that constrain and alter human experience. While on the one hand our society encourages drug-taking, it also argues that taking certain drugs is illegal. We have, with this example, an illustration of the four concerns of the social psychologists. Drug-taking experiences will change as a result of these controversies. New drugs will appear, and perhaps some will replace cocaine and alcohol. Some people will conform to the new laws, should they be written; others will deviate and not conform.

As this occurs, society through its laws will exercise power and constraint over those who deviate. Hence *new* forms of constraint will come into existence as the freedom to take drugs will be challenged, if not taken away.

BASIC SOCIAL PROCESSES

Four fundamental processes structure human experience. The first is material reality itself, including human needs, money, health, housing, work, and labor. The second process involves gender; a system of gender stratification organizes the relation between the sexes in any society. Language is the third process; it defines and mediates human experience. Subjective experience is the fourth major process that orders and gives meaning to human existence.

Language

Ferdinand de Saussure (1959), the Swiss linguist, gave the term *langue* to the system of language that exists for any speech community (i.e., English for Americans). He used the term *parole* to refer to the speaking side of language. Language is "the norm of all other manifestations of speech" (Saussure, 1959, p. 9). Languages are social institutions; they have their own systems of organization and their own history, and they are external to any given speaker. Speech is particular to each user of a language. However, the way any speaker uses a term will not alter its meaning within langue, or the larger language system.

Language refers to (1) a system of signs or words; (2) a set of rules that combines those signs into meaningful utterances (syntax); (3) a system of meanings attached to those words which arises out of use and speech; (4) speech behavior itself; (5) the institution of speaking and thinking for any group, culture, or society; and (6) the culture of a group (see Hymes, 1979).

Language exists over and above speech and can be studied separately from speaking. The science that "studies the life of signs within a society" is called semiology, from the Greek word sēmetô, or sign. Semiotics is a part of the field of social psychology (Saussure, 1959, p. 16, italics in original).

A sign has two parts: the *signifier* and the *signified.* These two terms refer to the *sound-image* that is heard and seen when a word is spoken (i.e., tree) and the *concept* that is seen as lying behind the sound-image. When I say the word "tree" you hear the sound "tree" and can imagine the picture of a tree in your mind. You have a concept that gives meaning to that word. Saussure (1959, pp. 66–67) called the sound-image the signifier and the concept the signified.

Language is a system of interdependent terms in which the value of each term results from the simultaneous presence of the others. Like a sheet of paper, thought is the "front and the sound is the back" (Saussure, 1959, p. 114). We cannot divide thought and sound; they depend on each other. The process of using signs, which are like words but mean more than words, is called *signification.*

Robert Perinbanayagam (1985, p. 9) has given the term "signifying act" to the act of articulating "a symbol by the initiator of a message." Humans communicate and interact through signifying acts, which rest on signs and their meanings.

According to Saussure signs are arbitrary and are understood as social facts which exist within the system of language of any social group. However, groups assign values to their terms; so that a sign not only signifies (points to) something in reality, but it gives a value to what is signified. Saussure (1959, pp. 115–16) offers an example:

Modern French *mouton* can have the same signification as English *sheep* but not the same value, and this for several reasons, particularly because in speaking of a piece of meat to be served on the table, English uses *mutton* and not *sheep*. The difference in value between *sheep* and *mouton* is due to the fact that *sheep* has beside it a second term while the French word does not. (italics in original)

We could offer additional examples. The French word *madame,* which refers to a married woman, can signify in English house-madame, meaning a woman who runs a house of prostitution. The English term carries two meanings. Many observers have noted that the English language is sexist and trivializes women (see Nash, 1985, pp. 234–36 for a review). An adult woman can be called a girl, hussy, spinster, broad, mistress, wife, mother, whore, and so on. As Nash notes, English contains thousands of words and phrases that describe women in sexually derogatory ways, but not nearly so many for men. Signs, then, signify reality and give a value, or meaning, to the unit of reality that is signified.

The language system of a society interacts with and reflects the gender stratification of the society, and this system in turn rests on the economic division of labor that exists in the society. Hence language, gender, and labor, together with subjective experience, constitute four fundamental processes which order social experience.

THE SOCIAL PSYCHOLOGICAL IMAGINATION

C. Wright Mills (1959) coined the term "sociological imagination" to refer to a form of sociological thought which attempts to speak to the promise of the social sciences. Borrowing Mills' term, we can call the "social psychological imagination" that perspective which attempts to grasp the larger historical context which shapes lived experiences. This view tries to come to terms with the personal and public problems of any given generation. It studies inner and outer lives, locating each person as a *universal singular* (Sartre, 1981) in their historical time. Each person's life is seen as having universal themes which are articulated in his or her experiences with self and others. Social psychology examines the dominant themes of each historical epoch. One social psychologist (Strauss et al., 1985) has studied medical technology and the influence of current medical practices on the experiences of the chronically ill. Lindesmith (1968) has studied the process of drug addiction. Denzin has recently completed a study of the American alcoholic (Denzin, 1986a, 1986b, 1986c). These kinds of investigations attempt to take common human experiences and reveal how they are given meaning by interacting individuals. They locate these experiences within their historical moment.

The person with social psychological imagination makes an effort to understand how the broader historical scene creates false consciousness, indifference, and insecurity for particular groups of individuals. This imagination promotes self-reflectiveness. It calls for a critical attitude toward history and

the world situation that enters one's life on a daily basis through the mass media. This perspective assumes that humans can influence how their histories are made. The social psychological imagination also attempts to identify the dominant themes and problems of any given generation; it then examines those problems as they enter into people's lives. If the 1960s focused on civil rights and the Viet Nam War, the 1970s focused on women's rights, the Equal Rights Amendment, and the like. The 1980s have taken on the threat of nuclear war, personal freedoms, health and medical care, worldwide terrorism, protection of the natural environment, family violence and child abuse, and alcohol and drug abuse as central problems. We will address these issues throughout this book, and in so doing will attempt to promote a sense of the social psychological imagination in you, the reader.

SYMBOLIC INTERACTIONISM

The term *symbolic interaction* refers to a sociological and social psychological approach to the study of human group life and human interaction (Blumer, 1969, p. 1).

Within American sociology, the work of Herbert Blumer (1969) has been most commonly associated with this perspective. The work of symbolic interactionists is routinely published in *Symbolic Interaction,* the official Journal of the Society for the Study of Symbolic Interaction, and in *Symbolic Interaction: A Research Annual.*

In 1937 Blumer coined the term *symbolic interactionism.* Philosophically, symbolic interactionism is most closely aligned with American Pragmatism (William James, Charles Sanders Peirce, George Herbert Mead, John Dewey), German Idealism (Hegel, Kant), and German and French Phenomenology (Husserl, Heidegger, Scheler, Schutz, Merleau-Ponty, H. Bergson, Sartre). The perspective has a certain compatibility with various forms of Marxist thought, psychoanalytic theory, phenomenological sociology, semiotics, ethnomethodology, and humanistic and existential psychology and philosophy (Rock, 1979). It is opposed to various "external" models of human experience, including behaviorism and functionalism.

Basic Assumptions

Symbolic interactionism rests on three basic assumptions. First, humans act toward things "on the basis of the meanings that things have for them" (Blumer, 1969, p. 2). Things are termed social objects and they may be as concrete as typewriters and pens, or as abstract as religious and philosophical systems of thought. Second, the meanings of social objects arise out of social interaction; meanings are not in objects. Third, meanings are "handled in, and modified through an interpretive process" (Blumer, 1969, p. 2). That is, people interact with and interpret the objects they act toward. As a consequence, the meanings of objects change in and through the course of action; meanings are not fixed.

For example, an American might well be attracted to a meal which features roast leg of lamb with young potatoes and garden salad. Few Americans would be attracted to "roast leg of sheep." The meaning of the term and the object lies in the interpretive process and in the meanings brought to the object and the word. To take another example, one which reveals how meanings change, the word-phrase PC (personal computer) would have little meaning to a person who knew nothing about computers and word processing. Ten years ago personal computers existed for only a few individuals; today they are commonplace. Computers have become personal possessions, and their meanings have drastically changed as a result.

The central object with whom one must deal with is oneself. Persons are both objects and subjects to themselves. The division between subjective and objective worlds of experience is removed in symbolic interactionist thought. The world is in the person, just as the person is in the world. The two are connected through the "circuit of selfness" (Sartre, 1956, pp. 155–58) wherein the person, the world, the situation, and self-consciousness interact, interpenetrate, and plunge through one another in a synthesis of being, action, meaning, and consciousness.

Language, as we have indicated, is the means for interaction and the medium through which it occurs. The term *symbolic*, in the phrase "symbolic interaction," refers to the underlying linguistic foundations of human life, just as the word *interaction* refers to the fact that people do not act toward one another, but *interact* with each other. Language, as a system of signs, symbols, oppositions, and meanings, permits people to enter into their own and others' activities and to make those activities objects of meaning and action. Through language, people enter into one another's ongoing lines of conduct. The study of language lies at the core of social psychology, and symbolic interactionism makes language a fundamental point of departure in the study of human interaction (Saussure, 1959).

By *interaction,* symbolic interactionists commit themselves to the study and analysis of the developmental course of action that occurs when two or more persons join their individual lines of action together into joint action, or into interactional sequences. Goffman's studies of encounters (1961), frame analysis (1974), and forms of talk (1981) at times emphasize this interactive feature of human conduct.

Studies of face-to-face interaction reveal its negotiated, situated, temporal, biographical, emergent, constructed, and taken-for-granted properties (Garfinkel, 1967; Strauss, 1978). The central object to be negotiated in interaction is identity (Stone, 1962; Strauss, 1969). The meanings of identity, one's own and that of others, lie not in people, but in the interaction itself. Hence the study of symbolic interaction requires constant attention to the study of a process—the process of interaction. This emphasis on process sets symbolic interaction apart from other points of view that stress the fixed, static, structural, and attribute-like properties of persons and their actions (Strauss, 1977, pp. 282–84).

The methodology of symbolic interactionism is naturalistic, descriptive, and interpretive (Denzin, 1988). The interactionist seeks to study symbolic interaction in the natural settings of the everyday world. Experimental methods and the use of social survey techniques are seldom endorsed by symbolic interactionists. The languages, meanings, actions, and voices of ordinary people—the verbs and nouns of the worlds they are experiencing—are captured in interactionist works. The prose of the world becomes the textual subject matter of interactionist work (Merleau-Ponty, 1973). Preferred methods include participant observation, life stories, unobtrusive methods, ethnographies, and thickly contextualized interaction episodes or behavior specimens; although any method which yields understanding is to be applauded. Thick description is a goal (Geertz, 1973). Interactionist interpretations seek to illuminate the phenomenon under investigation and to embed description in relational, interactional, historical, and temporal materials (Sartre, 1956). Causal explanations are set aside in favor of processual interpretations (Lindesmith, 1968).

Applications

Symbolic interactionists have contributed understanding to such diverse fields as social deviance and mental illness (Becker, 1973; Goffman, 1961), drug addiction (Lindesmith, 1968), collective behavior (Blumer, 1978), childhood socialization (Denzin, 1977), death and dying (Glaser & Strauss, 1965), aging (Unruh, 1980), illness and pain (Charmaz, 1980), and the sociology of art (Becker, 1982).

Symbolic interactionism is a perspective that demands that the study of human group life be grounded in the everyday natural world of interacting individuals.

Assertions

To establish the framework of symbolic interactionism, we can enumerate a number of key assertions that are central to this perspective. They may be stated as follows:

1. Biological variables do not determine behavior; they only influence it.
2. Interactional experience is based on self-indications and reasons for acting, called motives, which persons learn from others.
3. Motives explain past behavior and are used to predict future behavior.
4. Humans live in symbolic environments which are mediated by language and culture.
5. Self-reflectiveness is basic to human experience; it is learned through the socialization process and is influenced by gender and language.
6. Interaction involves the ability to take the attitude of others and to know how to define situations.
7. Interactional rituals contribute to the maintenance of the interactional order; rituals are ways of acting which confer status on self and others, and rules of etiquette are interactional rituals.
8. Everyday life is situated; it occurs in social situations.
9. Social situations are created through interaction.
10. Power and force are basic features of everyday life. Power is relational—it exists in social relationships and in social interaction. "Power is force or interpersonal dominance actualized in human relationships through the manipulation, control, and often destruction (both physical and mental) of one human by another human" (Denzin, 1983, p. 40).
11. Human experience is dialectical; that is, it rests on a logic that is conflictual, interactional, and emergent.
12. The self, defined as all that persons call their own at a particular moment, stands at the center of human existence. The self is a social

process; it consists of the "self-as-knower" and the "self-as-known" to others (James, 1890). The self rests on self-feelings which involve feelings of moral worth. The self is in the world of social interaction; it is not *in* the person.

13. Emotionality, the process of being emotional, is a central feature of social interaction (Denzin, 1984).

14. Intersubjectivity is basic to shared, human group life; it refers to the shared knowledge that exists between two persons regarding one another's conscious mental states. Intersubjectivity produces an intersection or intertwining of two fields of experience into a single shared experience. *Subjectivity,* in contrast, refers to a subject's knowledge of her own mental state (see Denzin, 1984, p. 283).

15. Time and how it is experienced is an integral part of human experience (Heidegger, 1927/1962).

16. Much of human experience involves careers, or movements through social positions. Careers have two sides, one of which is objective and the other which is subjective. The objective feature of a career refers to one's movement from one position to another; the subjective side of the career references the changes in self, self-feeling, and social relationships which follow objective career movements (Strauss, 1977, pp. 291–92).

These assertions point to the multifaceted features of human social experience of concern to the social psychologist. Thus no social psychologist should ignore the interactive relationship of biology, physiology, genetics, self-indications, motives, language, culture, self-reflectiveness, ritual, social situations, power, self, emotionality, shared experiences, temporality, and objective and subjective moral careers in the study of any interactional problematic. Sartre (1981, pp. 49–50) summarizes our position well:

In each particular case each individual must be seen like a man of *chance* . . . and yet the player acts, he casts his dice in a certain way, he reacts in one fashion or another to the numbers that turn up and afterwards tries to parlay his good or bad

fortune. This is to . . . integrate it (chance) into praxis as its indelible mark. . . . I apprehend myself as a man of chance and at the same time as the son of my works . . . soon the truth of my praxis appears to me in the obscurity of the accidents that make me what I must be to live. . . . We see this in lovers: for them, the object of their love is chance itself; they try to reduce it to their first chance encounter and at the same time claim that this product of an encounter was always theirs.

Sartre goes on to argue that the only way to make sense of a person's life is to reconstruct objectively that person's history; this will also involve understanding his or her family. The social psychologist must work forward through the person's life, finding the conditions and events that set the basic turning points, the contingencies that turned the person one way and not another.

Sartre is saying that every person has a moral career through life. This life is a product of chance from the outset, and is conditioned by one's family. We integrate our pasts into our lives and make who we were into projects to be pursued in the present and in the future. While Sartre brings our analysis down to the level of individual biography and life-history, his general perspective can be applied to the analysis of interactional experiences that pertain to social relationships, groups, and larger social structures.

RELEVANT ISSUES AND CRITICISMS

Some critics of symbolic interactionism think of it as a school of thought propagated by the wholly loyal disciples of its founding fathers (Huber, 1983). We reject this conception for several reasons. In the first place, many of the ideas it emphasizes have become commonplace and are widely accepted among sociologists working in a great many specialty areas. Since it is difficult to study any problem without forming ideas about the nature of humans—even in areas in which the primary focus is on analyzing statistical data—

any attempt to probe below the surface, to explain the interconnections of statistical variables, commonly leads investigators to adopt—at least in some partial or implicit and often unformulated sense—assumptions and theories about what humans are like and why they act as they do. These assumptions and theories have, in recent years, increasingly been drawn from the body of ideas and concepts with which we are concerned. In other words, we believe the term "symbolic interactionism" does *not* refer to a somewhat specialized or esoteric "school," but has become an integral part of sociology itself.

We must add, however, that persons who to some degree or another profess general adherence to the interactionist viewpoint, and critics as well, have widely different interpretations both of that position and its implications. Some believe that to say human behavior is decisively influenced by communication, language, and internal symbolic processes commits one to the exploration of "subjective" phenomena which cannot be handled rigorously in accord with the traditional standards of science. Opposing this view are those who reject the subjective-objective dichotomy, insisting that mental processes are, after all, behavior that involves the physical organism and its nervous system as indispensable participating elements, as does all other behavior. They argue that this behavior should not be dismissed from scientific study just because current methods and theories are inadequate to handle it; rather, one should directly confront the human organism's active organization of its own behavior, and develop better ways of coping with this phenomenon.

Some interpret the symbolic interactionist perspective as requiring the use of "soft" qualitative, as opposed to "hard" quantitative statistical data, but many interactionists are quite committed to the statistical method. This issue has been exacerbated in the controversy over whether interactionists take a determinate or indeterminate view of human interaction. Some, however, contend

that human activity is inherently emergent and indeterminate, hence not entirely open to fixed, quantitative-statistical modes of inquiry.

Also, we should note that symbolic interactionism is not the only "sociological social psychology" possible, and that interactionists by no means agree either on the priority of theoretical issues or even on all their sustaining assumptions. Some believe the general position is broad enough to include "exchange theory" (McCall & Simmons, 1981; Singelmann, 1972) or to permit genuine rapprochement with certain types of psychiatric theory (Sullivan, 1953). Others are critical or skeptical of those possibilities, yet believe the general position should be open to the findings and suggestions of compatible positions.

Some critics argue that symbolic interactionists contribute little or nothing to the understanding of organizations or of society as a whole. Often this criticism is couched in terms of a micro-macro (small-scale, large-scale) emphasis, but it fails to take account of the interactionists' assertion that organizations and societies are made up of the interactions of their respective members. This criticism continues in the form of an attack on the interactionists' supposed inability to handle larger interactive units, as well as the power arrangements that link those units to one another. Also, the critique leads to a view that institutional, group, and governmental affairs can be studied "on their own level," without reference to the individual participants and their interactions (but see Maines, 1977, 1979, 1982; Hall, 1986).

Another contention is that interactionists are compelled by their very methods of investigation (participant observation, especially) to become champions of outcasts, underdogs, and little people in general. This view is contradicted by the opposite contention that all social scientists who enjoy comfortable and easy living in our capitalistic system are thereby committed to the establishment view, and hence are really on the side of the "fat cats" (Gouldner, 1970). In our opinion, there is nothing intrinsic to the interactionist perspective that makes it politically conservative or liberal. However, symbolic interactionism is a radical approach since it requires firsthand knowledge about the empirical world before the researcher can begin formulating theories about that world. Few other approaches to human behavior put as much stress on this point. We are troubled by those who formulate grandiose theories about human behavior on the basis of intimate knowledge of the workings of computers or of the laboratory behavior of rats, pigeons, and monkeys, or by those who seek to generalize about the behavior of human beings whom they have never bothered to meet or observe.

The issue of politics and the political persuasions of symbolic interactionists leads directly into the question of relevancy: Does their perspective have anything to contribute to understanding the problems of human societies? Can it offer scientifically grounded suggestions concerning the control and amelioration of such diverse social problems as drug addiction, alcoholism, crime, marital discord, rioting and looting, corruption, and the political abuse of power and authority? Or does the interactionist perspective lead to yet another sterile academic enterprise? To those who claim its irrelevancy, we would say that it is hard to conceive of any situation involving policy issues that could not be better handled with greater firsthand knowledge of the materials with which one is dealing.

Certain observers have suggested a reconciliation between various versions of Marxist social theory and symbolic interactionism. Both traditions are interactional, historical, and concerned with language and culture. Ropers (1973, p. 44) has argued:

Marx and Mead . . . while focusing upon opposite ends of abstraction were in agreement as to the essential unity and prospective harmony between the individual and society . . . Marx the social structuralist and Mead the social psychologist can indeed "shake hands" in sociology. Both believe in

man as maker of society and history and share the conviction that free men in life-nourishing groups can build progressively more human and more just social institutions.

Mayrl (1973, pp. 44–45) has proposed:

On the one hand, if the social psychology of G. H. Mead is found compatible with the dominant assumptions of Marxism, and subsequently could lead to a development of Marxist social psychology, then a further reshifting of "Western" sociological assumptions may be precipitated. On the other hand, an incorporation of Mead's thought into a Marxist social psychology would lead to a sharpening and sophistication of the Marxist paradigm.

More recently, Stuart Hall (1981, p. 49), a leader of the British School of Cultural Studies, has noted that the interactionist emphasis on field methods, ethnographic study, qualitative analysis, and interpretation were important influences on the studies he and his co-workers conducted on the British working class and youth culture.

OTHER SOCIAL PSYCHOLOGIES

A number of recent observers (see Saxton & Hall, 1987) have argued that there are at least two and perhaps three types of social psychology. These have been called sociological social psychology, psychological social psychology, and psychological sociology (see Stryker, 1977; House, 1977). This classification of the field is obviously based on the discipline (sociology or psychology) in which the researcher is trained. Many scholars have attempted to integrate these versions of social psychology. Stryker (1977, p. 157) for example, suggests a merger of symbolic interactionism and attribution theory which is a psychological theory of social process. House (1977) believes that the three faces of social psychology should be merged through a confrontation with concrete research problems. Liska (1977) has suggested that sociological social psychology is in danger of losing its identity to psychology. Gergen (1973) and Gergen and Gergen (1984) argue for a fundamental reorientation of the field; they call for an interpretive, historical social psychology. Unfortunately their work reveals only a passing awareness of the symbolic interactionist and interpretive traditions. It remains for Gergen to integrate his proposals concerning a historical social psychology into the mainstream of interactionist thought.

It is our position that a truly sociological social psychology is one which builds on the following basic propositions concerning human behavior:

1. There is a psychic unity to human experience; that is, human behavior involves minded, symbolic, self-reflective conduct.
2. There is an extreme cultural variability to human experience.
3. Human experience is based on the creative ability of individuals to continually change and modify their behaviors to fit new historical circumstances.
4. Human beings are able to "feed back complex correctives" to their behavior, without engaging in trial and error, or conditioning, or new learning (Kuhn, 1964b, p. 82).
5. The ability of humans to produce and use symbols sets them apart from non-symbol–using organisms. Hence findings from the study of lower animals will have only limited usefulness for the field of social psychology.
6. Human experience is relational and influenced by the presence of other individuals.
7. Social psychology must be built up through the careful study of human experience. The methods of special psychology must be fitted to the lived experiences of human beings. Social psychology must be an interactional, interpretive field of study.

These seven propositions reflect our position on how the several social psychologies, or the several faces of social psychology may be integrated. *To the degree that a particular social psychological theory or method conforms with, or is compatible with these seven propositions, it contributes to the growth and development of the discipline called social psychology.*

With these considerations and reservations in mind, we must discuss "images of the social," and problematics within these images as they exist in contemporary social psychological theories. Once we discuss these images and problems, we will turn to a brief discussion of specific social psychological theories.

Images of the Social

On the one hand, there is what may be termed the *exterior model of humans and social order*. Here the scholar stresses the play of variables like role, status, norm, culture, social class, and value upon the human organism. Human society is lodged outside the individual and is seen as shaping his or her behavior in predictable ways. Various perspectives (social systems analysis, role theory, structural functional theories, and the cultural personality approach) emphasize one or another exterior structural variable in an attempt to explain the patterned regularities that are observable in all societies and social groups. The exterior approach says little about how individuals organize their behavior and seldom gives attention to the interaction process. In this sense, the individual is often viewed as a passive vessel through which flow the directives or commands of norms, values, roles, and statuses.

A second approach, which we term the *interior model of humans*, assumes that the organism enters the world with a set of built-in needs, drives, and psychic or physiological demands which call out fixed responses. Whether these are viewed as primary drives (the so-called thirst, food, shelter, and sexual drives) or as secondary drives (the need for a particular mate or lover, or for "psychic balance"), the interior model ultimately becomes tautological. The drive's existence is inferred from the behavior it allegedly produces, and this behavior is then explained by reference to the drive. (Other types of theory that provide interior models of man are those of stimulus-response or reinforcement, dissonance or balance, field or gestalt, exchange theory, and various versions of

Freudian theory.) An interactionist view stresses neither the interior nor the exterior influences to the exclusion of the other, but considers both as parts of a single dynamic process.

BEHAVIORISM AND MIND-BODY DUALISM

We assume that human behavior provides the primary data with which social psychology deals, and that the explanation of any particular form of behavior requires that its relation to other types be traced and demonstrated. Thus a given behavior is explained in terms of its interrelationships with other behaviors and not in terms of forces, drives, or anything else which lies outside the behavioral field or which is inferred from behavior. In accordance with this principle we reject the idea that behavior is "caused" by psychological states, desires, motives, states of consciousness, or unconscious motives when these are taken to refer to forces which "make" things happen. Such terms are only ways of naming various kinds of activity, and have no special explanatory value. We believe that it is entirely fallacious to explain the existence of science in terms of a "rational faculty" or innate "reason." It is much more plausible to look at reason not as a force of faculty, but as a complex and highly evolved form of symbolic activity that has emerged gradually as an historical product from other, simpler types of behavior. Similarly, "conscience" should not be thought of as a psychic force mysteriously implanted in humans, but as a special form of regulatory behavior by means of which other activities are inhibited or facilitated.

"Behaviorist" psychologists have emphasized ideas similar to those just stated, and on the basis of them have either rejected or redefined many of the old terms of the "psychology of consciousness." Practically all the lay terms used to refer to "mental" phenomena such as mind, idea, insight, imagination, reason, consciousness, and understanding have been conceived as activities rather than as entities or faculties, or have been dropped entirely as useful concepts. By this we mean that the words listed are, in effect, treated as verbs rather than nouns; and the behavior is usually described as precisely and unambiguously as possible. Behaviorists have tended to define these mentalistic terms by means of behavior that can be elicited from lower animals in the experimental setting and have rejected them entirely when this cannot be done (Zuriff, 1985).

We share some of the same assumptions but reach different conclusions. Behaviorists have unduly restricted their perspective by not taking a sufficiently broad view of behavior. They have paid too much attention to gross bodily movement and to lower animals, and have thus ignored language behavior or treated it as a minor matter. Such mentalistic terms as consciousness, conception, and reason need to be related to language behavior and conceived of as forms or aspects of symbolic behavior.

This implies that in order to understand how and why people do what they do, we must know how they think. The chief source of information about how people think is what they say. These conclusions, however, are not of the type which behaviorist psychologists endorse. In addition to the usual tendency to ignore language, they also avoid dealing with behavior that cannot be directly observed. Internal symbolic processes admittedly are not accessible to direct observation and for this reason among others, the behaviorists neglected them. Evidence of mental activity in human beings is usually secured through introspection or from verbal testimony (and the lower animals most often utilized in experimental work do not give verbal reports or engage in introspection!). Moreover, evidence so obtained is difficult to interpret. Nevertheless, if we agree that human thought is a vital feature of human behavior, no evidence concerning it should be passed over (see Ericsson & Simon, 1984).

The behaviorists have been reacting against a tradition going back to the ancient Greeks, which have been termed "mind-body dualism." Body and mind are viewed as separate and radically different kinds of reality. The body is physically real and tangible, while the mind is intangible, nonmaterial, and separate from the body. Once this separation is made, two separate vocabularies evolve to deal with each realm, and nonsensical questions (like "Which is more important, the mind or the body?" or "How can the mind influence the body?") arise. Our view of this position is also strongly negative: Mental activity is simply that activity of the human organism in which the central nervous system plays a central role. On this problem we agree with the French phenomenologist Merleau-Ponty (1963). The structure of human behavior is such that mind and body are intertwined processes whose meaning is given in the perceptual field that connects the individual to the direct world of lived experience.

Reductionism and Atomism

Sometimes the behaviorist becomes a biological determinist by seeking explanations of behavior in the biological mechanisms involved. A common expression of this tendency is to refer to the nervous system or to neural mechanisms to explain certain acts or kinds of behavior. The layperson may say that his "nerves are on edge" or "frayed." Neurologists and physiologists sometimes account for observed behavior by reference to some supposed neural or physiological process. Explanations of this type are called "reductionist" because they tend to reduce behavioral problems to the biological level.

The term "atomism," which is closely related to that of "reductionism," refers to the attempt to discover what things are like by taking them apart. The assumption is that "the whole is equal to the sum of its parts." The Greeks proposed the idea that all matter consists of tiny indivisible particles. The history of physicists' attempts to unravel the nature of matter is the prime example of the fruitfulness of this conception. The search for those ultimate "atoms" or building blocks of the universe has not turned out as anticipated, but it has given us modern nuclear physics.

The sociologist ordinarily opposes both the reductionist and atomist positions. She opposes the reductionist's contention that human behavior can be understood and explained in terms of physiological, neurological, anatomic, chemical, or physical concepts, and assumes instead that at each level of scientific concern, phenomena are and must be explained by reference to other phenomena at the same level. Chemical phenomena are explainable by reference to other chemical phenomena, and so on. Social behavior similarly must be analyzed and explained on its own level.

Sociologists ordinarily also reject the atomist approach. A whole, they argue, is definitely more than the sum of its parts. For example, a group may act as a unit and this involves, besides a number of individuals, a structured system of relationships among members and with other groups. Thus a nation continues to exist although all of its specific members ultimately will die. Conversely, a group may vanish or die without any of its members doing so.

This is not to say that the social scientist ignores the physical, biochemical, physiological, and neurological processes involved in all behavior. Consideration of such influences, although it cannot *account* for behavior, does contribute to understanding the physical and biological substrate that make behavior possible.

INTERPRETIVE VERSUS COGNITIVE SOCIAL PSYCHOLOGIES

While accepting the concept of a division of the field of social psychology into psychological and sociological camps, we feel that a further differentiation is required. Two broad categories organize social psychological theories of human experience. The first, termed *interpretive*, is closely aligned with our point of view. The second, *cognitive*, applies to the majority of the theories now holding sway in the field.

We must briefly discuss these two categories. An interpretive social psychology has the following characteristics: First, it stresses the interactional, historical, emotional, and interpretive dimensions of human experience. Second, it tends not to rely on experimental, statistical, quasi-experimental, or survey research methodologies. Third, its goal is the interpretation and understanding of human behavior, not its prediction or control. Fourth, interpretive social psychology tends to be humanistic, existential, and historical; it is always concerned with personal experiences. Fifth, the seven basic propositions concerning human behavior (outlined on p. 10) reflect the core assumptions of the interpretive perspective. Similarly, the 16 key assertions central to the interactionist point of view (discussed on pp. 6–7) describe the broader contours of the interpretive approach (see Douglas & Johnson, 1977; Douglas, et al., 1980; Kotarba, 1984).

Examples of interpretive social psychologies include Gergen's historical social psychology, Ron Harré's ethogeny (1982), Giddens' action theory (1984), hermeneutics, Douglas' sociology of everyday life, Lyman and Scott's (1970) sociology of the absurd, Garfinkel's ethnomethodology, the New Iowa School of Social Psychology (Couch, Saxton, & Katovich, 1986), our version of symbolic interactionism, and various variants of psychoanalysis, feminist, and Marxist thought. In the following pages we will discuss only historical social psychology and ethnomethodology. However, the reader is encouraged to explore the works of other interpretive social psychologists (see Secord, 1982).

Cognitive social psychologies have the following characteristics: First, we call them cognitive because they place special emphasis on the human being as a rational, thinking, planning organism. These theories often emphasize social exchange and economic factors in the study of human behavior. Second, these theories are the natural offspring of behaviorism in psychology. Third, they display a deep commitment to objective experimentation, quasi-experiments, and the social survey method. They often rest on the statistical analysis of data. Fourth, they are

often mechanistic and their "ideal" is to be scientific (Haugeland, 1985, p. 252). Fifth, they often emphasize external social factors which shape and mold human behavior (for example, roles and statuses); we call this variant structural, cognitive social psychology. Sixth, another version of this approach is seen in those theories which stress inner needs, drives, and cognitive states. These are also structural, cognitive approaches; they differ only in their emphasis on inner structural states. Seventh, these theories seldom develop the symbolic, emotional side of human experience.

Among the theories we include under the cognitive grouping are: exchange theory, dissonance theory, person perception theory expectancy-value theory, social reinforcement and learning theories, theories of artificial intelligence, role-identity theory, and certain dramaturgical theories. We will explore only exchange theory, attribution theory, situated identity theory, role-identity theory, dramaturgy, expectation states theory, and theories of artificial intelligence.

Obviously our preference is for interpretive social psychologies. We do not wish to dismiss the cognitive approaches, however, because they do point to sides of human experience that are not grasped or discussed by the interpretive approaches. A well-rounded social psychologist would have a knowledge of all these strains and versions of social psychological theory.

INTERPRETIVE SOCIAL PSYCHOLOGIES

Historical Social Psychology

Kenneth Gergen (1973, 1982) and Gergen and Gergen (1984) are closely identified with historical social psychology. Their view assumes that the field of social psychology is historical because it deals with facts that are largely nonrepeatable and which fluctuate over time. Knowledge cannot transcend historical boundaries, nor can it be based on purely objective methods. Building on the position that the social sciences differ from the natural sciences, Gergen calls for a dismantling of the unified science thesis (i.e., a single method unifies all the sciences). He wants social psychology to be based on methods and theories that derive from human experience. His view calls into question theories based on the mind-body dualism, atomism, reductionist, and exterior models of human experience discussed earlier. Gergen views knowledge as being socially constructed and historically embedded. Human action, he argues, is based on voluntaristic principles. He feels that research should illustrate and bring theory alive, rather than merely verify or test propositions.

Gergen and Gergen (1984, p. 174) make a series of proposals concerning the study of how humans give meaning to their experiences. They suggest that biographical narrative accounts, including life stories, and popular cultural texts (i.e., fiction) create for persons and social groups a coherence about social life that is connected, temporal, personal, and collective. These narratives may be tragic, romantic, or comic.

Historical social psychology is not new to the sociological tradition. *The Polish Peasant,* written by Thomas and Znaniecki in the early 1920s was historical, comparative, and interpretive. That Gergen would call for such a theory in the 1980s suggests that the field is returning to its roots (see Saxton & Hall, 1987). In 1959, Strauss (1959) called for a historical, biographical, interactionist social psychology. In many respects the Gergens' work continues this line of thought.

We must note, however, that a fully historical social psychology is one that could be grounded in any historical moment, not just the present. Like the new history associated with such scholars as Michel de Certeau (1984), historical social psychology would address the manner of women, men, and children produced, for example, in the Middle Ages, the Renaissance, the Industrial Revolution, colonial America, the post-bellum South, and so on. It would be politically historical, examining the power structures and

modes of economic organization that have existed in any given historical period. It would be subjective, written from the point of view of those who lived during the period being studied. It would rely upon letters, autobiographies, diaries, novels, and the cultural myths of the time. It would connect lived history to the human group and to the human family and it would do so from the standpoint of a political economy of interaction (see Foucault, 1980; Lefebvre, 1971; Sartre, 1960/1976; Mills, 1959).

Ethnomethodology

We should note that current formulations derived from the phenomenological perspectives of Husserl, Schutz, and Gurwitsch have been incorporated into the works of such scholars as Berger and Luckmann (1967) and into that loosely formulated school of thought known as *ethnomethodology* (Garfinkel, 1967; Heap & Roth, 1973; Sudnow, 1972, 1978, 1979; Cicourel, 1974; Garfinkel, Lynch, & Livingston, 1981; Garfinkel & Sacks, 1970; Heritage, 1984).

Central to this line of thought are the following assumptions: First, human behavior is to be approached subjectively from the standpoint of the phenomenological reality of individual actors. Second, there are as many phenomenological realities, or social worlds of experience, as there are individuals producing such worlds. Third, social action and social order are seen as problematic, yet taken-for-granted, productions. Society does not just exist; it has to be produced by interacting individuals. Fourth, in the course of interacting with themselves and others, individuals suspend many commonsense assumptions and act "as if" they understand one another, when in fact they may be talking past each other. Fifth, these taken-for-granted assumptions embody the very essence of social interaction and social order. The ethnomethodologist's task is to uncover these assumptions and show how they are routinely acted on or deliberately suspended.

While it is beyond the scope of this chapter to fully detail this approach, we note that recent work in psycholinguistics and sociolinguistics reflects the commitment to studying human behavior from the standpoint of native actors. Theorists such as Cicourel (1974) are trying to discover and chart the deep and superficial structural rules that native actors consciously and unconsciously employ in the organization of their behavior. Others (Sudnow, 1972) carefully study everyday conversations for what they reveal about the underlying dynamics of broader social structures.

A central figure in this line of thought has been Harold Garfinkel. The word *ethnomethodology* is used to describe what the practitioners of this approach see as the unique features of their perspective. *Ethno*, borrowed from Greek, means race, culture, or people. For Garfinkel and his associates, ethnomethodology refers to the practices of an observer who attempts to discover the methods that people use when they formulate definitions of a situation. An ethnomethodological investigation involves at least three steps. First, the observers suspend the assumption that social situations are governed by sets of rules; that is, they withhold judgment on the functions that roles, norms, rules, or culture may have in any particular setting. Second, they observe how laypersons and sociologists alike describe and explain what it is that they do. The third step requires treating these explanations as appearances produced so as to project the image that rules have been followed. The ethnomethodologist assumes that individuals explain their behavior in ways that fit everyday conceptions of what that behavior was all about. Zimmerman and Wieder (1970, p. 289) say that the ethnomethodologist is "concerned with how members of society go about the task of *seeing, describing, and explaining* order in the world in which they live" (italics in original).

The aim of such investigations is to discover the formal properties of everyday, commonplace actions; the method demands that the researcher look at behavior from "within" actual situations. Garfinkel, in an article entitled "What is Ethnomethodology?" developed this view of research activity (1967, p. 3):

Whenever a member is required to demonstrate that an account analyzes an actual situation, he invariably makes use of such practices of "et cetera," "unless," and "let it pass" to demonstrate the rationality of his achievement.... Much therefore of what is actually reported is not mentioned.... In short, recognizable sense, or fact, or methodic character, or impersonality, or objectivity of accounts are not independent of the socially organized occasions of their use.

For Garfinkel and other ethnomethodologists, all social interaction—whether it be husbands talking with their wives, students making purchases in stores, or interviewers talking with mothers about their birth control practices—involves individuals producing, describing, and explaining each other's accounts of their actions.

In one study Garfinkel instructed students to engage a friend in conversation and then press the person to clarify his or her remarks. Garfinkel presents the following case (1967, p. 43):

On Friday my husband remarked that he was tired. I asked, "How are you tired? Physically, mentally, or just bored?"

(S) I don't know, I guess physically, mainly.

(E) You mean that your muscles ache or your bones?

(S) I guess so. Don't be so technical.

(*after more watching*)

(S) All of these old movies have the same kind of old iron bedstead in them.

(E) What do you mean? Do you mean all old movies or some of them, or just the ones you have seen?

(S) What's the matter with you? You know what I mean.

(E) I wish you would be more specific.

(S) You know what I mean! Drop dead!

Garfinkel argues that people refuse to let one another understand what they are really talking about. They anticipate that others will understand them, and for this reason everyday conversations have a vague, ambiguous tone. They rest on a body of background assumptions taken for granted by the participants. Thus the husband in the above example assumed that his wife *knew* what he meant when he said he was tired.

Evaluation of Ethnomethodology

Ethnomethodologists claim to be concerned with the study of a phenomenon that has received little attention within the intellectual confines of traditional sociological perspectives. Their interest in "the elucidation of how accounts or descriptions of an event . . . are produced in interaction in such a way that they achieve some situated methodological status" (Zimmerman, 1976, p. 10) is taken to be a radical departure from traditional sociology. Furthermore,

Ethnomethodologists claim that the objective and constraining social structures of the world are constituted by "social structuring activities" (variously called "practices," "methods," "procedures," "reality work"). Ethnomethodology says that sociology ignores these structuring activities when they measure the degree of association between variables. One way of reading ethnomethodology is to see it countering this omission: ethnomethodologists study the social structuring activities that assemble social structures (Mehan & Wood, 1976, p. 14).

These structuring activities are not reduced to the psychological realities of solitary individuals. In fact, ethnomethodologists show no interest in probing the subjective individual or social experiences of the person. Following Garfinkel's lead, they study social phenomena that are "available in embodied, sensuous, human activity, in talk and actions. Though we may disagree on other matters, that principle binds ethnomethodologists" (Mehan & Wood, 1976, p. 15). Garfinkel states the principle as follows:

. . . there is no reason to look under the skull, since there is nothing of interest to be found there but the brains. The "skin" of the person will be left intact. Instead, questions will be confined to the operations that can be performed upon events that are "scenic" to the person (Mehan & Wood, 1976, p. 17).

Ethnomethodologists have been criticized on a number of issues. Some critics claim that ethnomethodologists produce research that is trivial and trite (Coser, 1975). Others argue that its focus on the mundane, taken-for-granted features of everyday life produces an ahistorical and amoral vision of human group life (Gouldner, 1970). In their concern for the systematic study of everyday life, ethnomethodologists have neglected to isolate, through a conceptual framework, the recurring features of interaction that any sociologist could examine and study. They have refused to define what they mean by everyday life; nor have they specified those properties of everyday life that are taken for granted. A symbolic interactionist would study selves, situations, social objects, social relationships, and rules of conduct as these processes are fitted together during the course of any interaction sequence. Ethnomethodologists have gone only as far as to state that their study would focus on talk, activity, and events that are "scenic" to the person. What are those events? What does "scenic" mean? How is to talk to be studied?

A general reluctance to probe the subjective, and at times private, side of social experience severely limits the ethnomethodologist's field of study and excludes from analysis an aspect of the social act that G. H. Mead and many symbolic interactionists have taken to be critical in their research.

Ethnomethodology is termed a radical perspective (not in the political sense) because it directs sociological attention to a neglected area—the everyday, commonsensical actions and interactions of laypersons and scientists as they produce the appearances of an existing social order. In this way, the ethnomethodological movement has produced a fresh, healthy, questioning outlook concerning many taken-for-granted views of social behavior and the proper methods for studying it.

However, it has also produced a considerable amount of philosophical fog (but see Hardin, Power, & Sugrue, 1986). To a substantial degree it appears to be an understandable revolt against current statistical methods and common assumptions concerning the nature of a science of human behavior, and, indeed, whether such a science is possible or desirable. Adherents of this school often give widely different interpretations of it. Many outsiders complain that they become more confused the longer they try to understand it. In time, perhaps, the issues raised may become clearer as ethnomethodologists make and publish more empirical studies that illustrate or demonstrate what their basic assumptions mean when translated into research actions. In this form the movement is likely to become more communicable than the philosophical position itself seems to be.

We are inclined to agree with the ethnomethodologists in their revolt against conceptions of scientific method of much of the sociological establishment and against the late, overwhelming dominance of what has been called the "Statistical Mafia" or the "IBM Lobby."

On the other hand, we are puzzled by assertions such as Speier's (1970, p. 190) that the major contribution of so-called ethnomethodologists to the history of modern sociology is in the discovery or emphasis on the "centrality of talk in the everyday organization of human activity." Speier goes on to argue that the sluggishness of sociology in recognizing this fact was, with the exception of Goffman, first noted by Garfinkel in 1967. We suspect, however, that this point was actually noted and recorded at least by the time of the ancient Greeks.

We quarrel with some versions of the ethnomethodological perspective on additional grounds. While the accounts that individuals give for their actions certainly must be taken seriously, these accounts cannot be regarded as the final or ultimate data for any sociological theory. Indeed, individuals seldom fully know why they acted as they did in a particular situation, and groups of individuals who have engaged in the same behaviors will seldom give the same explanation of their behavior. As Mead noted, often it is only after they have acted that humans give plausible retrospective accounts of their behaviors, and even these do not qualify as scientific explanations. To objectively study a social phenomenon requires a commitment to acquire a close, working familiarity of the individuals one is investigating. While we endorse a respectful stance toward the perspectives of those we study, we regard these perspectives as problematic data that require further ordering and analysis.

For ethnomethodologists, revealing how persons construct, or structure, definitions of situations has become an end, in itself. They argue that it is futile to attempt to generalize, and they occupy themselves instead with the classification and description of their subjects' views.

COGNITIVE SOCIAL PSYCHOLOGIES

Exchange Theory

In the last two decades, *exchange theory*—another general position developed especially by sociologists—has gained some adherents. It has even gained the approval of some sociological social psychologists (McCall & Simmons, 1981), who have found it compatible with their own conceptions of social psychology and human behavior. We disagree strongly with this assessment. We shall consider it here in more detail than the other positions just discussed because sociologists are more involved with its development.

As one critic of exchange theory has remarked, "The first difficulty one faces in trying to review exchange theory is that there is relatively little agreement among sociologists either on the definition of exchange theory or on the works which are supposed to be examples of it" (Heath, 1971, p. 91; Cheal, 1984). However, its most cited and influential works are by George Homans (1961), Peter Blau (1964), and Richard Emerson (1976, 1981). Homans, who had earlier rejected functionalism when developing his version of exchange theory, turned to behavioral psychology—mainly drawn from B. F. Skinner—and to elementary economics. He sees both perspectives as envisaging "human behavior as a function of its payoff: in amount and kind it depends on the amount and kind of reward and punishment it fetches" (1961, p. 13). And when what it fetches is the behavior of someone else, then one can refer to this "as an exchange of activity," which occurs between at least two people. It is exchange because rewards and punishments are being meted out.

In approaching the study and explanation of social exchange, Homans relies on general propositions borrowed from conditioning theory and from elementary economics. The following are examples of such propositions (1961, pp. 33–37). *The stimulus proposition:* "If in the past the occurrence of a particular stimulus, or set of stimuli, has been the occasion in which a person's activity has been rewarded, then the more similar the present stimuli are to the past ones, the more likely the person is to perform the activity, or some similar activity, now." *The success proposition:* "The more often a person's activity is rewarded, the more likely he is to perform the activity." *The deprivation-satiation proposition:* "The more often in the recent past a person has received a particular reward, the less valuable any further unit of that reward becomes to him." Homans uses three kinds of propositions to explain the more specific findings of studies of interaction and group behavior—what he calls "elementary social behavior." However, he does not merely apply the propositions drawn from neighboring disciplines, but elaborates them, since he deals with "social" behavior of considerable, although not the highest, complexity.

Blau goes further and turns his attentions to larger social structures and indirect exchanges (1964, p. 2). In a review of this book, Heath (1971) attempts to pull together some of Blau's major propositions, and we shall quote a few to give the flavor of Blau's approach. (Blau, in drawing explicitly on Homans' work, also relies on economics and conditioning psychology.) The examples of propositions are

1. The desire for social rewards leads men to enter into exchange relationships with one another.
2. Reciprocal social exchanges create trust and social bonds among people.
3. Unilateral services create power and status differences.
4. Power differences make organization possible.
5. The fair exercise of power evokes social approval and the unfair exercise of power evokes social disapproval.
6. If subordinates collectively agree that their superior exercises power generously, they will legitimate his power.
7. Legitimate power is required for stable organization.
8. If subordinates collectively experience unfair exercise of power, an opposition movement will develop.

In general, Blau's analysis moves from analyzing simple social relationships in terms of direct exchange processes to showing how complex social structures develop as networks of exchange become increasingly indirect.

Exchange theory, as exemplified by Homans and Blau, has been criticized on various grounds (Davis & Boulding, 1962; Robson, 1968): for example, that Homans' work is limited concerning any analysis of larger social organizations; that the content of both books is speculative; that many if not most of their propositions are untestable; that their approach is too "psychologistic" for the understanding of sociological phenomena. We agree with those criticisms but add, more specifically, the following remarks. The formulations border on tautologies; they are based on generalizations derived from the study of infra-humans and hence do not take into account human symbolic abilities. The reliance on rewards and punishments reflect simply one more variation of need-and-drive reductionistic psychology. The reliance on elementary economics—a presentation that most economists would reject—reflects a focus on aggregate analysis, which will not get us far in understanding either individuals or the complex social processes in which they participate. Aside from its assumption of rewards and punishments, the basic notion of "exchange" is amazingly simplistic, as contrasted with the full range of interactions that take place among humans (see Cheal, 1984). If the concept of exchange is to be greatly extended—to negotiation, coercion, competition, persuasion, and the like—then analysis needs to be done in terms of those and many other emergent kinds of distinctions, rather than foreclosed from the beginning by a preordained type of scheme (Strauss, 1978). In general, the simplistic and foreordained character of exchange theory renders it quite speculative and relatively uninteresting. It certainly cannot handle convincingly most of the phenomena that will be discussed in this text and does not purport to do so. The attempt to join it to a symbolic interactionist approach is fruitless.

We say this because of the deficiencies of exchange theory and because of the genuine incompatibilities between it and the approach developed here. However, not all symbolic interactionists would agree with us. In a recent attempt to assimilate exchange theory with symbolic interactionism, Peter Singelmann (1972) contends that there are "convergences" between the two approaches in four major areas. First, both "assume the operation of constructive mental processes when actors act toward their environment." Second, "exchange theory implies processes akin to G. H. Mead's 'self' and 'generalized other' in the sense that interaction in exchange requires persons imaginatively to assume the roles of others and view themselves in terms of the conceptions of others." Third, "in both perspectives social organi-

zation is viewed as emerging from constructed individual acts 'fitted' to one another." Fourth, in both, "social dynamics is conceived in dialectic terms, arising out of contradictions between micro- and macro-processes and inherent tendencies in social organization toward inconsistency, conflict and change." Singlemann is quite right to maintain that exchange theory and symbolic interactionsim share something. What they do not share are just those assumptions and stances which make the crucial difference.

Attribution Theory

Attribution theory is a psychological social psychology which draws upon the work of Heider (1958) and H. Kelley (1963). Recently Sheldon Stryker (1977) has suggested that this approach can be integrated into the interactionist theory of self and social process. There are two ways to read this proposal. The first sees a fundamental overlap between the two theories; under this interpretation they should be integrated. The second view sees them as resting on different underlying assumptions which make integration impossible, and if proposed, weak and unfruitful. We share the latter point of view and will indicate why in the following remarks.

Attribution theory rests on the key assumption that ordinary people operate with a naive psychology that leads them to make a causal sense out of their world. Ethnomethodologists would agree with this and so do we. We do not agree, however, with Heider's argument that humans have a "need" for a coherent understanding of their world, or that they have a "need" for control over their environments. We can only accept this position if "need" is interpreted culturally as a pattern of learned behavior. But Heider does not stress this point; hence attribution theory becomes a "weak" version of an interior need model of human behavior.

Nor can we accept the naive propositions that organize attribution theory. The principle of covariation argues that humans make causal inferences when two or more things occur together in more than one setting. This is an "associationist" argument. Its origins date to the Scottish and British philosophers of the 18th and 19th centuries (i.e., Hartley, Reid, Brown, Hamilton, Bain, Mill). Similarly the "discounting principle" of attribution theory argues that humans discount single causal explanations of human behavior when more than one cause operates.

These two propositions attempt to impose a causal order on human thought. Such an effort attempts to make sense out of the buzzing confusion of mental life by organizing it in terms of a few logical principles. This attempt yields few insights at the level of understanding.

Additional assumptions of attribution theory are (1) persons infer personality traits from overt behaviors; (2) individuals are influenced by the need to give causal explanations that support their own self-esteem; and (3) persons exaggerate their abilities to control their environments, including the belief that people get what they deserve.

This is a logical, individualistic social psychology. It reflects the attempt by psychological social psychologists to logically order human behavior so that it better conforms to the scientific norms of reason, logic, and causality. The theory simplistically treats the concept of cause. Its proponents would benefit from a closer reading of Schutz's (1964) conceptions of in-order-to and because motives and Scott & Lyman's theory of accounts (1968).

Situated Identity Theory

A variant of attribution theory is called situated identity theory (Alexander & Wiley, 1981). This theory is based on the idea that identity formation is a basic feature of social interaction. It argues that situated identities (self-meanings brought to bear upon persons in social situations), are attributed to persons on the basis of perceived dispositions they are seen as possessing. These at-

tributional definitions are evaluative and normative, and they serve to situate a person's conduct in concrete situations. This theory predicts that persons select socially desirable selves or identities to present in given situations. It has a great deal in common with Heider's attribution theory, although it draws upon the work of Gregory Stone (1962, 1981) on appearance and the self and Erving Goffman's (1959) dramaturgical sociology.

This theory tells us little about how people live and feel their identities. The theory is ahistorical and is based largely on experimental studies. It is not a theory of situated identities so much as a theory of how researchers impute identities to their experimental subjects.

Role-Identity Theory

Sheldon Stryker (1981) and McCall and Simmons (1978) have offered role-identity theories of interaction which bear some relationship to situated identity theory. These theorists view the self in terms of identities which correspond to a role the person plays. Role identities (identities attached to roles) vary by their salience, or importance for the person. They also vary by the degree to which persons are committed to them, and by the community of others also committed to them. The higher an identity in the salience hierarchy of persons and the more committed they are to the identity, the more likely they will be to seek out opportunities to enact the identity (Stryker, 1981, p. 24).

Both McCall and Simmons (1978) and Stryker (1981) assume that humans live in a symbolic world that is named and given meaning through interaction. A key feature of human interaction involves self-identification. Identities are based on the roles and statuses persons play and occupy in society. Behavior is the product of a role-making process (Stryker, 1981, p. 17).

These versions of identity theory give great stress to external social forces (roles, statuses); they can be termed "structural" identity theories. McCall and Simmons (1981, pp. 32–33) connect their formulations to exchange theory and to the work of Homans and Emerson. They argue that social exchange processes shape the negotiating and bargaining process that structures role-identities. They speak of humans as rational beings and they evoke the model of "economic man" in discussing the interaction process.

We applaud these efforts by Stryker and McCall and Simmons to produce theories of identity and self that are truly sociological. We quarrel, however, with their structural-exchange models of human experience. Our earlier criticisms of exchange theory apply to McCall and Simmons, and our earlier discussion of the problems of external models of human experience apply to Stryker as well. A structural theory of identity starts in the wrong place. It must begin with the lived experiences of the individual.

Dramaturgy

The parent theory which organizes all theories of identity is Goffman's dramaturgical theory of self and interaction. In *The Presentation of Self in Everyday Life* (1959) Goffman introduced a number of concepts from the stage to describe how persons present themselves to one another in everyday life. Goffman argued that everyday life is like the stage: Persons attempt to create impressions for others, play roles, assume characters, manage information, engage in collusion, keep secrets, think in terms of backstage and frontstage, treat others like audience members, and so on. This dramaturgical model has had a great impact on social psychological theorizing.

Perinbanayagam (1985) builds upon Goffman, while he uses Kenneth Burkes's theory of the pentad (act, agent, agency, purpose, scene) in his own theory of signifying acts. Perinbanayagam argues that the theatre is the primary source of meaning in everyday life. He sees the languages of self deriving from the myths, codes, religions, and ideologies of a society. He thus connects his

model with Goffman's dramaturgical theory and Burke's theory of drama and human society.

With the exception of Perinbanayagam, we find these dramaturgical theories too structurally restrictive. They attempt to explain human behavior in terms of external categories that do not derive from experience. They stretch the dramaturgical metaphor too far; they assume that persons can be called actors, and too often rest upon static views of the interaction process (see Glaser & Strauss, 1964).

To summarize this section: Identity theories are often frequently divorced from the actual world of interaction. They rest on metaphors and models that are too limiting. Because they are often ahistorical, they shed few insights into how selves and identities have been formed in earlier historical times. These formulations seldom speak to gender and power as pervasive features of human group life. While we applaud any theory that speaks to the self, we feel that such theories should be more in touch with how biographies create frameworks for selves and how biographies, in turn, are shaped by historical experience. We reject the structural versions of role-identity theory which still persist in seeing postmodern society in terms of roles and statuses.

Expectation States Theory

Expectation states theory is primarily associated with what has come to be called the Stanford School of social psychology. Berger, Cohen, Zelditch, Jr., and their colleagues and students have contributed to this theory, which is in fact a cluster of interrelated theories (see Molseed & Maines, 1987; Meeker, 1981; Berger & Zelditch, 1985 for reviews). The assumptions of this theoretical framework may be stated as follows: In small, problem-solving groups characterized by status inequality (i.e., differences in power and prestige) inequalities in interaction occur rapidly. That is, some persons emerge as leaders and others follow; some talk more, others listen; some are better liked, others arouse hostility, and so on. These inequalities tend to be interrelated; persons who are the most talkative also receive more talk than less talkative members. Once these inequalities appear they tend to be stable over time.

This theory attempts to explain the emergence and stabilization of these structures in small groups. It is argued that group members make evaluations of one another—evaluations which become consistent over time. They lead to expectation states, or anticipations of future performances. Once these expectations are formed they remain intact, somewhat independent of actual performances. Hence group behavior can be understood in terms of the expectation states that come into existence during interaction.

This theory has been subjected to criticism on a number of grounds. First, it is simplistic, for it does not take into account the complexities of group interactions that do not occur in laboratories. In the standardized experimental situation individuals have no contact with one another. Their status is assigned to them by the experimenter. Subjects sit on either side of a screen so that they cannot see one another. Subjects interact with the experimenter, but not with one another. Hence these studies do not study group interaction. The theory is based on contrived experimental conditions which bear little relationship to the real world of everyday group interaction.

Second, the theory is tautological; uniformities in behavior are explained in terms of expectation states which cannot be observed; and that state which is assumed to be the cause of behaviors is also the effect of the interactions that are created in the laboratory.

Third, the research excludes the realm of nonverbal behavior from group process (see Lee & Ofshe, 1981). When subjects are allowed to leave the laboratory cubicle they do not rely upon expectation states based on status characteristics as the basis for decision making (Molseed & Maines, 1987; Lee & Ofshe, 1981). Hence the key causal variable

in the theory appears not to operate in natural social situations.

Other problems with this theory include the questionable ethical practice of deceiving subjects about the task they are performing, and the flawed philosophy of science model the research program rests upon (Molseed & Maines, 1987). The Stanford group argues that they are building a deductive theory, expressed in terms of the rules of formal logic. They conceive of their research program as stemming from Lakatos' philosophy of science; a philosophy of science which Lakatos himself rejected. By failing to recognize the flaws and criticisms of the Lakatos program, the Stanford group has attached itself to a philosophy of science model that is no longer held in repute in the scientific community. While this theory has attracted much attention in the social psychological community we find it curiously out of touch with the world of lived experience.

Artificial Intelligence

Collins (1986, p. 1349) has proposed that one of the payoffs from microsociologists, ethnomethodologists, and cognitive sociologies of the last decade will be

a practical contribution to the development of Artificial Intelligence. It is becoming increasingly clear that individualistic psychology has not cracked the code that will open the way to a computer that can think and talk like a human being, and AI leaders are already turning to cognitive sociologists, including ethnomethodological ones, for a better lead.

Collins' remarks suggest that theories of artificial intelligence are drawing from the works of interpretive and cognitive social psychologists. Indeed, some argue that human beings are like computers. Hence to build a computer that thinks like a human and has humanlike intelligence has become a goal of many behavioral scientists, including Turing, von Neumann, McCarthy, Newell, Simon, and Minsky.

It is necessary, then, to discuss the concept

of artificial intelligence. Computers are becoming part of the American way of life, especially in the fields of business and education. Many have criticized the approach, including such philosophers as Taylor, Searle, Dreyfus, and Dennett. John Haugeland (1985) has presented a history and critique of artificial intelligence (AI); it is primarily from this text that we draw the following discussion. We shall see that AI raises many problems that relate back to our earlier discussion of mind-body dualism and reductionism (see Taylor, 1982, pp. 35–52).

There are many versions of AI, and theories of AI continue to change and evolve. Nonetheless the basic assumptions of AI may be stated as follows: 1) It must be understood that AI, like cognitive psychology and cognitive social psychology, is an off-shoot of behaviorism. It attempts to offer a logical, objective, experimental theory of the human mind, of talking, intelligence, and problem solving. 2) AI assumes that human thought is rational, orderly, and logical. 3) It is argued that if human thought is rational and orderly, then a machine which has these characteristics should be able to model and predict human thought. Because computers have these characteristics, they are like the human mind and brain; that is, computers can rationally and logically solve problems. 4) Computers have intelligence; this intelligence, however, is artificial, for it is not acquired like human intelligence. 5) It is argued that thinking and computing are the same. 6) Since thinking is rational, and like talking, AI argues that our minds operate on computational principles. Intelligence thus becomes the ability to say the right thing at the right time. 7) The computer is now seen as an interpreted, automatic, formal system which manipulates pieces of information, called tokens.

8) AI uses a formal language, which is not the natural language of everyday speakers. This formal language is a machine language, like FORTRAN or PASCAL. It was found that natural languages could not be reduced to a computer language. In 1960, linguist Yehoshua Bar-Hillel discovered that it was impossible to create a machine language that would encode all the facts of a natural language. He stated (1960, p. 160),

What such a suggestion amounts to, if taken seriously, is the requirement that a translation machine should not only be supplied with a dictionary but also with a universal encyclopedia. This is surely utterly chimerical and hardly deserves any further discussion.

9) As a result, computers work on a system of language that manipulates tokens, often organized in terms of oppositions, as in a digital system (i.e., positive-negative, present-absent, etc.). Computers are programmed to manipulate symbols/tokens so as to solve particular problems or puzzles. Tokens designate pieces of information that the system is able to interpret. As an interpreting, automatic, and formal system, the computer processes information within a meaning system that has its own rules of organization (syntax) and its own system of meaning (semantics).

AI works on the principle that there is a system of symbols/tokens/markers that operate in terms of a syntactical logic that is self-contained (i.e., programmed into the computer). Furthermore, it is argued that the meanings these symbols have exist in some relation to an external world. Haugeland (1985, p. 100) suggests that the formal tokens within an AI system have two lives: syntactical and semantic. The formalist motto of AI asserts that "if you take care of the syntax, the semantics will take care of itself . . . that is how the 'two lives' of an interpreted formal system go together" (Haugeland, 1985, p. 106).

10) The languages that computers use are, as indicated, based on symbol/token systems whose meanings are arbitrary. That is, the meanings of the words within a machine language are designated by the programmer. The ability of a computer to use a language and to form a correct solution to a problem is based on the coherence principle; the meanings of tokens within the system

must be logical, and must cohere and inter-relate in a rational, orderly manner.

11) Some AI theorists argue that computers can be seen as having a sense of inner consciousness, or as having introspective abilities. Dennett has suggested that introspection amounts to having a built-in ability to "tell" what is contained in our mental memory banks. Since computers can access information that as been stored, the argument goes, they can be seen as having introspective abilities.

12) Some AI theorists contend that computers have artificial egos, or artificial selves (see Haugeland, 1985, p. 245). This argument rests on the assumption that computers also have a sense of consciousness, or an ability to access information that has been stored. Haugeland goes so far as to propose (1985, pp. 230–38) that computers may have feelings, emotions, and moods, if by these terms we mean the ability of machines to sense their environment. He suggests that many fancy computer systems can sense pain (i.e., internal malfunctions, internal damage). He goes on to propose (1985, p. 235) that perhaps sensations do not matter when intelligent behavior is concerned. In this sense emotions are not a problem for a rational, cognitive system. Finally, Haugeland (1985, pp. 235–65) throws his hands up in the air, stating, "The more I think about this question, the less I'm persuaded I even know what it means (which is not to say I think it's meaningless)."

An Evaluation of Artificial Intelligence

Charles Taylor (1985, p. 127) has argued that AI, in its attempt to deal with the concepts that behaviorism excluded (i.e., mind, consciousness, intentionality, self, thought, language) has run into "difficulty a lot faster, and this is all to its credit." He suggests that AI rests on a naive representational theory of language and on a simplistic stimulus-response theory of meaning. Further, it lacks a theory of emotionality; its conceptions of self, ego, introspection, and consciousness are forced and empty. Furthermore the computer, as a thinking machine, contains no sense of interaction within a conflict-riddled, emergent social world. That is, it forces the external world, in the form of its user, to conform with its rules of syntax and semantics.

AI rests on a reductionistic, dualistic conception of mind, language, consciousness, self, and the human body. Remembering that reductionism refers to the tendency to explain human behavior in terms of physiological, neurological, chemical, physical, or mechanical concepts, we can see that AI is reductionistic. Computer programs are seen as having the same functions of human behavior. This reductionism is sophisticated, as Taylor (1985, p. 127; 1982, p. 36) observes, for it recognizes that "radically different forms of hardware (can) be programmed to represent the same process" (Secord, 1982, p. 15).

This reductionism is not just physicalistic; it rests on a distinction between the computing program that organizes the computer's "thought," and the physical realization of that program in terms of answers to questions. AI theorists contend that consciousness, or self-awareness, is always faulty and partial; yet their theories presume complex, inner processes that are involved in problem-solving activities. They "marginalize" consciousness to the fringe of awareness. They explain thought in terms of mechanistic, rational processes. Their model presumes the operation of higher mental processes that fall outside their reductionist, mechanical model; mental process is reduced to mechanical transformations. They do not explain thinking or thought on its own terms (Heidegger, 1977, pp. 341–67). The being or self that calls us into thinking stands outside AI's computer. By creating the illusion that computers can think like humans do, AI theorists engage in a form of "anthropomorphism" that has long been recognized as unacceptable in the human disciplines. Anthropomorphism, or the attributing of human characteristics to nonhumans, pervades all of AI theorizing. By stripping away the essential features of human experience so that a model of the human mind can be built, AI theorists end up with a grotesque caricature of what a human being is.

Dualistically, AI maintains a separation between mind and body as radically different realities. The two lives of the computer (the self-contained world of syntax and the outer world of semantics, meaning, and performance) speak to this dualistic bias. But more is at issue. AI works with a representational theory of mind which sees the computer mapping an external world; thus mind and world are separated, to be joined only through the computer's ability to produce truthful answers to the questions that are posed it. This model purges any bodily reality from mental processes just as it excludes any meaningful interaction between mind and world. The AI dualistic assumption posits, then, a physical world and a mental world; yet it has no way of bridging the gap between the two.

Consider shame. Taylor (1982, pp. 46–47) suggests that AI is unable to handle the fact that in the case of the human emotions it is impossible to push consciousness to the fringe of experience. Shame requires self-feeling, agency, purpose, and a language of emotionality (see Denzin, 1984). Shame cannot be reduced to physiological sensations; it requires self-reflection. Because computers lack the ability to engage in reflective self-thought, they cannot feel shame.

Consciousness and its meanings are basic features of human existence. Computers and AI theorists are unable to theorize consciousness, self, or emotionality. This is a decisive flaw in AI. Consciousness cannot be severed from human experience. A theory of minded, human behavior which is built on a mechanical theory of language, and which cannot speak to embodied emotional experiences, contributes little to our understanding of human behavior.

A second decisive flaw in AI involves its theory of language. Bar-Hillel's (1960) conclusion that a machine language could not recover all of the meanings in natural, every-day language set AI theorists in search of a machine language that would be completely self-contained. The systems of language that have been produced cannot handle the shifting meanings words take on in everyday conversations. In everyday life, speakers do not and cannot ignore meaning or semantics; nor can they just let syntax do the work of meaning. The AI assumption that syntax will do the work of semantics thus cannot be allowed.

Nor does the AI theory of language fit into the semiotic model of language produced by Saussure (1959). Words, as signs, have different values and meanings. Signs exist in both speech and language. AI's tokens and symbols exist in a never-never realm which is neither institutional nor interactional. Their languages have none of the features of language and speech as studied by Saussure; nor can their language deal with language games, signifying acts, and the rules of language use that Wittgenstein (1953) and Perinbanayagam (1985) have developed. Hence their position on language is ahistorical, non–social-psychological, and noninteractional. It is of little or no use when the problems of understanding how humans think and use language are raised.

Still, AI theorists are to be thanked for the careful way in which they delineate the limits of their models. Unfortunately, the very features of human experience and thought which AI excludes are those which are closest to what it means to be human.

CONCLUSIONS

We have covered a vast amount of material in this chapter. We have presented the basic features of our point of view and have contrasted it with other social psychologies. We spent much time on the "cognitive" social psychologies and have done this in order to expose the limits of a purely cognitive, rational, and logical approach to the study of human experience. We hope that our discussion of AI—the most sophisticated of the cognitive social psychologies—has successfully conveyed the limitations of these approaches.

In summary, we note that *all* social psychologies (of whatever theoretical variety) are concerned with the relationship between persons and groups or larger forms of social organization. All the theories discussed in this chapter share the following common assumptions: (1) Humans learn from experience. (2) Humans are symbol-producing and symbol-using organisms; this sets them apart, in one sense, from infrahuman organisms. (3) Human behavior is influenced by the presence of others. (4) Humans are capable of maintaining some control and consistency in their own actions. (5) Human behavior is constantly changing and adapting to new situations. (6) Some behaviors and influences are more significant than others. (7) Human behavior is meaningful; that is, it can be interpreted and understood. In short, all social psychologies employ some version of the scientific or interpretive method.

Despite these shared assumptions, each position tends to rely primarily on different kinds of research methods. Psychoanalysts employ in-depth interviewing, self-reports, and dream and fantasy analysis. Psychological social psychologists rely on laboratory and field experimentation as well as on psychological tests and questionnaires. Symbolic interactionists attempt to study persons in their natural locales and primarily use field observation, open-ended interviewing, life-history construction, and unobtrusive methods.

In this text we develop a view of human behavior which stresses that humans are social and symbol-using organisms. We attempt to cross the boundaries of sociologgy, anthropology, linguistics, psychology, political science, and history, and to utilize any and all data that elaborate our theoretical perspective. Our fundamental concern is to account for the structured regularity and irregularity of human conduct, and we assume that even deviance and deviant behavior are lawfully and predictably organized.

SUGGESTED READINGS

Berger, Peter and Thomas Luckmann (1967). *The Social Construction of Reality.* Garden City, N.Y.: Doubleday. Presents a lucid and informative treatment of a phenomenological and interactionist view of individuals and social structures.

Blumer, Herbert, *Symbolic Interactionism* (1969). Englewood Cliffs, N.J.: Prentice-Hall. This collection of papers offers a comprehensive review of Blumer's analysis of theory and method as seen from the interactionist perspective. Blumer has been the one sociologist most influential in defining the essential and unique implications of symbolic interactionism for the sociological community.

CHAPTER TWO
Sociobiology and Human Symbolic Behavior

In this chapter we will examine the behavior of lower species and indicate some of the major differences between it and various kinds of human, symbolic behavior. We will deal with the recent field of "sociobiology" (Wilson, 1975), which is the systematic study of the biological bases of all social behavior. Sociobiology primarily involves a study of animal societies, but it is also concerned with the "social behavior of early man and the . . . adaptive features of organization in the more primitive contemporary human societies" (Wilson, 1975, p. 4). Sociobiology is a branch of evolutionary biology; but it proposes a synthesis with modern sociology, for it attempts to isolate the underlying biological causes and functions of human, social behavior.

After discussing and evaluating sociobiology, we will discuss the behaviors of chimpanzees who have been taught a version of language. Then we will take up the topics of symbolic worlds and symbolic environments. Our intention is to secure firmly the importance of the "symbolic" in the study of human, social behavior.

THE EVOLUTIONARY SETTING OF HUMAN BEHAVIOR

The behavior of all animals (including humans) is social to some degree; even among the lowest species, organisms stimulate one another and may live in some sort of group. Social groups as we know them require organization, psychological unity, a communication system, and a division of labor—however simple—whereby group members cooperate toward group goals. Another type of group, exemplified by a mass of people waiting for a train, is known as an *aggregate,* or an *assemblage.* Members of the aggregate, whether it is composed of human beings or animals, do not act concertedly toward group goals or like members of social groups; they do affect one another's behavior, thereby making the behavior social to a limited degree. An aggregate thus is not a genuine social group because it involves only the most rudimentary social relations and lacks most of the features of social groups noted above.

While in our discussion we will place emphasis upon the evolution of forms of behavior, we should remember that cultural evolution presupposes and depends upon prior biological evolution. The evolution of the human brain, of course, has been of central significance. Specialists in this area generally emphasize that assuming an upright posture was of critical importance in the evolution of humans because it freed the hands for making and manipulating tools and for other fine manipulative behavior. This, in turn, changed survival conditions and helped produce the changes in cranial size and structure that distinguish homo sapiens from the human-apes thought to have been our immediate predecessors. The human brain is not simply a relatively larger one than that of monkeys and other primates; it is also qualitatively and structurally different. For example, the areas associated with the thumb (and with control of the hands in general), language, speech, and with higher mental functions are proportionately much more elaborate and specialized. In the ape's brain there is no counterpart to the specialized left-hemisphere language center characteristic of right-handed humans.

In the chronology of human physical and cultural evolution, it is significant to note that while the former no doubt sets the stage for cultural evolution by providing us with our human brain and physical form, the two forms of evolution seem to be unrelated after that point. Cultural evolution or change has, in recent times, accelerated at a geometric rate without any further significant evolutionary changes in the biological equipment of humans.

We must note, however, that not everyone agrees with this conclusion. Campbell (1975, p. 1123) states:

Urban humanity is a product of both biological and social evolution. . . Human urban social complexity is a product of social evolution and has had to counter with inhibitory moral norms the biological selfishness which genetic competition had continually selected.

Rossi (1984, p. 2) has argued:

. . . my assumption is that persistent differences between men and women, and variations in the extent to which such differences are found along the lift line, are a function of underlying biological processes of sexual differentiation as well as social and historical processes.

THE EVOLUTION OF SOCIAL BEHAVIOR

We turn next to different "levels" of organisms and behavior. Just where to draw the line between the social and nonsocial in the interorganismic contact of the very lowest animals is an indeterminate matter. Jennings (1942), the well-known student of protozoa, has confessed that in his younger days he concluded that aggregates of infusoria exhibited no social characteristics; he was reprimanded later by a critic who noted that the reactions he had described actually were social relations of the protozoan kind. Although the one-celled animal requires no other to aid it in performing its vital functions, it does nevertheless on occasion gather together with others of its kind. Dense aggregates may be produced by convergence toward a source of light or by movement against a current. These are aggregates in the literal sense of the term; there is no division of labor, no cooperative activity.

Two Aspects of Evolution: Continuity and Emergence

Although it is certain that various forms of group organization exist among the lower species, biologists find it hard to classify one as more complex or more social than another if the forms are not similar. Allee, for example, speaks of small but real differences of group organization (1931, p. 158):

We are confronted with a gradual development of real differences without being able to put a finger with surety on any one clearly defined break in the continuity. The slow accumulation of more and more social tendencies leads finally by small steps to something that is apparently different. If we disregard the intermediate stages, the differences may appear pronounced, but if we focus on these intermediates, it will be only for the sake of convenience that we interrupt the connecting chain of events at some comparatively conspicuous link and arbitrarily make this the dividing point, when one is needed, between the more and less social.

This statement brings out two aspects of evolution: One is the continuity of species and the other is the notion of distinct "levels" or the emergence of new properties. The latter has been stated in this way (Schneirla, 1949, p. 245):

The principle of levels has come into current usage through a recognition of important differences in the complexity, the degree of development, and the interdependent organization of behavior functions through the animal series. The evidently superior properties that appear on a new level of organization are not to be explained as due to a new kind of energy or new vital properties, but as functional properties arising from a new system of organization which differs in given ways from "lower" and "higher" systems.

The "levels" concept thus assumes the existence of continuity and similarity among species but stresses also the emergence of new properties of organization. The differences in levels have to do with "*what kinds of processes and capacities are available* to an animal and its species mates in adapting to their environments" (Schneirla, 1946, p. 57). Ants and bees live in organized colonies and operate at higher levels of capacity than do sponges or protozoa that live as individuals or in aggregates. Different animal aggregations reach the same general ends—such as providing food and shelter—but the organization of the aggregate, and the processes through which ends are attained, may be very dissimilar.

Anthropomorphism and Morgan's Canon

The concept of behavioral levels leads us to guard against anthropomorphizing. *Anthropomorphism* (from the Greek *anthropos*, "man," and *morphe*, "form") means the projection of human traits upon things not human, and it is a fallacy to steer clear of in studying the lower animals. We often make the anthropomorphic mistake of assigning human attributes to the behavior of an animal or species (for example, when a pet dog does something for which it is usually punished and is then viewed as acting guilty or looking ashamed).

In a sense, however, the human vocabulary must always be anthropomorphic. Suppose one makes a statement as simple as the following: "The chimpanzee placed the box so that by standing on it, he could reach the banana." Surely this sentence does not mean that the chimpanzee has verbally formulated his purpose within the framework of English or any other language, as might be assumed by a too-literal reader. We should remember that although we apply human words to the actions of animals, the animals themselves do not.

Asquith (1984, p. 138) has observed, in regard to the use of ordinary language and anthropomorphism, that

(Anthropomorphism) arises through qualitative or ordinary language description in which terms such as "threaten," "appease," "chase," "greet," "submission," and so on are applied to animal behaviour. These terms already carry meanings associated with human action (that is, purposeful behaviour).

Asquith's article contends that in ordinary language usage "metaphor" is the mechanism "which allows and in fact necessitates the semantic link between human action and animal behaviour" (p. 139). "It occurs simply as a result of our language, or more specifically, meaning in language" (p. 143).

Reynolds (1980, xxii) has summarized Weber's (1946) distinction between "be-

haviour" *(Verhalten)*, and "action" *(Handeln)* and a third term "meaning" *(Sinn)*, which links the two:

If we describe what people or animals do, without inquiring into their subjective reasons for doing it, we are talking about their *behaviour*. If we study the subjective aspects of what they do, the reasons and ideas underlying and guiding it, then we are concerned with the world of *meaning*. If we concern ourselves both with what people are, overtly and objectively, seen to do (or not to do) and their reasons for doing (or not doing) which relate to the world of meaning and understanding, we then describe *action*. (italics in original)

Drawing upon Harré and Secord (1972), Asquith writes (1984, p. 167),

. . . action has significance and meaning; it occurs in a social, not a physiological context; it is inextricably bound up with the nature and limits of language (and the fabric of society), and importantly there is no way of reducing action to movement and so of setting it within a physiological context.

Anthropomorphic ordinary language terms, then, when used metaphorically, may be a heuristically useful way to understand animal behavior. Asquith concludes (p. 169),

Because ordinary language terms for social behaviour have most often been used to express human action, they connote purposefulness in the animals to which they are applied. This occurs through metaphor and gives rise to generic anthropomorphism, or the treatment of animals as conscious agents. The usual connection we make between purposeful actions serves as a heuristic aid to interpretation of the animals' behaviour. The sophistication and applicability of quantitative description was argued not to replace our ultimate understanding of animal behaviour in terms of ordinary language.

It is not only in common speech that animal behavior is described and accounted for in human terms. Many years ago a comparative psychologist, Lloyd Morgan, attacked the then general propensity of both laypersons and scholars to find resemblances between the mental processes of human beings and those of lower animals. He enunciated a canon that has been quoted with general approval ever since by comparative psychologists (Morgan, 1894, p. 53):

In no case may we interpret an action as the outcome of the exercise of a higher psychical faculty, if it can be interpreted as the outcome of the exercise of one which stands lower in the psychological scale.

At the time of Morgan's writing, it was customary to prove similarities between animals and human beings by narrating anecdotes. The anecdotal method has long since disappeared from scholarly writing, but there are numerous references to animal reasoning, generalization, hypotheses, concepts, dominance, leadership, purpose, goals, neuroses, communication, and cooperation. The terms are often used within quotation marks to indicate that the reader is not supposed to take the analogy to human behavior too seriously; that many writers and readers *do* take the analogies seriously there is little doubt. Schneirla, who has attacked this kind of anthropomorphic writing, suggests that a distinction be drawn between the *description* of behavior and its causal *explanation*. We may speak loosely of protective behavior, food-getting, and courtship in various species, but a genuine causal description of the behavior will make clear that several processes are involved. For example, whereas intent and exchange of information and sentiment are involved in human courtship, none need be imputed to various of the lower species when they engage in sexual activity.

We believe that the concept of levels of behavior is particularly fruitful because it focuses attention both on the continuity of species and upon the differences among them. It requires that concepts and hypotheses concerning the behavior of any species be inductively derived from the study of that particular species—rather than, as is common, by extrapolation to lower species of the principles derived from mammalian investigation, or by the explanation of human behavior in terms of principles derived from lower mammalian types (*zoomorphism*). Morgan, advocating this view at the turn of the century, said cogently (1894, pp. 282–83):

When the doctrine of evolution was winning its way to acceptance, it was natural that its advocates should employ every means at their command to strengthen their position and to emphasize the continuity underlying diversity of aspect. But now that the position is secure, and continuity is generally admitted, it seems desirable to mark off, by restriction of the range of the use of terms we employ, the stages of differentiation.

A comparative psychology based upon this principle would be of great significance to social psychologists.

SOCIOBIOLOGY

Sociobiology is the study of the biological basis of social behavior in both animals and humans. Zoologist Edward Wilson, in his extensive book on sociobiology, writes, "One of the functions of sociobiology . . . is to reformulate the foundations of the social sciences in a way that draws these subjects into the Modern Synthesis" (Wilson, 1975, p. 4). According to Wilson, ". . . sociology, and the other social sciences, as well as the humanities, *are the last branches of biology* waiting to be included in the Modern Synthesis" (1975, p. 4, emphasis added). The "Modern Synthesis" is a neo-Darwinist evolutionary theory which examines each phenomenon under study (including human behavior) according to its adaptive significance and relates it to the basic principles of population genetics.

Sociobiology, then, applies natural selection theory to behavior. According to this theory, human social and cultural behaviors have biological, or genetic, determinants. That is, an individual's behaviors are at least partially determined by their genetic makeup (Ehrmen & Parsons, 1976). Wilson (1975) notes that prominent social scientists such as Chomsky, Piaget, and Kohlberg have theories of language, cognitive development, and moral development, respectively, that are consistent with sociobiology in that they posit an innate, genetic underpinning to child development. Children, they contend, go through certain stages in their development because they are genetically predisposed to do so. We regard this as a careless misreading of Chomsky, Piaget, and Kohlberg.

Assuming that behaviors have a biological basis, sociobiology maintains that genetic determinants of behaviors that are adaptive—in that they make the species fitter to survive and to reproduce—become more common in the gene pool of the population. To elaborate, individuals who behave in ways that enhance survival and reproduction will produce more offspring than those who behave in ways that impede survival and reproduction; therefore the genetic determinants of those adaptive behaviors will increase in the gene pool of the population.

Altruistic behavior has been a challenge to evolutionary theory because it seemingly results in a decrease in the reproductive success of the individual yet continues to be prevalent in both man and animal. A person who sacrifices himself for another will not produce more offspring, and the genetic determinant of altruistic behavior should decrease in the gene pool and eventually die out. This apparent contradiction has been explained through the process of *kin selection.* According to Greene, Morgan, and Barash (1979, p. 422):

Since natural selection operates through the representation of genes in succeeding generations, any one individual can pass on its own genes either by raising offspring or by helping a relative (with whom some genes are shared by common decent) to reproduce. Thus if two individuals are sufficiently related, then one individual may best further its own ultimate success by helping the other, even at some apparent immediate cost.

People, then, will be most likely to exhibit altruistic behavior toward those that are most genetically similar.

Altruism toward unrelated others has been explained in terms of the probability of reciprocity (Trivers, 1971). Given our lengthy lifetime and our high degree of mutual dependence, it is adaptive to be altruistic assuming that others will reciprocate at some future time.

Sociobiology has recently been used to help explain gender and parenting behaviors in humans. Alice S. Rossi, in her 1983 presidential address to the American Sociological Association, states (1984, p. 1):

This analysis of gender and parenthood begins with the judgment that none of the theories prevalent in family sociology—exchange, symbolic interaction, general systems, conflict, phenomenology, feminist, or development—are adequate to an understanding and explanation of human parenting because they do not seek an integration of biological and social constructs.

Rossi maintains that biology and sociology are interdependent and an understanding of both is needed to further our knowledge and understanding of social life. To study one and neglect the other "may doom efforts at social change to failure" (1984, p. 11).

Others are more critical of sociobiology. Vernon Reynolds is an anthropologist and ethnologist who posits a link between biological traits and social behavior. He maintains, however, that there is no reason to search for genetic factors in explanation of behaviors that can be explained as rational responses to recurring problems (Wallace & Wolf, 1986, p. 298). Bleier denies the biological-social dichotomy and maintains that the two are so intertwined that they cannot be separated (1984).

Donald T. Campbell, in his 1975 presidential address to the American Psychological Association, maintains that humanity is a product of both biological and social evolution but concludes that *"Human urban social complexity has been made possible by social evolution rather than biological evolution"* (1975, p. 115, italics in original). By social evolution he means, "a *selective* cumulation of skills, technologies, recipes, beliefs, customs, organizational structures, and the like, retained through purely social modes of transmission, rather than in the genes" (1975, p. 1104, italics in original). Both biology and sociology play a part in determining behavior, but the relative significance of each has yet to be determined.

Interpreting Sociobiology

What does sociobiology tell us about being human? How do sociobiological factors explain or account for language, culture, and those complex structures called societies? Wilson and others attempt to explain human, social, and cultural behaviors in terms of a general evolutionary model which stresses biological and genetic factors. While Campbell and others have raised problems with a strict evolutionary point of view, we need to note the following problems and criticisms of sociobiology.

Sociologist Bryan Turner (1984, pp. 1, 35, 41, 227) argues that sociobiology is reductionistic and a blind alley. He states that sociobiology suppresses the obvious fact that human beings have bodies, whose social presence is socially constructed and constituted through communal, cultural practices (Turner, 1984, p. 227). Sociobiology, he goes on to argue (1984, p. 35), suggests that the human body, in all important respects, has remained physiologically static over the last 2,000 years. This approach tells us virtually nothing about the history of the human body, its diseases, its illnesses, or its sexuality (Foucault, 1980, p. 185). It fails to see the body as a historical product whose meanings shift and change within social groups and cultures.

As a reductionistic perspective, sociobiology attempts to explain social behavior in terms of processes that operate below the level of the social. In this respect it is anthropomorphic and violates the levels of analysis principle discussed earlier. However, Wilson (1975, p. 30) predicates his entire program on the rejection of these principles. He argues with Morgan and Schneirla on precisely those points which served to estab-lish the boundaries of comparative psychology in the first place.

Wilson rejects the argument that the principles of selection and reproduction cannot be applied to group selection and higher social structures. He then proceeds to build his sociobiology on the premise that evolutionary processes will explain not only altruism, but language communication, aggression, caste systems, family organization and gender differentiation, parenting behavior, group formation, role playing, bonding, divisions of labor, culture, ritual, religion, ethics, and societies of the future.

Clearly, an interpretive social psychology cannot allow these assumptions. To do so blurs any distinction between human and nonhuman behavior. Furthermore, it distorts (if not destroys) any understanding of the complex structural and interactional processes that together produce social organization, culture, and human symbolic behavior.

In these respects sociobiology is also atomistic; it attempts to explain the whole in terms of its parts. Furthermore, it is dualistic; it posits a basic division between mind and body, body and nature, genes and culture, and so on. It is unable to offer a dialectical, processual theory of human, social structure (see Lewontin, Rose, & Kamin, 1984).

While Wilson speaks with the authority of a biologist, his theory of society and human nature is dubious. He assumes that there are universals in all societies, including athletics, dancing, cooking, religion, entrepreneurship, territoriality, warfare, and female orgasm (Lewontin, Rose, & Kamin, 1984, p. 243). He also assumes that these universal human characteristics are coded in the human genotype. He then contends that "these genetically based human universals have been established by natural selection during the course of human biological evolution" (Lewontin, Rose, & Kamin, 1984, p. 244).

Each of these assumptions is open to question. First, the universals that Wilson ascribes to all societies are themselves social constructs, or labels. They are not natural objects having a concrete reality universally agreed upon by all persons. Wilson arrives at his terms arbitrarily. There is no *a priori* way to determine whether in fact his categories of nature exist. He reifies these terms, giving them a force in human evolutionary history that they do not and cannot have. He also gives social metaphors and social concepts (i.e., caste, warfare, love), a force in primate and insect societies that is suspect. This is the anthropomorphic fallacy again. How is it possible to speak of "slavery" in ants (Lewontin, Rose, & Kamin, 1984, p. 249)?

Wilson's assumption that human social behavior is coded in the genes is also open to wide criticism. Lewontin, Rose and Kamin (1984, pp. 252–53) observe that up to the present time no scientist has been able to relate any aspect of human behavior to any particular gene. Wilson's simple determinative model of gene control is thus wholly fallacious.

The argument that natural selection has determined the evolution and origin of human traits has also been criticized. Lewontin, Rose and Kamin (1984, p. 261) state that

The combination of direct selection, kin selection, and reciprocal altruism provides the sociobiologist with a battery of speculative possibilities that guarantees an explanation for every observation. The system is unbeatable because it is insulated from any possibility of being contradicted by fact. If one is allowed to invent genes with arbitrarily complicated effects on phenotypes and then to invent adaptive stories about the unrecoverable past of human history all phenomena, real and imaginary, can be explained.

More deeply, sociobiology fails to offer an answer to the question of what it means to be human. It reduces the essence of the human being to the genetic level. It is unable to address how human beings live their bodies into existence. Sociobiology thus becomes a strangely static, mechanical theory. It drives all of human experience down to the level of the gene and becomes, in the process, unable to speak to those lived disorders of the body that include alcoholism, drug addiction, anorexia, and so on.

Sociobiology is a new version of Social Darwinism. It holds that the fittest survive and that populations display an adaptive capacity for reproduction which rests on the principles of natural selection (Wilson, 1975, pp. 1, 13–16). It is a conservative social philosophy which ignores the role of culture, religion, and political ideology in the production of the altruistic and conflictual forms of behavior that make up any society. We agree with Turner in his assessment of sociobiology: It is a blind alley. Lewontin, Rose and Kamin (1984, p. 264) are more harsh; they claim that Wilson, who has identified himself with American neoconservative libertarianism, has offered in his sociobiology a "vulgar Mendelism, vulgar Darwinism, and vulgar reductionism in the service of the status quo."

However, we are not willing to rule out biological and genetic factors. We merely see them as constituting a stratum or level of behavior that must be analyzed at its own level. They cannot be lifted to the level of social and cultural and made to do the work of truly social psychological and psychological concepts and theories. Sociobiologists, like AI theorists, clarify the assumptions and problems of social psychology.

In this respect, we find their work on animal communication and language systems important. We turn to a discussion of the "social" behavior of chimpanzees and the controversy surrounding their abilities to use language like humans.

THE BEHAVIOR OF CHIMPANZEES

The great apes, who of all the animals stand closest to us on the evolutionary ladder, offer perhaps the most interesting comparison with human beings, for they are unquestionably more intelligent than our usual house pets or farm animals. The great apes that have been most thoroughly studied are the chimpanzees. We shall attempt to show what sociable animals they are. In describing their behavior, we shall use language that will bring out their seemingly human qualities.

We shall then point to their limitations, which emerge when we compare them with the more complex human being.

Group Solidarity

"It is hardly an exaggeration to say that a chimpanzee kept in solitude is not a real chimpanzee at all" (Kohler, 1926, p. 293). This statement indicates the extraordinary extent to which chimpanzees are influenced by the presence of other chimpanzees. When forcibly removed from his companions or his group, this great ape "cries, screams, rages, and struggles desperately to escape and return to his fellows. Such behavior may last for hours. All the bodily functions may be more or less upset. Food may be persistently refused, and depression may follow the emotional orgy" (Yerkes & Yerkes, 1945, p. 45). The chimpanzee in these circumstances will even risk his life in an effort to return to his group. When he rejoins it, there is great rejoicing, and the one who has been isolated displays the deepest excitement.

A chimpanzee locked alone in a cage will stretch his hands out through the bars toward his companions, wave and call to them, or push various objects through the bars in their direction. If the isolated animal's cries are audible and his gestures visible to the others, they may embrace him through the bars of the cage and otherwise give evidence of what seems to be human sympathy for their unhappy fellow. But if they cannot hear him or see him, they show no awareness of his absence. If one of their number is taken away because of illness or death, there is usually no evidence that the others grieve for their missing companion or even know that he is no longer in their midst.

However, in the April 1985 *National Geographic,* Dr. Patterson reports on Koko, a gorilla who was taught American Sign Language:

Last year she (Koko) asked for and received a kitten. She attempted to suckle it and carried it tucked against her thigh, as gorilla mothers carry their babies. Tragically, All Ball, as Koko named the kitten, was killed by a car. When she heard the news, Koko remained silent for about 10 minutes, then began to cry—not with tears as humans do but with high-pitched soblike sounds (p. 409).

Chimpanzees have a characteristic cry of distress. When this cry is emitted in connection with some action taken by the human investigator, other chimpanzees tend to rally to the support of their companion and threaten or actually attack the offender. Sometimes it is difficult to train the animals when they are in a group because of this danger of attack, particularly when the chimpanzees are adults.

Limitations of Chimpanzees

When we consider the collective achievements of civilized humans, we are overwhelmingly impressed by the vast gulf between them and the apes. Chimpanzees do not weep. Although they have various ways of indicating pleasure, they do not laugh. Nor do they seem to have the slightest appreciation of human laughter; they tend to respond to it with bewilderment or rage. One could go on almost indefinitely enumerating specific kinds of human behavior that are beyond the ape. It is not so easy, however, to determine the exact sources of the chimpanzees' limitations or to define the precise limits of their accomplishments. Here we can indicate only some of the main types of differences between human and subhuman behavior that are to a degree substantiated by the work of comparative psychologists.

Animals Are Limited to the "Here and Now"

All subhuman behavior is sharply, although not absolutely, limited to the immediate, concrete situation. This limitation is one of time and space. Thus, Köhler states that a major difference between humans and chimpanzees is that the time in which the chimpanzees live stretches back and forth only a little way. The ability of chimpanzees to solve problems appears to be determined principally, Köhler says, by their "optical apprehension of the situation." Sticks and other instruments are most readily used as tools when they are in the immediate proximity of the problem situation. If they are moved away from it—as, for example, to the rear of the cage or into an adjoining room or corridor—the apes virtually cease to perceive them as potential tools, even though they may be perfectly familiar with these items and see them daily.

The assertion that animals are limited to the "here and now" requires some qualification: The limitation is not absolute, nor does it warrant overemphasis. Thus, if chimpanzees in a cage see bananas buried in the sand outside and are not allowed out of the cage until the next day, when they are released they run quickly to the approximate spot to search for the buried fruit. Other experiments clearly indicate that delayed responses of this type are well within the range of the chimpanzee's abilities. Moreover, a chimpanzee separated from a human being to whom he has been accustomed will give unmistakable signs of recognition when he sees him or her again after months of separation. But by and large, one may regard chimpanzees as limited to the here and now.

Quiatt (1984, pp. 34–35) complicates this conclusion slightly, stating:

That social strategies of monkeys and apes may be premeditated is suggested by both naturalistic observation and experimental research . . . a review of deceptive behavior in monkeys and apes convinces me that those animals do manipulate displays in complex and subtle ways. . . .

An interesting illustration is provided (Quiatt, 1984, p. 31) about a chimp playing a trick by keeping his mouth full of water until a human is in range and then squirting it at him.

Whether primate behavior displays planning and intentionality, as we understand those terms, is problematic. Harré and Reynolds (1984, p. 6) leave this topic open for discussion in the following statement:

Whether primate intentionality is the same as human intentionality is another matter, but there seems no reason to deny the possibility of some degree of overlap between primate intentions and some kinds of human intentions.

The Use of Tools

Although chimpanzees can use various kinds of objects as tools and can even construct certain types of tools, they show almost no tendency to store the tools for future use or to transport them systematically from place to place. Moreover, chimpanzees show practically no disposition to store or hoard food against future contingencies. Other animals, especially certain insects, do store and transport food in complex and systematic ways. Such behavior, however, does not have to be learned; it is biologically determined.

Chimpanzees have what seems to be an "innate destructive impulse," Yerkes states, that expresses itself in their tendency to break down into its constituent elements any complex object made up of various movable or removable parts. Chimpanzees, like small children, explore, pull, poke, and otherwise manipulate the object; they do not rest until it has been taken apart and the pieces strewn about. When chimpanzees do actually construct a tool—for example, by fitting two sticks together to make one long one—their action seems remarkable because it contrasts so sharply with their usual mode of behavior.

Moreover, unless they are continuously trained, there is a strong tendency for the animals to soon slough off most of the new behavior they have learned in the experimental training situation. As Köhler (1926, p. 296) says:

If one is able to produce a—very temporary—type of behavior which is not congenial to the chimpanzee's instincts, it will soon be necessary to use compulsion if he is to keep it. And the slightest relaxation of that compulsion will be followed by a reversion to type.

Yerkes exclaimed over the remarkable manner in which the chimpanzees of his laboratory colony learned certain human activities. Thus, when push-button drinking fountains were installed in their cages, only some animals were shown how to use them. The others learned from watching their fellows. Yerkes also observed that each generation became more tractable as experimental animals, certain of the activities required by the experiments being passed on from ape to ape "by imitative process" and from one generation to the next "by social tradition." These effects mentioned by Yerkes are the result of constant contact with human beings, and with an environment arranged by human beings. If the entire colony were returned to its native habitat, in a short time probably few, if any, traces of human influence would remain; a new generation would not profit from the older generation's contact with civilization. This is particularly so, as drinking fountains, hammers, keys, and the like are not usually found in the ape's native environment. It is clear that such transmission as may occur among trained chimpanzees is not the result of language communication as humans know it. "When Jane Goodall saw chimpanzees fishing for termites and sopping up water with crushed leaves, her mentor, Louis Leakey, remarked that we're either going to have to redefine tools, or redefine man" (Brownlee, 1985, p. 93).

The Absence of Language Among Lower Animals

Apes never learn to speak like human beings. Little success has been achieved in training them to imitate the sounds of human speech, although many investigators have tried. Relevant to this point are the reports of two experiments in which young chimpanzees were reared for a time in the homes of psychologists (Hayes, 1951; Kellogg & Kellogg, 1933). The Kelloggs (1933) report that they were entirely unable to train their chimpanzee, Gua, to utter any words or to imitate human speech. The Hayeses (1951), on the other hand, report that their animal, Vicki, acquired a vocabulary of three words—"mama," "papa," and "cup." From a demonstration witnessed by the authors, it was clear that the imitation was so crude that the sounds could hardly be identified, and could be called words only by a stretch of the imagination. It was also clear that Vicki used them in a mechanical and uncomprehending manner.

Psychologists continue to be preoccupied with the attempt to teach language to apes. Allen and Beatrice Gardner (1969) have taught a chimpanzee to communicate in American Sign Language, while Ann and David Premack have taught one of their chimpanzees, Sarah, a vocabulary of about 130 "words" which consisted of brightly colored plastic shapes that could be readily placed in various combinations (sentences?) on a magnetized language board (Premack & Premack, 1972). These recent endeavors do not seem to have created a new situation or discredited the idea that humans are the only animals capable of learning a language. They have, however, once more demonstrated the remarkable capabilities of one of our closest and most captivating primate relatives.

The Premacks trained Sarah by rewarding her when she chose the right plastic "symbols" in a given context. For example, in order to obtain and eat a banana, she was required to put the plastic "word" for banana on the language board. In later phases of her learning, the plastic symbols were combined to form "sentences," as for example, "Give apple Sarah." When Sarah did this correctly she was given a piece of apple. Sarah was also taught the names of various trainers who wore their plastic symbol-names on string necklaces. On one occasion when she put on the board, "Give apple Gussie," the trainer promptly gave the apple to another chimp named Gussie—and Sarah never again made the same mistake. In the more advanced phases of her training, Sarah became able, as the Premacks said, to make complex assertions and judgments such as the following: "Sarah take apple, if/then Mary give chocolate Sarah," "Red color apple," and "Red no color of banana." She was able to match the plastic word for apple with a real apple, and the plastic name for Mary (a trainer) with a picture of Mary.

The authors cautiously conclude (1972, p. 99) that "Sarah had managed to learn a code, a simple language that nevertheless included some of the characteristic features of natural language." They warn against asking of Sarah what one would require of an adult, but argue that Sarah holds her own in language ability when compared with a two-year-old child. The Premacks are able to say that Sarah has a language because their definition of language is too broad; they use it to refer to systems of communication in general, viewing human languages as particular "albeit, remarkably refined forms of language" (1972, p. 92). *They have thus conferred language upon chimpanzees by the very nature of their definition.*

Closer consideration of the highly interesting accomplishments of Sarah casts doubt even on the Premack comparison of Sarah with an ordinary two-year-old child. For example, children even at this early age use their language to talk with each other, while Sarah talked only with human beings. In contrast to how children acquire vocabularies, Sarah acquired her vocabulary exclusively or mainly in a laborious learning process, motivated by material rewards. While the Premacks say that Sarah mastered about 130 words, they also observe that her level of reliability was about 75 percent to 80 percent. This raises the question as to how well humans, even two-year-olds, would be able to communicate if, in the process, they said approximately the opposite of what they intended to about 20 to 25 percent of the time. One may further wonder how much a colony of chimps in their natural habitat, all trained to Sarah's level and equipped with plastic words and language boards, would be likely to use this language.

In general, as we have indicated, it seems improbable that the work of the Premacks and Gardners will result in any need to revise the belief that humans are the only animals capable of learning a language. The significance of this work is more likely to be felt in other areas, such as those that attempt to specify the basic points of difference that exist between human language and the lower-order system of communication. Anthropologist G. W. Hewes has recently reviewed this material in connection with a proposal he made concerning the possible origin of human language (1973). In the process of doing so, however, it seems clear that Hewes is not overly impressed with the idea that at least two chimpanzees in the world now have language, although they cannot talk to each other, since each uses a different one. While Sarah uses plastic symbols, the Gardners' chimp Washoe was trained to use the American Sign Language. We are more impressed by the ingenuity and creativity of the teachers than by that of their pupils.

Apes emit characteristic sounds of their own, but these do not constitute language in a genuine sense. This may easily be shown by considering three features of so-called ape language. First, the sounds are unlearned. This point has been proven conclusively by Boutan (1913), who raised an ape wholly isolated from other apes from birth until its fifth year. It uttered the same cries as those made by other apes. Second, the sounds emitted by apes, as various investigators have noted, are "subjective": that is, they merely express emotions; they do not designate or describe objects. In the words of one writer (Köhler, 1926, p. 85), "Chimpanzees can exclaim *kha* or *nga* over their food just as humans delightedly cry *yum-yum,* but they cannot say *banana, today.*" Their cries of enthusiasm are responses to an immediate situation: such cries "cannot be used between meals to talk over the merits of the feast." And third, ape sounds do not constitute a system of symbols. Yerkes has summarized this lack of system (Yerkes & Yerkes, 1945, p. 90):

Certainly chimpanzees communicate effectively with one another by sounds, gestures, facial and bodily expression, postures, and visible attitudes which function as meaningful signs. Symbols probably are rare and play a subordinate, if significant, role in their linguistic expression. Therefore, the composite language of the chimpanzee differs greatly from our own. They, for example, have no system, or even assemblage, of sounds which may properly be termed speech, and nothing remotely like a written language.

The sounds emitted by apes, or by any other animal clearly do not constitute systematized animal languages similar to human languages. Neither may one refer to animal sounds as words, for if one does, one is forced to recognize that human children also communicate their needs to one another and to their elders by means of cries—cries as natural for them as are chimpanzee cries to the chimpanzee. One would thus be led to say that children have language before they learn a language, and that they speak words immediately after birth. It is more in accord with accepted usage to restrict the term "language" to such conventionalized systems of sounds or words as those designated as English, French, German, Spanish, and other languages. All such systems have to be learned, and they vary by communities rather than by species.

Biologist J. Bierens de Haan has clearly and conclusively summarized the arguments against the possible existence of unknown animal languages. He notes, first of all, that human language has six characteristics (1919, p. 249):

... The sounds used in it are *vocal, articulate,* and have some *conventional meaning,* they *indicate something,* are uttered with the *intention* of communicating something to somebody else, and are *joined* together to form new combinations, so that phrases of various and different content are formed (italics in original).

On the relationship between primate sounds and objects, Cheney (1984, p. 58) reports:

Playback experiments of both the predator alarm calls of veret monkeys and the grunts used by verets during social interactions have indicated that nonhuman primate vocalization may effectively function to designate objects or events in the external world. . . . At present, our investigations of monkey vocalization are limited, in the sense that they can examine only the responses that calls evoke in listeners, and not the vocalizers' psychological or affective states. . . . However, whenever an organism communicates "about" objects external to itself, it effectively classifies objects in its environment, and in so doing reveals some of the cognitive processes that underlie its signals.

In her research, Cheney (1984, p. 58) investigates "the manner in which veret monkeys perceive and classify objects and events in the external world." She uses data on alarm calls and other vocalizations to argue that classifications made by verets both of one another and of other objects are complex and hierarchical, in many respects resembling the multilevel taxonomies created by humans to describe their own social organizations.

Harré and Reynolds (1984, p. 8) write, "The young veret gives a generalized alarm call to a variety of birds, later coming to restrict them to predatory birds only." Cheney suggests that the participation of the mother in cases where there really is a predator may be important in refining the call. We know that in humans, the broad categories of childhood are refined by learning and experience into the finer discriminations of adulthood.

Harré and Reynolds (1984, p. 8) state:

Many theorists of psychology would hold that there is a strict relation between the capacity to use concepts for thought and the acquisition of language, the latter conceived as an abstract and arbitrary system of signs. . . . In this context the issue of whether "signing" chimpanzees "have language" assumes great importance. If they have, there is at least a necessary condition satisfied for their having conceptual (intentions) thought ways. It seems that the question of whether some non-human primates "have language" does not admit a simple or clear cut answer. It looks now as though even the smartest "signing" chimpanzee lacks syntactical capacity, but does have semantical capacity of quite a high order.

Primate pseudo-language

Bierens de Haan (1929, p. 249) reasons that animals possess at best "pseudo-languages," since human language is of a decisively different order. We may summarize the evidence he offers for this judgment and invite the reader to compare this analysis with that of linguist Hockett presented in the next chapter:

1. *Vocal.* The great majority of animals—including most of the vertebrates—are mute.
2. *Articulate.* Syllables are joined together. This is impossible when sounds are produced by organs other than the mouth. Among the higher animals that possess voices, there is generally no joining together of syllables. Humans combine syllables into words.
3. *Conventional meaning.* With few exceptions, there is no direct relation between meaning and the nature of the sound. Even among the higher animals, sounds are innate and typical of the whole species.
4. *Indication.* With the aid of conventional meaning it becomes possible to indicate something—an object, situation, and so forth. Among the animals, sounds do not name objects or situations, but express "sentiments" and "emotions."
5. *Intention.* Animal sounds are generally uttered without reference to other beings. Although not made with intent to influence others, these sounds may be responded to by other animals.
6. *Joined together to form new combinations.* Combining words into phrases does not occur among animals; only humans do this.

We do not assert that there is no communication among the infrahuman species; quite the contrary. It is obvious even to the superficial observer that there is such communication. If communication is erroneously equated with language, then it is necessary to attribute language behavior to many lower species. But equating communication with language does violence to the usual meaning attached to these words and neglects the fact that there are many forms, or levels, of communication and that language is only one of these. If it is contended that lower animals have language like that of humans, it becomes necessary to explain the absence of behavioral effects of this fact upon them as

compared to the many profound effects of language on human behavior.

Just as there is no doubt of the existence of communication among the lower animals, there is also no doubt that humans are the only animals capable of language. We shall discuss the nature of language behavior in Chapter 3, but we may anticipate our discussion of it here by noting briefly that conversation is the fundamental form of linguistic intercommunication. Any intelligent person, given the proper training, can learn to converse with any other person on earth. However, one cannot converse with lower animals.

Consider the comments of Seyfarth (1984, p. 54), who with Cheney has studied primate communication systems in veret monkeys in their natural habitat in Africa. Seyfarth recorded an individual monkey's grunts such as the "grunt to a dominant" or the "grunt to another group" and then played these back to monkeys in the wild through a concealed speaker. The monkeys' responses to these calls were filmed. Seyfarth concludes (1984, p. 54):

Because veret monkey grunts transmit quite specific information, and because in some cases they clearly relate to external events, it is tempting to compare them with human words, where individuals often have a mental representation of some object or event they wish to communicate. Clearly, however, such a comparison is premature, since our experiments can only measure the responses evoked by grunts, and not what is going on in the mind of the vocalizer. . . . When a monkey hears a grunt, for example, he is immediately informed of many of the fine details of the social behavior going on, even though he may be out of sight of the vocalizer, and even though the vocalizer himself may not be involved. At this point, the monkey's system of communication, whatever its physiological or cognitive basis, begins to take on many of functional properties of a system of communication based on true representation.

Some Consequences of the Lack of Language

The fundamental difference between human and animal behavior, basic to and in a sense determining all other differences, is that humans can talk and animals cannot. Human possession of language symbols and our ability to produce them voluntarily enables us to overcome the time and space limits in which, as we have noted, subhuman organisms are enclosed. Indeed, it may be more accurate to say that the possession of language has enabled human beings to "invent" time and space—past, present, and future.

The differences between humans and the lower animals may be summarized by saying that the lower animals do not have a culture. The term *culture* is generally used to refer to behavior patterns—including beliefs, values, and ideas—that are the shared possession of groups and that are symbolically transmitted. A culture also includes artifacts or products that are handed down in a physical sense, but whose significance resides in their relationships with human behavior. As language is both an integral part of culture and the indispensable vehicle for its transmission, the assertion that animals do not possess it is a far-reaching one for comparative psychology.

Dolphins

Another type of animal that has received considerable publicity in recent years is the dolphin or porpoise (Kellogg, 1961; Lilly, 1961; Brownlee, 1985). The adaptability of this creature has been amply demonstrated, but the rash suggestions that it can talk and that it has a language are obvious examples of the way in which enthusiasm about the accomplishments of a given animal leads people to endow it with human qualities. It has been remarked that while humans may have some success in communicating with dolphins in "dolphin language," dolphins will probably have difficulty communicating with us in human language.

We say this despite the apparent efforts of some scientists to "demonstrate" the ability of dolphins to learn the names of objects and to respond to commands. Brownlee (1985, pp. 85–86), reviewing the evidence on this

matter, suggests that the question is not "so much whether animals think as what they have to do in order to convince scientists that what they're doing is in fact thinking."

Some have suggested that what is really happening with the lower animals is not the learning of language, but the learning of patterns of behavior that produce rewards. In 1973 the psychologist Terrance attempted to teach his own sign language to a young male chimpanzee named Nim Chimp-sky, after the name of the famous linguist Noam Chomsky. He hoped to disprove Chomsky's position that language is a uniquely human facility. After four years he gave up. Nim had learned 128 signs, but most of his sentences consisted of repetitive demands for food or play. Terrance (reported in Brownlee, 1985, p. 87) concluded that chimps do not use signs as words; they learn, instead, behaviors that are rewarded.

Terrance (1984, pp. 179–80) states:

The question of what language is has yet to be answered by linguists, psychologists, psycholinguists, philosophers and other students of human language in a way that captures its many complexities in a simple definition. Agreement has been reached, however, about one basic property of all human languages. That is the ability to create new meanings, each appropriate to a particular context, through the application of grammatical rules. Noam Chomsky and George Miller among others, have convincingly reminded us of the futility of trying to explain a child's ability to create and understand sentences unless one attributes to the child a knowledge of rules that can generate an indeterminately large number of sentences from a finite vocabulary of words. . . a rote learning of a string of words presupposes no knowledge of the meanings of each element and certainly no knowledge of the relationships that exit between the elements.

In his analysis of other chimp-language studies Terrance (1984, p. 196) argues:

Two films made by the Gardners of Washoe's signing, a doctoral dissertation by Lyn Miles . . . , and a recently released film of Koko, the Talking Gorilla, all support the hypothesis that the teacher's coaxing and cueing have played much greater roles in so-called "conversations" with chimpanzees than was previously recognized.

Summary

In this section we have sketched the chronology of human evolution, noting that after a certain point in time, biological and cultural evolution cease to be closely correlated. The enormous acceleration of cultural evolution in recent times is linked with language and especially with the invention of writing. The social and communicative behavior of a number of subhuman species, especially of chimpanzees, is considered in comparison with that of human beings.

The study of subhuman behavior has two general purposes for the social psychologist. First, it provides a picture of response mechanisms and adaptive devices that generally increase in complexity, sensitivity, and variability as one ascends the evolutionary scale to humans. The social insects live in societies based on principles altogether different from those that form the foundations of human groups; and these principles are instructive chiefly in a negative way, showing us what human behavior is not, rather than what it is. The second main purpose in studying subhuman behavior is to bring into sharper focus the differences among organisms of various degrees of complexity. As the organisms develop to more complex and more specialized levels, new behavioral possibilities and properties emerge. These new behavioral possibilities and properties, if they are to be investigated as such, must be conceived of as related to the previous possibilities and properties from which they have evolved. This does not mean, however, that they are to be identified with that from which they have evolved.

With reference to understanding human social behavior, the study of subhuman organisms enables us to form tentative conceptions (Allee, 1931a, 1931b) of similarities (common features) of human and subhuman behavior, and differences (unique elements) that distinguish human behavior from that of other living forms. We must give adequate attention to both of these aspects. Experimental and comparative psychologists frequently stress the similarities and underplay or altogether disregard the differences between humans and other animals; theologians and philosophers, on the other hand, often stress the differences to the point of failing to recognize that humans, after all, are animals themselves.

Social scientists are largely concerned with political, economic, legal, moral, religious, and other specific forms of behavior that are found almost exclusively in human beings living in groups. In other words, they are concerned with analyzing the unique phases of human behavior; therefore it is inevitable that they should seek explanations of this behavior in terms of something that human beings have and that other organisms lack. Such expressions as culture, mores, institutions, traditions, laws, politics, economics, philosophy, religion, science, art, literature, and mathematics all point to unique attributes of human behavior. These differences between humans and apes cannot be logically explained by referring to things that human beings and animals have in common.

Social psychology as the study of the influence of groups on the behavior of individuals is merely a part of the broader comparative study of species, each of which presents its own particular problems, but all of which share certain attributes in the sense that they are all living forms. It is unnecessary to insist either that only the differences be investigated and emphasized or that exclusive attention be focused on the similarities. It is understandable that economics, political science, and sociology, which deal with behavior that is not found outside of human society, should not directly concern themselves with subhuman behavior. As social psychology is a part of comparative psychology, it must concern itself with the behavior of lower animals in order to understand the evolutionary emergence of civilization, culture, reason, and intelligence.

SYMBOLIC ENVIRONMENTS AND COGNITIVE STRUCTURES

Earlier in this chapter we broadly outlined the study of humankind's physical and early cultural evolution and indicated some of the basic differences between humans and lower animals. We will extend the argument by noting that with the acquisition of language and conceptual thought, human reactions to the external social and physical worlds have become increasingly indirect. These reactions are increasingly affected by *ideas* that represent to humans an unknown and unknowable ultimate reality. Language—by enabling humans to be observers of their own actions, objects in their own thought processes—adds new dimensions to the simple and more direct consciousness of lower animals. It also ushers into awareness a private, incommunicable aspect of experience, commonly described as "subjective."

Symbolic Environments

In Chapter 1, we noted that language has several dimensions—including the institutional, the syntactical, the semantic, the cultural, and the interactional—and we argued that signs are fundamental features of language. We now need to introduce some additional terms. The word *symbol* refers to the ability of a sign to stand for something else—for example, the symbolic environment, or the world of symbolism in art. On occasion, we shall use sign and symbol interchangeably. Signs that refer to representations, like the "cross," will be called *icons*. Those signs which point to or measure something else will be called *indexes*. A barometer, for example, is an index of impending weather conditions. With these distinctions in mind we can now discuss symbolic environments.

Humans live in a symbolic environment because (1) they are responding directly to symbols, and (2) their relationships to the external world are indirect and organized by means of symbols. As Cassirer has aptly stated (1944, p. 25):

Man lives in a symbolic universe. . . . (He does not) confront reality immediately; he cannot see it, as it were, face to face. . . . Instead of dealing with things themselves man is in a sense constantly conversing with himself. He has so enveloped himself in linguistic forms . . . that he cannot see or know anything except by the interposition of this artificial medium.

The symbolic environment may be thought of as a substitute environment, but it is important to note that this environment is not a mere reproduction or reflection of the external world. Indeed, some believe that the "real" external world can never be known "for what it is"; what humans know of it, they know by virtue of their particular sensory equipment and their particular, socialized experience of it. The world in which human beings live and act is, in a sense, "constructed" by them in terms of the requirements of human conduct. That humans can invent symbolic structures and are affected by them introduces new dimensions and levels of interaction into the relations of humans to humans, humans to the external world, and humans to themselves.

The two types of relationships with the environment discussed here and shown in the illustration on page 43 can be illustrated by contrasting the relations of primitive and civilized humans to microbes. Primitive humans generally are unaware of the existence of microbes and thus have no symbols with which to designate, describe, and comprehend them. Nevertheless, microbes influence them and may even cause death. We therefore may say that microbes form a part of the nonsymbolic environment of primitive humans but that they are not represented in their symbolic environment. They are not, as Mead (1934) would have said, "social objects."

By contrast, civilized humans are aware of the existence of microbes and are able to formulate elaborate statements about them. Microbes today are represented in our symbolic environment, and this fact is of great significance. To have symbols for microbes means to be conscious of them, to comprehend them; it also means that microbes may be controlled and subordinated to human purposes. That civilized humans are able to make statements about these forms of life, which are invisible to the naked eye, is thus of utmost intellectual and practical importance. We may add that human conceptions of the world are rarely static or unchanging; thus, microbes have become linked by biologists in new and complex ways with each other, with viruses and cells, and with physiological and genetic processes.

Humans also use language to describe themselves, devising terms and concepts for the human body and its parts and finding various means of describing processes that go on within the body. Humans, in short, become objects to themselves; they become conscious of their own thought processes and of consciousness itself. They learn not only to make and be influenced by statements about their physical world; they also learn to formulate verbal propositions about themselves and to be influenced by them. Insofar as humans are aware of their own responses, those responses become part of the human environment too.

The human environment, therefore, does not consist merely of natural and external events and processes; it also includes the symbols by means of which humans name, classify, and form conceptions of things as well as of the world of ideas and values. These symbols are products of group living; they reflect the fact that the members of groups—in the process of intercommunication and adaptation—devise linguistic schemes for classifying, describing, and responding to persons, objects, and events. These schemes form part of the social heritage and are the most significant aspects of the human environment. It is not just a matter of complexity that is involved (as the astronomer's world is more complex than that of most lay star gazers) but quite literally that the world is differently constructed by different groups. *In a sense, most of this text illustrates not only that point, but how those different constructions affect interaction between particular groups of human beings.*

Humans as Actors and Observers

From the foregoing discussion an important point emerges: namely, that humans engage in activity while simultaneously observing their own actions. It is as though human beings, acting out parts on the stage, are also sitting in the audience watching their own performance and evaluating it as it unfolds. Sometimes these two processes interfere with each other, and people tend to switch from one activity to the other. They may become so absorbed in what they are doing that they fail in their observer role and do what they had not intended to do. Or, as observers, they may become so preoccupied in watching their own performance—or that of the others involved in the real-life drama—that they distract themselves in their role as actors and forget their lines or miss their cues.

This aspect of human behavior arises

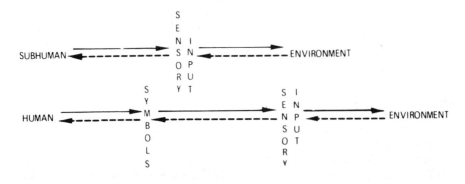

from the fact that humans live largely within a symbolic environment of their own creation. We can describe this in general terms by saying that humans become both subjects and objects; that they become conscious of consciousness; that through their conceptualizations they establish a distance between themselves and their experiences of the real world. This distance, or detachment, enables them to deal conceptually with their own experiences and gives them a new dimension by making them objects within their own thought processes. Presumably, lower animals are incapable of this activity; they may be conscious, but they are not conscious of their own consciousness. They obviously have experiences of a direct sort but are unable to observe their own actions. For such reasons, a distinction is made between the one-dimensional consciousness of lower animals and the two- or more-dimensional humans, which is often called *reflective self-consciousness* or, more simply, *self-reflectiveness* (see Chapter 1).

Subjective and Objective Reality

It has been said that human beings live simultaneously in three kinds of worlds: the real world of things and events; a subjective, private world; and a symbolic or cultural world of shared beliefs, accepted ideas, and *objective* knowledge which are distilled from experience and observation and transmitted via language.

Concerning the first of these worlds—reality as it really is—little need be said here, although philosophers have said much about it. As physical beings we are part of this reality, deny it or not, no matter how imperfectly we understand it. Presumably, this world exists independent of our intellectual grasp of it.

The second world—the private subjective realm—is one in which we are alone. All our experiences have a unique personal reference in the sense that they are ours and no one else's, and that we alone have direct access to and awareness of them. This is true

regardless of whether the experience is artistic, religious, or of any other kind.

The third realm is the cultural world of belief, ideas, knowledge, theories, and logic. It has the appearance of objectivity because—as we shall note more fully in Chapter 4—it is communicated and shared within groups which act toward the presumed real world of objects, people, and events in terms of it. The cultural world actually is created through "a process of consensual validation of experiences" which in their origin are inherently subjective; that is, unique experiences of unique individuals. The connection between "objective knowledge" of the real world and the real world itself is always problematic, as Henri Poincaré, the famous French mathematician and scientist, indicated by posing the question: What would happen if an omniscient being were to appear on earth and go from one scientist to another telling them the final truth about the problems they were investigating? Poincaré's answer was that nothing would happen because the scientists would be unable to comprehend what they were told. Indeed, one might wonder whether the omniscient being would be able to state the absolute truth in any existing language (or be able to stay out of jail or a mental institution long enough to complete the mission).

The term *subjective* is commonly misused to designate events that transpire in the heads or brains of humans and presumably of other animals. These events, however, can no more be called subjective than those that presumably occur in the interior of the sun. Both events occur in a real, material world; those in the human brain are material events that involve a substratum of complex interlocking neural, chemical, and electrical occurrences that use up energy. It is therefore erroneous to call mental processes subjective merely because they are internal and relatively inaccessible to observation, as are those inside the sun.

Clearly, "subjective" means something other than simple inaccessibility. What it actually refers to must be not the material occurrences themselves, but some aspect of how these occurrences are perceived by the organism. Our analysis suggests that the term refers to the communicability of experiences; there are aspects of all experience which escape the communication network and cannot be fully shared with others because they are the peculiarly private property of unique individuals. This aspect of experience can properly be called subjective.

We may, for example, tell a friend that we have a toothache, and because she has had similar experiences, she understands what we are saying. Nevertheless, the toothache remains our own personal experience. This latter aspect is the private, or subjective, part of the experience; it is difficult to describe because it is essentially incommunicable. We know that it is there—"in ourselves"—by introspection and infer that it can also be present in others, but beyond that we can do little else beyond advising other people that they will not understand all of what we are trying to say unless they have had exactly the same experience themselves. For example, how does it feel to die? We suppose there is only one obvious way to find this out for oneself. In matters like this, the languages of poetry and art come closer to communicating than does the precise, didactic language of science.

It is thus meaningless to assert that falling in love is a subjective experience, since there are no other kinds. By the same token, it is equally meaningless to claim that weighing an object is an objective experience. The difference between these two experiences is simply that the latter is more readily transmitted to others than the former. The terms in which both are conceived, perceived, and communicated are intimately related to the symbolic coordinates of the speaker's world. We turn now to this topic.

SOCIAL WORLDS, SYMBOLIC COORDINATES, AND FICTIONS

The idea of a symbolic environment implies that all humans live in what can be termed *social worlds*. These can be thought of as groupings of individuals who are bound together through networks of communication—whether the members are geographically proximate or not—and through the sharing of important symbols. Groups also share common or similar perspectives on reality. For simple societies, as described classically by anthropologists, one might think of the society as equivalent to a single social world whose members have essentially a single organized outlook on reality. But as Shibutani notes (1962, pp. 128–37): "Modern mass societies . . . are made up of a bewildering variety of social worlds. . . . Each . . . is a cultural area, the boundaries of which are set neither by territory nor formal group memberships but by the limits of effective communication." In short, a nation is not the equivalent of a society—there are many societies, many social worlds, within each nation; and people may have membership in international communities (such as the community of biologists or Jehovah's Witnesses) regardless of where they live.

The members of social worlds conceive of reality in terms of certain basic *symbolic coordinates*. To grasp the notion of "symbolic coordinates," consider the early Christians' ideas of reality following from their interpretations of the teachings of Jesus—ideas linked with concepts of God and His son and the implications of those concepts; then compare this view of reality with that of the modern atheist who accepts a strictly materialistic, "scientific" view of the universe; or compare both with the Nazis' conceptions during the 1930s. One philosopher has suggested that perspectives on reality can be represented by quite different metaphors: a prison, battlefield, stage, garden, and so on. Each metaphor has different implications as to how reality is conceptually organized. Each metaphor also has perspectives on what space looks like and what time feels like—indeed what time periods (past, present, future) are most important or how they relate to each other. The basic items concerning all these are what we mean when we refer to the social coordinates of a given social world.

From the individual's standpoint, the symbolic environment that he or she thinks of as "reality" itself seems like an objective "thing." Berger and Luckmann have phrased this in similar terms (1967, pp. 22–23):

I apprehend the reality of everyday life as an ordered reality. Its phenomena are prearranged in patterns that seem to be independent of my apprehension of them and that impose themselves upon the latter. The reality of everyday life appears already objectified, that is, constituted by an order of objects that have been designated *as* objects before my appearance on the scene. The language used in everyday life continuously provides me with the necessary objectifications and posits the order within which these make sense and within which everyday life has meaning for me. . . . In this manner language marks the co-ordinates of my life in society and fills that life with meaningful objects.

Berger and Luckmann add that this reality presents itself to the individual as a world that he or she shares with others. And—a very important point—this "reality" is taken for granted *as* reality. It does not require verification over and beyond its simple presence; it is simply *there*.

This reality, the symbolic coordinates and symbolizations, may be regarded by later generations as mistaken, misguided, or dreadfully immoral. Obviously, the same judgments can be made by contemporaries. Insofar as the members of one social world are concerned with the views and actions of people from other social worlds, they will take corrective action: This can be argumentative, rhetorical, persuasive, or directly coercive, giving rise to fights, imprisonment, or warfare.

Prejudices and Stereotypes

Social scientists and language students have mistakenly referred to the "incorrect" symbols of others as *fictions*. A striking contemporary example is that of commonly held ideas of *race*. Whatever scientists may say about the pitfalls attending the classification of humans by biological characteristics, certain socially important classifications of race still exist. Just as humans classify objects into categories and act toward them on the basis of class membership, they classify other humans into racial groupings and behave toward them on the basis of presumed racial membership. The ways in which one perceives other humans as black or white are as much part of social heritage as the words *Negro*, *black*, and *white*. The same individual may be classified differently in different places on earth or in different social groups in the same place, and behavior toward him or her will vary accordingly.

In the United States some people have held truly nonsensical attitudes about "black blood." Since in America it is customary to regard a person as black if he or she has any "black blood," "mulattoes" are described as "blacks having some white blood"—never as "whites having some black blood." During World War II, "black blood" and "white blood" were sometimes kept in separate blood banks. The idea underlying this practice was that if white people received a transfusion of "black blood" then their skin color might change, or they might have been said to have "black blood" in their veins. It was sometimes supposed that this would affect the individuals or their progeny.

These conceptions are absurd. In the first place, the blood of a pregnant woman does not flow through the vessels of the unborn child; hence, we are not justified in saying that we have our parents' blood in our veins. Moreover, there is no difference between the blood of blacks and whites; all blood types are found in both races. Neither the physical nor mental traits of parents or their future offspring can conceivably be affected by blood transfusion. Popular thinking on these matters is based on certain misconceptions— the scientist would say—about the nature of races, blood, and heredity. These ideas have no biological foundation; indeed, scientific evidence points to the essential biological unity of all human types. Not only are all blood types common to all racial groupings, but the human organism is so uniform throughout the world that for experimental work in physiology and anatomy, the "race" to which the subject belongs does not matter. But as long as the members of some social world regard other persons as belonging to a genuine race, then they will act toward them accordingly.

Another term that is similar to *fictions* (especially racial ones) is *stereotypes*. Sociologists have long and customarily used the term to refer to certain oversimplified, fixed, and usually fallacious conceptions that people hold about other people. Etymologically, the first part of the term is derived from the Greek word *steros,* meaning solid or firm. Historically, it is derived—at least in American technical usage—from a book on public opinion by Walter Lippmann (1922), who used it to refer to "the pictures in our heads." Lippmann asserted that because people approach facts with preestablished classifications, they do not see the facts clearly or in unbiased fashion. "For the most part, we do not first see and then define, we define first and then see." There is stereotyped imagery of races, nationalities, national groups, occupational groups, social classes, and the sexes; but it is in the racial area that stereotypes have most often been studied. It has been found that although the practice is changing, our movies, radio and television programs, and popular literature have rarely portrayed blacks in any role other than that of servant or low-class person—roles that fit the old white stereotype of blacks. Similarly, stereotypes influence the depiction of females in the mass media. Until recently, women have been cast only as wives and mothers in situation comedies and television commercials.

Once formed, the stereotype tends to persist even in the face of contradictory evidence and experience. So long as one classifies certain persons as belonging to a group or race and attributes certain characteristics to the group in general, those who do not have these characteristics are dismissed as exceptions to the norm; and we are told that "exceptions prove the rule." The rule, as we have already seen, is what the group is supposed to be "by nature."

The notion of stereotypes has been useful for the social psychologist in the investigation of intergroup hostility, but it is not really a special and distinct concept. It provides an effective means of calling attention to erroneous and oversimplified concepts that people have about other people. By their very nature, all classifications are selective responses to a complex environment, and thus are necessarily somewhat simplified versions of reality. Stereotypes often are strongly tinged with emotion, but this is also true of many other conceptions. Likewise, as classifications are embedded in systems, many of them resist easy change even when confronted with contradictory evidence.

Some students of language phenomena advocate that such fictions—*all* fictions—should be eliminated from the language, as they refer to nothing real and are socially harmful. "No other animal produces verbal monsters in his head and projects them upon the world outside his head (Chase, 1938, p. 14). Such a proposal, of course, demonstrates a radical misconception of the nature of language and associated forms of symbolization.

Sociologists Kluegel and Smith (1985) and Reskin (1984) have added new dimensions to our understanding of racial and sexual discrimination and segregation in American society. Their findings extend our discussion of the uses to which prejudice and stereotypes are put by members of society. While the civil rights and women's movements have led to *some* improvement in socioeconomic status for women and blacks, the problems that prompted these movements still exist. Many people apparently believe that discrimination against blacks and women ended in the 1970s.

Reskin's research indicates that women currently earn 63¢ on every dollar that men earn; sex segregation accounts for nearly half of this wage gap. Segregation against women operates at three levels: in industry, at the occupational level, and at the departmental level. Many industries still exclude women (i.e., construction). Occupationally, women still occupy positions below men (i.e., clerical versus managerial). At the departmental level—for example, retail sales—women are more likely to be given lower-priced items to sell, with lower commissions.

Kluegel's investigations into inequality in American society reveal that while federal regulations have attempted to eliminate overt racial prejudice, they have not addressed the basic problems of education, training, and equal pay. Still, most whites believe that the socioeconomic status of blacks has vastly improved, and see no need to continue affirmative action programs. Why is this so?

Kluegel offers several reasons. Modern racism is subtle; anti-black feeling in this country is seldom overtly expressed. It takes the form of the belief that blacks shirk traditional white values: hard work, individualism, and delayed gratification. Another belief is that blacks stay in low-paying jobs because they lack the motivation to lift themselves out of poverty. Modern racism holds blacks responsible for their socioeconomic inequality. Some whites believe that those blacks who do succeed do so because of reverse discrimination.

The public remains uninformed concerning the actual pay, work, and living conditions of women and minority members. Prejudices and stereotypes maintain these public fictions concerning the progress women and minorities have made since the civil rights movements of the 1960s and 1970s. These stereotypes and prejudices constitute problems for millions of Americans. The social psychologist who studies prejudice and stereotypes can thus shed light into how our society maintains its structure of inequality. The fictions that structure these beliefs, and the functions that these fictions perform, carry important implications for all of us.

CONCLUSION

The reactions of humans to their surroundings are mediated ones. They are not based on reality, but on ideas of that reality expressed mainly by means of linguistic symbols. Hence the symbolic environment of humans, the names, words, terms, concepts, categories, fictions, stereotypes, prejudices—in short, the symbolic meanings—are social, interactional productions. They are the means by which humans make sense of the world around them. The acquisition of language habits generates the motivation to name, classify, and explain the significant aspects of one's environment.

In this chapter we saw how human biological and cultural evolution have set the boundaries for the development of language. We presented and criticized the sociobiological point of view which attempts to reduce human experience to the level of genes and to universal evolutionary principles. We also discussed the behavior of chimpanzees and indicated how their experiences reflect the absence of language, as we understand language at the human, group level. It should be clear from our discussion that it is impossible for chimps to have prejudices, form stereotypes, or mediate their worlds with the complex structures of meaning that language provides. In the next two chapters we discuss in greater detail language, social structure, and groups.

SUGGESTED READINGS

HARRÉ, ROM, AND VERNON REYNOLDS (EDS.) (1984). *The Meaning of Primate Signals*. Cambridge: Cambridge University Press. A highly informative collection of research studies on the latest findings on primate communication systems.

KOHLER, WOLFGANG (1926). *The Mentality of Apes*. New York: Harcourt Brace Jovanovich. The author's study might be described as one of participant observation, it remains an early classic account of the behavior of chimpanzees.

WILSON, E. O. (1975). *Sociobiology: The New Synthesis*. Cambridge, Mass.: The Belknap Press of Harvard University Press. The controversial source that sparked the recent debate over sociobiology.

CHAPTER THREE
Language: Theoretical Perspectives

The symbolic interactionist perspective demands an immediate and direct focus on various forms of symbolizing activity. Chief among them and central to an understanding of human conduct is *language*.

In this chapter, however, we will consider only one general aspect of language: its nature and the various theoretical perspectives that have been brought to its study. (In Chapter 4 we will take up language's relation to group life, culture, and social structure.) We will consider recent developments in the field of semiotics as they relate to the symbolic interactionist view of language.

SEMIOTICS AND SYMBOLIC INTERACTIONISM

Semiotics, as we noted in Chapter 1 is the science of signs within a society. It is an integral part of social psychology because social psychology is, in part, the study of the social foundations of language. This social aspect of linguistics is called *sociolinguistics* (Grimshaw, 1981), whose aim is the study of language in use in social contexts, and "in how speech (and other language in use) simultaneously influences social interaction and has its 'meaning' constrained by its interactive context" (Grimshaw, 1981, p. 201). Semiotics and sociolinguistics constitute integral parts of the field of social psychology.

We need to give careful meaning to a number of terms. A linguistic *sign,* as we noted in Chapter 1, is a two-sided psychological entity, represented by the terms signifier (sound-image) and signified (concept). *Signification,* we said, is the process of using signs in speech. Perinbanayagam (1985) has given the term "signifying acts" to this process. *Language,* we proposed, is a social institution and a system of values that give meanings to words. *Speech,* in contrast to language, is essentially an individual and interactional production of selection and actualization. Extended speech, in any context, is called *discourse.* Language and speech exist in a dialectical relation to one another; each

achieves its full meaning only in relation to the other (Barthes, 1964/1967, p. 15).

Language can be seen as existing on three planes: First as a structure, form, framework, or institution; second as a norm—that is, as an ideal; and third, as usage. Every social group has its own norm-usage-speech pattern. After Barthes (1964/1967, p. 21), we will use the term *idiolect* to refer to the speech and language of a specific linguistic community or a particular speaker. Others have used the words "argot" and "special languages" to refer to idiolect.

The term *code* refers to how a message, or spoken utterance, is formulated in terms of the syntax of speech, numbers, writing, etc. All messages are coded, wrapped in a framework that allows the speaker and hearer, or writer and reader to comprehend and define what is being communicated. Some codes are formal and logical (i.e., a computer program), while others are based on commonsense frameworks (i.e., where there is smoke, there is fire) (see Manning, 1985, p. 80).

Sign Systems

Within any social group there are a number of different sign systems which extend beyond the language-speech distinction. A sign, then, need not refer just to the *words* of a language; anything that can be represented by a group can be organized into a sign system. Barthes (1964/1967, pp. 25–31) discusses such sign systems as the garment system, where clothes are (1) written about, (2) photographed, and (3) worn. Other sign systems include the food system of a society where there are rules which (1) exclude certain foods from being eaten, (2) specify how certain foods are to be associated, and (3) rituals of use. The menu in any restaurant can be interpreted as a sign system—for example, (1) appetizers; (2) main course items; (3) a la carte items; (4) dessert items; (5) drink items.

Any sign system is organized in terms of a set of rules and a set of oppositions and similarities that are somewhat arbitrarily organized. The automobile system in American society is organized this way. Each American automobile manufacturer distinguishes their model from other models, and models are presented in terms of the status they will confer on the buyer. Freedom in choosing models is severely restricted, that is, only a few different models are available for purchase. The car system turns cars into objects, and the meaning of the object is given in ownership and in the act of driving.

Barthes (1972) has analyzed the worlds of wrestling, films, soap powders and detergents, children's books, ornamental cookery, and striptease performances as sign systems which he calls *mythologies*. Myths are sign systems that are based on everyday phenomena (i.e., advertisements for new soaps). These myths convey a sense of naturalness about our world that masks reality or hides meaning. Myths tend toward proverbs; they attempt to quantify quality (i.e., "our soap" is *this* much better than "their soap"; "Excedrin cures headaches 10 times faster than aspirin"; etc.). Myths are often presented as self-evident truths and present objects in a kind of timeless historical moment.

Myths attempt to rid viewers of prejudice. Consider the following example from Barthes (1957/1972). He is describing an advertisement for margarine in a French magazine:

The episode always begins with a cry of indignation against margarine: "A mousse? Made with margarine? Unthinkable!" "Margarine? your uncle will be furious!" And then our eyes are opened, one's conscience becomes more pliable, and margarine is a delicious food, tasty, digestible, economical, useful in all circumstances. The moral at the end is well known: "Here you are rid of a prejudice which cost you dearly!"

Barthes contends that myths are language systems which convey a particular set of meanings about our contemporary world. He began his analysis of these myths in order to understand how the media, books, art, and common sense present things and experiences with a "naturalness" that dresses up reality and hides the history that exists behind these representations.

The Classification of Signs

We must distinguish signs from other related terms. According to various authors, *sign* can mean the same thing as *symbol, cue, signal, index, icon,* and *allegory* (Barthes, 1964/1967, p. 35). All these terms share a common characteristic: They refer to a relation between two or more things. We cannot distinguish these terms on this ground, and must turn to other considerations. First, does the relation between the two terms (i.e., symbol and thing, sign and thing), imply the mental representation of one of the terms? Second, does the relation imply an analogy between the terms? Third, is the link immediate? Fourth, does the relation imply an existential connection with the user? (That is, does it refer directly to the user?)

Use of these terms varies by author (see Harman, 1986, p. 149 for a comparison of Mead, Peirce, Saussure, Barthes, Baudrillard, and White; and Barthes, 1964/1967, p. 37 for a comparison of Wallon, Peirce, Hegel, Jung, Walton, and Saussure). The controversy centers on the difference between sign and symbol.

Saussure (1959, p. 68) for example, rejected the term *symbol* in his semiotics. He felt it was restrictive because its meanings were never arbitrary. The symbol of justice—a pair of scales—cannot be easily replaced by another symbol, a car, for example. Peirce (1960, vol. 2, p. 135) offered a semiotic which defined sign, the basic concept in his system, as "something which stands to somebody for something in some respect or capacity." Icons, indices, and symbols were different types of signs. Mead (1934) used the term *universe of discourse* to describe how language works in interaction; his significant symbols were gestures that call out consensual meaning in another person. Meltzer (1972, p. 8) suggests that signs are directly linked to immediate situations, while symbols have arbitrary meanings that transcend situations.

MacCannell (1976, p. 102) proposes that a symbol is a sign that lacks a syntactic component, while a sign lacks a semantic component.

Following Barthes (1964/1967, p. 38), we will adopt the following set of meanings for these terms:

1. *Signal:* a term which establishes an immediate, existential relation between two terms, for example, a traffic light and a moving automobile.
2. *Index:* a term that is a measure of something else, for example, a barometer.
3. *Icon:* a figure or image that represents something else (e.g., the cross in Christianity). An icon implies an analogy, the link is indirect to the thing being represented, and it must be existential.
4. *Sign:* a term that is unmotivated and exact; there is no analogy implied. The word ox and the image of ox implies a direct relation which is not existential.
5. *Symbol:* a term that implies a relation that is analogical and indirect ("Christianity 'outruns' the cross") (Barthes, 1964/1967, p. 38).
6. *Learned cues:* a term that carries an immediate and direct relation between two things, for example, the sound of a gong which triggers a dog's salivation. Animals respond to learned cues.
7. *Natural sign:* a term and what it relates occur in the same space-time framework, for example, the sound of a siren and the passing of a fire engine on the street.
8. *Conventional sign:* a term that derives its meaning from social consensus and is arbitrary.
9. *First-order sign:* a sign that operates for lower animals, like a natural sign and a learned cue.
10. *Second-order sign:* a sign applied to visual or auditory data, for example, the word *box* applies to our sense impressions of a box. Second-order signs are like conventional signs.

In this text we shall try to maintain the sign-symbol distinction as much as possible. A sign and a symbol both represent something which stands for something to somebody. A sign refers to relatively unmotivated representations, while symbols are motivated and nonarbitrary. When we speak of the "symbolic environment," we are referencing all the meanings (given in the list on p. 40) which have been applied to language. Similarly, when we discuss the categorical, or language attitude, we are assuming all of these meanings.

Components of Signs

Before turning to the language attitude and human experience, we must note the following features of signs and symbols. First, it is impossible to separate a sign or a symbol from the object it represents. We cannot, for example, think of the object *automobile* without immediately giving that object a set of meanings (new, old, American) that are contained in the sign we attach to the object. Signs have invaded the objects they represent (Baudrillard, 1972/1981). When we attempt to unravel how signs give meanings to objects, we must ask how signs have come to be connected within any sign system. For example, we might ask how it is that Cadillac automobiles have come to carry such prestige and status in American society. The sign "Cadillac" immediately confers status on a person who owns a car so labelled, just as the signs "BMW," "Audi," and "Jaguar" do for other individuals.

Second, the objects upon which signs and symbols are conferred are cultural in nature. Cultural objects are organized in terms of four overlapping logics, or meaning systems. Every object (car, table, TV, stereo) has (1) a use value, (2) a market value (i.e., how much it costs), (3) value as a gift, and (4) value as a status or prestige marker. Objects that are signified can thus have meanings as instruments, commodities, gifts, and prestige markers.

Third, we live in an age of simulation. Baudrillard (1983, p. 146) calls this the age of the hyperreal, in which "the very definition of the real becomes: *that of which it is possible to give an equivalent reproduction*" (italics in original). Disneyland is a perfect example of this. In such settings, one finds a perfect model of simulation: the worlds of Pirates, the Frontier, the Future, and so on. Each of these worlds is presented in perfect simulations or representation of the real thing—but they are *not* the real thing. We live in an age where objects and meanings are mass-produced. We find, as symbolic interactionist Harvey Farberman has argued (1980, p. 18), that

The subject matter that now confronts us supercedes symbolic interaction; rather it is the process surrounding the autonomization of signs; signs that stand for—and refer to—nothing but themselves.

The commodity that is now bought, sold, and signified within our language and sign systems is experience. How that experience is lived and given meaning is the subject matter of the symbolic interactionist and the semiotician.

THE CATEGORICAL, OR LANGUAGE, ATTITUDE

We organize or adjust our behavior toward things and persons by means of symbols, and these symbols come to embody a plan of action. "A category . . . constitutes a point of view, a schedule, a program, a heading or caption, an orientation" (Dewey, 1938, p. 237). Thus if one hunter shouts to another, "A duck!" the second hunter immediately looks into the sky and makes the appropriate preparations for shooting at a bird on the wing. If the first hunter shouts, "Rabbit!" his partner responds in a different manner. Language symbols do not merely stand for something else—they also indicate the significance of things for human behavior, and they organize behavior toward the thing symbolized.

Some writers have gone further, pointing to a general attitude toward the world that is implicit in language use and therefore common to all those who use language. They have called this general attitude the *categorical attitude*. In its simplest terms it can be described as the realization that (1) things can be named and talked about; (2) events and objects may be grouped or classified; and (3) by naming and classifying the features of our environment, new modes of behavior—as well as new possibilities of manipulating that environment—are brought into existence.

Children first demonstrate this attitude when they learn that everything has a name; they soon exasperate their parents by persistent questions: "What's this?" "What's that?" At first they are satisfied with mere names, as they identify the name with the things named; they have acquired an initial appreciation of the importance of language symbols. Later, when they start to ask "Why?" children exhibit a second, more mature phase of the categorical attitude.

We can illustrate the adult categorical attitude by giving an analogy. Let us suppose that a boy who has lived all his life in an isolated rural section of Africa is suddenly placed in the middle of Johannesburg. He sees large numbers of people hurrying past, hears a chaotic jumble of sounds, and sees a bewildering array of buildings, billboards, neon signs, automobiles, and other objects. The people he encounters respond to him in ways that utterly confuse him. He does not know what to do or where to go. To him, the city is merely an immense buzzing confusion.

We can compare this boy's view of Johannesburg with the view of the world that a man without language would have. The longer one lives in a large city, one grows accustomed to it; "things" gradually become classified or categorized. Most of the sounds that assail the ear are disregarded as irrelevant, simply forming part of the roar of the city. The countless motor vehicles are ignored; they are hazards that one must consider in crossing a street. The newcomer is astounded by the skyscrapers, but soon grows used to them and thereafter may scarcely look at them. The attitude of a city dweller compares with the attitude that humans acquire toward the world in general through their use of language symbols: Things have been organized into systems or categories in terms of their significance for one's behavior.

Consider Mark Twain's comments on "Two Ways of Seeing a River" (1897/1976, p. 41):

Now when I had mastered the language of this water and had come to know every trifling feature that bordered the great river as familiarly as I knew the letter of the alphabet, I had made a valuable acquisition. But I had lost something, too. I had lost something which could never be restored to me while I lived. All the grace, the beauty, the poetry, had gone out of the majestic river!

The terms "concepts" and "categories" will be used almost synonymously here, although they have different connotations that should be kept in mind. *Concept* has a broader meaning which includes "categories" as a special kind of concept. To have a concept of something means to be able to picture it, to describe or represent it to oneself or another, or to grasp it intellectually. A concept is a way of thinking about something—therefore it is also usually a way of talking about it; conceptual thought is communicable thought. Concepts of classes or types are called *categories*. Through the use of such categories of classification, we are able to group things together and to distinguish one type of thing from another and, ultimately, to see the world as orderly. Indeed, without categories one could not think in a sophisticated human sense. The expression "categories of thought" refers to basic concepts (such as space, time, substance, and motion) that are regarded as fundamental in human reasoning about the material world.

We have indicated that the categorical attitude impels human beings to group things into classes. By categorizing or conceptualizing our experiences we are able to analyze them and respond selectively to some aspects of experience while ignoring others. By using of categories and concepts we are able

to picture the world as relatively stable, predictable, and orderly, and to find unity in its limitless diversity.

An example indicates the connection between concepts and the language attitude. There is a certain animal that we call a "cow." When we use the word "cow," we refer to all the cows in the world and also, in a sense, to all the cows that have ever existed or ever will exist. But no two cows are ever exactly alike; they vary greatly in size, color, and disposition. Nevertheless, we lump all cows together, disregarding their differences. In this way we identify them, thus indicating to ourselves and others their significance for human beings. By means of the concept "cow," we have created unity out of diversity and multiplicity. There are millions of cows, but one single concept refers to all of them.

Still another implication of the categorical attitude then follows. When we see objects, we see them not only as concrete entities, but also as representatives of the classes to which they belong. Every time we see and recognize an animal as a "cow" we bring into the picture, in an implicit or indirect way, all the other cows in the world that we cannot see and have never seen. For these reasons, language concepts are called "universals."

One should not suppose that any given object can be classified in only one way. It can be placed in a number of different categories according to the way in which it is being viewed or used. Thus, it may be classified in a series of classes on an ascending scale of abstractness so that each is more inclusive than those preceding it and less inclusive than those following it. The more abstract the classification, the fewer and more general are the criteria of classification.

According to Alfred Schutz, classification is a process of typification and the sign system of language is the "typifying medium par excellence" (1964, p. 96). Typification is based on a generalized knowledge that categorizes objects or events, into like groups. Each object, although recognized as unique, is classified as similar to other objects. This typification process provides people with a frame of reference from which to deal with the object. A person does not need to fully understand the unique differences surrounding each object or event; it is sufficient to recognize the general type and act toward it on the basis of previous experience.

Meaning, for Schutz, can be attributed to a sign insofar as both the person using the sign and the person interpreting it can rely on similar past experiences in understanding what the sign represents. This sharing of meanings for signs leads to reciprocal perspectives between people. Language, then, allows us to classify similar objects within the same category and develop recipes for interaction that enable us to manage our social worlds (Stone, 1982, p. 101; Schutz & Luckmann, 1973, p. 146).

Conversely, the more concrete the classification, the more numerous and specific are the criteria. For example, a particular cow may be classified on an ascending scale of abstractness as follows: Farmer Jones's cow, cow, mammal, animal, living form, material object. Cows can also be classed as four-legged creatures, objects weighing over 100 pounds, edible animals, economic assets, sources of milk, livestock, and so on. Each classification carries its own connotation of point of view and potential use. None of them is "natural," or inherent in the nature of the world, although some are obviously more effective than others for certain purposes.

To complicate matters further, a cow can also be seen as a composite—not unitary—object. To a butcher, it is made up of sirloin, porterhouse, T-bone, and other cuts of meat. A biochemist, a physiologist, and an anatomist would each describe and classify the cow's components in wholly different ways. Farmer Jones himself might well think of his cow as something compounded mainly of hay, corn, grass, water, and a little salt.

Dale, discussing the child's growing understanding of the concept of "dog," has made much the same series of points that we have in discussing cows (Dale, 1954, p. 31):

One of the child's earliest learnings is the name for the shaggy thing that barks. It is called *Rover*. Next he learns that *Rover* is like *Sport* and *Shep*, and finally that things that look and act like them are called *dogs*. Once he has the *dog* classification, he may move in either or both of two directions in further classification. He may learn that there are terriers, St. Bernards, shepherds, and poodles; and then subdivide terriers into wire-haired, rat, Boston, and so forth. He can also go in the direction of more general classification—a dog is a quadruped, an animal, a vertebrate, or a mammal. If he continues, he may arrive at classifications used by the zoologist, involving abstractions that are extensive, precise, and increasingly complex. There are, of course, a variety of other paths that criss-cross the two chief directions . . . indicated, in the course of which his concept of *dog* grows richer.

That humans have concepts and categories with which to classify, subclassify, and cross-classify the objects of their environments is thus greatly important. Our concepts and categories give us a flexible point of view and a multiplicity of perspectives, enabling us to see connections among things that otherwise would be impossible; they also enable us to think of things in terms of their constituent parts rather than as undifferentiated wholes. They are therefore indispensable tools in any analytical procedure. This implies that concepts alter our behavior by making it more discriminatory, selective, and flexible (that is, more intelligent).

Some students of human behavior object to the implication of the term "meaning," which is often thought of as a metaphysical essence residing in symbols, a person's brain, or objects themselves. In this book, we use *meaning* in a behavioral sense. *The meaning of an object or a word is determined by the responses that are made to it: That is, meaning is a relationship and not an essence.*

It is easy to fall into the habit of locating a word's meaning in the word itself. But, as noted previously, meanings arise out of group activities, and they come to stand for relationships between actors and objects.

Our position has been stated clearly by Lee (1954, p. 74), who says that language

. . . is not a system of names for passively sensed objects and relations already existing in the outer world; but neither does it fit experience into predetermined molds. It is a creative process in which the individual has an agentive function; it is part of a field which contains, in addition, the world of physical reality, the sensing and thinking individual, and the experienced reality. In this way each word, each grammatical formation, is not an empty label to be applied; it has meaning, not because meaning has been arbitrarily assigned to it, but because it contains the meaning of the concrete situation in which it participates and has participated, and which it has helped create.

Thus, a concept implies a unitary mode of action; it enables people to act the same way toward a variety of objects. There are many types of foods, for example, but once a substance has been identified as belonging to the food category, a common mode of behavior toward it is established. Thus, every class concept is also a generalization, as it "generalizes" behavior toward everything included within its boundaries. The invention of generalizations never ends; as long as group activity and experiences continue, members of the group will discover and transmit new meanings to one another.

Symbols, or conventional signs carrying meanings upon which there is consensus, are by their nature open to manipulation. *Signs* operate upon signs as in algebra, mathematics, or in argument. Concepts breed new concepts as they are manipulated in handling problem situations. In group action, differences of opinion and position that are expressed in conversation and debate produce new perspectives and meanings.

Symbols enable us to escape the narrow confines of the immediate natural world and participate in the artistic, religious, moral, and scientific worlds created by our contemporaries and ancestors (Brown, 1958, p. 41):

Without symbolism the life of man would be . . . confined within the limits of his biological needs and his practical interests; it could find no access to the "ideal" world which is opened to him from different sides by religion, art, philosophy, science.

THE NATURE OF LANGUAGE: SIGNS AND SYMBOLS

Classifying and analyzing symbols are exceedingly complex, controversial tasks. Generally acceptable concepts and a stable working vocabulary have not yet been achieved, although various attempts have been made to establish them. Recognizing the difficulty of the problem and the possibility for confusion, we will present a greatly simplified account and confine ourselves to only a few fundamental distinctions.

All living creatures learn to respond to environmental cues. Inevitably, some stimuli come to stand for other stimuli. "The sound of a gong or a whistle, itself entirely unrelated to the process of eating, causes a dog to expect food, if in past expeience this sound has always preceded dinner; it is a sign . . . of his food" (Langer, 1948, p. 23). The dog also learns to respond to visual cues (a stick), movements (raising a hand), odors (that of a cat), and so on. Psychologists call such learning of cues "conditioning," and in the laboratory they have conditioned many animals to respond to "substitute stimuli." The world of any animal (human or subhuman) is full of such cues, and behavior is largely accounted for in terms of responses to them. Hereafter we shall refer to *learned cues* as "signs."

Sign behavior runs the gamut from the simple to the complex; it ranges from the most elementary forms of conditioning to the most complex verbal behavior. A simple sign response can be produced in an animal by repeatedly sounding a buzzer and always feeding him immediately after. This situation can be made more complex in various ways—such as by delaying the reward, introducing the factor of punishment, giving the animal multiple-choice problems, or requiring him to respond to two simultaneous signs. Thus an animal can be taught to obtain food by pressing a lever; later he can be taught that pressing the lever will yield the usual reward only when a green light is on and not when a red light is on. Experimental psychologists who study the conditioning processes in animals can investigate only the nonverbal sector of the sign range because there is no verbal sign behavior among subhuman animals.

All psychological behavior probably involves sign behavior at some level. Perhaps more correctly, psychological behavior is sign behavior. Let us consider a simple psychological act—the perception of a box. If we ask a physiological psychologist to describe what happens when the box is perceived, she will begin by noting that light reflected from the box reaches the eyes. From that point on, the account will be concerned entirely with descriptions of how the light impinges on the retina of the eye, how the retina is connected with the central nervous system, and how impulses pass through the nerves. The act of seeing is described as occurring entirely inside us. In short, the process of seeing is a representational or sign process in which the things that occur within us function as signs of the real box. However, this account does not explain why we see the box outside of us, or why we see it as a box and not as an image of our retina or as something in our heads.

Human beings display a tremendous range of sign behavior, from the simple thought processes of the mentally retarded to the complex thinking of the genius. Almost any object, act, occurrence, or quality can function as a sign of something else. The red glow of wood indicates that it is hot; a gesture may reveal anger; a cross is a symbol of religious sentiment; a falling barometer forecasts a change of weather, and so on, endlessly. Words are our most versatile signs, for by means of them we can talk of anything, whether or not it is before us, and whether it is in the past, future, or only in our imagination.

From such examples we can see that signs are related to the thing signified in a variety of ways. The relationship of the falling barometer to the impending weather change is different from the relationship of the cross to the sentiment to which it refers, and both of these differ from the relationship between words and their meanings. Signs of the type represented by the cross have been called *icons;* those represented by things like the barometer, *indexes.* Note that what is signified may be even more varied in nature than signs; besides referring to all kinds of real acts, events, and objects, signs can also indicate nonexistent things that can only be imagined, and they can also indicate other signs.

The Second Signaling System

To further complicate things, signs may be classified as *conventional* or *natural,* and in other ways as well. A *natural sign* is a movement, sound, smell, gesture, or any other stimulus that is perceived to be connected with something else. The natural sign and what it indicates occur together in the same space-time framework, and both are thus parts of a concrete situation. For example, the dog that follows the rabbit's trail connects the scent with the actual rabbit because he has learned that the two go together. By contrast, the *conventional sign* derives its meaning from social consensus and is "movable," or arbitrary, in the sense that different signs (for example, in different languages) can mean the same thing, and that the sign (for example, a word) may be used in situations in which the object referred to is not present. Conventional signs relate to social groups or language communities in which the same signs are interpreted in the same ways by a number of persons.

Natural signs are not "natural" in the sense that they occur only in nature; they also can be human artifacts such as the psychologist setting up a sequence of buzzes (food in a dog's experience), or the lines in a spectrum being taken as evidence of the presence of certain elements. Similarly, the click of a Geiger counter is a natural sign of the passage of an electron. Symbolic analysis enables humans to notice and respond to much more subtle cues than the natural signs which the lower animals are able to master.

Another way of expressing the ideas developed in the preceding paragraphs is that signs may also represent other signs; for example, when we use the word *box* to refer to the visual data relayed to our central nervous system when confronted with a boxlike object. For lower animals, these sensory experiences are natural signs of an external but unnamed object. When we call the object a box, this word functions as a *second-order sign* to designate the sensory experiences which in their turn are *first-order*, or direct, signs of the actual boxlike object before our eyes. An essential difference between natural signs and conventional signs is that the latter are always at least second-order signs, which are related only indirectly to physical reality through the mediation of *lower-order* signs (that is, sensory experiences or natural signs). This idea was expressed succinctly by Pavlov, who called the simple sensory cues the *first signaling system,* and language and speech the *second signaling system.*

While signs function in place of the objects they represent, keep in mind that the word *box* is not the box itself, and that the light reflected from the box (which enables us to see it) is also not the box itself. When we see the box, we respond to the light waves that it reflects; when we name it, we respond to the sound waves that constitute the spoken word. All organisms respond to the external world not as it really is, but in accordance with the information they have about it. They respond to signs that *represent* external objects. While the organism's information may be adequate for its specific behavioral needs, it is always highly schematic, incomplete, and inaccurate when judged by the standards of, for example, the physicist, who does not claim to tell us what the world is actually like but only tries to indicate how it

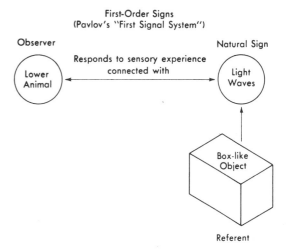

An animal is enabled to act with reference to the object it sees.

can be represented or conceived (Morris, 1946, pp. 3–5).

In the accompanying figure, the fact that there are no arrows linking the box directly with the observer indicates that, in a profound sense, the observer never can have any direct communication with a box as it really is, whatever that may mean. All his contacts with it are indirect, mediated, and shaped by the nature of the sense organs and the sensory input from it, be it visual or tactile. Lower animals with different kinds of eyes, for example, may see objects without color or in simplified color schemes, while others attend primarily to movement and evidently perceive stationary objects only vaguely.

Determining the precise effects of symbolic behavior, and the differences between human and animal behavior, is thus the study of the interrelationships of different levels or systems of sign behavior. One basic consequence of the existence of second-order signs such as words is that they make sensory experience a subject of discourse and an object of reflective thought and analysis, thus establishing the behavioral foundation for all the higher cortical functions in humans. Being human social inventions, they are basic to human society.

As Soviet psychologist Luria (1976, p. 9) has observed:

Language, which mediates human perception, results in extremely complex operations: the analysis and synthesis of incoming information, the perceptual ordering of the world, and the encoding of impressions into systems. Thus words—the basic linguistic units—carry not only meaning but also the fundamental units of consciousness reflecting the external world.

We shall return to this point about consciousness when we discuss the relationship between thought and language.

In this book we designate all conventional signs by the term *symbols,* recognizing that the characteristic forms of human symbolic activity have to do with language or are derived from it. Three important characteristics that distinguish language symbols from other kinds of signs are briefly summarized:

1. They constitute symbol systems, so that the meaning of any single symbol cannot be grasped in isolation but must always be understood within the system. For example: "Wife" is intelligible only in terms of a wider linkage of symbols like "husband," "marriage," and the like.

2. Language symbols are inherently social in character and meaning. They evoke from the person who produces or uses them the same or similar responses as those elicited from the person to whom they are directed. If communication is faulty or if the speaker talks past the listener, the words do not function as symbols.

3. They can be produced voluntarily even when the external events or objects to which they refer are absent or nonexistent. We can thus say that although people carry their symbolic systems around with them, the fact that one makes assertions about an object does not prove that the object is present or that it even exists.

However, we should not think of language merely as a system of words, a combination of phonemes, or the contents of a dictionary. Language is, first of all, a form of behavior. It is not merely a system of symbols, but the activity of using and interpreting symbols. Speech is often said to be the most primitive form of language behavior, but speech is meaningless unless it is addressed to an understanding listener. Hence,

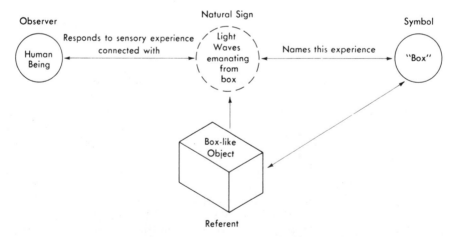

Second-Order Signs
(Pavlov's Second Signal System)

A human being is enabled to act toward, use, remember, imagine, and conceptualize boxes and to reason, talk, and plan about them with other human beings.

conversation is the essential and original form of language; language behavior not only originates in cooperative social action, but it *is* such action. This is why parrots are not given credit for language behavior, even when they produce words.

Viewed in this manner, language becomes at once more significant and complicated. The act of listening and comprehending, for example, does not itself involve an act of speaking, but only appropriate response to the other's verbalizations. The response evoked by the other's utterances may be a bodily act or it may be a covert or internal response, perhaps leading to a reversal of roles in which the listener becomes the speaker and vice versa.

Conventional signs or symbols are not necessarily linguistic, as a brief reference to such cultural items as flags, rings, pins, uniforms, monuments, and music makes clear. However, all nonlinguistic symbols of this sort—as well as all ceremony and ritual—have meanings based on group consensus and are deposits of collective experience; hence they fall into the general category of conventional signs. If we return to the triadic relationships of observer, sign, and thing signified, the added element appearing in conventional signs is this: Instead of a single observer, we have a group that interprets the sign in the same way and gives it its meaning. For this reason, conventional signs, unlike natural signs, always involve a group reference and communicability.

We should not assume that humans operate exclusively on the level of linguistic symbols although that is their most characteristic mode of behavior, or that this symbolic behavior is itself a single, unified process: It falls into many different types which in turn represent a scale graded from most simple to most complex. The use of proper names is a simple symbolic process, as the person's name refers only to a single object and can be fairly adequately defined by pointing. Using a class name like "human being" is more complex, because the name refers to many objects and involves differentiation between "human" and "non-human." The use of terms like "tautology," "contradiction," "truth," "generalization," and "abstraction" is even more complicated, because these symbols refer to other symbols and to the way in which they are interrelated. The manipulations of abstract orders of symbols by mathematicians, logicians, philosophers, and other scholars are among the most complex kinds of symbolic behavior.

Analyzing language from the viewpoint of modern linguistics, Charles F. Hockett (1965, p. 574) has enumerated key properties of language as follows: (1) *duality*, the combination of a relatively small number of basic sounds—meaningless in themselves—in a relatively large number of meaningful words (for example, "tack," "cat," and "act," which are composed of three sounds in different combinations); (2) *productivity*, referring to the fact that words can be combined in completely new ways to say something that has never been said before and can nevertheless be understood; (3) *arbitrariness* of linkage between symbol and what is signified, a feature that delimits what can be talked about; (4) *interchangeability*, which refers to the ability of speakers of a language to reproduce any linguistic message they can understand, and which is closely associated with the fact that speakers hear what they themselves say; (5) *specialization*, the sharp functional distinctions between words even poorly pronounced—in contrast, for example, to the gradations of anger expressed by raising one's voice; (6) *displacement*, the ability to talk of things remote in time and place from where the talking occurs; and (7) *cultural transmission*, transmission by learning rather than transmission through the genes.

Nonverbal Communication

Those who dispute the importance that we attach to language behavior sometimes emphasize that a lot of communication between people occurs on the nonverbal level—without speech. For example, the communication could be *touch*. In romantic attachments of past years, young people were expected to go through a long preliminary dating period during which they first got to know each other solely through verbal communication. At a certain point, if everything seemed to be going well and if he was encouraged to do so by the young woman, the young man was supposed to clasp her hand. If she responded positively by squeezing, there followed a predictable period of handholding and mutual squeezing and stroking, leading to a new gambit—the first kiss. Assuming a positive response from the young woman, the young man would put his arm around her waist, and then would follow a series of warmer and closer embraces along with kissing and considerable body contact, leading to breast manipulation, then genital manipulation, and sometimes to the culminating act. In any case, gestures and "tactile communications" took precedence over verbal ones, or if verbal, they were expressive rather than representational.

This series of steps was quite clearly prescribed, as was the order. "There is usually a well-established code for these communications, with degree of intimacy of direct tactual contacts" (Frank, 1966, p. 209). The boy who omitted a step was regarded as "fast," while one who was unable to read the signs given by his partner to signal the next step was seen as "slow." As the process proceeded, other senses besides tactile—such as taste and smell—entered into the interaction.

To be systematic about nonverbal communication, we should make the following distinctions: Words themselves can be used expressively to designate additional or contradictory meanings in addition to their "actual" meanings. Thus Pittinger and Smith remind us that words can be drawled or clipped; they can be spoken loud or soft, with raised or lowered pitch, with a spread or squeezed register, with a rasp or with openness, and with increasing tempo (Pittinger & Smith, 1967, pp. 61–78). There is also *body language,* which as commonly used, refers to several kinds of phenomena. It can include gestures (made in the air or against someone else's body), which can either replace words or accompany verbal language. They can be highly stylized or they can be idiosyncratic, but they are generally readable by anyone from the same general social background. There is also a class of highly stylized gestures, like salutes or nose thumbing. Finally, there is an iconic sign language connected with the body, consisting of the messages flashed by one's posture, grooming, hairstyle, facial expression, eye movements, and so on.

Most of these nonverbal gestures of body movements are not natural signs. If a person involuntarily squirms in pain or moves restlessly in hot weather, we might speak of these movements as uncontaminated by symbolism, but it is difficult to do so with most other body movements. Birdwhistle, one of the most sophisticated researchers in the area of *kinesics* (nonverbal communication), is highly instructive (1970, pp. 182–83):

Early in the investigation of body movement patterning, I had to deal with that deceptively transparent set of phenomena commonly called *gestures.* A considerable body of ethnographic data was extant demonstrating that these varied from culture to culture. An even larger body of philosophical and psychological literature maintained that these could be understood as "signs" as distinct from less transparent or easily translatable "symbols." Examination of these phenomena in context, however, soon revealed that this was at best a dubious interpretation of their activity or function.

What Birdwhistle means is that gestures are no less "conventional signs" (in our terminology) than are words themselves. One must know the interactional context in which the gesture is made. "A 'salute,' for example, depending upon the integrally associated total body or facial behavior, may convey a range of messages from ridicule and rebellion to subservience or respect." This is true of a smile, wink, wave, or bow. "To call these 'signals' is to indicate a specificity such behavior lacks in actual practice" (Birdwhistle, 1970, p. 183).

One proviso needs to be added to Birdwhistle's general point: the possibility that there are a few cross-cultural facial expressions of emotion. Research by Ekman (1973; 1970, pp. 151–58) and Eibl-Eibesfeldt (1970) evidences that similar facial expressions are used across cultures for expressing happiness, sadness, anger, fear, surprise, and disgust. Ekman notes, however, that "universals in facial expressions of emotion can be explained from a number of nonexclusive viewpoints as being due to innate neural programs or living experiences common to human development regardless of culture"—and notes that future research is needed to determine this matter. Ekman severely criticizes an extreme view like LaBarre's that "there is no 'natural' language of emotional gesture," because it does not distinguish facial gestures from facial expressions of emotion. However, Ekman does admit that many facial gestures are independent of facial expressions of emotion and that these "may well be culturally variable."

In another study, Ekman (1972) illustrated how emotional displays vary from culture to culture. He compared Japanese and American adults viewing a distressing film alone and in the presence of an interviewer. When they were alone, both the Japanese and the Americans showed similar reactions to the film; but when the interviewer was present, the Japanese showed less distress; they appeared to be masking their emotions behind a polite smile.

Ekman (1980. p. 99) further maintains:

Having taken some time to explain a number of different ways in which culture and various experimental factors could shape facial expression, let me say that I don't think there is complete plasticity. . . . It seems unlikely that experience will be organized and maintained directly in opposition to biological predisposition. However, there is ample room for enormous cultural differences in emotional expression.

This discussion deals only with facial expressions as they express rather basic emotions—as compared with all other gestures that may stand for less basic matters and even for finely differentiated emotions like love of country or embarrassment over a spouse's behavior.

Let us return to Birdwhistle's point about the conventional-sign aspects of gestures, which he illustrates in an interesting description of the various types of gestures (he calls them *markers*) that accompany verbal communication. He notes that markers may be used to indicate the specific person(s) referred to when the pronouns he, she, and them are used; in this case, the markers may be slight movements of the head, finger, hand, or eyes in the direction of the person referred to. When the reference is to I, me, us, or we, the gestural markers are different. The markers indicating future events are likely to be different from those used in speaking of past occurrences. Verbal communication including such words as *in, behind, on top of* ("area markers"), or *quickly, lightly, roughly* ("manner markers") is also accompanied by characteristically patterned gestures; such markers sometimes replace speech rather than merely accompany it, as, for example, when one is in the dentist's chair and unable to talk but wishes to tell the dentist to "take it easy."

This information is relatively simple compared to what Birdwhistle calls the total body language used, say, when one woman tells another about the intricacies of dressmaking. The concept of gestural markers, he says, is insufficient to describe the various processes involved, adding that he is inclined to view total body language "as examples of derived communicational systems"—derived, that is, from prior verbal communication.

The ways in which nonverbal communication as interaction occurs can be schematically represented by indicating whether the messages are transmitted or received knowingly or unknowingly. Thus, a speaker who arouses an audience's hostility may feel a vague discomfort without knowing why. The audience members, on the other hand, without consciously doing so, may lean back in their seats with folded arms and blank faces. Here, the message is transmitted unintentionally and received without clear awareness.

To illustrate another of the four possibilities: At a class reunion, one of the authors met a former classmate who told him that many years earlier, during their student days, she had tried for a year to attract his attention—a fact of which he had been totally unaware. In this case, the messages were deliberately sent but were not grasped by the person to whom they were directed. The opposite situation (unknowing-knowing) is demonstrated when someone becomes irritated but is unaware that this irritation is apparent to bystanders, who easily read his or her gestures and facial expressions.

The last situation, where both sender and receiver are quite aware, hardly needs illustration, but we might note that a particularly pleasant example from the theater is the elaborate but shared facial and body movements made by a skilled mime like Marcel Marceau. This French artist can be understood by Americans because he draws upon social situations and gestures that are cross-cultural. On the other hand, some of the cultural limitations of mime are suggested by an American student of French culture, Laurence Wylie, who attended a Parisian school of mime. He remarked that when Americans were required to act out what happens when fire meets water, rubber meets glass, and glass meets steel, "they could not prevent themselves from getting involved in the idea of winning a contest. They become a street gang defending its territory" (Wylie, 1973, p. 2).

In sending these messages, the Americans were drawing not only on national imagery, but undoubtedly on what Ekman would call wittingly sent and culturally shared "emblems" and "illustrators." When emblems are used, the receivers usually know not only the message but also that it was deliberately sent to them. Such emblems are most often used when verbal discourse is prevented by agreement (as in miming), by external circumstances, or by distance. Thus, an emblem for sleeping might be moving the head into a lateral position perpendicular to the body, while bringing both hands below the head to represent a pillow. According to Ekman, many messages are emblematic in more than one culture, but often "a different movement is used in each culture." To represent suicide, an American places a finger at his or her temple, the hand arranged like a gun; in New Guinea, the emblem to represent hanging is to grab the throat with an open hand and push up; in Japan, one plunges the fist into the stomach to represent hari-kari, or draws an index finger across the neck to represent throat-slitting.

Ekman's illustrators are essentially the same as Birdwhistle's markers; they are "used with awareness and intentionality, although . . . usually in peripheral, not focal, awareness" (Ekman & Friesen, 1972, pp. 358–59). Referring to hand gestures, Ekman distinguishes the following types of illustrators:

batons—movements which accent or emphasize a particular word or phrase.
ideographs—movements which sketch the path or direction of thought.
deictic movements—pointing to an object, place, or event.
spatial movements—depicting a spatial relationship.
rhythmic movements—depicting the rhythm or pacing of an event.
kinetographs—depicting a bodily action, or some nonhuman physical action.
Pictographs—drawing a picture in the air of the shape of the referent.

These illustrators are intended to further explain what has already been said verbally.

Receiving	Sending	
	Knowingly	Unknowingly
Unknowingly		
Knowingly		

They are socially learned and culturally derived. Their interactive function—and that of emblems too—are suggested by Ekman's finding that they are hardly ever used when the person is alone or not actually communicating with someone. American Sign Language (ASL), which is taught to the deaf, represents an attempt to standardize a nonverbal gestural system; every letter in the English alphabet is given a different gestural configuration.

Our own interactional scheme—the four cells—does not take into account either the misreading or the failure to receive an intended message, or the simple failure to recognize that there is anything to read, like the professor so involved in her subject that she is oblivious to students' impatience after the bell has sounded. These interactions too, although nonverbal, fall within the realm of the symbolic, of "communication." Without shared understandings from prior verbal communication or from participation in common culture, nonverbal communication would be primitive indeed.

INTERNALIZED SPEECH AND THOUGHT

From Egocentric Speech to Thought

From the ages of about three to seven years, the speech that growing children redirect at themselves becomes more and more abbreviated and less and less intelligible to outsiders. (See Chapter 9 for a critique of this formulation.) Their self-directed remarks may become increasingly truncated, and they use various abbreviating devices (for example, the subject of the sentence tends to be omitted because it is implicitly understood).

What happens to the egocentric speech of children is interesting. It does not simply disappear without a trace but gradually becomes internalized, becoming transformed in the process. It ceases to be speaking and becomes thinking.

Using some ingenious experiments, Vygotsky (1939, pp. 29–52) has discovered and described some features of the gradual transformation. His evidence indicates that the internal speech of adults retains many of the characteristics of childish egocentric speech. For example, it is highly abbreviated, much concerned with self, often highly fragmentary and disjointed, and filled with irrelevancies. It should be emphasized that the egocentric speech of the child is not mere verbal play; like the adult thought which grows out of it, it serves an adaptive function. Thus, if children are alone or in a noisy room, or if they think they are not being understood, their egocentric utterances diminish. However, when they are faced with problems, both their references to self and assertions of their own ego increase in number. Speaking aloud apparently helps them solve problems by "thinking them through" aloud.

The process which transforms external language into thought is illustrated by how we learn to count. Children at first count aloud, touch, or point with hands or head to the objects they are counting. If they are prevented from pointing or saying anything, they are usually unable to count at all. They begin also by counting similar objects, for their counting depends on external features and overt processes which are not essential to the adult. As children grow, the external props are discarded one by one. They learn to count dissimilar objects; it becomes unnecessary for them to point; and later it becomes unnecessary for them to count aloud. They may continue to move their lips and count inaudibly to themselves, but eventually this external activity also may disappear. For the person with mathematical ability, the very awareness of number-words may vanish, so that mathematical thought often appears to proceed without any dependence upon language symbols.

A similar process of internalization is involved in learning to read. Here, as in learning to count, children first learn to read aloud, progress to reading inaudibly to themselves, and end by following a sequence of ideas with relatively little attention paid to specific words.

The Dualistic Error

Many people erroneously conceive of thinking as independent of the more overt forms of language behavior that precede it and make it possible. Laypersons are not the only ones who commit this dualistic error; as Vygotsky has written (1939, p. 29):

The fundamental error of most investigations in thinking and speech, the fault which was responsible for their futility, consisted in regarding thought and word as two independent and isolated elements.

Language behavior is erroneously supposed to have a material or behavioristic basis, whereas thinking is regarded as something separate, distinct, and of a purely "mental" or "spiritual" character—in short, disembodied. The "mental powers" involved in thinking are viewed as seeking external means of expressing themselves, and language becomes merely their external agent or tool. Language is said to be "a vehicle for the transmission of ideas"; it is a way of transferring the ideas occurring in one person's mind to the mind of someone else. Thus the indissoluble unity of language and characteristically human thought is destroyed and placed outside the realm of empirical research.

While it is generally agreed that language and thought are interconnected processes and forms of human behavior, specifying the precise nature of the interrelationship is a moot point among philosophers and scholars. We cannot enter into the detailed arguments that are advanced on this question by numerous schools of thought except to indicate that they exist, and that they constitute a considerable body of literature.

As a working conception suitable to the limited purposes of this discussion, language behavior and thinking can be pictured as two intersecting circles with considerable overlap. This scheme oversimplifies and to some extent misrepresents the situation, but makes the points that lower animals and infants have some sort of thinking processes, and that language behavior may sometimes be relatively mechanical in nature and have little or no communicative significance. We think that behaviorist John Watson's idea—that thinking is sim-

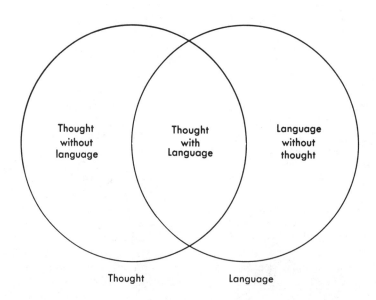

ply talking to oneself—is a considerable overstatement, and that the opposite position—that thinking and talking are two radically separate and independent kinds of activity—is demonstrably false. For socialized human beings, we postulate that there are levels of psychological activity (similar to those in the lower animals) that do not not enter into explicit awareness; Freudian psychologists place heavy emphasis upon this type of subliminal thinking. On the other hand, it is also plausible that in some of its most complex manifestations, thinking may occur in some sense without language, and transcend the limitations of existing language structures. Without the latter assumption, it would be difficult to understand human creativity. The creative drive of human imagination and inventiveness constantly tends to outrun the capabilities of existing formal symbolic devices; as a result, new forms of language, mathematics, and other notational or coding systems are constantly being produced.

Symbols cannot represent the real world completely and exactly, nor can they convey the full content of human experience. If thinking were completely confined within the limits imposed by language, there would be no way to account for the progressive expansion of knowledge and the emergence of new ideas.

At this point we should consider the thought processes of creative artists. Do painters or musicians have to use language as they paint or compose? Do sculptors use language as they shape a stone figure with a live model before them? From the subjective reports of artists and musicians, it is clear that they can manipulate musical and artistic symbols with or without verbally formulating their means and ends to themselves. When artists are asked what a given picture "means," they often reply in what seems to be gibberish—or they refuse to talk at all, stating that the picture should speak for itself. The symbols they create and use are nondiscursive and nonlinguistic; they cannot be translated into verbal symbols. Some people naively believe that such nondiscursive thought is purely recreational when compared

with the strenuous thinking of the scientist or mathematician. Dewey, among others, has countered with the following (1934, pp. 45–46):

The idea that the artist does not think as intently and penetratingly as a scientific inquirer is absurd. A painter . . . has to see each particular connection of doing and undergoing in relation to the whole that he desires to produce. To apprehend such relations is to think, and is one of the most exacting modes of thought. . . .

Soviet psychologist L. Vygotsky represented the interrelationships of language and thought by two intersecting circles (see Figure on p. 66). He went on to say (1962, pp. 125–53),

Thought is not merely expressed in words; it comes into existence through them. Every thought tends to connect something else, to establish a relationship between things. Every thought moves, grows and develops, fulfills a function, solves a problem. . . .

The relation between thought and word is a living process; thought is born through words. A word devoid of thought is a dead thing, and thought unembodied in words remains a shadow.

Interestingly, Vygotsky's ideas and the research conducted by him and his followers (Luria and Yudovich) takes its point of departure from an aspect of Pavlov's thought that has received little attention in the United States—that is, his description of language as the second signaling system. Soviet psychologists and physiologists, led by Vygotsky and Luria, have reported on the results of extensive observation and experimentation concerned with the relationship between complex mental and cortical processes and language behavior. The conclusions are practically identical to the theoretical perspective developed here. Luria and Yudovich discuss the significance of the point of view that links complex mental activity with language and the processes of social interaction (Luria & Yudovich, 1959, p. 15):

Perception and attention, memory and imagination, consciousness and action, cease to be regarded as simple, external, innate mental "properties." They begin to be understood as the product of complex social forms of the child's mental process; as complex "systems of functions" which appear as a result of the development of the child's activity in the process of intercourse; as complex reflective acts in the content of which speech is included, which, using Pavlov's terminology, are realized with the close participation of the two signal systems—the first signal system being concerned with directly perceived stimuli, the second with systems of verbal elaboration.

A similar position has been developed by Werner and Kaplan (1963).

When we discuss aphasia (Chapter 5), we note that these patients can perform acts of direct reference but not acts of symbolic reference—in other words, they characteristically fail to organize their activities on the highest level of abstraction. Such simple dichotomies as "concrete attitude" and "abstract attitude" or "direct reference" and "symbolic reference" merely suggest the immense range of sign behavior from the simplest to the most complex. No human thinks systematically, logically, and on the highest planes of abstraction at all times; nor do all matters require abstract thought. Some people may never learn to think consistently at the highest levels—that is, similar matters may be dealt with on varying levels of abstraction. Various classifications of sign behavior and thought have been suggested as preliminary to investigation of the full range of thought. Dewey and Bentley (1949, p. 16) offer a tentative hierarchy. The idea that thinking covers a range of sign behavior is

likely to be a fruitful one; study of this range is a task for the future.

CONCLUSION

We have covered much theoretical material in this chapter. We have attempted to elaborate and develop the general relationship between language and other forms of social behavior and have indicated how semiotics, the science of signs, bears directly on the symbolic interactionist view of language. We have dealt at length with the language of categorical attitude and have shown how a word's meaning lies in its relationship to human experience and human action.

We have also discussed signs and symbols and different levels of signal systems (first and second). Nonverbal communications, internalized speech and thought, and the dualistic error were also analyzed. In the next chapter we will more firmly anchor language in the human group.

SUGGESTED READINGS

BARTHES, ROLAND (1957/1972). *Mythologies.* New York: Hill & Wang. A very readable presentation of Barthes semiotic approach to contemporary culture.

CASSIRER, E. (1944). *An Essay on Man.* New Haven: Yale University Press. This work by the eminent German philosopher presents a view that pertains directly to the materials in this chapter. Those interested in his approach should read his more elaborate work, *The Philosophy of Forms.*

SAUSSURE, FERDINAND DE (1959). *Course in General Linguistics.* New York: McGraw-Hill. The classic statement on semiotics—the science which studies the life of signs in a society.

CHAPTER FOUR
Language, Groups, and Social Structure

In this chapter, we will be concerned with the ways in which human group life structures language, its use, and its meanings. The emphasis on group life is both a necessity and a virtue—a necessity because all languages are rooted in groups, and a virtue because groups are at the core of the interests of sociological social psychologists.

CONSENSUS AND HUMAN GROUPS

Coordinated group activity presupposes communication, shared goals, and shared perspectives. It is obvious that group activities are consequences of linguistic communication. Membership is essentially not a physical matter, but rather a question of how people think, how they conceptualize their social worlds and themselves, and how they relate themselves to others through the communication circuits available to them.

Communication among members of social groups and the sense of belonging to a group may vary greatly. For example, there may be little direct communication among the members of an audience. In a *primary group*—to use Charles Horton Cooley's term—such as the family, communication is on an intimate face-to-face basis. A sense of intimacy, solidarity, and "we-ness" characterizes primary groups. In more formal groups and associations, however, communication often takes the form of written correspondence, telephone calls, or highly formal notices and announcements disseminated from a central office. These may be supplemented by annual conferences ordinarily attended by a relatively small proportion of the total membership or by small seminars of exclusive groups.

The Small Social Group

The small social group is a network of one-person, two-person, and three-person social relationships. Groups exist within a symbolic structure or framework of experiences, and are characterized by a sense of supraindividuality which connects one-person, dyadic, and triadic relations into a complex structure that encompasses all the members. Groups have a common interest—often, a desire to combat loneliness—and they may be fused and pledged to a set of meanings that brings the members back to one another. (An Alcoholics Anonymous group, for example, is pledged to the concept of sobriety. Recovering alcoholics keep coming back to A.A. groups out of a commitment, in part, to this pledge) (see Denzin, 1986b).

In small groups, interpersonal biographies are joined. Each member brings a unique personal history that becomes part of the group's culture and emotional life. Every group has its own "emotional frame of reference." This framework may include the periodic or regular production of togetherness, horror, fear, dismay, joy, reverence, love, intimacy, and warmth. Emotions, which are self-feelings, are social processes that join group members into felt mood-states.

A group's special language, or idiolect, contains words and references that give meaning to the selves, emotions, and relationships which combine to make each group unique to its members. This language is woven into the cycle of group life and serves to give each group its own special sense of history and temporality (Denzin, 1984, pp. 35–48).

THE GROUP BASES OF LANGUAGE

Anthropologists' study of primitive cultures demonstrates that all human societies have language. While there are hundreds of different languages in the world, and often numerous dialects within each, linguistic behavior as such is universal. Differences among languages are apparent, as any traveler to a foreign land can attest. Not so apparent, although equally true, is that the language of every human society is complex, intricate, and systematic—the carrier of a great wealth of experience and attitude. "The mechanics of significant understanding between human beings," writes linguist Edward Sapir, "are as sure and complex and rich in overtones in one society as in another" (Sapir, 1942, p. 78). Every existing language contains at least five thousand words. As examples of primitive language complexity, we might note that in the speech of the Abipones, a South American Indian tribe, the verb can take more than 400 endings to indicate mood, person, and tense; and in some Australian aboriginal tongues, dual, triple, and even quadruple forms of nouns are in use (Hiller, 1933, pp. 401–15). Sapir has perhaps overstated the case for the equal complexity of all languages; but all linguists agree that speech is highly developed throughout the world. For this reason, one writer has referred to language as humankind's "fundamental institution" (Sapir, 1942, p. 78).

The social heritage of any society consists of its traditional ways of acting, believing, and speaking. This social heritage—often referred to as *culture*—is distinct from biological heritage, which is transmitted from parents to infant by way of parental genes in the chromosomes. (The genes determine such physical characteristics as hair color and eye color.) A basic difference between biological and social heritage is that social heritage is never passed on biologically; the child must acquire social heritage through some process of learning. This simple fact is a disadvantage in that transmission by learning is fallible and imperfect; it is an advantage because, being fallible and imperfect, it provides for the possibility of rapid evolutionary change.

Traditional ways of acting, thinking, speaking, and handling the language vary widely from country to country, and from place to place within the same country. The language of a given nation or segment of it is part and parcel of its social heritage; for example, Muslims, Christians, and Jews who have lived in close contiguity in Baghdad for hundreds of years nevertheless speak three quite different versions of Arabic. Like other

traditions, language is passed down from generation to generation nonbiologically. Newborn babies are unable to speak their parents' tongue, nor do they acquire the ability to do so as a result of later bodily maturation. They must learn word order, pronunciation, and—if they learn to write—spelling and punctuation.

The language learned by children is not primarily *their* language so much as it is that of their society and of their primary group. Adults have linguistic standards to which the child must conform. Although different individuals may set unique distinctions of pronunciation, enunciation, and meaning upon established ways of speaking and writing, there is nevertheless a common core to all these individual treatments. Language is a group product that, like every other part of the social heritage, must be learned (Judd, 1926, p. 195):

The child playing in the sand invents a word for the pebbles that fill its hand. The new word is "pocos." Does society adopt this word . . . ? Not at all. Society has an expression of its own for the designation of pebbles, and it does not look with favor on the exercise of further inventive genius. So the child's word "pocos" lingers for a time in the tolerant memory of the immediate family and then passes into oblivion.

Many children invent a baby-talk of some complexity which the parents learn, participating for a while in a bizarre linguistic game. But if children are to be understood by persons outside the family, if they are to become adjusted members of society, they must eventually employ generally accepted linguistic forms (see Chapter 7).

Indeed, marked individual deviation from the accepted language meets with disapproval. To be sure, a certain amount of latitude is allowed—all Americans do not pronounce, enunciate, or construct sentences identically— but one must not stray too far from certain linguistic patterns. Generally speaking, a future tense cannot be substituted for a past tense to indicate something that has happened. In the United States, American word order must be used; German word order is scarcely permissible. In France, inflection and intonation must approach a common French standard; they must not be appreciably American or Chinese. Marked deviation from the community's linguistic norm will fall stridently upon the ears of one's friends and associates; they are likely to respond with expressions of distaste, amusement, or ridicule. Deviants may even be punished: Witness how "bad" grammar may deprive a person of career opportunities or prevent college students from passing freshman English.

The meanings of correct American speech in the world of the immigrant have been beautifully recaptured by the writer Alfred Kazin (1951, p. 22):

A "refined," "correct," "nice" English was required of us at school that we did not naturally speak, and that our teachers could never be quite sure we would keep. This English was peculiarly the ladder of advancement. Every future young lawyer was known by it. . . . It was bright and clear and polished. We were expected to show it off like a new pair of shoes. When the teacher sharply called a question out, then your name, you were expected to leap up, face the class, and eject those new words fluently off the tongue.

Reactions to the violation of linguistic rules are no different from reactions to transgression of other customs and rules. Linguistic ways are public property and must not be grossly violated. Like other items of social heritage, individuals can use language to private ends; it can be made to fit the pattern of unique personalities. But individuals must operate within a framework of what is deemed permissible. Language is essentially a group product, the outcome of the common experiences of members of social groups.

The social character of language may be underscored by noting what linguists call *special languages* (Vendryes, 1925, p. 249):

By the term "special language" we mean a language which is employed only by groups of individuals placed in special circumstances. The language of the law is a case in point. In the exercise of their profession lawyers employ a language very far removed from that of ordinary speech; it is a special legal language. Another example can be found in ecclesiastical language. A special language is often used in addressing the Deity. . . . All forms of slang are special languages. Students, artisans, and thieves all use a language of their own. . . . They all have this in common . . . when their structure is examined they are found to be the outcome of a common tendency to adapt the language to the functions of a particular group.

Each special language is based upon and utilizes the framework of the larger society's language. Yet people who are outside a group are aware of being strangers to that group's ways when they encounter its distinctive vocabulary. All of us have probably undergone experiences in which we felt like strangers to some group in our own society because we did not possess its language.

Language and Group Experiences

It is said that the history and interests of a people are reflected, to an astonishing degree, in their language. The British have a language rich in nuances and expressions for the sea; Eskimos make minute distinctions among numerous kinds of snow and snowfall (Hiller, 1933, p. 115). Klinberg comments on the Arabs' concern with the camel (1954, p. 50):

There are said to be about six thousand names connected in some way with "camel," including words derived from the camel and attributes associated with it. These include, for instance, names and classes of camels according to function—milk camels, riding camels, marriage camels, slaughter camels, and so forth; names of breeds of different degrees of nobility of lineage, derivation from different lands, and so forth; names of camels in groups, as several, a considerable number, innumerable, and with reference to their objectives—grazing, conveying a caravan, war expedition, and so forth; as many as fifty words for pregnant camels, states of pregnancy, stage at which movement of the foetus is first felt, mothers who suckle and those who do not, those near delivery, and so forth.

The special languages of any society's subgroups provide additional examples of this mirroring of interests. The idioms and vernacular of sociologists, journalists, bankers, college students, and football players all reflect their respective dominant interests and concerns.

Language is also the carrier and the embodiment of environmental features that group members feel are important. People's words designate, refer to, and select aspects of the world relevant to their lives. "For not everything in the world has a name. . . . Language singles out for specification only those features which are, in a peculiar sense, *common* to the social group" (deLaguna, 1927, p. 272). As Lewis says (1948, p. 224):

Among the Solomon Islanders . . . there are nine distinct names for the cocoanut, signifying stages in its growth, but no word corresponding to our general term "cocoanut." On the other hand, they have only one word which covers all four meals of the day—breakfast, dinner, tea, supper—but no special name for each of these. It is of practical importance to them to distinguish the nine stages of the cocoanut but not to discriminate between "dinner" and "tea." . . . *A concept is a means of preserving distinctions which are of practical importance in the life of a community.*

Examples taken from the argot of the confidence man illustrate concretely how the members of a group develop concepts that refer to matters of group interest. The confidence man is a criminal who lives by his wits and tongue; his stock-in-trade is to relieve people of their money by deceiving them. This is done by persuading the victim to invest money in a fake enterprise. Here are some terms in the confidence man's vocabulary (Maurer, 1940, pp. 256–96):

Mark: A victim, or intended victim. Synonyms for mark are apple, Bates, egg, fink, John Bates, Mr. Bates, savage, chump.
To put the mark up: To locate a good prospective mark.
Tow: A bank roll.
To rumble: To excite a mark's suspicion.

The send: The stage in a big con-game at which the mark is sent home for a large amount of money.
To sting: To take a mark's money.
Touch: The money taken from a mark.
To tear off: To cheat one's partner out of his share of a touch.

Many social groups develop concepts or categories that refer to major or dominant statuses and positions in the life cycle. They are likely to have words designating sex, age, and marital and economic status, and they may have complex vocabularies indicating one's position in the kinship structure of that group. The socialization of children into the group requires that they learn that group's language. Furthermore, a group's standing in the broader society is in part reflected in the degree to which their private or peculiar languages are spoken by the members of that society.

Thus, black standard English is seldom spoken by white school-age children, and central Hebrew phrases have seldom become incorporated in our national vocabulary. Colonializing nations have long recognized that language control leads to group control; the British, for example, were quite skilled in making the English language *the* language for the countries they controlled. As a group or a nation gains control over its own fate, one of its first actions is to require the learning of its "native" language. Indeed, it may insist on conducting all public business in that language, and ban the languages of its prior oppressor from its schools in the process.

LISTENING AND COMPREHENDING

Conversation is a complex activity, as each participant is engaged almost simultaneously in a number of distinct processes. Thus while *A* speaks to *B*, *B* listens to *A*. But *B* is also busily engaged in formulating the remarks that she intends to make as soon as *A* stops speaking. *B* also may be commenting to herself upon what *A* is saying. Some of these comments may not even be explicitly formulated, and generally they will not be uttered aloud. Thus, *B* may silently remark that *A* is stupid or confused or dishonest; but, when her turn to speak comes, these comments are suppressed in favor of others that meet the conversational requirements of courteous social intercourse. To complicate matters still further, *A* not only speaks to *B; A* also listens to what he is saying to *B*—correcting, revising, retracting, and evaluating as he goes along. Both *A* and *B* alternate between listening to their own speech and to the speech of the other. The remarks made by each are called forth by, and adapted to, remarks made by the other as each assesses the other's intentions and motives. Each is involved both as a participant and as an observer.

Comprehension of someone else's speech presupposes mastery of the language and is the counterpart of speech. The other person's words act as stimuli that produce in the listener an internal symbolic process that constitutes the act of comprehending. When we listen attentively to another person, our own word schemes are not directly involved, as we temporarily ceded control to the other. Speech and comprehension of speech are not so much different processes as they are different phases of the same process. None of us can communicate linguistically with others unless we comprehend our own remarks. Conversely, we do not adequately comprehend others' ideas until we are able to formulate them for ourselves. The crucial test of comprehension of a word is the individual's ability to use the word correctly; that is, to be able to evoke on the part of the listener the same response it evokes for the speaker.

As we will see when we discuss aphasia (Chapter 5), if we shift our attention to the neurological and physiological levels and ask what goes on in the brains of two people engaged in conversation, the situation becomes infinitely more complicated. Only some of these internal processes have been roughly

identified. It is impossible, for example, to provide a meaningful description, in neurological and physiological terms, of the simplest conversational episode or to distinguish one type from another. Thought, speech, and conversation unquestionably require the participation of various neurological and physiological mechanisms and processes. They are not, however, identical with these processes. They must be viewed in a broader sociohistorical perspective (Luria & Yudovich, 1959). Nevertheless, sociologists, psychologists, and other behavioral scientists share, with biological scientists, a profound interest in the nature of the functioning of the human brain.

Although some hold that dogs and other animals "comprehend" things said to them, the standard of comprehension is not the same as that of human beings. Parents, for example, do not assume from isolated correct responses that their children understand all the words directed to them. The child is subjected to another, more crucial test: he must be able to use the words correctly—not just once or twice, but in a wide variety of situations and in various combinations. If we remember that *the fundamental prototype of language behavior is conversation*, we shall not be confused by the fact that lower animals such as dogs seem able to comprehend verbal cues. As we have seen, children show a similar subverbal comprehension before they have learned to speak.

Writing and the Literate Tradition

It is virtually impossible to exaggerate the importance of the invention of written symbols in the evolution of culture (Couch, 1984b, p. 302). Primitive writing systems developed early in the evolution of the ancient civilizations, arising out of the practical necessities and problems that arose when human beings first began to live together in large permanent settlements and form political units. The term *civilization* implies the existence of literacy, political organization, and city life. Cultures that lack writing are located in an oral tradition. Without writing, history gives way to myth, and organized intellectual activity is limited, there could be no mathematics, algebra, science, or any of the other numerous disciplines incorporated within the literate tradition. In preliterate societies, customs, practices, and beliefs are passed down through the generations essentially through long chains of person-to-person conversations. This method of transmission is sharply limited in the kinds of information that can be transmitted, and it also tends to distort the past because of people's tendency to reinterpret and understand the past in terms of the present (Goody & Watt, 1972).

Writing probably began as pictures or drawings representing external objects, people, and animals; marks were used to indicate numbers. From the latter, various types of number systems were invented and elaborated; from the former, the modern alphabet was created, primarily by the Phoenicians and the Greeks during the first millennium B.C. The earliest writing systems were cumbersome, hard to master, and restricted to elite segments of the population. The emergence of a phonetic alphabet not only made it much easier to become literate, but also radically altered the function of writing. This function, at first, was to represent the world by means of pictures or simplified drawings. In contrast, the alphabet permits us to describe and record the sounds people make when they speak, regardless of what they talk about. It took several thousand years after the first appearance of primitive forms of writing for humans to develop the modern phonetic alphabet.

Writing was initially a response to the practical necessities created by the development of commerce, trade, agriculture, and organized government. The earliest writers wrote laboriously on stone or clay. The Egyptians later learned to write on papyrus; paper was first produced about A.D. 200 in China, whence its production and use was acquired centuries later by the rest of the civilized world. The Arabs introduced paper making into Europe in the 12th century A.D., and in 1452 Gutenberg invented the printing press. These advances added revolutionary new dimensions and possibilities to the social and intellectual significance of writing and literacy.

The invention of writing has a more subtle intellectual implication in that it converts language and the thoughts it expresses into material objects in the external environment. Oral speech, in contrast, consists only of sounds or events that occur and vanish except as they may be remembered by individuals. Recorded speech or writing invites sustained attention and analysis, both with respect to the structure of language and the structure of thought. Writing also facilitates thinking; try to imagine what mathematics would be like without it. Because of writing, talk about talk and thinking about thought are stimulated and facilitated.

In view of this discussion, it is probably no accident that the flowering of Greek civilization during the first millennium B.C. was preceded by the adoption of the modern phonetic alphabet and accompanied by an expansion of literacy in Greek society (Goody & Watt, 1972; Couch, 1984b). It also makes sense that the Greeks invented logic, cultivated rational discourse, speculated on human nature and the nature of the world, practiced mathematical reasoning, and wrote plays and poetry.

The development of writing in a society creates a complex literate tradition that contributes to an accelerated rate of cultural evolution, the accumulation of knowledge, and the development of science and technology. Recorded history begins and a new sense of the past emerges. New modes of symbolic operation become possible and new conceptions of the world, of humans, and of the past and the present emerge. The literate tradition does not displace the oral tradition, but rather supplements it. Writing differs drastically from oral communication in that (1) it is not supplemented by the wide variety of nonverbal signs that routinely accompany conversations; and (2) what is written acquires an objective public character which ordinary conversation lacks. Writing is thus a purer example of linguistic communication than oral communication, and by the same token it is more exacting. Thoughts tend to evolve and change as one tries to represent them on paper and, sometimes, they may simply evaporate.

The oral and literate traditions coexist in modern societies; they also interact with each other, and items pass from one to the other. The oral tradition is the carrier of what is called "practical common sense," while the literature is represented by what is learned from books, and advanced training and education. There is often conflict between the two traditions. No one in our society can avoid the influence of the oral, but it is quite easy to minimize that of the literate tradition.

LANGUAGE AND THE SOCIAL STRUCTURE OF THOUGHT

The social environment affects the content of a person's thoughts, as well as the form of his or her thinking. Sapir (1949b), making a point akin to that made earlier concerning symbolic environments, suggests the importance of particular languages for the construction of thought and environments (1949, p. 120):

Human beings do not live in an objective world alone . . . but are very much at the mercy of the particular language which has become a medium of expression for their society. It is quite an illusion to imagine that one adjusts to reality essentially without the use of language and that language is merely an incidental means of solving specific problems of communication or reflection . . . the "real world" is to a large extent unconsciously built upon the language habits of the group. No two languages are ever sufficiently similar to be considered as representing the same social reality. The worlds in which different societies live are distinct worlds, not merely the same worlds with different labels attached.

The influences of language structure upon the structure of thought are illustrated by the problems of translation. The translation of other languages into English involves more than merely finding equivalent words; the translator must try to convey meanings and nuances of meaning that may be practically impossible to express in English. The translation of non-European languages into English is even more difficult, because the modes of thought are likely to be even more divergent from ours. Consider Chinese and American thinking. The differences between these two styles of thinking are suggested by the following quotation (Brynner, 1929, p. 27):

Chinese poets seldom talk about one thing in terms of another. . . . If a metaphor is used, it is metaphor directly relating to the theme, not something borrowed from the ends of the earth. . . . For our Western taste, used as we are to the operatic in poetry, that is, the spectacular or shocking effect produced by some unusual analogy or metaphor, the substance of Chinese poems seems often mild or trivial.

This newspaper account suggests some of the problems conscientious translators encounter when they try to interpret English expressions into Chinese (Vinacke, 1953, p. 37):

Some of the great difficulties among the diplomats sitting around the international table (at the United Nations) arise from the differences in languages, alphabets, and, consequently, ways of thinking; and in no tongue is more ingenuity required for accurate, precise translation than Chinese.

The Chinese ideograph script is one of the world's oldest written media, but the talk at Lake Success is so brimful of new ideas, new concepts and new words that, to translate even the basic Charter itself into Chinese, it was necessary to devise almost 2000 new combinations of characters.

A perfect example of the troubles faced here by Chinese translators is the word "uranium," which has a persistent way of cropping up with a decision to call the atomic base "U-metal." That, however, only started their headaches.

The symbol of "U" was found in the Chinese word for grapefruit, which in literal translation is the "U-tree." What was just as disturbing, from a purist point of view, was the discovery that the symbol for metal was contained in the first part of the world for "bell," which literally translated meant "metal boy."

After some cudgeling of brains, however, the calligraphers came up with the proposal to shave off the "tree" part of the "U-tree" character, discard the "boy" part of the "bell" character, and then in the best manner of diplomatic compromise, join the severed remains to form a new symbol: "U-metal" or, as we would say, uranium.

Although new words can be added to a language with relative ease, the language's basic structure is highly stable and resists change. Most people who speak a given language are unaware of its structure as something that differs from the structures of other language systems. Consequently, the uniform modes of thought imposed upon them by their native tongue are not recognized, but are accepted as part of the "real nature of the world" or as among the elements of "common sense."

Since most Americans are acquainted with only the general family of Indo-European languages, they are likely to view skeptically the contention that thinking is not essentially the same the world over. They know that the content of thought varies from group to group; nevertheless, they are likely to believe that the form of all "correct" thinking is the same everywhere. The divergent modes of thought of other peoples—which actually do exist—are often regarded merely as varieties of error.

It would be revealing to know what effect the English language has on our thinking processes. It is probably impossible for anyone operating within the framework of our language to become aware of the influences it exerts upon her without first being acquainted with other languages (preferably non-European ones). For this reason, we shall illustrate our point with material from the Navaho Indian language, which is quite different from our own (Kluckhohn & Leighton, 1946, p. 149):

(Navaho language) delights in sharply defined categories. It likes, so to speak, to file things away in neat little packages. It favors always the concrete and particular, with little scope for abstrac-

tions. It directs attention to some features of every situation, such as the minute distinctions as to direction and type of activity. It ignores others to which English gives a place. Navaho focuses interest upon doing—upon verbs as opposed to nouns or adjectives. . . . The important point is that striking divergences in manner of thinking are crystallized in and perpetuated by the forms of Navaho grammar. Take an example of a commonplace physical event: rain. . . . To give only a few instances of the sorts of discrimination the Navaho must make before he reports his experiences; he uses one verb form if he himself is aware of the actual inception of the rain storm, another if he has reason to believe that the rain has been falling for some time in his locality before the occurrence struck his attention. . . . Similarly, the Navaho must invariably distinguish between the ceasing of rainfall (generally) and the stopping of rain in a particular vicinity because the rain clouds have been driven off by the wind. The (Navaho) people take the consistent noticing and reporting of such differences . . . as much for granted as the rising of the sun.

The author points out that Navaho is a very literal language which gives concreteness and specificity to everything that is said. The result is that Navaho thought is more exact and particular than English. This is demonstrated by the way the Navaho express the meaning conveyed by the English verb "to go." The Navaho specify precisely whether the journey was made on foot or by horseback, wagon, auto, plane, or train; they also indicate whether they are starting to go, going alone, returning from somewhere, or arriving at a point; and, if they make a trip astride a horse, different verb forms indicate whether it was at a walk, a trot, or a gallop (Kluckhohn & Leighton, 1946, pp. 197–201).

The study of nonEuropean languages makes it evident that there are different modes of reasoning. Every child is introduced to a system or systems of language embodying certain peculiar and nonuniversal conceptual distinctions. Thus the child is inducted into traditions of thinking—traditions consisting not only of certain kinds of ideas but of certain ways of thinking. The point is made particularly clear by a consideration of time divisions. If certain temporal distinctions are not made by one's language, one cannot think in terms of them. Behavior can scarcely be organized, systematized, arranged, defined, regulated, or coordinated in terms of temporal categories of which the person is unaware. While our own language

. . . always expresses tense with perfect definiteness there are languages . . . which are incapable of doing so . . . in Samoyedic (Siberian) only two temporal forms of the verb are recognized . . . one of these . . . signifying present and future . . . the other indicating the past . . . The minute temporal distinctions which we recognize as "present," "present perfect," "past," "past perfect," "past future," "future perfect," and "past perfect" are impossible in these languages.

A number of languages clearly reveal the efforts which have been made to render intelligible the elusive and abstract nature of time by interpreting it in terms of space . . . (In Sudan language for example) the locations in space are crudely expressed by means of body-part words, and these spatial expressions then serve as indicators of time . . . here the fundamental institution of time is quite different from that to which we are accustomed . . .

(For) some people future and past fuse linguistically into what might be called a "not-now" . . . in Schambala (African) the same word designates the distant past as well as the distant future. For them there exists only a "today" and a "not today" (Werner & Kaplan, 1963, pp. 126–29).

Other critical categories (such as number, action, and quality) also differ in various languages.

Since the language people use is largely an inheritance from previous generations, the modes of thought it conveys are also derived from the past. This has disadvantages as well as advantages, for the experiences of past generations are not always comparable to those of later ones. The errors of the past are tenacious because they become embedded in the language and popular thought—so much so that they become unquestioned assumptions. Note, for example, the sayings that the sun rises in the east, and that members of a race are related to each other by blood. Scientific progress often depends upon freeing oneself from the implications of popular speech. Sapir reminds us that "language is at one and the same time helping and retarding us in our exploration of experience" (Sapir, 1949, p. 11).

In setting forth the general hypothesis that profoundly influences the forms of thought, we are not saying that a given language rigidly determines the form of thought of the society in which it is spoken. But language so thoroughly penetrates the modes of experiencing that at the very least it limits the possibilities of perception and thinking.

Componential Analysis

During recent years, anthropologists who take a position close to our own have begun to develop what has been termed *componential analysis*. This is a sophisticated linguistic analysis undertaken in an effort to avoid projecting the ethnographer's modes of cognition and perception onto his or her subjects, and instead attempting to discover *their* modes. Charles Frake, a leading exponent of this view, expresses the position in terminology that will sound familiar to our readers (1962, p. 54):

A successful strategy for writing productive ethnographies must tap the cognitive world of one's informants. It must discover those features of objects and events which they regard as significant for defining concepts, formulating propositions, and making decisions. The conception of an ethnography requires that the units by which the data of observation are segmented, ordered, and interrelated be delimited and defined according to contrasts inherent in the data themselves and not according to prior notions of pertinent descriptive categories.

Frake then points out that anthropologists customarily do what he suggests when they study kinship systems. No ethnographers describe social relations in an alien society by referring to the doings of uncles, aunts, and cousins; however, when they describe utensils, trees, shrubs, and other features of the environment, they customarily do so "solely in terms of categories projected from the investigator's culture" (p. 59). Frake suggests that if the investigator were to follow the sensible strategy used when studying kinship, "then the problem of describing a tangible object such as a plant may become rather more complex than the relatively simple task of defining contrasts between categories of kinsmen" (p. 59). Why? Because the plant world is frequently differentiated in the amazingly complex ways that we have noted. Frake gives the example of a Philippine rain forest agricultural society whose members "exhaustively partition their plant world into more than 1600 categories."

What Frake suggests ethnographers should do is not an easy task, but the componential analysts believe that it must be done. That task is not necessarily easier when investigators study a group within their own nation if that group's symbolic worlds are markedly different from their own. Investigators cannot simply stop with penetrating the symbolic worlds of their subjects; as social scientists, they must develop their explanations *after* grasping these other worlds.

Sociolinguistics

Sociolinguistics, as we noted, studies the social organization of language behavior in social situations. Sociolinguistics examines how such structural factors as age, sex, social class, race and, ethnicity mold the talk that occurs in social situations. Their research indicates that the dominant power structures in society come into play in the talk that occurs between people. Thus West's (1984) study of encounters between doctors and patients found that (1) male doctors interrupt patients more than female doctors do; (2) male doctors interrupt blacks and females more than whites and males; (3) doctors ask more questions than patients; and (4) patients' questions are not preferred.

Sociolinguistics has taken several turns. Some analysts perform what is called *discourse analysis* (see Manning, 1987, for a review). These scholars examine the stories and texts produced in institutional settings like the courts, hospitals, physicians' offices, and clinics. They study linguistic units that are larger than utterances of sentences.

The problem with discourse analysis is that too frequently, analysts assume that meaning is given in the rules of procedure that organize the texts under analysis. Manning (1986) suggests that meaning and its interpretation remain unresolved issues within discourse analysis.

Conversational analysts focus on naturally-occurring units and forms of talk—including openings, closings, turn-taking, next speaker selection, repairs, and question-and-answer sequences. Manning (1987) regards this as a highly sophisticated technique of sociolinguistic analysis. Much of the work in this area draws on the original work of Harvey Sacks, Emanuel Schlegoff, and Gail Jefferson. West's (1984) study, mentioned above, is an example of conversational analysis in an institutional setting.

Conversational analysis involves a transcription system for converting recorded speech into written texts (Manning, 1987). Conversational analysts assume that speech as heard is the object of study, and such speech can be converted into printed texts. It is unclear how these analysts are able to record and transcribe speech "as it is heard" and given meaning in an interactional situation. This mode of analysis also assumes that what is heard, and then transcribed, is what is meant. An orderliness is given to spoken speech which may not be actually present in "talking situations"; indeed, Manning (1987) notes that analysis of messy conversations and group sociable talk is avoided by these analysts. The context-dependent features of conversation remain to be explored in detail (Manning, 1987).

SYMBOLIC BEHAVIOR AS SHARED BEHAVIOR

Let us suppose that a dozen dogs have been conditioned so that whenever a buzzer sounds, each produces saliva and otherwise behaves as though he anticipated being fed. Then suppose that all twelve dogs are together in one room and that the buzzer is sounded. Presumably, all would respond in the same way to the same stimulus. Can we say that all of them are responding as a group to a sign which all understand in the same way? To answer this question, let us compare such a situation with that existing in an Eskimo settlement where the food supply is running low. A hunting party sets out to kill seals to replenish the food supply. Can we say that the Eskimos, like the dogs described above, are making similar responses to the same stimulus, and that therefore the two types of activity are the same?

A moment's reflection will show that there is a fundamental difference between these two situations. Through intercommunication the Eskimos respond as a group, acting collectively rather than individually. Their behavior is shared; that of the dogs is not. Each member of the Eskimo community grasps the common purpose. In terms of that common purpose, which each understands and knows the others understand, they respond in different ways in order to attain the common goal. Some members of the settlement stay at home and prepare to take care of the kill; others form the hunting party within which all may play different but coordinated roles. It is no accident that the Greek word *symbola,* from which the word "symbol" is derived, referred to "the two halves of a broken stick or coin which were kept as tokens of a contract. Thus the word came to mean an item—such as a word—employed as an instrument of communication (Lorimer, 1929, p. 83).

Gestures as Shared Symbols

We can emphasize the shared character of language by noting how conventional gestures are utilized and understood. Gestures such as shaking hands in greeting, showing affection by kissing, and waving good-bye, all seem "natural" to Americans. Yet these acts do not seem natural to the people of other countries and societies. A Palaung woman in

Southeast Asia said, after several Englishmen had heartily shaken her hand: "I suppose that they mean to be kind, but what a strange custom. I am very glad it is only my hand that they wish to shake and not my head!" (Hiller, 1933, p. 121) Most human gestures are highly conventionalized and stylized, taking on their meaning through cultural definition. The same gesture may stand for very different meanings in different lands; conversely, different gestures may stand for the same meanings. Only if both people—the one who makes the gesture and the one who sees the gesture—attach the same significance to it can there be communication between them. An "outsider" will attach the wrong meaning (or no meaning) to the gesture; hence communication will be impaired. The following cross-cultural mixture of gestures representing "greeting" illustrates the shared and conventional character of human gestures (Hiller, 1933, pp. 101–102, 119):

Among the Wanyika, people meet by grasping hands and pressing their thumbs together; dwellers in the region of the Niger join their right hands and separate them with a pull so that a snapping noise is made by thumb and fingers. The handshake of the Arab seems to be a scuffle in which each tries to raise to his lips the hand of the other. The Ainus draw their hands from the shoulders and down the arms to the fingertips of the person greeted, or they rub their hands together. . . . Polynesians stroke their own faces with the other person's hands. . . . The Fuegians in saluting friends hug "like the grip of a bear." Some people greet by placing one arm around the neck of the person saluted and chucking him under the chin, or encircling his neck with their arms. . . . (Among the Ainu a distinction is made) in the manner of greeting appropriate for men and women . . . men rub their hands together, raise them to the forehead (palms up), and then rub the upper lip with the first finger of the right hand. . . . In some Eskimo tribes . . . the courteous way of greeting a stranger is to lick one's own hands, draw them first over one's own face and then over that of the visitor. . . . Among the Polynesians, Malays, Burmese, Mongols, the Lapps, and others—a usual salute is that of smelling each other's cheeks.

Even gestures of assent, dissent, and beckoning—which most Americans probably assume to be among the most natural and nonconventional gestures—are conventionally defined. Hiller (1933, pp. 103–104) notes that inhabitants of the Admiralty Islands express a decided negative reaction by making a quick stroke of the nose with a finger of the right hand. If the reaction is doubtful, the finger is rubbed slowly across the nose. To beckon a person, the hand is held half erect with the palm forward, moving in the direction of the person addressed. By contrast, the beckoning approach for the Bahima of eastern Africa involves a reversal of the palm in a manner that, to an American, would indicate repulsion. The Niam-Niam of central Africa wave their arms when they beckon.

New Zealand natives indicate assent by head elevation and with the chin, instead of by nodding as Americans do. Turks show negation by throwing the head back and then by making a clucking noise with the tongue. Such gestures would have either no meaning or the wrong meaning to us; we do not share these peoples' gestural symbols.

Pseudo-Communication

Often, two people will become involved in an argument in which both use the same words, but the words have different meanings for each person. When this occurs, a genuine interchange of ideas does not take place, as each individual makes remarks inappropriate to the meanings that the other has in mind. They talk past each other and grow angry at what each feels to be the other's stupidity. If the two parties do not realize that they are using words in different ways, communication is seriously impeded or made impossible; this is called *pseudo-communication*. They are interacting *at*, rather than *with*, one another.

If the disputants grow aware of the different meanings possessed by common terms, their discussion often develops into a consideration of proper linguistic usage. Thus it is apparent that citizens of the United States

and of the Soviet Union use the word *democracy* in different senses. Once this fact is appreciated, it becomes necessary to distinguish between "American democracy" and "Soviet democracy" if communication is to take place. Unless there is agreement as to the meanings of terms, people who believe they are discussing the same thing may actually be talking about different things.

Up to now, we have been discussing language symbols as symbols whose sole function is to refer to objects or to designate meanings. If someone says, "We are having lovely weather," we have treated such a statement as an indication by one person to another that the sun is shining and that it is pleasant outside. Obviously, however, this statement may mean something entirely different: Speakers may be in a social situation in which they are expected to talk whether or not they feel they have anything to say. As all the people present are generally aware of the weather that day, there is really no point in saying anything about it; nevertheless, all are likely to feel more at ease if there is conversation. Here the purpose is not to tell people something they do not already know but rather, by uttering certain sounds, to give evidence of good will and sociability. Hiller has called this kind of conversation "social ritual." Language so used may be termed "expressive" rather than "representational." Another example of purely expressive speech is swearing—although swearing *at* someone usually also involves some communication. Words used expressively cannot be understood by referring to the dictionary; they can be understood only as conventionalized ways of giving vent to certain feelings. Thus, the nervous woman at a tea discusses the weather; an angry mean swears; two people greet each other by saying, "Hello." In these situations, the function of language is not so much communication as expression—though of course some meaning is definitely being communicated.

The expressive use of language may seem to be much the same as the use of sounds made in certain situations by chimpanzees or dogs, but there is a difference. The dog's growl is a biologically natural sound for it to make, but "hello" and other expressive human sounds are conventionalized forms of utterance. In certain situations, all human beings tend toward expressive verbal behavior, but the vocalizations vary immensely from society to society and are socially defined. Thus expressive human speech, although on a lower symbolic and cognitive level than speech designating and describing objects, is nevertheless on a higher level than the expressive utterances of animals. Chimpanzees, for example, can no more be taught to say "hello" appropriately than to use the word "papa" correctly.

In Chapter 5 we shall discuss *aphasia,* the loss of power to use language symbols. Studies of aphasia and other speech disorders offer experimental evidence that expressive speech is more primitive than representative speech. Aphasics whose powers of speech are nearly gone and who cannot name even the most familiar objects in their everyday environment, nevertheless usually retain the ability to swear and to exclaim (Head, 1926; Luria, 1972; Sacks, 1985).

HUMOR, INTERACTION, AND THE RESOURCES OF LANGUAGE

It is sometimes said that humans are the only animals who talk, weep, and laugh. We should take that statement with skepticism, since animals certainly exhibit playful behavior, and chimpanzees, at least, seem to engage in practical jokes. Yet as Wolfenstein (1954, p. 11) observes, "humor is a distinctively human achievement: among living things only human beings laugh." Whether humans learned to laugh before they learned to talk is an open question, but there is little doubt that once they developed language they probably laughed and joked a great deal more. Even in the face of disaster, humans satirize their oppressors and make bitter jokes about their own plight. Humor—in the form of jokes, puns, and witticisms—has often been compared to dreams.

Like dreams, jokes have latent meaning; they also disguise hostile emotions and may reflect underlying definitions of the sect or of social relationships. Through humor, people reflect their responses to problematic situations. A dramatic example is that of the criminal who is led to execution on Monday morning and remarks: "Well, this is a good beginning for the week" (1954, p. 212).

There are so many forms of humor that one can hardly begin to list them: satire, irony, gallows humor, ethnic jokes, sex jokes, puns, slips of the tongue, misprints, spoonerisms, "in jokes," black humor, jibes. Whatever its form, humor usually draws directly on the resources of language—even when the humor is gestural (as in takeoffs) and does not involve actual speech.

To say that humor depends on language means much more than merely that words and sentences are used to create humor; it also presupposes a common universe of discourse and shared experiences. To take the most obvious example: understanding the humor of a foreign country is one of the last and most difficult accomplishments of newcomers to its culture. What they do understand quickly, of course, is humor about those matters which they share with its citizens. But the subtleties and styles of a country's humor depend on the intricacies of its social relationships and the linkages of its social groups. On the other hand, certain jokes, such as sex jokes, are more readily transferable from country to country—although even in this case they tend to carry a particular cultural stamp or style. This is illustrated by the contrast between British and American styles, which often leads Americans to think the British lack sense of humor—to the amazement of the latter.

Insofar as a universe of discourse is widely shared, the audience of a given bit of humor can be huge; for instance, jokes about leading politicians. Every informed Englishman during the days of Gladstone and Disraeli understood the following exchange between the two men: Gladstone said Disraeli would either be executed on the scaffold or die of a loathsome disease, to which Disraeli replied that this depended on whether he embraced Gladstone's principles or his mistress.

Certain types of puns and other sayings can be understood and used by citizens of very different backgrounds, again because they can share certain general perspectives. For instance, the conundrum: "What did the ram say as he fell off the cliff? Answer, "I didn't see that damned ewe turn." The phenomenon of *in jokes* exists because the universe of discourse, the shared communication, is limited in scope. In jokes are always related to some social world—be it ethnic, sexual, occupational, or recreational. Each social world has its particular stock jokes, humorous sayings, and fabled humorous stories about personages, social types, or important concerns in that world. For example, golf: a newcomer to the game, looking for his ball that strayed in the midst of trees and underbrush, rises with the ball in his hand and says to his partner: "Here's the ball, now where's the course?"

In reviewing the jokes just given, it is apparent that their effectiveness as humor depends not only on language as a body of words, but language as sets of meanings—and the interaction that sustains these meanings. Humor's persistence and pervasiveness—as well as its many forms—suggests that in the face of taboos and threats, humor is a vital and basic form of human behavior. The few social psychologists, psychiatrists, and philosophers who have tried to analyze humor as a phenomenon have tended to restrict their foci to the so-called functions of humor, or have simply classified its forms, or have attempted to account for humor by remarkably overgeneralized theories. The conditions for and the consequences of telling jokes, laughing at slips of speech, creating irony, and other settings for humor are multitudinous; no simple theory could possibly account for them all. For the social psychologist, the important task is to get humor back into the interactional picture as an essential and important part of human behavior.

Being Humorous

Lynch (1982), Flaherty (1984), and Fine (1984) have contributed to our understanding of how humor and playfulness in everyday life are constructed and given meaning. Following Bateson (1979), Lynch notes that playful humor involves a process of creative exploration in a relationship. Consider the following excerpt from his field notes. The occasion is a sociable gathering attended by seven people. The principal interactants are Shan, a 40-year-old professor of social psychology from Japan; Paul, a 45-year-old professor in the social sciences; and Rob, a graduate student. During an evening of sociable talk, it is proposed that Shan and his wife have a veranda sale to sell their furniture before they return to Japan. The following conversation was recorded:

SHAN: "Actually, garage sale is an interesting phenomenon—we don't have such a recycling system in Japan. . . ."

PAUL: "That's right—garage sales have much cultural significance!"

SHAN: "I think that *in garage saleology*, there is also great economic significance.

PAUL: "What we really need then is a department of *garage saleology* to study this important phenomenon seriously" (Lynch, 1982, p. 51).

In this playful, humorous interactional episode, the participants create a new concept—garage saleology. They produce this concept out of their earlier talk about a veranda sale (itself an instance of humorous playfulness); they then turn this concept into a department and a field of inquiry. The talkers have pushed the boundaries of their relationship into new realms of playfulness, and they have done this by turning talking and language into resources for interaction. Lynch shows how talkers construct play in social situations. He shows how play originates, gains momentum, becomes serious, breaks down, changes course, builds on itself, suffers disruption, and then fades away (Lynch, 1982,

p. 60). He shows how participants signal one another about the play they are engaging in. In play and humor, interactants take a step outside literal reality and enter the realm of make-believe.

Flaherty (1984, p. 75) suggests that humorous interaction is reality play; by this he means that interactants play at not taking reality seriously. Normal interactions are organized in terms of what he calls "reality work"; the attempt to organize interaction and talk in terms of taken-for-granted rules regarding proper interaction. In reality play, interactants trifle with, alter, and change the normal expectations which are themselves "constitutive of reality work. In turn, this leads to a formal definition of humor as 'every event which manifests itself as reality play'" (Flaherty, 1984, p. 80).

Compare an actual interview between a patient and a psychiatrist, and the following account from a Woody Allen monologue in the film *Annie Hall:*

A boy goes to a psychiatrist, and he says "Doctor you must help us, my brother thinks he's a chicken." And the psychiatrist exclaims, "You must have him committed at once." But the boy retorts "We can't, we need the eggs" (Flaherty, 1984, p. 76).

This short strip of humor challenges normal expectations concerning a patient-psychiatrist dialogue. The joke releases us from the ordinary world of reality work and makes us laugh. This is what reality-play-as-humor is all about. Flaherty suggests that reality play exists everywhere. With Lynch he would suggest that in reality play and humor, people step back from literal reality and creatively insert playfulness into their ordinary routines.

Fine (1984, pp. 83–101) has suggested that humor in social interaction plays an important part in shaping how people define themselves and their situations. Jocular or humorous interaction has, he argues, three features. First, it demands an immediate reaction from its listeners. Second, it allows the

person who is joking to place some distance between themselves and the joke they tell. Third, humor carries deep, often metaphorical meaning which extends beyond what is overtly intended.

Fine (1984, p. 94) gives an example of how humorous talk is used to justify one's action, especially when the action might be questioned. A girl (Bev) makes the following statement after she throws some food from a car window:

I littered, but it's biodegradable. A peanut butter and jelly sandwich. (Bev laughs.) No big threat to ecology. (Bev is giggling while she says this.) (All laugh.)

In this episode Bev presents a humorous denial of any deviance or harm she might create as a result of littering the roadside, and places distance between herself and her action by calling the sandwich biodegradable. This account elicits an immediate reaction from her listeners.

DAYDREAMING AND DREAMING

How do our previous discussions of thinking, shared symbolic behavior, expressive verbal behavior, and humor contribute to our understanding of such related mental and interactional phenomenon as daydreaming, fantasy, and dreaming? These processes—unlike *thinking,* which involves conscious and reflective attempts to enter into the activities of another individual—represent, as Singer (1975, p. 3) suggests:

a shift of attention *away* from some primary physical or mental task we have set for ourselves, or *away* from directly looking at or listening to something in the external environment, *toward* an unfolding sequence of private responses made to some internal stimulus.

The inner processes that the daydreamer attends to involve "pictures in the mind's eye" which may anticipate future experiences in which the thinker will take part, or the pictures may recall past experiences of some significance to the person. Daydreaming is a normal mental process.

In psychological writing, it is common to make a distinction between objective, rational thought and autistic, or fantasy, thought. The former is supposed to be more or less impersonal, systematic, objective, and logical; the latter is supposed to occur because it satisfies the subjective wishes and desires of the person and so is more or less irrational, illogical, and out of touch with reality. The assumption that fantasizing is a process apart from rational or systematic thinking, is associated with the belief that daydreamers substitute the satisfactions of the daydream for those denied them by the exigencies of actual life. It is said that they derive three main types of satisfactions: compensation, escape, and release. Compensatory daydreams allow the person to imaginatively attain goals that are otherwise unattainable. The Cinderella legend has its counterpart in the fantasies of anyone who wishes for something he or she cannot get. Daydreams of escape occur under such conditions as anxiety, boredom, hardship, and fear; the fantasies temporarily transport the dreamer into more pleasant surroundings. Daydreams of release function as safety valves by allowing the individual to dissipate anger, hatred, resentment, or jealousy in a harmless imaginary form.

Although fantasy is supposed to serve the functions of escape, compensation, and release, it is not easy to prove that these are its only functions. It is hard to determine the function of a given daydream merely by examining its content; even if one knows a great deal about the personality and background of the daydreamer, the fantasy activity may still not fit into any of the three conventional categories.

The attempt to uncover the function of daydreams is based upon the assumption that fantasizing is something apart from rational thinking; it is assumed that it must yield special satisfactions or it would not occur. Hence, daydreaming is supposed to occur mainly in connection with situations of stress, anxiety, boredom, and the like. This is underscored further by the vivid and elaborate fantasies of the psychotic, and the excessive daydreaming of maladjusted people. However, a closer scrutiny of daydreaming (without previous commitment to a dichotomization of "reality thinking" and a substitute for it) brings some other relevant matters into focus.

Normal adults know perfectly well when they are daydreaming, and they will sometimes set aside time to engage in this often pleasant activity. Young children often have difficulty distinguishing between reality and fancy; they sometimes get them mixed up, to the amusement or exasperation of their elders. The requirements of adult life eventually make it necessary for the child to draw a strict line between fact and imagination. The severe psychoses and the condition of senility cause their victims to lose the ability to make this clear separation, at least in their less normal moments. In the psychotic, various types of fantasizing seem to constitute "thinking" and "reasoning." These commonplace observations do not lead to a separation of fantasizing and reasoning but suggest quite the opposite—namely, that fantasizing is a type of reasoning.

As fantasizing is not a single process but embraces many types of covert activity, we can say that reasoning of various kinds may occur when anyone fantasizes. The fantasy life of young children may be one of their dominant lives; They have not yet been sufficiently socialized into correcting their perspective by checking them against the facts or comparing them with the views of other people. Severe psychotics, for the most part, do not operate with *consensual validation* (public verification) in mind; the various types of fantasizing in which they engage constitute their modes of handling social relationships and responding to the physical world. Maladjusted persons get "absorbed in their fantasy life"; this is the way they meet the impinging world. Normal adults, although they know the difference between reality and fancy and between public knowledge and private secret, are not constrained to reason only in socially sanctioned and verifiable modes or in systematic or rational ways. It is well known that even though scientists present their findings and check them for public appraisal in systematic ways, their guiding ideas may have occurred to them through processes that are like reveries.

A *stream of consciousness* or of *associations* is likely to be a peculiarly rich mixture of covert mental processes. Visual and auditory images, subverbal comments, daydreaming dramas, recollection, reviewing past scenes, self-judgments, internal dialogue, and many more elements jostle each other. Even a daydream with a fairly tight plot or progression may have intrusions in the form of the daydreamer's comments or judgments. A certain amount of control may be exerted over daydreams by repeating and reviving them. Many daydreams appear to be fragmentary and of short duration, and are preceded and followed by conscious, rational thought processes. Like the latter, the fantasizing may be absorbing enough to exclude external stimuli that might otherwise impinge upon the awareness of the person (or the stimuli may break the line of reasoning or fantasizing). It is easier to daydream when other people are not around to break the reverie, but this is perhaps true for any kind of thinking (except that which depends upon immediate reciprocal stimulation and verification).

Some writers have contended that it is "more plausible to consider it (daydreaming) as preparation for hypothetical activity than as consummation" (Faris, 1952, p. 100). This is certainly a function of all thinking, and there is little doubt that it is the function of much fantasizing. It should be noted that interaction between humans is dramatic in character, and thus a dramatic imagery is required for both actual and imaginary participation in it. For example, a man prepares for such interaction when he pictures to himself various ways of getting acquainted with a

woman who attracts him. In order to imagine the play of gestures and to judge the effects of conversational lines, he plays out various dramas in his imagination. Out of these, a plan may emerge.

It is a moot point whether persons about to enter knowingly upon a new status, or about to embark upon any enterprise involving new interpersonal relationships, can initiate their lines of behavior without daydreaming of themselves in their new role. Cues for actual behavior seem to be derived from this kind of thinking, which is also intertwined with less pictorial reasoning. Anticipatory fantasizing can even occur in an overt or shared form, as when husband and wife plan an exciting trip or anticipate the birth of a child. The preparatory functions of fantasizing—rather than the merely wish-fulfilling functions—can be suggested by the experience of immigrants who imagine what the new land will look lie and what will happen to them there. Visionaries, utopians, and leaders of social movements do not merely plan, organize, and execute; *dreamer* can be applied to them literally. In order for the symbolism of a movement to recruit members and help retain them, it must be kept vivid and rich. Retrospective fantasizing may occur when an individual reconstructs a particular pleasurable act. Indeed, as we suggest in Chapter 13, the sexual act may be grounded in retrospective and prospective fantasy.

Like other forms of thinking, fantasizing may turn to the past. It is true that one may help eradicate shame and other unpleasant feelings by refurbishing a past conversation or incident in daydreams; but it is also characteristic of humans to seek explanations of the past and to "rethink" incidents and discover new meanings in them. Some of this reinterpretation and reconstruction presumably goes on in the form of reverie. Reveries abound in times of personal crisis, when individuals are questioning themselves about where they are going and must consequently consider where they have been.

These processes are also implicit in any thinking or imagining in which people seek to establish relationships with real or imaginary people. Some people clearly get pleasure out of imagining meeting celebrities, and they may daydream long conversations occurring in such improbable situations. This kind of fantasizing may not merely be pleasurable; it may transform the individuals in their own eyes. Such shifts of self-conception occur even though the dreamers are aware that they are fantasizing. Another kind of vision is that sought by Eastern mystics who fast in order to achieve an elaborate reverie, or series of reveries, in which sacred animals and gods appear. Here there is social sanction both for the vision and its lifelong effects upon the individuals, and perhaps upon their social group. This last example suggests the close connection between ritual and reverie. Ritual, when it is not merely routine, represents a collective acting out of hallowed dramatic sequences, and these, like reverie, may orient one for future conduct. In Langer's felicitous phrasing (1948, p. 128):

(Rituals) are part of man's ceaseless quest for conception and orientation. They embody his dawning motives of power and will, of death and victory, they give active and impressive form to his demoniac forms and ideals. Ritual is the most primitive reflection of serious thought, a slow deposit, as it were, of people's imaginative insight into life.

Seen in such wider contexts, fantasy processes are multiple in kind and function, and are orienting as well as wish fulfilling.

Most of the literature on autistic thought and fantasizing behavior has been produced by psychiatrists and clinical psychologists who are impressed with the great amount and truly fantastic quality of the reveries of their patients. This latter fact, combined with certain assumptions about the nature of humans and their relationship to reality that are made by many psychiatrists and psychologists, leads to an undue stress upon the crippling or merely compensatory effects of fantasy life. Excessive fantasizing does not lead to maladjustment, but may be a symptom of it.

DREAMING

The meaning of dreams has long intrigued and sometimes worried humans; as far back as the Old Testatment, Joseph was rewarded for correctly interpreting Pharaoh's troubling dreams. for books on dreams go back as far as the second century A.D. There are "dream books" that purport to offer guidance in interpreting dreams by supplying the meanings of dream sequences and events, usually in terms of predictions for the future of the dreamer. Eating cheese in a dream, for instance, is said to portend good fortune. The symbols interpreted in dream books are universal in the sense that anyone eating cheese is in for happy times. The question of what specific dreams "mean" and whether a universal symbolism exists have had lively treatment by scientists during the past century, largely in the fields of psychiatry and psychoanalysis. Social psychologists seem less interested in dreaming, presumably because they do not utilize dreams for obtaining insights into the mental and emotional processes of patients; but dreaming is an interesting and important psychological phenomenon in its own right.

Many studies of dreaming deal with physiological correlates, duration, speech, and frequency of occurrence of types of imagery (visual, auditory), as well as with the dream imagery of the blind or the deaf-blind, with sex and age differences, with types of dreams, and so on. Psychiatric literature is replete with examinations of the meanings of dream symbols and with the roles of certain kinds of dreams in the lives of certain types of neurotics. Despite the considerable bulk of this literature, both empirical and theoretical, the nature and significance of dreaming are areas of dispute.

The most influential theory of dreaming is that of Sigmund Freud. Freud's dream theory is part of a much wider and elaborate theoretical system concerning the psychological nature of humans in general. For our purposes, we need stress here only a few of the chief features of his views on dreams. Freud believed that various wishes threaten to disturb the sleeper's rest, and dreams perform the function of seeming to fulfill these wishes. Usually the wishes are unacceptable in the sense that the person does not care to admit that he or she has them. Hence they tend to be *repressed,* or excluded from consciousness, during waking hours. In sleep they appear as dreams, but in disguised forms, since even during sleep the person's psychic mechanisms are operating. The obvious, or *manifest,* content of the dream is an expression of its *latent,* or real, meanings. Freud writes that "we have got to turn the manifest dream into the latent dream, and we have to show how the latter became the former, in the life of the dreamer (1933, p. 19). Through the technique of evoking the patient's free associations, or nonlogical linkages, the patient and analyst eventually arrive at an interpretation of latent content and a knowledge of the connections between this and the manifest content.

The transformation in the dream of latent content into manifest content is termed *dream work,* and it proceeds through a process termed *secondary elaboration*—that is, the person *attempts* to give a rational account of her otherwise unaccountable and unfathomable dream. Dream work is an example of primitive modes of operation, which are characteristically unconscious. These modes are not rational and objective, and furthermore, they do not involve logical connect between propositions. Their hallmark is associations or nonlogical linkages. Freud termed this type of mental functioning *primary process,* and the sharply contrasted logical type he considered to be a *secondary process.* The primary process of mental functioning manifested in the dream is *regression.* The reason that dreams are visual is that there is censorship of undesirable wishes and of *instinctive impulses* which causes these wishes and impulses to emerge in disguised forms. "On account of the . . . process of re-

gression ideas are turned into visual pictures in the dream; the latent dream-thoughts are . . . dramatized and illustrated" (Freud, 1933, p. 31). Some associations which appear in the dream are not unique to the dreamer but are universal or at least common.

Freud pointed out that there were certain possible objections to his wish-fulfilled theory of dreams in the form of contradictory data. People who had had serious traumas reexperience these in their dreams. Freud questions what possible satisfaction of impulse can be had by this painful experience. Likewise, the reappearance in dreams of exceedingly unpleasant incidents from early childhood causes pain to the dreamer. Freud tentatively accounts for this partly contradictory evidence by stating that (1938, p. 18)

The sleeper has to dream, because the nightly relaxation of repression allows the upward thrust of the traumatic fixation to become active; but sometimes his dream-work, which endeavors to change the memory traces of the traumatic events into a wish-fulfillment, fails to operate.

The Freudian theory of dreams has been considerably amended by American psychoanalyst Thomas French, who has contended that the mode of mental functioning exemplified in the dream is neither Freud's secondary process nor primary process (1952, pp. 35–39):

In fact, it is not associative thinking at all . . . but rather thinking in terms of a practical grasp of real situations: "If I act upon this wish, then I must expect such and such consequences. Shall I renounce the wish or suffer the consequences? Or is some compromise possible?" The dream's solution may not be very good from the point of view of waking life, but it is always intelligible, once we grasp the nature of the conflict.

French sees dreaming as much like ordinary processes of practical thought, which generally are neither overly logical nor verbally formulated. He rejects the associational psychology that was prevalent in Freud's day, suggesting that the connections between specific latent and manifest meanings are related to dreamers' attempts to reconcile their conflicting wishes. We should note particularly in French's account that although the notion of wishes is retained, the nature and functioning of dreaming are conceived of quite differently.

The psychoanalytic conception of dreaming as wish fulfillment has been attacked repeatedly. Faris, for instance, contends that dreaming is an effort to solve problems, although the nocturnal effort is far less efficient than those of waking life (1952, pp. 101–104). A more systematic attack has been launched by C. Hall (1953), who argues that dream symbols are not disguised, but are merely representations of ideas: "Dreaming is pictorialized thinking; the conceptual is more perceptual. . . . A dream symbol is an image, usually a visual image, of an object, activity, or scene; the referent for the symbol is a conception." Since different people may have different conceptions of "woman," for instance, the dream symbols for woman vary accordingly. Hall, who has counted 102 symbols for the male organ in psychoanalytic writing, concludes that "since the referent is not an object, person, or activity, but a conception, the 102 different phallic symbols represent 102 ways of conceiving of the male genitals" (1953, p. 186). Of course, the dreamer may hold different conceptions, and hence he may utilize different symbols referring to these conceptions. Dream symbols, consequently, are not universal, although they may be widespread in a given culture. Hall's criticism of Freud seems to stem mainly from two objections: (1) that Freud's "disguise" theory of dream symbolization makes sleep a more active period than seems likely on the basis of studies and observation; (2) that Freud's associational psychology is "passé."

H. Sullivan, a thoughtful psychiatrist whose views we shall encounter again, criticized any account of dreaming as cognition on the grounds that dreamers cannot help distorting their reports of what happened during their dreams; there is an impassable barrier between the covert process of dreaming and the verbal formulations of waking life. Even if dreamers wish to remember the exact details of their dreams, they cannot (Sullivan, 1953, p. 343):

People who feel that they should analyze . . . a dream . . . into what it stands for, seem to me to be in exactly the state of mind of the person who says to a child of two-and-a-half, "You ought to show more respect for your mother because God on Mt. Sinai said to Moses, 'Honor they father and they mother.'" . . . The psychiatrist is dealing with the type of referential operation which is *not* in the syntaxic (verbal) mode, and one merely stultifies himself . . . by trying to make this kind of report syntaxic.

For Sullivan, dreaming is like other mental processes which go on in waking life but outside of awareness, and which have to do with the avoidance of severe anxiety. During sleep, people have less need to defend themselves against anxiety-arousing events, so that dreaming functions to guard against anxiety during sleep and (symbolically) to satisfy needs unslaked during the day. Sullivan imputes no regression to dreaming, and he is wary of interpreting symbols in any but a purely personal context. In Freud's defense, we must note that he too was sensitive to the fact that dreamers could never have direct access to their own dreams, and his concept of secondary elaboration refers to this.

These alternative treatments of dreaming suggest the controversy surrounding the topic. Is dreaming like logical reasoning—that is, practical, everyday thinking—or is it vastly different? Is it problem solving, or wish fulfilling? Are the symbols unique to individuals or groups, or are many of them universal? We shall not try to mediate in this free-for-all; however, because we generally reject many of the Freudian assumptions about motivation (and make this explicit in Chapter 6), we do reject the view that dreams are disguises for unsanctioned and unconscious instinctual impulses and wishes, and that there is unvarying correspondence between a given manifest content and the latent content of a dream. In our view, the living organism is engaged in covert symbolic processes even when asleep or unconscious. The processes involved in dreaming are on "lower levels" than those involved in self-conscious rational thought, particularly when the latter is being prepared for public appraisal. It is unlikely that the modes of sign manipulation employed in dreaming should differ much, if at all, from those employed in waking hours, particularly when the person is at a low point of self-awareness.

As for reporting dreams, we agree with Sullivan as to the great difficulty or impossibility of reporting dreams accurately; no one can possibly remember a dream without converting the dream sequence into words and so distorting and probably oversimplifying it. For the social psychologist, an important aspect of dreaming is that a dream, like any other private experience, can be responded to by self-conscious persons afterward. They may be pleased or ashamed of themselves for dreaming what they did; they may accept the view of their analyst or another person, including a fortune teller or the author of a dream book; and, as with all other interpretations, they may change their mind about it at a later time.

METAPHOR, ANALOGY, FLEXIBILITY OF THOUGHT AND METONYMY

Events and objects can be classified in many different ways. We can make a game of this by trying to see some common object—an apple, for example—from as many different perspectives as possible. Besides thinking of it as an edible fruit one may imagine it as a ball, a table decoration, a magical object, a pupil's gift to a teacher. Each idea leads us to view the apple from a different perspective and to act as if it were what we assume it to be or what we use it for. This ability to switch perspectives and regard the same event or object in many different contexts is uniquely human.

When something is treated linguistically as if it were or might possibly be something else, we employ *simile* or *metaphor*. In this way, a novelist might describe a helicopter hovering over an airfield as if it were an insect. Metaphorical language is not merely poetic, not simply a colorful embellishment, but is necessary to communication. If it is said that a party was "like a funeral" or that a man's speech was "like the braying of an ass," it is understood that the analogy is to be taken descriptively, not literally. Metaphors are often used in humor and satire: For example, in the occupational lingo of funeral directors the person in charge of cremation is called a "chef." And during the 1973 Watergate hearings, one columnist described how Dick Tracy (the great fictional detective) had been called into the White House the previous year to handle matters threatening our national security and had engaged in all the activities under investigation—bugging, burglarizing, and political "dirty tricks." Then, at the end of the story, it was revealed that Dick Tracy was the president himself.

According to German linguist P. Wegener (Langer, 1948, pp. 111–15), all discourse involves a context which is well known to speaker and listener, and also a novel element. To express the latter, the speaker will utilize a metaphor or analogy—if precise descriptive terms do not already exist—and the context tells the listener that the analogy is not to be taken at face value. It is impossible to strip explicit or implicit metaphor from speech, for many novel elements cannot easily be handled with extant vocabulary; so the speaker must hint, suggest, and evoke. The same is true of speech to oneself. In other words, *analogy* is at the heart of new perspectives, new orientations, vision, and advance in thought.

However colorful and "concrete" metaphors and similes appear, they betray a process of abstraction. As Langer (1948, p. 113) has pointed out, a word like *run,* when used in connection with rumors, brooks, and competition for political office, has nothing to do with leg action. She suggests that originally all the uses of the verb were probably metaphorical, but now "we take the word itself to mean *that which all its applications have in common*, namely, *describing a course*." Wegener has termed such a word a "faded metaphor"; he hypothesizes that "before language had any faded words to denote logical subjects, it could not render a situation by any other means than a demonstrative indication of it in present experience." We need not agree with Wegener's account of the development of language to see that abstraction rests in some part upon analogy. "The spontaneous similes of language are our first record of *similarities* perceived," Langer writes. But *analogical thinking* is integral to abstract cogitation of even the most abstract and systematic sort. Of course, it is used constantly in developing new political and social positions and in justifying them.

We are properly advised against taking an analogy too literally, as in relying upon analogy in order to prove a point in an argument. "The great danger of analogy is that a *similarity* is taken as evidence of an *identity*" (Burke, 1936, p. 128). However, as economist John Maynard Keynes argued, one must always generalize by analogy from a sample of a class to the entire class, because in many respects each instance is unique and there is no absolute identity of all instances in the class. Keynes' point, as well as our previous discussions of the nature of categories, make clear that all abstraction and generalization are inevitably oversimplifications of reality. Hence all analogies, however fruitful, will be questioned sooner or later.

The danger and necessity of analogy are the danger and necessity of language itself. No classification covers all qualities of the objects it embraces. Yet without classification and metaphor there would be limited flexibility of behavior, and our attention would be focused directly upon immediate situations. The danger and fruitfulness of metaphor can be epitomized by a strategy—an old and necessary technique often used by philosopher John Dewey. Dewey would take two sharply opposed philosophical positions and show that from yet another and "tran-

scending" position, the opponents were really rivals on the banks of the same local stream. In turn, we can be sure that Dewey's position could be lumped with many that he attacked. From a historical perspective, the positions of even the bitterest opponents often appear to be much closer than the rivals would have thought possible.

Metonymy

Metonymic thinking and speech, in which the name of one thing is used for that of another related to it—for example, the effect for the cause, the bottle for the drink—parallel metaphorical thinking. Metonymy reveals how events and objects can be classified in different ways. While metaphor relates things that are similar, metonymy relates things that are closely associated with one another in a contiguous manner. Both are figures of speech which establish equivalences in that they "characteristically propose a different entity as having 'equivalent' status to the one that forms the main subject of the figure" (Hawkes, 1977, p. 77).

Generally speaking (Hawkes, 1977, p. 77), metaphor exploits a proposed similarity or analogy between a literal object and its metaphorical substitute, for example, a car's movement compared to the beetle's movement. Metonymy, on the other hand, is based on a sequential association between the literal object (the president) and its adjacent replacement (the White House, where the president lives).

Jakobson and Morris (1956, pp. 69–96) have proposed that language use reveals a tendency toward one of two polarities. Romantic poets, surrealist paintings, Charlie Chaplin films, and Freudian dream-analyses tend toward metaphor. To the metonymic order, in which associations of a linear (syntagmatic) nature predominate, belong heroic epics, narratives of the Realist school, and Griffith and Hitchcok films (see Barthes, 1964/1967, p. 60).

Jakobson and Morris propose that certain types of aphasia (see Chapter 5) tend toward either metaphor or metonymy—that is, similarity disorders versus contiguity disorders. Patients suffering from similarity disorders preserve metonymy (i.e., fork for knife, table for lamp, smoke for fire). Patients with contiguity disorders organize speech in terms of metaphors (see Hawkes, 1977, p. 78).

Lacan (1977, pp. 158–59) has suggested that in the unconscious, dreams are organized in terms of metaphor and metonymy. He sees the unconscious dream processes of condensation and displacement as structured by metonymy and metaphor. Metonymy, with its word-to-word movement, is like displacement (Coward & Ellis, 1977, pp. 99); metaphor, which combines things that are similar, is like condensation. Thus Lacan argues that language is organized in the unconscious, as it is at the conscious level, in terms of the two great poles of language identified by Jakobson—metaphor and metonymy.

This formulation extends Saussure's (1959) position that the mental activity that takes place within language occurs along two dimensions, which he calls the *syntagmatic* and the *associative* poles. Word and thought combinations supported by linearity are syntagams, for example, "God is Good" (Saussure, 1959, p. 123). On the other hand, words also acquire meaning by virtue of their association in memory. The French word "enseignement" (teaching) will "unconsciously call to mind a host of other words (enseigner 'teach,' renseigner 'acquaint,' etc. . . ." (Saussure, 1959, p. 123).

Jakobson consolidated Saussure's two poles of language (syntagmatic and associative) into the metaphoric, metonymic polarity; these then become the "two great poles of language." Lacan then argued that the unconscious, structured like a language, is organized in terms of these two processes.

More work needs to be done on metaphor, metonymy, and the everyday thought processes that these terms organize. Clearly, Lacan has metaphorically redefined two Freudian terms (displacement and condensation) and reasoned, by analogy, that they operate in terms of metonymy and metaphor. Jakobson has made similar moves in his studies of aphasia and in his classification of modern art, literature, and film. In these efforts we can see attempts to join semiotics with literary criticism, psychoanalytic theory, film theory, and the study of disturbed thought processes. Metz (1982) has systematically applied these concepts to the semiotic, psychoanalytic analysis of film.

CONCLUSION

We have shown how human groups form the basis for language, thought, symbolic behavior, humor, daydreams, and dreaming, and we discussed the various forms of analysis that constitute sociolinguistics. Language behavior is universal among all human groups, although each separate group tends to develop a special language of its own as an expression of its particular points of view, interests, and way of life.

Concern with human groups is a central focus of social psychology. Groups vary widely in size, duration, and complexity. Individuals who are born into groups or join them must learn the appropriate behavior and beliefs of each. A basic characteristic of groups is that they exist because of and through communication, especially spoken and written language. Language is always a group product, it is both an intrinsic part of the social heritage and the mechanism by which this heritage is transmitted from one generation to the next.

SUGGESTED READINGS

COOLEY, CHARLES HORTON (1902). *Human Nature and Social Order*. New York: Scribners. This book contains the essential thought of a forerunner of contemporary symbolic interactionist thought.

MEAD, GEORGE HERBERT (1934). *Mind, Self and Society*. Chicago: University of Chicago Press. Mead, along with Cooley, laid the foundations for much of the material in this chapter.

CHAPTER FIVE
Emotions, the Naming Process, and the Internal Environment

In this chapter we will take up the following topics: (1) the body and pain, (2) emotional experience, (3) madness, the uncanny, aphasia, and Alzheimer's disease, (4) body images, medicine, AIDS, and anorexia nervosa, (5) opiate and other addictions. We intend to explore the internal environment of the human so that we can gain a deeper understanding of how language and symbols structure human experience. The above topics reflect points of entry into the inner, symbolic world of the human body.

THE BODY

The human body, or the "lived body" as Merleau-Ponty (1968, p. 256) called it, is a complex structure. At one level, it is a physiological body and a sounding board for bodily sensations. At another level, it is a source of experience for the person, as when we feel fatigued after a long day at work. The body is also a source of information about the person; as others gaze upon us, or catch us in a glance, they gather and make inferences based on our body's appearance (Stone, 1962).

Persons have a threefold relation to the body. They are their bodies. They live, so to speak, inside their bodies, and they can get outside their bodies, and view themselves, sometimes objectively, as when they consider their reflections in a mirror. The lived body is the point of reference for the person's social and emotional experiences in the social world; it is also the symbolic and physical extension of the person in the situation. No dualism is implied in this statement, for the body and the self are intertwined presences in the world of experience.

French physiologist Claude Bernard has said that the stability of the internal environment is an indispensable condition for a free life. This statement points up the fact that in the routine business of living we tend not to pay much attention to our bodies as long as they remain healthy and respond properly in their customary manner. Our attention is focused much more on the outside world and on external events. In certain situations, however, we receive from the body unusual types of messages to which we are not accustomed. These experiences include pain, anxiety, and other types of problematic or extraordinary sensations, such as those involved in sexual activity or those experienced by a psychotic or drug user. Experiences of this kind require that we learn how to respond to them, cope with them, label them, and interpret what they signify. For example, a person who first uses marijuana must commonly learn both how to identify the effects and how to enjoy it.

PAIN

The preceding points are vividly attested to by that pervasive and seemingly quite physiological phenomenon known as pain. Most of us are likely to recognize that "pain is subjective"—despite its physiological sources. Pain is rooted in the body, of course, and in its internal malfunctioning or in the wounds received from the outside. People with different physical constitutions appear to have different capacities to withstand pain, as well as different thresholds for feeling pain. Also, people from different ethnic backgrounds reveal varying propensities to define and act on pain and illness. Nevertheless, there is no one-to-one relation between some physiological experience and the sensation of feeling a particular pain. In short, the messages coming from within the body which we label "pain" are interpreted just as any other perception is. Like other perceptions, pain has a private coloration but its meanings are deeply social in nature; and as with other meanings, we act upon them.

Among pain's properties are its (1) placement (where within or on the surface of the body); (2) frequency of appearance; (3) duration; (4) degree of intensity; and (5) quality—as described by adjectives like burning, searing, flooding, annoying. These properties seem "natural" to pain, but they are also matters of definition and social experience.

If knowledge of internal organs is imperfect or vague, then pain will be attributed to "the stomach area," "in there," or "down there" (pointing). Children and adults whose vocabularies are inadequate to describe certain pains will use crude approximations, and we may wonder, whether they have that intense a pain, or if they really experience it as "searing" rather than as just "burning" or as "lots of pain." Experience plays a part, too, as when a sufferer of occasional backaches gets to recognize the beginnings of a severe and lengthy "session" if she does not quickly correct her sitting position.

Pain rarely is just pain; it is set within a context of meanings. Thus a new or unexpected pain brings about an etiological search—Why this pain? An expected and socially legitimate pain—for example, the experience of childbirth—needs no such search, for its interpretation is obvious. Evaluations as well as interpretations are placed on various pains, as when a dentist angrily reproved a friend of ours, telling him he deserved his toothache because he had neglected his teeth for at least a decade. On occasion, pain can be received joyfully because it stands for something valuable, as in circumcision rites or other rites of passage wherein the pain signalizes passage into manhood. Pain can be endured and accepted as inevitable, as when someone needs an operation which she knows will be followed by a few days of postoperative pain.

In terms of the complexities of "the naming process and the internal environment," the search for etiological meaning is among the most interesting. Ordinary pains get self-diagnosed. However, extraordinary or persistent ones bring the sufferer to some presumably knowledgeable agent—a physician, faith healer, or druggist. Through the person's experience, or through diagnostic procedures, the agent will arrive at some decision about what in the body is causing the pain. If the agent cannot find a reasonable explanation, there are various options: to say so, to give a false answer, to refer the client to another agent, or to suggest a psychological

rather than a physiological cause. Modern medicine frequently employs technology and a complex division of labor to obtain a proper diagnostic answer—requiring the drawing and examination of blood, taking and reading X-rays, and examinations by specialists. Some diagnostic procedures themselves inflict pain, so that the patient must undergo further pain in order to be rid of a major pain. Of course, procedural pain is usually of short duration; but sometimes, as with bone biopsies, it is exceedingly hurtful.

Thus in discussing a phenomenon like pain, the social psychologist moves from considerations of "naming" internal bodily occurrences to quite external considerations involving interaction, social relationships and alternations in identity and self-image.

EMOTIONAL EXPERIENCE

Emotional experience provides an excellent example of a type of behavior involving an unusually complex combination of events and processes of different natures occurring at different levels. Thus, an emotional response may be triggered by an external social situation; as it occurs, it often conspicuously involves visceral and glandular changes that are accompanied by psychological processes. Emotional reactions traditionally have been regarded as distinct from other types of response (such as the cognitive), probably because they are not readily communicable and seem, therefore, to have a distinctively private aspect. Different aspects of total emotional response have tended to form the basis for mutually incompatible theoretical formulations found in different disciplines.

The nature of emotion has been a controversial question for centuries, and there are countless theories concerning it. Students of emotion have written about it in terms ranging from the physiological to the cultural. Most of the efforts of psychologists have been concerned with the physiology of emotion; for example, attempts have been made to determine what muscular and glandular patterns of response accompany specific emotions, whether the sources of emotional awareness are in bodily movement or in attitude, and what part of the brain is involved in emotional behavior (see Scheff, 1979; Kemper, 1978).

Like many other aspects of human behavior, our emotions are profoundly affected by the fact that we live in complex societies. To the student of human behavior who seeks to take into account the types of feelings and emotions that are found in various societies, the situations that call them forth, and the many-sided conventionalized ways in which they are expressed, it appears that they are to an amazing extent regulated, prescribed, and even defined by groups (Lofland, 1985; Hochschild, 1983).

What arouses a given emotion is determined by social situations rather than physiological processes. For example, embarrassment is caused by different situations in different societies. Similarly, shame is an emotion aroused in accordance with prevailing social definitions. Even an emotion like fear is not invariably kindled by specific situations; in one society fear may be aroused by the occurrence of a bad omen—such as an eclipse—and in another society, by anticipation of collapse of the stock market. As we shall see, the emotions connected with even such commonly assumed biological drives as sex and hunger are also aroused by different situations in different societies.

The expression of emotions is also socially influenced, for the physiology of any emotion does not determine how the emotion will be expressed. In our society, anger is likely to be shown by sudden, impatient, or violent movements; but may be expressed differently in other societies. The Chinese, for example, are likely to show anger by staring with wide-open eyes. Klineberg (1940, p. 186) has noted that "the Chinese find that the faces of Europeans seem constantly to be expressing anger or irritation; this is probably due to the fact that the normally larger and rounder eyes of the Europeans resemble the Chinese eyes in anger." In the United States, one may express love in one way in the bedroom and in another way in public; anger is manifested differently in private and in the presence of company; expressions of hate are not supposed to be shown before children, but may be displayed when children are not present.

Much anthropological research has pointed to another and more subtle aspect of emotional patterning. Each society provides differential conditions of life for its members, so that certain emotions are aroused more frequently and intensely in one society than in another (see Ekman, 1980).

Many emotions are undoubtedly universal, but since the conditions of life vary so widely and the experiences of groups are so diverse, allowance must be made for variation from society to society. In societies where there is not an elaborate organization of social classes, emotions that have to do with class mobility and the maintenance and change of status can scarcely exist. The very language of such societies lacks a vocabulary for indicating the experiences and the events around which these emotions occur. Americans cannot easily imagine how it would be to experience a medieval sense of religious awe; they cannot appreciate the abasement of self that a caste system implies; nor can they feel the anticipation of the Brahmin as he looks forward to death and reincarnation (see Perinbanayagam, 1985).

THE LINGUISTIC ASPECT OF HUMAN EMOTIONS

The arousal and expression of emotion may be categorized into three phases, in their order of occurrence:

1. A stimulus or situation that is defined or interpreted in certain ways.
2. An internal response to the defined situation, involving both physiological and symbolic processes.
3. An outward conventionalized expression (by means of words, gestures, facial expressions,

and the like), that serves to indicate the emotion to others.

A given external situation or act does not call forth an emotion until it has been interpreted in a certain way. The emotion is a response not to a raw stimulus as such, but to a defined, classified, and interpreted stimulus, to signs with meanings that vary according to situation, as shown in the accompanying table. The physiological aspects of emotional response (such rising in blood pressure, a changed heart beat, and increased activity of the ductless glands) are not learned forms of behavior. On the other hand, the symbolic processes involved in emotion are learned. The third phase of emotional behavior has sometimes been called the "mimicry" of emotion because persons may voluntarily utilize the conventional means of emotional expression without actually experiencing the genuine emotion. The actor does this constantly, but the same sort of mimicry is commonly used in ordinary life as people strive to conform to the polite usages of social intercourse.

The actual learning of emotional behavior considerably reverses the chronology of the arousal and expression of emotion just discussed. The child is first encouraged to imitate the outward manifestations of adult emotions—for example, at a funeral—even though he may not grasp the significance of the situation. Only as the child acquires a better understanding of the significance of death will he be able to actually feel the expected emotions and conform inwardly as well as outwardly. The table below outlines this process.

An adult who moves into a new social group may find that the modes of emotional expression of the group seem strange at first. The pressure to conform causes the person to quickly adopt the external forms of behavior, even though at first this may be merely playacting. As the person adopts the group's perspectives and begins to see the world as other people see it, her playacting becomes instead a genuine expression of experienced emotions.

We have been speaking of the first phase as if the stimulus that aroused the emotional response always comes from outside the organism. Actually, in humans the stimulus may lie within the symbolic processes. This can be seen plainly if one considers the arousal of emotion through daydreaming. A soldier may dream of going overseas and become fearful at the "thought" of it. Fantasy may also revolve about past events. While fantasizing, a person may recall a past insult and undergo emotions similar to those that were aroused by the actual insult; or he may reinterpret the event, perhaps laughing once he realizes no insult had been intended. Whether in daydreaming forward or backward in time, the stimulus to emotional arousal is not externally present.

Humans are aware of their own emotional responses, and they name, evaluate, and interpret them in accordance with definitions provided by the groups to which they belong. People not only experience anger, but they label their feelings as such and are able

Act	Situation	Definition	Resulting Emotion in the Victim
Slap in the face	Two quarreling people	Insult	Fury and resentment
Slap in the face	In a play	Playacting	None or simulated
Slap in the face	Father slaps child for lying	Punishment	Shame
Slap in the face	Twenty-month-old child slaps father	Good spirits	Amusement

to tell other people about them. Because of this capacity, humans have the power to control and inhibit their own feelings to some degree. Thus, a devoutly religious person who recognizes that she is becoming angry may check her response and seek a new interpretation of the situation that will allow her to respond, for example, by feeling compassion for the person who has insulted her. An almost uncontrollable impulse to laugh in church at a minister's gesture may be stifled by a quick redefinition—taking the form perhaps of "this is church, laughing would be awful," or of acute fear of embarrassment or shame (see Hochschild, 1983).

Cognitive-Social Aspects of Emotion

As the preceding discussion indicates, it is difficult to conceive of an experience that is purely emotional or an emotion that is purely physiological. Apart from the difficulties inherent in the idea of a purely physiological experience, Skinner (1953, pp. 161–62) has observed that the scientific study of emotional behavior which is based on the idea that each emotion has its own characteristic pattern of emotional response offers a far less reliable basis for identifying emotion than does common sense.

A decisive consideration here is that many of the physiological accompaniments of emotion can be produced by drugs. When this happens in a situation that has no emotional significance, the subjects do not report that they feel "angry," "afraid," or "unhappy," but rather that they feel as though they were experiencing one of those emotions without actually doing so. This suggests that rapid heart action, increased blood pressure, and other such phenomena do not signify emotion except when they are part of an appropriate behavioral context. In short, even if all the biological aspects of feeling terror were to be artificially produced, an individual evidently would not actually *feel* terror unless there were something in the environment that might cause this feeling. In absence of the appropriate situation, the physiological accompaniments of emotional behavior produce only "mock" emotion, not the real thing.

Schachter and Singer, taking their point of departure from the general idea that the interpretations of internal physiological processes that intrude on consciousness depend on how people view them or what they know about what is happening to them, have performed experiments of special significance in this argument (1962). Subjects were given a drug in a variety of ways for control purposes. Some subjects were grossly misinformed as to what to expect from the drug. The drug given was adrenalin, which normally produces palpitations, hand tremors, and a warm, flushed face. The misinformed subjects who experienced these unexpected effects were then put into different types of emotion-producing situations. The results indicated that they were more prone to become emotionally involved, but that the same state of physical excitation led to different and contradictory types of emotion, depending on the situations in which the subjects were placed. In contrast, subjects who were correctly informed as to the drug being given and its effects tended simply to explain how they felt as a consequence of the drug. The investigators concluded that when individuals experience physical excitation they do not understand, they tend to account for it with whatever cognitive schemes are available to them.

The situation faced by the subjects was much like that of persons who experience unusual abdominal symptoms and pains that do not fit into any pattern they know about. They are not only likely, but virtually bound to explain them with whatever cognitive terms are available or make sense to them. If they are perplexed, their friends cannot help them, and their symptoms are serious and persistent, they will normally consult a physician who will diagnose their ailment (name it, explain it, indicate its probable cause, apply a cognitive structure to it, and issue prescriptions and instructions to deal with it).

If the essentials of emotional behavior are not physiological, it is incongruous to think of them apart from the cognitive features with which they are inseparably entwined. How, for example, can people be expected to experience fear in a situation in which they are unaware of danger? How can people feel anger at an insult if they do not know they have been insulted? As new knowledge accumulates, new threats and new emotion-creating situations are created. For example, fear and anger have been generated by the reported level of strontium in the milk or water supply, and by second-hand reports of high radiation levels produced by fallout from distant atomic explosions.

Our discussion suggests that emotion should be viewed as an aspect of certain types of behavior rather than as a distinct form of behavior in itself. The specifically emotional portion of behavior is elicited by the relationship of the emotion-provoking situation to the values of the person as seen by that person.

If we accept the idea of emotion as an aspect of a behavioral sequence within a situation that is cognitively grasped, it is easy to understand that the emotional responses of any two people may be radically different in the same situation. *A,* for example, devoutly religious, believes that his immortal soul is in jeopardy; *B* is certain that she has no immortal soul and cannot, therefore, be worried about it.

It is also interesting to note that, perhaps because the involved multiple phases of emotional experience are sometimes spread out over an appreciable interval of time, the process may be interrupted so that during a dangerous event no subjective feeling of fear may be noticed. Victims of automobile accidents often report that when an accident begins, events seem to slow down in a curious way. They may have attended only to this and to the strange sensations created by the spinning or rolling car. The feeling of fear may not appear as a completed experience until after the accident. Other self-observations by individuals indicate the same points;

it is often remarked that one may observe the first surges of an emotional reaction with a certain detachment and even surprise, and have time to remark to oneself about it. Another observation is that a person can experience strong reactions without knowing for certain what the emotion is—whether it is anger, fear, embarrassment, or self-consciousness.

EMOTION AS SYMBOLIC INTERACTION

We can extend these remarks on emotional behavior by arguing that the processes of symbolic interaction organize all emotional experiences. By this we mean that the process of self-reflection, the organization of social acts, the meaning of time, and the labels we bring to our emotional experiences are themselves based on the interactional process. We suggest that emotions are *embodied self-feelings which arise from emotional social acts persons direct to self or have directed toward them by others* (Denzin, 1983, p. 404). Emotions are social acts and self-interactions; self-feelings refer to any emotion the person may feel—including bodily sensations, intentional feeling-states like grief, and feelings of self, such as shame or guilt. Every feeling a person has unfolds within a process that first involves a sense of feeling in terms of awareness; second, a sense of self feeling the feeling; and third, a set of self-feelings (for example, guilt, shame) in relation to the emotion.

Linguistically, we can see how every emotional word in our language contains hidden referents to self and to other people. We feel embarrassed, for example, in situations where we have acted in a way that causes others to react negatively to us. Emotional terms and labels, then, are interactional words; they locate persons in emotional situations. We can never have a completely private emotion, nor can we have an emotion or self-feeling that is not felt in the real or imagined presence of others.

Types of Emotions

We can distinguish four types of lived emotional experience. The first form is called *sensible feelings;* these are sensations felt in the lived body (pain, for example). They are not deliberately produced by the person. The second form is termed *feelings of the lived body.* These are feelings captured by such phrases as sorrow, despair, happiness, or anger. Lived feelings communicate an emotional definition of the person in the situation. People, for example, can see our grief or "feel" our sorrow about the loss of a loved one.

Intentional value-feelings is the third form of lived emotion. These are feelings which reference ways in which we intend or want to feel in a situation, but they are not the actual feelings we will feel. These are feelings about feelings, so to speak. If a person is ill and vomits, and then turns back on this experience, a feeling of self-anger may be felt—"Why did I eat that last piece of rich dessert anyway?" In this example the person intends a feeling about an emotional experience that has just been felt.

Intentional value-feelings can reference feelings that will occur in the future or events that have happened in the past. These feelings are produced through self-conversations, and they may or may not be accompanied by sensible feelings, or feelings of the lived body.

Feelings of the self, or the moral person, are the last form of lived emotion. Unlike intentional value-feelings, which originate in values that lie outside actual emotional experiences, feelings of the self originate from within the self, and are located in the inner stream of experience of the person. These feelings may carry deep implications for how we feel about ourselves. Consider the following statement by Malcolm Lowry (1947, pp. 223–89). A deep wrenching of the self from its inner moral meanings is offered in this statement by Lowry's protagonist, the Consul:

That bloody nightmare he was forced to carry around with him everywhere upon his back, that went by the name of Goffrey Firnin . . . deliver me from this dreadful tyranny of self. I have sunk low. Let me sink lower still, that I may know the truth. Teach me to love again, to love life. . . . Let me truly suffer. Give me back my purity, the knowledge of the mysteries, that I have betrayed.—Let me be truly lonely that, that I may honestly pray. . . . Destroy the world! he cried in his heart.*

Here we see a lonely, frightened individual, feeling a series of self-feelings which cut to the core of who he sees himself as being. Self-feelings are part of being human. In studying and interpreting emotional experiences, it is important to keep in mind the following points: First, all emotions have a linguistic foundation. Second, all emotions are interpreted by the self, at some level of awareness. Third, the way in which the self and the lived body enter into the experiencing of emotion varies by whether they are sensible feelings, feelings of the lived body, intentional value-feelings, or feelings of the self.

INTERPRETING DRUG EXPERIENCES

Increasing attention to the effects of drugs has accompanied the increased popularity of marijuana, cocaine, and other drugs among persons of the middle class. The effects of a drug are not easy to communicate to those who have not experienced them. In order to conceptualize what such an experience is like, one must either talk with and observe those who know from direct experience or try it oneself. The final authority on the question of how drug effects are experienced by a given user is the user and no one else.

Carrying the argument further, we can note, as Becker has pointed out with respect to marijuana, that users must generally learn

---

*From Malcolm Lowry, *Under the Volcano* (New York: Harper & Row, 1984). Reprinted by permission of the publisher.

how to "smoke pot," how to identify the effects and how to feel "high" or "stoned" (1953, 1973). The most common report of the beginner who tries marijuana is that he feels nothing; the first experiences may also be unpleasant. This may be due to faulty technique or false expectations—and if one's expectations are based on reports in the mass media, they are almost certainly wrong. Because the beginner looks for effects that marijuana does not produce, he fails to notice those that it does produce. This error is quickly corrected by the user's associates, who assist users in learning and validating in their own experience the viewpoints and shared conceptions that cause marijuana users to experience the effects as pleasurable.

A fairly elaborate ideology and mystique grows up around the drug from its collective use and from the sharing of experiences with it. Its dangers, techniques of dealing with uncommon effects, ways of counteracting excessive doses, and the effects of drugs on various activities—all become part of an ideology that carries the authority of a considerable tradition built up by generations of users. Just as with alcohol, marijuana users are instructed in what to expect under various circumstances and therefore are not alarmed by what the drug does to them.

Similar points can be made concerning alcohol, but in this case there are many millions of people who have experienced various possible effects and have described them to others. Because knowledge of alcohol's effects is widespread in our culture, the alcohol experience seems less mysterious and less subjective than the LSD, cocaine, or marijuana experience. The person who gets a hangover for the first time and takes it too seriously is promptly reassured by the laughter and advice of associates who instruct her about hangovers and what to do about them. If, while drunk, she has done things that would otherwise be viewed as proof of a psychotic condition, or if she blacks out and cannot remember what happened the night before, this too is explained as ordinary and

unalarming. At higher levels of sophistication, such as those represented in Alcoholics Anonymous, other more advanced phenomena such as the "shakes" and delirium tremens are similarly handled by group definitions consensually validated by the experiences of other members.

This kind of reasoning has also been applied by Becker (1967, pp. 163–76) to LSD, which is a drug of greater potency than alcohol or marijuana. Being a new drug in the 1960s, LSD had not been thoroughly explored as a pleasure-producing agent. Consequently there was uncertainty even in the minds of users as to what to expect, what the dangers were, and how they might be dealt with. It is noteworthy, however, that users already emphasized that before taking a "trip" one should be briefed and coached on what to expect and what to do when the effects took hold. Techniques for dealing with bad trips were reported. We suspect that similar processes are now occurring for cocaine users, especially in light of the growing numbers of deaths associated with its use.

MADNESS, THE UNCANNY, AND APHASIA

French psychiatrist Charles Blondel, speculating some years ago on the uncanny impression that the psychotic creates in the nonpsychotic, has proposed an interesting and relevant interpretation of this type of mental abnormality (1928b). Some of his ideas were derived from Durkheim, who has been an influential figure in the development of American sociological thinking.

According to Blondel, the ordinary activity of an individual presupposes a smoothly functioning internal psychological and biological environment, and goes on against a background of internal stimuli arising from various parts of the body and from normal psychological reactions. He calls these internal stimuli, which are larely ignored except when they signal a disturbance of bodily equilibrium, or homeostasis, the "kinesthetic mass." In the nonpsychotic person these processes are the setting within which the higher functions occur. The socialized individual responds to these internal stimuli in terms of the categories provided by the society of which he is a member. Thus, people respond to certain types of internal stimulation by reporting, "I am hungry" or "My foot is asleep."

Blondel believed that in the psychotic, this kinesthetic mass is disturbed; he or she becomes aware of internal stimuli that cannot be identified with the usual labels. Psychotics develop the notion that curious and fantastic things are happening within them, and when they attempt to describe their experiences to other people, they are not understood. Others regard the psychotic's remarks as queer or crazy; their response leads the psychotic to withdraw, and this in turn accentuates the break in communication.

Finding themselves rebuffed by others, psychotics withdraw into their own private world but continue to attempt to adapt themselves verbally to their strange sensations. In their struggle to assimilate their essentially unique and unassimilable experiences, they build up ideas that seem fantastic and senseless to others. The curious speech and distorted reasoning of the psychotic as conceived of by Blondel is an attempted symbolic adaptation to an organic disturbance. Blondel does not account for the origin and nature of this organic disturbance; presumably, however, the disorder would be in the central nervous system, whatever its causes might be.

Blondel's theory, whether or not it will stand the test of verification, has interesting implications because it avoids the usual mind-body fallacy. Even if all the psychoses should turn out to have organic causes, the study of psychological symptoms would not be irrelevant to the study and understanding of psychotics.

H. S. Sullivan's conception of schizophrenia resembles Blondel's, for he too stressed the crucial role of the uncanny and of the inability to communicate and designate it. But he does not make physiological stimuli the cornerstone of his analysis (1953, p. 327):

In the schizophrenia state, very early types of referential process occur within clear awareness, to the profound mystification of the person concerned. And since many of these referential processes are literally historically identical with the composition of the not-me components in personality, their presence is attended by uncanny emotions . . . (These) schizophrenic processes which we encounter represent attempts on the sufferer's part to communicate types of processes that most of us created to have within awareness by the time that we are two and one-half.

According to Sullivan, there are three modes of experience: the prototaxic, the parataxic, and the syntaxic. These terms refer to the manner in which experience is registered and to the nature and degree of inner elaboration that it is accorded. In the prototaxic mode, there is an absolute minimum of inner elaboration, and experience consists mainly of discrete series of momentary states which can neither be recalled nor discussed. The syntaxic mode, in contrast, involves a maximum of inner organization and elaboration; because it is fully encompassed by symbolic formulation and is logically ordered, it can be discussed and completely communicated to others. In the parataxic mode of experience, which lies between the two, experience is partially organized or organized in a quasi-logical manner, but there are also elements of which the individual is unaware. Parataxic experience can be discussed by the adult human subject, but Sullivan states (1953, p. 29):

The mode which is easiest to discuss is relatively uncommon . . . experience in the syntaxic mode; the one about which something can be known, but which is somewhat harder to discuss, is experience in the parataxic mode; and the one which is ordinarily incapable of any discussion is experience in the prototaxic or primitive mode.

Children's earliest experiences (as we note in Chapters 7 and 8) are in the prototaxic mode, but they quickly progress to the parataxic once they start to make sense out of their environment and note certain interconnections and simple sequences. Lower animals also are capable of reaching the parataxic level, according to Sullivan. The syntaxic mode appears with the learning of language and is hence confined to human beings, although Sullivan emphasizes that it is rarely possible for us to express all aspects of an experience in words. Roughly, we can say that the three modes represent the incommunicable or ineffable (prototaxic), the partially communicable (parataxic), and the wholly communicable (syntaxic). This scheme allows a considerable place for unconscious behavior without positing an "unconscious mind" or instinctual urges as the mainsprings of behavior.

While Sullivan's account stresses childhood experiences as the probable origin of some psychoses, he does not rule out organic causes in other psychoses. Blondel, on the other hand, emphasizes organic causes but leaves open the question of the nature and causes of these organic conditions. Both stress that the psychoses conventionally said to be characterized by a radical detachment from reality—or, in our terms, by a breakdown in the communication mechanisms—are linked with disturbances within the internal environment that are as uncanny and incommunicable. The symptoms of psychoses are conceived by both psychiatrists in terms of the individual's efforts to grapple with this situation. These conceptions are clearly related and applicable to certain types of effects produced by drugs such as those we shall discuss later.

Interestingly, strange internal experiences of the type that Sullivan and Blondel were concerned with, and those produced by certain drugs, are often interpreted in religious or mystic terms. There are numerous cults and religious groups in different parts of the world that are either organized around the use of substances that change mental func-

tioning or that include the use of such substances as an integral part of their ceremonies and rituals. The psychedelic movement that focused on LSD is only one example; the peyote religion that flourishes among American Indians is another prominent example (Aberle, 1966, p. 28). In Mexico the "sacred mushrooms" from which psilocybin is obtained have been used for centuries, and were known to the Aztecs as "God's flesh" (Solomon, 1964, p. 153). In India and the Middle East, hemp or marijuana has been linked for centuries with religious beliefs and practices (Carstairs, 1954; Ebin, 1961). Some writers have suggested that the origins of religion may perhaps be traced to experiences of the type that scientists today label as "psychotic" or "drug induced."

Aphasia and Related Neurological Disorders

We have noted how various forms of madness and the uncanny illuminate the complex relationship between the internal environment of people and their speech and language abilities. We shall now briefly discuss aphasia—a language disturbance produced by lesion or disease in the brain—and related neurological disturbances which alter the "normal" relationship between speech, thought, and the internal environment.

Aphasia is often, though not necessarily, brought about by cerebral injury. Aphasic conditions may also be produced under hypnosis or by traumatic experiences. The loss of function associated with aphasia can assume various forms, including the inability to read, write, or name familiar objects.

Consider the following statement from a young Russian soldier who during World War II sustained a severe brain injury which altered his ability to read, think, speak, and write. He is discussing his attempts to write with a pencil (Luria, 1972, pp. 71–72):

I'd forgotten how to use a pencil. I'd twist it back and forth but I just couldn't begin to write. I was shown how to hold it and asked to write something. But when I picked up the pencil all I could do was draw some crooked lines across the paper and finally moved the pencil across the paper. But looking at the mark I'd made it was impossible to tell where I'd started. It looked something like the scribbling of a child . . .

Often, in the aphasic's world, there is no memory of the past. This means that the patient has difficulty connecting internal, bodily processes with the words that represent those processes. Luria (1972, pp. 87–88) describes the Russian soldier trying to relieve himself. Here are the soldier's words:

After dinner, when the other patients were going to sleep, I suddenly had to relieve myself. To put it plainly, I needed the bedpan. But what a complicated thing it was for me to remember the word and call the nurse. For the life of me I couldn't think of the word *bedpan*. . . . I saw the nurse . . . I yelled . . . calling her *sister,* a word that suddenly entered my mind: "Sister . . . I also . . . need the . . . what's it!"

Oliver Sacks, (1985) professor of neurology at the Albert Einstein College of Medicine, discusses a patient who had suffered a lesion in the visual cortex. The patient had difficulty converting sensations into recognizable objects. When shown a glove, he described it as a continuous surface unfolded on itself with five outpouchings. When by accident he put it on his hand, he exclaimed, "My God, it's a glove!" At the end of one consultation session he attempted to put his hat on and instead seized his wife's head, tried to lift it off, and attempted to put it on his own. He had "mistaken his wife for a hat!" (Sacks, 1985, p. 11).

The patient's wife made the following statement about his condition:

He does everything singing to himself. But if he is interrupted and loses the thread, he comes to a complete stop, doesn't know his clothes—or his own body. He sings all the time—eating songs, dressing songs, bathing songs. . . . He can't do anything unless he makes it a song (Sacks, 1985, p. 45).

The patient was a doctor of music, he learned to use melody, sound, and rhythm as a guide that gave meaning to his actions, but had lost the ability to connect his thoughts with words and the actions of his body.

In the 1890s, Charles Sherrington, a British neurologist, discovered what he called our sixth sense, which he named "proprioception." By this he referred to our normal ability to know where our bodies are, what position or posture we are in, and so on. We know this subliminally, without looking. Some aphasics appear to lose this proprioceptive sixth sense.

Sacks had a patient named Christina, who, after routine surgery, developed an acute infection in her nerves which permanently destroyed her proprioceptive nerve fibers. She became, and remains, disembodied. She lacks all instinctive sense of her body, its position, its posture, and its movements. She feels that her body is dead, not-real, not-hers, blind and deaf to itself.

There are a number of different ways to classify aphasia. Head (1926) distinguished four main types: verbal, nominal, syntactic, and semantic aphasia. More recently, in a review of the latest research on aphasia, Wallace (1984, p. 80) suggests that there are two basic types of aphasia. The first involves language disturbances that primarily affect the ability to speak (expressive, or Broca's aphasia), and the second involves the ability to understand language (receptive, or Wernicke's aphasia). Broca was the first to link types of aphasia with areas of the brain. He demonstrated an association between damage in the left hemisphere and aphasia. Patients who suffer brain damage in this area of the brain usually show disturbances in the ability to produce written and spoken language. They often speak slowly and with difficulty. They display poor articulation, improper sentence structure, and omission of small grammatical words and word endings. They may, however, understand written and spoken speech and often have the ability to sing familiar songs.

Wernicke identified another type of aphasia which results in disturbances involving how language is understood (receptive aphasia) as well as in speaking (Wallace, 1984, p. 80). Patients often have fluent and rapid speech, but their utterances are devoid of meaning.

Other types of aphasia have also been identified. Word deafness, for example, refers to a patient's inability to understand spoken language, even though he or she can hear normally, read, and write.

Wernicke proposed a theory of language production which is still held to be valid (Wallace, 1984, p. 80). This theory argues that an underlying utterance originates in Wernicke's area (the temporal lobe of the brain), and then is transferred to Broca's area where a coordinated program for the utterance is produced. This program is then passed to the motor cortex, which "activates the appropriate motor sequences required for the specific utterance" (Wallace, 1984, p. 90).

We noted in Chapter 4 that Jakobson had distinguished those aphasic disorders involving contiguity disorders and those involving similarity disturbances. Jakobson proposed that the two poles of language (syntactical and associative) were revealed in metonymy and metaphor. It is not entirely clear how Jakobson's classification scheme fits with the more recent distinction between expressive and receptive aphasia. However, those theories which explain aphasia in terms of disturbances to specific brain areas are called localization theories (Schutz, 1962, p. 263).

The Nature of Aphasic Experience

In analyzing the aphasic's experiences, we must maintain a distinction between inner speech and external speech performances (Schutz, 1962, p. 264). Inner speech finds its expression in thought and in the selection of words and word categories which fit the subject's ongoing flow of experience, including how she interprets bodily sensations. External speech performances, or speech acts, locate the inner speech and thought of the subject in a social conversation. In aphasia, this connection between inner thought and outer speech is broken, thought and speech become problematic, and furthermore, words are no longer immediately and directly linked to experience. Clearly those theories of aphasia which explain it in terms of localized injuries to specific areas of the brain speak not to language disturbances per se, but rather to a disturbance in memory. The aphasic loses the ability to deal with concrete, immediate experience. However, localization theories have problems explaining how the same word, spoken by different people in different contexts, is understood as the same word (Schutz, 1962, p. 270).

Merleau-Ponty (1962) has developed this point. The normal mind is able to spontaneously organize its perceptual field and its symbolic structure. It experiences no break or gap between sensation, perception, memory, thought, speech, and action. These accomplishments occur in the lived present. The aphasic is incapable of doing this; for him, the world suddenly becomes strange and problematic. A theory of aphasia which accounts for these disturbances solely in terms of the localization of brain function becomes a mechanistic, physiological account which does not account for how the person engages the world in a continuous process of interaction. Localization theories fall into the dualistic trap of separating mind from body. We can illustrate these points by taking up the introspective reports of aphasics.

Introspective Reports of Aphasics

Some of the most significant materials on aphasic thought are found in Head's work. The comments of his patients are interesting and provide some insight into their condition. One of them said (1926, p. 256):

When I think of anything, everything seems to be rolling along. I can't hold it . . . I can see what it is. I seem to see it myself, but I can't put it properly into words like you ought to. I can see what it is myself like. My mind won't stop at any one thing. They keep on rolling. Myself, I imagine when you're talking you're only thinking of what you're talking about. When I'm talking to anybody it seems a lot of things keep going by.

Another patient, attempting to explain the difficulty he had in finding his way about London, said, "You see it's like this: with me it's all all in bits. I have to jump like this," marking a thick line between two points with a pencil, "like a man who jumps from one thing to the next. I can see them but I can't express. Really it is that I haven't enough names" (1926, p. 371).

A number of comments by these patients indicate that images and the flow of imagery are profoundly affected by the loss of language that occurs in aphasia. Head always asked his patients to draw pictures, both from a model and from memory. One of the patients who had drawn a jug from a model could not do it from memory. He commented as follows (1926, p. 193):

I was trying to see the glass bottle: the picture seemed to evade me. I knew it was a bottle, and I could describe the drawing. But when it came to seeing it as a picture, I was more or less nonplussed. I often seem to have got the picture, but it seemed to evade me.

When this patient was questioned further it became clear that he experienced images, but that they appeared to be unstable and could not be controlled or evoked at will. He said, "The more I try to make them come the more difficult it is to get in touch with them, as one might say" (1926, p. 193).

Head performed the following test with one of his patients: He rolled bits of paper into wads and had a contest with the patient to see who could toss the improvised balls more accurately into a basket placed some distance away. The aphasic proved more adept than Head. Then a screen was moved in front of the basket so that the basket was not visible, and the contest was repeated. This time Head did far better than the patient; the patient was at a loss as to what to do. He explained his difficulties (1926, p. 208):

When I could see the basket I could follow the line of vision; when it was in the same place . . . I'd seen the basket before you put the screen there; I knew you hadn't changed the position, but in some odd way I didn't feel perfectly confident in my own mind that it was in that position.

We noted in Chapter 3 that through the internalized use of language, humans are able to imagine objects and events that are removed in time and space. This point is corroborated in the study of aphasia, for the aphasic's flow of imagery is so disturbed that he or she is unable to visualize objects adequately when they are not in view.

The inability of some aphasics to deal with objects they cannot see or touch is brought out in a curious manner by their inability to strike an imaginary match on an imaginary matchbox, to drive an imaginary nail with a nonexistent hammer, or to demonstrate with an empty glass how one drinks water. These same patients can strike actual matches, drive actual nails, and drink water from a glass when they are thirsty. Goldstein (1940) described these and other inabilities of the aphasic as a regression from an abstract or categorical attitude toward the world to a more concrete attitude.

DISTURBANCES OF VOLUNTARY ACTIVITIES

Clearly, aphasics appear to have lost a certain flexibility of orientation so that they no longer seem at home in the world. We can put this descriptively by saying that aphasics are not self-starters; they cannot talk effectively to others or to themselves about things that are not actually present. Their inner life is impoverished and simplified, and freedom of thought and action is largely lost. Aphasics are more or less at the mercy of the external stimuli that play upon them.

The aphasic is often able to function normally in simple concrete relations. But when required to act on the basis of long-range goals or abstract principles or merely of remembered events, objects, or persons, as all people constantly are, aphasics tend to fail. This limitation to the concrete present makes impossible much of the voluntary, "creative," kind of human behavior—behavior that seems normal because human beings think about things, events, and people and adapt their behavior to these verbal formulations or interpretations. Aphasics are unable to make these verbal formulations; therefore their responses are piecemeal and unintegrated. Aphasics respond to each concrete situation as such; and when no immediate demand is made upon them, or when excessive demands are made, they tend to lapse into inactivity or anxiety, realizing that there is something wrong with their inner life.

Goldstein has shown how drastically aphasia affected the intimate social relations of one of his patients. The patient, a husband and father, prior to his affliction had been devoted to his family. During his stay at the hospital, however, he appeared to show neither concern nor interest in his absent family and became confused when any attempt was made to call his attention to them. Yet when he was sent home for brief visits, he warmly displayed his former interest and devotion.

Goldstein concluded that this patient's "out of sight, out of mind" attitude toward his wife and family grew directly out of his inability to formulate his relationships to his family when it was physicially absent. He could not imagine it adequately, and consequently he could not engage in internalized thinking about it. In short, when his wife and children were not visible to him he was unable to think of them, because he could not produce and manipulate the necessary verbal symbols.

Failures of Projection

In one of the most significant tests he administered to aphasics, Head required the patient, seated opposite and facing him, to imitate his movements. Head placed his left hand to his right ear, his right hand to his right eye, and so on. Then he repeated the tests while the patient observed and imitated these movements as they were reflected in a mirror.

The patients either had great difficulty with the first part of this test or they found it altogether impossible to imitate Head's movements, whereas they were generally able to imitate the movements correctly when they observed them in a mirror. The reason was not difficult to find: When the doctor and patient sat facing each other the patient could not imitate directly, but had to transpose directions (remembering that his left hand corresponded to the investigator's right hand, and so on). When Head's movements were reflected in the mirror, this action of transposition was unnecessary; all that was required was direct mechanical imitation.

Significantly, this simple but exceedingly effective test demonstrates that the person lacking language cannot project himself or herself into the point of view of another person. Patients are unable to guide actions by imagining them to be in some other position than the one in which they actually are. In a fundamental sense, normal adult social interaction rests upon a person's ability to anticipate and appreciate the actual and possible reactions of other people—in short, to assume the role of another person. The loss of this ability in aphasia (to varying degrees, depending upon the severity of the disorder) thus provides powerful experimental and clinical evidence to support the thesis that language is the basic social and socializing institution.

Direct and Symbolic Reference

Head made a distinction between what he called "acts of direct reference" and those that require some sort of symbolic formulation between the initiation and the completion of the act. This distinction is roughly equivalent to Goldstein's distinction between the "concrete" and the "abstract" (categorical) attitudes (1941). Acts of symbolic reference imply a complex adaptation involving the recognition of signs, logical symbols, or diagrams. Acts of direct reference are organized on a simpler level.

The aphasic generally functions adequately in acts of direct reference but has trouble with acts of symbolic reference. The accompanying table provides a few illustrations of the difference between the two classes of acts.

Acts of Direct Reference	Acts of Symbolic Reference
Imitating investigator's movements as reflected in a mirror.	Imitating investigator's movements seated opposite, facing him.
Shaving.	Gathering together in advance the necessary articles for shaving.
Selecting from a number of objects before him the duplicate of one placed in his hand out of sight.	Selecting from objects placed before him the duplicates of two or more objects placed in his hand out of sight.
Tossing ball into a basket that he can see before him.	Tossing a ball into a basket concealed behind a screen.
Exact matching of colored skeins of yarn.	Sorting and arranging colored skeins of yarn in a systematic way.
Pointing to familiar objects in his room.	Drawing a ground plan of his room that shows the location of familiar objects.
Swearing.	Giving the name of the Deity upon command.
Recognizing familiar streets and buildings of a city.	Following directions within a familiar city.
Repeating, fairly correctly, the numbers up to ten and sometimes beyond that if he is given a start.	Carrying out arithmetical operations, particularly those involving numbers of several digits.

Not all types of behavior listed in the second column are beyond the capacity of all aphasics. There is considerable variation ac-

cording to the severity of the disorder and the type of aphasia involved. Moreover, aphasics often learn over a period of time to perform some of the more complex acts listed, although usually with difficulty, by resorting to more primitive methods than those used by normal persons. Thus a patient who cannot follow directions in a city may learn a route by sheer repetition and memorization of landmarks. Similarly, he or she may learn to make change properly by repetition and memorization rather than by calculation.

Unreliability of Introspective Evidence

The data on aphasia indicate that introspective evidence of the role of language must be interpreted cautiously. Just as other functions drop out of consciousness when they become automatic, so may language fade out of the picture when many apparently purely motor and other types of skills of which it is the basis are fully established.

To illustrate our point, we can ask if the game of billiards presupposes language ability. Offhand, there seems to be no possible connection between the propulsion of billiard balls on a green table and the ability to talk. If we ask billiard players about the game, they tell us only that when they aim they make a sort of geometrical calculation and have in their "mind's eye" a kind of geometrical image of the path they wish the cue ball to take, striking first one and then the second of the two other balls involved. It would appear that language plays no part in this activity.

However, such introspective evidence is contradicted by the facts. The aphasic, even though she may have been skillful at billiards prior to the onset of aphasia, usually loses that skill along with language ability, reporting an inability to visualize the three balls simultaneously. The aphasic does not know at what angle to strike the second ball and may even hit it on the wrong side.

Similarly, one would suppose from introspective evidence that the ability to draw a picture of a cow is totally unconnected with language and thus would be unaffected in aphasia. This is not so, as we see from the following example. It was Head's practice to ask his patients to draw pictures of familiar objects from memory. He requested an English army officer, for example, to sketch an elephant. Prior to his illness, this officer had spent many years in India and had once shown rather good amateur ability at drawing. Nevertheless, the drawing he produced was exceptionally poor. It lacked some essential parts, such as the trunk and tusks; some of the parts were in wrong relation to one another; and, in general, the whole picture was scarcely recognizable. Later, when the bullet wound that had caused the aphasia had healed and the patient had recovered much of his language ablity, he drew upon request a detailed, accurate picture of an elephant.

These two examples point to the conclusion that language may play a vital role in an activity without the individual's introspective awareness of that fact.

Language Impairment and Thought

We have said a great deal about language and thought in past chapters, emphasizing that the latter cannot exist without the former. Thought without language is reduced to the level of thinking—if we may call it such—that is characteristic of lower animals. Those who study aphasia sometimes erroneously conceive of thinking and language as two entirely distinct and separate processes. Thinking, speaking to others, and speaking to oneself are inextricably interrelated and dependent processes. Head has compared the aphasic with a man in solitary confinement whose only contact with the outside world is a defective telephone. While this comparison is picturesque, it is incomplete, when the aphasic tries to talk to himself to formulate his own thoughts, he uses the same defective telephone.

Neurologists who study speech-related functions in the brain generally agree with

Russell and Espir that in the brain, speech cannot be separate from thought. Luria (1966, p. 34), also comments: "The reorganization of mental activity by means of speech, and the incorporation of the system of speech connections into a large number of processes, hitherto direct in nature, are among the more important factors in the formation of the higher mental functions, whereby man, as distinct from animals, acquires consciousness and volition."

Aphasia and related disorders in their almost bewildering variety of manifestations serve to bring home the enormous complexity of the language function and its interconnections with other processes. Russell and Espir observe that severe aphasia destroys the individual's capacity to enjoy reading a book; he may read slowly, absorb the meaning with difficulty, and lose the train of thought because the previous pages are inadequately remembered. They observe that there are a number of storage systems that he must use in reading: (1) visual patterns acquired much earlier for the recognition of letters and words; (2) the associations that give meaning to the words; and (3) "the capacity to hold something of what he reads for long enough to correlate it with later pages" (1961, p. 105).

These writers observe that intelligence and personality are disorganized in severe aphasia, adding that some of the long-range effects of aphasia are loss of memory, difficulty in concentration, mental fatiguability, irritability, and change of personality. "The scaffolding on which speech is developed," they add, "is built up in relation to hearing, vision, and the sensori-motor skill involved in uttering words." However, this scaffolding "is concerned with much more than speech for it seems to provide a basis for the psychological processes of thinking and learning" (1961, pp. 170–71).

The normal human finds it difficult to imagine how it feels to be an aphasic. There is little in our experience that enables us to project ourselves, as it were, into her position, or to see and experience the impairment of thought that hinges upon her speech difficulties. To better understand, suppose we pretend that we are in a foreign land whose language we know only moderately well. Conversation with others is reduced to simple concrete levels, as considerable facility in the language would be required in order to exchange views on complicated, abstract, or philosophical matters. It is easier to talk—with the aid of gestures—about concrete objects that are present, such as the immediate scene and the weather. If we try to speak of events long past or far in the future, or of objects out of sight, our vocabulary is insufficient. However, if we try to carry on such a slightly involved conversation, the effort is likely to prove exhausting. As an acquaintance of the authors once said:

I went to bed exhausted every night from trying to speak German; particularly when I was with a lot of German people who were engaging in a cross-fire of conversation. It was simply exhausting—after a while you felt you wanted to sit down and recuperate. And you felt absolutely frustrated and bottled up; you wonder if you're ever going to think a complex thought again in your life. You can ask for beer and coffee and potatoes, but when you have to discuss a complex feeling or reaction or analyze a political situation, you're simply stalled. You struggle to speak, but you're reduced to the level of your vocabulary.

Suppose that in addition to conversing with others in the foreign language, we also had to converse with ourself (that is, think) using only this same restricted vocabulary. How difficult it would be to carry on internalized conversation that had any semblance of complexity!

ALZHEIMER'S DISEASE

It will be instructive to briefly compare aphasia with Alzheimer's disease, which has been called the disease of the century for it is now the "single most devasting illness of old age" (Gubrium, 1986, p. 38). This disease leads to a progressive decline in mental functioning; victims experience forgetfulness, depres-sion, disorientation, confusion, and an inability to plan and organize activities, including simple daily tasks. It is often called the disease that "dims bright minds" (Gubrium, 1986, p. 39). A patient's spouse describes her husband's actions:

I just don't know what to think or feel. It's like he's not even there anymore. . . . He doesn't know me. He thinks I'm a strange woman in the house. He shouts and tries to slap me away from him . . . he makes sounds more like an animal than a person. Do you think he has a mind left? . . . Sometimes I get so upset that I just pound on him and yell at him to come out to me (Gubrium, 1986, p. 41).

This disease has two victims: the person with the disease and the caregiver. In a particularly insightful interaction analysis, Gubrium (1986, pp. 37–51) has described how caregivers struggle with the meaning of mind and agency in the Alzheimer patient. Especially distressing for the caregiver is the fact that the patient, often a spouse or parent, no longer displays actions which indicate that they know who they are, how they feel, or how they feel toward the caregiver. This leads caregivers to impute a "hidden mind" to the victim, and behind that hidden mind they impute a biographical theory of "agency" which assumes that the victim still loves them and cares for them. The following two accounts (Gubrium, 1986, p. 42) indicate how caregivers struggle to maintain the belief that the victim still has a mind. A man named Jack is discussing his spouse, who he says is just like the living dead:

That's why I'm looking for a nursing home for her. I loved her dearly but she's just not Mary anymore. No matter how hard I try, I can't get myself to believe that she's there anymore. . . . I just know that's not her speaking to me but some knee-jerk reaction. . . .

Another caregiver, Sara, replies:

Well, I know what you've gone through, and I admire your courage, Jack. But you can't be too sure. How do you *really* know that what Mary says at times is not one of those few times she's been able to really reach out to you? You don't really know for sure, do you? . . . I face the same thing day in day out with Richard (her husband). Can I ever finally close him out of my life and say, "Well, it's done. It's over. He's gone"? How do I know that the poor man isn't hidden somewhere, behind all the confusion, trying to reach out and say, "I love you, Sara"? (she weeps)

Gubrium's analysis reveals how the spouses and children of Alzheimer's disease victims impute a theory of minded, intentional, loving conduct to them. Such beliefs keep alive the hope that a "mind is still inside," and that that mind still cares for them. In these ways caregivers indicate how mind is a social, interactional process.

There is no known cure for Alzheimer's disease; however, victims of aphasia can be treated and in many cases there is hope of recovery. These two disorders reveal how disturbances in language ability strip from humans their basic abilities to be feeling, thinking, expressive beings.

BODY IMAGES AND MEDICINE

As in other areas of symbolic behavior, one must distinguish carefully between the *ideas* that people have of their bodies and the *concepts* of biological scientists of anatomy and physiology. Scientific views, in their turn, should be distinguished from objective reality, which is always somewhat problematical. We are concerned here with popular images of the body and with some of the behavioral consequences that follow from them.

People have always had conceptions of what was inside their skins and how those insides might function. Inasmuch as the study of anatomy arose only recently and then only in Western cultures, the anatomical ideas of even sophisticated early societies like that of the ancient Greeks seem crude. Their conceptions of physiology also seem ludicrous and primitive when judged by our standards.

It follows that conceptions of the body's insides and functions vary greatly from society to society. The Chinese practice of acupuncture exemplifies this point. In recent years, some anthropologists studying underdeveloped countries have been concerned with the theoretical and practical consequences of native medical beliefs. Their research reveals how tremendously varied are conceptions of the body, its functioning, and the manner in which it should be treated when it does not function normally. The research also indicates that people believing these ideas tend to form conceptual systems that are related to other conceptual systems, such as those concerning the supernatural or those having to do with people. Popular medical ideologies also specify the persons who are viewed as capable of diagnosing and dealing with the disorder.

Charles Frake has reported that among the Subanun of Mindanao, there are 186 names of diseases that classify specific illnesses, symptoms, or stages of illness. The diagnostic criteria that distinguish one disease from another are conceptually distinct. Every person is his own herbalist, as there is no separate status of diagnostician or curer. Each person diagnoses and names his own illness and then turns to appropriate remedies (Frake, 1961). Elsewhere in the Philippines, another anthropologist reports that both natural and supernatural causes of illness are recognized, and that one way of staying well is to not violate the mores. Five types of practitioners exist, each with his own qualifications, modes of treatment, and types of illness in which he specializes (Nurge, 1961). In still another Philippine community where sorcery is recognized as a cause of some illnesses, the sorcerer is called upon to cure the supernaturally caused sickness, while other types of curers are called on to handle illnesses regarded as biological malfunction (Lieban, 1966).

Perinabanayagam (1982), in a study of self, society, and astrology in Jaffna, the northern peninsula of the island of Sri Lanka, found that astrologers were key medical personnel in the treatment of mental and physical illnesses. For example, a young woman, aged 20, is brought to an astrologer with her horoscope. Perinbanayagam (1982, p. 143) reports:

Once the calculations have been made, the astrologer inquires about the patient, and is told that she is a recent mother (two weeks), suffering from sleeplessness, loss of appetite, "fear," "anxiety" . . . "indifference." Now the astrologer proceeds to do a horoscope for the newly born and then gives the following discourse: "According to the child's horoscope, this period is one of danger to the mother. There is a fault in the child's horoscope—it is, however, temporary, and there is really nothing to worry about. It will pass in time. But go to the temple and do a Navagrapha pùja— pùja to the nine planets." The subject leaves, and subsequent inquiries establish that such a pùja was in fact performed and that the medicine prescribed by the Ayurvedic physician was also taken. In any case, subject recovered from her "postnatal depression."

Here astrology blends with a theory of self, society, and illness. The astrologer prescribes specific lines of action for the patient to take. These actions are believed to be valid treatments for the illness in question. The patient, after all, was relieved of her postnatal depression.

From the viewpoint of modern science, such systems of concepts and the therapies based on them are often erroneous. Indeed, one reason for the increase in research in medical anthropology is that in the underdeveloped countries of Asia, Africa, and South America, various governments are trying to effect some transfer of native allegiance to whatever Western medicine may exist within their countries. Even in the most technologically and scientifically advanced nations, however, ideas generally accepted by the scientific or medical community compete with many other systems of conceptualization.

Manning and Fabrega (1973, pp. 251–301) have summarized the differences between modern, technologically impersonal medicine, and the personalistic medical systems that exist in the so-called "underdeveloped" societies. They contend that the differences between these medical systems revolve around conceptions of self, society, and the body. Impersonal, modern medical systems have the following characteristics: (1) body and self are seen as separate entities; (2) bodies and/or selves may be sick, or normal; (3) the body is described within a biological framework and is seen as a biological machine; (4) the body is partitioned into parts, systems, and functions. In contrast, personalistic medical systems (1) do not treat the body and the self as different entities; (2) see health and illness as part of the same process; (3) use few biological terms to describe the body; and (4) view the body as a unified whole that is responsive to the social environment of the person.

Western medicine tends to be atomistic, while non-Western medicine is holistic. Entirely different ways of perceiving and defining the body (and its illnesses) thus derive from these two conceptual schemes. Westerners have medicalized the body and the mind (O'Neill, 1985, p. 123). Health engineering has produced an industrialization of the lived body; medical technology now provides life-support systems to keep bodies alive long after many patients and their families desire.

The Morality of Medicine

Modern medicine is a decidedly moral enterprise; the consequences of its practices extend far beyond the treatment of illness, disease, and pain. Indeed, many have argued (Foucault, 1980; Turner, 1984; O'Neill, 1985) that modern medicine takes a distinctly moral position on defining normal behavior. Furthermore, medicine has shaped the history of the human body and the meanings that have been brought to our bodies.

Take the case of AIDS. This is partly regarded as a sexually transmitted disease; some view it as the "black plague" of the 1980s. Homosexuals have been singled out as the population most likely to get and transmit the disease. In many cases, this disease is associated with illicit or promiscuous sexuality. Professional pronouncements on the disease have approached the level of hysteria, and the public response to AIDS has been likened to medieval attitudes towards leprosy (Turner, 1984, p. 220). AIDS victims have been systematically isolated and excluded by the public. Some have been fired from their jobs because they had the disease. In one state in 1986, a political party campaigned on the slogan of killing all AIDS victims.

One result of the AIDS epidemic has been the emphasis on monogamy, sexual fidelity, and celibacy. Clearly, modern medicine has been anything but morally neutral about AIDS. Indeed, some have suggested that modern medicine has contributed to the latent "homophobic" attitude that already existed in American and other Western societies.

Anorexia nervosa is another example of how medicine moralizes. Foucault (1980, p. 104) argues that one of the consequences of modern medicine has been the "hysterization of women's bodies." He means that certain "disorders" of the body were found to be peculiar to women. In many cases, the mental illnesses that women suffered were found to be caused by their sexuality and their relation to their sexual bodies. Thus in the late nineteenth century, women became hysterical and were even hospitalized for it. Like hysteria, anorexia is a disorder almost entirely specific to women. French psychiatrist Charcot, in the late 1880s, found that hysterical women were anorexic.

Anorexia is an illness found mainly in young women, and has become a popular diagnosis among medical practitioners. Sociologist Turner (1984, pp. 183–84), following the lead of feminists, suggests that anorexia is an "illness" that reflects the contraditory expectations of beauty in a consumer society where male criteria of aesthetics predominate. The clinical symptoms of anorexia include at least a 25 percent loss of body weight, a distorted attitude toward food and eating, and no prior medical illnesses which could account for the disorder.

There are several interpretations of anorexia. Some argue that it is an attempt by middle-class daughters to exert greater control over their lives. By not eating and by attempting to conform to a cultural concept of thinness and beauty, such women conform to the ethic of consumer beauty. Because anorexia disrupts and often delays the menstrual cycle, extreme dieting may be "associated in puberty with a rejection of sexuality through the suppression of menstruation" (Turner, 1984, p. 185). However, anorexia can end in death. It has been described as (MacLeod, 1981, p. 88, quoted by Turner, 1984, p. 186):

a disease in which the concept of the whole person is so confused, so dialectically divided, that "I" can at the same time be choosing to live, as the self, and choosing to die, as the body, however unconscious those choices may be . . . both suicide of the schizoid type and anorexia nervosa involve a denial of reality which depends upon an acceptance of a split between self and body.

From a social psychological perspective, the labels of scientific medicine are not statements about "real" disease entities (Turner, 1984, p. 182). They are the effects of particular power-knowledge structures within our society regarding women, sexuality, beauty, health, and illness.

OPIATE AND OTHER ADDICTIONS

The phenomenon of drug addiction provides a complex example of the way in which behavior is shaped and directed by the way inner experiences are defined. The patterns of use connected with addictive drugs such as the opiates, barbiturates, and alcohol contrast sharply with those connected with non-physically addictive drugs like marijuana and cocaine.

The Fixation Process

An outstanding characteristic of addictive drugs is that withdrawal from them after regular use over a period of a few weeks or more produces an automatic painful physical reaction. Opiate drugs (those derived from the opium poppy) and their synthetic equivalents are the most important drugs of this type. However, alcohol and the barbiturates also produce physical dependence and withdrawal distress. Barbiturate withdrawal is more severe and dangerous than opiate withdrawal. Barbiturates are widely prescribed by physicians for insomnia and other ailments; addiction to this type of drug, however, requires that it be used in much larger quantities than those ordinarily prescribed by doctors. The withdrawal distress connected with opiates varies with individuals, and its intensity depends upon duration of use, amount used, and other factors. Withdrawal symptoms form a characteristic pattern which in its severe form is unmistakable. These symptoms begin about four or five hours after the last injection; if no further drugs are taken, they increase in intensity for about seventy-two hours and the more noticeable ones disappear only gradually over a period of about two weeks. An injection of drugs during the withdrawal period causes all symptoms to vanish in a matter of minutes. Withdrawal distress occurs in newborn infants whose mothers are addicts, and in various animal species when drugs are regularly administered. This shows that the withdrawal reaction is biological in nature; this has led some students to declare that drug addiction is essentially an organic condition or disease.

In view of the publicity given in recent years to teenage addiction, it is unnecessary to describe addiction or withdrawal distress in detail. It should be noted that much of the popular literature is aimed at frightening or warning young people; this has led to inaccurate and exaggerated descriptions of the alleged evil physical effects. The facts are that with the full establishment of addiction after several weeks of regular use, a bodily condition of tolerance or "drug balance" is acquired. When this has occurred, the main effect of the drug is to maintain this balance, to prevent withdrawal symptoms, and to cause the addict to feel normal. The user may experience a physical "kick" when he or she takes a shot, especially if it is a "main liner" (an injection into the vein), but during the several hours between injections it is exceedingly difficult to determine with certainty whether or not the person is under the influence of the drug. People who take drugs by means other than hypodermic injection (for example, orally) may never have experienced physical pleasure from taking them; this is especially true when the initial uses occurs during an illness.

During the initial period of use, several radical changes occur that amount almost to a reversal of the drug's effects. Thus the original depressing effect on bodily functions tends to vanish and to be replaced by a stimulating one. Also, the euphoria of beginning use vanishes and is replaced by the negative effect of relieving withdrawal distress and achieving approximate normality between the shots. Bodily functions originally disturbed by the regular injection of drugs generally return to an approximately normal level when tolerance has built up. The long-continued use of such drugs as morphine or heroin, contrary to popular belief, does not lead to major tissue destruction or to insanity; tooth decay, constipation, and sexual impotence—which are relatively frequent among drug addicts—are not necessary consequences of addiction, and some addicts, especially those who are well-to-do, do not experience them. The principal deleterious effects are psychological in nature and are connected with the tabooed and secret nature of the habit, with the extreme cost of obtaining a supply of drugs at blackmarket prices, and resulting changes in self-conception, occupation, and social relationships.

In asking why people become addicted to the opiates, we might also ask what is the nature of the experience in which the craving for drugs is generated. It will not suffice, as we shall see, to say that it is the pleasurable sensations or inner experiences that occur when the drug is used. Marijuana, cocaine, and other substances produce such pleasure without many of the unpleasant consequences associated with opiates, but they are nonaddicting (in a physical sense, that is).

A crucial element in the fixation of addiction appears to be the user's understanding of what is going on. If drugs are received without knowledge, a craving for them will not develop. Even if persons know that they have been receiving morphine regularly, they will still evidently not get "hooked" if they do not grasp the nature of the withdrawal distress that occurs when they stop regular use.

It is the repetition of the experience of using drugs to alleviate withdrawal distress (when the latter is recognized and properly identified) that appears to lead rapidly to the changed orientation toward the drug and to the other behavior that constitutes addiction. Addicts do not get hooked on the pleasures of opium, but on the experience of relief that occurs immediately after a shot. This effect depends on cognitive elements and is absent when the person does not understand the withdrawal distress that is suffered. Psychologists who rely on reinforcement explanations might describe the process as one in which a response pattern is established by negative reinforcement (that is, the removal of an unpleasant stimulus). These psychologists would leave out the cognitive and emotional aspects of the situation which, from our point of view, are crucial as they probably account for a number of aspects of addiction that otherwise appear paradoxical.

To clarify, let us assume that the beginner, on the way to addiction, takes a shot every four hours. The theory we present here is that addiction is established in the experiences that occur approximately ten minutes after each shot, and not by the way the user feels during the other 230 minutes. Those who think of drugs in terms of being "high" or "stoned" are likely to emphasize the 230

minutes rather than the ten, and to think of addiction in terms of an ecstatic pleasure that is often presumed to extend throughout the interval between shots and to be renewed by the next one. A major problem with this view is that addicts (who are, after all, the only real authority on how they feel) uniformly deny it. Between injections they feel normal or, as one user remarked on a television program, the way one feels after a good breakfast.

The Pleasure Theory

Those who try to explain heroin addiction in terms of pleasure ordinarily emphasize that the pleasure of the "high" is the key to addiction. They may admit that between shots during the steady state—as opposed to impact effects immediately after—the fully addicted individual may feel normal. Nevertheless, they insist—and many addicts also contend—that the "high" is the key motivating factor. Addicts often describe this experience in ecstatic terms (see McAuliffe & Gordon, 1974; Lindesmith, 1974).

What is wrong with this view? It is essentially a tautology, like a person saying a disease is caused by a high fever or a lover's explaining that he is in love with a woman because she makes him feel wonderful. In these instances, the condition that is said to explain the phenomenon is simply a part of it. The addict's assertion that she "loves" the "high" that heroin produces is only an indication that she is addicted; it does not tell us why she loves the heroin high or what was the learning process through which she acquired this attitude.

To explore this line a bit further: The initial experience with heroin is often perceived as unpleasant or unimpressive, or may not even be noticed, almost exactly the same as with initial marijuana use. Even when the first experience is pleasurable, the attitude it then engenders scarcely compares to what it later becomes in addition. This is readily demonstrable by noting the contrast between the reports on heroin or morphine effects given by the same person before and after her addiction. This means that falling in love with the heroin-impact effects does not occur prior to addiction, and therefore cannot be viewed as a causal factor since causes must precede effects, not follow them.

What happens to heroin addicts can be represented by contrasting their attitude with that of a hospital patient. We may represent the total of an individual's life activities and concerns by a large circle. The hospital patient who has, let us say, received morphine for three weeks regularly without knowledge and been withdrawn from it, may be represented as follows:

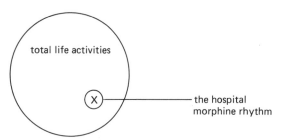

Hospital Patient's Experience with Morphine

The hospital experience for such persons remains an isolated minute item of experience, which they occasionally may recall or talk about, but which has little influence on the remainder of their life, despite their having been physically dependent on the morphine and having experienced its effects.

In contrast, the addict's situation appears as follows:

Addict's Experience with Heroin

The rhythm of regular "fixes" of the drug moves into the center of the person's atten-

tion, as he or she becomes addicted, or falls in love with, or learns to crave the drug. All other activities tend to be progressively drawn into the orbit of the heroin rhythm, organized around it, and subordinated to it.

At this point, those who assume that heroin must produce intense pleasure to be as powerfully addicting as it is have problems explaining the apparent absence of such pleasure in the addict between shots. Far from being a happy person, the addict is one of the most miserable and unhappy types in our society. Strategic devices used to salvage the pleasure theory are to deny the addict's claim that he or she feels normal between shots, and to argue that the addict continues to use drugs in a futile attempt to recapture the original euphoria of early use during the "honeymoon" period. This comes to an end after a number of weeks, like other honeymoons.

Relapse

If we ask why people who have been "hooked" tend to relapse after they have been apparently "cured," the answer implied by the viewpoint presented here is clear in its broad outlines. To be hooked on drugs means to be pervasively changed by experience, to acquire new conceptions and attitudes as well as new knowledge of one's own body and its capabilities and the effects of the drug. This experience in many respects is comparable to that of acquiring one's first sexual experience or going to war. These are not experiences of which one can be readily "cured," even when they lead to unhappiness or disaster. Similarly, after people have been hooked on a drug like heroin or morphine, their changed conceptions and new knowledge remain after the drug is taken away, and create in them an impulse to relapse. This impulse is sometimes resisted for varying periods of time, but it is doubtful that it can ever be wholly eradicated.

Paradoxes and Problems

Among the many paradoxical aspects of opiate addiction are the apparently contradictory reports on the subjectively experienced effects of these drugs. Nonaddicts, given single shots of heroin and placebos without their knowing which, report greater pleasure from the placebos than from the heroin. Hospital patients who are given morphine regularly over periods of time sufficient to establish physical dependence, as we have indicated, may be prevented from becoming addicted by being kept ignorant of the drug they are receiving and of its effects. When this is successfully done, and the patient who is physically dependent upon morphine without knowing it is asked about the effects of the medicine, he reports nothing out of the ordinary. He may merely observe that it reduces the pain and discomfort connected with his ailment, makes him feel reasonably comfortable, and makes it easier for him to sleep. Should this same patient later become addicted, his description of the drug's effects will change dramatically, for he will now talk of it in terms generally used by addicts. He will do so even when the quantity of drugs and the methods used are exactly the same as when he was a patient. This indicates that, like Becker's marijuana users, opiate users learn how to react to the drug; their subjective experiences are profoundly altered by the fact that they have learned to crave it. Similar processes appear to work for cocaine addicts.

Another facet of addiction which is of interest to the social psychologist and poses interesting theoretical problems, is the fact that addicts can—under certain circumstances— be deceived into believing that they are under the influence of drugs when they are not, and vice versa. During the 19th century, for example, it was customary to take addicts off drugs by a gradual withdrawal method over a period of weeks. Under this system the user might be placed in a hospital and given the drug every four hours in diminishing doses, so that after a couple of weeks the drug would have been wholly withdrawn without the patient's knowledge, and he would be receiving an inert substance instead. Under this system the withdrawal distress was reduced and spread out over time, and the patients did not ordinarily realize that they were off drugs as long as the placebo doses continued to be given regularly.

Conversely, addicts who are accustomed to intravenous injections may be given heroin or morphine by other means (such as in solution or by suppositories) without their realizing it. When the administration of drugs is taken out of a user's hands and the intravenous injection method is replaced by others, the addict may become uncertain or confused about whether he is receiving drugs and, if so, in what quantity. This confusion appears to stem mainly from the fact that when the intravenous method of administration is not used, the addict cannot "feel" his shots. If from its inherent pharmacological nature the drug automatically produced great euphoria or pleasure, the addict would surely not be confused. The fact that he *can* be suggests that his state of mind between injections is not sufficiently extraordinary to explain the power of the habit (Lindesmith, 1947, 1966, 1974).

CONCLUSION

People react to their bodies, and the processes that occur in them, on the basis of sensory cues that are assimilated in conceptual schemes that include ideas of the nature of the body and its functions and malfunctions. Like cognitions of the external world, these ideas are socially derived and vary from one society to another. The interpretations of the bodily changes associated with emotional reactions are an example of the manner in which internal processes are brought into the social sphere by being named, explained, and talked about. Experiences induced by drugs like marijuana, LSD, cocaine, and the opiates are other examples. Subjective experiences that cannot be shared or communicated, such as those of the psychotic, are felt to be "uncanny" and are often interpreted by oneself and others as evidence of insanity or as religious or mystic experiences. The measures that people resort to in order to cure their illnesses depend upon their ideas of the nature and sources of their ailments, and vary widely from group to group even within Western societies.

We have examined such related phenomena as the body and pain, emotional experiences, madness, the uncanny, aphasia and Alzheimer's disease, body images, medicine, and opiate and other addictions. Our extended discussion of aphasia revealed how disturbances in language processes can alter and change an individual's relationship to the internal environment of the body and the external world of social experience. We have seen how relatives of Alzheimer's disease victims input a sense of mind and emotion to victims. We contrasted modern medicine with the treatment of health and illness in "underdeveloped" countries, and we discussed the morality of medicine, as seen in the treatment of AIDS. We also spoke briefly about the phenomenon of anorexia nervosa. Finally we took up the topic of opiate addiction and indicated how behavioral theories of addiction are unable to explain the addict's addiction to the opiates and other drugs.

Our purpose has been to show how language structures and shapes our interpretations of what goes on inside our bodies. The naming process is absent in the lower animals. In the next chapter we will continue this line of thought by showing how humans learn and construct explanations for their actions in problematic situations.

SELECTED READINGS

DENZIN, N. K. (1984). *On understanding emotion.* San Francisco: Jossey-Bass. An interpretation of emotion as symbolic interaction.

EHRENREICH, B., & D. ENGLISH (1978). *For her own good: 150 years of the expert's advice to women.* New York: Columbia University Press. A history of medical practices as related to the treatment of women.

LINDESMITH, A. R. (1968). *Addiction and opiates.* Chicago: Aldine. A detailed presentation of the views of opiate addiction briefly presented in this chapter.

O'NEILL, J. (1985). *Five bodies: The human shape of modern society.* Ithaca: Cornell University Press. A critical discourse on the tyranny of modern technology and its effects on our bodies and our lives.

TURNER, B. (1984). *The body and society.* London: Basil Blackwell. A sociological theory of the body and its relation to society, medicine, religion, and modern cultural practices.

CHAPTER SIX
Perception, Memory, and Motives

In this chapter we will explore the language and group foundations of human perception, memory, and motivation. The temporal foundations of human experience—as seen in those behaviors directed to the past, present, and future—will be examined. In other parts of this book, we have dealt with the other consequences that follow from the internalization of language. Here, *perception, memory, planning,* and *motivation* are grouped together because they are interpretive adjustments to the past, present, and future. When we consider how these four fundamental processes differ in human (and nonhuman) subjects, the importance of language internalization becomes evident.

We will take up, in order, the following topics: (1) the social and cultural patterning of perception; (2) the social and historical basis of memory and remembering; (3) the planning of human behavior; (4) motives, accounts, and human activity.

PRELIMINARY CONSIDERATIONS

It is pertinent to remind the reader of Pavlov's distinction between the first and second signal systems which we already touched upon in Chapter 3. We noted that sensory input or stimulation is transmitted to the brain in the form of "messages" that are coded in terms of impulse frequency. These messages serve a representational function when they are processed in the central nervous system so as to orient the organism within its environment. In other words, sensory input from seeing, touching, hearing, tasting, and smelling provides both human and nonhuman organisms with *signs,* or *cues,* representing the environments of these organisms. This is what Pavlov called the first signal system.

At the neurological level, what Pavlov referred to as the second signal system consists of the new or additional neural circuits established in the central nervous system when humans acquire language. These new neural patterns are established largely within the left, or dominant, hemisphere of the brain in those areas in which the most complex and least understood regulatory and integrative processes linked with voluntary behavior and consciousness are believed to take place. The processes involved are viewed as second-order signs or symbols, since they represent the lower-order sign processes involved in simple sensory experience. Since these language-derived sign processes of the second signal system merge with, absorb, or dominate many of the lower-order neural patterns, and since the second signal system is social in nature and origin, the existence of the latter has the effect of making many of the psychological activities of human beings subject to social influences transmitted symbolically in a communication or interactional process.

Perception and memory, considered here as symbolic activities, have often been viewed as though they were mechanical, while planning is usually not thought of as a separate activity. Thus, visual perception has been treated as though it were a process of photographing, and the human visual apparatus has been treated as though it were a camera. Ignored by this view is that the past experiences of the organism influence its perceptions, and that cameras do not have experiences, desires, aspirations, or attitudes. The same mechanical approach has been used to reduce human emotions to purely physiological functions located in the viscera or in some part of the brain. Memory has been treated in a similar manner; it has been conceived of as a mechanical record akin to the "memory" attributed by some to electronic calculating machines. Although this has shed light on some aspects of remembering, it has not clarified other important aspects.

Motives and Activity

One especially perplexing aspect of the study of humans arises from the fact that they, unlike any other objects of scientific study, have ideas of their own about why they act as they do. Consideration of what people say in explanation of their behavior inevitably leads to a consideration of motives and motivation. The concept of motivation is especially applicable to human behavior. It is less applicable to the lower animals, and when applied to them is usually translated into biological terms. It is, of course, entirely inapplicable to inorganic matter and plant life. In this chapter we shall be concerned with the concept of motivation as it is applied to human behavior, and we shall see that it poses some of the most difficult and controversial problems in the social sciences.

The issue of motives and motivation, as we shall show, is often confused in the social and psychological sciences. It is useful at the outset to state one's position in this matter. We assume that the human organism is active from birth to death. Accordingly, activity per se is a constant factor across all human situations. The explanations for the direction, shape, and form that activity takes, however, are varied and variable. The explanations that persons give for their behavior we shall call *accounts,* and these accounts are often subsumed under what Mills termed *vocabularies of motive.* As humans act, they may alter their reasons for acting. In this sense, accounts and motives are embedded in ongoing activity. This suggests that "What motivates human behavior?" or "What are the motivations for a particular action?" are erroneous and misleading questions. *Motives,* not *motivations,* are what concern us here. We turn first to common conceptions and misconceptions concerning these points.

When specific acts are explained in ordinary discourse, the explanations rest upon assumptions about behavior in general. Systems of philosophy also require that assumptions be made concerning the nature of behavior and its motives. In this connection, the problem of motivation is an old one; and it has been handled in many different ways. The various hedonistic philosophies have tended to conceive of pleasure-seeking and the avoidance of pain as the bases of most action. Another approach has been to think of humans as motivated by certain powerful drives or combinations of drives, such as sex, hunger, love, self-interest, and self-preservation. The sources of the purposes which move human beings have been found also in supernatural beings or superordinate structures such as God, the state, community, economic system, or class system.

Since humans have a curiosity about and a deep interest in the "why" and "how" of behavior, every generation makes a fresh attack on the problem of motivation. Nevertheless, we are struck by the tenacity with which certain classical conceptions reappear in new guises. The terminology may be new, but the themes are not.

The imputation of motives to others is an integral aspect of human interaction. It is inconceivable that social life could exist if people did not make guesses or assumptions about the purposes of others. The mark of human behavior, as opposed to animal behavior, is that it is organized around anticipation of others' responses to one's own actions. Anticipation involves assumptions as to how and why others will react. It also involves judgments about previous acts of others, as they have bearing upon their possible future acts. A knowledge of the purposes of others is the most effective basis for understanding what they are doing now and knowing what to expect from them in future.

Incorrect assessment of such purposes has important consequences, since it may lead to embarrassment, misunderstanding, loss of money and time, or other even more unfortunate effects. When acts are familiar, traditional, and routinized, the assessment of motivation is easy and taken for granted. No one questions why people walk erect, build houses, or wear clothes, although the question of motivation is brought into sharp focus when they do *not* do these things. If the reasons for customary behavior are inquired after, usually by an outsider, the person who is questioned may be at a loss for an answer. In relatively homogeneous societies, the questioning of motives is relatively infrequent, because the bases of customary behavior are infrequently challenged.

As Lewis (1948, p. 175) puts it:

There are societies . . . with little or no group-awareness of group incentives; they have few, or no, formulated ideals of conduct, and they do not attempt to bring their group incentives into the light of day in the guise of accepted motives. Their problems of group behavior are problems of *how* and not *why*. They learn how to behave in this or that contingency; and if ever they ask why—and they rarely ask this unless some [anthropologist] asks them—the answer is, This is how we have always behaved. The society is unified and integrated by the sharp clarity of its techniques coupled with the obscurity of its motives.

In heterogeneous societies, actions more frequently raise questions because the behavior is unfamiliar to some, or because it is performed in contexts which make it unclear. Then some guesswork, and sometimes some sleuthing, is called for on the part of the investigator. The difficulties of correct assessment are further increased by the fact that people very often do not clearly formulate to themselves the purposes of their actions and so can give little help to others who wish to understand them. There may also be several purposes, or levels of purposes, involved in the same act. The importance of clues to future behavior is further underlined by the existence of duplicity in interaction. The concealment of motives and the deliberate misleading of other people is sometimes cultivated as an art, and appears to be necessary for smoothly functioning social relationships, even relationships among friends, lovers, and kin. "Nothing but the truth" would thoroughly disrupt human relations.

SOCIAL PATTERNING OF PERCEPTION

Selectivity in Perception

Perception refers to the ways in which organisms respond to the stimuli picked up by their sense organs. It refers to processes of immediate experience. Perception has often been distinguished from *cognition* and *interpretation,* which refer to how perceptual experiences are ordered and given meaning, often in terms of symbolic, individual, group, and cultural meanings and categories (see Tajfel, 1969, p. 317; Dougherty, 1985, p. 4). The disciplines of cognitive psychology and cognitive anthropology study the relationship between perception, cognition, meaning, culture, and language.

The subject of visual perception has traditionally covered such topics as the perception of space and form and on the "close mapping of stimulus and experience" (Kolers, 1983, p. 130). Over the past 20 years, research has shifted from these traditional interests to such phenomena as iconic memory, backward masking, apparent motion, and imagery (Kolers, 1983, p. 130). We shall briefly discuss two of these phenomena. *Iconic memory* describes the ability of people to describe various features of letters and digits that were briefly presented but are no longer in view. It is seen as a first stage in the process of information extraction in perception. *Backward masking* refers to how an event perceived later in time interferes with the perception of an earlier event. Kolers (1983, p. 136) describes this process thus:

When the time interval separating two flashes is appropriately brief, the two stimuli tend to be seen as a single object. As the interval increases T (the original flash) is seen less distinctly; later still, during the recovery stage, they are often seen as two temporally distinct objects. Not only was the "backward" aspect of masking counterintuitive, the fact that visibility of T first decreased and then recovered as time between T and M (second flash) increased violated many assumptions about visual perception; particularly it violated the assumption that perceptions were coded immediately and were realistically faithful to stimulis events.

It was once thought that perception was something analogous to such mechanical processes as photographing an object or recording sound on a record. That analogy to a mechanical sequence is inadequate, however, since it ignores the fact that perception is influenced by interests, needs, and past experiences. The analogy also does not take into account the fact that the total volume of physical stimuli reaching us both from sources within our body and in the environment is so great, most of them must be ignored and therefore can neither function as cues nor enter significantly into the determination of behavior. Physical illness sometimes reminds us painfully of some of the multitudinous processes that normally go on inside of us without our being aware of them. The hypochondriac illustrates par excellence preoccupation with stimuli originating in bodily processes. Ordinary healthful living requires that we be highly selective of the stimuli to which we pay attention and, at the same time, that whole ranges of stimuli be consigned to the background and ignored.

Response to environmental cues constitutes the reality orientation of the organism. The data which are supplied by the sense organs and the receptor nerves are interpreted and acted upon as signs of the nature, location, size, movement, and quality of objects and occurrences. The degree and nature of inner elaboration or "interpretation" of experience varies among species and among individuals. It reaches its peak in humans in whom the elaboration may be very great, and in whom it assumes a symbolic form. Individuals' reports of what they perceive, and their ideas of what they see or hear, include matters of inference, interpretation, and judgment—in short, they do not discriminate between what may be called direct perception, or physical stimulus, and the meaningful elaboration of the perception that occurs when it is classified, named, analyzed, and judged (Bartlett, 1932, p.31):

On the face of it, to perceive anything is one of the simplest and most immediate, as it is one of the most fundamental, of all human cognitive reactions. Yet . . . it is exceedingly complex. . . . Inextricably mingled with it are imagining, valuing, and the beginnings of judgment.

This point is illustrated graphically in Dougherty and Keller's (1985, p. 162–63) discussion of how blacksmiths organize their tools in their shops. A person unfamiliar with how a blacksmith works might organize the tools by size, by common labels (i.e., hammers, including ball-pen, claw, sledges, mallets)—saws, including hacksaws, coping saws, Japanese carpenter's saw, rip saws, and so on. Tongs, clamps, and chisels might be categorized as well.

One blacksmith who saw this organization stated: "We could sort them into tools with wooden handles, single pieces of metal, pivoted metal tools, and multicomponent tools, too . . ." (Dougherty & Keller, 1985, p. 163). The question this smith asked was "What do you want to make?" Thus one linguistic sorting of the perceptual objects in the blacksmith's shop—that done on the basis of common labels—was found to be unsuited to how working smiths organize their work. In this case, perception and cognition are based on the task-at-hand and what the perceiver is doing. Perceiving, naming, categorizing, and labeling are individual and cultural matters. The meaning of the perception of an object is not just given, as in a camera's image of the object perceived.

Stimuli viewed as purely physical events are presented to us by our environment and are not changed in any way by being named, classified, or interpreted. Stimuli become cues, however, when attention is paid to them or when they are responded to. The individual learns to select and interpret the stimuli relevant to her actions and interests, and to ignore others or take them for granted.

It is easy, but fallacious, to conceive of perception as a single passive act, as if an organism looks out upon an environment and receives impressions of it through the sense organs. This *copy conception* was attacked by Dewey (1922, 1925) and others who stressed that perceiving is part of a larger organization of activity. Some persons do sit idly and allow stimuli to flow in upon them, but usually they are engaged in some sort of activity. What is noted and how it is interpreted affect the course of action. As the action enters new phases, new kinds of cues are sought and evaluated. Lines of activity are typically intermittent and extend over periods of time, as for example when an individual is buying a house, planning a vacation, or making a garden. When a given line of behavior is temporarily suspended, we have time to ruminate over the past and anticipate the future. Both past and future may influence our perceptions when we resume the earlier activity. Perceiving as part of the larger pattern of activity is necessarily focused on the future, even though it occurs in the present. As Ittelson and Cantril, following Dewey's general position, say (1954, p.27):

Perception certainly seems to be of the world as it is right now, or, perhaps, as it was a few minutes ago. Indeed, the definition of perception frequently appears in psychology texts as "the awareness of immediately present objects.". . . [But] While present and past are involved in the perceptual process, the chief time-orientation in perceiving is toward the future. The primary function of perception . . . is prediction of the future.

The facts are that perception is selective; motivation and needs sensitize us to specific stimuli or sometimes lead to distorted perception; stimuli are often misinterpreted; and perceptions of the same situation may vary from individual to individual. But these facts should not cause us to ignore the further fact that reality sets limits to perception. People who persistently see nonexistent objects like pink elephants or who hear voices when no one is speaking are out of touch with reality; they are hallucinating. Perception therefore, is not arbitrary, but is limited by what is actually present in the environment. None of us can live in the real world if we see only what suits us.

Learning to perceive causes behavior to become more discriminating and flexible with respect to environmental reality. It does not, however, free behavior from reality. Admittedly, the complications introduced into the perceptual processes when they become linked with high-order conceptualizations and symbolic systems (such as one's conceptions of self) increase the probabilities of distortion and error. The perceptions of the lower animal or the child are probably less

subject to error than those of the sophisticated adult.

Selectivity of perception is especially marked in social interaction in which the person's self-esteem is at stake. Psychiatrists and clinical psychologists have long noted the human tendency to ignore or misperceive things that would be damaging to their egos if correctly noted. Psychiatrist H. S. Sullivan coined the expression *selective inattention* for this process in which "we fail to recognize the actual import of a good many things which we see, hear, think, do, and say, not because there is anything the matter with our zones of interaction with others, but because the process of inferential analysis is opposed by the self system" (1953, p.374). Some experimental studies by psychologists have shown how perceptions are distorted because of the perceiver's needs and motives; and this work supports, if it does not greatly amplify, the observations of psychiatrists and other trained observers. Some years ago Henry Triandis, in summarizing work on "cultural influences on perception," suggested that members of given societies may see object A rather than object B, when presented with both, "because of (1) the greater meaning of A than B . . . ; (2) the higher frequency of occurrence of A relative to B; and (3) the more pleasant associations with A than B." Therefore, he concludes, "cultural experience may enhance the availability of a category and depress another" (1964, p.13).

The same point is supported by research on cross-cultural differences pertaining to perception of optical illusions. Thus, Segall and his associates studied 1,878 subjects from fourteen non-European cultures and three European cultures. The experimenters used versions of the Muller-Lyer, The Sander Parallelogram, and the Horizontal-Vertical illusion. Their "results strongly support the hypothesis that the perception of space involves, to an important extent, the acquisition of habits of perceptual inference" (1964, p.14). For instance, Europeans experience the first two illusions much more sharply than do non-Europeans, but experience the Horizontal-Vertical illusion less sharply.

Social Factors in Perception

Social or cultural influences affect perception in a marked way. Laymen, of course, have noticed this phenomenon. The poet Carl Sandburg (1936) made the point effectively in a poem entitled "Elephants Are Different to Different People," as shown in the excerpt below:*

Wilson and Pilcer and Snack stood before the zoo elephant. Wilson said, "What is its name? Is it from Asia or Africa: Who feeds it? Is it a he or a she? How old is it? Do they have twins? How much does it cost to feed? How much does it weigh? If it dies how much will another one cost? If it dies what will they use the bones, the fat, and the hide for? What use is it besides to look at?"

Pilcer didn't have any questions; he was murmuring to himself, "It's a house by itself, walls and windows, the ears came from tall cornfields, by God; the architect of those legs was a workman, by God; he stands like a bridge out across deep water; the face is sad and the eyes are kind; I know elephants are good to babies."

Snack looked up and down and at last said to himself, "He's a tough son-of-a-gun outside and I'll bet he's got a strong heart. I'll bet he's strong as a copper-riveted boiler inside. . . ."

Three men saw the elephant three ways. . . .

One might object that each man saw the same elephant but interpreted it differently; but interpretation is involved in all acts of perception.

A real-estate broker looking at a house is not likely to observe the same details as does an artist, a fire-insurance agent, or an architect. When viewing a landscape, artists will perceive details and relationships of line, space, light, and color that escape ordinary "seeing." What is selected and emphasized in perceiving is connected with the observer's perspective, with her value system, interests,

---

*From Carl Sandburg, "Elephants are Different to Different People," *Home Front Memo* (San Diego: Harcourt Brace Jovanovich, 1943), Copyright © 1943 Carl Sandburg, renewed 1971 by Lillian Steichen Sandburg.

needs, and the like. Perception is clearly dependent upon previous experience, interests, and concerns. These in turn are related to such factors as the perceiver's occupation, class, and age—in short, to his social background.

PERCEPTION, LANGUAGE, AND GROUPS

We have noted that humans act toward objects in light of their classification of them. The term schemata (Bartlett, 1932; Casson, 1983, p. 430; Agar & Hobbs, 1985, pp. 413–31) has been employed by cognitive psychologists and anthropologists to describe the conceptual abstractions that mediate between stimuli received by the sense organs and behavioral responses. Schemata "are abstractions that serve as the basis of all human information processing, e.g. perception and comprehension, categorization and planning, recognition and recall, and problem-solving and decision-making" (Casson, 1983, p. 430).

Schemata are based on group languages and group perspectives. Group influences on perception are well-illustrated in a recent study by Boster (1985, pp. 177–97) of the Aguaruna Jivaro, a forest-dwelling tribe in the northern Peruvian *montaña*. Boster studied how the Aguarunas classified and named manioc, a starchy root that contributes about 60 percent of the calories in the daily diet of this group. It is also used for making beer, and is the source of tapioca pudding.

In order to investigate Aguaruna manioc identification, two experimental gardens were planted; the first had 61 different varieties of manioc, the second had 15 common varieties of the plant. Fifty-eight women participated in the identification of the manioc in the garden which had 61 varieties. Boster called this the hard task. Forty-three women and 21 men participated in the easy task—the garden with 15 varieties of the plant. The findings from this study may be summarized as follows: (1) all women, in both tasks (hard and easy), with only two exceptions, had higher overall agreement on the classification of manioc, than did men; (2) younger women, who had gone to school, were more likely to disagree with others in their classifications; (3) women from the same kin group were more likely to agree with one another, when compared to women from different kin groups.

How do we interpret these findings? First, we must note that in this cultural group men do not garden. Hence the fact that women were able to classify manioc better than men is explained by this sexual division of labor in the group. Second, a woman who leaves the group to go to school is deprived of her "education as a horticulturalist with her mother in the garden" (Boster, 1985, p. 189). Third, women within the same kin group share intimate knowledge about manioc that is not shared in other kin groups (Boster. 1985, p. 193). Fourth, "different layers of agreement corresponded to different layers of social identity and also to different modes and intensities of communication about manioc" (Boster, 1985, p. 183). Fifth, the variation between individuals can be explained by each of these layers and forms of social identity.

We can see that different cultural schemata are associated with the sexual division of labor and the organization of women within kin groups in this culture. These schemata lead to differences in the perception of the object manioc. Boster's study points out the implication of different learning situations for the way in which objects and concepts are organized (Dougherty, 1985, p. 175).

As the above example suggests, objects are perceived characteristically not as isolated items, but as members of a class. The class to which an object is fitted is in turn related to the task-at-hand of the perceiver. We do not perceive bare, unnamed isolated objects. Glance around the room, making note of what you "see." Do you not see class representatives such as walls, books, pencil, chair, and flowers? Linguistic classification is not external or incidental to such perceiving, but is an integral part of it. What we term "perceiving" involves linguistic distinctions, for objects cannot be perceived as class members unless the observer's language has already designated these classes or enables her to invent new categories. As J. Gibson says (1953, p.136):

The factor which makes for the socializing of perception in human organisms, we may suspect, is the process of word-making. Presumably, since only human beings make words, only human beings show the phenomenon of a cultural stereotyping of their percepts. . . . The phenomenal world of a language community is partly determined by its language, that is, people see what they have words for. A promising explanation of this fact is that the entities of stimulation that get identified, the variables that get discriminated and abstracted, are very much determined by the verbal responses which accompany perceptual and motor activity. Words tend to fix or freeze the objects and qualities which become differentiated out of the stimulus flux; words tend to determine a man's repertory of perceptions. . . . Since people must reach a kind of consensus of mind-reactions in order to communicate, they tend to reach a consensus of individual perceptions.

The linguistic character of even rather simple adult perception is shown in a study by L. Carmichael (1932). Visual outline drawings were presented to subjects, and as the drawing was shown, a word categorizing it was spoken by the investigator. Thus

was called either "sun" or "ship's wheel." Reproduction of the outline drawing shortly afterward (from memory) varied according to the word spoken. Carmichael attributed this variation to certain processes initiated by the word that affected perception of the drawing.

F. Bartlett's (1932) careful work, which is still a point of reference for current research in this area (Casson, 1983, p. 430), indicates also how linguistic elements influence perception. Subjects briefly shown the figure

sometimes thought the rectangle was completely drawn in. In such a figure as

, naming was of great importance in helping to shape perception. Subjects looking at this figure who saw "picture frames"

perceived an object that looked like

or . The figure was called a "pick-ax" by one observer and reproduced with pointed prongs; another person called it a "turf cutter" and drew it with a rounded blade. Several persons called it an "anchor" and exaggerated the size of the ring on the top. Only one person correctly perceived the pointed blade; he had seen it as a prehistoric battle-ax. Bartlett noted that if a figure seemed odd, disconnected, or unfamiliar it was usually seen in terms of an analogy—that is, in terms of the identity of a known object. He concludes that "a great amount of what is said to be perceived is in fact inferred."

A commonsense maxim holds that in general, "people see what they are looking for." This is not always true, but the phrase indicates that verbal frames of reference organize perceptual responses. A person's perceiving is likely to follow along the lines of familiarities and expectations. The illustrations taken from the work of Bartlett and Carmichael demonstrate this well, as does the existence of some types of "suggestion." Thus, when Binet (Murphy et al., 1937, p. 173) showed subjects "a series of lines of gradually increasing length, but with occasional 'catches' where the lines did not lengthen as expected . . . not one of his forty-five pupils completely escaped the suggestion of increase in length in all lines." This kind of suggestion can be accounted for very simply by supposing that Binet's subjects were *set* to see successively longer lines.

Complex Social Perceptions. If simple perception such as that studied by Carmichael and Bartlett involves naming, analogy, and inference, it can be assumed that more complex acts of perceiving will involve more complex uses of language. To illustrate, let us consider a cross-cultural exam-

ple. Among the Murngin, a primitive Australian tribe, every man shows respect to his mother-in-law by strict avoidance, so that if the mother-in-law is seen coming down the path, both he and she must avert their eyes and turn aside. An American observer might perceive this act on at least three increasingly complicated levels. On one level the observer might see only a man and a middle-aged woman walking toward each other, then turning aside and not looking in each other's direction. The second level, assuming the observer knows only how the two persons are related to each other, would involve seeing the son-in-law and the mother-in-law avoiding each other and refraining from looking at each other. The observer would not know what was being expressed—shyness, guilt, hatred, mutual punishment, or fear. The third, most complex level would involve a comparatively thorough knowledge of Murngin family relationships, including recognition of the meaning of "avoidance for respect." In this instance the observer would "see" the son-in-law paying respect to his mother-in-law by respectfully "avoiding" her.

Complex Perceptions and Codability. The Solomon Islanders have a complex and detailed perception of coconuts, Eskimos make fine discriminatory classifications of snow, and Arabs have many words for camel (including fifty that describe various stages of the pregnancy of camels). These fine discriminations make it possible for those who make those discriminations also to make the associated perceptual distinctions. It can be said that without the linguistic distinctions, people can still make the same perceptual distinctions (for instance, Brown has argued that Americans distinguish as many kinds of snow as Eskimos [1954, p. 455]). But the Eskimos' categories have what has been termed *high codability*. High codability means that the classes of things to be talked about have established single names permitting the members of a language community to respond quickly and consistently from one situation to another, both to the names and the things. Such terms are especially useful in communicating perceptual distinctions, and probably in making them.

Possibly, there may sometimes even be a link between social structure, norms, and specific categorical distinctions. For instance, the Pawnee Indians have an identical word for mother's brother's wife, ego's wife, and the sister of ego's wife. Lounsbury's study showed that an adolescent Pawnee first has sexual intercourse with his mother's brother's wife; when he marries, he may have intercourse with his wife's sisters. "The designation of all these women by a single kinship term is consistent with these customs, though such correspondence between category content and social structure is itself arbitrary and may occur in one culture but not in another" (Berkowitz, 1964, p. 20). Social structural considerations may easily be seen to affect category content, hence perception in our society. We have only to recall the discussion of special languages to realize that categorical distinctions made by some groups are related not only to efficiency and pertinent interests but to the moral judgments they make about types of persons.

THE SOCIAL BASIS OF MEMORY

Perceiving involves the response to or interpretation of signs in the form of sensory stimulation resulting from the organism's contacts with the external environment or arising within the organism. *Remembering* is a response to signs of past experiences, which in some form or other are preserved within the organism. In the one case the sign bridges a spatial gap, in the other a temporal gap. Thus, remembering, like perceiving, is a complex form of sign behavior. Like perception, memory is profoundly influenced by the communicating we do in the groups to which we belong.

Content of Memory. An illustration of how memory is affected by group mem-

bership is a story told about a number of Swazi chiefs from South Africa. The chiefs visited England, and after returning home discovered that their most vivid memory was that of a British policeman regulating traffic with uplifted hand. The vividness of this particular memory was related to the Swazi custom of greeting one another with the same gesture.

Bartlett (1932), who has studied remembering among these people, writes that they have the reputation among their neighbors of possessing excellent memories. After testing the memories of several representative Swazi, he concluded that this reputation was unfounded; but he later discovered that Swazi memories connected with cattle and cattle raising were almost phenomenal. As Bartlett explains, cattle raising is a central concern of Swazi society.

It is common knowledge that an individual's interests are a good key to what he will remember. If a woman is inclined to gossip, she is likely to remember gossip tidbits, although her memory for other items may be far from superlative. People who like poetry may be able to recite dozens of stanzas yet fail to remember algebraic proofs or the names of people whom they have met. Numerous small boys in the United States astound their elders with their ability to remember the batting averages of favorite baseball players. These same boys may be the despair of their teachers because of deficient memory in classroom work.

Most people could point to instances in their own lives where certain vivid memories were linked with interest and attitude. The studies cited above demonstrate that even run-of-the-mill memories are dependent upon perspective and interest. As our examples and these various studies show, perspective and interest are not merely individual matters, but are much affected by group membership and the kinds of communication that flow among the members. The circumstances involved in those situations where one's self is transformed will also be remembered. (See Chapter 12.)

HUMAN REMEMBERING AS A SYMBOLIC PROCESS

Remembering Depends Upon Categorization. Humans without language, like animals, would be tied down to concrete situations. They would have no conceptions either of history or of a personal past. On reflection, it becomes clear that much of our remembering revolves around memorable events, holidays, and dates. We cast back "in our memories" to last Friday, last summer, the weekend before last, the day we entered college, or our sixteenth birthday. We often recollect by means of such notational devices. If we are asked where we spent last Thanksgiving and what we did, the task of recalling is made relatively easy. If, on the other hand, we are asked what we did last November 6 (unless that is some memorable date, such as a birthday), recollection is likely to be either weak or totally absent.

To hear a melody and recognize vaguely that you have heard it somewhere does not perhaps clearly depend upon language. However, to say to yourself, "How does the first movement of Beethoven's Fifth Symphony go?" and then by an act of "concentration" to call up themes from that movement, is clearly dependent upon a linguistic framework. Music is so closely linked with language that attention could not be kept focused upon that symphony and that movement if the linguistic framework were missing. Similarly, if you ask, "What is the color of my house back home?" it is by virtue of language that you can call up that house and name its color. Without language categories, such an act of remembrance would be impossible. Again, we are asked to meet a friend for lunch at twelve o'clock in such and such a restaurant, and at a quarter of twelve we remember our engagement. Could we have remembered without the aid of the appropriate names—time categories—which we verbalize to ourselves, perhaps repeatedly, or which we actually write down on a memo pad? Moreover, how would we remember

the past or keep appointments in the future without our systems of time notation?

The psychology of legal testimony supplies an interesting instance of the organization of memory around verbal plans or labels. People may erroneously remember details as having happened, provided that the details fit into a frame of reference. An instance of this is provided by early litigations over patents on the telephone (Judd, 1939, p. 354):

Certain people in a little town . . . gave at a second court-hearing testimony totally different from that which they had given several years earlier at the first hearing. The first testimony was vague and uncertain. In the interval between the two hearings the major subject of discussion in the town had been the apparatus in question. At the second court hearing the people recounted as fully established facts incidents which had apparently been generated by their discussions.

Studies of distortion in the transmission of rumors show the same sort of inaccurate remembering. As it is passed from one person to another, the content of the rumor undergoes alteration, according to how the transmitting person hears and remembers the rumor—both activities depending upon the person's frame of reference (Allport & Postman, 1947; Shibutani, 1966).

Not only does society provide the linguistic and other devices used by the individual in registering an event, recalling, identifying, and placing it, but human memory has other important social dimensions as well. French psychologists and sociologists, particularly, have elaborated the idea that the things people remember form interlaced and mutually reinforcing systems organized around group situations. Thus, Halbwachs (1925, 1950) noted that the student's memory of a given professor, and the course he took with him, is different from the professor's recollection of the student and the course. The student's memory is generally much more precise, Halbwachs deduces, because his experiences are part of a unique group situation shared with others. Professors, on the other hand, experience each class and the individuals in it primarily as one of a series of similar situations occurring in their professional activity. They have met successive classes in the same room or in similar rooms; class follows class, and, as the professors have no special group framework for each of them, they retain only the haziest ideas of what they did, what happened, who was present in any of the classes, or in which buildings and rooms they were held.

Most of our memories, Halbwachs observes, are organized in this way within a framework provided by the group to which we now belong and by those to which we have belonged. When we are within a given group (for example, our families) over a period of time, the members talk about past experiences and keep them fresh in our minds. Familiar faces and old haunts become linked with memories of past events. When we leave the group for a long time or permanently, the memories fade along with the faces, places, and names until only a skeleton or almost nothing remains. If we return after many years to the old group and the old environment the memories are revived, although they are not the same. As we remember and reconstruct the past, according to Halbwachs, we project ourselves into a group framework and use it to revive and organize past experiences. This argument is used to explain the tendency for memories of experiences in temporary groups—for example, the kind formed on board an ocean liner—to shrink and disappear quickly. This is especially true if no lasting relationships are established and if one does not again meet any of the persons involved. Human memory, Halbwachs contends, is therefore *collective*, or social, in nature. We are able to think of memory as individual only because we overlook or take for granted its group connections.

Amnesia for Childhood Memories. Why is it that there is such a dearth of recollections of childhood experiences, and a virtually total amnesia for the period of infancy? Some writers have hypothesized that repression of memories takes place. This is an unsatisfactory explanation, since it neither accounts for the forgetting of pleasant happenings nor for the complete absence of memory of the earliest experiences of a fully sentient infant.

Schachtel (1947) has argued that infants and young children live in a world of feeling and fantasy in which their experiences are such that they quite literally cannot be formulated in words. Hence they cannot be recollected, for infants lack symbolic means to retain them and adults do not have the proper mentality to recapture them later. Schachtel lays great stress upon the stereotyped, abstract, and schematic character of adult language that transforms growing children in socializing them and renders them in a sense unfit to be a child even in remembrance. We need not adopt Schachtel's nostalgic attitude toward the richness and vitality of childhood imagery, but his emphasis upon the crucial import of symbolic structures for remembrance is important. Infants, lacking these symbolic structures, have nothing to record them with so that they can recapture them later.

A subsidiary, but also important, point is that the transformations of children during the course of their socialization make recollection difficult or impossible. The Luria (1928) experiment has suggested this same conclusion. In a study of the development of children's concepts of money, Strauss (1952) found that it was unusual for the children to recollect any of the concepts held at earlier ages. In fact, they rejected notions once firmly believed with no awareness that they had once accepted them—rejected them with ridicule, laughter, and incredulity. This is precisely what one would expect if it is assumed that development implies genuine transformation of behavioral organization. In his studies of children, Piaget also has observed that when children are asked where they learned their most recent conceptions, they often remark, "I have always known that."

Halbwachs (1925) has suggested that although certain childhood memories can be recaptured, at least in a gross sense, certain others cannot because perspectives have changed. For example, one can often remember the name of a book read as a child, conjuring up the look of the print and some of the imagery of the pictures and possibly even recapturing some of the overtones of the feeling experienced while reading the book. (However, it takes a rare person, like novelist Marcel Proust, to recapture feeling.) But, as Halbwachs shrewdly notes, it is literally impossible to divest oneself of the experiences of the intervening years so as to feel exactly as one did when reading the book as a child. He remarks that the effort to recapture feelings poses the same problem as the effort to recapture the spirit of preceding periods in history. We may add that even Proust, dredging up minute and poignant details of his childhood, gives only the illusion of an accurate recollection. Recollection is active, not passive. Proust's *Remembrance of Things Past* is an artistic and artful reconstruction, a creative act, not the record set down by a passive watcher as his memories file by like a parade. Adults, moving through the life cycle to new perspectives and abandoning old ones, can be expected to find it difficult to recapture any but the grossest or most static, or poignant, moments of their past.

The Child's History

Taking our lead from Proust, we can argue that the resources for producing a childhood history are present in most children by the age of three years. By this age, children (see Chapter 8) have mastered language, and are capable of self-reflective thought and action. They are able, that is, to produce events which can and could be remembered at a later date (Denzin, 1982, pp. 29–46). How-

ever, as our remarks on childhood amnesia suggest, children lack the complex symbolic equipment necessary for grasping or recapturing any but the most vivid events of their past.

Nonetheless, families keep histories on their shared and significant experiences. Family photo albums, mementos from vacations, souvenirs, and gifts all mark significant moments in historical time. They serve to locate the child's self in the memories of this past. We may ask, what things from childhood are remembered? Alice James (Edel, 1964, pp. 127–28), sister of William and Henry James, considers the question in the following passage:

I wonder what determines the *selection* of memory, why does one childish experience or impression stand out so luminous and solid against the, for the most part, vague and misty background. The things we remember have a *firsttimeness* about them which suggests that may be the reason of their survival . . . I remember so distinctly the first time I was conscious of a purely intellectual process.

One's remembered childhood may hinge, then, on the experiencing and the cataloguing of first time, significant events. In between these first time events are chains of repetitions, habitualized routines and daily doings. One establishes the credibility of their childhood by remembering it well and in vivid detail.

Henry James (1913) offers the following remembrance of one of his early childhood perceptions. It involves his temporal standing in the James family, behind his older brother William:

. . . One of these, and probably the promptest in order, was that of my brother's occupying a place in the world to which I couldn't at all aspire . . . as if he had gained such an advance of me in his sixteen months' experience of the world before mine began that I never for all the time of childhood and youth in the least caught up with him or overtook him. He was always round the corner and out of sight, coming back into view but at his hours of extremest ease. We were never in the same schoolroom, in the same game, scarce even in step together or in the same phase at the same time; when our phases overlapped, that is, it was only for a moment—he was clean out before I had got well in. How far he had really at any moment dashed forward it is not for me now to attempt to say; what comes to me is that I at least hung inveterately and woefully back, and that this relation alike to our interests and to each other seemed proper and preappointed. (pp. 9–10)

Now consider the following statement from another member of the James family. Robertson James, the youngest of the James sons, said of himself in a fragment of an autobiography (Burr, 1934, p. 25):

I was born in the year 1846, in Albany, N.Y. I never remember being told anything extraordinary about my babyhood but I often like to contemplate myself as a baby and wonder if I was really as little appreciated as I fully remember feeling at that time. I never see infants now without discerning in their usually solemn countenance a conviction that they are on their guard and in more or less hostile surroundings. However that may be, in my own case, at a very early age the problems of life began to press upon me in such an unnatural way and I developed such an ability for feeling hurt and wounded that I became quite convinced by the time I was twelve years old that I was a foundling. (p. 25)

We have, in these statements, painful remembrances of childhood. Henry James felt that he was always behind his brother William, no matter where they went or what they did. Robertson remembers himself as feeling hurt and wounded, and not fully appreciated. He generalizes this childhood memory to all infants and young children. These accounts from the James family suggest that memories of childhood can take on an influence that is still felt in adulthood.

The Symbolic Nature of the Past

Maines, Sugrue and Katovich (1983, pp. 161–73), commenting on Mead's (1929,

1932, 1934, 1936, 1938) theory of the past, suggest that four dimensions to the past may be identified. These are (1) the symbolically reconstructed past, (2) the social structural past, (3) the implied objective past, and (4) the mythical past.

The symbolically reconstructed past involves "redefining the meaning of past events in such a way that they have meaning in and utility for the present" (Maines, Sugrue, & Katovich, 1983, p. 163). We have seen how members of a family symbolically reconstruct past events so as to give them meaning in the present.

The social structural past refers to how events in the past *structure* and *shape* experiences found in the present. In the preceding account, Robertson James explains how his experiences in early childhood led him to see infants in the present with the conviction that "they are on their guard." His past experiences structure and shape his present perceptions and actions.

The implied objective past is the third dimension of Mead's theory. Mead states, "The past is that which must have been before it is present in experience as a past" (Mead, 1929. p. 238). He refers here to the existence of previous events; to the fact that they must have existed in order for them to exist in the present as a past. Mead is suggesting that past events have an implied, objective existence in that "they exist in the present through memory" (Maines, Sugrue, & Katovich, 1983, p. 164). The present structures what is remembered from this implied past. Henry James gives an implied objective past to his relationship with his brother William. He states that William "was always round the corner and out of sight"; this is how he objectively remembers William.

The mythical past is Mead's fourth dimension. These pasts are "creations, rather than re-creations, because they are not empirically grounded." They are fictitious. However, they are "empirical in their consequences because they materially affect relationships" (Maines, Sugrue, & Katovich, 1983, p. 164). Returning to Henry James' biography once again, he creates a mythical past that includes his brother and their relationship. Mead is suggesting that we create myths (a story, the origin of which is forgotten, ostensibly historical, which usually serves to explain some practice or belief) because they have practical value in solving problems.

Each of these dimensions of the past flow through the "specious," or immediate, present. The existence of these events which occur in the past is never doubted, because they are given meaning in the present. What is problematic is their meaning in the present (Maines, Sugrue, & Katovich, 1983, p. 165). We will develop these points in the next section.

Historical Communication, Perception, and Memory

We have shown how perceiving and remembering are selective processes. Selectivity is socially influenced. Schemata are social constructions. Because groups, organizations, and institutions exist for long periods of time, memories of past events and dead personages are passed along from generation to generation. Each generation, however, symbolically reconstructs, structures, and creates its own versions of the implied objective past, and weave these pasts through their myths. Let us consider several instances of collective heritage, historical communication, and collective memory.

A relatively simple instance is the common garden variety of remembrance that most of us have about the relations between American Indians and white Americans during the nineteenth century. Unless we have heard or read specifically to the contrary, we tend to believe the mass media's version of *How the West Was Won.* Indians tend even to be equated with the West! A more complete version would include the idea that rarely have a group of natives been so completely swept clean off their land and with such cruelty. Our individual memories of these events are nonexistent, so our views of this past, and to a large extent our views of Indians today, are

rooted in our induction into channels of communication represented mainly by the mass media. Since European children also may read the same stories and see the same movies, they too may be inducted into the standard set of legends. Various Europeans have described this induction (Grosz, 1946; pp. 18, 32–33). Recently, some Indians have been trying—with difficulty, for collective memories are tenacious—to refashion Americans' conceptions of the past relations of whites with Indians.

With more passion and perhaps more face-to-face interaction, most Southern whites have images both of what the "War Between the States" was like and what followed directly thereafter during the Reconstruction period. The present generation has heard about these events from their parents through folk tradition. Southerners who were not born in the South have been inducted into the intense communication about these events through friends and acquaintances, perhaps from teachers, as well as through the various mass media that circulate in the South. Indeed, some of the nonnatives may have sharper and more passionately held images than Southerners whose forefathers fought in the Civil War. These collective memories have helped to shape the subsequent course of events in the South and in the North also. Attempting to answer this legendary tradition, black and white historians have done firsthand research that shows that both popular and scholarly historians (mostly Southern whites) have often made errors in fact and in interpretation (Franklin, 1956; Jordan, 1968; Beringer, Hattaway, Jones & Still, Jr., 1985). More recent emphasis on black pride and other attempts to counter the destructive effects of being black in a white-dominated society have also sought to rectify the remarkably inaccurate history of race relations in the United States.

We need not attribute deliberate distortion to historians, press, or ordinary conversationalists as they reshape the past through their interpretations of it. Quite enough distortion occurs through the selective processes of perceiving, remembering, and retelling without the necessity of our assuming deliberate manipulation, although assuredly falsification of history often does occur. The selective processes can be seen at work in "house organ history," whether it is a history of a corporation, voluntary organization, religious denomination, city, or profession. These accounts are almost certain to be "slanted" in the direction of self-aggrandizement, if only because those who write the histories are either biased in the direction of "progress" or have seen events from a particular position, or both.

Continuity of the legendary tradition of any group is broken when the communication channels either disintegrate or are captured by people who wish to change the information transmitted by those channels. The latter strategy is shown by what happens when authoritarian governments begin to beam different interpretations of national history over the mass media, blocking out as completely as possible all competing versions of the past. The disintegration of communication channels generally means either the disappearance of the communication-bearing group itself, or the disappearance of persons who acted as key transmitting agents for the old days. Another possibility is the transformation of the group itself so that in some sense the original group has disappeared, as happens with minority groups that become assimilated into the mainstream of a nation's life. Its members are likely to forget much of the ethnic heritage—such as foods, religious beliefs, and customs—whereas an embattled minority group, as in the Balkan countries, may persist for centuries with collective memories of its distant past as vivid as those of yesterday.

A new group, organization, or social structure may also appropriate as part of its functioning heritage various events and objects that either were forgotten and are now rediscovered, or which genuinely had little connection with its actual past. History is full of such events. The rediscovery by Renaissance scholars of the Greek past, and how this past was interpreted in contemporary terms, is one of the great stories of Western civilization. In turn, this story becomes part of *our past*—if we know about it. A contemporary instance of the same type of rediscovery is how Americans and Europeans are learning about the great pre-Greek civilizations that contributed to the rise of the Western world. The proliferation of best-selling archeological books is not to be overlooked, for they are sources for transmitting this information to new audiences. They are present as remarkably visible elements in the actual and conversational baggage of travelers in the Near East. In Israel, each new archeological discovery is front-page news, avidly read about by everyone, as it is likely to have direct bearing on ancient Jewish history and symbolic bearing on the identities of Israeli citizens.

An even more striking and momentous contemporary instance of discovering the past is the search for national identity that is exhibited by newborn nations as they comb their tribal and regional pasts in an effort to get a national past of which they can be proud. As Everett Hughes remarked some years ago, it would be interesting to see what elements they would choose to incorporate into their national memories; and he was quite right. Many European nations, of course, went through a similar process during the last century (Hayes, 1926). The pasts they constructed and reconstructed are immensely relevant to the perceptions, memories, and actions of contemporary citizens. Stalin himself bowed to the persistence of older national memories when, during World War II, the question of the Soviet Union's survival was at stake. Communist symbols were minimized, and the older national symbols were reinstated into public favor. They had never really disappeared from the more private channels of communication.

THE PLANNING OF BEHAVIOR

As we have stressed repeatedly, the human is a planning animal, making continual references to the past, present, and future. As the person moves through the present into the future, the past is recast and reformulated to fit the images of the future. This merger of the past and future in the present constitutes what G. H. Mead termed the *specious present*. That is, as we act in the present, we bring our previous actions to bear upon our anticipated actions in the next moment. These anticipations, in turn, shape our actions in the present. In the specious present, past, present, and future flow into a single temporal phase of experience. William James described this as the *stream of consciousness* of the person. In their plans, however ill-defined and vague, humans reveal an ability to take control over their own behavior so as to give it the semblance of organization and predictability. Plans, then, take many forms: They can be well-thought-out, written down, and made public, as when a president or head of state lays out a ten-year economic plan. They can refer to private affairs or public affairs, and they can refer to individual actions, to the actions of large collectivities, to the plans of families, or to the plans of two lovers. People vary in their ability to formulate plans. Young children, for instance, seldom have any control over when they will enter school, be taken on a vacation, or be permitted to open a savings account. Furthermore, people vary in their power—legitimate or illegitimate, institutionalized or informal—to formulate plans. This ability and authority to make plans varies by one's location in the power networks that make up social groups and complex bureaucracies. We can also see that individuals' plans vary by where they see themselves in their overall moral career. The plans of the aged and the elderly, which reflect some attempt to control their last years of life during retirement, are quite different from those of a person just beginning a work career. Plans are always about the future, even when formulated in the present, for they refer to how individuals will organize their action in the next moment, day, year, or decade. Finally, we can note that some plans are hidden from others—embezzlers, for example, seldom make their plans known—while other plans are matters of public infor-

mation—a phase of an economic anti-inflationary plan, for example. These aspects of plans, and the human's ability to plan, are not often considered in the social and psychological literature. To illustrate this conclusion, we will make brief reference to the stimulus-response view of planning as a form of human activity.

The S-R Model and Its Critics

Having indicated that planning, perceiving, and remembering are interrelated intellectual processes of great complexity, we can approach the matter in another way by reminding the reader of an older psychological model of behavior that stressed *S-R* (or *stimulus-response*) *bonds* as something like the basic elements of all behavior. Stimuli were said to "elicit" (cause) responses, and complex behavioral patterns were said to consist simply of multitudes of such S-R bonds organized in sequences and patterns. The model was largely derived from observing lower animals.

This conception came under fire from other psychologists and others interested in human behavior on the grounds that it presented an overly mechanical view of human behavior and that it tended to ignore problems raised by the fact that—in human behavior in particular—there is often a vast time gap between stimulus and response—that is, a *delayed response*. Critics suggested that one ought to know what was happening during this interval. It was observed that perhaps a basic and radical difference between lower animals and humans was that the latter were capable of checking or inhibiting their responses in order to gather further information and to allow time for processing and evaluating them, and also to formulate plans for an eventual response on the basis of anticipated consequences and contingencies and on their assessment of the stimulus situation. From this viewpoint, the most important parts of human behavior are precisely those that the S-R model omits—namely, those events that transpire in the time interval between the S and the R. It can be argued that it is during this interval that a given event or situation becomes a specific stimulus by virtue of whether or not it is noticed at all, and, if noticed, how it is interpreted. An automatic S-R connection is comparable to an automatic electronic control device like a thermostat, but we do not say that latter has *plans* to keep our house warm in our absence, although we might say that it is "programmed" to do just that. In this case, it is the programmer, not the thermostat, that plans. We argue that social scientists should focus on the programmer rather than the thermostat.

By virtue of their higher mental processes, then, humans can, on a symbolic level, engage in true deliberation—which is, as John Dewey notes with his usual emphasis on behavior, "a search for a *way* to act, not for a final terminus" (1922, p. 193). Dewey also emphasizes, as we have, the unified character of past, present, and future, reminding us that we judge present "desires and habits" in terms of their probable consequences, with which knowledge is linked (1922, p. 207). "We know . . . by recollecting what we have observed, by using that recollection in constructive imaginative forecasts of the future, by using the thought of future consequences to tell the quality of the act now proposed."

Planning, Feedback, and Probabilities

The process of deliberation referred to by Dewey is actually much more complex and delicate than it seems at first glance, especially when plans involve the presumed reactions of other people. One way of illustrating this point is by referring to what are called *self-fulfilling and self-negating* predictions. The former are exemplified by the person who seeks to make money in the stock market by following some of the well-known formulae disseminated in financial circles. If there are many investors who believe that stocks should be sold when stock averages behave in certain ways that are believed to constitute sell "signals," then stock prices will fall when the signal occurs, simply because there are enough people who heed the signal to force prices down. The

self-negating prophecy, or prediction, is one which induces the person whose behavior has been predicted to prove that the prediction is wrong. Some years ago, before going barefooted was as common as it is now, a professor arguing before a class said that it was easy to predict human behavior and made his point by predicting that everyone would be wearing shoes and stockings at the next meeting of his class. At the next class a number of students arrived barefooted to prove him wrong.

These examples indicate some problems of planning and predicting that are introduced by the fact that people tend to seek information about the plans that others make concerning them and to alter their own accordingly. As activity proceeds, information concerning its effects and the reactions of others tends to flow back to the persons involved in what is called a *feedback* process. Feedback data are then interpreted and utilized to confirm, negate, or alter the ongoing course of action.

Another example from the legal field illustrates other aspects of planning. How do individuals decide whether or not they should take the risk of violating the law? Obviously, this may involve a very complex set of considerations, one of which is the probability of being caught. Suppose the question is that of driving an automobile when drunk. Two questions may be raised: (1) from police statistics, what are the objective probabilities that a drunken driver will be arrested?; (2) how does the person feel about his or her own chances of being caught? This is the difference between *objective* and *subjective* probability, and the two may be quite unrelated. A similar example is to consider how people in big cities might plan their movements within it in relation to their estimates of the dangers of being victimized by a criminal. A further question is raised as to how such persons make their assessments of danger. Is it from the criminal statistics, from the reports of their friends and associates, from what they hear and see from the mass media, or do they simply draw on their imagination?

Because there is an inherent uncertainty

about the future that increases geometrically with time, probability judgments weigh heavily in virtually all planning. Sometimes this uncertainty is dealt with by planning a series of lines of action in case the unexpected should happen. For example the thief expects not to be caught, but she takes along a sum of money to bribe the victim, policeman, or other official in case she is caught. If all this fails, she may have made advance arrangements with a "fixer" who will perhaps be able to get the case dismissed. Respectable citizens do not face the same hazards that a thief does, but despite all the planning we may do, the uncertainty of the future remains.

Kristin Luker, in *Taking Chances: Abortion and the Decision Not to Contracept* (1975), interviewed over 600 women who had abortions. Her findings illustrate our points on planning and probability. She found that for all the women she interviewed, the decision to "seek an abortion has been serious, thoughtful, and carefully considered" (Luker, 1984, p. 285). She found that many women had unwanted pregnancies (because of their age, health status of their spouse, number of children, job situation, personal health and goals, and so on). These pregnancies occurred because the predictions they made about getting pregnant were incorrect. Her respondents made subjective probability predictions about not getting pregnant, and these predictions underscored their decision not to contracept. Their decisions, and the consequences of those decisions, then led them to form accounts (explanations) of their conduct, in which they justified their actions to themselves and to others, including abortion counselors. They were required in many cases to (1) have reasons for not contracepting and (2) have reasons for seeking an abortion.

MOTIVES, ACTIVITIES, AND ACCOUNTS

At the start of this chapter we suggested that human beings have a deep interest in the "how" and "why" of behavior. We will now examine three theories which address these questions. The first theory is the Freudian conception of human behavior; the second is the Marxist position; and the third is the social psychological point of view we hold in this text.

FREUDIAN CONCEPTIONS

Probably the most influential motivational scheme of this century is the Freudian, which was most popular in sociology between the years 1930 and 1939. Some variant of it is utilized by most clinical psychologists and psychiatrists. Social workers, child psychologists, and anthropologists have often found it useful or acceptable, although sociologists far less so. Fragments of the Freudian terminology and conceptual scheme have also found their way into popular thought. It is difficult to set forth current Freudian ideas in a form that would be subscribed to by all Freudians, because there are considerable differences in viewpoint, formulation, and emphasis among them. Whatever these differences may be, there is a fair amount of agreement on a number of basic points and assumptions. (See also Chapter 8). The psychoanalytic view has also gained a great deal of interest in literary criticism in recent years. The work of Lacan (1977) has been especially influential in this regard (Coward & Ellis, 1977; Ragland-Sullivan, 1986).

Some Basic Points

Among the basic assumptions underlying the Freudian view of motivation are the ideas that all human behavior is motivated, that the explanation of any behavior requires that its motives be analyzed, that the energy sources of motives are biological in nature, that motives range from those which are entirely conscious to those which are altogether unconscious, that most important ones are either unconscious or partly so, and that the conflict of motivational forces plays a dominant role in personality development. Thus, according to the Freudian position human behavior is activated either by innate biological needs or by elaborations of them. Human culture is conceived of both as an agency which frustrates and disciplines primitive urges, and as a consequence of such frustration, the basic sources of energy are undirected and goalless and are channelized through cultural forms. Freud says (1933, p. 151):

... Our civilization is built up at the cost of our sexual impulses which are inhibited by society, being partly repressed but partly, on the other hand, made use of for new aims. However proud we may be of our cultural achievements ... it is by no means easy to satisfy the requirements of this civilization and to feel comfortable in its midst, because the restriction of the instincts which it involves lays a heavy psychological burden on our shoulders.

However complex the social proliferation of instinctual demands may be, these demands are nonetheless a "facade behind which the function of the underlying innate drives are hidden (Miller & Dollard, 1941, p. 19).

Freudian emphasis on unconscious drives and motives involves a corollary skepticism concerning the purposes which people consciously assign to their acts. Psychoanalysts believe that not only is there much duplicity and concealment about motives, but most people actually know very little about their own motivations. They also point to the difficulty of assessing the motives of others because one's own repressions and motivations get in the way. "The obstacle which one's own repressions constitute against understanding others can be appreciated if one realizes that the uniformity and harmony of the conscious mind are guaranteed by repressions" (Alexander & Ross, 1952, p. 20). In training psychoanalysts, great stress is placed upon the understanding of one's own motivations so that they will not be allowed to interfere with the effort to understand the patient.

The Freudian scheme of motivation applies to human behavior the *conservation of energy principle*, which holds that energy can be neither created nor destroyed. Repressed wishes carry energy charges, and this energy much be discharged in some way or other. Hence the occurrence of such processes as *sublimation*, in which forbidden sexual impulses obtain indirect gratification through acceptable modes of behavior such as artistic creation, intellectual pursuits, simple labor, or other not obviously sexual outlets.

Some psychiatrists conceive of their professional task primarily as that of understanding the unique individuality of the patient. Others place a relatively greater stress upon generalizing about classes of individuals and types of behavior and seek to make psychoanalysis a generalizing science. Allport has designated these two ways of approaching behavior, respectively, as the *idiographic* and the *nomothetic* (1937, p. 22). As to the generalizer's point of view, it is interesting to observe that the various individuals who engage in a given form of behavior (for example, heavy drinking) usually give a wide variety of contradictory reasons for doing so. For the Freudian who seeks to generalize about the particular form of behavior under scrutiny, the problem thus posed is resolved by searching for the underlying unconscious motives which the individuals themselves do not and cannot give.

The Freudian therapist attempts to give patients insight into their repressions and unconscious wishes. This is accomplished in the "prolonged interview" in which the patient tells the psychiatrist about himself and the psychiatrist attempts to make the patient conscious of the real (or unconscious) sources of his behavior. Though Freudian theory places a pronounced emphasis upon the primacy of the unconscious, Freudian therapy emphasizes consciousness as the primary agency through which personality integration is achieved.

Evaluation

The Freudian system is complex, and as we have stated, it has many variants. We will therefore content ourselves by commenting critically upon those aspects which have to do most explicitly with motivation.

We have already critically examined the idea that all human behavior and all cultural forms stem directly or indirectly from primal biological sources. We may add that Freudian theory is an especially elaborate form of a modified biological determinism. Despite the ample allowance that contemporary analysts often make for social or cultural factors, the theoretical scheme still presents an extremely oversimplified view of the relationship of humans to groups. This is perhaps to be expected from the fact that this body of theory arose from therapeutic practice with individual patients, and that its main focus is still perhaps on therapy.

Because orthodox Freudian psychoanalysts view society and its functions as growing out of individual biological urges, they are compelled to view the urges which derive from group life as entirely secondary. The sociologist's position is usually that groups by their very interaction generate new "needs"—that is, wishes, aspirations, ambitions, ideals, values, and goals—and that these needs constantly change and proliferate. This is a pervasive feature of group life which need not and cannot be explained in terms of primal urges. Individuals are born into or join groups which are already going concerns, often with long histories, and learn the appropriate motives for action in them. As groups change and develop new interests, individuals change with them, dropping old motives and acquiring new ones. The Freudian idea that culture is a dependent variable, that it merely reflects the psychology of the individual, does not square with history and has led to strained and improbable interpretations of many institutions and historic events—war, social movements, marriage, drug addiction, the Nazi revolution, and international affairs, for example. Freud himself set this pattern, and his statement about the origin of religion gives an idea of the flavor of some of these interpretive efforts: "Psychoanalysis . . . has traced the origin of religion to the helplessness of childhood, and its content to the persistence of the wishes and needs of childhood into maturity" (1933, p. 229).

One feature of Freudian psychology which still is relatively popular, despite its stress upon instinctive drives, is that it does assign an important role to learning. The instincts that are recognized are only two in number: Life and Death (Eros and Thanatos), and they are seen mainly as energy sources having no implicit direction or goals. The direction, form, and content of the resultant pattern of behavior, as well as the objects toward which it is directed, are regarded as a matter of learning. In the actual acquisition of specific behavior, primary stress is placed upon the interaction between a child and his parents and siblings. Although the behavioristic psychologist and social scientist usually do not accept the whole Freudian scheme, some are receptive to the idea that organic drives become harnessed to social motives through a conditioning or learning process.

At the heart of Freudian psychology lies *the energy postulate,* which asserts that individuals have fixed quantities of energy at their disposal. What this means is that all socially learned motives are merely transformations of basic urges and do not have autonomous status of their own. The energy postulate leads Freudians to assume further that motives acquired in adult life are merely complex permutations of old ones. As Piaget, criticizing Freud, says: "When there is transfer of feeling from one object to another, we must recognize that in addition to continuity there is construction of a new feeling through the integration schema" (1951b, p. 186). Allport made much the same point when he insisted upon what he called the *functional autonomy of motives* (1937, pp. 190–212). By this he meant that a form of behavior, first performed as a means to a given end, may become an end in itself when the original purpose has long since disappeared. The error involved in the Freudian view of motivation is that of confusing historical continuity with functional continuity. The motives of acts being performed now obviously must be operative in the present. The fact that these motives have a history does not mean that they are determined by early childhood antecedents. Some analysts, heeding this type of criticism, qualify Freudian theory—in practice, at any rate—to place more stress upon current functioning.

The concept of energy makes no distinctions between types of energy; for example, physical, psychological, moral, and intellectual energy are not distinguished. The inadequacy of this concept is obvious if we consider a person like Mahatma Gandhi, the great Indian leader. One of his most energetic and influential actions consisted of going on hunger strikes, thus depriving himself of all energy intake. Excess intake of energy often leads not to productive and creative activity, but to the deposit of fat and to general torpor.

Tempting as it is to think of human behavior in this way, we should keep in mind that when we do so, we are making use of an analogy—the energy postulate—borrowed from the physical sciences. It invariably turns out that such borrowings do violence to the subtle aspects of human behavior.

One major objection to the Freudian system hinges on the conception of "the unconscious" and unconscious motives. There is no question that people are often unable—or unwilling—to give adequate grounds for their acts or that there is much irrationality in human behavior. Considering the complexity of human interaction and personal life histories, individuals can hardly be expected to account fully and accurately for their behavior and all its antecedents. This fact had been recognized for generations before Freud.

However, the Freudian view of unconscious functioning is open to question on a number of points. First, it exaggerates the extent of unconscious motivation. A great deal of human behavior certainly appears to be routine, standardized, planned, or otherwise rational. The Freudians have been accused—we think rightly—of taking a dim view of the rational processes and tending to seek for motivational complexities where they do not exist. In the hands of a novice, this can be a form of "motive-mongering." At best, such an analytic approach tends either to reduce complex phenomena to terms of individualistic motives or shies away from these phenomena, many of which, like the establishment of the United Nations, are of a conscious and planned character. When analysts write about a complicated social phenomenon like crime, they invariably allow their theory to dictate the selection of cases in order that they may stress the irrational and unconscious. Their case studies of criminals, for example, focus on what might be called individualistic crime or the pathology of crime, such as sadistic murder, rape, and other sex offenses. Another criticism often made of the Freudian conception of the unconscious is that the term is so loosely used, it confuses issues. It can be used to indicate an experience which an individual has forgotten, or to designate an innate drive. It can designate an experience that individuals have never had, in the sense that they failed to notice that certain things were happening. It can also designate simple ignorance about themselves and their acts, or it may refer to their failure to analyze their own behavior. Miller has listed sixteen different usages of the term, pointing out that the writers are not always explicit about how they are using it (1942, pp. 271–85).

An examination of any one portion of Freudian theory tends to lead to a consideration of the whole system. However, we shall confine ourselves to a few comments on the Freudian theories of repression, memory, and unconscious purposes.

One does not have to deny the existence of repression, or something like it, to quarrel with the Freudian interpretation of it. People sometimes do bury memories so deeply that they are entirely unconscious of their existence; and they are often unaware of impulses and desires which influence them. In much of Freudian theory, however, the concept of repression is overextended, as when it is used to explain why people do not recall experiences during infancy. The total volume of anyone's experience is so great and behavior is so complex, it seems inevitable that everyone should forget much and that none of us should be fully aware of the reasons for our actions. As Cameron and Margaret say: "We all learn to practice selectivity among our own reactions, to accept what fits in with our ideal picture of ourselves and to reject that which seems at variance with it" (1951, p. 13). Sullivan refers to *selective inattention,* which enables us to maintain our self-esteem by not noticing things that may threaten it (1953). The concept of repression calls attention to an important psychological process, but a satisfactory description of the process remains to be formulated.

Researchers seeking to check the theory that unpleasant experiences are more often forgotten than pleasant ones have found only a relatively slight tendency in this direction. As Faris says: "These studies . . . do not furnish crucial proof of any operation of repression. An efficient repressing mechanism should work better" (1952, p. 127). Since the differences noted are average group differences, it appears that some people also have an opposite tendency to recall unpleasant experiences.

The Freudian conception of repression rests on a particular view of memory. "For Freud, the whole of the past is preserved in the unconscious . . . another conception of memory has been opposed to it, that of reconstruction-memory" (Piaget, 1951, p. 187). The latter concept, as we stated, interprets memory as a reconstructive act, dependent upon the nature and organization of the material and the linguistic categories available to the person. Forgetting is regarded as a complex and not necessarily repressive process. It is clear that repression is often associated with anxiety and threats to self-esteem, but the precise nature of the connection is not clear.

A final point concerning unconscious motivations: By definition they are inaccessible to the individual. This means that evidence concerning their existence cannot be obtained by direct testimony, but their existence must be inferred from what the person says and does. Evidence of this sort is subject to interpretations that differ according to the school of thought followed by the interpreter. The acceptance or rejection by the patient of a specific interpretation in itself proves nothing concerning the correctness of the interpretation. Taken with other evidence, the patient's rejection of an imputed motive is often viewed as proof of its existence, as is the patient's agreement with the analyst in other circumstances. We can even ask if a wholly unconscious motive can exist at all. As we have indicated with respect to oxygen deprivation, a person may desperately need oxygen and be entirely unaware of it; as long as this is the case, no appropriate behavior to satisfy the need occurs, and thus the biological need can scarcely be called a motivational force. Vitamin deficiency, withdrawal symptoms connected with drugs, calcium deficiency, and many other similar conditions illustrate the same point. (Appropriate behavior is mobilized only through some sort of recognition or consciousness of the condition, and the corrective behavior may be inappropriate if the condition is misnamed—that is, if it is not recognized for what it is.) So-called unconscious motives should probably be called by some other name than "motives" to indicate that they are not like the ordinary conscious ones for which the term might well be reserved.

We have offered this long, detailed analysis and criticism of the basic Freudian position on motivation because of its continuing influence upon contemporary thoughts. (For example, a revised version of Freudian thought has resurfaced in recent years in the statements of feminist scholars who are reassessing Freud's and Lacan's theories concerning sexuality, gender, and the family.) There is no doubt that it has provided a needed corrective of rationalistic and static psychologies and suggested new depths and dimensions of behavior. It has fostered a well-warranted skepticism about easy explanations of behavior in terms of its face value. As Langer said (1948, p. 18): "The great contribution of Freud to the philosophy of mind has been the realization that human behavior . . . is a language; that every *move* is, at the same time, a *gesture*."

THE MARXIAN VIEW

Another very influential motivational terminology in the contemporary world is that provided by Marxism. Most American social psychologists pay scant attention to it, although in other social sciences—anthropology and political science, for example—it is more influential. Also, among some younger sociologists there has been considerable reliance on, or stimulation from, Marxism. European social scientists give considerable attention to it, and in communist countries, of course, Marxist ideas of motivation are dominant. A brief general consideration of the Marxist view offers an interesting contrast to the Freudian scheme.

The Marxist social scientist conceives of the individual as the product of institutions, whereas the Freudian scheme considers institutions to be the product of individuals. The Marxist locates sources of motives in the social structure rather than in the individual. Like the Freudians, Marxists do not take seriously the expressed purposes of people, regarding them as mere surface manifestations or rationalizations of fundamental economic and class interests which may go unrecognized. In Marxist theory, these interests have nothing to do with primal biological urges but are seen as arising from the social structure and its particular historic past.

The details of Marxist theory are complicated; however, the major theme is that the economic system is the source from which the important motivations flow. An individual's position within the economic structure has a pervasive effect upon most of her thought and action. Since individuals share or have similar positions, they form different social classes and other somewhat less massive and important interest groups. The course of history is seen as the struggle for power among these groups.

According to this view, all thoughts, beliefs, philosophies, writings, art, and the like are determined by the basic economic facts of the society and reflect the position in the class structure of those who have formulated or created them. In Marxist terminology, mental products are *superstructure*. Marxists have used the term *ideology* to discredit their opponents' arguments and suggest that these arguments are mere reflections of class interests. The Marxist use of the term "ideology" is not identical with the Freudians' use of the term "rationalization," since the former refers to a collective, or group, rationale. Since ideas are held to be derived from class position, Marxists theoretically disparage as "idealistic" any psychology which attaches much importance to the motivational aspect of ideas, although they make practical use of this aspect in the political sphere.

The Marxist position is radically environmentalistic and hence comes into conflict with views stressing hereditary or biological factors in the determination of behavior. In the Soviet Union, the antiheredity bias is so strong that under Stalin it was a political issue, and there was danger in taking the opposite stand. Soviet writers—the nondissident ones, at least—are generally contemptuous of psychologies which place the mainsprings of human behavior in the individual organism, and Freudianism has been castigated as bourgeois and evidence of the degeneracy and immorality of capitalist society. Russian physiologist Pavlov, famous for his studies of conditioning in dogs, is held up as a worthy model in preference to Freud, as are Vygotsky and Luria.

The Marxist recognizes a difference between the real interests of a person or class and the perceived interests. Thus in the Marxist view, the real interests of white-collar clerks may be identical with those of factory workers because both stand in opposition to an oppressing elite. However, white-collar workers usually ally themselves with their employers and thus, according to the Marxist, betray their own class interests. They do this because their eyes have not been opened to the way in which society really functions; in this sense they have a *false consciousness*. Marxists explain white-collar attitudes by referring to the special occupational position of this group of workers. They contend that only through Marxist analysis—that is, analysis in terms of class structure—can white-collar workers see their true position and recognize their affiliation with the working class. This distinction between real and perceived interests is paralleled by the Freudian dichotomy of unconscious and conscious motives. Like the Freudians, Marxists try to help their adherents to bring the real sources of their behavior into the open (Laclau & Mouffe, 1985).

Marxist theory involves some ambiguity, as many critics have pointed out. However, the theory of historical epochs, which predicts alterations in symbolic, cognitive skills, has guided the research of Luria, and earlier, that of Vygotsky. Paradoxically, however, "Marxist materialism" as reflected in the work of some Soviet psychologists turns out to be the approximate equivalent of American "behaviorism."

Although they profess to regard ideas as mere reflections of the basic economic facts of life, Marxists nevertheless use and manipulate ideas as powerful tools of action when they try to get people to acknowledge their real interests. In the practical political arena, Marxists have the greatest respect for the importance of ideas. More consistent with the theory is the belief that the basic economic changes following the seizure of power by a revolutionary elite will bring pervasive ideological changes.

There is some significance and truth in the idea that occupation and class position are important sources of motivation. The Marxist theory is much too one-sided, but it has played an important historical role in social science by counteracting individualistic assumptions concerning the motives of humans. It has placed a needed emphasis upon institutionally derived loyalties and has called attention to economic interests, group allegiances, and intergroup conflicts as determinants of individual action (Althusser, 1969; Anderson, 1984; Giddens, 1981).

A SOCIOLOGICAL CONCEPTION

Rationalization and Interpretation

As we have seen, both Freudians and Marxists regard as suspect the verbal accounts which individuals give of their own purposes. The Marxists often regard such accounts as a cover-up of real economic motives or as evidence of ignorance. Freudians calls them "rationalizations" and heavily discount them. Although they admit that some statements of purpose of a rational and conscious sort are in accord with reality, they are mainly concerned with irrational and unconscious motivations.

A technical definition of *rationalization* is that it "is a common technique by which the ego keeps certain tendencies repressed. . . . Emphasis upon the acceptable motivation allows the ego to keep the unacceptable repressed, since the selected motives can sufficiently explain the act in question" (Alexander & Ross, 1952, p. 13). The psychoanalytic concept of rationalization implies that when acceptable motives are substituted for unacceptable ones, individuals are actually unable to think of the latter: when they deny their existence, they are not being dishonest or "kidding" themselves. In popular discourse, the term "rationalization" is usually taken to mean "giving socially acceptable but 'phony' reasons instead of the socially unacceptable but 'real' reasons for one's acts." Thus, a woman quarrels with her husband in the morning and throughout the day deals harshly with her daughter on the grounds that she needs discipline. This conception implies that the real reasons for one's acts are usually known, and hence tends to equate rationalization with dishonest or deluded thinking. It is a common belief that honest people do not rationalize, or do so infrequently.

Strictly speaking, dishonesty has nothing to do with rationalization, for if a person deliberately makes false statements he is not rationalizing at all, but merely lying. A genuine rationalization is a formulation which the individual believes to be true even though it may be labeled self-deception by outside observers. The concept is probably used so widely by laypersons because it allows them to disregard or discredit the opinions of other people. As Burke has said (1936, pp. 19–20):

Much deep sympathy is required to distinguish our reasoning from another's rationalizing. . . . As people tend to round out their orientations verbally, we sometimes show our approval of their verbalizations by the term reasoning and disapproval by the term rationalizing. Thus these words also serve as question begging words.

The central sociological conception of rationalization is that people interpret their behavior and the entire situation in which it occurs either before or after the act—or both. Such interpretations sometimes represent distortions of the facts, however subtle, so that one's face or self-esteem is preserved. Concerning the interpretations that are made after the act, they may have to do mainly either with "purpose"—that is, motive—or with "the objective situation" in which the act occurred. For example, suppose that a man shows cowardice when he is attacked or threatened at a party by another man. He may avoid the implications of cowardice, either in his own eyes or those of others, by a rationalization in terms of motives ("I didn't fight because I wanted to wait until a better moment to answer him"); or he may rationlize by interpreting and perhaps distorting the objective situation ("He had a number of friends there and they would have helped him"). Whether the interpreta-

tion after the act is chiefly concerned with purpose (of the self or of others) or with the objective situation, distortion or inaccuracy may creep in because of the person's self-involvement. In order to obtain a true or correct interpretation of an event or situation, one thus attempts to rule out all bias stemming from personal involvement and to base interpretation upon genuine evidence, so that if possible all disinterested observers may agree on "the facts." Procedure in courts of law is the classic example of a formalized, if not always successful, attempt to accomplish this. No sharp line can be drawn between a rationalization about a situation and a description of it, for it is difficult to rule out the influence of all personal interest and bias.

Accounts

Scott and Lyman (1968) have pointed out that these rationalizations, which they term *accounts,* are called forth when the social actor needs to explain unanticipated or untoward behavior—that is, problematic rather than accepted routine behavior, whether past, present, or future. They note that in general there are two types of accounts: *excuses* and *justifications.* They also distinguish five linguistic styles that "frame the manner in which the account will be given" and that often indicate "the social circle in which it will be most appropriately employed." First, there is the *intimate style,* used among those who share deep, intense, personal relationships. There is a tendency to use single sounds or words, and jargon for the communication of ideas. An example given by Scott and Lyman: A husband caresses his wife in bed but gets no endearing response; the wife just says, "pooped." Second is the *casual style,* used among peers, in-group members, and insiders: Typically, words are omitted and slang is used. Thus, among regular users of cocaine, the question "Why did you sell your stereo?" might be answered simply, "Coke." Third is the *consultative style,* which ordinarily is used when the amount of knowledge available to one interactant is unknown or problematic to the others. In response to the question "Why are you using cocaine? Don't you know it's addictive?" the individual might reply, "You don't know anything about addiction; cocaine's not addictive because there are no physical withdrawal effects, like there are for alcohol." Fourth is the *formal style,* for groups perhaps larger than six persons, where listeners must wait their turns to speak. The formal style typically occurs in bureaucratic organization, the courtroom, and organized meetings. Fifth, there is the *frozen style,* an extreme version employed among people required to interact while yet remaining strangers—for example, telephone operators speaking to customers and air pilots talking to the airport tower.

Scott and Lyman also emphasize that accounts may or may not be honored, so each person must learn a repertoire of proper accounts for appropriate audiences as well as proper styles of wording the accounts. When an account is not honored, it will most frequently be viewed as illegitimate or unreasonable.

In common experience, many acts are interpreted more than once. Indeed, if the act is important, it may receive several interpretations, sometimes distributed over a number of years. Individuals usually are not aware of this reinterpretation. This kind of reseeing of the past we have already discussed as *reconstructive memory.* It should be apparent that a large proportion of the later interpretation is not concerned with the preservation of self-esteem—that is, it is not rationalization in the narrower, Freudian sense of the word.

Interpretations of an act may also be made before the act takes place. Such *preinterpretations* include an estimate of the situation in which behavior is called for—including the possible actions, intentions, and expectations held by others—and some judgment of how and why one proposes to act with regard to the situation. The *how* and *why* of the coming act have to do with people's purposes; and if they should happen to phrase the matter

aloud to someone else and explicitly to themselves, they will generally use the word *because* when referring to these purposes. For example, someone is asked what he is going to do next summer and answers, "Go to Europe." When asked "Why?" or "Why next year?" he offers a statement that includes purpose: "Because I am getting to the age where I feel I can spend my savings and because I have never been there." The initial statement of purpose is likely to be somewhat condensed; if he is encouraged, the person may present his reason in more detail. "I have never been there" may be expanded to an explanation that he wants to go to Europe so that he, too, can talk about Paris when others speak of their experiences there.

Purpose, as we use the term, is synonymous with motive; and Mills (1940, pp. 904–13) has called statements about purpose *motivational statements,* whether offered to others or to self, since they are formulated, at least partially, in verbal terms. When others ask us to account for an act, either forthcoming or past, we usually give them a motivational statement so that they may understand the reasons for our act. The statement that we offer them may—but certainly need not—be quite false. We may couch it in terms that appear reasonable to them so as to "get by," or we may conceal our real motives for various other reasons. As Schwartz and Merten have remarked (1971, p. 294), "The ease with which people shift from what [Alfred] Schutz calls 'in order to' to the 'because of' motivational explanations gives the actor considerable latitude in the way he can construe his actions."

Disclaimers

Hewitt and Stokes (1975) and Hewitt (1984, pp. 167–68) discuss a second form of motive talk, the disclaimer. A *disclaimer* is "a verbal device people employ when they want to ward off negative implications of something they are about to do or say" (Hewitt, 1984, p. 167). A person might say, "I'm not prejudiced, because some of my best friends are Jews, but ... ," or "This may seem strange to you, but. . . .", or "I'm no social psychologist, but. . . ." (Hewitt, 1984, p. 167). In these statements, the individual introduces an act or statement that contradicts the premise of the disclaimer. A person claiming not to be prejudiced makes a racist statement; a self-proclaimed nonexpert makes an announcement that only an expert would be trusted to make (Hewitt, 1984, p. 167). Disclaimers are *prospective social acts;* they reveal how people attempt to protect their identities in the eyes of others. In some cases, disclaimers support prejudice and stereotype.

Motive, Disclaimer, Purpose, and Cause

Motive, disclaimer, and purpose should not be confused with *cause. Cause* and *causation* have backward references, while motive, disclaimer, and purpose have forward references in time. They are concerned with the anticipated consequences of acts; cause refers to antecedent processes which precede an event and which influence it decisively or determine it. (Motives are in a sense personal and private, whereas causes are general and public.) Causation applies to classes of events, and causal explanations are subject to public verification. The causation of human behavior is poorly understood, but it is known that much more than motives is involved.

Motives appear or are mobilized at the beginning of an act and indeed are a part of the act, since they persist throughout its course. They may, of course, change during the act by becoming more complicated or more simple; they may be joined by other motives; or they may even be replaced, particularly if the act has considerable duration. Hence, in describing any complicated event in a person's life, reference must be made to the purposes the individual had in mind. But in addition, a whole range of other conditions must be taken into account—namely, the motives of others and the material or objective situa-

tion. Individuals themselves are in a sense the final authority on their own purposes, since they know better than anyone else what they had in mind, even though the mechanisms of repression or rationalization may have operated to distort their knowledge of their actions. With respect to the objective situation, on the other hand, individuals usually cannot be well informed, since it is impossible for them to possess all the information concerning their own nervous system, physiological state, and past experiences which might be relevant to an explanation of why they performed a specific act exactly as they did at exactly the time they did.

Before an action is completed, the purposes of the behavior are likely to loom large to the person engaged in it. After the action is completed, second thoughts often occur and the person may then wonder whether her reasons were as simple as they seemed. When asked to account for past actions, people often give commonsense, causal explanations rather than motivational ones. For example, a husband may scold his wife at the breakfast table, believing that he is scolding her because she has spoiled his coffee. He may later explain the quarrel by saying that neither he nor his wife had enough sleep the previous night.

Since motives appear at the beginning of acts or in preparation for action, and since each individual feels his own motives in a direct way, it is easy to understand how they have come to be viewed as causes of the behavior of which they are a part, and indeed as "forces" which "make" the behavior occur. It was common earlier in the 20th century for sociologists to explain institutional and other cultural behavior in terms of the operation of wishes, interests, needs, and other "social forces." However, the idea of causation no longer includes the conception of force in this sense. There are many different ideas of causation in the philosophy of science, but on this particular point there is general agreement.

Scientific Cause. The scientific concept of causation, of course, is a general feature of many scientific fields in which no problem of motivation exists. Indeed, in view of the instability and variability of human purposes and of the fact that purposes are really part of behavior rather than mysterious forces lying behind it, motives are not so much explanations of behavior as they are behavioral problems, themselves requiring analysis and explanation. From this viewpoint, explaining such behavior as stealing, for example, includes the problem of accounting for the fact that people steal from so many different motives.

We have seen how Freudian psychoanalytic and Marxist "scientific" theories attempt to offer causal analyses of complex forms of human behavior. We have also shown how individuals construct their own "casual" interpretations of their conduct. It is therefore useful to distinguish, as Alfred Schutz (1962, pp. 3–5) did, between commonsense and scientific thinking on causal matters. Commonsense causal explanations are based on matters which lie outside, but may draw upon, scientific formulations. They tend not be strictly logical; they are often based on unclear meanings or vague definitions given to words, and they are not predicated on scientific knowledge (Garfinkel, 1967, p. 271). Scientific explanations are derived from scientific theories. They are based on knowledge that has been scientifically verified and they are typically logical and semantically clear. Accounts and disclaimers are examples of commonsense causal interpretations. The Freudian and Marxist schemes are examples of scientific causal interpretations.

These examples point up the truism that people and groups may do the same things for different reasons, and different things for the same reason. Since causal generalizations are based upon elements that are common to various instances of a given form of behavior, in problems like the above these generalizations cannot be stated in terms of motive. Psychoanalysts have attempted to meet this difficulty by looking for uniformity and common motivations on the unconscious level. What is suggested here is that

the matter may be dealt with in another way, provided that one conceives of motive as something other than a specific determinant of behavior. It may be conceded that most significant human behavior is and must be motivated, but this is a far cry from contending that any given form of behavior must always be motivated in the same way.

SOCIAL SOURCES OF INDIVIDUAL MOTIVATION

As Mills (1940, p. 906) says, "Motives are of no value apart from delimited societal situations for which they are appropriate vocabularies. They must be situated. . . . Motives vary in content and character with historical epochs and societal structures." One implication of this statement is that although our motives generally appear to us as peculiarly personal and private, many of them are learned from others and are furnished to us tailor-made by the society or the groups in which we live.

When one joins a group of long standing, she finds that the proper codes of conduct, including the ends and means of group activity, have been spelled out in considerable detail. They may even be formalized and embodied in written documents such as the Hippocratic oath, an oath of allegiance, or in constitutions, contracts, or codes. When persons leave groups and join new ones, they must learn new motivations. As Weber has pointed out in connection with work, for instance, "The motives which induce people to work vary with different social classes. . . . When a man changes rank, he switches from one set of motives to another" (1936, pp. 316–17). Even when people live rather stable lives, changing their group memberships very little, some of their motives nevertheless change with advancing age according to prevailing social definitions. Although the physical processes of aging are much alike in all cultures, the motivational adaptations to them are endlessly varied.

These statements by Weber and Mills point to a phenomenon immensely important to the social psychologist. How a person sees his own behavior and how he may explain it to others, as well as how they may see it and interpret it to others—including him or her—is crucially important. It is important for understanding their interaction, as well as for understanding their thoughts about themselves. But social psychologists cannot comprehend the full significance of this accounting, interacting, and thinking unless they link them with both the personal biographies of the individuals and the social biographies of the groups to which they belong. This point closely relates to our earlier discussions of the group contexts of language and thought as well as to the group and historical contexts for remembrance. Said another way—although the quote pertains to identity rather than to motives— "personal identity is meshed with group identity which itself rests upon an historical past" (Strauss, 1959, p. 173).

The fallacious commonsense imputation of motives has its academic counterpart. For example, psychoanalysts have reinterpreted the private lives of famous people such as St. Augustine and Leonardo da Vinci in terms of twentieth-century sexual symbols, thus ignoring the fact that these historical characters viewed the conduct of others and themselves in very different terms than do people of our own era. Such scholarly interpretation is equivalent to translating other rationalizations into our own. Since humans are interested in the lives of past generations, such translating is inevitable. The only corrective to a superficial handling of the past is an adequate understanding of the period under consideration through exhaustive examination of historical sources. The accuracy of the account should rest upon an understanding of the actual symbols available to the historical personages; it should not rest upon the degree to which their motives appear plausible to us in the light of our own motives at the present time.

It follows that individuals cannot express purposes or rationalize behavior in terms they have not learned. We cannot motivate

people to act by using terms outside their comprehension: we must appeal to purposes which they understand and which make sense to them. Conversely, it is incorrect to impute rationalizations to an individual when these involve motivational terms which she does not possess. Nevertheless, such imputation is a common recourse when it is found to be impossible to assess behavior in one's own terms. There is almost always a tendency to explain other people's behavior in terms of one's own vocabulary of motives. This form of incorrect assessment is called *projection* and is seen in a crude form in most romantic historical novels. The characters, supposedly living a century or two ago, are made to rationalize their activities according to the symbols of the twentieth century. Likewise, in American movies, heroes and heroines dress in the clothes of other eras but act as if their incentives were those of twentieth-century Americans. But the projection of motives may take more subtle forms.

Apropos of motives and explanation, Alan Blum and Peter McHugh (1971, pp. 98–109), influenced by critical positivistic tendencies in ethnomethodology, have also severely criticized symbolic interactionist conceptualizations of motivation. They reject, as we do, the idea of motivation as simple "cause," but contend that symbolic interactionists accept the actor as "a research informant, whose report acquires analytic status because the actor is thought to be a privileged and exclusive source on questions of his motives." They argue that the researcher ought to systematically try to learn how a motivational statement is generated to begin with—how, for example, the actor is constrained to cite a reason at all; how it takes the form it does (giving a reason for, say, telling a joke); how it comes to be acceptable to the hearer as an answer. We believe that Blum and McHugh have badly misread the conceptualizations of motive and motivation by symbolic interactionists. However, they make an excellent point, provided one mutes their criticism, when they say that there is often an inadequate formulation of the "conditions" under which specific types of motivational statements are given, chosen from alternatives, offered or given to others, or accepted or rejected by those who give them as well as by others. This leads us into considerations touched on in the next section.

Motives, Morale, and Social Structure

The stability and endurance of social groups or structures depends upon getting the members to carry out necessary lines of action. This means that persons must be motivated to perform these actions. When a structure recruits "from the inside," as when persons are born into it, the problem of motivation is handled early through the socialization of the young. But when members are recruited, as in an army or a vocation, the new member must be taught to act in accordance with the essential purposes of the body or group. Since many recruits join voluntarily, some learning of appropriate motivations starts beforehand; for example, future doctors learn something about the aims and aspirations of the medical profession long before they go to medical school. Involuntary membership may present the group with the problem of apathy or lack of enthusiasm, since the purposes of the organization may seem irrelevant to the new members, or they may even be antagonistic. These attitudes are exemplified by political apathy among citizens and "going AWOL" among soldiers. Insofar as good citizens and good soldiers decry unmotivated or badly motivated colleagues, they exemplify their own attachment to the long-range functions of the state and the army. Considerable variation in personal motivation may exist among the membership of any group, but in general, motivations must be geared in with, or at least not antagonistic to, the group purposes.

Social structures vary tremendously in the amount of latitude permitted to their membership in this regard; and the degree of latitude is related intimately to the nature of the structure. For instance, if an embattled religious sect is to survive, it must arrange matters so that group and individual motivations are virtually identical. The very existence of a revolutionary or radical political elite, such as the communist party leadership in a capitalist country (or at least in earlier years when the party was revolutionary), also requires that individual and institutional motivations be closely intermeshed. The concept of "party discipline," as the communists use it, requires that individuals make the party's decisions and policies their own, regardless of how they may vary from week to week or how they may appear to the individuals personally. They are required to sacrifice personal comforts and immediate personal desires in the long-run interests of the party, and they are willing to do this because they identify their own essential interest with that of the party. A group characterized by this attitude is said to have a *high morale,* or *high solidarity.* This is equivalent to saying that even in the face of setbacks, the membership persists in pursuit of group aims, and, indeed, may thrive upon a certain amount of opposition or suppression, since this adversity supplies additional justification for revolutionary ardor. Self-interest and group interest coalesce so completely in groups of this kind, whether political or otherwise, that the person may sacrifice her own life for the good of the cause and may do so not only willingly but with elation.

Most organizations, of course, allow more latitude between individual and group purposes, and demand lesser degrees of allegiance and sacrifice. For these groups to function effectively, there must be a certain amount of consensus concerning matters relevant to group survival. Individuals may retain membership for a variety of reasons, some of them quite peripheral: For example, people belong to churches for business and social reasons as well as for religious ones.

In any society, some parts of the total structure are generally recognized as more vital than others. There is a corresponding difference in the pressure upon individuals to conform to the controlling norms. People who "buck the system" because they do not value it or because they will not support the group endeavors are liable to severe punishment. Court martial, imprisonment, and so on are deterrents to deviance; but positive allegiances operate more efficiently.

When a social structure fails to elicit the minimal allegiance necessary for its proper functioning, then we speak of *poor morale, or low solidarity.* Presumably, there are different types of poor morale, depending on the kind of group structure, but essentially it comes down to a lack of effective coordination because of discrepant individual aims. To take the simplest case first, there may be so little consensus about group values and such diversity of individual purposes that the group cannot act in concert. A more complicated form of poor morale stems from discrepant definitions of group ends on different social levels represented in the group. Whenever the structure is complex, there is a problem of obtaining a working consensus shared by the various echelons. This condition can exist in a political party, industrial corporation, religious organization, or university. Of course, some segments of the organization may have excellent morale, others poor morale, since they evaluate differently the way matters are progressing.

CONCLUSION

The distinctive qualities of human mental activity are the consequences of humans' incorporation and use of language symbols. *Goal behavior* involves response to signs representing the future; *memory* is response to signs representing the past; and *perception* is response to signs representing the present environment. Skill in interpretation of and response to signs on any level is *intelligence. Reason* involves the interpretation and use of symbols and is the equivalent of conceptual thought. It is a peculiarly human activity.

Such complex mental functions as perceiving and remembering are examples of complex human sign behavior. Individual human beings take over language symbols as part of their repertoire of behavior. This incorporation of group-created conventional signs creates new complexities of response and makes human mental functions different from (and superior to) those of the lower animals. Mental processes in the lower animals parallel the higher functions in humans but are of a lower order of complexity, being based on simpler forms of sign behavior. Perception and memory in the lower animals are more closely tied to biological conditions than they are in humans. Unlike the lower animals, human beings are able to assimilate socially developed symbolic systems that transform their psychic life, add new dimensions to their behavior, and make it possible for them to profit from the experience of past generations and to anticipate and plan for the future in ways unparalleled in the rest of the animal world.

Motivation presents an old and thorny problem for the student of human behavior. The manner in which it is handled by social theorists is likely to determine the way in which they will deal with a great many other problems. Through the course of group interaction, individuals develop *accounts,* or linguistic explanations, of their behavior. These accounts are lodged in ongoing interaction. A common conception of motives, which we reject, gives them a biological base, as when hunger is identified with the contractions of the walls of the stomach and other bodily conditions. A biological condition by itself has little motivational significance, except as it is perceived or interpreted by the individual in whom it exists. The influential Freudian conception of motivation, which emphasizes unconscious wishes and desires, has serious weaknesses arising mainly from the fact that no theory about the content of the "unconsicous" can be proved because the unconscious is, by definition, virtually unknowable. Marxist theory presents an interesting comparison with that of Freud, for in the former the emphasis is placed upon unconscious economic, rather than sexual, motivations. A conception of motives held by symbolic interactionists treats them as essentially verbal in nature, as part of behavior, but as something other than causes of behavior. Knowledge of motives, in this conception, is used primarily to enable a person to project himself or herself into the outlook of another person; that is, for "understanding," rather than for "explaining," behavior. Motives are learned in social experience, vary from group to group, and are relative to a social context. A consideration of group morale, or solidarity, gives some indications of the way in which persons are motivated by their group identifications. The research implication of our discussion is that the accounts people offer for their own behavior, far from explaining it, themselves require analysis and explanation. Motives are social and interpersonal products. They emerge and may be observed in the interaction process. They are often "after the fact" explanations of human conduct.

SUGGESTED READINGS

BURKE, K. (1945). *A Grammar of Motives*. Englewood Cliffs, N.J.: Prentice-Hall. A sensitive and sophisticated discussion by a literary critic of the linguistic nature of motives and the functions of motivational accounts.

PERINBANAYAGAM, R. S. (1985). *Signifying Acts*. Carbondale, IL: Southern Illinois University Press. A seminal presentation of the symbolic interactionist theory of motives.

CHAPTER SEVEN
Acquisition of Language and Concepts in Early Childhood

We turn now to the topic of childhood socialization. Here, we take up the acquisition of language and concepts in early childhood. We hope this analysis will provide a framework for better grasping our earlier discussion of language. As social psychologists, we are obliged to devote a considerable amount of time to childhood socialization; the nexus between self and society lies in the socialization process. Any theory of how society is possible must be able to account for the social and socializing experiences of the young child. The term *childhood socialization* refers to those experiences and interactive relationships that build human nature into the child (Denzin, 1977, p. 3). Central to this process is the acquisition and use of language (Markey, 1928).

The learning of language is not merely a matter of mastering the mechanics of speech. The symbols that make up a language are concepts, and represent ways of acting and thinking. Infants must learn to classify objects and to act appropriately toward them. They must also learn that some words refer to things that do not exist as material objects, but only as ideas, abstractions, or relationships. To teach anyone the conventional meaning of a word is to teach him or her how to act or think with reference to the object or the concept to which the word refers. The meanings of words are not locked up in dictionaries, but are found in people's acts. In this chapter we will review the growing literature on language acquisition, paying particular attention to the speech patterns of young children. As language is acquired, the child develops the ability to be consciously self-aware, as we shall discuss in Chapter 8. Language acquisition is basic to the genesis of self in early childhood. The research and theory of Piaget, Vygotsky, and Chomsky will be discussed. We shall argue that the "universal" features of language usage may reflect "universal" characteristics of the primary group and may not, as Chomsky has argued, be based on innate, inherited biological, or neurological tendencies.

The child's learning of language is not merely an intellectual process. Language puts children in touch with their parents and peers in new and significant ways and initiates their acquisition of broader and more socialized perspectives. It introduces them to new pleasures and satisfactions and also creates a great many new needs and problems. Through learning a language, children learn the rules and standards that regulate social relations, and they develop ideas of mortality and religion. Language is also the means whereby children are gradually prepared for and later inducted into the roles in which they are destined to play, and through which they learn to grasp the viewpoints and understand the feelings and sentiments of others. Through language, they become aware of their own identity as a person and as a member of groups in which they seek status, security, and self-expression, and which in turn make demands upon them.

Since newborn babies cannot be aware of their caretakers' symbols, they remain relatively unsocialized for some time. Socialization begins even before infants begin to learn language, since they are responding to all kinds of stimuli. On the other hand, until they begin to comprehend and use conventional speech, their humanness is only partial. Children become socialized when they have acquired the ability to communicate with others and to influence and be influenced by them through the use of speech. This implies socially acceptable behavior toward named objects.

However, learning concepts one by one in piecemeal fashion is not enough, for concepts are interrelated. A word such as *spoon* refers to more than a piece of shaped metal, although "metal" and "shaped" are themselves complex concepts. The meanings of *spoon* (that is, modes of response toward it) are linked with and contingent upon a whole system of related meanings (for example, what foods are eaten with spoons, how spoons are handled, what they are made of, where they are placed as part of a table setting, and so on).

Just how the child passes over to a consistent and conventional use of words is a crucial problem for social psychology. We do not really know the full details of this transformation (from babbling and initial imitation to adult verbal behavior) in which the spoken word is used with a conventional meaning. We shall consider materials that are available.

INSTRUMENTAL USE OF GESTURES

Children make meaningful as well as sheerly expressive bodily movements long before they speak conventionally. Such gestures may be accompanied by vocalizations. At first these may not be understood by even extremely solicitous parents, but gradually their meanings are discovered so that an approximate interpretation is readily made. As late as eighteen months, babies communicate needs largely through gestures and expressive utterances rather than through actual words. *Neologisms,* or made-up words, may be used (Brown, 1970; Taine, 1877; Denzin, 1977; Cook-Gumperz, 1975; De Villiers, 1979).

The infant's gestural communication gradually recedes and becomes secondary to his or her other gradually evolving vocal language. Some children are retarded linguistically because they develop an elaborate gesture "language" so well understood by their parents that there is neither incentive nor urgent necessity for learning genuine speech. Parental refusal to respond usually results in the abandonment of such a system of gestures.

The most important point about infants' use of gestures is that it is instrumental. They use gestures—although they are not aware that they are using them—to reach for something, avoid something, or call for something. Children's expressive bodily movements occur within a context of social relations; that is, people react to their gestures and children respond both to people and to their actions with still further gestures. Although at first children make expressive movements toward a brute physical environment, the responses of their parents soon transform their environment into a thoroughly social one in which their early expressive movements become endowed with a social significance.

The foregoing considerations suggest that language might best be viewed as a *conversation of gestures.* Language and speech behavior are processes that vary by context, speakers, listeners, and their intentions. Any language contains a set of rules, however implicitly organized and recognized, which governs the expression and interpretations given both to spoken utterances and nonverbal gestures. This view of language is crucial for understanding early childhood speech, for infants speak in a highly personal, often nonverbal language. Indeed, the family must be viewed as a complex language community. The child must master the language of all family members before she can successfully take their perspectives in any speech encounter.

Children learn to speak before they learn to think (in a verbal sense), for their first utterances bear no meaning for them and are unlikely to have clear, conventionalized meaning for their caretakers (Vygotsky, 1962). Their verbal sounds begin to get attached to concrete objects and concrete movements. Initially, the young child may develop a complex "crying" vocabulary, as Roger Brown (1958) has noted, with as many as seven different cries designating diverse states like happiness, pain, anger, discomfort, hunger, and frustration. Often a verbal utterance is combined with a particular nonverbal gesture. The sound "jeewsh" (which the parent translates as "juice") may be accompanied by pointing to the refrigerator or a container filled with juice. The child has elaborated the contextual meaning of his or her nonconsensual utterance with an unspoken gesture. While many have argued that the family is basically a monolithic speech community, our remarks suggest that each speaker in the family has a unique mode of speaking and gesturing. Each will have an unique style of pronunciation, accent, gesture, and particular patterns of intonation and resonance.

LEARNING TO USE AND COMPREHEND SYMBOLS

Bilingual Children

Bossard and Boll (1960, p. 265) suggest that at least one of every five white Americans has grown up in a home where language other than English was dominant. Such persons may adopt a set of *protective devices* which aid them in the production of their speech acts. They may speak in restrained fashion and attempt to be inconspicuous speakers, seldom talking in "mixed linguistic" company. On the other hand, they may overcompensate and adopt a meticulous mode of talking. As bilingual children, they may develop a stigmatized view of self based on their linguistic status. This is especially so if they come from a disadvantaged ethnic or racial group which is stigmatized by the broader society. Labov (1968) has gone so far as to argue that many American blacks speak a form of "nonstandard" English which gives them a distinct linguistic disadvantage in public schools.

If one of every five Americans comes from a bilingual family, the above remarks suggest that indeed all Americans are socialized into multilingual speech communities—if nonverbal features of language are incorporated into the definition of "language." The problems of the bilingual child are simply more complex than those of the child who comes from a family where only standard English is spoken. Both kinds of child speakers, however, must learn complex sets of verbal and nonverbal languages.

Learning the Speech Act

The *speech act,* to paraphrase Searle (1970, p. 16), can be defined as the production of a set of sounds that are understandable to at least one other person. Such acts are the basic units of linguistic communication and may be verbal or nonverbal. The infant, of course, enters the world with no conception of the speech act and must be taught how to speak. Initially its utterances—the cry, the whimper, the giggle—are not attached or linked to an internal second signal system that would give a referent to the sound. The child must learn how to produce speech acts which are meaningful for others. In this context, it is useful to recollect Vygotsky's (1962, p. 17) distinction between vocal speech (verbal utterances) and inner speech (silent thought). Thought is "soundless" inner speech. The child's first speech acts are global, social utterances that (1) are understood by the recipients of the sounds but not by the child, (2) are undifferentiated sounds which, (3) are not attached to internal symbolic or categoric referents. As children acquire a speech act repertoire, their talk becomes increasingly egocentric, or self-centered, in nature. *Egocentric* utterances progressively merge with *sociocentric* formulations such that children are increasingly able to place themselves in the perspectives of others and to view action from their standpoints. *Sociocentric speech* is possible because of the emergence of inner speech, or thought. Vygotsky's remarks (1962, p. 19) summarize our position on this point.

Vygotsky's model can be contrasted to the proposals of Piaget. Vygotsky views speech as having a social origin that stands outside the infant. The infant's speech is first social in nature, and then becomes egocentric in nature. Egocentric speech progressively translates into inner thought and speech. Piaget, on the other hand, views the origins of speech and thought as first arising within the infant. His model works from the individual to society. Vygotsky's model works from the social environment to the individual. Thus, he reverses the more traditional psychological views of speech and thought development. Piaget's choice of the term *egocentric* to describe the child's thought was perhaps unfortunate. (See Chapter 9.)

For children to become credible and understood members of the family speech community, they must relinquish their private, autistic speech for the differentiated symbol system consensually understood by all members of the family.

The Characteristics of Baby Talk

We have noted that the child's speech acts tend to move from undifferentiated utterances to progressively refined categorical statements. In an intriguing study of baby talk in six languages, Charles A. Ferguson (1964) has noted that baby-talk words are modifications of normal adult words; the child, for example, says "choo-choo" for train or "itty bitty" for little. Ferguson's research revealed the following features of this form of speech. First, baby-talk items consist of simple consonants, stops, and nasals, and only a few vowels. Second, there is a predominance of reduplication (repetition) of particular sounds. Third, in each of the six languages studied (Arabic, Marathi, Comanche, Gilyak, English, and Spanish) there was a typical morpheme form of talk. The most typical was a sound that began with a monosyllable and ended with a consonant. Given those cross-cultural commonalities, Ferguson maintains (1964, p. 110):

In view of this similarity one is tempted to make the hypothesis that every language community provides a stock of baby-talk items which can serve as appropriate material for babies to imitate in creating their phonemes but which do not interfere with the normal words of the language and can gradually be discarded as real words emerge in the children's speech. . . . The baby-talk lexicon of a language community may thus play a special role in the linguistic development of its children.

Thus, by differentially rewarding or through showing indifference, adults contribute to the child's progressive speech skills. They may encourage excessive baby talk or talk to the child in more adult language. If the latter, then the use of baby talk will be at a minimum. However, it must be noted that the human's ability to make certain vocal sounds is a function of the

speech apparatus itself, and certain sounds are easier to make than others. Furthermore, cultures vary in the kinds of sounds they emphasize. As a consequence, the character of the child's speech acts are to a certain degree conditioned or influenced by its physiological development—for example, the size of the tongue and the ability to move the lips or to bring the tongue to bear against the teeth, as when the "f" sound is made. The ease with which some sounds are produced may account for the remarkable similarity in baby talk across cultures that Ferguson observed. All cultures, for example, had a word for mother, and it assumed the "ma-ma" form. The "m" sound is an easily produced sound. Thus, while mothers may delight in their infants' first utterance of "ma-ma," this sound is really one of the most simple phonological sounds that the infant can make.

Indeed, the first word spoken by infants the world over is usually a syllable or repeated syllable such as "mama," "dada," "bebe," "nana," "wawa," or "papa." The word is expressive of either pleasurable or unpleasurable states. These syllabic phonetic forms become stabilized in the infant's speech with the help of delighted elders, who pick out certain ones and repeat them to the baby until he uses them correctly.

The use of other words soon follows, especially when the infant somehow makes the momentous discovery that things have names. When children have managed to discover that every object has a name, they have taken a conspicuous step toward learning parental speech.

Besides discovering that things have names, children may also be said to discover that names have things—that the words they learn correspond to aspects of the real world. In complex types of learning especially, the progression may be from words to things rather than the reverse. The fact that racial prejudice can be learned before contact with the racial group in question is an illustration of this point. The acquisition of vocabulary sensitizes individuals to certain aspects of the environment which they may encounter later, and predisposes them to notice those which correspond with or confirm what they have previously learned through verbal communication alone. It is in this sense that we may say that the world is not made up of ready-made, discrete objects, events, and qualities waiting to be perceived and named, but is rather built up through collective experience and crystallized in linguistic forms. As learning proceeds, this type of movement from words to things tends to become more and more important.

Usually the infant's first words are employed as sentences rather than as single words; they do duty as one-word sentences. Analyzed merely as parts of speech, they are characteristically nouns or interjections. The infant, however, uses these words as complete—although by adult standards, crude—sentences. Thus "mama" will have to be interpreted by parents in a variety of ways, depending upon the situation in which the word is spoken as well as the intonation and gesturing that accompany it. "Mama" may mean that the infant "wishes" the mother to come, or that she is hungry, or content, or that she sees the mother enter the room. "Ball" may mean "there is a ball," "where is the ball?" "I want the ball," and so forth. These earliest word-sentences cannot be understood out of context nor without noting associated inflection and gesture.

At this stage of language development, children possess words that have only a partly socialized meaning (that is, they have learned to employ words conventionally) with approximately the same meanings that their parents attribute to them. Their use of words is close enough to conventional adult usage so that from the context in which the word is spoken their parents are able to understand them.

Children are able to use words in an amazing variety of ways because they have not caught on to their full public meanings. As de Laguna has written (1927, p. 270):

It is precisely because the words of the child are so indefinite in meaning, that they can serve such a variety of uses. . . . A child's word does not. . . designate an object *or* a property *or* an act; rather it signifies loosely and vaguely the object together with its interesting properties and the acts with which it is commonly associated in the life of the child. The emphasis may be now on one, now on another, of these aspects, according to the exigencies of the occasion on which it is used.

Adults, who are much more conscious of the "real" (conventional) meanings of words, cannot employ words so irresponsibly or variously.

Children use these early words as a way of responding to a situation. A child does not merely name an object with a word (such as naming mama by using the word "mama"). "Mama" means "mama come here" or "I'm glad to see you," and so forth. As Lewis (1959, p. 91) has noted: ". . . when he speaks the sounds it is his way of dealing with the situation." The child's words are instruments; they are means of handling the environment. We shall see how children progress rapidly to the point where words become very effective means for managing the environment and manipulating certain key environmental objects.

DECLARATIVE AND MANIPULATIVE FUNCTIONS OF LANGUAGE

We previously noted the instrumental use of gestures and word-sentences; its implications now call for further analysis. The work of M. M. Lewis will be closely followed here, since in our judgment his is the most careful inquiry into this aspect of our problem.

Children use their early "conventional" words instrumentally in ways that are either *declarative* or *manipulative*. Declarative use involves drawing adult attention to some object. By uttering such words as *chair* or *doll*, the children direct adult attention to those items. Manipulative use of words by children involves, in addition to drawing attention to some object, a demand that their needs with regard to that object be satisfied by the adult. For example, the word *cookie*, when used in manipulative fashion, is equivalent to a demand for aid in reaching the cookie jar and getting a cookie. The words *tick-tock,* used manipulatively, might mean, "Papa, show me your wrist watch."

The child's instrumental use of language, whether declarative or manipulative, results in drawing other people within his or her circle of activity (Lewis, 1936, pp. 147–49):

In the declarative use he attracts another's attention and so assures himself of company. If he is delighted, the presence of another person enhances his delight; if he is afraid the presence of another person alleviates his fear. . . . In the manipulative use the child is again using the word as a social instrument; this time as a means of securing the help of others in satisfying his practical wants.

Even before infants learn any real words, they have used their own vocalizations for declarative and manipulative purposes. But when they learn real words, those two instrumental functions become more effective because they enable children to point more precisely to the objects which attract their attention.

A series of significant points is involved here. (1) Children's instrumental use of sounds is rooted in the children's past, and his instrumental use of sounds merges imperceptibly into their acquisition of conventional speech. (2) Children's learning of conventional speech rests upon their using it as an instrument; that is, upon their calling adult attention to more specific objects and aspects of their environment than was possible with their ambiguous baby vocalizations. (3) Finally, children's gradual approach to conventional speech presupposes the cooperation of adults. If adults paid no attention whatsoever to them, or if children could not use words as social instruments, it is difficult to imagine how they could ever learn conventional usage.

Initial Use of Words is Inaccurate. When children discover adult words, they do not employ them to specify precisely the same objects that are referred to by adults. To put this into commonsense terms, children do not at first use adult words with their correct adult meanings. To the adult, the child'a application of words often seems haphazard and frequently amusing.

Infants, in fact, apply sounds and homemade words to objects long before they master adult words. It is out of these initial vocal references that the infant's ability to use adult words correctly eventually develops. Taine has given us an instructive description of how children begin to apply vocalizations to the objects of their infantile world (Taine, 1877, pp. 254–56):

She was in the habit of seeing a little black dog belonging to the house, which often barks, and it was to it that she first learnt to apply the word *oua-oua.* Very quickly and with very little help she applied it to dogs of all shapes and kinds that she saw in the streets and then . . . to the bronze dog near the staircase. Better still, the day before yesterday when she saw a goat a month old that bleated, she said *oua-oua.* . . . *Cola* (chocolate) is one of the first sweetmeats that was given her and it is the one she likes the best. . . . Of herself and without or rather in spite of us she has extended the meaning of the word and applies it now to anything sweet; she says *cola* when sugar, tart, a grape, a peach, or a fig is given her. . . . In the same way the above little boy of twenty months used the word *teterre (pomme de terre)* to designate potatoes, meat, beans, almost everything good to eat except milk, which he called *lolo.* Perhaps to him *teterre* meant everything solid or half-solid that is good to eat. . . . Once more education produced an unexpected effect on her; the general character grasped by the child is not what we intended; we taught her the sound, she has invented the sense.

From this description it is clear that when children first apply learned words to objects, they do so with different meaning than does the adult. Although Taine thought he had taught his daughter the essential meanings of the word *baby,* he had not. Similarly, although the child applied the word *cola* to the correct object, she also applied it to other, incorrect objects. The child sometimes uses adult words to designate objects outside the adult definition, and sometimes he or she does not use the word to designate enough objects. "Some words he uses more widely than we do, others more narrowly" (Lewis, 1936. p. 210).

Inaccurate Usage Reflects the Child's Point of View. Why is the child at first unable to grasp the correct adult meanings of a word? For an answer, we may refer to our discussion of language in Chapter 3, where we noted that the vocabulary utilized by any given society or social group necessarily reflects its interests and preoccupations. To state this another way, the distinctions implicit in a society's words are distinctions that members of the society consider important and relevant.

It may be assumed that infants, before becoming overly influenced by human association, will make distinctions of importance to themselves. They choose features of their world that appear similar and group them together under an identical word. Where adults make a distinction between prunes and carrots—as fruit and vegetable—infants at first may use the same sound (say, "teter-re") to pick out similar features of a solid-something which tastes good.

Children cannot very well group together the same objects as does an adult, for the latter sees the world from points of view derived from participation in certain social groups. Children have yet to acquire these standardized categories. Features of their environment that strike them as similar are features that grow out of their own experiences.

Thus, since chocolate tasted sweet, peaches tasted sweet, and grapes tasted sweet, Taine's daughter called them all by the same name, "cola." A young acquaintance of ours came to call a small doll "putzibabe"; he then extended the name to other small objects, including small dogs, and later to his baby sister. Similarly. when an infant touches a rose, the infant's mother may carefully call it "rose," whereupon he or she is likely to apply "rose" to all flowers. The child's need to deal declaratively or manipulatively with an object—calling our attention to it, or to his or her needs with reference to it—often leads the child to make naïve and unique use of words.

The child's adoption of adult words is encouraged by the adult's readier response to conventional sounds than to the child's private vocalizations. The conventional sound proves to be a more efficient instrument for calling attention to an interesting object or to one's desires with regard to the object; hence the child has an incentive for appropriating the conventional sound.

Perhaps this is an instance of social pressure. But children do not automatically conform to social pressure; their choices and use of words are selective. Their experience determines the range and extension of words; the decision does not lie with the adult. For a time, children may stubbornly resist the adult's word, so that even after they are aware of the conventional word and have imitated it correctly, they may continue to use their own unique word form. Or they may alternate, sometimes using the adult word and sometimes their own. The conventional term has to be accepted by the child as the more efficient instrument of the two before he or she will finally adopt it.

Contemporaneously with and, undoubtedly, as a partial result of adult intervention, children learn to make increasingly adequate distinctions among classes of objects. For instance, they begin to discriminate between a solid-something eaten with a spoon (potato) and a solid-something eaten by hand (bread). The adult encourages the child to make such distinctions and helps to crystallize and fix them by supplying the necessary conventional words. Growing discrimination and adult intervention-cooperation go hand in hand; it is fruitless to inquire which contributes more. Both contributions are crucial to the gradual convergence of child and adult symbols. Children thus stand on the threshold of mastering their native language; they are becoming capable of employing voluntarily the symbols of the society to which they belong.

LANGUAGE ACQUISITION ACCORDING TO CHOMSKY

Linguist McNeill has commented on the character of early childhood speech (1966, p. 34):

At the age of about one, a normal child, not impaired by hearing loss or speech impediment, will begin to say words. By one-and-a-half or two years, he will begin to form simple two and three word sentences. By four years, he will have mastered very nearly the entire complex and abstract structure of the English language. In slightly more than two years, therefore, children acquire full knowledge of the grammatical system of their native tongue. This stunning intellectual achievement is routinely performed by every preschool child, but what is known about the process underlying it?

Thus, by the age of four, children have acquired the major linguistic categories and meanings of their social groups. Children quickly become masters of their own behavior. That this linguistic ability appears so early in the developmental cycle is the subject of considerable controversy. Chomsky, a linguist whose writings have had a great impact on other linguists and on psychologists, argues that language may be, in some sense, an innate ability. He makes this point quite explicit in the following passage (1965, p. 59):

. . . On the basis of the best information now available, it seems reasonable to suppose that a child cannot help constructing a particular kind of transformational grammar to account for the data presented to him, any more than he can control his perception of solid objects or his attention to line and angle. Thus it may well be that the general features of language structure reflect, not so much the course of one's experience, but rather the general character of one's capacity to acquire language—in the traditional sense one's innate ideas and innate principles.

The suggestion that innate ideas and principles, as part of a general capacity to acquire language, may be inherited, poses formidable difficulties if one tries to imagine how it might be translated into specific genetic mechanisms, as Piaget (1970) has pointed out. However the problem is conceived, it should be formulated so as to bring it, theoretically at least, into the realm of empirical inquiry. The human brain and nervous system are without doubt amazingly complex structures that unquestionably play a central role in the easy acquisition of language in early childhood, but it is extraordinarily difficult to conceive of their being programmed with innate ideas and principles, or with what some call an underlying *language acquisition device* (*LAD*). It is possible that better understanding of the brain and its functions, coupled with further study of the nature of language and how it is learned, may take the mystery from this problem. Another point that might be made concerning those who, like Chomsky and McNeill, are so impressed by the child's ability to acquire language, *is that small and seemingly insignificant causes fairly commonly produce large and even revolutionary effects.* The invention of writing may be taken as an example. Spoken language had been in existence tens of thousands of years before the absurdly simple idea of a primitive form of writing came into practice. Those who participated in and contributed to the early evolution of writing would surely have been incredulous if they could have been told of the revolutionary consequences that were to follow from their invention. (See Brown, 1958; Couch, 1984)

We ourselves adopt a "constructionist" view of language acquisition. From birth, the infant is exposed to linguistic experiences, and these experiences are progressively adopted by the developing child. The regularity of speech behavior is contingent on the symbolic environment to which the child is exposed. In this respect we side with Sullivan (1953, pp. 178–79), who suggests that

The learning of gestures, by which I include the learning of facial expressions, is manifested by the infant, certainly well before the twelfth month, in the learning of the rudiments, one might say, of verbal pantomime. And this learning is, in good measure, learning by trial-and-error approximation to human example. . . .

As the foregoing suggests, we need not resort to an innate, "deep-structure" interpretation of how language appears in the child's behavior. Sullivan's observations suggest that the infant is constantly involved in the process of mimicking the languages and sounds of the adult world. Sullivan's remarks can be framed in terms of two propositions. *"The more complex the linguistic community of the primary group, the more elaborate and complex will be the speech patterns of the young child."* And, again: *"The greater the complexity of this community, the more rapid will be the child's acquisition of speech."* These propositions are consistent with our earlier discussion of social isolation. If social behavior is not directed toward the child, his or her rate of social development will be correspondingly retarded or impeded. The basic similarities between languages (similarities that impress Chomsky), rather than being the result of inheritance, may simply be a reflection of the basic similarities of primary groups throughout the world. In the primary group, speech is acquired by infants, just as Charles Horton Cooley suggested that "human nature" is derived from this source.

The Syntax of Thought and Speech

Sounds, gestures, and thoughts are organized and made intelligible through using a set of syntactical rules that are specific to language communities. Written speech is governed by a set of rules that are quite precise and rigorously governed and studied by grammarians. Thought, on the other hand, has its own set of rules that may bear little

relationship to the specifications governing the printed word. Finally, spoken vocal utterances are governed by another set of rules. Speakers, for example, develop their own styles of punctuation, exclamation, and interrogation.

Of concern in this context are the peculiarities of inner speech. Many students of early childhood thought and speech have erroneously judged the child's speech behavior from the standpoint of the syntax of formal, written utterances. Furthermore, when they claim that the child thinks "egocentrically," they are making that judgment on the basis of adults' thought and speech rules. There is no "thought rule" governing the organization of a thought, nor is there a rule concerning the prominence of the thinker's self in his or her own thoughts. We turn then to a further elaboration of *thought*, following Vygotsky's formulation (1962, pp. 146–47). We note that (1) thought is truncated, abbreviated, and often abstracted from concrete experience; (2) its meaning is embedded in a larger context of perhaps unformulated thoughts; and (3) it is grounded in words that flow together. The word *love*, for instance, merges into a number of other images and experiences that are involved in the love relationship. Unlike vocal speech, thought does not fall into separate categories or units. We quote Vygotsky's remarks on this point (1962, p. 150):

When I wish to communicate the thought that today I saw a barefoot boy in a blue shirt running down the street, I do not see every item separately: the boy, the shirt, its blue color, his running, the absence of shoes. I conceive of all this in one thought, but I put it into separate words. A speaker often takes several minutes to disclose one thought. In his mind the whole thought is present at once, but in speech it has to be developed successively. A thought may be compared to a cloud shedding a shower of words.

Thus, as Vygotsky notes, there is no direct transition from thought to speech. The same relationship holds for the various transitions that move thoughts into printed or written sentences, sentences into paragraphs, and paragraphs into books. To understand another speaker's speech, "it is not sufficient to understand his words—we must understand his thought" (Vygotsky, 1962, p. 151). In other words, the subjective side of speech must be penetrated if listeners or readers are to comprehend and place themselves in the perspective of the utterer or the writer. One author (Hulett, 1964) has noted that the message that is sent is seldom, if ever, the message that is received.

Rather early in the process of acquiring language symbols, children begin to use them to influence their own behavior. Lorimer has described an amusing instance of this (1929, pp. 134–35):

A child of about eighteen months was warned not to put her hand into a certain open chest and not to take out things in the chest. The inhibition was clearly established, but the original impulse was strong. For ten enormous minutes I watched with fascination the battle between the impulse and inhibition, as the little hand reached forward toward the things in the chest and withdrew to the verbal accompaniment "no, no, no!" uttered by the child herself. Then the battle subsided, called to a close by the distraction of other interests.

Such a self-command (the beginnings of what is commonly called "will power") derives from previous adult commands and prohibitions.

Children will eventually internalize their self-directed words so that they will say "no" to themselves silently, or will merely think the command. But at an early age, self-directed language is not completely internalized. Let us take another example: Ask young children to say how many pencils are lying on a table. They are likely to touch each pencil, counting aloud "one, two, three" as they touch. If you hold their hands, thereby preventing them from touching the pencils, they either cannot tell you the total number, or they will nod their heads in the direction of the pencils and count "one, two, three." Youngsters at play are often overheard giving themselves commands like "put this

block there." As the child grows older, language becomes internalized so that counting, commanding, and expressing desires can be carried out silently. The external conversation of gestures-vocal-speech merges into inner thought, or into "the internal conversation of gestures."

THE LEARNING OF CONCEPTS

Learning language, as we have stressed, requires that the child master systems of interrelated concepts. A number of investigators have studied how children's conceptions of time, space, movement, shape, weight, and numbers progressively become more sophisticated and differentiated. Ames (1948), for example. has traced children's use of terms for time (day, minute, and so forth) as these become detached from concrete actions and grow increasingly abstract and inclusive in scope. Studies of children's notions of social relationships, such as those bearing upon social class and race, also show in a general way how knowledge of these matters gradually becomes more discriminative and more systematic.

For instance, C. Stendler (1949), in a study of American small-town children, found that awareness of social class differences develops slowly, passing through four states: (1) preawareness, (2) the beginning of awareness, (3) the acceptance of adult stereotypes of class, and (4) the recognition of individual differences among people, regardless of social class. Likewise, it has often been pointed out that young children are not attuned to racial differences, especially to their more subtle aspects. J. Moreno (1934) has reported that when young schoolchildren were asked whom they would like to have sit beside them, there was no apparent color discrimination in the first three or four grades. Likewise, Horowitz and Horowitz (1936), in a study of a small Tennessee community, noted that black and white children attempted to carry on friendships despite parental admonitions and injunctions. One of the chief causes of punishment for the white children was that they continued to be friendly to black children.

Most studies of children's learning of concepts are of the very general kind described above. Emphasis is upon revealing what children of varying ages know about certain topics, rather than upon the exact tracing of stages and mechanics involved in the development of that knowledge. Our discussion of the nature of symbols and of concepts indicates that change in a given concept is clearly linked with the development of related concepts. As new classifications are found or learned, the child's old concepts are revised, qualified, or assimilated by the new ones. The refinement of concepts waits upon the development of related concepts. Later meanings are built upon and absorb earlier and simpler ones, although the children themselves do not usually recollect most of their earlier conceptions. Children at the same stages of conceptual development tend to commit similar types of errors.

Conceptions of Money

These points can be illustrated by a consideration of some steps through which children pass when learning about money and its uses (Strauss, 1952). Concepts of numbers, coins, monetary transactions, and associated persons like customers and storekeepers are all related in systematic, if immature, ways for the young child. At the beginning, children play with money as with other objects, piling it and pushing it. They make no connection between buying and money. Money is a "penny." At about age 5½, American children also recognize nickels, but cannot consistently match the silver coins put before them to test their discrimination. The child's preferences for coins are based on their size or upon rote memory of relative significance. Money buys goods, but any coin buys anything. Primitive rules cover exchange; four coins are given for four pieces of candy. As the child sees it, both customer and storekeeper pay each other.

At about age 6½, children begin to name

all coins correctly and recognize that nickels buy more than pennies and less than dimes. But a given coin buys only its exact equivalent, no more and no less; a nickel will not purchase a penny piece of candy. Money now has a more genuine function than formerly; it does not merely accompany each transaction, but in some sense makes it possible, since things are not merely bought—they are worth something.

The child may develop a finer sense of mathematics at this stage. A nickel cannot buy a ten-cent piece of candy—not merely because ten is not exactly five, but because it is more. How much more is yet unknown, for the child's mathematics is simply in terms of "more" or "less." In a vague way the child is beginning to sense that there is a connection between the amount of money paid by and to the customer. Money now buys services as well as objects, so that the storekeeper's employees—whose existence has now been recognized—can be paid. Storekeepers, who need money to buy things for their families and for their employees, now sell "to make money" rather than merely to service the customer.

Children at this age (about 6½ years) may also reason that customers must pay for the goods because simple taking of them means a loss to the storekeeper. Previously, they said one paid "just because," or because "you'd be punished" for taking goods. The owner of a store is still paid directly by a customer, and must actually sell in order to be paid. Something like absentee ownership is not grasped.

At about 8 years, children finally get the arithmetical details straight. Sales transactions are now impersonal, nonwhimsical, and arithmetically ordered. But it is not until almost a year later that certain other relationships become depersonalized. For instance, at the 9-year-old level, the child understands that a customer who is disliked nevertheless receives the same change as one who is well-liked. The child also understands now that some of the customer's money goes to the manufacturer and some goes to the

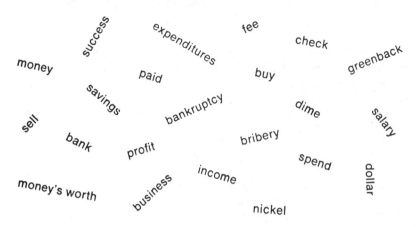

How many different connections among these words has a child learned by the time he or she is an adult?

employee, and that the storekeeper gets some of the remainder. (But the contradiction in this notion is that owners are believed to sell goods for exactly the same price that they paid for them; to do otherwise would not be "fair".) Around the age of nine some children are vaguely aware that goods may, perhaps, be sold for more than cost, but moral considerations plus rigid application of change-making principles confuse the issue. It also occurs to some of the children that the owner pays proportionate amounts to him- or herself and to the employees: "He'd get about fifty dollars, his helpers twenty." Absentee ownership is beginning to appear as a concept. Finally, at about age 10, children grasp the concept of profit. They also finally understand that neither the customer nor the storekeeper gets the better of the bargain when the one gets change and the other is paid. It is not until about a year later that the possibility of shortchanging is seen.

Learning Concepts of Gender

Lacan (1977, pp. 151–52) suggests that young children enter or learn language as "sexed" or "gendered" beings; that is, they learn language from the standpoint of being boys or girls. Many authors have suggested (Joffe, 1971) that children learn gender concepts early—in the primary socializing agen-

cies of the family, day care, and preschool. We will review some of these findings in Chapter 9. At this point we wish merely to note that of all the concepts young children learn, perhaps gender is the most important. This is the case because the gender stratification system in any society rests on the gender concepts a group passes on through the socializing process. We understand gender to refer to the cultural and social patterning of maleness and femaleness, and gender encompasses concepts like sex role. In later chapters, we shall use the term *sexuality* to refer to the actual sexual experiences associated with gender identities in this or any other society.

Boys and Dolls

In a series of ingenious studies, William Damon (1977, pp. 240–81) asked children of different ages to respond to the following scenario: A little boy, named George, likes to play with dolls. His friends think he is silly to play with dolls. His parents tell him that little boys don't play with dolls; only little girls play with dolls. His mother has purchased all kinds of other toys including model airplanes, trucks, and baseballs. Damon then phrased the following questions (1977, p. 242):

1. Why do people tell George not to play with dolls? Are they right?
2. Is there a rule that boys should not play with dolls?
3. What will happen if George keeps playing with dolls?
4. Should George's parents punish him?
5. What if George wore a dress to school?

He asked these questions of 56 boys and girls between the ages of 4 and 9. Here are representative statements from children of different ages; their answers reveal different conceptions of correct gender behavior for young boys.

Jack, 4 years old, said that it was okay for George to do these things because there are no rules against it. Jack did not think that George should wear a girl's dress "because boys don't wear them" (Damon, 1977, p. 240).

Jane (4 years, 6 months) stated that she didn't think George should play with dolls "because he's a boy . . . and he'll get in trouble" (Damon. 1977, p. 254). She said that "dresses can only be for girls" (Damon, 1977, p. 254).

Eugene (7 years, 4 months) is firmer on these understandings. He stated that George can't play with dolls "because it's not right for boys to play with dolls because boys play with other toys like cars and girls play with dolls" (Damon, 1977, p. 256).

Laura (7 years, 9 months) argues that "boys play with boy's stuff and girls with girl's . . . because girls don't like boys' stuff" (Damon, 1977, p. 262). Laura went on to say that boys should be allowed to play with dolls if they want to because it's not fair to say they can't.

Damon proposes that there are four levels or stages of children's reasoning about social regulations like gender (1977, pp. 246–47). These stages are:

Level 0: All types of social regulations are seen as situationally specific and to be followed only if the child wants to.

Level 1: Social regulations are seen as constraining and as conflicting with personal preferences.

Level 2: Social conventions are seen as being arbitrary and may be rejected because of this.

Level 3: Social conventions are respected and followed.

At Level 0 the child only respects those conventions that conform to his or her desire. At Level 1 there is an appreciation of the importance of conventions that extend beyond personal desire. In Level 2 the conventions are seen as being arbitrary and in Level 3 they are seen as being necessary.

The children quoted above (Jack, Jane, Eugene, and Laura) span Levels 0 to 2. Here is a child at what Damon, following Turiel (1975), calls Level 3: Todd (9 years, 6 months) states that George "should tell his mother that he likes to play with them (dolls), and then if his mother says he can't play with them, then he can't play with them" (Damon, 1977, p. 270). Here the convention is followed because it is respected.

We can extract several points from this discussion. First, children from the ages of four through nine do have firm gender understandings regarding "correct" male and female behavior. Second. these understandings are gender-specific; that is, connected to boys or girls. Third, the fact that there *appears* to be a general movement from personal-situational views of gender conventions to a more abstract, less personal position, suggests that as society gets inside children, the arbitrary nature of rules becomes more and more acceptable. Fourth, there is some suggestion that girls grasp these understandings faster than boys do. Fifth, it is clear that there are two gender codes operating in early childhood, and these codes are tied to the acquisition of language and the group's point of view.

REASONING AND CHILD DEVELOPMENT

Sensorimotor Intelligence. It is incorrect to maintain that babies and very young children do not give evidence of intelligent behavior, for even prior to the acquisition of language they are capable of primitive kinds of "mental" activity. Following Piaget (1950), we may term this activity *sensorimotor,* because through touch, sight, and movement the infant locates and relates objects in space and time. Sensorimotor intelligence has nothing to do with language; it develops partly as a result of biological maturation and partly as a result of the child's experiences with objects. At a crude cognitive level, the infant begins to make distinctions between her own body and objects that are external to it.

At first, infants do not even realize that objects which have disappeared from their field of vision still exist. The objects do not have any temporal permanence. Thus, if one covers an objects with a cloth while the 5-month-old infant is reaching for it, he will cease reaching and lose interest (1950, p. 27).

The primitive world is not made up of permanent objects . . . but of moving perceptive pictures which return periodically into non-existence and come back again as a functional result of the proper action.

Nor does the young infant have any clear idea of objects in space. Through exploration of objects—rotating and touching them, seeing their various sides—she soon arrives at some elementary notions of space and of the permanence of objects.

The sensorimotor "reasoning" of infants eventually makes them vaguely aware of their body as one among many stable objects. This represents a considerable advance over their initial picture of the world as made up wholly of impermanent objects.

Logic in Children. Many child psychologists believe that "the child's reasoning processes at the age of six are [not] essentially different from his reasoning processes at the age of twelve or eighteen" (Jersild, 1947, p. 380). This belief involves several assumptions. First, children's logic is essentially the same as that of adults. Second, the more frequent errors committed by the child are a consequence of false premises rather than inferior logic or inability to reason abstractly. Third, these false premises exact because the

child has had inadequate experience with the given subject matter. Fourth, adults, when confronted with unfamiliar subject matter, also are likely to commit errors in logic and judgment. This belief in the general equivalence of child and adult reasoning can easily lead to a subtle form of anthropomorphism concerning the child. Our earlier discussion of the evolution of sign behavior implies that children should be expected to acquire mastery of the higher orders of symbolic activity only gradually. This is obvious if we consider some of the difficulties with logic that children encounter. Casual observation of the child's speech reveals some of these, but others are not apparent unless the child is trapped into revealing his thought process through clever questioning and verbal testing. Some of these deficiencies in logic are shown in the table on p. 167, in which we paraphrase Piaget (1950).

The ability to reason abstractly has a lengthy developmental history. The authors observed an episode in which a child could not describe correctly the kinship relations between his mother and his two maternal aunts, nor could he indicate how many sisters each had. When questioned about this in the women's absence, he fell into the confusions and contradictions typical of a five-year-old. However, when all the women were seated at the table and he was asked how many sisters each had, he was able to answer correctly. The effort that this task cost him was unmistakable: He looked fixedly at his mother, then turned and looked at her two sisters one by one, naming each as he did so. Then he repeated the same process for each of his two aunts. The child's behavior clearly represents a phase in learning to understand relationships. At five years of age, the child's comprehension of abstractions tends to be on a relatively low level—his comprehension is concrete rather than abstract, as Goldstein would say.

The persons or objects must be physically before him if he is to solve even the simpler kinds of questions concerning their interrelations.

Difficulties in	*Illustration*
Classifying abstractly (generalizing)	Four trays, each holding a small wooden dog and one other object, are shown to the child. She is asked to name the common element (the dog). Few children under four or five years of age could name it by saying "All trays have dogs."
Realizing that the class name is only a convenience	The young child believes the name is "in" the object—is inseparable from it. For example, the sun's name is "in" the sun.
Understanding the relativity of relationships	The child maintains that a pebble is light and that a boat is heavy. He does not realize that a pebble is light for him and heavy for the water in which it sinks, or that the boat is light for the water, but heavy for him. Another example: the child cannot grasp the following set of abstract relations. "Edith is lighter than Suzanne. Edith is darker than Lily. Who is darkest—Edith, Suzanne, or Lily?"
Imagining the merely possible	Asked to suppose that the sun is really called the moon and vice versa, the child is likely to argue that that is impossible. Asked "If your brother is a year older than you, how old is he then?" a child with no brother will protest that she has no brother.
Avoiding logical contradictions and inconsistencies	The child will maintain that big bodies are heavier than small ones, but that a small pebble is heavier than a large cork. He will state that rivers have strength because they flow, and a moment later maintain that rivers have no strength because they can't carry anything.
Understanding logical necessity	If asked why water goes down and smoke goes up, the child answers that heavy bodies fall and light ones rise. Her answer is based not on logical necessity, but moral obligation: The object must rise or fall because it is morally obliged to, rather than because it is lighter or heavier than air.
Dealing simultaneously with several logically related matters	The child is asked the following question: "If the animal has long ears, it is a mule or a donkey; if it has a thick tail, it is a mule or a horse. Well, this animal has long ears and a thick tail. What is the animal?" The child cannot answer correctly. Example: "The animal can be a donkey because you say that if it has long ears it is either a donkey or a mule. But it can be a mule, for you say that if the animal has a thick tail it is either a mule or a horse."

Here is an illustration of how children may apply what they learned in a relatively concrete situation to one in which a higher degree of abstraction is required. The child has learned, by purchases in stores, that the more pieces of gum were bought the more pennies were needed. He or she is then shown one stick of gum and asked what it costs—"one penny." Then the stick of gum is broken in halves in full view, and the question is repeated—"two cents." Another half is divided, and the answer is "three cents."

Piaget has analyzed the failures of children on certain tests dealing with concepts of space, number, movement, and the like. His technique is suggested by the following (1950, p. 133):

To study the formation of classes we place about twenty beads in a box, the subject acknowledging that they are "all made of wood," so that they constitute a whole, B. Most of these beads are brown and constitute part A, and some are white, forming the complementary part A'. In order to determine whether the child is capable of understanding the operation A plus A' equals B, *i.e.*, the uniting of parts in a whole, we may put the following simple question: In this box (all the beads still being visible) which are there more of—wooden beads or brown beads, that is, A < B?

Piaget has suggested that there are four fairly clear stages in the learning of logical operations. We do not need to describe these stages; but the import of his theory is that as children move from stage to stage, the organization of their behavior changes accordingly.

Vygotsky's (1962) very interesting experimentation has influenced American research and theory about child development. One of Vygotsky's most general findings was that children reason according to *chain complexes*. This term means that in putting together objects that "belong" together, children do not use a consistent classificatory system, but instead use a succession of similarities (they look yellow, then they look blue); but the successive similarities have no constancy. Bruner and Oliver (1963), influenced by both Piaget and Vygotsky, also concluded that children form chain complexes. Thus, children were offered pairs of words (for example, *peach* and *banana*) and then were asked in what ways those two objects were alike. Next, additional words were presented (*meat* and *potato*) and the children were then asked how all the words were alike. They gave answers such as that the banana and peach are yellow, the peach and potato are round, and the potato and meat are eaten together.

Roger Brown has questioned these kinds of experiments (1965, pp. 385–88). He agrees that children in such experiments tend to sort objects on a part-whole basis and form chain complexes; also that they seldom are able to formulate rules that accurately describe the classes they form, and they do not fully understand the relation of class inclusion. He argues, however, that even adults cannot always give the rule describing their use of words; and while it is probably true that adults understand class-inclusion relations and children do not, knowledge of these relations is not required for referential use of a word, nor for most propositional purposes. He asserts, therefore, that the "intellectual characteristic of children that seems most likely to be reliably characteristic and to have general implications for their understanding of words is their use of chain complexes." Brown cautions against supposing that because adults seldom reason with chain complexes in the experiments, that they also seldom do so in real-life solving of problems.

SUMMARY

In the child's acquisition of language—from her earliest babblings and simplest vocalizations to the final convergence with adult speech—the progression is from the instrumental use of words, word-sentences, and gestures to the more complicated forms of speech. Ways of speaking are intimately connected with ways of thinking, and we have emphasized the ways in which the child's assimilation of language is related to self-control and to the development of logical thought. The rules governing speech are much different from those that control thought. The child's growth of logical comprehension is illustrated by the way in which black children acquire concepts of race and the way in which children's ideas of money and the process of exchange are developed. One's patterns of speaking and thinking reflect one's location in the social structure. Further study is needed of the relationship between language behavior and socialization. On the whole, this has been a neglected research area, but it is a field that deserves serious social psychological attention.

SUGGESTED READINGS

BROWN, R. (1970). *Psycholinguistics*. New York: Free Press. This is an important collection of papers by an eminent linguist and social psychologist who cogently reviews the theories of Chomsky and presents his own highly original research on the "first" language of young children.

CHOMSKY, N. (1975). *Reflections on language*. New York: Pantheon. Further reflections on the controversial theory of language acquisition and language competence of this important linguist are sketched in the essays in this volume.

KLEIN, W. *Second language acquisition*. New York: Cambridge. Offers a general model of language acquisition in first and second languages.

PIAGET, J. (1970). *Structuralism*. New York: Basic Books. Piaget offers a critical review of currently popular theories of language behavior.

VYGOTSKY, L. (1962). *Thought and language*. Cambridge, MA: MIT Press. A classic statement of this author's position on language and thought in early childhood.

CHAPTER EIGHT
The Origins and Development of Self

Consistent with our symbolic interactionist orientation, we hold that any theory of socialization and interaction must ultimately consider the question of how the newborn human becomes a self-conscious participant in the interaction process. In this chapter, we review the social conditions that give rise to the development of self in early childhood. We conclude with a discussion of various developmental theories, including those of psychiatrist Harry Stack Sullivan, who in our judgment offers the most coherent interactional treatment of the rise of self-consciousness in the human organism that is currently available. Chapter 9 will extend our analysis, focusing on the social worlds of early childhood. We begin with a general view of socialization and interaction.

SOCIALIZATION AND INTERACTION

Humans have to develop self-control and a sense of self; the infant is born with no sense of self, other, or social situation. The cardinal task of the child's caretaker is to transform this socially neutral infant into a symbolically functioning human being. The child enters an ongoing world of social interaction that is presented through the symbolic and behavioral actions of its most immediate caretakers, typically those persons who make up the primary group of the family. Assuming there are no organic or neurological deficiencies, the object called "child" possess at birth the necessary equipment to become social and self-conscious (Damon, 1977; Richardson, 1969; Zigler & Harter, 1969; Bullock, 1987).

We assume that the child immediately after birth is exposed to the necessary interactional experiences that will eventually become incorporated into her behavioral repertoires. In short, before socialization can occur, the child must be exposed to face-to-face interaction. Once interaction begins, every succeeding exchange between the child and the mother can be viewed as an instance of socialization. Should interaction cease, or be deflected for a period of time, the child symbolically will regress to an earlier level of development.

Attachment, Bonding, and Deprivation

The research on maternal deprivation, pioneered by John Bowlby and his associates in the mid-1950s, clearly revealed that infants in orphanages who were not exposed to face-to-face interaction rapidly began to lose weight, and many were so understimulated, interactionally, that they began dying at the ages of three and four (1953).

Attachment is an affectional bond that ties one person to another over an extended period of time. Following Bowlby's pioneering work, attachment—as it is used in developmental theories—typically refers to the bond between mother and child. Children can, and do, form attachments to persons other than their mothers, but this attachment is usually primary. Through behaviors such as smiling, gazing, touching, talking, crying, and physical proximity a person promotes and maintains interaction with someone to whom they are attached. Distress often occurs when attached infants are separated from their mothers. It is widely believed that healthy mother-infant attachment is essential to normal child development.

One reason for this is that children learn about their worlds through exploration and play. It appears that children who have developed a healthy attachment use their mothers as a secure base from which to venture forth and explore their physical and social worlds. As these children's sense of security strengthens, they feel more comfortable leaving their mothers for longer periods of time. Healthy attachment, then, can foster later independence.

Recent research by Klaus and Kennell (1982) indicates that there may be a sensitive period shortly after the birth of a child that is important for mother–infant attachment. They contend that when mothers are separated from their babies during the first hours and days after delivery, they may have difficulty forming an attachment. They recommend that whenever possible, mother, father, and infant be left alone for about 30 minutes after birth to facilitate bonding. The duration of this sensitive period has not been determined, and it seems that under appropriate conditions attachment can occur after this phase.

According to Ainsworth (1973), the amount of mother-infant interaction determines whether the infant becomes attached, while the kind of interaction shapes the quality of the attachment. Pediatricians, psychologists, and social workers see scores of children who are strongly attached to abusive parents. The quality of attachment is largely determined by maternal responsiveness. The mother, however, is not solely responsible for her ability to respond to her infant, some infants are easier to respond to than others. Premature and handicapped infants, for instance, do not make as much eye contact with their mothers and are slower to respond to maternal cues—which make it more difficult to be appropriately responsive to these babies.

Maternal deprivation implies inadequate or insufficient maternal care, and under these circumstances attachment often does not occur. It has been found that infants that are maternally deprived often develop abnormally, these infants have lower IQ scores, exhibit social deficits, and have poorer health than infants with normal attachment to their mothers. One of the most profound long-term effects of extensive deprivation in infancy and early childhood was found to be inability to establish and maintain deep and significant interpersonal relations—that is, inability to become attached.

Childhood as Status Passage: Children as Optional Objects

We must make clear, however, that there is nothing intrinsic to the object called "child" that makes it more or less human. Accordingly, depending on the actions taken toward it, different types of selves will be produced. When a society does not have a status called "childhood," "children," in a sociological sense, will actually not be produced; consequently, childlike behavior as it is known in current scientific theory will not be found in those societies and social groups that have no conception of childhood (Goodman, 1970). It would be expected that their children would be permitted to engage in the behaviors normally reserved for adults only. They would own property, exercise political power, make sexual contracts. and engage in the vices of that group (Van Gennep, 1960; Linton, 1942).

A group's stance toward the desirability and inevitability of childhood will determine whether or not that group produces children. Six categories are suggested. Childhood may be viewed as desirable or undesirable (as is claimed to be the case for the Parisian French, by Wolfenstein, (1955). Next, childhood may be regarded as inevitable, optional, or it may not exist. Middle-income Americans regard childhood as desirable and inevitable. The French (according to Wolfenstein) view is as undesirable and inevitable and think one should move through it is rapidly as possible. The Amish view it as optional and desirable, although for those studies by Kuhn (1954) it ceased to exist after age two. The Balinese have no period called childhood and immediately transform their children into adults (M. Mead, 1955).

The Changing Value of Children

Some recent authors (Packard, 1983; Postman, 1982; Winn, 1983; Elkind, 1981; Skolnick, 1977; Suransky, 1982; Zelizer, 1985; Degler, 1980) have asked if children are becoming emotionally dispensable in the 1980s. They point out that women are delaying childbirth, and that an increasing number of children are cared for by someone other than the parents. In 1981, approximately 50 percent of American children were in some form of daycare setting (Caldwell & Feyer, 1982). Suransky (1982, p. 189) has suggested that the feminist movement resulted in the oppression and commodization of children. Zelizer (1985, pp. 223–28) sees a shift in American society back toward the view of children as useful participants in family life. She sees a changing world of childhood emerging within the new egalitarian ideologies of male-female relations in the 1980s. Still, to the degree that day care centers become institutionalized in our society, children will be treated as commodities whose time, emotions, and experiences are managed by others (Power, 1985, p. 221). Clearly, the meanings of the social object called "child" are changing. Whether a new place for children in the family unit will be found remains to be seen (Zelizer, 1985, p. 228).

Groups that view childhood as undesirable produce adults at a much faster rate than do those who define it as desirable. This suggests that distinct cultures of childhood and adulthood will exist in those groups which prolong entry into adult world. Thus, while we would argue that "childlike" behavior as it is known in current scientific theory will not be found in those societies and social groups that have no conception of childhood, nonetheless we contend that the steps or phases by which the self develops are universal in nature. Their specific contents will vary from group to group, but the forms are universal. With the foregoing reservations and points in mind, we can turn to a discussion of the self and its emergence in early childhood. We must first treat the general place of the concept called "self" in the literature of social science.

The Concept "Self"

A concept such as *self* or *ego* is essential to any account of human social nature or the socialization process. Humans characteristically act with self-awareness, exercise self-control, exhibit conscience and guilt, and in the great crises of life make decisions with reference to some imagery of what they are, what

they have been, and what they hope to be. The wider social community enters the person through its language, which in turn furnishes the foundations for the self.

Proponents of the "self" idea have gained the advantage in the controversy in the last few decades. The concept was never entirely rejected in all fields of psychology; it was granted some validity, particularly in child and social psychology. Then, with the increase of the influence of psychoanalytic theory upon studies of personality and in the psychological clinic, there has come a revival of interest in problems of self. Since the 1960s, there has been a considerable amount of research involving or focused on the idea of self. One reason for this has been a growing discontent with theorizing about self, which is done without some empirical base in research; another reason has been a growing awareness that the concept has implications that can guide significant research provided those implications are followed through. Our view is that some of the most significant research is that which focuses on implications of the self-concept. We concur with Theodore Newcomb and his colleagues (1965. p. 142) that the original emphasis on the self as a product of social interaction has been reinforced rather than altered by the more recent investigations. As they say, now we "know much more about the psychological processes by which children learn to perceive themselves, but the earlier conclusion that the self is a social product has scarcely changed at all."

DEVELOPMENT OF SELF-AWARENESS

Observers of child behavior have long noted that the child develops a kind of crude self-awareness within two or three years; and that it takes many more years before full adult self-awareness comes into being. The abilities to think of oneself as an object and to have feelings about oneself evolve throughout the childhood years. The observation that self-awareness has a gradual development misled many philosophers as well as laypersons into thinking of this development as a biological process. It was assumed that infants lacked self-awareness because they were physically incapable of experiencing it; bodily maturation was supposed to provide the capacity to conceive the self. Self-consciousness, in other words, was seen essentially as a natural outgrowth of innate physical endowments. Although this hypothesis was completely disproved by studies made in the 19th century (Sherif & Cantril, 1947, pp. 156–78), it is easy to see how it could have been formulated (Baldwin. 1897). Now, however, there is general agreement that socialization, over and beyond mere biological maturation, is essential to the development of self-consciousness. Deprived of human association, the biologically developing infant could scarcely develop a sense of self (Bowlby, 1953; Schaffer, 1971).

Body Awareness and Body Display

The infant at first has no conception of what belongs to his body and what does not, but seems rapidly to develop several patterns (Murphy, Murphy, & Newcomb, 1937, p. 207):

At six or eight months he has certainly formed no notion of himself. He does not even know the boundaries of his own body. Each hand wandering over the bedspread for things which can be brought into the mouth discovers the other hand and each triumphantly lifts the other into his mouth; he draws his thumb from his mouth to wave it at a stranger, then cries because the thumb has gone away. He pulls at his toes until they hurt and does not know what is wrong.

This is not to say that others in the immediate environment of the newborn do not make social judgments about the child's body and its relative degrees of perceived attractiveness. The newborn enters the world with a physical body which, given the presence of others, is constantly on display and under evaluation. At the outset, the infant passively enters into the display rituals that surround the presentation and inspection of its body. At this age, the child lacks any ability to adorn, dress, or systematically manipulate her own body. As a sense of self is grasped, the child more actively controls these ritual elements of self-presentation.

Slowly. infants learn the boundaries of their own being and learn to make distinctions between what is part of their body and what is part of something else. M. W. Shinn has described two incidents in this process (1891, p. 143):

The 181st day her hand came into contact with her ear; she became at once very serious, and felt it and pulled it hard; losing it, she felt around her cheek for it, but when her mother put her hand back, she became interested in the cheek and wished to keep on feeling that. . . . To the end of the year, she would. . . feel over her head, neck, hair, and ears, the hair she discovered in the eighth month, 222nd day, while feeling for her ear, and felt it over and pulled it with great curiosity.

This lack of differentiation between body and surrounding environment is merely a specific illustration of the infant's generally blurred perceiving (Piaget, 1967, pp. 236–37). Piaget has used the term *indissociation* to describe this undifferentiated perception.

In considering the case of the blind child, the following findings emerge (Scott, 1969, p. 1032):

While the environment of the blind child may fade in and out of his awareness, his own body remains constant. The child may be unable to experience the impact which his manipulations have on the toy which he holds, but he can experience the impact which he has upon his own body . . . his own body becomes the vehicle for feedback.

Compared with the sighted child, "the blind child explores his own body whereas his sighted counterpart" can more directly explore his environment as well as his body (Scott, 1969, p. 1032).

This lack of differentiation, as we discussed in Chapter 7, exists because the child has yet to acquire the necessary linguistic skills which permit him to differentiate self from others. To have a sense of self—to be able to objectify his own activity and separate it from that of others—the child must be able to see himself as a distinct object and realize that the self is not the same as the material-body self. Further, as Mead (1934) argued, the child must be able to see himself from the perspectives of others. The genesis of self involves an awareness that other perspectives outside the child's direct control exist and must be taken account of. The child's knowledge of self is contingent on a separation of self from others.

Naming the Object Called "Child"

Central to the creation of the self as a social object is an identification of that object which will be termed as self. Identification, as Stone (1962), Strauss (1969), and Allport (1961) have argued, involves naming. Once an object has been named and identified, it can be acted toward. This is true for children, as well as for any other object—whether it is a chair, cigarette, or scientific theory. For children to acquire a sense of self, they must be named and singled out from other objects; they must be labeled as distinct objects. Such an identification permits a differentiation from other persons or selves. As Allport (1961, p. 115) has argued, the most important linguistic aid becomes the personal name. Elaborate rituals surround the selection of first and middle names for American children. Rossi (1965) has shown that kinship, generational, and religious processes enter into the selection of names for newborns. Similar events have been observed in other countries. Thus, Young and Willmott (1957) have shown that lower-class London families also employ rather complicated rules in the selection of names for their children.

Allport has commented on names and the emergence of a separation of material-body self from the social self (1961, p. 115): "By hearing his name repeatedly the child gradually sees himself as a distinct and recurrent point of reference. The name acquires significance for him in the second year of life. With it comes awareness of independent status in the social group."

Confusion of "Self" with "Nonself"

Even after infants learn to distinguish between their bodies and the world, they do not have full self-awareness. The child continues for several years to have difficulty in properly locating processes that go on "within his or her own mind" and in keeping them separated from external processes. Thus, Piaget (1967) noted that if the child were asked: "Where is the dream when you dream?" he or she would say that it is "in the room" or "beside the bed." Asked by Piaget where the name of the sun is located, children usually answered that it was very high in the sky. Conversely, they attributed to words qualities signified by the objects or events. Thus the word *elephant* was declared to be a very "strong" word in comparison to *mouse*. Children, of course, also project human attributes onto various animate and inanimate objects. They may believe, for example, that fish eat three meals a day; that if a pin is poked into a tree, the tree feels it; that it hurts a rock to be broken by a hammer. They assume that all people are like themselves, that animals are like humans, and that inanimate objects are alive. They may even identify themselves with material things.

Young children have a particularly difficult time learning to use personal pronouns correctly. Their initial use of *I, me, mine,* and *you* may be confused and inaccurate. They hear their mother use the word *you* toward themselves and will address themselves as *you* instead of *I*. They may speak of themselves in the third person instead of the first person; for example, "Donnie wants that." As Allport says, (1937, p. 161), "The two-year-old often confuses quite sadly the first, second and third persons. He may be overheard to say to himself, 'You be careful, William get hurt. NO! I won't get hurt.' He is first, second and third person all at the same time."

Cooley has suggested that young children misuse pronouns because they cannot directly imitate them. Ordinary words such as *apple* or *doll* can be easily imitated, whereas words like *you* or *I* have to be reinterpreted by the child rather than copied directly (Cooley, 1930, p. 200). Actually, as we have seen, children at first do not imitate such words as *apple* or *doll* very directly. However, they have their chief difficulties with relationship terms such as *brother, father, I,* and *you,* since during their early years they are unaware of perspectives other than their own.

Increasing accuracy in the use of pronouns shows children's maturing conception of their own existence and individuality. This is reflected also by the acquisition of new pronouns. Before age 5, first-person pronouns in the plural (*we, us, ours*) appear infrequently in children's vocabulary; they increase as children grow older and become more conscious of their own participation in groups.

Bain (1936, pp. 767–75), following Cooley's lead, studied his young daughter's acquisition of pronouns. The first pronoun appeared at the age of 15 months, but she did not systematically employ it until the age of 20 months. By the age of 2 years and 9 months, she was using 71 proper nouns (persons) and fourteen pronouns (*I, me, my, mine. myself, we, us, your, something, it, both, any, none*). By the age of 10 months and 20 days, she was answering to the question. "Where's Sheila?" with "She-e! She-e!" Although she also had a term for mother and father, she did not make these designations until aged 1 year.

The Looking-Glass Self

There is a close connection between self-awareness and imagining how one looks to other people. To illustrate, we can consider what is properly termed *self-consciousness.* Almost every one of us has been placed in a situation in which we felt an acutely heightened sense of self; that is, in which we were extremely conscious of our existence and appearance. Consider, for example, a student making her first speech in a public speaking class. She perspires, fidgets, feels tense, and may even have "butterflies in her stomach." Although she may be on good terms with everyone in her audience, she concentrates on such thoughts as: "What are they thinking of me?" "How do I look?" "What kind of impression am I making?" Nor does our imaginary, fright-stricken student have to face an audience to feel acutely self-conscious; she need only think of facing the audience to experience some of the same symptoms. "Mike-fright" has been known to happen to radio speakers before a "dead" microphone. *Self-consciousness* is an extreme example of being self-conscious; it illustrates well the connection between self-awareness and imagining what one looks like to others.

Cooley had this connection in mind when he coined the phrase *the looking-glass self*. His analysis is worth quoting (1902, p. 184):

As we see . . . our face, figure, and dress in the glass, and are interested in them because they are ours, and pleased or otherwise with them according to as they do or do not answer to what we should like them to be; so in imagination we perceive in another's mind some thought of our appearance, manners, aims, deeds, character, friends, and so on, and are variously affected by it.

A self-idea of this sort seems to have three principal elements: the imagination of our appearance to the other person; the imagination of his judgment of that appearance; and some sort of self-feeling such as pride or mortification. The comparison with a looking-glass hardly suggests the second element, the imagined judgment, which is quite essential.

This emotional-affective response of self-feeling, which appears when people present themselves in front of others, is not present in the early stages of self-awareness.

As we have noted, newborn infants lack the ability to visualize themselves through the eyes of others. They must acquire this ability through learning; essential to this is language acquisition, which permits children to take the roles of other individuals.

Learning to Take the Attitude of the Other

Language is necessary to the development of self-awareness. Many writers have recognized this relationship and expressed it in various ways. Some have suggested the importance of linguistic anchorages like address, salutations, and property. Others have regarded parental use of the child's name as an important factor. Still others have assumed that the use of pronouns by both the child and his elders helps fix the child's idea of self-reference. But none of these views is as concrete or convincing as that of G. H. Mead (1934).

Mead notes that among the most significant adult vocalizations, from the standpoint of children, are those that have to do with themselves. These are picked up, imitated, and gradually incorporated in the evolving system of signals, or cues, which children use to stimulate themselves. They hear their name repeated over and over by others who accompany it with appropriate gestures and activities to indicate what it means. The remarks that they are able to remember and repeat to themselves gradually increase in complexity: At first they can use only simple words, then groups of words, and later simple sentences. Finally, they become capable of rehearsing in their imagination entire conversations in which they have been involved. They learn to ascribe motives to their actions, and become concerned over others' reactions to their behavior. As the person converses with herself, an inner dialogue can be observed: The person takes the attitude of another person and judges that attitude in terms of her own response to the situation at hand. Mead described this as an exchange between the "*I*" (the person) and the "*me*" (the reflected attitudes of the other).

Through this process of self-stimulation, children learn to think of themselves as persons, with personal points of view, feelings, ambitions, and goals. Such recognition necessarily means that they recognize or conceive of themselves along lines similar to the conceptions that others have of them. In this inner forum, this personal rehearsal and dramatization of roles, young individuals learn to apply symbols to themselves and to their behavior. As Mead has pointed out, young children are characteristically less adept on the "me" side. They respond directly to stimuli, but do not have the means—or have inadequate means—of taking the other's attitude.

In the course of responding to themselves, children (1) develop an awareness of their own responses, (2) learn something of their consequences, and (3) achieve a certain objectivity about them. Fundamental in the process is the medium of language. Individuals become aware of objects when they are able to name and classify them; similarly, they become aware of themselves when they learn to apply symbols to themselves and to their acts.

To the necessity of symbolization for the realization of selfhood, we should emphasize the turmoil that may accompany this development of self-symbolizing. This was succinctly noted by Baldwin (1897), who pointed to the fact that self-conceptions depend upon assessments of others' perspectives toward one; and since wrong assessments as well as correct ones are made, children learn about themselves without some turmoil. In the writings of Freud and other psychoanalysts, this point is raised to a central theme. Children identify closely with one of their parents, take over some of the parent's moral perspectives, and apply these to their own behavior. But the identification is fraught with peril, and the internalization of parental views may result in a harsh control over basic attitudes.

INDIVIDUALITY AND THE SOCIAL CHARACTER OF THE SELF

The preceding discussion indicates that the self is a social product; it is a consequence of the individual's incorporation within his own emerging sense of self of a social process, which involves ongoing conversations between the "I" and the "me." Indeed the self is just this process of intraindividual communication. Selves do not exist except in a symbolic or social environment from which they cannot be separated. Intraindividual communication is only a part of the total communication network, which extends also to relations between individuals and between individuals and groups. The very idea of an isolated self as an atomistic unit is an error. Symbolic behavior is shared behavior; "self" therefore implies "others" and is inseparable from them. The meanings of the symbols by which selves are organized are based on the responses of others. The fact that a self always seems to belong to an autonomous biological organism should not cause us to neglect the fact that it is built upon a social foundation and that it continues to draw its sustenance from its roots in social relations. As Mead (1934, p. 164) has said: "No hard-and-fast line can be drawn between our own selves and the selves of others, since our own selves exist only insofar as the selves of others exist."

However, a commonsense idea of individuality runs counter to this. It is thought that because persons have unique bodies and somewhat unique experiences, they are quite autonomous products. There is no need to deny individuality in affirming the basic social nature of self. As Cooley (1930) has said, the use of the word "I"—which expresses individuality—would be inconceivable in the absence of an audience to address or exert power over. But in an even more subtle sense, the social nature of the self necessarily implies, rather than denies, individuality. The *generalized other*, the organized community of attitudes to which the person responds—the "me,"—is not a mere importation into the person; it is an assimilation attended—with anguish, anxiety, concern, and care. In a report of a series of observations of his young daughter, Cooley contended that a sense of appropriation was crucial to the development of a sense of self. He pointed to the early and passionate use of

pronouns like "mine" and "my." In a limited way Cooley was getting at a much larger point—namely, that people are not compliant automatons.

The Nature of Self

The use of such expressions in common speech as "self-consciousness," "I hate myself," "I hurt myself," "I am a problem to myself," and "I will be here myself" are indications of the self in action. However, popular usage of self-words is often inconsistent and confusing, particularly because the self is sometimes identified with body and sometimes not. *Self* has both an objective and a subjective reference. Using *self* as a noun seems to imply the existence of a corresponding entity or object. This, however, is an erroneous conception—as erroneous as it would be to think of *speed* in the same manner. Both terms refer to events and relationships, rather than to entities having a definite location in space. For these reasons the self has been described as a "grammatical illusion."

If the self is thought of as a thing, it is reified; that is, it is either conceived of as the body or is thought of as an entity somewhere within the body. It is universal to refer—at least poetically—to some part of the body that is especially favored because it is the seat of selfhood (perhaps particularly the heart, the eyes, the breath, and the brain). Horowitz (1936) has reported some amusing answers by subjects to a request that they locate their selves: They named such varied zones as head, face, brain, eyes, heart, chest, lungs, teeth, hands, and genitals. Kluckhohn and Murray's (1948, p. 9) definition of the personality as "the organization of all the integrative (regnant) processes in the brain" is a sophisticated example in technical literature of the tendency to locate the self in a part of the body.

In order to have a self, one must first have a body. Hence some psychologicsts have spoken of the "physical self" as apart from "the social self." Little is gained by this, since we already have a word to designate the body, namely *body*. The self is not in the body as a physical part; neither is it a spiritual or mystical entity located somewhere or everywhere in the organism; yet the body is implicated in the very notion of self.

The Self as Organization

A Definition. We will note in Chapter 11 how persons' conceptions of themselves serve to evoke and organize appropriate responses and, as part of the same process, inhibit other responses. Such conceptions have a much greater effect on the control of behavior than a simple verbal command or a single inhibiting response. In the same way, at a higher level of integration, one may think of *self as* (1) *a set of more or less consistent and stable responses on a conceptual level that* (2) *exercises a regulatory function over other responses of the same organism at lower levels.*

This definition of self does not imply that the self is a "motivating force." It is not the ultimate vital source of behavior and energy; neither is it a suprabehavioral court to which all behavior is somehow mysteriously referred. Dualistic notions of this kind often pervade popular thinking about human behavior and are also found in scientific literature.

The self is an organization or integration of behavior imposed upon individuals by themselves and by societal expectations and demands. Social requirements and pressures impose limitations upon the degree of inconsistency tolerated in the behavior of individuals and impel the person to eliminate or reconcile such inconsistencies. The organization and integration of lines of activity that appear contradictory or inconsistent to the outsider are essential parts of what is referred to as the self. For the person, they merge together in the conversations between the "I" and the "me." Clearly, people have multiple "I's" and multiple "me's."

The self, as we have defined it, does not enter significantly into all behavior but is differentially involved in various acts; at one

extreme, involvement is slight. Psychological experiments dealing with "level of aspiration" have shown that when involvement in a task is increased (that is, when the individual is appropriately motivated), performance is improved or changed. In many involuntary and automatic activities, little of the self is implicated, although even in these the action may have significance of which individuals are not aware. Moreover, an automatic action, like tapping the table with your fingers, may acquire significance if it is singled out for attention or criticism by other persons so that it takes on meaning for yourself.

Self and Self-Control. Self-control is usually thought of in connection with self-awareness; for example, we speak of people controlling their appetites or curbing their passions. However, regulatory functioning is not necessarily accompanied by acute self-consciousness; for example, a driver may pilot a car quite skillfully for many minutes while engaged in conversation or sunk deep in thought. Any physical skill tends to assume an automatic character, although when first acquired it is at the forefront of attention. Some skills may become the basis of self-esteem, as in persons who use them professionally or competitively, so that they continue to be at the center of attention in a somewhat different way.

The Mechanism of Control. Self-regulation is inseparable from social control. The language mechanisms by which self-control is exerted are derived from social sources, and the regulatory process itself occurs largely in the form of internalized conversation. Mead has distinguished two phases of internalized conversation, the "I" and the "me," which can be made clear by means of a simple illustration. Let us suppose that a man walks into a bank and finds himself in a position where he can make off, without fear of detection, with a large sum of money. We shall suppose that our hypothetical man is not above temptation in this particular situation. Something like the following inaudible and greatly abbreviated conversation might take place:

Phase One—"I"	*Phase Two—"Me"*
I could use that money.	But it's stealing.
So what! Everyone steals if they have a chance to.	You know it isn't so.
I could get a new car.	No. Better be honest.
No chance of getting caught.	Dishonest.
Banks make lots of money; they won't feel it.	Isn't right to take it. Isn't theirs either.

If he is above temptation, Phase One does not exist and the conversation does not occur.

Internal conversation does not go on in terms of complete sentences or words alone, but rather as a kind of mental tug-of-war between conflicting impulses interspersed with visual and auditory images and daydreams, and accompanied by corresponding feelings. Such conversations are not necessarily short, nor do they always take place in a single episode. The battle against a particular temptation may be a sporadic and long one that is brought alive periodically by external circumstances.

Much of our thinking, particularly when we are dealing with difficult or problematic situations of a moral or volitional kind, involves these two general phases of conversation. Mead called Phase One the "I" and Phase Two the "me." The "me" in his scheme represents internalized group standards; that is, the "me" is the community in the individual. To Mead, the "I" represented impulses which are supervised by the "me," either being squashed as they get underway or afterward, or diverted into acceptable channels.

The widespread popular conception that the impulses of the "I" always require supervision and are of a negative and unsocialized character requires considerable qualification. Impulses may be perfectly socialized, but nevertheless judged inappropriate to the

situation after brief consideration. Such judgments are continually being made, since life is anything but routine. Control is not necessarily a matter of stemming ignoble temptation or putting the lid on passions; it may be quite the reverse, as when one checks overgenerous impulses in favor of other considerations. Furthermore, control may be positive in the sense that we have to urge ourselves to do things, the urging representing the regulatory side of our action. We shall draw a sharp line between negative and positive self-control, since lines of action necessarily involve both the eliciting of certain responses and the negation of others. Puritanical traditions emphasize the repressive aspects of control and disregard the fact that the "I" may become socialized and need not be an expression of the brutish side of human nature.

Social control is not based exclusively—and certainly not primarily—upon coercion. Neither can effective group action be based upon the continuous direct surveillance of individuals. If this were false, humans would revert to sheer brutality and opportunism whenever they were out of sight or earshot of others, or whenever the chances of detection were slight. Orderly social controls are based on contract, obligation, trust, and responsibility. Even limited alliances involve these.

Theories of human nature that postulate opposition between individual and society, picture society as a kind of police officer watching over the individual. Self-interest is seen either as being in opposition to collective interest or as utilizing the latter to gain its primary ends. This is a misconception of the nature and function of ethical codes and of the requirements of group life. Compliance with community norms and with contractual obligations is not only a requirement of effective collective action, but is a necessity for the creation and fulfillment of individual aspirations. There is no natural opposition of humans and society. Asch (1952, pp. 320–21) made a similar point when he suggested that the accentuation of self is often a response to social failure:

When the possibilities of entering into appropriate relations with others are barred, the ego turns its potentialities for care upon itself. Avarice, greed, and ruthless ambition often are the answer the ego gives when it fails to find in the surroundings the opportunity for its outgrowing needs.

Conscience, Guilt, and Shame. Internal control in moral matters is referred to as *conscience*. What is regarded as right and wrong varies widely among societies, among groups, and even from situation to situation within a homogeneous population. Also, as Cameron and Magaret (1951, p. 285) point out, "The behavior which one man views within an ethical context of 'right' and 'wrong' may be for his neighbor a matter of expediency, taste, or arbitrary cultural control." Naïve judgments are sometimes made about another person's acts because the varied content of consciences is not taken into account. Sometimes conscience is identified with religious precepts; religion and mortality are frequently so closely interwined that a coalescence of ethical and religious teaching seems part of the natural order of things. However, in some soceities large areas of morality lie outside the religious sphere.

In Western theological writing and in commonsense thinking, transgressions of the dictates of conscience are associated with guilt. One stands alone before her God—or conscience—and suffers remorse for what she has done or left undone. The subtleties of guilt and self-judgment and the means of expiation hardly need be dwelt upon.

THE SELF IN EARLY CHILDHOOD

The child is not born with a sense of self. The self develops out of the matrix of experiences to which the child is exposed. The foregoing sections have implicitly presented a number of notions central to a social psychological theory of self-development. We shall review the work of Cooley and Mead, contrast it with the psychosexual formulations of Freud, Lacan, and Erikson, and conclude with an appreciative statement of Sullivan's *The Interpersonal Theory of Psychiatry*.

Cooley and Mead

Mead and Cooley presented views of early childhood that could be termed interactional and developmental. They argued that the self emerged in three sequential phases. For Mead, these phases were termed *play, the game,* and *the generalized other*. In each phase, the child was progressively better able to differentiate self from other. In the play phase of self-development, the child was seen as unable to take more than one role at a time. In the game stage, multiple roles could be segregated but they could not, as in the generalized other phase, be combined into a consistent symbolic perspective. The generalized other describes persons' interpretations of their experience with others who make up their world. They need not be an actual group per se. In the generalized other stage of self-development, individuals were capable of standing over and against the outside community and capable of clearly seeing themselves in terms of the moral and symbolic expressions of others. This is what Mead meant by the terms "I" and "me." The "I" component of the self described the individual's distinctly personal views of self, whereas the "me" referred—in Sullivan's terms—to the "considered and reflected appraisals" of others. The self, for Mead and Cooley, reflected constant interaction between (1) the individual's definitions of situations, and (2) the definitions reflected to the individual by others. Cooley located the emergence of the self in the primary group of the family. *Self-feeling* was basic to his theory. Mead, on the other hand, argued that the genesis of self was based not on self-feeling per se, but upon the child's ability to *reflexively* respond to the attitude of the other.

Stages of Selfhood

We may call these three phases of selfhood the *preparatory stage,* the *interactional stage,* and the *participatory stage.* In the pre-paratory stage, the child imitates and mimics the words, actions, and feelings of others. In the interactional stage, he is able to take the attitudes of specific others, and a process of anticipatory socialization begins to occur. The child is learning the languages, feelings, emotions, and ways of acting that are shared by other family members. In the participatory stage, the child learns to take the attitudes of the family and play group, and can grasp the generalized outlook of the group. Socialized speech of a nonegocentric nature is produced (see Mead, 1934; Meltzer, 1972, pp. 9–10; Stone, 1981, pp. 200–201).

Gender and Selfhood

In Chapter 7, we discussed gender codes and conventions and noted how young children quickly acquire understandings of gender-specific behaviors. We can now note that selfhood is directly connected to gender. The self that emerges in childhood is not gender-free. An axis of value and mood (Stone, 1981), or instrumental and emotional attachment (Gilligan, 1982, pp. 8–9), differentiates males and females in our society. These may be termed *gender codes;* one is masculine, the other feminine (Erikson, 1950; Kohlberg, 1981). The masculine code in our society represses emotionality; the feminine code releases emotion. To the degree that males and females in our society are socialized into these two codes, the emotional experiences for the two gender classes will differ. At the same time, the ability of each gender to take the attitude of the other gender member will vary and be differentially difficult or easy. Thus it is easier for boys to understand boys than it is for them to understand girls. The same holds for adult males in their relations with other males and with females. Kohut (1977), a psychoanalyst, has suggested that the goal of socialization is to produce a human being who is cohesive and responsive to the needs of others, irrespective of gender. This may be a utopian goal, given the current arrangement between the sexes in our society.

Recently, Lever has noted a sex difference in children's play and games. She found that while boys tend to participate in more formal games, girls are more often involved in small group play which mimics primary group relationships. She writes (Lever, 1978, p. 481), "In Meadian terms, it may be that boys develop the ability to take the role of the *generalized other* while girls develop empathy skills to take the role of the *particular other*" (italics in original). When children live in a shared environment and are part of the same community, they tend to take the attitude of the same generalized or particular order, and thus respond to the same set of rules—including feeling rules.

Thorne and Luria (1986, pp. 176–90) have observed that 11-year-olds form separate gender play groups, and these groups foster ritualized and asymmetric relations between boys and girls. Hence, sexual scripts for adolescence are learned in these play groups. This finding is consistent with Sullivan's theory, which we discuss later.

Early Selfhood

Wiley (1979, pp. 87–105) has outlined a theory of infant selfhood. He indicates three stages in the genesis of self in the first year of life. The infant's first sense of self-awareness emerges in the "me" stage, when she defines herself through her mother. This stage flows into the second, the "we experience," in which mother and child merge in a field of shared social experience. The third stage is the "I" stage, which develops when the infant can turn back on her behavior from the standpoint of the "me" and the "we experience" and see herself as a "psychological I," or self. In the "I" phase of self, the infant is able to temporally and interactionally reflect upon her own conduct from the double standpoint of her and her mother's points of view in the social situation. Wiley's formulations locate selfhood earlier in the life cycle than do many other theories. His emphasis on the "me," "we," and "I" phases strengthens Mead's theory, which did not locate a social relasionship in the center of the self-experience. That is, Mead's "me" was not closely joined to the self in a "we" relationship.

OTHER DEVELOPMENTAL VIEWS: FREUD, LACAN, ERIKSON, SULLIVAN

While Mead and Cooley saw self-reflexivity as a problematic element in every interactional episode, other theorists take a more deterministic view. We term them the *psychosexual* or *psychosocial developmentalists*. The two most prominent theorists in this tradition are Freud and Erikson. Each, in a somewhat different fashion, stressed age, sex, and family experiences as crucially determining variables in the emergence of the self and personality. Each adopted a relatively fixed sequence of stages through which the infant must pass on the way to adulthood. Each assumed that processes internal to the organism significantly entered into the developmental process. We turn first to Freud, whose work is still highly influential in the fields of psychiatry and clinical psychology. (See also our discussion in Chapter 6.)

Freudian Developmental Theory

The general Freudian thesis of personality development has been concisely stated by Benedek (1952, p. 100):

The integration of the *sexual drive* from its pregenital sources to the *gential primacy* and to functional maturity is the axis around which the organization of the personality takes place. From the point of view of personality development, the process of interaction is the same in both sexes. Men and women alike reach their psychosexual maturity through the reconciliation of the sexual drive with the superego and through the adjustment of sexuality to all other functions of the personality. . . . *The sexual drive is organized differently in men and women, in order to serve specific functions in procreation.*

In our presentation of Freudian developmental theory, we shall rely mainly on Benedek's summarization. We should remember that there is some divergence of opinion among Freudian psychoanalysts and others who subscribe to the general outline as Benedek gives it. She herself indicates some of the points of divergence (see Mitchell, 1983; Rose, 1983; Coward & Ellis, 1976; Benjamin, 1981).

The Stages

The early developmental history of the child is described in terms of the dominance of certain sensitive—or *erotogenic*—zones, such as the oral, anal, and genital regions. Infants' earliest libidinal pleasures are connected mainly with their mouths. They suck at their mother's breast and their own fingers, and they also use their mouths to explore and test the objects they encounter in the external world. The oral phase of development occupies approximately the first year. The psychoanalyst Abraham distinguishes two phases of this stage: the *passive-receptive,* in which children merely have things done for them, and the *active-incorporative,* in which children are able to reach actively for objects. During the oral period, if the infant's instinctual needs are not adequately met, insecurity, anxiety, and conflict develop. Throughout this period, children are "narcissistic," deriving most of their gratification from themselves and their own bodies, with little reference to external objects. However, children are learning what causes them pain and which of their actions bring disapproval and withdrawal of love. The differentiation of id and ego has begun, as children begin to establish relationships with their mother and with objects.

In the second phase, the anus becomes the dominant erotogenic zone. "Its double function—retention and elimination—becomes the center of interest and the source of pleasure" (Benedek, 1952, p. 71). Toilet training then becomes critical. Parents, in a fashion that depends on their cultural and personal backgrounds, attempt to teach the child sphincter control. By this time, the child understands adults well enough so that he can cooperate with or resist them, depending upon the kinds of relationships that have been established. "Toilet training," Benedek says, "is the ego's first conscious struggle for mastery over an id impulse" (1952, p. 72). The mother's approval is balanced against the instinctual pleasure of soiling. When mastery of the impulse becomes a goal in itself, a new phase begins. The ego, even in the absence of the mother, resists the id impulse. This represents a big forward step in building personality structure. One of its immediate results is that the child is now vulnerable to threats from id impulses which may break through against the controling ego. This conflict also represents a clash between the *pleasure principle* and the *reality principle*. The former, in the service of the id, strives for immediate gratification; the latter postpones immediate gratification for later gratification through a mastery of the reality situation.

The particular method of toilet training employed is important, since it causes the child to react in certain ways. Thus, over-severe training seems punitive to the child and may lead him or her to rebel and become hostile toward the mother. This creates a vicious circle as the mother reacts to this rebellion. When sphincter control is secure, the conflict situation diminishes and the child is ready for the next step. During the anal period, differences in learning between the sexes begin to appear. Benedek remarks that mothers generally recognize that girls are more easily trained than boys. This is because the girl identifies with the mother more readily, whereas in boys a good relationship with the mother is merely preliminary to self-assertion and eventual identification with the father. The roots of competitive behavior are said to lie in the achievement of sphincter control. A British analyst, Jones, even stated that the model for competitive behavior among men derived from boyish competition in urinating.

The third general stage is called *oedipal,* or *phallic,* because the child's sexual urges, originally directed toward his own body, now become intensified and directed toward the parent of the opposite sex. For obvious reasons, boys become aware of genital gratifications earlier than girls. The mother is the object of the boy's first heterosexual interest. The girl's development is slower and more complex; her sexuality remains more diffusely located in sensations of the skin and in motor coordination rather than focusing on the genitals. As we noted in Chapter 6, Freud postulated that the sight of the male genitals arouses "penis envy" in the girl, and that this is instrumental in breaking the girl's attachment to her mother and directing her erotic impulses toward the father and eventually to other males. Freud believed penis envy to be the key to feminine psychology. (This is one point at which some analysts disagreed with Freud.) In any case, the girl is said to turn toward the father, thus arousing an instinctual conflict between attraction to the father and the potential loss of gratification of needs by the mother. However, sometimes after lengthy conflict and vacillation, the girl develops her own kind of oedipus complex—the *electra complex.* The boy's oedipal development is more direct, yet there is a crucial conflict associated with it. The boy is in competition with his father for the mother, but cannot win. Although he cannot actually consummate his urges, he feels guilty and "expects retaliation to be directed toward the organ from which he receives pleasure. The fear of castration—mutilation—develops in varying intensity, even if a threat of physical punishment was never uttered" (Benedek, 1952, p. 82). Fear of castration brings about ambivalence toward the father. The boy tries to please him by identification with him in nonsexual areas of behavior and tends also to idealize him. Identification with the father leads to internalization of the father's moral code, although the working out of the oedipus complex, and the associated development of a mature superego, takes many years. In the meantime. genital urges may find expression in masturbation or other substitute activities and attachments. Benedek also lists various ego defenses against sexual tendencies which help to repress and resolve the oedipus complex. These include the intellectualizing of curiosity about sex, development of infantile sexual theories, denial of sexuality in the parents, and identification with the opposite sex. The latter is a defense against the dangerous heterosexual urge. This is known as a "negative oedipus complex" and is usually temporary, since it is not a feasible solution of the sexual problem. The various phases of the resolution of the oedipus complex do not occur in a fixed time sequence, but may occur more or less simultaneously.

During the oedipal period, the structure of the personality becomes much more complex and differentiated. The superego is developing and is in conflict with the id. The ego now undertakes the function of mediating between (1) the id and the superego, and (2) the id and reality. At this stage, the ego represses the sexual tendencies, thus initiating the latency period.

The beginning of the latency period coincides, in our society, with the beginning of school. "The desexualization of the child's interest enables him to comply with environmental requirements and thus to expand in mental and social growth" (Benedek, 1952, p. 88). The basic biological tendencies of giving and taking, retaining and eliminating, and other tendencies from the anal and oral stages continue to develop into more complex forms. Oral receptive pleasure continues in the form of pleasure in the reception of material and spiritual gifts. During latency, children learn how to share. Aggressive incorporation appears in the form of envy, jealousy, and maliciousness. Passion for collecting betrays the retentive tendency. Boys characteristically collect masculine objects (stones, strings, keys) and girls accumulate feminine objects (beads, dolls). If either sex evinces much interest in the wrong kind of objects, this is an index of bisexuality. The existence of the latency period as a biologically determined stage is another point upon which all Freudians do not agree.

The next phase is brought about by the onset of puberty and is coterminous with adolescence. The physical maturation which occurs in this period reawakens latent conflicts, and the ego must again master them. Girls, for example, become sensitive to the changes in their bodies and may become ashamed or shy. In both sexes, attempts are made to master sexuality through repression, a technique which was successful in the earlier oedipal stage. As the sexual drive becomes more urgent, "all the available resources of sublimation are mobilized, and expansion of interests and achievements is generated" (Benedek, 1952, p. 97). Safe ego gratification is afforded by these interests. Yet "the ego . . . cannot withstand for long the pressure of the instinctual impulses; the defenses yield and the instinctual tension is released" (Benedek, 1952, p. 97). During adolescence the child discovers new values and ideals and appraises those of the parents, thus reactivating the old conflict with them: The boy quarrels more with his father, the girl with her mother. As the child becomes more independent of the parents, the superego becomes less rigid, and a more complex level of personality integration is reached. Sexual maturity requires a personality which accepts both the sexual drives and the social regulation of them.

The systematic account of development offered by Freudians ends at this point. Later events tend to be interpreted as a working out, in relation to an adult environment and advancing age, of earlier genetic occurrences. This account of development must be viewed as an ideal, or average normal, picture. Children, it is said, vary in the rates at which they pass through some or all of the phases; some experience one or more phases only in dreams or fantasies. Sometimes part of a phase may be repeated as a consequence of regression, which is in turn a consequence of disappointments. Adolescence is such an especially tortuous process that some analysts refer to the "normal psychopathology" of the period. It is also noted that some individuals do not go through adolescence to the final stage but remain fixated at earlier points, and that if the process goes awry, libidinal urges may find expressions in a wide variety of curious or abnormal ways.

Criticism and Appreciation

In criticizing this account, we can quote Benedek herself to show what is left out of it. In discussing the anal stage, she comments briefly on the development of speech during the second and third years (Benedek, 1952, p. 74):

It is in another area of maturation that the child learns to speak. . . . This complex process is considered to be the result of the progressing maturation of the speech apparatus and of intellectual accomplishments and is, therefore, not usually discussed in connection with the psychodynamic aspects of personality development.

She touches briefly upon initial learning of words and sentences, noting that the child "has stored in his mind symbols related to . . . experiences" that occur before the development of language, and that these experiences and symbols may never reach the level of verbalization, but may form the content of the unconscious (Benedek, 1952, p. 76). This is virtually all that is said of language behavior. The separation of "emotional experience" from cognition, which is implied in Benedek's quotation, is characteristic of psychoanalytic thinking. It stems from the classical tripartite distinction between cognition, conation, and affect (intelligence, will, and emotion). Those who make this distinction neglect the fact that emotional experiences do not exist as pure states, but are shot through with cognitive elements. The fiction of the separation of intellectual development and personality development can be maintained only if one disregards or underrates the role of language in the organization of behavior, including emotional behavior.

A second major criticism is that a *genetic fallacy* is persistently maintained when the last event in a chronlogical series is identified

with the first, as illustrated by Benedek's frequent use of the term "model" (as in the suggestion that urinary competition provides the model for all later male competition). The attribution of sexuality to both newborn infants and adults is another example. Some analysts have made note of the resulting confusion, and have differed with Freud on this point. The same type of fallacious genetic reasoning is evident in the conception of the biologically rooted drive as the theme which unites all processes throughout the developmental sequence. Although learning is given an important place, its primary function is seen as the harnessing of the id drives in socially acceptable ways. The genetic approach of Freudian analysts gives their explanations a narrative character. If they are asked why two persons whose childhood experiences appear to be substantially the same turn out very differently as adults, the analysts' answers will frequently consist of two biographical narratives.

A third problem arises from the general character of analytic theory itself, which makes it difficult or impossible to subject it to empirical tests at crucial points. In a review of psychological studies of children, Koch (1954, p. 22) has pointed out that there is virtually no evidence of a nonclinical sort on which to base an evaluation of psychosexual stages. With respect to some minor points, it has been possible to check the implications of the analytic account. The existence of the latency period, the validity of the concepts of sublimation and repression, and the oedipus complex itself, as described by Freud, have been made questionable through checking. Anthropologists, by using comparative data, have raised serious doubts of the alleged universality of some of the central factors in the developmental process, such as Freud's concepts of the superego and oedipal attachments. The assumption that development is virtually over—except for minor variations—when adulthood is reached, is questionable to sociologists. (See Chapters 11 and 12.)

Despite the many objections that have been raised concerning it, Freudian developmental theory also has some clear-cut virtues. The fact that it is a general theory concerning areas of human behavior which are vital to self-esteem makes it significant and challenging. It at least proposes explanations for many forms of behavior which are ordinarily passed over by other psychological systems. Analytic theory has also performed the function of calling attention to the subtlety of human interaction and the existence of concealed factors which subjects themselves are unable to report. It has sought to isolate and analyze crucial experiences in the life of the child and has described, with much clinical detail, various significant processes, such as identification with parents and other mechanisms of interaction and ego defense. Close contact with patients provides the analyst with a continuous flow of clinical data of great value to anyone interested in childhood development, regardless of how it may be interpreted. Some suggest that Freud's theory should be read as a myth, and others regard it as supporting male dominance over women.

LACAN

Jacques Lacan (1977), a French psychoanalyst, has undertaken a complete rereading of Freud's works. In the process, he has modified and changed a number of the key Freudian concepts. Positing that language is central to an understanding of the unconscious, Lacan has produced a semiotic–psychoanalytic framework that has become quite controversial. Lacan's works are difficult and are subject to many different readings (see Ragland-Sullivan, 1986; Metz, 1982; Coward & Ellis, 1977). We will now discuss his theory of the "mirror stage" and the phases of development the young child moves through on the way to resolving the crisis of identity Freud located in the oedipal phase.

Sensorimotor Phase

To borrow Piaget's term (1953), the sensorimotor phase sees the infant like a "homolette," or a little man, spreading without hindrance in all directions (Coward & Ellis, 1977, p. 101). The infant moves around its environment, crawling here and there. In this phase, the child experiences a sense of "oneness" with the mother. This is like Wiley's "we" phase.

Splitting Phase

In this phase, the infant begins to detach from the mother. The mother receives all the infant's demands, and is the object of its desires. In this splitting phase, the infant divides the world into two categories: self and world. An emerging sense of prelinguistic self-awareness develops in this phase; this may begin as early as three months, although some say it appears at birth (Feld, 1979; Martin & Clark, 1982).

Mirror Phase

In the mirror state, the infant sees his image in the mirror and forms an ideal, unified picture of himself. This image splits the child from the mother because it provides a picture of self that is no longer dependent on the mother's attention. Simultaneously, it unifies the child's sense of self and creates an ideal, imaginary self. Soon the mother becomes another "mirror" for the child, for the infant sees himself mirrored back in the mother's actions.

Lacan argues that the mirror stage creates an ideal yet fictional self-image for the child. It gives the child a false sense of unity. The mirror stage is critical to all later experiences of self because it establishes the infant's first reflective relationship with the external world on an error, or on what Lacan terms *méconnaissance*. Because the "I" of the infant is ushered in under imaginary, false circumstances, the underlying social foundations of the self are unstable and fragmented. This genesis of the self in the mirror stage prefigures later personality disorders which appear in adulthood, including narcissism, aggression, neurosis, and madness (Lacan, 1977, p. 7). For Lacan, the mirror stage means that there is no firm, steady center to the self.

Language and Subjectivity

Lacan (1977, p. 2) argues that the child emerges as a subject when the pronoun "I" is acquired. However, he argued that the "I" of language is a false ego ideal, for the "I" has no real permanence in the child's world. Arguing that children enter language as gendered beings, Lacan proposes that the mother is the first ego-ideal of the child. The child attempts to become like the mother, but always fails. Finding her place in language, the child confuses herself with the mother. This means she has an imaginary ego that is located in the mother; she has another imaginary ego that is located in the mirror phase. These two ego-ideals create confusion and ambiguity. Ultimately the child's subjectivity is located in language; but language separates the infant from herself. Hence, language gives a false sense of self-unity. The infant's self exists in a vacuum; it is neither in language, nor in the mirror and the mother. In no sense is self connected to validating self-experiences that would promote security and self-assurance.

Identity Crisis

As the infant is detached from the mother and acquires language, another crisis occurs. She is unable to identify with the ideal type of her sex. She is not her mother and she is not her father. But she is a gendered individual; that is, she is called a girl. In the triadic family drama with the mother and the father, the child experiences what Lacan, after Freud, terms the "castration complex." The male child cannot use his penis to express his desire for his mother because of the incest ta-

boo. The female child is deprived of a penis, as is her mother. She experiences herself as a lack or an absence. Her sexual desire is repressed, and she is forced to submit to language and to the symbolic order of the family where her subjectivity and sexuality are regulated. A similar process occurs for males.

Lacan's image of the infant and young child suggests that this period is filled with anxiety and fear. His emphasis on gender and sexuality suggests that the self-genesis experiences for males and females will be considerably different, although the broad outlines of the identity crisis surrounding the "castration complex" will be the same for males and females. His suggestion that language mediates and structures self-awareness fills out a part of Mead's theory that was only hinted at by Cooley's study of the pronouns in early childhood. The discussion of the splitting phase and the mirror phase is also useful, for it points to experiences that are missing in Mead's play, game, and generalized other phases. Whether the mirror stage lays the foundation for unstable self–other relations later in life is problematic. Clearly, however, Lacan's mirror is not like Cooley's looking-glass. Important here is that both authors see the child's identity being reflected back not only through mirrors, but also through the actions of other people—most especially the mother.

Erikson's Model of Developmental Stages

Another Freudian approach to developmental stages that has gained a wide audience in recent years is that proposed by Erik Erikson (1965, 1950, 1969, 1959, 1962).

Although a psychoanalyst trained in the Freudian tradition, Erikson's experiences while doing research among American Indians and in treating patients in the United States have led him to still another approach to developmental stages. His scheme has gained great popularity, principally among child and adolescent psychiatrists and among clinical psychologists. Many enthusiasts take it as a rather definitive picture of developmental reality, although Erikson himself apparently meant it only as a suggestive guide. We shall not outline this scheme in any detail, for it is not very different in some important assumptions from the Freudian one.

Erikson rethought Freud's theory of infantile sexuality, developed a diagram that emphasizes the step-by-step (progressive) nature of the mind's development, and stressed the ways (modes) that the body's sensitive zones (openings, organs) work (Coles, 1972, p. 75). He linked this with a sequence of social experiences, emphasizing critical periods that the child must manage, either doing well or failing in some degree (Coles, 1972, p. 137). Later he added additional stages and developmental tasks, eight of each in all. Erikson does not regard these stages and tasks as rigidly sequential, but remarks (Coles, 1972, p. 138):

If the chart . . . lists a series of conflicts or crises, we do not consider all development a series of crises. Development proceeds "by critical steps—critical being a characteristic of turning points, of moments of decision between progress and regression, integration and retardation."

In a sense, the developmental tasks run all through the adult years. perhaps in any individual never being accomplished for once and for all.

An interactionist must view such a scheme as not remarkably different from the Freudian, to which Erikson was reacting. Thus, there still is a great emphasis on psychosexual linkages, and despite the disclaimers, it attempts to give a "stage" picture of development. The earlier stages, in which the family is implicated, receive much more emphasis and are discussed in greater detail than the later, or adult, years. And Erikson focuses considerably—understandably, since he is a psychoanalyst—on psychic health: hence the abilities to become trustful, autonomous, industrious, and to become truly able to exhibit initiative and to share intimate relations are crucial. There is nothing "wrong" with emphasizing these things, but this focus on psy-

chic health tends to restrict unduly the scheme for more wide-sweeping social psychological purposes. Certainly it tends to restrict focus—despite Erikson's own interest in history and in famous figures like Gandhi and Luther—to individuals rather than to interlocking social biographies.

The point is underscored by the largely clinical use to which Erikson's chart and writings have been put. A painful example is given by Charlotte Green Schwartz and Merton J. Kahne (1973), who document how college psychiatrists have picked up Erikson's scheme and applied it faithfully to college students as a "real" explanation of adolescence. Consequently, when the campuses felt the effects of the events of the 1960s, beginning with the civil rights movement, college psychiatrists simply translated students' memberships in all the emergent social movements into Eriksonian language. The scheme allowed them to discount the students' complex memberships and commitments to political movements, and almost totally allowed them to misread the students' participations in a variety of other social worlds. Indeed, Parsons (1970), in his efforts to elaborate the Freudian and Eriksonian schemes, has suggested that between adolescence and early maturity is a clearly discernible developmental stage which he terms "studentry." In this sense, Erikson's scheme may be restricted to only certain classes of individuals. Finally, with his emphasis on sequential *identity crises* in adolescence, Erikson often gives less attention to the transformations in self which occur in middle and late adulthood. The foundations of these identity crises are also not fully clear. They, too, may be relevant only to certain groups of individuals.

Sullivan's Developmental Theories

We turn now to the developmental scheme of Harry Stack Sullivan. His approach, in our judgment, overcomes many of the flaws of Freud and Erikson.

Theorists who do not subscribe to the cen-

Erikson's Eight Stages of Psychosocial Development

Stages	Psychosocial Crises	Significant Social Relations	Favorable Outcome
1 First year of life	Trust versus mistrust	Mother or mother substitute	Trust and optimism
2 Second year	Autonomy versus doubt	Parents	Sense of self-control and adequacy
3 Third through fifth years	Initiative versus guilt	Basic family	Purpose and direction; ability to initiate one's own activities
4 Sixth year to puberty	Industry versus inferiority	Neighborhood; school	Competence in intellectual, social, and physical skills
5 Adolescence	Identity versus confusion	Peer groups and out-groups; models of leadership	An integrated image of oneself as a unique person
6 Early adulthood	Intimacy versus isolation	Partners in friendship; sex, competition, cooperation	Ability to form close and lasting relationships; to make career commitments
7 Middle adulthood	Generativity versus self-absorption	Divided labor and shared household	Concern for family, society, and future generations
8 The aging years	Integrity versus despair	"Mankind"; "My kind"	Sense of fulfillment and satisfaction with one's life; willingness to face death

Source: Erikson (1963), modified from original. E. R. Hilgard, R. L. Atkinson, R. C. Atkinson. (1979) *Introduction to Psychology* (7th ed.) p. 95. (New York: Harcourt Brace Jovanovich). Used with permission.

tral tenets of the Freudian position are disposed to locate the critical junctures in development at other points and ascribe somewhat different significances to them. This is true even of formulations that focus exclusively on children. One of the most systematic and thoughtful accounts of personality development—and which differs in important ways from the Freudian position—is that of Sullivan. Like Freud, Sullivan developed his position mainly out of his experience with psychiatric patients. Through his close association with anthropologists and other social scientists, he placed more emphasis on the social environment than Freud had. He repudiated much of the Freudian vocabulary and developed one of his own. The *interpersonal theory* of psychiatry he formulated has found expression in an influential journal and has also been disseminated through the work of his students. Perhaps because of the great difficulty of communicating with schizophrenes, he early became concerned with the nature of communication. Sapir, who markedly influenced Sullivan's thinking on communication, was a pioneer anthropological linguist. The roles in development which Sullivan ascribes to communicative processes and the cultural milieu give his work special significance for the social scientist. Our discussion of his position will be based primarily on Sullivan's posthumously published lectures (1953).

Some Central Concepts

For Sullivan, the avoidance of severe anxiety is central to human behavior, and he argued that a *self-system* starts to develop in infancy as a protection against over anxiety. The process of *selective inattention* was mentioned in this connection. Sullivan formulated several other concepts that require elaboration before an account of his developmental stages will make much sense to the reader.

From the first moments of life, infants interact with adults—mainly with their mothers, who are concerned particularly with satisfying the infant's initial bodily needs. The mother also has needs, which in turn are met by her general activity in caring for the child. Sullivan thus says that the situation is *integrated* insofar as it is meaningful for both organisms. In adults, a mutually satisfying friendly conversation would exemplify an integrated situation. Situations may be *resolved* when the needs are met. There is then no longer any reason for continuing the immediate interaction unless new bases immediately arise. Situations *disintegrate* when they are terminated before they are resolved. Anxiety may play a large role here: it arises, for example, when one makes friendly overtures to a desirable person and is rebuffed.

According to Sullivan, there are three types of experience: the *prototaxic, parataxic,* and *syntaxic*. These terms refer to the manner in which experience is registered and to the nature and degree of inner elaboration which it is accorded. In the *prototaxic mode* there is an absolute minimum of inner elaboration, and experience consists mainly of discrete series of momentary states which can neither be recalled nor discussed. The *syntaxic mode,* in contrast, involves a maximum of inner organization and elaboration, and because it is fully encompassed by symbolic formulation and is logically ordered, it can be discussed and completely communicated to others. The *parataxic mode* of experience lies between the other two; in it, experience is partially organized or organized in a quasi-logical manner, but there are also elements of which the individual is unaware (1953, p. 29).

The child's earliest experiences are in the *prototaxic mode,* but he quickly progresses to the parataxic as soon as he begins to understand the environment and notes certain interconnections and simple sequences. Lower animals also are capable of reaching the parataxic level, according to Sullivan. The syntaxic mode begins to appear with the learning of language and is hence confined to human beings, although Sullivan takes pains to emphasize that it is rarely possible for us to express all aspects of an experience in words.

Roughly, the three modes represent the incommunicable or ineffable (prototaxic), the partially communicable (parataxic), and the wholly communicable (syntaxic). This scheme allows a considerable place for unconscious behavior without positing an "unconscious mind" or instinctual urges as the mainsprings of behavior.

Sullivan's treatment of needs is a fluid one. The infant quickly develops new needs in addition to the initial bodily ones, both through experience and maturation. Needs appear chronologically, some not until several years have passed. Thus the sexual drive—or as he terms it, the *lust dynamism*—does not arise until puberty. (Here Sullivan explicitly departs from Freud, who views the sexual drives as present from birth.) The various needs are given sophisticated treatment and are not regarded as inner forces. Apart from elementary biological needs of the infant, most of the needs with which Sullivan is concerned arise in interpersonal interaction and have nothing to do with biology. Needs are satisfied in highly complex ways through interaction. Much satisfaction, Sullivan holds, must take place through *sublimation*—that is, by indirect means. This is because the initial means adopted are met with reactions by significant others which arouse anxiety in the person.

Stages

Sullivan's designation of stages is a clue to important differences between his position and that of orthodox Freudian psychoanalysts. *Sullivan distinguished seven stages of personality development: infancy, childhood, the juvenile era, preadolescence, adolescence, late adolescence, and adulthood* (1953, pp. 33–34).

Infancy extends from birth to the appearance of speech. *Childhood* covers the period from the onset of articulate speech to the appearance of a need to have playmates. The *juvenile era* covers the period of grammar school through, as a result of maturation, the desire for an intimate relationship with a companion of the same sex. *Preadoles-*

cence ends with the display of sexual awareness and the desire for an intimate of the opposite sex. *Adolescence,* which varies from culture to culture, ends when the individual has developed some social relationship and pattern of activity which fulfills his or her lust, or desire, for sexual activity. *Late adolescence* extends the individual's attempts to form a socially acceptable pattern of intimacy and sexual behavior. At *adulthood* the person enters into a love relationship (which may or may not satisfy the person's sexual desires). During this era the person establishes a relationship with another person who is regarded as a significant other. That person becomes highly important to the individual and his concerns may take precedence over the individual's own view of her life situation.

Sullivan's account of *infancy* and *childhood* covers much of the same ground that has been covered in chapters of this text that deal with the development of language, thought, and self. He emphasizes the role of anxiety in the origin of the self-system. The Freudian concepts of the ego, id, and superego are not included, and there is no discussion of instinctual drives or the oedipus complex. In childhood, along with the gradual learning of the syntaxic use of language, children may also use language as an anxiety-reducing instrument. as when they verbally disown certain of their actions—"I didn't do that, it was my hand," or "I did it. I am sorry." Parents' demands for apologies and explanations further this use. During childhood the need for tenderness, which appeared during infancy, is manifested and elaborated in the desire for play and physical contact with others, particularly the mother. If the mother is consistently unable to respond with tenderness, children may be compelled to sublimate the need or they may give it up. Like other observers, Sullivan remarks upon the fact that children learn to deceive adults and so escape rebuff and anxiety. Sullivan is constantly concerned with inadequate means of handling issues that may be taken by the child, and notes a number of appropriate modes of concealment which may lead to trouble later. One of them is the use of *verbalisms,* or *rationalizations,* to ward off punishment.

Vicious cycles of malevolent development may start through interaction of the sort that occurs when the mother continually disparages the father and explains the child's behavior by saying he is like his father. This may establish the conviction in the child that he is detestable and unworthy and must expect always to be treated badly. This unfortunate turn of events may "very easily prevent a great deal of profit from subsequent developmental experiences. . . . There is literally a slowing down of healthy socialization" (1953, p. 217). Important to Sullivan is the idea that any developmental mishap may prevent or slow up the learning process. The arrest of development is not a static thing, for the person continues to change and develop; however, "the freedom and velocity of the constructive change are very markedly reduced" (1953, p. 218).

In *late childhood,* children become more aware of their identity as males or females and begin to adopt appropriate behavior. Their knowledge of other cultural perspectives also broadens. Like Piaget, Sullivan emphasizes the necessity—imposed by the requirements of others—for the child to begin to distinguish between reality and fantasy (autism, or autistic thought). Toward the end of this period, children have learned to sort out that which they must conceal from that which they can talk about because it will make sense to adults.

Even when malevolent or other inappropriate personality organization has developed, the transition to the next stage introduces a real possibility for correction. Sullivan is impressed by the amount of change that can occur "as one passes over one of these more-or-less determinable thresholds of a developmental era" (1953, p. 227). This means that children, to some extent, are given the choice of a fresh start, although the older they grow the more they become the heirs of their own past.

The *juvenile era* starts approximately the time the child begins school. School plays a key role in various ways. Many more "authority figures" appear on the child's horizon—teachers, playground bullies, traffic police, and other parents—and she has to learn to live with all of them. By the end of this era, authority figures—including the parents—are being compared with one another as persons. The parents are no longer regarded as the most perfect people on earth, nor are they any longer endowed with omniscience. At the beginning of the era, children typically begin to desire contact and play with other children; this sociability contrasts with the greater egocentricity of younger children. Hence, schoolchildren are open to tremendous influence from their peers. They learn that their peers have points of view, and they discover how many perspectives there are. Through interaction with their peers, some of it brutal and antagonistic, they learn a great deal about how to handle themselves without suffering unduly from anxiety. They must face the possibility of ostracism. Toward the end of the period, especially, they begin to be sensitive to their reputation—that is, their general self-conception deriving from juvenile groups. Sullivan notes that mobility of the parents may be disastrous by causing children to continue to be strangers as they go from one school to another.

The juvenile era is given tremendous weight by Sullivan as a determinant of future development. It is "the time when the world begins to be really complicated by the presence of other people" (1953, p. 232). Through rough-and-ready interaction with these new people, children's misconceptions of self are corrected, and they acquire a wider grasp of selfhood and their place in the community. If they are fortunate in their development, they emerge with an "orientation in living"—that is, an idea of how to satisfy their needs without arousing too much anxiety (1953, p. 244). This represents their first and most important socialization experience; if they have not learned this, they are in for trouble. They may, for example, use the technique of disparaging others as a protective device: This is equivalent to saying "I am not as bad as the other swine." This does not give a secure base to a sense of personal worth.

Preadolescence is ushered in by an interest in a new type of personal relationship: friendship with a person of the same sex. This is quite different from previous relationships, for it turns upon intimacy and collaboration in satisfying each other's expressed needs (1953, p. 248):

Because one draws so close to another, because one is newly capable of seeing onself through the other's eyes, the preadolescent phase . . . is especially significant in correcting autistic, fantastic ideas about oneself or others.

Participation in preadolescent gangs has a similar desirable effect. The need for chums arises both as a result of interpersonal development and of maturation. Sullivan emphasizes the great therapeutic effects of these preadolescent intimacies in saving persons from previous unfortunate courses.

However, the preadolescent period is also an era of danger because of differences in rates of development among friends. Children reach puberty at different ages; variation within the same sex may be as much as three or four years. Hence, some preadolescents lag behind the others. Some still require intimate chumship when the others no longer do, or one child may not yet need these intimate relationships when most of his or her peers do, and so later may have to establish such relations with a much younger or much older person.

The early stage of adolescence is defined "as extending from the eruption of true genital interest, felt as lust, to the patterning of sexual behavior which is the beginning of the last phase of adolescence" (1953, p. 263). Sullivan considers lust as the last of the maturation needs, drawing a sharp line between it and the need for intimacy. *The need for intimacy* starts much earlier and has an independent development. At the onset of adolescence, there is a significant change in the object of intimacy. *If there has been no very serious warp in development, the child begins to seek increasing intimacy with a member of the other sex,* the pattern of intimacy being much like that of preadolescence. In America, the fulfillment of this need faces serious obstacles, since it runs into the sex taboos. The obstacle which prevents access to intimacy leads to *reverie* and *fantasy,* and in "the gang," children may engage in discussion pertaining to it. The discussion of "who's who and what's what" in the heterosexual world is of great profit for those of the gang who are already in the adolescent stage.

In adolescence, life becomes tremendously complicated by the elaboration of potentially conflicting needs. The appearance of lust—a powerful need—adds greatly to the problems of the period. There may be collision between the requirements of lust and the maintenance of self-esteem. Genital urges may create acute self-doubt, puzzlement, embarrassment, and other unpleasant reactions. Because of the way sex is viewed in Western society, the desire for sexual activity often clashes with a sense of security in interpersonal relations. This is true in adolescence and in later life as well. Intimacy and lust requirements may also conflict with each other. A common manifestation of this conflict is the separation of persons into two mutually exclusive classes: those who can only satisfy one's lust, and those who can only satisfy the need for intimacy and friendship. The distinction between "good women" and "bad women," "sexy girls" and "good girls," conveys this idea (1953, pp. 269–70).

Thus satisfying one's lust must be at considerable expense to one's self-esteem, since the bad girls are unworthy and not really people in the sense that good girls are. . . . The trouble . . . is that lust is a part of personality, and no one can get very far at completing his personality development in this way.

The shift in the sex of the desired object of intimacy may also clash with security needs. For instance, the parents may disparage and ridicule the adolescent's interest in the opposite sex; The parents may be jealous, may not wish the child to grow up too fast, or may fear sexual accidents. The various collisions of needs may lead in this stage to homosexual play, but more usually produce autosexual behavior (masturbation).

Sullivan points out (1953, pp. 271–72) that the "number of wretched experiences connected with adolescents' first heterosexual attempts is legion, and the experiences are sometimes very expensive to further maturation of personality." They may be destructive to self-esteem and may erect permanent barriers to satisfactory heterosexual consummations.

Several unhappy long-term outcomes include the following: Some people feel pursued by the opposite sex and expend a great deal of energy trying to avoid them. Lust may be dissociated from consciousness and may be expressed only in fantasies. Lack of potency may be connected with failure to resolve the lust-intimacy problem. In some persons, the appearance of lust may be accompanied by the continuation of intimacy needs on the preadolescent level, leading to transient or persisting homosexual tendencies, with the genital drive handled in a variety of ways—homosexual reverie, homosexual relations, autoeroticism. In some persons, lust may mature, although they remain chronically juvenile. The ladies' man, and the persistent "tease," are often chronic juveniles, according to Sullivan. These people need to be envied by others of their sex, and hence often boast of their conquests.

Sullivan indicates the extreme diversity of alternatives which face the adolescent. He or she has to discover (1953, p. 297) "what he likes in the way of genital behavior and how to fit it into the rest of life. That is an achievement of no mean magnitude." The range of alternatives is demonstrated by showing that there are about 45 patterns of behavior that are "reasonably probable." Sullivan reaches this figure by setting up classifications of intimacy, kinds of objects of lust, and types of sexual activity.

Late adolescence, for Sullivan, is the period when the mode of sexual activity is decided upon. In addition, he stresses the great growth of experience in the syntaxic mode of communication. Through formal education and work experience, persons acquire greater insight into their own and others' behavior and may develop enormously in knowledge and maturity. Many adults, because of their developmental heritage, are greatly restricted in what they can learn from a potentially enlightening environment (1953, p. 306): "Large aspects of living are, as it were, taboo—one avoids them." As for truly mature persons, Sullivan confesses that psychiatrists have very little to say, since they do not meet them in their offices as patients. With the progress of patients toward maturity, the psychiatrist loses sight of them (1953, p. 310).

Evaluation

Sullivan's view has much in common with the Freudian conception. Both give considerable attention to unconscious features of behavior, and both focus attention on the dynamic interplay of personal relations. Both have a place for bodily maturation and posit a close relationship between this maturation and the development of personality. They are also alike in that they are mainly derived from clinical experience with adults rather than from a firsthand, intensive study of children. One further point of similarity is that both more or less terminate their systematic accounts of development at the threshold of adult life. The differences between the two conceptions will become apparent as we review some of the main features of Sullivan's scheme.

Sullivan's account provides an important place for needs which arise sequentially. Sex appears late—rather than early, as in Freud's account—and is not given supreme priority. Many of the important needs arise from interpersonal relations rather than biological bases.

Those needs that are of biological origin, such as the infant's need for "tenderness," quickly become transformed as they are felt and interpreted and as they enter into progressively more complex interpersonal patterns. Even what Sullivan calls "lust," with its obvious biological concomitants, is of this nature. The needs which arise in interpersonal relations, although associated with biological maturation, are essentially consequences of the development complexity of the communicative processes and the self-system. Instinct is not inevitably in conflict with society—indeed, Sullivan explicitly rejects the instinct theory and the id concept which makes humans essentially evil beings held in check by social proscriptions. The "unconscious mind" in which Freud located the instinctual impulses does not appear as such in Sullivan's theory, although he makes ample provision for the unwitting aspects of behavior.

The crucial experiences of each period are specified clearly by Sullivan and in such a form that empirical testing of his views is possible. He presented his position as a tentative one, recognizing the need for empirical validation. He acknowledged that many of these critical experiences, and even the stages themselves, might vary from culture to culture. The role of various adults as representatives of culture, rather than as unique personalities, is always recognized and often specified. Like other writers, Sullivan has emphasized the important fact that the differential rates of biological and experiential development of children may crucially affect personality development. His treatment of some of these consequences, as in his discussion of the transition to adolescence, shows great insight. Following a line of thought which has generally taken hold in recent years, he also emphasizes the uselessness and possible danger of training children before they can assimilate the training experience.

The scheme is genuinely developmental in the sense that no genetic fallacy is introduced. No stage is a repetition of a preceding one, and in each stage genuinely new behavior emerges. A tremendous possibility of change is acknowledged by Sullivan, particularly during transitions into new stages.

So-called arrests of development are not viewed by Sullivan as "fixations" or "regressions." The capacity to learn from experience is greatly reduced by such arrests, but change and development go on. This change is not conceived of as merely a new form of an old personality organization, but as a genuine, if unfortunate, innovation.

A central concept in Sullivan's system is *consensual validation,* by which he means the manner in which the meanings of symbols and the validity of ideas, including ideas of self, are confirmed in the process of communicating with others. (We have discussed this idea in numerous places in this text.) Sullivan notes that symbols do not carry meaning, but evoke it in user and listener, and that consensual validation makes symbols precise and powerful instruments in handling both people and ideas. Through his emphasis on the effects of the communication process upon the developing personality, Sullivan introduces a social dimension to the center of individuality. This is in line with his explicitly stated idea that the scientific analysis of interpersonal relations requires a *field theory* rather than an elementaristic or atomistic approach. Sullivan's main contribution has not been in the analysis of what he called the *syntaxic mode,* or public communciation, but in his more discriminating treatment of the "unconscious." He has reinterpreted the unconscious as a distortion of the communication process through such mechanisms as (1) selective inattention, (2) dissociation, (3) misinterpretation, and (4) masking processes. Cottrell and Gallagher have said (1941, pp. 23–24):

Sullivan attempts to show the influences within a given culture which channelize awareness. . . . If we accept [G.] Mead's analysis of the way in which meaning emerges from an incorporated verbal structure of rights and duties, Sullivan's work suggests an important amendment. The meaning that is borne by verbal interchange in interpersonal relations can be completely distorted by the dissociated elements which are at work to set the tone and color of the situation.

Our criticism of Sullivan's developmental scheme is based mainly on what it leaves out. The omissions can be partly attributed to Sullivan's explicit psychiatric interests and partly to the scantiness of his actual writings. The gravest omission is the lack of consideration of personality change after the initiation of adulthood. By implication, the importance of such change is suggested, but it is not discussed. The consequence of this is that such influences as the following are left out: occupational status and other adult statuses; the shifting of age memberships, including the effect of children on parents; adaptations to the approach of death; the handling of slow or abrupt changes of statuses of many kinds.

The developmental account itself, insofar as it deals with children, must be amplified, as Sullivan himself recognized. It can be extended, of course, by actual investigation of children. Cultural variation as well as variation by sex, and the general influence of social structures, must be more extensively taken into account. A wider range of psychological processes also needs to be included.

One major reservation about the account itself is justified. Sullivan makes anxiety virtually central to—actually, the basic motive of—human behavior. No one, of course, should deny its great importance. Despite his great sophistication about the ramifications of anxiety and the associated needs for security and intimacy, Sullivan's treatment of this central concept is like that of the older motivational theories. In his defense, it should be said that he was tentative about the centrality of anxiety (1953, p. 8):

In discussing the concept of anxiety, I am not attempting to give you the last word; it may, within ten years, be demonstrated that this concept is quite inadequate, and a better one will take its place.

The research on children that has been done by anthropologists and sociologists since the 1950s considerably amplifies our knowledge of cultural variations in child-rearing and child development. However, this research does not—except as it accepts and details the psychoanalytic developmental account—provide an overall systematic developmental theory; Sullivan's does.

SUMMARY

In this chapter we have surveyed recent research bearing on the process of self-development. The human infant enters the world with no self-conception. Exposure to interaction produces the socialization experiences that progressively mold and build an emerging self-conception. The self is not a part of the physical body, but is rather a set of symbolic indications that individuals make to themselves on the basis of their interpersonal experiences with others. The formulations of Cooley and Mead were reviewed and contrasted with the developmental schemes of Freud, Lacan, Erikson, and Sullivan. Of the Freudian models, Sullivan's was found to be the most satisfactory. Freud's original scheme lacked any systematic view of the self, and Erikson's formulations stressed individual crises that must be surmounted if a "healthy" personality is to form. Both Freud and Erikson heavily stressed sexual experiences, and Freud posited that the sexual drive was the major motivating force for the human organism. Sullivan's theory, on the other hand, located the origins of the self in interpersonal relationships. Thus, his views extended the statements of Cooley and Mead and presented testable hypotheses which can be subjected to empirical examination. This fact makes Sullivan's theory more attractive than either that of Freud, Erikson, or Lacan.

SUGGESTED READINGS

Erikson, E. H. (1950). *Childhood and Society*. New York: W. W. Norton & Co., Inc. Contains a treatment of the author's well-known child developmental stages and presents the research on children which led to his theoretical modification of Freud.

FREUD, S. (1938). *The Basic Writings of Sigmund Freud*, trans. and ed. with an introduction by A. A. Brill. New York: Random House. Contains all the basic elements of Freud's theory, including *Psychopathology of Everyday Life, Totem and Taboo*, and *The Interpretation of Dreams*.

LACAN, J. (1977). *Écrits: A Selection*. New York: W. W. Norton & Co., Inc. This book contains a number of important essays detailing Lacan's departure from Freud. It also contains his essay on the "mirror stage."

MEAD, G. H. (1934). *Mind, Self, and Society*. Chicago: University of Chicago Press. Contains Mead's most important essays on the emergence of self out of interaction.

SULLIVAN, H. S. (1953). *The Interpersonal Theory of Psychiatry*. New York: W. W. Norton & Co., Inc. This book presents the most comprehensive picture of Sullivan's developmental theory. Students are encouraged to explore these readings by Erikson, Mead, and Sullivan and to draw their own conclusions concerning which theory is most viable for an understanding of the emergence of self in childhood and adolescence.

CHAPTER NINE
The Social Worlds of Childhood

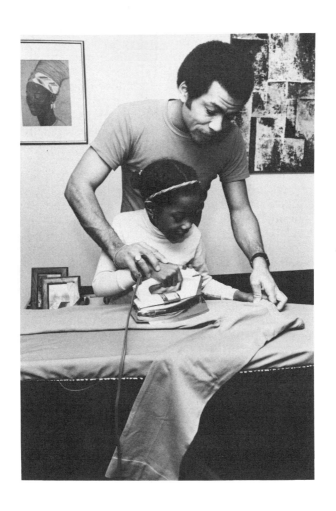

A major consequence of children's linguistic socialization is that they become involved in increasingly larger systems of social relationships. The acquisition of the verbal and nonverbal languages that make up the family speech community permit children to become more adept participants in complex social situations. As they become increasingly more self-reflexive, they are able to stand outside their own behavior and view it from the stances of others; they begin to move from the *play* stage of social awareness to the *game* and *generalized other* modes of social interaction. In this chapter we examine the complex social worlds that make up childhood. Social worlds consist of groupings of persons bound together by networks of communication and common understandings. Often widely distributed in geographical space, members of the same social world share similar views of reality. The social worlds of childhood embed children in common interactive experiences with significant others. Like members of other social worlds, children come to develop their own patterned ways of thinking and acting. In examining these patterns, we shall employ a developmental, or sequential, model of analysis to lay bare the underlying processes that make the child a more competent interactant. One of the more popular theories which has gained increasing interest in recent years is that of the Swiss psychologist, Jean Piaget. While we have drawn upon his work in earlier chapters, we shall depart from his specific developmental scheme and offer a set of criticisms of his perspective. In the last section we discuss sex role socialization.

THE CHILD'S EGOCENTRISM

In a series of books, Piaget (1937, 1948, 1951a, 1951b, 1952a, 1952b, 1952c, 1959, 1960, 1969) has documented what he has called the *egocentric* character of childish thought. The entire intellectual development of children—from the time at which they can speak with relative adequacy to the point at which they

acquire an approximately adult view of themselves and the world—is described as a gradual process of overcoming this initial egocentric tendency. It is unfortunate that Piaget selected the term *egocentric* to describe the child's early thought patterns, for it implies that such thought is not social in nature and origin—although it decidedly is. James F. Markey, in his long-ignored work *The Symbolic Process and Its Integration in Children*, suggested that Piaget's "encumbrance with the psychoanalyst's conception of . . . autistic . . . thought . . . permits him to ignore its essential aspects" (1928, p. 152).

Children are at first enclosed in their own point of view and see all things from within it. They are, as Markey noted, the centers of that universe. Their perceptions and judgments tend to be absolute or egocentric, because they are unaware of any other points of view and perceptions. Thus, Piaget points out that most young children of five or so believe quite firmly that the sun and moon follow them as they walk about. At this age, children are not troubled by the logical difficulties that would confront adults. They do not attempt to account for the many sudden changes in direction of the movement of moon and sun, or to account for the way in which these bodies may appear to other people who are moving in various other directions. Their conviction arises from their own perception of movement. Because perspectives other than their own are not taken into account, children's own perceptions appear absolute—the only possible ones.

Another example is furnished by the child's difficulty in properly using such terms as "brother" and "sister." Thus, John and Paul are brothers aged 4 and 5, respectively. If we ask Paul how many brothers he has, he may say "One," or "Two, counting me." If he has decided that he is not his own brother, and is asked how many brothers his brother John has, he usually denies that John has any. By questioning Paul, we may sometimes induce him to say that there are either one, two, or three brothers in his family.

Paul's confusion over the significance of the term "brother" arises because the word refers to different persons when he and John use it. Paul is fairly clear about the fact that John is his brother. But because he views the situation absolutely rather than relatively, he becomes confused when required to take any point of view other than his own. He cannot view the family of which he is a part from John's standpoint.

The following is another illustration of the young child's egocentricity (1937, p. 32):

What will happen when it is a question of imagining distant objects, and of coordinating the perspectives of different observers? . . . The child is placed opposite a small model of three mountains, and given a certain number of colored pictures of these mountains; he is then asked which of the pictures show the mountains from the positions occupied successively by a doll on the mountains in the model. The function of age in this development of these reactions is very clear. The little ones do not understand that the observer sees the same mountains quite differently from different points of view, and hence they consider their own perspective absolute. But the older ones discover the relativity necessary to objectivity after a number of systematic errors due to the difficulty of coordinating the relationships in question.

The egocentrism of young children is also reflected in their play activities. Parten (1932, p. 263) has asserted that "since the young children lack the power of expressing themselves with language, they have difficulty in playing in cooperative groups." Young children playing in the sandpile usually do not play *together*, although they are fond of playing in company; older children, however, are likely to play together cooperatively. Another investigator, Bridges (1931, p. 72), has noted that "two-year-olds usually play or work by themselves with little reference to others except to claim their toys or otherwise interfere with them. . . . Older children engage more often in group play than younger ones and seldom play alone." These and other investigators have asserted that as children grow older they learn to play

cooperatively; and that in the earlier years, although children may like to play in the presence of others, they do not in a genuine sense play *with* them. Because children do not at first grasp the roles of others, and because they lack an adequate time perspective, they tend to act in terms of short-range egocentric goals. Their ideas of fair play and of the "rules" are inadequate or absolute (see Corsaro, 1981; Selman, 1981).

A CRITIQUE OF THE EGOCENTRIC PERSPECTIVE

Vygotsky has remarked that psychology owes Piaget a great debt, for he revolutionized the study of children. Vygotsky observes (1962, p. 9):

Like many other great discoveries, Piaget's idea is simple to the point of seeming self-evident. It had already been expressed in the words of Rousseau, which Piaget himself quoted, that the child is not a miniature adult and his mind not the mind of an adult on a small scale.

Piaget assumes that the child is unlike the adult, and this difference sets the tone for early egocentric thought. It is on this point (and others to be elaborated below) that we part company with Piaget. As we have argued earlier, there is ordinarily little—if anything—intrinsic to the human organism which upon birth will make it more or less responsive to the symbolic environment to which it is exposed. In short, we argue for a model of social development that begins from ongoing social worlds of experience, not from traits and attributes that the infant brings into the world at birth.

This point warrants elaboration. Piaget isolates three modes of thought: *autistic, egocentric,* and *rational.* As Vygotsky (1962, p. 13) notes, Piaget's conception of development is psychoanalytic in origin, for it assumes the child is initially autistic and will change to rational thought only after a long and arduous process of socialization. Furthermore, Piaget repeatedly implies or asserts that autism and egocentrism are tied to the child's psychic nature and are impervious to social experience. He asserts that until age 7 or 8, real social life does not exist among children. They engage in open monologue conversations; they are incapable of placing themselves in the perspective of others; they are essentially self-centered and egocentric in nature.

We reject the two assumptions underlying this formulation. First, there is nothing intrinsic to age that makes a 7- or 8-year-old child more or less egocentric. Second, the degree of egocentric thought present in the child's behavior repertoire will be a direct function of the complexity of his social environment. Consequently, thought and its complexity are *not* a function of organic and psychic factors but are inextricably bound up in the world of social experience. In short, thought is a product of social interaction. To argue otherwise, as Piaget does, is to construct a psychologistic, not a sociological model of thought and development. Piaget assumes, then, that thought moves from inner, autistic experiences to outer, sociocentric utterances which are mediated by a lengthy period of egocentric thought. As outlined in Chapter 7, in our discussion of the Chomsky formulations, our model of linguistic development assumes that thought follows vocal utterances, that initial utterances are global and nonspecific in nature, and that thought and speech progressively merge into one.

We wish to make two more points concerning egocentric speech. First, we concur with Vygotsky that egocentric speech quickly joins with inner thought. Furthermore, egocentric, or self-centered, speech and thought always involve the utilization of a social perspective. The dialogue between the "I" and the "me" is a social process. Egocentrism, or the primacy of the "I" over the "me," is always a matter of degree and is not as clearcut as Piaget's work would imply. But more importantly, the presence of egocentric speech in the young child can be taken as

evidence that the self as a distinct object is starting to emerge in the child's thought patterns; this is Markey's point also. The presence of pronouns in the 3-year-old child's vocabulary is unequivocal proof that a linguistic conception of self as actor is forming. In this sense we wish to reverse the usual meanings of egocentric and argue that (1) all individuals are egocentric from someone else's perspective, and (2) young children who think and talk egocentrically are in essence separating themselves from others, however unsuccessfully, and in that process are making distinct objects of themselves.

The following excerpts from one of the authors' studies (Denzin, 1972, pp. 299–300) in a preschool underscore this position.

Two girls are standing below the large doll house inside the preschool.

FIRST GIRL: They're people up there. (Points to three girls playing upstairs.)

SECOND GIRL: Shall we go up there?

FIRST GIRL: No, they'll say "you can't come up here."

A three-year-old girl has just finished working at the painting table. She gets up and goes across the room to get a book. An instructor confronts her:

INSTRUCTOR: Are you through painting? Don't you want to hang up your painting?

GIRL: No, I don't want to!

INSTRUCTOR: Don't you really?

GIRL: No. (Shakes her head and walks off.)

INSTRUCTOR: I'll do it for you. (Grimaces.)

These examples reveal that young children, at least in preschools, use personal and impersonal pronouns with ease, and in direct reference to ongoing activity systems. There are few elements of egocentric thought in either episode. The examples also suggest that the children were capable of placing themselves in one another's perspective and formulating lines of action on the basis of that role-taking process.

It would be expected that the more familiar the situation to the children, the more reflexive and accurate they would be in separating themselves from the selves of other individuals. In those worlds that children control—sectors of preschools, their own bedrooms, and playrooms—greater levels of reflexivity will be observed. The argument to this point can be quickly summarized. *The child actor is a sophisticated interactant. Many theories of child development gloss over children's interactional skills by either studying them in unfamiliar test-taking situations, or focusing on solitary individuals without attempting to catch them in moments of serious play.* Too many students of early child development, as Markey observed in 1928, have failed to check their findings out in nonlaboratory settings; this situation has not changed significantly since 1928. Piaget's view of the egocentric child may hold for those children he observed in his institute, but our position is that if left to their own devices, and if exposed to a sufficiently rich and complex interactional environment, three- and four-year-old children will act in ways that are essentially adultlike. Perhaps the point can be underlined with one more field observation done by one author of this book. A very alert 4½-year-old child was observed making quite adultlike remarks in which she made clear distinctions of "mine" and "mummy's." A few minutes later, watching her mother turn the pages of a book of art reproductions, she "dropped" to the level of pointing at objects and naming them ("tiger," "mother," "baby"). Later in the afternoon, she tried to explain to the author that her mother and she had looked for his parked car—where they thought he would be but was not—and did it not have something blue in it (a coat)? And several minutes later, when the author said, "Let's go get your parents," she objected that they were not her parents, but her "mummy and daddy"—denying that she knew what "parents" meant! Interviewed à la Piaget about what was a "mummy" and a "daddy," and how did they get to be that (and was the author without children a dad-

dy?), her thought processes perfectly fitted Piaget's descriptions of children of that age. They gained that status by passing the age of seven—which she counted up to—and becoming grown-up, then became "daddy" or "mummy."

THE CHILD'S NETWORK OF SIGNIFICANT OTHERS

Infants, as Mead and Cooley observed, are born into an ongoing network of interconnected social worlds which are filled with individuals who will later become their *significant others*. That is, these people will stand in some position of influence and authority over the children, and they will come to view those people as influential in organizing their own behavior.

Six categories of significant others can be identified. The child is likely to confront and interact with his various significant others at predictable times and in predictable places. The first class of significant others are those termed *sociolegal*, and they are the child's parents or guardians, his siblings, and other members of the kinship system. The second class of significant others are *socio-others*, drawn from the sociability network that surrounds the primary group of the family. These individuals assume fictional "kinship" in the family and may be called "aunts" and "uncles"; babysitters also fall in this category. Third are the *coequal*, or *compeer*, significant others. These may include siblings, but more importantly, playmates and children in the neighborhood and at school who come to assume a high degree of socializing influence over the child. By age 3 or 4, compeers may rival parents and other sociolegal significant others in their influence over the child. Certainly by the first grade, and by age 7 or 8, he may have moved nearly entirely into a peer-oriented world of social control.

The fourth class of significant others are *child care experts*. These persons have attained some legitimate authority over child care and child evaluation. Pediatricians, child psychologists, child care workers, psychiatrists, teachers, lawyers, politicians, and social workers dictate and shape the broader process by which a society produces its children. A fifth class of child caretakers and significant others is drawn from the mass media: *Media others* enter the child's world through television, radio, record players, movies, storybooks, and nursery rhymes. These others may view themselves as experts on childhood; but more importantly, they staff and populate the child's world of fantasy and entertainment. Captain Kangaroo, Mr. Rogers, and Big Bird and Cookie Monster on "Sesame Street" represent such fictive and real others who daily enter the child's world of interaction. Media others may have more contact with the child than do any of the aforementioned classes of individuals. A typical American television station, for example, programs up to 7 hours of children's television six days a week. Surveys suggest that "the television in an average household is turned on for about seven hours every day" (Messner, 1986, p. 218), and recent research (Denzin, 1977) indicates that four- to six-year-olds may watch up to four hours of television a day. This exceeds the interactive experiences they may have with one or both of their parents.

The last major class of significant others comes from the world of public places. *Public place others* include police officers, firefighters, mail carriers, clerks and strangers in stores, and individuals normally met by the children or their caretakers when in the public arena. These others fall into a residual category, and their influence on the child is likely to be specific to particular situations or services. These six categories of significant others constitute what may be termed the child's interactive world. The two most important categories of significant others will be drawn from the sociolegal and compeer sectors of the child's social world. These persons make up the child's primary group, and they provide the sources of self-worth and self-awareness that the child first experiences. They are, as Kuhn argued, *orientational*

significant others. They shape conceptions of self, provide vocabularies of motive, furnish symbolic environments, and promote a sense of "we-ness" and solidarity. Depending on the stances that these others take toward the children, their rate of social development and their lingerings within the egocentric mode of thought will be hastened or retarded. We turn to the decline in egocentrism in early childhood.

The Decline of Egocentrism

As a consequence of entering into more extensive and complex social relations, children become increasingly and more systematically aware of the points of view of other persons. They learn that these are often at variance with their own and that they must be taken into account. The young boy learns that though he has a brother, his brother also has a brother (himself); that a pebble is light in weight from one point of view but heavy from another point of view; that an object may be to the left of one object but at the same time to the right of another. Children's thinking becomes increasingly relativistic. They come to realize that the sun follows neither them nor anyone else; they learn to conceive of it as the center of a solar system and think of the earth as one of several spherical bodies revolving about the sun. When they have achieved this mature point of view, they have, in a sense, synthesized virtually all conceivable views of the sun as a physical object and can assume the perspective of anyone in any location with respect to it. The age of transition, learning to grasp other points of view—learning to become nonegocentric—is placed by Piaget at approximately seven, but some English and American investigators have challenged this. In accordance with our own position, as stated earlier, presumably the age of transition besides being different in different individuals also varies from society to society, from social world to social world. Presumably a young child might remain relatively egocentric in some respects and achieve somewhat greater social awareness in others. The important point is not the exact age at which egocentricity disappears, but that the disappearance is gradual. Of equal importance is children's *interactional age,* which is the amount of time they have spent in exposure to a given social experience. *Chronological age,* as such, is often superseded by interactional age. Hence, rates of cognitive development cannot be predicted simply on the basis of how old a child is.

Mead has described graphically how children playfully imitate the roles of elders or associates, thus gradually developing an ability to see objects, other persons, and themselves from a nonegocentric standpoint. Mead emphasizes what Piaget merely noted in passing—namely, that language is basic in the development of the ability to play roles (1934, pp. 150–51, 364–65):

[There are] countless forms of play in which the child assumes the roles of the adults about him. . . . In the play of young children, even when they play together, there is abundant evidence of the child's taking different roles in the process; and a solitary child will keep up the process of stimulating himself by his vocal gestures [spoken words] to act in different roles almost indefinitely. . . . A child plays at being a mother, at being a teacher, at being a policeman; that is, it is taking different roles. . . . He has a set of stimuli which call out in himself the sort of responses they call out in others. He takes this group of responses and organizes them into a certain whole.

The children's playing at being people other than themselves is paralleled in actual life in their interactions with parents and playmates. One theory of play is that it is a preparation for later adult activity wherein individuals apply the skills they have acquired (Denzin, 1977). Thus the standards of fair play and the proper attitude toward defeat in competition are often said to be learned on the gridiron or on the "playing fields of Eton." No doubt it is from considerations of this kind that the widespread absorption of children (and adults) in comic strips and comic books concerns and alarms

some who feel that constant identifications with comic-strip characters of doubtful virtue may lead the children to emulate these fictional "heroes." Without accepting this position, one may recognize that this kind of play activity and fantasizing gives the child a repertoire of roles and practice in switching from one to the other.

The initial role taking of young children (placing themselves in the perspectives of another person) is simple and limited, involving only limited and brief fragments of behavior and the imitation of a few specific persons. As the child's circle of acquaintanceship is enlarged, as her mastery of communication develops, and as her real roles multiply in number and become more complex, the role-taking processes become more complicated (Opie & Opie, 1969; Selman, 1981).

PERSPECTIVES AND THE GENERALIZED OTHER

When children have developed the ability to grasp the role or attitude of one other person at a time, they are on the road to becoming social beings. However, before they can participate in organized adult activity, children must be able to systematically conceive their own role from the standpoint of all other participants.

An illustration will clarify this: Suppose that a group of Air Force men are on a bombing mission. Each man has a definite, assigned general role that involves certain duties and obligations. Each man has a clear conception of his general role, as he imagines it from the points of view of all the others. He also has a clear picture of how his own role fits in with the role of each of the other men.

Mead asserts, by contrast, that the very young child is able to take the role of only one other person at a time. From this simple kind of role taking, the child eventually develops the ability (1) to take the roles of others in the situation, (2) to organize these roles into an integrated whole, and (3) to view his or her own behavior from this standpoint. Mead's suggestion of how this learning takes place is as follows (1934, pp. 151–52, 154):

If we contrast play with . . . an organized game, we note the essential difference that the child who plays in a game must be ready to take the attitude of everyone else involved in that game, and that these different roles must have a definite relationship to each other. . . . In a game where a number of individuals are involved . . . they do not all have to be present in [his] consciousness at the same time, but at some moments he has to have three or four individuals present in his own attitude.

Through their participation in organized games, play, and other activities, children learn to take the role of the participants and grasp the fact that the roles of others are intertwined. At the same time, they begin to see how their own activity within the situation looks from the standpoint of the others. They see their own actions as part of a whole pattern of group activity.

Mead has coined a term for this organization of the roles of others; he calls it the *generalized other*. He used this expression because it means that one is taking the related roles of all the other participants rather than the role

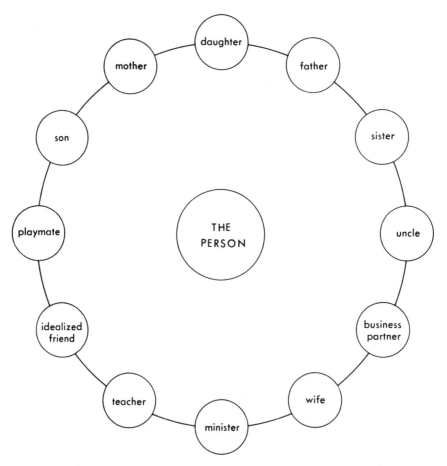

Persons learn to look upon their own behavior from the points of view of all these people. They learn the various points of view at different periods of their life, and these points of view have varying importance for the organization of their behavior.

of just one other person. This concept of the generalized other applies to the organized roles of participants within any defined situation.

The term *generalized other* does not refer to an actual group of people, but rather to a conception or an interpretation that persons derive from their experiences. They then regulate their behavior in terms of these supposed opinions and attitudes of others. They stand outside their own behavior and view it from the perspective of these others. They imagine what people would say "if they knew" or what they will say "when they know." The term "people" may not have any specific reference to actual persons, but may merely represent the child's conception of abstract moral standards. These standards widen as role playing becomes more generalized. Internal "I"-"me" conversations become increasingly more complex.

We disagree with Mead's view on one important point. If one observes them closely, young children will take the role of multiple others (mother and father, for example) quite nicely in some situations but regress in other situations to Mead's "able to take only one person at a time." Some children take the role of multiple others quite easily. Mead's points about their increasing ability to do that, along with the general direction of their development, seem accurate enough.

As children's conceptualizing ability approaches the adult standard, their concepts become more numerous, and the interrelationships of those concepts become more complex. Children's ability to play roles and to be different persons, and to understand the actions and motives of others developed in a parallel course.

The earlier role conceptions of children are, from the adults' viewpoint, rather curious and often amusing, although in their own way they represent a primitive if incorrect systematization of how roles (behavioral expectations) vary for different individuals. Thus, very young children know there are storekeepers and customers, but they think that the customer buys goods and both customer and storekeeper pay each other. Only

the customer buys goods; the storekeeper never does. Monetary activity is confined to buying and selling. Although one storekeeper may help another sell, the distinction between owner and employer is unclear and is not involved in the buying-selling transactions. There are no other roles such as that of manufacturer (Strauss, 1952, p. 278).

The work of Hartley and his associates (1948) shows that the young child is unable to organize certain perspectives properly. Thus, a young child can conceive of a mother only from one perspective, and deny that mothers can play other roles (that of a salesperson, for example). Older children widen the positions from which role players are viewed until they are able to conceive of any individual as momentarily or permanently playing one role but potentially capable of playing many others. The inflexibility of the very young child who (like Gertrude Stein) may insist that a mother is a mother is a mother, represents an inability to slide in imagination from perspective to perspective or to organize perspectives into a more inclusive whole.

Hartley's discussion is deficient in that it does not bring out the fact that the young child who cannot conceive of the mother as a salesperson nevertheless can conceive of her as a daughter or her grandmother. Children can do this because in their immature systematization of role concepts, certain roles seem compatible with each other while others do not.

At one step of concept development, children will deny that two roles are compatible; later, having grasped their relationship, they will agree that they go together. Thus, a child at a young age will deny that a teacher can be a storekeeper or vice versa, because each belongs to a different world. Later the child agrees that a teacher could be a storekeeper "after school," but still denies that a storekeeper can be a customer. Still later he sees that a storekeeper can buy in a store and still in a general sense be a storekeeper. He does not yet perceive that the storekeeper must be a customer of manufacturers.

Much of children's early learning about

role relationships occurs in concrete situations in which the roles are played out before their eyes. However, most role relationships are rather abstract. Even those relationships that seem most concrete and visible—for example, those between a teacher and a pupil—involve much more than is visible on the surface. Greater maturity and breadth of experience are necessary before the child can be expected to understand the subtler aspects of such relationships.

The Generalized Other and Moral Behavior

That generalized others are learned conceptions has two important implications: (1) children do not acquire moral views automatically or mechanically, and (2) even persons belonging to the same groups cannot have identical generalized others. Children are rewarded, punished, and exhorted so that they will conform to adult expectations. However, every parent knows that learning is not a rubber-stamp process and that one cannot mechanically or forcibly inculcate adult ideas into a child.

The concept of the generalized other has been mildly criticized by Mills (1939, p. 672) on the grounds that it implies too great homogeneity and does not account for the multiplicity and heterogeneity of modern societies. It is argued that the generalized other of a given person is always relative to particular groups and persons, and that not all participants in a given social act have equal influence. A person is said to build up her moral and intellectual standards only in terms of significant other persons rather than all others in the situation. There is obvious truth in this. The standards of the criminal, for example, do not enter into the generalized other of the law-abiding citizen except to reinforce them by negative example. Even significant others are significant in different ways and to different degrees. A student's intellectual orientation may be described in a gross way by relating it to a specific university, specific subject, and specific department. Closer scrutiny may reveal, however, that really decisive influence has been exercised by certain professors, or perhaps by one professor. The same can be said of moral standards, which are perhaps most usually acquired from parents. The mother's and father's influences upon the child may be very different, and in some cases, neither of them may exercise the dominant influence—that is, the child may acquire moral conceptions from peers, a well-liked teacher, or someone else. (See the discussion of child development as conceived by Freud and Sullivan in Chapter 8.)

Social Structure, Membership, and Self-Conception

As children become adults, self-conceptions undergo a variety of patterned types of changes and become increasingly anchored in the groups and broader societal structure in which they participate. Kuhn (1960, p. 40) has developed this point in a study in which people of various ages were asked to make twenty statements in answer to the question, "Who am I?" It was noted that children's answers to the question tended to scatter over a wide range of focused on particular, individualistic, or idiosyncratic aspects of their lives. With increasing age, the conceptions of personal identity funneled into the kinds of broad social categories that also are employed to describe the social structure. Adults identified themselves more often by occupation, class, marital status, sex, age, race, religion, and other similar criteria. Thus, when a very young child who has lost his parents in a crowd is asked who he is, he may be able to supply his first name and a variety of irrelevant information that does not give much help to those who are trying to return him to his parents.

Two examples from Kuhn's study underline the point. A fourth-grade girl replying to the question, "Who am I," wrote a series of negative statements about her behavior, obviously reflecting parental discipline and admonition: "I boss too much. I get mad at my sisters. I am a show off. I interrupt too much. I waste time. Sometimes I am a bad sport. I fiddle around. I am careless at times. I forget."

In contrast, the response of a university senior included the following items among others: "I am of the female sex. My age is 20. I am from (city and state). I have two parents. My home is happy. I am happy. I am of the middle class. I am a (sorority name). I am in the Waves Officer School. I am an adjusted person. I am a (department major). I attend church." It is apparent that the latter series tells us much about the person's position in society, whereas the former tells us about almost nothing except the parental discipline imposed upon a fourth-grade child.

As children are processed through the educational system and drop out of it at various stages to assume adult responsibilities, they are distributed in a variety of jobs, places, and positions. This process of distribution is complex but not haphazard; it is regulated in a general way with respect to occupation by the number of job opportunities existing in each field and by price mechanisms that offer differential economic rewards for different occupations in rough proportion to the balance of supply and demand.

In order for a job, rank, office, or any other status to exert a pervasive and decisive influence upon a person, it must become linked with her self-conception and with the networks of social relationships that make up her social worlds. At the heart of this linking of self-regard and social position is a fateful commitment to doing well as "that kind of person." A civilian soldier is not insulted by being told that he is not a soldier, but a professional military man is. The latter's behavior is largely oriented around his being a soldier. It is therefore a matter of some importance to him to believe that he is a good one, in a good army, preferably one of the "best soldiers in the best damned army in the world."

We say that a person's commitment to central statuses—those roles that are important to him as a person—is fateful because failure to uphold the standards will be read by the individual as failure and will cause him to feel guilty or ashamed, lose self-respect, and make efforts at redemption. When conception of self is based on a simple central status, all other statuses tend to become subordinate to this one and to be judged by reference to it. To continue the example of the professional military man, he will tend to judge many nonmilitary phases of his life in terms of the bearing they have or are likely to have upon his military career. The higher his status, the greater will be the demands of his profession on him for more total commitment, and the greater will be the probability that this commitment will eclipse or take precedence over any others. In discussing morale, we have already seen that certain social organizations demand almost total devotion and allegiance of members, even to the exclusion of familial and other roles that may cut athwart the group purposes. Even family roles may become impossible to maintain, or may become subordinate to and subtly colored by more essential loyalties.

Morality and Objectivity

In an interesting study, Lerner (1937, p. 546) asked children between the ages of eight and twelve the following question: "Is it worse to tell a lie to your father or to your mother?" Typical reasons given for naming the father were "because he can punish harder" and "because you can't get away with it with him." Those who thought it worse to lie to one's mother reasoned in such terms as "she is sweeter" and "she is the best friend you have."

Murphy, Murphy, and Newcomb, in commenting upon Lerner's study, remark that (1937, p. 546)

Moral judgments . . . are clearly *not* simply assimilated readymade from the preceding generation, but are reworked in terms of the child's needs and degrees of identification with, and respect for, other individuals. . . . Many moral judgments of children are in violent conflict with those of their parents and, indeed, of the whole social world around them, if a line of conduct close to their own needs is involved. The parent who has tried to teach the small child that caterpillars, bugs, spiders, and other "pests" must all be exterminated knows that even when the whole world backs him up the child may protest that the destruction of some tiny animal friend is wrong, and that in fairy stories, despite the universal condemnation of the wolf or the tiger, the child may alarm the parent by wholeheartedly assuming the wolf's point of view. Thus Boeck found a dependable stimulus for protest or tears to lie in the destruction of the wolf at the end of the Red Riding Hood story. . . . The moral responses . . . depend not only on the world of culture, but on the individual's own needs.

The needs to which these authors refer are not simply biological ones, but the outgrowths of social experience. It should be evident that just as the needs of any two children are not identical, so their moral experiences cannot be the same.

Studies of the development of children's moral ideas and judgments demonstrate that the child moves from predominantly egocentric to increasingly relativistic moral standards. Piaget (1948) has analyzed this aspect of childhood. In his study of lower-class children of Geneva, Switzerland, he discerned a series of transformations in their moral conceptions. The young Genevan up to four or five years of age is characterized by "moral realism." Right is right and wrong is wrong: if a person does wrong, he or she should be punished regardless of motives. Later the child realizes that moral rules are not objectively real but reflect group values—a realization based upon the recognition of multiple perspectives. Geneva children remain at this stage until nine or ten, when a third level is reached at which the rules are allowed to be altered by considerations of equity; for example, a lame boy may be given a head start in a race. Piaget believes he has demonstrated that the child's conception of moral rules changes from the belief that rules are absolute to the knowledge that they are agreed upon. Other studies of children support Piaget's conclusions (Lerner, 1937; Strauss, 1954).

Studies like those made by Macaulay and Watkins (1937, p. 650) also point to the gradual growth of wider moral meanings. Children were asked to make a list of the most wicked things they could think of. Their answers showed that up to nine years old, children's moral conceptions are rather definite and concrete and are formulated in terms of their own personal relations. After this age, moral conceptions appeared to grow more generalized. Stealing and fighting in general were beginning to be regarded as wrong at age nine. From eleven years, conceptions began to show the influence of conventional adult notions of sin, although only the children in late adolescence wrote of such sins of the spirit as hypocrisy and selfishness. As Murphy, Murphy, and Newcomb have noted about the elementary-grade child: "Abstract conceptions of justice and 'fairness' are not yet very clear. 'Ideals' and general rules of the institution have little weight."

Piaget's specific explanation for the direction of moral development is dubious. He hypothesized that the early conceptions of moral rules are absolutistic because of the authoritarian relations that exist between parent and child; and that conceptions grow more relativistic, general, and systematic as cooperative relationships spring up between the child and others, particularly her peers. Neither does it seem adequate to explain the growth of moral conceptions merely as a consequence of reward and punishment or of learning from specific direct experiences "to recognize a common element in a variety of situations" (Erikson, 1950, p. 438). Conceptions of roles and of rules grow side by side. Built into role conceptions are the justifications and canons appropriate to the roles. When children are young, their moral standards lack relativity and generality because they cannot grasp the fuller meaning of acts as seen from wider perspectives. It is therefore worthwhile to distinguish between the full and general comprehension of moral values and the learning of a specific rule.

These remarks are supported by some imaginative research reported by Lawrence Kohlberg, a psychologist who has been stimulated by both Piaget and Mead (1966, 1963a, 1963b, 1969, 1971, 1976). To children varying in age from seven to seventeen, Kohlberg (Brown, 1965; Kohlberg, 1966) posed stories that embodied moral dilemmas. For instance:

In Europe, a woman was near death from a special kind of cancer. There was one drug that the doctors thought might save her. It was a form of radium that a druggist in the same town had recently discovered. The drug was expensive to make, but the druggist was charging ten times what the drug cost him to make. He paid $200 for the radium and charged $2000 for a small dose of the drug. The sick woman's husband, Heinz, went to everyone he knew to borrow the money, but he could only get together about $1000, which is half of what it cost. He told the druggist that his wife was dying, and asked him to sell it cheaper or let him pay later. But the druggist said, "No, I discovered the drug and I'm going to make money from it." So Heinz got desperate and broke into the man's store to steal the drug for his wife. Should the husband have done that? Why?

Such dilemmas can be resolved by subordinating a rule of law or authority to a higher principle. Kohlberg's results concerning moral judgment are much more complex than Piaget's; he found six stages of development and distinguished thirty aspects of morality. His evidence does not support Piaget's conclusions about the origins of absolutism (authoritarian relations) or the sources of relativism (peer group cooperation). Kohlberg studied children as old as 17, and found that developmental stages continue through the entire age range. In the sixth stage, children judge their conduct in accordance with their own internal standards, doing right to satisfy their own conscience. Although an operating conscience exists earlier, only considerably later do children explain conduct to themselves in terms of their conscience.

Roger Brown comments on Kohlberg's findings, comments with which we agree. He remarks that to speak a language the speaker must have a system of general rules, and so also must a person in order to act morally. But parents "do not provide lessons in what to do if your wife needs a medicine you cannot afford or in how to resolve the conflicts that may arise in a bombing raid. We have no rote answers to Kohlberg's dilemmas" (Brown, 1965, p. 407). Such dilemmas can only be resolved by reference to general rules. Brown's comments are in accord with our previous contention that it is worthwhile to distinguish between learning specific rules and comprehending general moral values.

Criticisms of Kohlberg: The Case of Gender

A number of authors have criticized Kohlberg's formulations of moral judgment. Lever (1978), whom we cited in Chapter 8, found that gender differences operate in the games that boys and girls play. Boys are fascinated with the legal aspect of the rules that apply to their games, while girls are more pragmatic and tolerant of exceptions to the rule. While Lever does not elaborate the implications of her work for all of Kohlberg's theory, she does suggest that the interactional contexts for the learning of morality differ for males and females.

Gilligan (1982, p. 10) suggests that Lever's work is colored by a bias which judges moral development in terms of a male model. She quotes Virginia Woolf (1929, p. 76), who stated, "It is obvious that the values of women differ very often from the values which have been made by the other sex . . . yet it is the masculine values that prevail." Gilligan contends that the traits contained in Kohlberg's moral development scale mark women deficient because they reflect a male view of morality, judgment, and responsibility. She states (Gilligan, 1981, p. 18):

the very traits that traditionally have defined the "goodness" of women, their care for and sensitivity to the needs of others, are those that marked them as deficient in moral development.

Kohlberg's conception of moral development is derived from the study of men's lives, not women's. Women, Gilligan argues, define and judge themselves in terms of such moral values as care, responsibility, helping, and nurturing. Men, on the other hand, emphasize individuality, achievement, legal rights, instrumentality, and control. These two moral domains are often in conflict in male-female relationships, and they continue the gender stratification system in our society. Clearly, any model of moral development that stresses the male over the female model is deficient. It is apparent, however, that these two models clash in the social worlds of childhood (Damon, 1977; Thorne & Luria, 1986).

THE SOCIALIZING OF EMOTIONALITY*

Emotions play a central role in childhood socialization, for it is through their emotions that children come to understand themselves, others, and situations.

The socializing of emotionality means the process by which socially constructed meanings for emotions vis-à-vis situations are passed on to the members of a social group (in this case, children), and the ways these persons interpret and construct meanings into self-feeling such that they can share their emotions with each other interactionally. Children are born into a social and emotional world and quickly learn to order, interpret, and understand their experiences, including their emotional experiences. In learning about emotions, they must learn when and where they "should" experience, and how they "should" express various emotions. They must learn to manage their emotions in the interactional arena (Hochschild, 1979, 1983).

Central to emotion management is a knowledge of feeling rules and the ability to do emotion work. According to Hochschild, feeling rules are "guidelines for the assessment of fits and misfits between feelings and situation" (1976, p. 566), and emotion work

is "the act of trying to change in degree or quality an emotion or feeling" (1979, p. 561). Feeling rules tell us how we should feel in a particular situation, and emotion work enables us to change our emotions so that they will fit the situation's social expectations. Hochschild also maintains that "feeling rules are the what guide emotion work by establishing the sense of entitlement or obligation that governs emotional exchanges" (1983, p. 74).

The socializing of emotionality occurs through interactions with *emotional associates*, using *emotional talk*, in *emotional situations*. These three components, which provide the basic structure of emotionality in early childhood, will be developed next.

Emotional Associates. Emotional associates are those persons who, both directly and indirectly, share in an emotional experience (Denzin, 1984, pp. 92–93). In the socializing of emotionality in early childhood, caregivers facilitate a child's understanding of emotions in several ways. Lewis and Michalson (1983) contend that parents overestimate their children's emotional development. They note, ". . . to teach children . . . the socializing agent must 'preview' such capacities in order to promote the children's acquisition of them. Previewing may involve attributing skills and capacities to infants before they actually exist" (p. 221). In support of previewing, they cite an article by Panabecker et al. (1980), in which mothers were asked to report on the emotions of their children from birth to eighteen months: 66 percent of the mothers reported that interest, joy, surprise, anger, disgust, and fear appeared in the first three months. Important here is not how the mothers made this assessment or even if these emotions actually existed in their babies, but that the mothers saw these emotions and acted "as if" they existed.

Another way that adults might facilitate a child learning about emotions is through the way they respond—or don't respond—when a child is expressing an emotion. Brooks-Gunn and Lewis (1982) found that, as their

---

*This section was written by Martha Bauman Power.

children get older, mothers respond less to their crying, but they increase their responsiveness to positive expressions of emotion. Seemingly, mothers are facilitating their children's emotional socialization by teaching them that it is more appropriate to express positive than negative emotions.

Caregivers can also influence children's emotional experiences by trying to manage when children will be exposed to various experiences. Hartup (1979, p. 949) writes: ". . . parents manage the social lives of their children directly. Mothers and fathers consciously determine the timing and circumstances under which their offspring will have contact with individuals outside the nuclear family." Parents often attempt to manage their children's emotional lives as well; typically, they try to prevent their children's exposure to experiences that will have a negative emotional impact (e.g., experiences that will upset or frighten them). This can include restricting their television viewing to nonviolent shows, or restricting their contact with other children, such as the "neighborhood bully" or a child with a mental or physical handicap.

Emotional Talk. Language, in the form of emotional talk, is the means by which the socializing of emotions typically occurs. Adults, both intentionally and unintentionally, use emotional talk to express and explain emotions to children. It is through emotional talk that the child comes to develop emotional intersubjectivity. They come to identify and confer meaning on their recurring self-feelings, and concurrently come to interpret and understand emotions in others. This gives people a way of sharing their emotional meanings.

Using emotional talk, a child gradually comes to recognize and use the commonly held linguistic labels for emotions. By acquiring this socially shared knowledge, the child is able to join her subjective meanings for her self-feelings with others. Through intersubjectivity, based on language, she is able to take the perspective (including the emotional perspective) of the other. Through interactions with others, the child comes to recognize expressions of emotions in self and others, comes to assume these expressions are indicative of recurrent, identifiable self-feelings, and learns the commonly held linguistic labels which often are attached to these self-feelings. Consider the following example of a young boy learning to label and share his feelings (field notes, Sept. 7, 1984):

A mother and father are talking with their 5-year-old son about his day in kindergarten.

Mother: Did you play with Sam today?
    Son: No. I'm not playing with him anymore.
Mother: Why not?
    Son: Because he said he didn't want to be my friend anymore.
Mother: How did that make you feel?

The son looks puzzled by the question, so the mother elaborates.

Mother: Did it make you feel happy or sad or something like that?
    Son: (pausing, apparently groping for a word): It made me feel truant.
Mother: (looking confused): "Truant? What do you mean?"
    Son: You know. That's between sad and mad. First there's happy, then there's sad, then there's truant, then there's mad.
Mother: I think I know how you felt, but that's not the right word. A truant is someone who doesn't to go school when they're supposed to be in school. I don't know of a word that means between mad and sad.
Father: Maybe bitter's the right word.
Mother: Yeah. Bitter sounds like it might be between sad and mad.

This boy is trying to share his self-feelings with his parents, but before this can be accomplished, they must agree upon a commonly held linguistic label for his emotions. This problem is compounded by the fact that our vocabulary of sharable emotional terms does not have a definitive, unambiguous label for his emotional experience. This is always the case, but as we become emotionally socialized we learn to typify our emotions; we attach to them a label that approximates what we feel. In so doing, we tend to group potentially different self-feelings under the same rubric.

Emotional Situations. Emotional situations are those socially structured, constructed, and emergent interactional episodes in which emotions are recognized, interpreted, managed, hidden, shared, or defined. Emotional situations are structured by rules and rituals.

Through emotional talk with emotional associates, a child comes to recognize smiles, frowns, and grimaces; comes to assume these expressions are indicative of recurrent identifiable feeling-states; and gradually learns the commonly held linguistic labels which can be attached to these feeling-states and their expression. We teach our children both the linguistic labels for their self-feelings and various linguistic rituals that may accompany emotions in self and others. *Linguistic emotional rituals* are those gestures, words, and phrases that children (and adults) use to acknowledge regard toward or confer respect on another. We teach children the social niceties, the rules of "polite" interaction, such as saying "please" and "thank you." The significance of this ritual can be seen in the deference (Goffman, 1967, p. 56) that saying "please" and "thank you" affords another. If a child (particularly an older child) does not show deference to an adult, the adult may feel upset by the child's "lack of manners." Further, parents frequently become distressed by their children's lack of interactional skills, and are pleased when they "behave appropriately."

Another linguistic ritual that we teach our children is the *apology ritual*. This includes saying such things as "excuse me" and "I'm sorry." The "I'm sorry" ritual can take several forms: The most common form, especially for very young children, is adult-initiated, in which the adult prompts the child to make

the apology. Another form is the misdirected apology, where the wrong child initiates the actions. A variation of this form is when both children respond simultaneously. Regardless of the direction of the apology, it provides a satisfactory close to the episode.

Temporal rituals involve teaching children when they should exprience or express different emotions. They can be seen as attempts to control children's behavior through the use of time, thereby influencing children's emotional interactions with others.

We tell children when to get up, go to sleep, get dressed, eat, go outside, come inside, even go to the bathroom. Day care centers further rigidify their time; here, children's activities and interests are typically subordinated to the teacher's agenda of scheduled activities. Often a child's day is scheduled according to what activity it is time for—snack time, story time, potty time, nap time, play time. Efforts are made to control children's disruptive behaviors by telling them it's not "time" for that—"it's not time to be running around—we do that during gym time—now it's time to sit still and listen to the story."

We need more research on the socialization of emotion in childhood. We need to connect children's games with emotional experiences and with the rituals that structure emotional expression. Gender should be located centrally in our studies of childhood emotion.

GENDER DIFFERENTIATION

No society fails to embody in its practices and language the fundamental biological distinction between the sexes. Many societies recognize still further categories, which include men who act like women and women who act like men. These in-between persons are sometimes taken for granted, sometimes looked upon as biological abnormalities. Scientists and sophisticated laypersons recognize another intermediate hermaphroditic class of persons who at birth have some of the genital apparatus, and perhaps physical traits, of both sexes (Edgerton, 1964).

Regardless of these intermediate classes, we can take for granted that humans universally recognize the existence of polar biological types—that is, men and women. It is easy to understand why the incorrect assumption is frequently made that infants "naturally" know to which sex they belong. Every child must not only (1) learn the meanings of "male" and "female," but also (2) classify himself or herself with both or neither.

This poses a problem. How do children learn to identify themselves as members of one or the other sex? The reader who seeks a detailed, exact answer to this question will be disappointed, for pertinent scientific data are meager. However, the larger outlines of the process of sex identification are clear enough.

Recognition of Sex Differences

When young children start to learn sex distinctions, they employ criteria that betray rudimentary conceptions of the differences between men and women. These criteria vary according to opportunities available to children for observing and conversing about sex behavior. In the United States, such experiences vary widely according to social class, social worlds, conditions of housing, number of siblings in the family, sibling position, moral philosophies of the parents, and other relevant factors.

In an outstanding study, Conn and Kanner (1947) have analyzed the criteria which children use to differentiate the sexes. Although their sampling is deficient—the study covers children of many social classes ranging from ages 4 to 12—it offers valuable hints about the learning of sex differences.

One item which the children mentioned most frequently as a sign of sex membership was clothing. Their data indicate that this sign is learned, accepted for a time, and then discarded (1947, p. 13). A few children under age seven equated sex differences with differences of attire, apparently recognizing no other distinctions. Clothing was most important for children ages nine to ten. When asked if there would be any difference between undressed boys and girls, these young children were "either puzzled by the questions, or declared categorically that removal of clothes made a distinction impossible" (1947, p. 13). Apropos of this finding is a story involving a 5-year-old acquaintance of the authors who attended a party at which children of both sexes bathed in the nude. When asked how many boys and how many girls were at the party, she answered: "I couldn't tell because they had their clothes off."

Hair was frequently mentioned as a differentiating characteristic of the sexes (1947, p. 13). Many children thought that differences of hairstyles are inherent—though helped along by scissors and the barber. As another young acquaintance of the authors confidently asserted: "Boys have straight hair and girls have curly hair." Differences of urination posture were mentioned spontaneously by 44 children. Although breasts were generally recognized as belonging only to women, only nine of the 200 children spontaneously included this distinguishing sign. The method used by the investigators is not open to the charge that children did not mention breasts because of inhibiting taboos. "There were so many other things closer to the children's interest and immediate awareness" (1947, p. 17).

An interesting finding is that (1) older children spontaneously mention other criteria such as shape of face, complexion, hands, strength, and gait; but that (2) children below certain ages did not mention these criteria. The investigators conclude that many younger children do not possess the requisite language necessary to see these sex differences; Their summarizing table is as follows (1947, p. 16):

Difference	*Youngest Age of Naming*
Hair	4
Clothes	5
Eyes	5
Hands	5
Face	6

Complexion	7
Hands and feet	8
Figure	8
Strength	8
Gait	9

That the child has learned to identify persons correctly as male or female does not mean that she has gained an adult conception of sex differences. The meanings of *male* and *female*, like those of other symbols, cannot be fully grasped by youngsters. Children have neither the requisite experiences. nor—in the case of the very young—the mentality necessary to understand adult concepts of sex contrasts.

On the learning of sex differences, Conn and Kanner (1947) present helpful data. Older children from urban centers generally recognized and mentioned genital difference between the sexes, but did not always realize that such differences also characterized animals. Consequently, varying conceptions of sex differences were offered. A common notion was that all animals of the same species were of the same sex; that all cats are females and all dogs are males. Some children regarded ribbons as a distinguishing sign, and other children regarded names as evidence of sex. Farm children, of course, are likely to be more sophisticated about the sex of animals.

Involved in adult conceptions of sex differences is an awareness of the sex act and its conventional socialized meanings. In some countries and classes, children may be allowed to engage in sex play with others of their own age and have frequent opportunities to witness adult coitus. These conditions prevail among the Trobriand Islanders, a South Sea people. Consequently, this part of the adult symbolization is learned earlier than it is by American children. The Conn and Kanner figures, which seem relatively trustworthy, indicate that only a small proportion of a total of 200 children under age 12 knew of the existence of coitus. There are no grounds, however, for assuming that even these relatively sophisticated children had adult concepts of the act. The Conn and

Kanner research is over 40 years old; while their study is a landmark investigation, it must be regarded with some caution. Recent changes in the sexual arena (see Chapter 13) are likely to produce earlier awareness in children about sexual behavior and sex role identification.

The point is vividly illustrated by Richard Wright's (1945, p. 36) account of how, at the age of six, in a bar where he had insisted on hanging around, he had been taught numerous sexual terms and obscenities. Two or three years later, he unwittingly enraged his grandmother when, after his bath, she was scrubbing " . . . my anus. My mind was in a sort of daze, midway between daydreaming and thinking." Before Wright knew it, "words—words whose meaning I did not fully know—had slipped out of my mouth. 'When you get through, kiss back there.' . . . Granny became terribly still, then she pushed me violently from her." Later still, Wright was playing in front of a neighboring house with another child when an older girl said, "They gonna make a lotta money in there today. . . ." Richard asked why, and the girl asked if he didn't know what they were selling in there." " 'They don't sell nothing in there,' I said. 'Aw, you just a baby,' she said slapping her dingy palm through the air at me in a contemptuous gesture."

The institutions that any society assembles for the production and rearing of children differentially stress sex role attributes as they structure the socialization process (Aries, 1962). This is particularly evident in the education arena, where males and females are segregated in the bathroom and physical education activities. Perhaps more critical are the lessons in sex role socialization young children receive in preschool and day care centers. Bathroom interactions in nursery schools may provide occasions for conversations about anatomical differences between the sexes; the bathroom becomes a "social place." One observer in the Columbia University Nursery School in 1929 noted that "As the children grow more efficient in taking care of themselves, many interesting conversations are carried on [there]. And, the teacher often adds bits of information in response to natural questions." Observers such as Joffe (1971, pp. 467–75) and Henry (1963) have noted that many preschools are explicitly organized so as to set males and females against one another. Teachers expressly value and reward appropriate "male" and "female" behavior and often discourage "female" behavior on the part of boys and aggressive "male" behavior on the part of girls. One of the authors observed a preschool teacher in a racially mixed middle-class preschool repeatedly embarrass a four-year-old boy who insisted on dressing each day in the garments of a bride. Joffe reports the following episode drawn from a parent-cooperative nursery in Berkeley, California, in 1970 (1971, p. 470):

L. and N. have been arguing over the use of a spade. N. pushes L. and L. responds by delivering a solid punch to N.'s chest. A mother who has witnessed the scene says to the observer (within hearing of L.), "Did you see the punch L. gave N? He really can take care of himself like a man."

Young children find that they are rewarded when they act on preferred sex role stereotypes, and often bring "sexual rhetorics" into their games. Joffe observed the following exchange between two girls and a boy (1971, p. 472): "C. and two other girls are playing on top of a large structure in the yard. A. (male) comes over and C. screams, 'Girls only!' to which A. screams back, 'No, boys only!'"

Phrases like "Your hair looks nice today," or "What a pretty dress you have on," inform girls that they will be positively addressed and identified if they look nice—to be dressed nicely and have one's hair and other physical features properly in order. Thus, by the early age of three, young children begin to assign to themselves and others quite specific self-identities with sexual dimensions.

Learning the Meanings of Sexual Behavior

The meanings associated with sexual activities must be learned by children. They do not in any significant degree invent them; nor do they acquire them through biological endowment or maturation. They may not understand the full adult significance of many sexual words and acts until they are well into adolescence, or later.

Although humans everywhere recognize the existence of sexual excitement, coitus, masturbation, sex organs, and the like, they nevertheless take dissimilar attitudes toward these objects, acts, and events. Words convey or mirror attitudes—that is, they have meanings. When the child—whether American, Japanese, or Marquesan; upper or lower class; boy or girl; rural or urban—learns words, he learns also the conventional points of view which they express.

Kinsey (1948) asserted that at the time of his study there were differential American class attitudes toward the meaning of sexual behavior. We summarize a few in the accompanying table.

Motivation and Learning

Kinsey found that sexual vocabularies varied tremendously by region, class, race, age, and other groupings. These differences of vocabulary, of course, mirror differences of attitude and constitute important data for anyone interested in understanding, explaining, and predicting human sex behavior. When the child learns these idiomatic terms, she also internalizes the meanings they express. American middle-class parents recognize this fact implicitly, since they teach their children euphemistic expressions for sex organs and sex acts rather than the "vulgar" terms children pick up later from others of their own age. Public use of technical sex terminology is permissible, whereas the use of corresponding "Anglo-Saxon monosyllables" is taboo. Although the one-syllable words refer to the same objects and events, they convey very different attitudes. Because words evoke attitudes, such Anglo-Saxon terms have been considered inappropriate in public discussion, but this taboo has been considerably relaxed in recent years.

Anthropologists agree that although great

Event or Object	Upper Classes	Lower Classes
"Heavy Petting"	Part of the sex act or a substitute for it.	Not much practiced. As a substitute for the sex act, a perversion.
"Clitoris"	Many recognize its function in sexual foreplay as exciting to female. A function emphasized in widely read marriage manuals.	Word not in common use, nor any equivalent for it, since few know the organ exists. This is true particularly of males, but also to a lesser degree of females.
"Foreplay"	Widely regarded as an important preliminary to coitus.	Generally not considered important.
"Positions"	Some sophistication about possible variations.	Only one position is natural: the "American one."

variations in sexual codes exist, no society sanctions all aspects of all sex behavior, and every society frowns upon and forbids certain sex acts. These taboos rest upon basic assumptions concerning the nature of the world, of humans, and of the sexes and their relations.

Misconceptions of Child Behavior

Laypersons and even students of child behavior frequently make the mistake of anthropomorphism; they project adult attitudes and conceptions onto the child, or regard children's ideas and modes of thought and behavior as curious forms of error. This tendency to interpret the behavior of children with concepts derived from and appropriate to adults is also noticeable in the study of the child's sex behavior.

The fallacy is aggravated by using the same terms to describe child and adult behavior, or by using such hazily defined terms as "libido" and "sexual." While the popularization of psychoanalytic theories and concepts has undoubtedly swept away many of the puritanical and mid-Victorian misconceptions about children, it has opened the way to errors of another kind. Thus when one states that the infant masturbates, it is usually assumed that infant and adult mas-

turbation are equivalent acts—a dubious assumption indeed. The rebellion against the reluctance of past generations to face sexual facts has led to excessive zeal in discovering sexuality in the behavior of children. It must be emphasized that *children live in a world of their own; they have their own concepts, their own ways of acting, and their own perspectives.* It is just as erroneous to judge children's behavior by adult standards or to read adult motives into it as it is to measure African Bantu behavior by American standards.

Illustrating an extreme example of this type of error, Isaacs (1933, p. 160) writes: "Penelope and Tommy were playing 'mummy and daddy' and Tommy insisted upon being the mummy." The boy's act is interpreted as an attempt to quiet his fear of castration—yet no data are presented regarding the actual state of the child's sexual knowledge or how he may have obtained it. The child analyst Klein (1932, pp. 42–46) provides an even more flagrant example: Her patient was a three-year-old boy who between the ages of 18 and 20 months slept in his parent's room and had occasional opportunities to witness coitus (if one can stretch the meaning of the word "witness"). The child, writes Klein, is therefore fearfully jealous of his father, feels inferior because of his own lack of physical potency, fears that his mother was hurt by coitus, wishes to smash his father's genitals, wishes to kill his father, and so forth. How can such complex ideas be attributed to young children?

Other child psychologists and psychoanalysts have been much more circumspect in their interpretations. Cognizant of the social origins and learned nature of sexual behavior, many psychoanalysts have pointed out weaknesses in Freud's theory that feminine character may be largely explained in terms of "penis envy" (see Chapter 8) and reactions to it. According to this theory, when the young girl discovers that every boy has a penis, she is disappointed and shocked at her own lack of the same organ (see Chapter 8). Hence she develops a sense of inferiority or penis envy. The traits of character she develops in her childhood and adult years are, according to Freud, the consequences of her attempt to adjust to her sense of inferiority. But the sociologist is inclined to note that reactions of this type are associated with the patriarchal organization of Western European society—that is, a society in which men and masculine values are relatively dominant. This patriarchal situation, however, is by no means universal, even in Western society.

Disinterested investigation of girls' reactions to the discovery of genital differences, such as that by Conn and Kanner (1947, pp. 44–48) shows without question that girls do not always respond with penis envy; some girls exhibit envious feelings, but most do not—instead they accept these differences matter-of-factly or react with amusement. In the light of the learned character of such behavior, one would not expect all girls to react identically. Freud's overstatement of the case should make us wary of equating children's sexual responses with those of their elders.

By word or act, punishment or reward, and through the various media of communication, the young boy and girl learn the sex behavior associated with their roles; they learn to avoid those acts which will evoke reactions of ridicule, disgust, or anger. The taboos are internalized in children to the extent that they become angry and ashamed if they break them.

CONCLUSION

Early childhood is made up of a complex set of *significant others* who take part in the process of socializing children into the complicated areas of causal understanding about the physical world, as well as into the more intricate topics of morality and sex role behavior. Children quickly relinquish an egocentric conception of their surrounding world, replacing that biased view with a more relativistic perspective that is grounded in the multiple perspectives of their generalized others. Children enter the world with no knowledge of sex role differences. Through their interactive experiences with peers, parents. and other adults, they soon develop sophisticated images of proper "male" and "female" behavior. A society's educational institutions take on the major assignment of teaching children what these differences between the "sexes" are.

We have considered the importance of gender and moral judgments, noting that different moral codes appear to hold for males and females in our society. These codes are located in Western religion, culture, and philosophy; they are also deeply intertwined in the economic and stratification systems of our society. A crucial phase of childhood socialization involves emotion. We have shown how children's caretakers teach various emotional meanings, rituals, and understandings. The topics of gender, morality, and emotionality remain important areas of social psychological study.

SUGGESTED READINGS

DAMON, W. (1977). *The social worlds of childhood.* San Francisco: Jossey-Bass. An important collection of papers detailing the developmental experiences of young children in such areas as the emotions, friendship, morality, and knowledge.

DENZIN, N. K. (1977). *Childhood socialization.* San Francisco: Jossey-Bass. An analysis of early childhood from a symbolic interactionist point of view.

PIAGET, J. (1983). *Intelligence and affectivity: Their relationship during child development.* Palo Alto, CA: Annual Reviews, Inc. A statement of this important psychologist's studies on intelligence and affect in child development.

SURANSKY, V. P. (1982). *The erosion of childhood.* Chicago: University of Chicago Press. A critical reading of current practices and policies concerning children in American society.

CHAPTER TEN
Interaction and the Self

The everyday world of social interaction is this chapter's topic. We will discuss the following topics: rules and roles; social situations; social relationships and identities; status passage and interaction; awareness contexts; small groups; interaction rituals and the interactional order; mesostructures, collective behavior, collective protest, and social unrest; and power.

TWO APPROACHES TO INTERACTION: RULES AND ROLES

Two approaches have dominated the study of social interaction: one in which the emphasis has been on regulated and patterned interaction; and the other in which the emphasis has been on relatively open-ended, albeit patterned interaction between self-reflexive interactants. Here we will attempt to achieve some balance between these two views of interaction.

Very little (if any) interaction occurs even between total strangers, without some element of code, norm, or rule entering into the interaction. This is true even when conflict exists between individuals or where interaction actually takes place around a conflict—as in warfare or an athletic contest. Rules, as prescriptions for conduct, come closest to determining interaction when it is ritualistic—as exemplified, say, by religious ceremonies. Anthropologists and sociologists some years ago employed a loose terminology of "rights" and "obligations" when analyzing such repetitive and standardized forms of interaction; they also used terms like "roles" and "statuses" and applied them to situations where the interaction was either relatively narrow or quite wide in scope (as in the institution of slavery, master and slave having reciprocal rights and obligations associated with respective statuses). These concepts were often combined with others, like contract, custom, codes, and mores. A newer generation of social psychologists and sociologists has sustained this interest in socially regulated and patterned behavior, but has abandoned most of the older terms—except for role and status—and substituted ones like "negative sanctions," "positive sanctions," "norms," "reciprocity," "distributive justice," "the exchange process," and the "rules of conduct."

The second traditional approach to interaction emphasizes that it is often "fluid" and that even when standardized, it can break out of bounds into the unexpected, the surprising, and the novel. As we shall see, social psychologists in this tradition talk about "the self in interaction" and about role taking. They are wary of confusing patterned regularity in interaction with rules, norms, and roles—which supposedly determine that regularity. They tend to think of interaction as Blumer does—in terms of interactants working out their relationships (1962, p. 190): "Interpretations have to be developed and effective accommodation of the participants to one another has to be worked out." Or, as Blumer (1962, p. 188) also takes the position: "In modern society, with its increasing criss-cross of lines of action, it is common for situations to arise in which the actions of participants are not previously regularized and standardized." Social psychologists who take this position tend to think that those who represent the other viewpoint remove the self from the interactional process while assuming that "their" structural or psychological variables cause humans to act in relatively fixed and predictable ways.

Our own position is that: (1) rule-guided, or influenced behavior is extremely important, but not *all* important; (2) that a simple vocabulary, such that offered by sociologists who are functionalists and by many social anthropologists, is not useful for examining or researching how interaction actually might be affected by rules which the interactants are "following"; and (3) an analysis of rules and interaction is empty if it ignores the place of the self in the negotiation process.

Interactional Repertoires

In light of these considerations it can be argued that in most, if not all, interactional episodes persons orient their behaviors toward the emerging standpoint, or line of action, of those whom they confront. These standpoints represent unique configurations of meaning and interpretation and may be termed "interactional repertoires." Such repertoires are characteristic lines of action associated with a particular self or person. When a class of individuals share the same or similar repertoire across situations, then it is appropriate to speak of a common interactional role. However, all interactants are obliged to assess the special line of action taken by any individual whom they confront, and in such assessments they must turn some amount of attention to the special features of the other's definition of the situation. All interaction, and all interactants, display some complex mix of self and role taking. Individuals take one another's perspective, and to term that "role taking" has meaning only if it is remembered that it is selves interacting with one another—not roles, not role sets, but networks of interactional repertoires. To divorce the self from the interaction process is to produce an empty, mechanistic view of human behavior.

The Social Situation

All interaction occurs in social situations. These situations have three components: The physical aspects of a room, hallway, playing field, or street corner refer to the objective features of a social situation. The definitions people bring to a situation and work out inside it reference the subjective side of the situation. The third feature of a situation consists of the people who interact in it. We can see how the same objective situation can take on different meanings depending on who is interacting in it. Compare, for example, the meanings brought to a house by a real estate agent versus the meanings of that house to the people who are selling it. For the realtor the house is a piece of property to be sold; for the people who live in it, the house is "home," and it has the meanings of a personal space where important transactions and experiences have occurred. Sociologist W. I. Thomas suggested (1928), "If people

define situations as real they are real in their consequences." This oft-repeated sociological dictum speaks to the subjective side of social situations.

Situations exist, then, only insofar as people define them and make them real. All human experience is situated and every situation is unique. However, situations have historical meanings, as well; these meanings are passed on from one generation to the next and they shape the interactions that occur within them.

In addition to the objective, subjective, interactional, and historical features of situations, we may note that situations may exist only in persons' imaginations; for example, the dream world of a child. Other situations are completely objective and push themselves into the person's world of experience. When two cars collide at an intersection, there is no way to avoid the fact that an automobile accident has occurred.

In social situations, individuals enact and play out interactional repertoires. Situations provide the point of contact for the person and social structure. This brings us to our next concept: the two streams of experience. The accompanying figure describes the process of interaction in the social situation.

In any situation, there are two streams of experience flowing alongside one another. The first is the interactional stream, which references the face-to-face interaction that occurs between two parties in a concrete or imagined social situation. The second stream, the phenomenological stream, describes the inner side of interaction that occurs when the person interacts with himself and with another in a social situation. In the phenomenological stream the person takes his own attitude toward self (A-A), toward the other (A-B), and turns the imagined attitude of the other toward himself (B-A).

Interaction in any situation will involve person A initiating a line of action toward B that calls out in B a significant emotional and cognitive gesture that is present in A's action and thought. Person A turns this emotional and cognitive gesture inward, judging and interpreting the meaning of B's actions in

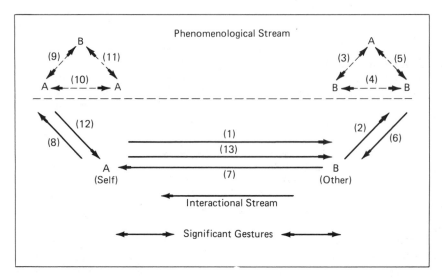

Interaction in the social situation. (Adapted from N.K. Denzin, *On Understanding Emotion* (San Francisco: Jossey-Bass, 1984), p. 55. Used with permission.

light of A's own incipient emotional and cognitive attitudes (A-A, A-B, B-A). This interpretation becomes part of A's emotional and cognitive self-feelings and is then incorporated into A's next gesture or statement to B. Thus A's self-feeling and self-definition become part of an emotional, cognitive, social act that enters B's inner phenomenological stream and becomes part of B's emotional social act (toward both B and A).

A circuit of selfness (Sartre, 1956, pp. 155–58) attaches each person to the social situation and to the other person(s) in the situation. In this circuit emotion, meaning, and self are joined. This field of experience anchors the self and the interactional repertoire in the other's phenomenological and interactional streams.

Defining the Situation

Implicit in our discussion is the fundamental idea that role playing occurs in episodes, scenes, or situations. These have to be recognized, named, and catalogued by the individual so that appropriate action may be taken. No two situations are exactly alike, but there is often enough resemblance between the present situation and one formerly encountered to permit it to be recognized, and thus give rise to orderly and regular behavior. Many situations can be immediately "tabbed" because they are routine, traditional, or familiar. "Sensing the situation" means that one immediately gears herself to it. At the other pole, many situations are problematic and subject to different interpretations. Definition of situations, both familiar and new, involves the interpretation of a multitude of cues.

In a problematic situation, action may have to be delayed while one searches for the relevant clues as to its nature, or one may act tentatively without committing oneself in order to elicit further clues. In any case, one never sees the total situation as an omniscient being or a playwright might see it. The individual can only perceive what his abilities, categories, and interests lead to or enable him to see. As MacIver (1942, p. 296) indicates, the situation is not a mere physical inventory of external data:

The situation he assesses is one that he has selectively defined, in terms of his experience, his habit of response, his intellectual grasp, and his emotional engrossment in it. The dynamic assessment limits the situation by excluding all the numerous aspects that are not apprehended as relevant to the choice between alternatives. At the same time it includes in the situation various aspects that are not objectively given, that would not be listed in any merely physical inventory . . . it envisages the situation as impregnated with values and susceptible of new potential values.

It includes, besides one's own values and motives, those imputed to others. No hard and fast lines can be drawn between the definition of a situation and the behavior thought to be appropriate to it. Any definition necessarily implies and carries with it a plan of action. One does not usually name the situation and then sequentially decide what to do; defining the situation and exploring alternative courses of action usually occur simultaneously. These processes are often tied up with a review of preceding events and a reinterpretation of them and of past lines of action.

To illuminate these points, consider the following excerpts from Raymond Carver's short story, "The Calm" (Carver, 1981, pp. 115, 121):

I was getting a haircut. I was in the chair and three men were sitting along the wall across from me. Two of the men waiting I'd never seen before. But one of them I recognized, though I couldn't exactly place him. I kept looking at him as the barber worked on my hair. . . . The barber turned me in the chair to face the mirror. He put a hand to either side of my head. . . . We looked at the mirror together, his hands still framing my head. . . . He ran his fingers through my hair. He did it slowly, as if thinking about something else. He ran his fingers through my hair. He did it tenderly, as a lover would.

That was in Crescent City, California, up near the Oregon border. I left soon after. But today I was thinking of that place, of Crescent City, and of how I was trying out a new life there with my wife, and how, in the barber's chair that morning, I had made up my mind to go.*

Several processes are working in this story. Carver is interactionally and phenomenologically connected to the barber, to him-

self, to the barber's movement of his hands through Carver's hair, to his own emotions, and to his recent past. The circuit of selfness joins Carver to the barber and to the emotions he feels and remembers in the situation.

Now reflect on William Samson's (1955, pp. 230–32) description of Preedy, a fictional Englishman, on vacation. Here we see an interactional repertoire fitting itself to a social situation.

But it was time to institute a little parade, the parade of the Ideal Preedy. By devious handlings he gave any who wanted to look a chance to see the title of his book—a Spanish translation of Homer, classic thus, but not daring, cosmopolitan too—and then gathered together his beach-wrap and bag into a neat sand-resistant pile (Methodical and Sensible Preedy), rose slowly to stretch his huge frame (Big-Cat Preedy), and tossed aside his sandals (Carefree Preedy, after all).†

Preedy is interacting with the situation. He is presenting himself to any who will look. He has an interactional repertoire—the way he walks, the book he is reading, his beach-wrap, his sandals, and so on. He is set on making an impression (Goffman, 1959, p. 6) on others. He has turned the beach into a personal situation, thereby making it a public place for the presentation of himself. Preedy is preparing himself for a *social relationship*—our next topic.

Social Relationships

Gregory P. Stone (1984, p. 5) has divided social relationships into interpersonal and structural relationships. The difference between them consists of the fact that the structural relationship exists for the lifetime and participation of the individual member (Stone, 1984, p. 5). An example reveals the difference between these two types of relationships: University students assemble for courses and are taught by members of the faculty, who have been appointed by members of the administra-

---

*From Raymond Carver, "The Calm," *What We Talk about When We Talk about Love* (New York: Random House, 1982). Used with permission.

†From William Samson, *A Contest of Ladies* (Honolulu: Hogarth Publishers, 1955), pp. 230–32. Used with permission.

tion. In the case of the university, we are dealing with a real social structure which outlives any given member.

Now look at a small group of friends who live in the same rooming house. They have come together through the exchange of personal names. No external social structure brought them into the rooming house. When they leave, or when one moves out and another person takes her place, new names will be exchanged and a new informal, small social group will be formed.

Stone argues that the key difference between structural and interpersonal relations lies in how one enters them. In structural relations, the person exchanges a name for a title which refers to a position in a social structure (i.e., student, physician, nurse, etc.). In interpersonal relations, the individual exchanges only a name or nickname (Stone, 1981, p. 189; 1984, p. 7).

Stone (1981, p. 189) distinguishes two other types of social relations. *Human relations* are those based on such universal identities as age, gender, race, ethnicity, or community membership. Social relations which occur for members of the *larger public* (i.e., the masses) are anonymously entered. Social relationships can now be viewed as ongoing social interactions between two or more persons which are classified according to the "identities which must be placed and announced to permit entry into the transaction" (Stone, 1981, p. 189).

Human and mass relations can form the basis for interpersonal relations—as when strangers meet at a political rally, exchange names, and form a friendship. Similarly, structural relations can lay the basis for interpersonal relations; Office co-workers can become friends. Furthermore, interpersonal relations can introduce persons into structural relations; friends, for example, can sponsor friends into exclusive clubs or fraternities (Stone, 1984. p. 7).

Identities

Following Stone (1981), Strauss (1959),

and Maines (1978), we can define identities as "social categories through which people may be located and given meaning" in some situational or interactional context (Maines, 1978, p. 242). When "one has identity, he is situated—that is, cast in the shape of a social object by the acknowledgment of his (or her) participation or membership in social relations" (Stone, 1981, p. 188).

Identity is established as a result of two processes. The first situates the person with other persons in a situation, and the second separates the person from others.

We can see that identities are created in social situations. Furthermore, identities involve social relations. Larger interactional forms (groups, organizations) give persons identities and locate them in social relationships. There is a close relationship between self, identity, names, titles, interactional repertoires, social situations, and social relationships.

To return to our earlier example, Preedy appears quite willing to be situated in the identity of a handsome man looking for interactions with members of the opposite sex. He will exchange his name for an interpersonal relationship. He is prepared, in a sense, for a status passage.

STATUS PASSAGE AND INTERACTION

Social structure is often conceived of as a system of interrelated "offices," "statuses," roles, or other designations that stand for social positions. People are said to act in accordance with the requirements of those social positions—insofar as they play those roles, fill those offices, occupy those statuses. In short, social positions carry with them guidelines for those who are "in" them. The guidelines can be in the nature of generalized expectations by others (and often internalized, so that the actor has those expectations, too); but sometimes they are rather rigorously prescribed, being more in the nature of rules and regulations and even of law. Offices, statuses, and roles can therefore be conceived as somewhat independent of the specific individuals who happen to be filling them. This also implies that people must be induced to fill those positions, as well as leave them at some appropriate time (Glaser & Strauss, 1971, pp. 2–3). "Insofar as every social structure requires manpower, men are recruited . . . to move along through social positions or statuses. Status is a resting place for individuals. But while the status itself may persist for many years, no matter how long an individual remains in, say, an office, there is an implicit or even explicit date when he must leave it."

The movement of individuals in and out of statuses has long been referred to as "status passage." A great many such passages (into and out of the presidency of the United States; into and out of the statuses of "accused" or "witness" in a court trial) are governed by fairly clear rules concerning when and how the passage is made, who is involved in it, what the prescribed sequences of steps that must be gone through are, and the like. If all passages were so neatly governed, then there might not be much change in the social structure of any group, organization, or nation. However, a large share of passages in modern societies are much less regulated, prescribed, and organized. American passage into marriage, while guided by implicit rules of dating and more explicit ones pertaining to the wedding itself (the woman's family pays) may have many ill-defined features: the length of the engagement, whether there is an engagement, whether the couple lives together before, even what the details of the wedding will be. Similar unstandardized features mark the passage into the divorced status. Probably most status passages leave those who pass, and the agents who help in the passage, with a fair degree of latitude about a great many details, including major ones that relate to sequences of steps and timing.

We can see also that the interaction during a passage will vary considerably in accordance with other properties of the passage. Sometimes the passage is undesirable to the person

passing or to others involved in her passage. Sometimes the passage is not very important to her, but sometimes it may be central in her life. Some passages are reversible (studenthood), but some may be irreversible (parenthood). Other conditions of passages include whether they are inevitable (childhood to adulthood), voluntary or involuntary, and whether the person goes through the passage alone or with others (classmates). Also, some passages are left to the person passing to initiate or consummate; others are actually initiated and controlled by agents, rather than by her. All these properties affect how the participants will act toward each other. In turn, their actions will have consequences for self and other evaluations, which then will affect some of the next steps of the passage.

This general manner of looking at the relations among statuses, offices, or roles brings out two important points. First, one can see the processual or more dynamic side of social structures. Even if given statuses do not change in character, there is a good deal of movement going on into, through, and out of them. Second, it is clear that social interaction has two sides: the structural side and the self–other side. We cannot understand interaction without taking both into account.

TWIN PROCESSES: PRESENTING AND ASSESSING

We noted previously that in interaction, each actor necessarily is assessing—not necessarily with full consciousness—the other. The assessor has various cues to go on: verbal, expressive verbal accompaniments, nonverbal (including posture, gesture, management of body in space, eye gaze), and also stylistic cues related to how the other dresses, arranges his hair, or surrounds himself with household or decorative objects. The type of people with whom he surrounds himself is a cue too (Argyle, 1969; Goffman, 1959).

The counterpart of this interactional assessment process is what Goffman has called "impression management"—that is, the organization of the presenting person's cues so as to elicit desired responses in the assessing other. This management of the other's assessment may be completely sincere or coldly manipulative; it may be done deliberately and consciously, or virtually without awareness. Impressions are created by a large variety of communicative devices and interactional tactics and by the use of external props. Many of these involve teamwork, as when husband and wife collaborate to give a party for the boss, or when several members of a confidence mob separate a mark from her money.

Gregory P. Stone (1962) has further developed the analysis of self-display strategies by looking closely at clothing. He notes that people select what clothes they will wear, and how they will wear them, in an effort to get others to form the desired impression. In a general statement of this, he remarks that (1962, p. 90): "Identifications of another are facilitated by appearance and are often accomplished silently or unverbally." Stone's analysis indicates that the use of clothing to create an appearance is quite complex (1962, p. 101): "By appearance, a person *announces* his identity, *show* his value, *expresses* his mood, or *proposes* his attitude."

Of course, people not only display aspects of themselves, but attempt to suppress or hide those aspects they do not wish to reveal. They do this, for instance, by arranging clothes to hide a potentially stigmatizing disease system or by using perfumes or deodorizers to disguise or suppress smells (Largey & Watson, 1972).

The phenomenon of "passing" of blacks for whites, Jews for gentiles, spies for ordinary citizens, necessarily relies both on suppressing give-away signs and emphasizing signs which represent the desired appearance. Thus John Griffin, a white journalist (1962), for some weeks passed as a black in the South, having first taken the precaution of having his skin color changed temporarily with chemicals. We need not think of such

suppression of signs of "true self" as being so esoteric; we all engage in such suppression from time to time. Indeed, to use Stone's terminology, depending on how we feel today, we may wish to "appear" that way, choosing clothes appropriate for that appearance, simultaneously suppressing those signs, including clothing styles, which are inappropriate to today's desired appearance.

Such analyses as those by Stone and Goffman are valuable extensions of the self-presentation idea. These examples bring us to the assessor's tasks. He has to read the other's signs accurately or face the consequences of his misreading. Thus, if the other is seeking to present a false appearance, the assessor has to be able to "see through" that fiction or to have developed countertactics to elicit important giveaway signs. Some countertactics for recognizing persons who are suppressing their identity depend on passing as a member of their group—an FBI agent posing as a communist—or on getting information from others within the group. Persons of similar status may use conventional signs, both to avoid a mistaken recognition of the assessing person and to further recognition if their own assessment of him is accurate: thus homosexuals flash signs readable only by those who are either homosexual or "wise" (sympathetic insiders). Usually there are places where the gathered insiders can forego their efforts to disguise or suppress identifying signs; but they may need, as with drug addicts, countertactics to avoid betrayal even in such secluded places (Goffman, 1969).

The assessing person is aided not only by astuteness. experience, and slips of control by the presenting other; he is aided by the latter's flashing of cues of which he is not even aware. Only practiced actors, like spies, are intensely aware of all those features of their nonverbal behavior which act as potential revelations of selves, or aspects of selves, that they would rather not be seen. Freudians would term these "unconscious" slips, that is, loss of control of which the presenting person is not even aware. Examples would be slips of the tongue, too-rapid breathing, and blushing. It is notable, however, that everyone is flashing cues all the time—most of which she cannot notice because her attention is somewhere else. The assessing person may happen to notice them, or make it his business to notice them. Those are the same nonverbal cues which we mentioned before: posture, gesture, eye gaze, verbal expressivity, movement in space, and the like. One must also recognize that skilled actors, intent on presenting a desired appearance, may flash cues in such a way that the assessor falsely interprets what he assumes are unwitting signs. The entire question of "accurate" interpretations turns out to be very complex (Icheiser, 1949; Weinstein & Deutschberger, 1963).

Awareness Contexts

In considering the strategies and problems of self-presentation and of the assessment of others, it is relevant to introduce the concept of "awareness context," as developed by Glaser and Strauss (1964, 1969). Awareness context refers to "the total combination of what each interactant in a situation knows about the identity of the other and his own identity in the eyes of the other. The total awareness is the context within which are guided successive interaction . . . over periods of time—long or short." Four principal types of awareness context are relevant to the presentation and assessment which goes on in interaction. An *open* awareness context prevails when each interactant is aware of the other's true identity in the eyes of others. A *closed* awareness context prevails when one interactant does not know either the other's identity or the other's view of his identity. Examples would be: a spy whom the other believed to be an ordinary person; a virgin who either is deliberately passing as or is mistakenly assumed to be a sexually experienced person; or more simply, an American-Japanese visiting Japan

who is mistaken for a native. A *suspicion* prevails when one interactant suspects the true identity of the other, the other's view of his own identity, or both. A *pretense* context prevails when both are fully aware, but pretend not to be.

The concept of awareness context is applicable in a great many interactive situations, for those situations have the potential for deliberate misrepresentation of self as well as honest presentations of self; likewise, mistakes are inherent in both presentation and assessment despite each actor's attempts at honest presentation. Moreover, the need for fictional acting, through what everybody can see through but feels the need not to state bluntly, is inherent in many situations. Some social philosophers, as well as lay persons, have been so impressed by the fictional and misrepresentation as to believe most human relations are governed by hypocrisy. Others have merely emphasized the Machiavellian character of interaction.

McCall and Simmons have expressed this similar pessimistic view, although mitigating its full implication with a last qualifying phrase (1966, pp. 195–96): "Owing to the very peculiar nature of knowledge about other persons, relationships necessarily turn on somewhat misguided and misleading premises about the other parties, social order rests partly on error, lies, deception, and secrets, as well as upon accurate knowledge." A more balanced characterization of interaction, and the social order which it both expresses and makes possible, is that *all* types of awareness context are potentially operative in interaction.

Furthermore, the types are not mutually exclusive but tend to move from one to another, depending on the stage of development to which relationships have evolved (Icheiser, 1970). Thus, in the early stages of friendship formation, it is likely that pretense and suspicion awareness contexts predominate; but as the individuals acquire more information about one another, they can more easily and more fully reveal their perceived ambiguities about each other and about themselves as well. Indeed, friendship formation may be contingent on breaking out of the pretense and suspicion awareness contexts.

To illustrate the shifting character of awareness contexts, as well as to locate interaction in a larger institutional setting, we briefly sketch what may happen to a person who lies dying in a hospital (Glaser & Strauss, 1968).

1. Hospitalized patients frequently do not recognize their impending death, while the staff does. Thus interaction between the staff and patient occurs within a closed awareness context about the patient's true identity.

2. At least four major structural conditions determine this closed awareness context. First, most patients are not especially experienced at recognizing the signs of impending death. Second, the hospital is magnificently organized, both by accident and design, for hiding the medical truth from the patient. Records are kept out of reach; the staff is skilled at withholding information from him; medical talk about him occurs generally in far-removed places, and the staff is trained or accustomed to act collusively around patients so as not to disclose medical secrets. Third, physicians are supported in their withholding of information by professional rationales: "Why deny them all hope by telling them they are dying?" Fourth, ordinarily the patient has no allies who can help him discover the staff's secret; even his family or other patients will withhold such information if privy to it.

3. To prevent the patient's comprehension of the truth, the personnel utilize a number of "situation as normal" interaction tactics. They seek to act in his presence as if he were not dying, but only ill. They talk to him as if he were going to live. They converse about his future, thus enhancing his belief that he will regain his health. They tell him stories about others, including themselves, who have recovered from similar or worse illnesses. By such indirect signaling they offer him a false biography. Of course, they may directly assure him that he will live, lying with a clear purpose.

4. In such collusive games, the teamwork can be phenomenal, but the dangers of disclosure to the patient are great. Unless the patient dies quickly or becomes permanently comatose, he tends to suspect or even to understand clearly how others identify him. Patients do overhear occasional conversations about themselves. Personnel unwittingly may flash cues or make conversational errors which arouse the patient's suspicions. Day and night staff may give him contradictory information or divergent clues. The frequent practice of rotating personnel through the hospital services, or adding new personnel through the hospital services, may add to the danger of disclosure.

5. Some interactants may wish to move him along into other types of awareness contexts. If so, they can employ certain interactional tactics which are, for the most part, merely the opposites of the nondisclosure tactics. Intentionally, a staff member may give the show away wholly or partly, by improper management of face, by carefully oblique phrasing of words, by merely failing to reassure the patient sufficiently about a hopeful prognosis, by changing all talk about the future into concentration upon the present, or by increasing avoidance both of conversation and the patient himself. Of course, personnel occasionally may just plain tell him that he is dying.

6. The closed awareness that "surrounds" the dying patient has many significant consequences for patient and staff. The patient, unaware of the other's view of his identity, cannot act as if he were aware of dying. Thus, he cannot talk to close kin about his fate. He cannot assuage their grief. Nor can he act toward himself as if he were dying, by facing his expected death gracefully—or with panic and hysteria.

What this analysis of the dying situation brings out apropos of awareness contexts, is that the interactional features can be very different. Thus, the signs or indicators of the dying person's status, or condition, may vary in visibility to the other interactants. Different numbers of interactants can be involved in any interactional episode. Different numbers of groups—family, nurses, physicians—can be represented by the interactants. The ratios of insiders and outsiders present during the interaction may vary (one patient and dozens of staff members). The positions of interactions may also vary hierarchically, that is, they may be on the same or different levels of the hierarchy. And, of course, the stakes of the interaction may vary tremendously for the respective participants. Like the situation of dying persons, most interactions are not merely interpersonal (two-person) affairs; they frequently involve persons as representatives of groups and almost always in some kind of groups or institutional setting. That is why social psychologists cannot get very excited over the idea of, or studies of, interpersonal relations.

SMALL GROUPS AND PROBLEMATIC INTERACTION

There is voluminous literature about "small groups." While this literature reports research that is far from homogeneous in character and intent, the investigations share three features. First, the groups are newly formed, for the members have little or no previous relations with each other. Second, the groups are formed under the aegis of the investigator who brings them together for her own purposes. Third, the research almost always takes the form of an "experiment."

We will avoid the temptation to present a "classic" experimental small-group investigation, offering instead a brief account of how interaction occurs in natural social groups. We shall draw our example from the interactions of the groups which form the basis of how Alcoholics Anonymous works (Denzin, 1986b). In so doing, we will attempt to draw together our previous discussions of identities, situations, social relationships, awareness contexts, and selves.

The Alcoholics Anonymous Group

There are over 50 thousand Alcoholics Anonymous groups in the United States. They range in size from five persons to thirty or more. A.A. groups meet at least once a week. Every group has a chairperson who calls the meeting to order, announces him or herself as an alcoholic, asks for a moment of silence, and then asks the members present to say the "Serenity Prayer." The chairperson then asks a member to read "How It Works," which is a statement from the text *Alcoholics Anonymous* (1976) that contains A.A.'s Twelve Steps. After this text is read, another member reads A.A.'s Twelve Traditions (A.A., 1953). After this reading, some A.A. groups ask a member to read from a thought-for-the-day book that contains a prayer, a meditation, and a thought for the day.

After these three texts are read, the chair asks (1) if there are any visitors to the group; (2) if anyone has an A.A. birthday (i.e., has been sober for one year or more); (3) if there are any announcements; (4) if anyone has a Step, problem, or topic to be discussed.

At this point in the meeting a member may raise his hand and make the following statement: "My name's Bill and I'm an alcoholic. I'd like to talk about not drinking today." The chairperson will typically say something like, "OK, Let's talk about the First Step. Who would like to go first?" A member will raise his or her hand and begin speaking, always with the announcement, "My name is _____ and I am an alcoholic." After each group member has talked, the chairperson will ask, "Does anyone have seconds?" At this point a member may speak again. Having given everyone this option, the chairperson then closes the meeting. This is done by asking everyone to join in the saying of the "Lord's Prayer." All members of the group rise, join hands, and say this prayer in unison. This ends the meeting.

A.A. meetings last one hour on the average. Each member typically speaks for no longer than two to five minutes. When a member speaks, she speaks only for herself, not for A.A. or for the A.A. group.

Group Ritual and Interaction

We can extract several social psychological processes concerning how small groups operate from this description of the A.A. group meeting. First, we can see the operation of ritual. Reciting the Serenity Prayer, the Lord's Prayer, and the readings from A.A. texts ritually organize the group; they draw it together and create moments of ritual solidarity at the beginning and end of the meeting. Thus ritual, as a social act which confers special status on one or more persons, is central to the organization of the group. Second, the group exists in and through talk. Communication in the form of talk represents the central activity of the A.A. group. Third, the group is organized in terms of a "pledge," or a larger purpose that encompasses every member. This purpose is twofold. First, it tells the members that their primary purpose is to carry the message of A.A. to the alcoholic who still suffers. Second, it subordinates individual purposes to a larger group goal.

Fourth, the A.A. meeting is organized in terms of a shared identity, which is contained in the word "alcoholic." Every member of the group identifies him or herself in terms of the label alcoholic. This shared identity locates every member within the ritual structure of A.A. This identity is passed on the merger of quasi-formal title (I'm an alcoholic) and on the personal name; thus the A.A. meeting merges structural and interpersonal relationships. This is underscored by the fact that A.A. members seldom exchange last names; hence the word "anonymous" in the title of the organization.

Fifth, every member shares an open awareness context, involving the identity of alcoholic, although members may suspect that they are not alcoholics. They may pretend to be alcoholic by announcing themselves as "alcoholic," but they may not believe this about themselves. They may also suspect others of not really being alcoholic. Sixth, the A.A. group, through its meeting, is a temporal production. That is, action and talk within the meeting are based on shared pasts, a shared present, and a common projected future (Couch, 1984b, p. 1). Members share past experiences with alcoholism.

They locate themselves in the now of the present as they take part in the A.A. rituals. When the meeting closes with the phrase "Keep coming back," the members project a future which will be shared at the next A.A. meeting. The A.A. meeting is a coordinated production, resting on shared identities, interpersonal relationships, and a shared perspective on the past, the present, and the future.

Emotional Understanding

There is an additional feature of the A.A. experience (Maxwell, 1984), the phenomenon of *emotional understanding*. By this term we refer to knowing and comprehending through emotional means, including sympathy and imagination, the intentions, feelings, and thoughts expressed by another (Denzin, 1984, p. 282). Alcoholics understand one another emotionally because they have had similar experiences with alcohol, including being drunk, hung over, depressed, remorseful, guilty, fearful, and dependent upon alcohol for courage. By sharing these experiences with one another in A.A. meetings, alcoholics build up a form of emotional understanding that is unique to the A.A. experience. This form of understanding brings them back to meetings.

We are suggesting that every social group, at a basic level, rests on a form and type of emotional understanding that is unique to the group. Because every social group organizes itself around this phenomenon, we can argue that this is a universal feature of ongoing human groups. In and through emotional understanding, groups and their members form attachments of a long-standing and often intimate nature.

Interaction Rituals and the Interactional Order

Goffman (1983) has suggested that a neglected area of sociological study is the interactional order, which is the world of interaction that occurs whenever persons come into one another's presence. This is the world of face-to-face interaction, encounters, and behavior in public places. We will briefly discuss Goffman's analysis of interaction rituals and the interactional order; throughout his work he has directly confronted how etiquette rules or ceremonial prescriptives enter into interaction (1956, 1959, 1961, 1967, 1971, 1974, 1981, 1983).

The core of Goffman's position is that social regulations subtly govern interaction. This conception of regulated interactions is clearly illustrated in his paper, "On Face-Work, An Analysis of Ritual Elements in Social Interaction" (1955). Goffman begins by noting that everybody "lives in a world of social encounters" that involve face-to-face contacts with others. During these encounters, people tend to act out "lines"—whether deliberately or not. A line is a pattern of verbal and nonverbal acts by which the person expresses both his view of the situation and the participants in it, including himself. The term "face" is "the positive social value a person effectively claims for himself by the line others assume he has taken during a particular contact." The person "may be said to *have*, or *be in* or *maintain* face when the line he effectively takes presents an image of him that is internally consistent," supported by others' gestures, and confirmed through "evidence conveyed through impersonal agencies in the situation."

Goffman emphasizes that the line "maintained by and for a person . . . tends to be of a legitimate institutionalized kind." During certain socially defined situations, "an interactant of known or visible attributes can expect to be sustained in a particular face." A person is "out of face" when he is not ready with a line of the kind that the participants in given defined situations "are expected to take." When a person is out of face, the ordinary regulated interaction is out of balance: "expressive events are being contributed to the encounter which cannot be readily woven into the expressive fabric of the occa-

sions." Thus the person may be embarrassed, shamed, or confused, and may show these reactions. If she can control or conceal these reactions, she has "poise."

All participants in these encounters share the responsibility of maintaining face. Concerning his own face, "each person takes on the responsiblity of standing guard over the flow of expressive events. . . . He must ensure that a particular *expressive order* is maintained—an order which regulates the flow of events, large or small, so that anything that appears to be expressed by them will be consistent with his face." Rules of considerateness and self-respect help him conduct himself to maintain not only his own face but that of the other participants. Consequently, these encounters embody much "face-work," which "serves to counteract 'incidents'—that is, events whose symbolic implications threaten face."

Goffman has focused on one class of rules—"rules of etiquette" or "ceremonial directives." Other rule-based categories, such as those that protect the civil-legal order, or those that are specific to intimate relationships, go basically unnoticed in his studies. Thus he offers a restricted account of interactional rules. Furthermore, his model of interaction assumes a "threat-based" view of human interaction. His individuals genuinely are actors, always on a stage, rarely if ever able to relax and "drop their guard." In this sense an uneasy dramaturgical analogy underlies a good deal of his work. He offers insights into the drama of action in public places, but seldom takes the student into the "safe" regions of comfortable, at-ease interactants; nor does his perspective suggest leads for studying a common everyday situation—the case of two interactants, experienced in working together, who are now working on a common task.

Goffman's analysis is primarily concerned with *stabilities* in interaction. This is made quite clear by his closing points, which touch on the relation of face saving to social relationships. When a person enters an encounter, "he already stands in some kind of social relationship to the others concerned, and expects to stand in a given relationship to them after the particular encounter ends." That is how social contacts among people are linked with wider society. Much of the activity during an encounter is understandable as an effort by everyone to get through the encounter "without disrupting the relationships of the participants." What about relationships that happen to be changing? "And if relationships are in a process of change, the object will be to bring the encounter to a satisfactory close without altering the expected course of development." Understandably, this kind of accommodative behavior requires the socialization of all the participants. This view of interaction pictures interaction as governed or guided by not only explicit rules, but implicit rules. The informal control that society exerts on individuals is not rigid or mechanical, but subtle, resulting in a corresponding subtlety of interaction.

MESOSTRUCTURES AND INTERACTION

We shift our attention from social relationships, small groups, encounters, and interaction rituals to another level of social interaction. Following Maines (1977, 1978, 1979, 1982), we term this next level of interaction *mesostructure*. The mesostructure refers to interactional processes that mediate between the world of immediate social interaction and larger institutional and organizational structures. An example of a mesostructure would be the homecoming celebrations on many American college and university campuses where students engage in rallies, parades, game attendance, and after-game celebrations. In these activities, their experiences are mediated by larger structures (i.e., the university, their dormitory, fraternity, sorority, the athletic contest, the

stadium, and so on); yet their activities occur in face-to-face and larger interactional contexts (i.e., as spectators at the homecoming game).

Another example of a mesostructural process would be negotiators at a bargaining table, attempting to mediate between labor and management over a wage contract. Here the negotiations represent the intersection of two larger orders—union and management.

Other instances of mesostructure would include small- and large-scale social movements (see Zurcher & Snow, 1981), in which participants attempt to call attention to alternative views of a current public issue. The anti-nuclear movement, ERA, protests on behalf of South Africa, and Mothers Against Drunk Drivers, all reflect processes that mediate between the world of immediate, private interest and the world of public issues, public policy, and public opinion.

As we use the term mesostructure, it encompasses earlier concepts like *negotiated order* (Strauss, 1978; Maines & Charlton, 1985) and the various forms of *collective behavior* that have been studied by sociologists. Thus crowds, public opinion, and social movements are all forms of mesostructures in process (see Lofland, 1981, p. 412). Similarly, collective protest and instances of social unrest speak to mesostructural processes (see Blumer, 1978).

The various negotiated orders studied by Strauss (1978), including interorganization negotiations, the Nuremberg trials, the international negotiations between the United States and the Soviet Union over the Balkans, and the power struggles between various ethnic groups in Kenya, are themselves instances of mesostructures in process (Maines, 1982, p. 277–78). Negotiated orders occur within any social order or social world when common understandings break down and have to be reconstituted or renegotiated. Negotiations occur within all social orders, even the most repressive (Strauss, 1978). Negotiations and negotiated orders thus connect mesostructures with larger institutional forms (e.g., the U.N.)

and the world of immediate negotiated inter-action.

In this section we will discuss two meso-structural forms: (1) the war games that oc-cur in the U.S. military and (2) the social un-rest and collective protest that erupted into the storming of the Bastille in Paris in 1789. This will allow us to speak about collective behavior as a form of social interaction, and will also serve to make our point that meso-structures constitute important social psy-chological phenomena.

The War Game

Zurcher (1985) has described the workings of the war game on a military reserve exer-cise—this particular game, a three-day exer-cise in August 1983. It involved approximately 200 navy, marine, army, and National Guard reservists—most of whom were medical per-sonnel—who were required to make an am-phibious and helicopter landing on a small is-land occupied by "hostile forces," a few miles from the Mississippi coast. The "hostiles" were to be attacked and overcome by the Marines. Medical personnel were set up to deal with sim-ulated casualties. Participants were expected to demonstrate medical expertise, combat behav-ior, and a "gung ho" emotional attitude (Zurcher, 1986, p. 192). Units were ranked on their performances in this exercise. Zurcher suggests (p. 203) that:

the immediate situation interfaced empirically and analytically the macro-organization and mi-cro-interaction influences on the Reservist's emo-tional expression. In this sense, the immediate sit-uation was a mesostructural phenomenon.

Zurcher supports this conclusion through the following analysis. First, the war game was scripted and prepared in advance by mil-itary authorities. The scenario outlined key players, gave a script for action on the field, suggested how the exercise was to be staged, and specified how the participants were to look, act, and feel. This first phase of the exercise included game preparations and travelling to the war game. By the time they arrived, participants were expected to have learned their parts.

The second phase of the game involved the actual performance in the field. In this stage the members enacted, modified, and negated the organizational script. In the be-ginning of this phase, participants behaved mechanically, with little show of emotion. The "gung ho" emotional script was clearly absent. Members grumbled about what they were doing while supervisors exhorted them to move faster and to get with it. The tem-perature was in the high 90- to 100-degree range and the humidity was 95 percent, and members were sweating profusely. They complained about their food rations during the meal break.

As soon as the break for lunch was over, the major component of the war game be-gan. Participants fired small arms loaded with blanks. Helicopters swooped into the exercise area in simulated attack; the landing crafts on the beach fired heavy weapons; smoke bombs were set off. Designated ma-rine casualties fell on the field, and medical units retrieved and treated the wounded. Wounded marines had been dressed in "moulage" simulations—"rubber and plastic molds of bodily injury . . . protruding bro-ken bones, exposed entrails, or brains—am-putated limbs, charred flesh, and spurting artificial blood" (Zurcher, 1986, p. 197). En-thusiasm ran high during the first two hours of the conflict; then members began to com-plain of fatigue. At the conclusion of the war game afternoon, senior officers complained that the troops had not performed up to the appropriate emotional level. During the eve-ning meal, reservists "bitched" about being tired, about not being able to take this stuff seriously, and about the senior officers. Re-servists left the war game the next morning; when they arrived at the naval staging base they joked about the war being over and about going home, and expressed pleasure that the exercise was over.

The war game, as analyzed by Zurcher, was a mesostructural phenomenon. It connected the larger military social structure (macro-level), with the immediate world (micro) of face-to-face interaction. We turn to a discussion of collective behavior.

Collective Behavior: Crowds, Movements, and Protests

Collective behavior traditionally has been defined as "emergent and extra-institutional forms of behavior" (Lofland, 1981, p. 411) which involve a "suspension of the attitudes of everyday life" (Lofland, 1981, p. 414). Instances of collective behavior include rumor, panic, angry or joyful crowds, mass fears which grip a society, fads, social movements, and instances of collective protest and social unrest.

The literature on collective behavior is diffuse and at times contradictory. Various theories—resource mobilization, value-added, frustration-aggression, emergent norm, psychoanalytic, behavioral, deprivation, alienation, circular interaction, cognitive-emotional—have been offered to account for the forms and functions of collective behavior (Zurcher & Snow, 1981; Miller, 1985; McPhail & Miller, 1973). It seems useful to present an empirical example so that we can make better sense out of what occurs in those situations defined as exhibiting collective behavior.

The Storming of the Bastille

Sartre (1976, pp. 351–63) has described how, in July 1789, the people of Paris revolted against monarch Louis XVI. This revolt, which was part of the chain of events that have become known as the French Revolution, mobilized the citizens of Paris and France against the monarchy and contributed to a rewriting of French civil code concerning the rights of the state in relation to the citizens of France. It signaled a wave of democracy which was to sweep Europe.

Sartre's analysis encompasses the major concepts which exist in the collective behav-ior literature. Panic and rumor were everywhere; joyful and angry crowds assembled in the streets; mass violence occurred; the king surrounded the city with his armies; newspapers were shut down; citizens met in small secret groups to protest what was occurring; a reign of terror existed. In the end the citizens won; they stormed the Bastille and brought down the government.

How did this occur? Sartre suggests that the king and his forces constituted a third party or force which organized the alienated French citizens into fused and pledged groups. At first the citizens were disorganized: They appeared in the streets in gatherings or crowds; they were unstructured and had few leaders. As they continued to meet more resistance, they organized into pledged groups; that is, they agreed to fight the king and his forces. The pledge that they took, which consisted of phrases like "Freedom for all," organized them into solidarities. They had a purpose—to overthrow the government. Soon the pledged groups became more rigorously organized. Leaders and divisions of labor appeared; schedules and agendas were formed; motives for acting became slogans; a group purpose came into existence. Before long, the revolt consisted of public protests, organized crowd actions, and institutionalized groups. New members were recruited and became committed to the cause.

As a form of social unrest, the revolt challenged the existing social structure. It was an aggressive and collective protest against the king and his powers. It was a form of collective protest that "centered on persistent aggressive efforts to change social arrangements irrespective of the opposition" (Blumer, 1978, p. 31). As such it had the following features: First, it was a continuing affair—it was not short-lived. Second, it had no clear-cut goals, other than bringing down the king; its goals emerged as it unfolded. Its main focus was on dissatisfaction with the existing social order; and its participants were preoccupied with immediate issues.

Third, the collective protest of the citizens took on *expressive, unifying, symbolic,* and *coer-*

cive purposes. The protest became a way of *expressing* forms of feeling and emotion that had been built up and repressed. The protest released emotions (Blumer, 1978, p. 41). The *unifying* function of the protest has already been suggested; it created new forms of solidarity and group awareness among the French citizens. *Symbolically,* the protesters used their actions as a way of influencing public opinion. Their protest activities were symbolic displays. *Coercively,* the protesters tried to force the French authorities to meet their requests and demands.

Fourth, as the protest developed, a polarization of opinion emerged. The protesters and the authorities entered into a warlike relation—which, fifth, created the place for violence and terror to emerge. This violence served, sixth, to crystallize the protestors into an organized movement (Blumer, 1978, p. 49). Once the collective protest became an organized movement, it came to assume the framework of "a working organization" (Blumer, 1978, p. 50). A stable leadership appeared; a secretariat was set up; members were organized and given rights and duties; rules for guiding action were put in place; long- and short-term goals were developed; an ideology was put in place. The protest began to lose its spontaneous features; it became a social structure.

This discussion of collective protest and social unrest reveals how the social psychologist analyzes forms of social behavior that are larger than face-to-face interactions. We have shown how groups and their organization lie at the heart of collective protest and collective behavior. The concept of mesostructure suggests an interplay between larger institutional structures, groups, and immediate interactional experience. Within mesostructures, negotiations occur; thus a negotiated order, whether based on violence and terror or mock war games, lies at the heart of all social orders. Following Hall (1986), we can argue that the study of social organization and social interaction involves a consideration of how collective activities are organized in terms of interactional networks,

conventionalized practices, resources, temporality, and power. This brings us to our last topic.

Power

We define power as force or interpersonal dominance which involves the manipulation, control, and often destruction of one human by another. As force, power often translates into violence, which is the attempt to take back by force something that has been lost. Power always exists in social relationships; hence the study of power involves the study of power relations. Power relations (i.e., master-slave, parent-child) rest on interactional practices which place persons in authority relations over one another. Power exists as a process in social interaction. Behind power lie ideology, political belief, and systems of truth and knowledge. All systems of power assume theories of truth. For example, some say that it is right and proper that parents have more power than their children because they know more.

Systems of knowledge which support power structures often rely upon scientific knowledge for their support. We have seen how Freudian and Marxist theories support various theories of human motivation and action. The knowledge structures that support power arrangements are constantly changing, and are in constant demand by a public which accepts theories of sexuality, drug addiction, and alcoholism on a large scale. More and more, theories of knowledge emanate from the university (Foucault, 1980, p. 51). We shall say more about power later when we discuss gender, self-control, and social control.

CONCLUSION

Interaction is rule-guided, and in many situations rituals organize how persons present themselves to one another. All interaction occurs in social situations; how situations are defined is a problem that especially concerns the social psychologist. In social situations, social relationships—structural and interpersonal—are established. Identities are located in social settings, and changes in identity accompany status passages through the social structure. Small group interactions are often organized in terms of the sharing of emotion; emotions are also shaped by the awareness context of interaction. At the mesostructure level, collective behavior, social protest, and staged social dramas occur. Power, knowledge, and force are basic features of the interaction process.

SUGGESTED READINGS

BLUMER, H. (1962). Society as symbolic interaction. In A. Rose (Ed.), *Human behavior and social processes* (pp. 179–92). Boston: Houghton Mifflin. This article forcefully contrasts the structural view of society with the symbolic interactionist conception developed in this chapter.

BLUMER, H. (1969). *Symbolic Interactionism.* Englewood Cliffs, NJ: Prentice-Hall. The classic symbolic interactionist statement on self and interaction.

GOFFMAN, E. (1974). *Frame Analysis.* New York: Harper & Row. Goffman's most difficult book on the problematic and ritual nature of interactional experience.

STONE, G. P. (1962). Appearance and the self. In A. Rose (Ed.), *Human behavior and social processes* (pp. 86–118). Boston: Houghton Mifflin. Stone offers a view of interaction and the self that stresses the place of communication and appearance in social discourse. An important contribution to the symbolic interactionist view of the self and the individual in the socialization process. A revised version of this article appears in Stone & Farberman (eds.) (1981). *Social psychology through interaction* (2nd ed.). New York: John Wiley.

McCALL, G. J., AND SIMMONS, J. L. (1978). *Identities and interactions.* (rev. ed.). New York: Free Press. An important analysis of self, identity, and interaction from a perspective somewhat different from our own.

CHAPTER ELEVEN
Self-Control, Social Control, and Identity Transformation

The self is not fixed at the conclusion of childhood, as Freud might have implied. In Part Four we examine the transformations of self which occur in later phases of the life cycle. Some have divided the life cycle, without great success, into the phases of *infancy, childhood, adulthood, middle age, old age,* and *death.* We intend to demonstrate that the self changes as its social relationships and social worlds undergo transformation.

In earlier chapters, we considered how the internal environment of the individual is categorized, perceived, and brought into systematic relation with the outside world. Central to this process are the development of self-awareness, the acquisition of language, and the ability to put the self in the perspective of another individual. Society, as Cooley (1902) argued, exists inside the individual in the form of language and thought. Society and the individual, to use his term, are "two sides of the same coin." We wish to develop this point one step further by examining in greater detail the links between self-control, social control, and the transformations of self that emerge during the interaction process.

In Chapter 8 we noted that individuals act in ways to salvage and enhance their self-conceptions. Here, we shall examine those situations where individuals often find themselves denied the rights of esteem. Few individuals voluntarily submit to derogation, embarrassment, or self-mortification. Such activities do occur, however, and with a patterned regularity that crosscuts small groups, total institutions, and intimate friendship circles. We will examine the circumstances that give rise to these interactional experiences.

We propose the following model of analysis. Individuals can *cede self-control*—that is, give up a degree of autonomy over their thoughts and actions—voluntarily (as in hypnosis); involuntarily (as in a mental hospital or a prison camp) or they can find, quite unexpectedly, that in the course of an emergent interactional episode that their fellow individuals have suddenly turned against them.

Or they may find that the compounds they have ingested suddenly leave them with no immediate control over their own thoughts and actions.

If we examine the sources to which self-control can be ceded, the following distinctions are relevant. First, individuals may voluntarily give over control to another individual, perhaps a psychiatrist or a physician. Second, they can place themselves in the hands of a small group. Third, they may find that they are in the clutches of a complex organization, perhaps the military or a mental hospital. Fourth, they may commit themselves to, or find that they are under the control of an ideology or an abstract cause, such as communism or a deviant cult. In a strict sense, commitment to a cause leads the individual into direct interactions with other individuals who may be caught up in organizations or small groups. This set of distinctions produces twelve possible relationships between the source of ceding control and the mode of ceding control. It is beyond our scope to discuss these twelve ideal-type cases; we only note in passing that the relationship between who controls the individual and how that control has been gained is quite complex. Further, we must indicate that in some situations single individuals gain control over broad segments of the population, as politicians do. Finally, throughout this discussion the question of what is given up continually must be raised. Few individuals find themselves in situations where all aspects of their life have fallen under the complete control of another individual or group. Some slices of the self inevitably remain free from the control of others, even the decision to die. That is, coercion is seldom complete; only parts of the individuals' activities and self-conceptions come under the control of others. Even during instances of potentially total coercion (prison camps, solitary confinement), individuals attempt to keep control over the "deepest" and most sacred parts of their selves. They will fight to the bitter end to maintain segments of self-respect, preserve control over their own thoughts, and protect the sanctity, privacy, and inviolability of their physical bodies.

Our discussion in this chapter is guided by two central questions: How is an individual's control of her own actions related to societal control of her actions? And how can an individual's actions be controlled by others? To answer such questions, we shall discuss several topics that may seem quite unrelated; however, each bears on the issues of self-control and social control. We shall discuss the nature of voluntary behavior, the phenomenon of hypnosis, the loss of self-control, and the institutionally induced changes in individuals that cause them to either cede a measure of their own control to others, or change radically the social bases of their own self-control. We also will examine the circumstances of group commitment, embarassment, degradation, and paranoia.

VOLUNTARY BEHAVIOR

The popular conception of voluntary behavior is that it involves control of behavior by an internal psychological force called "will" or "will power." This force is seen as independent of any specific biological or neurological structure and is usually believed to be "free" and, therefore, essentially unpredictable. Its most typical manifestation is in choosing among alternatives.

The discerning student will recognize in this common but naïve view the same dualistic distinction that is generally made between thinking and language. Just as language supposedly expresses thinking and is its vehicle, so voluntary behavior is supposed to be merely an expression of the person's will.

A sounder, more scientific view is the conception of voluntary behavior as an activity that depends upon the internalization of language. We have noted that as one ascends the evolutionary scale from the simplest forms of life to humans, the central nervous system assumes greater and greater dominance. Internal cortical processes are not solely determined by stimuli from outside the nervous system, but depend also upon stimuli that originate within the system. Voluntary behavior, from this point of view, depends upon the ability of people to initiate responses within themselves which in turn inhibit or facilitate other responses. These controlling responses are verbal in nature or are derived from verbal behavior.

Views of volitional behavior that are remarkably alike in some of their basic outlines have been developed by Hull (from the study of hypnosis and suggestibility); Luria (through the experimental study of child psychology and of hypnotism); Head and Goldstein (from the study of aphasia, as discussed in Chapter 5); and Hudgins (from experiments on voluntary control of the pupillary reflex).

Hull (1933) finds that there are two fairly distinct levels of human behavior: "an upper or symbolic level, and a lower nonsymbolic or instrumental level." Symbolic acts are described as "pure stimulus acts, acts that function purely as stimuli to evoke other acts." The most common form of symbolic behavior is speech. Hull applied this scheme to hypnotism and voluntary behavior. He indicated that in the hypnotic situation the symbolic stimulation is (1) produced by one individual, and (2) carried out on the instrumental level by another. In voluntary behavior, however, the same person performs both the symbolic act and its instrumental sequel. For example, a hypnotized man drinks a glass of water because he is told to do so by the hypnotist, whereas in ordinary life he drinks a glass of water because he tells himself to do so. The "will" is thus conceived by Hull as a symbolic process or as control of one's own behavior through self-stimulation (what he calls "pure stimulus acts").

Hudgins (1933) has demonstrated experimentally that individuals' control of their own responses by verbal mechanisms can be extended even to some reflex activities that are ordinarily beyond voluntary control (for example, the pupillary reflex). The way in which the result was accomplished throws a great deal of light on what is sometimes called the "will." Subjects were first conditioned to produce the pupillary reflex when a bell was sounded through the simultaneous flashing of a light into their eyes. An electric circuit was then arranged so that when the subjects closed their hands at the vocal command of the investigation, the light and bell circuits were closed, thereby causing the bell to ring and the light to go on. Finally, all other stimuli except the verbal command were eliminated and the subjects' pupils were observed to contract when the experimenter gave the command. The next step in developing voluntary control of this conditioned response was to require the subjects themselves to repeat the verbal cue. The commands were first repeated aloud, then in a whisper, and last subvocally. The subjects were finally able to cause the pupils of their own eyes to contract merely by thinking of the verbal command.

Luria (1960), approaching the study of voluntary behavior from another perspective, also emphasizes that it involves the use by the individual of auxiliary verbal cues. He notes that people do not control their behavior directly by the exertion of "will power," but can do so only indirectly through the mediation of verbal self-stimulation. For example, if a despondent woman is urged to "buck up and be cheerful," she cannot do so merely by wishing it. However, if her attention can be directed to more cheerful subjects by talking with her or by inducing her to engage in some recreational activity such as a game of tennis, the desired result may be accomplished. Similarly, as Hudgins' experiment indicates, people cannot cause the pupils of their eyes to contract merely by concentrating or exerting "will power." Intermediate steps, such as those used by Hudgins, must be included.

From this point of view, will power ceases to be conceived as a psychological force and becomes a number of complexly interrelated central processes deriving from the inter-

nalization of language and speech. Just as memory may be jogged by tying a string around one's finger, so do the culturally derived language mechanisms function as mediating and structuring devices through which self-regulation is achieved. *Self-control and voluntary behavior are thus conceived as products of external influences emanating from the cultural environment, rather than as the unfolding of vague, disembodied innate propensities of the organism.* Some sort of conception of this general nature seems to be required to make sense of the kinds of phenomena considered in this chapter.

The views of Hull and Luria, and the experimental results obtained by Hudgins and others, all point toward the same conclusion.

Like the notion of will itself, the idea of "free will" is based upon a false view of symbolic behavior. As a corrective we may note several points. To begin with, "free will" is not entirely free, for it is bounded, restricted, and limited by the culture of the actor. Thus, it does not occur to the readers of this book to make choices involving the values of the Bantu or Balinese, or to act like these people. This may appear to be a trite observation, but its truth is often ignored; for example, it is commonplace to blame persons who, from an objective point of view, ought not to be blamed. Thus, children are often held responsible for stealing before they know what stealing really means. Our blaming rests upon the assumption—often false—that these persons know better and have a genuine choice of attitude and act. Whatever "will" may be, it cannot operate outside the confining limits of the actor's system of symbols.

Human social behavior is not mechanically determined by immediately given external events and situations; it is organized symbolically. Human freedom is thus a relative matter. Humans are not entirely bound by the physical conditions of space and time, but they are enclosed within symbolic systems. The thoughts of a prisoner in solitary confinement cannot be controlled by his jailers, but they are controlled and limited by the social groups that have imposed their standards, moral codes, and symbols upon him.

One of the authors once listened to a passionate plea for individual freedom addressed to a class of several hundred students by one of its members. The speaker argued that "the individual" should free him- or herself from all "herd" influences, from all groups and institutions; that he or she should think and act as a free individual. This view represents a logical consequence of the popular misconceptions of "freedom," "free will," and "individuality." Its essential absurdity will be clear to anyone who reflects upon it for a moment. In the first place, if this student desired to be free of all institutions, he obviously should not have learned English or any other language; he should not have attended a university or spoken to a class as he did. The obvious implication of his view is that humans can be free only if they avoid all human contact and civilization.

Many years ago, French sociologist Durkheim opposed individualistic notions of freedom and autonomy by pointing to the body of moral and social rules that are chronologically antecedent to the birth of every individual. Durkheim saw these group rules as largely controlling the behavior of individual members, duty and voluntary behavior being closely linked. Durkheim stressed that concepts and categories are supraindividual, the product of collective activities, and that since individual thinking necessarily utilizes concepts, the idea of individual volition apart from norms is illusory. Blondel (1939) has modified this position by arguing that it is not necessary to deny genuine individual autonomy merely because a person must always make choices within a framework provided by society. Freedom of the individual, he contends, is itself a social product. Human beings, in contrast to lower animals, are free precisely because they are social animals living primarily in a symbolic world. To this should be added a point which we already made in another context—namely, that no two situations are ever completely identical; hence, all behavior possesses some degree

of novelty, and some of it requires genuine decisions. The discovery of values and the consequent organization of behavior along new lines free humans from slavish obedience to tradition; at the same time, tradition enters into the organization of new as well as customary behavior.

Social Control and Commitment to Groups

Social control is often erroneously seen as something that is achieved by formal governmental agencies and officially promulgated rules and regulations. Actually, most people do what they ought or have to do simply because they want to. It is only against this background of willing conformity that the formal agencies of control can be effective.

This argument can be summarized by saying that social control and self-control are interlocked and interdependent processes. This interrelationshio is brought about because people find self-fulfillment, self-expression, and a sense of identity and personal worth primarily through commitment to various kinds of groups and the standards of those groups. This point is well stated by Kanter, who, on the basis of her study of communes, remarks (1972, pp. 65–66):

For communal relations to be maintained, what a person is willing to give to the group, behaviorally and emotionally, and what it in turn expects from him, must be coordinated and mutually reinforcing. This reciprocal relationship, in which both what is given to the group and what is received from it are seen by the person as expressing his true nature and as supporting his concept of self, is the core commitment to a community.

In terms of this statement, we can say that social control can be effective only when persons identify with the group and internalize its values so that it becomes essential to their own sense of self-esteem and personal worth to act so as to support the social order. They hold a sense of involvement and belonging; they think of the group as an extension or part of themselves and make its values and rules their own personal values and rules. The group has become a part of them; it exerts its influence over them in symbolic as well as in direct behavioral ways. Again quoting Kanter (1972, pp. 66–67): "Commitment links self-interest to social requirements. . . . When a person is committed, what he wants to do is the same as what he has to do, and this gives to the group what it needs to maintain itself at the same time that he gets what he needs to nourish his own sense of self." As Kanter says (1972, p. 66): "A committed person is loyal and involved; he has a sense of belonging, a feeling that the group is an extension of himself and he is an extension of the group." That is, in social control there is always self-control, and in self-control there is always social control. By the same token, lack of self-control is often a reflection of an absence of social control. But without individuals committed to their maintenance, social groups would collapse. In this sense, persons create and contribute to the very situations that control their own lives, fates, and careers.

Embracement and Distance

When individuals have committed themselves instrumentally, emotionally, and morally to a social group, they may be said to have *embraced* that group's universe of discourse. Embracement produces both moral solidarity and a solidified group perspective. It is a mistake, however, to assume that all members of any group mutually and with equal enthusiasm commit themselves to the group's demands. In a different context, Goffman (1961) has introduced the concept of *role distance* to describe those moments when individuals place a wedge between themselves and the role they are playing. Adults riding merry-go-rounds, for example, typically act as if they wish they were not seated on the wooden horse, while young children vigorously throw themselves into the activity of horse rider. In the present context, we can propose that on occasion members of all groups place a wedge be-

tween themselves and the demands that their groups place on them. These "self-distancing" activities may include refusals to meet the requests of other group members, or may be displayed in a progressive withdrawal from the group entirely. There is, then, a constant tension between the demands of the group and the demands individuals place on themselves. Total, complete, and continuous commitment and embracement to social groups is an infrequent occurrence. More typical are moments of heightened involvement, followed by periods of disinvolvement, disengagement, and self-distancing.

Propaganda

The problem we are concerned with now is the relationship between self-control and propaganda. For example, consider the man who implicitly believes what he reads in his favorite newspaper, what the latest government handout says, or what a particular television commentator announces. Is this person really a free agent? Or is the dupe of propaganda comparable to the hypnotized man who says, does, and apparently believes whatever he is told to say, do, or believe? If the latter answer is accepted, then it is probably necessary for us to admit that we are almost continuously, in varying degrees, being manipulated by outside persons, agencies, and forces which shape our symbolic environments, our conceptions of the world. They do this in ways that often have little relationship to the real objective world— whatever that may be. Granting this situation, the important point really may be whether we are permitted to cherish the delusions of intellectual mastery of our environments and of being free and autonomous individuals. These, by the way, are delusions that the subject who acts our posthypnotic suggestions also ordinarily entertains.

Persons who are relatively unaware of the pervasiveness of propaganda—having committed themselves to a general political or social philosophy—tend to select media sources that present them with views that they are predisposed to accept. They also tend to have friends and belong to groups that reinforce their opinions and that rely on the same sources for support of their opinions. In this process of mutual reinforcement, there is selective inattention to information and interpretations not in harmony with the person's basic social and political assumptions, which may be anywhere on the political spectrum from the extreme left to the extreme right (Blumer, 1978; Smelser, 1963; Altheide, 1985). Some persons commonly have the comfortable illusion that they have valid and reliable information about, and are responding rationally to, their environment and have it under control in an intellectual sense.

On the other hand, there are people who feel that they are being manipulated by external forces that control events, social policy, and the flow of information. They tend to emphasize the unreliability of mass media reports and interpretations. They commonly assume the existence of extensive behind-the-scene news conspiracies by rich and powerful persons, corporations. or organizations to manipulate people, events, and information in their own interests for the sake of wealth, power, or other material advantage. People with such views tend to feel a sense of futility and helplessness with respect to the broad social and political issues and often simply ignore them and commit themselves only to small, restricted groups like the family. Others, who believe that things can be changed, may commit themselves to reform groups or "revolutionary" movements.

INTERACTIONAL LOSS OF SELF-CONTROL

In the preceding section we discussed the situation where individuals cede self-control to a group or cause. Often voluntary and positive in consequence, these exercises in self-exchange involve planning and reciprocal commitments by the persons ceding control and by those who receive their goods, resources, and self-identities. They gain something positive for what they give. The tenuous, yet complex relationship between selves and others can be further elaborated by examining the situation of *interactional loss.* Such moments, which may be planned or unplanned, collusively based or emergent in tone, self-initiated or other-initiated, describe those occasions when individuals find their fellow interactants have either unexpectedly turned against them or now define them as less-than-competent selves. While on occasion planned—as when a person is a defendant in a divorce case—most typically these moments arise unexpectedly and catch them off guard. Incidents of this kind range from the deliberate embarrassment or harassment of individuals, to degradation ceremonies, self-mortification rituals, and collusively based conspiracies to drive someone from an organization. Then, people find that their ability to control and protect their valued self-identities have been denied, if not suddenly taken away.

In this section we examine the conditions that give rise to this interactional loss of self-control. For purposes of simplicity we focus on three forms of interactional loss: (1) emergent loss, as seen in embarrassment; (2) preplanned exclusion and self-loss, as witnessed in the degradation ceremony; and (3) emergent exclusion, which is common in instances of imputed paranoia or mental illness.

Embarrassment: The Case of Emergent Self-Loss

Any instance of emergent or planned self-loss requires time. Some moments are preceded by events which unfold in a serial fashion. That is, an individual is not just mortified, embarrassed, or degraded; a set of mutually held definitions of the situation must be brought into play if an instance of self-loss is to occur. In a sense, individuals cooperate in their own mortification, and they act so as to sustain or justify definitions in which they have been judged as less than competent. It is a mistake to assume that when self-control is ceded over to others, this ceding involves only one set of actors—those taking from the individual in question. It involves at least two parties: one to offer a definition, and another to accept or fight off that definition. Such moments are interactional productions.

Consequently, we can see that it takes two parties to produce an instance of embarrassment—one party who acts in a less than propitious manner and another party who acts on those untoward actions. In this sense we agree with Gross and Stone, who argue that (1964, p. 1):

Embarrassment exaggerates the core dimensions of social transaction, bringing them to the eye of the observer in an almost naked state. Embarrassment occurs whenever some *central* assumption in a transaction has been *unexpectedly* and unqualifiedly discredited for at least one participant. . . . Moreover embarrassment is infectious. It may spread, incapacitating others not previously incapacitated. It is a destructive disease. In the wreckage left by embarrassment lie the broken foundations of social transactions.

According to Goffman's (1961) formulations, embarrassment produces moments of "flooding out." Individuals lose control over themselves, their occasions, and their respective involvements. Action stops, and attempts to smooth over the flawed episode only acknowledge that something untoward has occurred. In short, to act on an instance of embarrassment can be as embarrassing as the original episode itself. Hence, individuals employ elaborate avoidance or defensive techniques to act as if an instance of embarrassment had not occurred. But these strategies need not concern us now. More to the point are those actions that produce the interactional discomfort of embarrassment. Following Goffman and Gross and Stone, we can note that any of the following acts or activities can cause an embarrassing incident in the flow of interaction. First, individuals can display a lack of poise. They stumble,

spill a drink, unaccountably touch another person, or perhaps give off an odor that discredits their claim of respectability. A person may also lose poise when he intrudes into the private settings of others, dresses improperly for a particular social occasion, or is the host of a cocktail party with an inadequate supply of food and drink.

By failing to measure up to the demands of the occasion, the individual calls into question the actions of all those who have conformed to social expectations. To be in the company of an embarrassing actor not only challenges one's own credibility, but raises the question of why that individual's actions should be regarded as embarrassing; and if they are so judged, why are her actions so judged and not those of another person. In these instances, embarrassing actions provoke both sympathy and discomfort. All individuals can recall moments when they acted, or could have acted, in a similar fashion. For this reason, actors typically cooperate to pull one another through the embarrassing transaction. But for the individual in question, shame, guilt, and a lack of self-respect are produced. Credible individuals ought not to embarrass others.

If loss of poise produces embarrassment, then we can see that presenting an inappropriate identity, or incorrect identification, can also disrupt the flow of interaction. Instances of misnaming, forgotten names, forgotten titles, and mistaken kinship affiliations are in this category. A divorced woman may be asked, innocently, how her former husband is doing. A college president may be misidentified by a member of the police. A faculty member may be mistaken for a janitor, perhaps because he dressed like a janitor. Misidentifications intermingle with actions that disturb the sequential flow of sociable gatherings. Individuals may attend a party thinking they have been invited because they are friends of the host or hostess; however, they find they have been invited not as guests, but as actors who might contribute to the status of the party givers. Having misread the character of the occasion, they may then act so as to quickly bring their role in it to conclusion. They may refuse to talk, talk to excess, exaggerate the effects of alcohol, or demand to be placed center stage, thus juggling the career and development of the party. They actively intrude into the gathering so as to gain some control over their place in it. Feeling that they have been embarrassed because of their own misidentifications, they make no attempt to turn the tables.

Deliberate Embarrassment

The foregoing examples of embarrassment were focused on unanticipated acts and actions that challenge the credibility of someone in a concrete situation. These accidental acts are less consequential than those that are deliberately produced; for if the individual does not anticipate such an activity, she is less accountable for its consequences. Deliberate embarrassment (Gross & Stone, 1964) is more severe. Here members of a group plan in advance to discredit one of their members. They may do so to facilitate socialization into a role or a preferred activity or identity—for example, hazing in the military or the college fraternity discourages one set of actions and rewards another set—or to halt the performance of an individual who is challenging the social group. Scapegoating, identity slurs, misrepresentations of integrity, and charges of malfeasance set the offended party off from other members of the group. Thus, embarrassment serves as a social control device for social groups. This suggests the third function of embarrassment: It reasserts and reaffirms power alignments, since only certain categories of individuals can legitimately embarrass others. Thus, embarrassment typically flows from the top down. It is bad form for a low-status actor to embarrass a superior, and he has less interactional power to command.

Degradation Ceremonies: Preplanned Loss

With the exception of planned embarrassment, most embarrassing incidents emerge unpredictably; neither their definers nor their actors anticipate their occurrence. These incidents are haphazardly, rather awkwardly accepted instances of status-forcing. The problematic individual is forced to accept an otherwise unacceptable definition of self. Degradation ceremonies describe planned and anticipated instances of status-forcing in which derelict individuals know in advance that they will lose self-credibility. Indeed, they may be shamed and openly required to plead guilty. Garfinkel (1956) has described the conditions that give rise to successful degradation ceremonies. Persons who are being degraded must be placed outside the everyday moral order and defined as a threat to that order. They may be defined as political criminals, "sex" fiends, child molesters, or murderers. Their actions must be cast in moral terms which threaten the existence of the social group, and their accuser must be defined as a person who is morally superior. The accuser will evoke higher moral values which witnesses accept, and he will be defined as a legitimate upholder of those volume. If the accuser is successful in his attempts, the accused individuals have no options open; they must accept their new status. Degradation ceremonies force them to yield to the wishes of others. They give up control over their own moral career, finding that their fate now lies in the hands of others.

Paranoia: Emergent Exclusion and Self-Loss

Planned exclusionary rituals are set up in advance and give the charged actor little control over her fate. They are to be contrasted with emergent exclusion. Often individuals begin to sense a wedge between themselves and others. They become uneasy, hypertensive; they overreact to the thoughts and actions of others. Such persons are often termed *paranoid*—their behavior is out of line with the realities of social interaction. Lemert (1962), in a series of case studies of paranoid individuals, has come to different conclusions. He suggests that paranoid individuals indeed may be accurately reacting to the specifics of their social situation. His analysis is instructive and may be utilized as an instance of a situation in which neither the individual in doubt (a man, say) nor his fellow interactants wish to alter their social relationships. He has no desire to be excluded, and they have no desire to exclude. However, through a course of events, both parties come to reject one another. The person who loses the most is the actor defined as paranoid. He may have nowhere to turn and may be unable to pinpoint accurately the causes of his exclusion; nor can his fellows accurately recount exactly why it was they came to feel uncomfortable in his presence. The emergence of exclusion rituals follows a relatively predictable career. First, there is an alteration in ongoing relationships. Persistent interpersonal difficulties between the individual and his interactive others lead to a collapse in trust and common understanding. The death of a relative, a threatened status loss, or a failure to be promoted produces a sense of uneasiness on the part of the "pre-paranoid" individual. This uneasiness, in turn, produces a series of overreactive behaviors toward superiors and close intimates. Arrogance, insults, and exploitations of the weaknesses of others may occur. Third, the individual begins to act in ways judged to be unreliable and dangerous to others. At this point he undergoes a set of redefinitions of both himself and others; he feels they are belittling him. A set of *spurious interactions* emerges. He avoids others and they avoid him; conversation drops to a minimum, and he begins deliberately to exclude himself from their company. At the same time, they are gossiping behind his back and excluding him from their sociable interactions. Conspiratorial actions now develop. Others openly plot to remove the deviant from their presence and he, correspondingly, may plot to have them removed or seek relocation elsewhere. Delusion sets in. The individual is denied interactional feedback. He has no reliable "reality" check for his inferences and his hunches. No one will talk to him. Soon

the individual moves into his own social world, and he may, as Goffman notes, produce an insanity of place both for himself and for others (1971, p. 390):

The manic declines to restrict himself to the social game that brings order and sense to our lives. Through his antics he gives up "his" self-respect, this being the reward we would allow him to have for himself as a reward for keeping a social place that may contain no other satisfaction for him. The manic gives up everything a person can be, and gives up too, the everything we make out of jointly guarded dealings. His doing so, and doing so for any of a multitude of independent reasons, reminds us what our everything is, and then reminds us that this everything is not very much. A somewhat similar lesson is taught by other categories of troublemakers who do not keep their place.

In the end, what began as a minor disturbance in interpersonal relationships produces a massive realignment of self and others. A new deviant appears. He loses, as does everyone else. Emergent self-loss of the exclusionary variety vividly highlights the points made earlier, namely, the social order is a symbolic order that must, however tacitly, be jointly maintained by the actions of cooperating individuals.

Recapitulation: Losses and Gains

Embarrassment, degradation, and the dynamics of organizational exclusion are descriptions of three situations where individuals lose more than they gain in their contracts with their outside social worlds. Whether fleeting, as with embarrassment, or preplanned, as in degradation, or emergent and long term, as with paranoia, agents of social control—who after all are fellow interactants—deliberately and unwittingly deny one another's claims of self-worth and self-esteem.

This is not to imply that all instances of self- and social control imply losses for one or more parties. Indeed, our earlier discussion of communes suggested that on many occasions individuals gain a great deal by giving themselves over to a social group, a cause, or an organization. Also, crowdlike collective behavior often produces serious alterations in the social structure (Le Bon, 1916; Rude, 1964). In the next section we discuss hypnosis, which describes a situation where the individual may enter into a relatively neutral relationship with an agent of social control, the hypnotist (Miller, 1986).

HYPNOSIS: THE CEDING OF SELF-CONTROL

The phenomenon of hypnosis provides striking examples of symbolic control over a wide range of human behavior. The hypnotized subject may be viewed as one who, in a peculiar sense, is relatively lacking in self-control, because behavior (ordinarily evoked by the person) is evoked by the hypnotist. A whole range of behavior may be elicited from a subject by simply ordering him to act and feel in certain ways.

Hypnotic Phenomena

The behavior elicited in hypnosis is unusual and puzzling. We shall therefore begin our discussion by describing some of it, turning then to the theories that have been proposed to account for it, and finally considering its implications in relation to less extreme behavior of a somewhat similar nature (Evans, 1984; Blum, 1984; Watkins, 1984; Edmonston Jr., 1984).

The *hypnotic trance* is induced in subjects primarily by talking to them. A variety of specific devices may be used; a woman may be placed in a relaxed position and told that her eyelids are heavy and that she is becoming sleepy. She is also told that as the hypnotist slowly counts to 50, her sleepiness will increase until, on the count of 50, she will be in a deep sleep. The subject may be asked initially to fix her eyes on a bright, rhythmically moving object to facilitate the process. Whatever the specific devices used, the essential factor is communication, usually verbal. Hypnotists cannot, however, induce the trance in anyone with whom they cannot

communicate verbally. Lower animals, for example, cannot be hypnotized. *Trance logic* (Orne, 1970) is the term given to the ability to hypnotized subjects to tolerate logical incongruities. For example, a hypnotized subject will converse with a hallucinated friend who is not present; or if told to hallucinate his friend Joe sitting in a chair on his left, when he is really sitting on the right, he will do so.

Susceptibility. Susceptibility to hypnosis, contrary to popular belief, is not correlated with lack of intelligence or "will power." Persons who follow the commands of the hypnotist and who succeed in focusing on her to the exclusion of anything else may be hypnotized even though they do not wish to be, and even though they believe that hypnotic phenomena do not exist or are merely "faked." Persons who are overcome by amusement, who think of other matters, or who react in opposition to the commands naturally do not make good subjects.

Eysenck tells of an experiment with a boastful young man who came to the laboratory telling everyone that he did not believe in hypnotism and that no one could hypnotize him (Eysenck, 1964, pp. 40–41). He continued to make such remarks while the hypnotic suggestions (for example, that he would fall into a deep sleep when the table was struck with a hammer) were being made to him. When the experimenter rapped the table the young man fell at once into a trance, leaving incompleted a sentence in which he had begun to say that he did not believe that a person with strong will power like his could be hypnotized. This subject remained under hypnosis for more than two hours. When he was awakened, he completed the sentence that he had started more than two hours earlier and refused to believe that he had been hypnotized until he consulted his watch.

Distortion of Perceptions. When the subject has been hypnotized, she can be induced to do, say, and apparently, believe many things that are contrary to her ordinary behavior and beliefs. She can be made to report seeing and hearing things that the hypnotist tells her she will see and hear, such as thirteen strokes of a nonexistent clock. She will squirm uncomfortably when told she is sitting on a warm radiator, and will reach out happily to gather in coins supposedly raining from the skies. She will eat make-believe fruit, carefully peeling a fictitious banana. Told that a lemon is an apple, she may agree that it tastes like one. Lewis and Sarbin (1943) have shown that when a subject eats a make-believe meal under deep hypnosis, her gastric hunger contractions are apt to be inhibited as though she were eating real food. Actual perceptions can be "wiped out." Thus, the subject is told she cannot see a pack of cigarettes lying before her, and so will not reach for them when ordered to smoke. She can be told that some person in the room is absent, and when asked to count the people present will omit this person, although she will collide with the person if she walks about the room.

One of the most impressive features of hypnosis is the inhibition of pain reactions. As is well known, subjects under hypnosis who have been told that they will feel no pain neither report pain nor flinch when a pin is stuck into their hand or a flame is applied to their fingertips. Although rarely used since the development of anesthetics, hypnosis has been used in surgical operations, dentistry, and childbirth. For purposes of entertainment, hypnotists often demonstrate that hypnosis affects the memory. Some subjects can recite poetry once learned but apparently forgotten, or are able to recall events of early childhood. The subject may reenact the first day at school or the tenth birthday, with seeming fidelity.

Posthypnotic Suggestion. Posthypnotic action can be suggested during the actual trance. When the subject is being taken out of the trance, it is standard practice to suggest that she will remember nothing that occurred during the session; she will report that she does not remember, even when later urged to try to do so. The subject may be told

that five minutes after walking she will feel intense thirst, but will not know why. Five minutes later she will get herself a glass of water. It was reported that one subject was told that when reading the even-numbered pages of a book he would breathe twice as fast as usual, and half as fast as usual when reading the odd-numbered pages. Several weeks later he was still doing this. Some persons have tried to break habits (such as smoking) by means of hypnosis, but this technique is not particularly successful, since the effects of hypnotic suggestion fade out unless they are renewed.

Moral Behavior Under Hypnosis. A controversial question is whether hypnotic subjects can be made to do anything that will harm them or that is counter to their moral ideas. Affirmative evidence is provided in a report of an investigation by Rowland (Eysenck, 1964). He asked and eventually persuaded one of his subjects to reach out to touch a rubber rope (actually a coiled rattlesnake under glass). After hesitating, some subjects followed his command that they throw acid at him (he was protected by an invisible sheet of glass). It has been argued that the subjects knew they were in an experiment and that therefore the proof is inconclusive. However, of 42 unhypnotized subjects, 41 refused to follow instructions about reaching for the snake; the one person who complied did so because she thought it was an artificial snake, but she became frightened when told it was not. Experimentation to determine the limits of this kind of suggestion is beset by obvious difficulties.

Eysenck has made important contributions to the discussion of this aspect of hypnotic phenomena by citing instances that he believes demonstrate that serious infractions of rules, involving severe punishment, can be produced by hypnosis. Thus, by posthypnotic suggestion a soldier assigned to military duty was induced to desert (Eysenck, 1964). A private was hypnotized in the presence of a number of senior army officers and was told by a lieutenant colonel stationed about ten feet in front of him that when he opened his eyes he would see before him a "dirty Jap soldier" determined to bayonet him. The private was told that to save himself he would have to strangle his aggressor with his bare hands. The subject, when he opened his eyes, crept toward the lieutenant colonel, brought him down with a flying tackle, knocked him against the wall and began to strangle him. Three persons were needed to separate the two men. The victim of the attack reported that without immediate help he was sure he might have been killed or seriously injured. An assault upon an officer is, of course, a very serious offense in the army (Barber, 1961; 1969).

Conceptual Control in Hypnosis. Some writers have characterized hypnosis as a kind of enthusiastic faking. The argument is that subjects, although they appear not to experience pain or various sensations, or to see objects manifestly present, actually are merely reporting what they think they are supposed to report. This point has been explored in experiments by Pattee (1935). He designed a box with two openings (one on the left covered with red glass and one on the right with green glass). Inside the box were prisms that actually reversed the lines of vision. A hypnotized subject was told that he could not see with his left eye; he was then told to look through the box with both eyes open and to report the color that he saw. The subject thought that he saw green and denied seeing the red because he thought that it was his right eye that perceived the green; actually, because of the prisms, it was his left or "blind" eye. Similar experiments indicate the same sort of results for hearing. Other investigations on the capacity of hypnotized subjects to regress to childhood show conclusively that they do not actually regress, but merely reenact the gestures or simulate the performances that they believe to be appropriate. The performances on this kind of test (including writing, drawing, and IQ test performances) are about the same as those of nonhypnotized persons who are asked to

playact (Hull, 1933; Wolberg, 1947; Young, 1940; Evans, 1984).

Skepticism about the actual perceptions of the hypnotized subject is warranted in the light of the aura of mysticism which surrounds the topic in everyday discourse; but this skepticism misses the point. Since hypnotism involves control by the central nervous system (that is, through concepts), it is to be expected that the subject acts in terms of her own conceptions. An old demonstration will illustrate the point nicely. When she is told that her hand is numb up to the wrist, a subject reports that this line of numbness is there and responds accordingly. She reacts, in other words, according to the conceptions of neurology suggested by the hypnotist, and not in accordance with actual neural structure.

Hull found that although his subjects reported no pain when burned or stuck with pins, in fact automatic emergency reactions were occurring, because changes were observed in pulse rate, respiration, and galvanic skin response. The central problem of hypnosis then has to do not with whether the subject's conceptions or reports are accurate, but why she acts as though they were.

Hypnotic compliance with outside commands, requests, or "suggestions" carries an aura of the fantastic or mysterious. Yet conformance with commands, requests, or suggestions under normal waking conditions seems to most people an ordinary fact of life. This is so even when the suggestions and demands are fairly extreme. Even the phenomena of hypnosis find their parallels in normal behavior. To illustrate this, you might stretch out your arms before you, parallel to the ground, and then imagine that an iron bar runs through your right arm from shoulder to hand. Your right arm is likely to become, as it does in many people, rigid and heavy. Some people, if asked to clasp their hands tightly and imagine them to be stuck together, have momentary difficulty in wrenching them apart. All of us recognize that we can deliberately and imaginatively transport ourselves into certain social situations and so temporarily lose contact with reality. Much behavior is determined by what one believes, fantasizes, or imagines to be true. The mystery of hypnosis arises largely from the fact that the source of control in hypnosis is another person.

THEORIES OF HYPNOSIS

Theories of hypnosis center around explaining how the outsider gets control. Ordinarily, individuals who receive commands or suggestions make some evaluation of them before translating them into commands that they give themselves. Of course, if you are crossing the street and someone shouts "Look out!" you react without thinking it over; but usually self-stimulation is requisite to action, and involves the regulatory self-system described earlier.

The Conditioned-Response View. One theoretical explanation of hypnosis is that it is a form of conditioned response. This theory is embodied, for example, in the writings of Hull (1933, p. 397). The central idea is that words become linked with acts and tend to call forth these acts. Hence, "the withdrawal of the subject's symbolic activities would naturally leave his muscles relatively susceptible to the symbolic stimulation emanating continuously from the experimenter." Viewed as a conditioned response, the response to hypnotic suggestions, or indeed to any suggestion, involves no new principles. Pavlov makes this point when he says (1927, p. 407): "We can . . . regard 'suggestion' as the most simple form of the typical conditioned reflex in man." The verbal suggestion of the other person is but an external stimulus acting to arouse a conditioned response or a set of such responses. Asch (1952, p. 420) has pointed out that the older speculations on the nature of hypnosis were often much like present-day conditioning theory.

The stimulus-response conception of hypnosis, like general conditioning theory, is subject to criticism for avoiding the issue of how self-control operates or fails to operate. It assumes that language behavior and all intellectual processes are reducible to stimulus-response mechanisms. By regarding hypnosis as merely another instance of conditioning, this view denies that the phenomenon of hypnosis raises any special problems or that it, in itself, requires any explanation at all.

Freudian Interpretation. Although Freud used hypnosis in therapy in the early part of his career, he later abandoned it in favor of free association and other psychoanalytic techniques. However, hypnosis is still used in therapy to some extent. Freud viewed the hypnotic relation in terms of dominance and subjection. Other analysts, such as Ernest Jones and Paul Schilder, conceive of it as a kind of sexual response. Analysts generally do not pay much attention to hypnosis or propose specific theories to account for it.

A variant of the Freudian approach is represented by the view of Guze (1953). He notes that different hypnotic subjects respond differently to the same command. He interprets this as due to "their typical manner of dealing with their desires and drives." Hence, Guze hypothesizes that "all hypnotic commands become 'wishes' (that is, desires and drives) in the subject's thinking." Subjects handle them as they handle their other wishes; they may accept the wish enthusiastically, resist it but carry it out, reject it, carry it out and feel remorse, and so on. The point that individuals behave differently in response to the same stimulus, whether under hypnosis or not, is well taken. But Guze's account does not particularly advance our knowledge of what hypnotism *is*, neither is his description of hypnosis as a heightened state of emotion illuminating.

A Role Theory. Another attempt to explain hypnosis is that it is goal-directed behavior, the object of which is to behave like a hypnotized person, "as this is continuously defined by the operator and as this is understood by the subject" (Weitzenhoffer, 1953,

p. 503; and see Orne, 1979). This conception implies complementary roles of hypnotizer and hypnotized, and Sarbin (1950) has made this view more explicit. The subject, he says, attempts to enact the role of a hypnotized person, and the success of the attempt is a function of three factors: favorable motivation, role perception, and aptitude for role taking. The subject is likened to an actor on the stage, who also strives to act a fictional, or "as if," role. The hypnotizer is analogous to the stage director. Both actor and hypnotized subject may lose themselves in the excitement of the role. in the sense that they focus full attention on it and fail to notice many events that occur concurrently. Sarbin's account is designed to explain the differential ease with which persons can be hypnotized. Correlation of role-taking ability with susceptibility to hypnosis is not an easy matter to test, since the former ability is a fairly vague one. Sarbin's formulation, however, makes the subject an active participant in the hypnotic process rather than a puppet, and it does point to an overall organization of behavior. On the other hand, calling hypnosis "role playing" does not explain it; such a definition merely says that the behavior is organized much like other behavior and involves a process of interaction. In a sense, hypnosis is explained away by first noting how subjects act, and then suggesting that they act this way because they think they should.

Sarbin's role theory of hypnosis and the view that hypnotic phenomena are somehow fabrications have been satirized by H. J. Eysenck, a hard-nosed, empirically oriented British psychologist. He reports, for example, that when hypnotized subjects are successfully made to regress to earlier birthdays, a simple test of the validity of their experience is to ask them what the day of the week is. Of course, children are usually keenly aware of the day of the week on which their birthday falls, but hardly any adult can remember the day on which the tenth, seventh, or fourth birthday fell. Eysenck states that when regressed under hypnosis, 93 percent of the subjects correctly stated the day of the week of their tenth birthday, 82 percent were correct for their seventh birthday, and 69 percent for their fourth birthday. It is absurd to account for such results by saying that the subject was trying to enact the role of a hypnotized subjects (1964). The same is true of the subject who goes on talking and does not bother to look at his hand when a needle is pushed through it by the hypnotist. Eysenck suggests that persons who think hypnotic phenomena can be imitated should try such experiments on themselves. A hypnotized subject will drink a glass of soapy water with every sign of enjoyment, Eysenck notes, if it has been suggested that he is drinking champagne. This is another self-experiment recommended for skeptics (Eysenck, 1964, p. 37).

Hypnosis and Speech Mechanisms

While hypnosis has been employed primarily in therapy and as a source of entertainment, it is obvious that hypnotic phenomena have great theoretical significance and that hypnosis presents a potent research device. Eysenck suggests that perhaps 85 percent of the population can be hypnotized to some degree. If this potential exists so widely in human beings and is altogether absent in animals, this fact would seem to constitute a theoretical issue of top priority. This is all the more true because it is commonly stated that hypnotic phenomena resemble, or are at least related to, a considerable range of other common human behavioral phenomena, such as those discussed in psychology texts under the heading of suggestibility.

Nevertheless, as the psychologists who explore this area themselves say, there has been relatively little serious scientific effort expended in the attempt to formulate even provisional explanatory theories. Eysenck (1964, p. 65), in a brief review of current theories, characterizes the idea derived from Pavlov that hypnosis is like sleep, as "almost certainly false." The conditioned response view, he remarks, ". . . fails completely to account for many of the phenomena associated with hypnosis. . . . Certainly by itself it is not sufficient." Other theories are similarly characterized, and the role theory is called the "weirdest of all."

Since hypnotic behavior is triggered by the hypnotist's verbal cues and suggestions, a theoretical approach based on the analysis of speech mechanisms is indicated. It is logically impossible to explain behavior that occurs in humans and not in lower animals in terms of mechanisms and processes that are present in both. The neglect of hypnosis by American psychology and social psychology is probably closely related to the fact that dominant current theories, especially those derived from the study of lower animals, do not handle the existing data (see Orne, 1979).

From the standpoint of experimental research, the potentials of hypnosis are great because the investigator can induce a wide variety of behavioral and organic manifestations, the sources of which the subject does not know. At the same time, although researchers may not know *how* the effects are produced or what brain mechanisms are involved, they do know that they were triggered by their own commands or suggestions. From the symbolic interactionist viewpoint, hypnotic phenomena point emphatically toward a general conception of humans as creatures in which the higher cortical functions associated with speech and language are dominant and pervasive influences throughout virtually the whole structure of behavior, so that, as Luria (1960. p. 428) has said, "we find them literally in every movement of the fingers."

One may perhaps speculate that there may be something like a command center within the neurological structure of the brain, from which emanate messages that stimulate or control other parts of the structure (Luria, 1973). Two pervasive complementary aspects of the functioning of the nervous system are *inhibitions* and *excitations*. The entire system cannot be equally excited all at once; when one part is in a state of excitement, certain cell assemblies become active, while others are inhibited. The phenomena of hypnotism and

other forms of ceding or losing self-control may, on the neurological level, represent this balancing of excitation and inhibitions. Thus, while the command, or self-stimulating, part of the brain seems to be inhibited and inactive in a hypnotized subject, other central functions, such as memory, are apparently facilitated. In loss of control under the influence of alcohol, the inhibition is brought about by chemical influences which interact with self-perceptions and the definitions of others brought to bear upon the drinking individual. It has been observed with respect to alcohol that there is a patterning of effects as drinking proceeds, with the most complex and recently acquired controls being the first to deteriorate or weaken. Drinkers often begin to show this effect by becoming uninhibited in their speech, laughter, and actions and ending up in a state of general stupor.

INSTITUTIONALLY INDUCED CHANGES IN SELF-CONTROL

Ceding Control

People may also deliberately cede over a measure of their own self-control under quite regulated institutional conditions. This is what happens when students allow a psychologist to convert them into experimental hypnotic subjects. However, there are less equivocal and more ordinary instances of this very complicated social process. We shall select one from a great many possible instances to clarify the point.

Under certain conditions, people allow physicians and nurses to do things to their bodies that otherwise they would not permit. The physician says to a man: "I must operate on you." The patient then allows the physician to use drugs that render him temporarily insensible. He allows the physician to remove a bodily part. He also allows the hospital staff to control some other sectors of his life and behavior. They regulate his movements by confining him to his bed or room. They regulate his waking hours by taking away his control over when he will sleep (giving him drugs to induce sleep), or when he will eat (feeding him in accordance with a given schedule), or how he will eat (feeding him intravenously). All these events are fairly institutionalized, regularized, or routinized because the hospital is organized for this purpose. If the patient's condition warrants different kinds of control, he may be sent from one medical service to another within the same hospital.

If we observe closely, we also note that the ceding of control from patient to hospital staff is not a static phenomenon. As the patient's condition worsens he may agree, explicitly or implicitly, to further loss of control over his own activities. As he gets better he is given, or requests, or demands that some of that control be ceded back to him. Disagreements occur daily between staff and patients in hospitals over just this matter, and a considerable amount of negotiation within hospitals pertains to setting these matters straight. A study of cardiac patients with "infarctions" has shown that after patients have been hospitalized, they tend to judge their condition by the amount of pain they still experience. If there is considerable pain, they will not wish to recover as much control as the staff wishes them to regain, and the staff may be annoyed at their overanxiety. More frequently the annoyance runs in the opposite direction, because the staff will not allow patients to act as they feel they have the right to act. Since most illnesses run a course (upward or downward), the negotiation over control between patient and staff is potentially, if not always actually, an explosive process.

This explosiveness is dramatic in situations in which patients are dying (Glaser & Strauss, 1965). Suppose that a man thinks he is quite sick, but the staff has informed his family that he is dying. Everyone controls his or her own responses so as to prevent the patient's coming "into awareness." When patients finally understand their real condition, they sometimes drastically change the conditions of control. Some give up and refuse to

do anything to prolong their lives. Some escape all control by signing themselves out of the hospital or by committing suicide.

It is interesting to note what happens when sick patients return home from the hospital or from a clinic visit. The physician commonly gives the patient a set of directives that she is supposed to follow. The patient may or may not follow this regimen, depending on such conditions as whether she trusts or believes the physician, or whether she thinks the regimen is too difficult and can be altered without too much harm. More to the point of this chpater are those instances in which patients think they are following the physician's directives but actually do not understand them. They act in accordance with the control ceded to the absent physician, but when the physician discovers what the patients have been doing, he may accurse them of departing from instructions because of laziness, insufficient trust, or some other unworthy motive. In virtually any clinic where patients of lower income groups are treated by middle-class nurses and physicians, one can hear those accusation either fired directly at the patients or merely noted among the staff itself. In many instances, however, patients simply do not understand the orders; they act in accordance with the orders as they have heard them.

These relationships between patients and hospital staffs are not independent of group affiliations and positions in a nation's social structure. Middle-class Americans have learned to cede over to physicians degrees of control that lower-class Americans have not yet learned to cede—a matter related to higher education, and meanings of health and body, as well as "health education." In a country like Greece, many citizens still regard the hospital as a place to die and will not go there when sick (Blum & Blum, 1965). Consequently, when Greek patients or their family discover that they are no longer regarded by the staff as dying, they will be whisked out of the hospital; they will cede nothing else to the medical people. Conversely, when Malayans discover that one of their sick kinfolk is actually dying within a hospital they will take him or her home, disregarding all protestations of the hospital staff, because now a series of religious and other ritual actions must be performed both before and after the person's death. These would not be performed by the hospital staff, and thus great spiritual harm would be done to the dying person.

"Brainwashing" or "Thought Reform"

The preceding section dealt with institutionalized forms of ceding control. We turn to a related phenomenon wherein a person retains self-control, but changes both behavior and the bases of controlling behavior under the guidance of others. Commonly, we recognize that any person who enters a new organization and begins to believe in what it stands for may then begin to "conform" to its standards. Even skeptics may thus be converted after they have entered a group just to scoff at it. Naturally, there are many obstacles to these kinds of conversions, especially to well nigh total conversion, as when an Episcopalian joins a radically different religious group like Jehovah's Witnesses.

Radical changes require that adult persons undergo turmoil. If some group or organization wishes them to change the bases of their self-control and thought in some given direction, they must be thrown into turmoil or self-doubt while simultaneously being led to new ways of seeing themselves and the world. Thus, if their loyalties to colleagues, friends, and parents are to be loosened, these people must be impugned, attacked, shaken from pedestals, and questioned. A certain amount of self-doubt and doubt of others can be induced by verbal means, but it is also essential that crucial situations be established wherein the persons see themselves and the others, if possible, acting in ways that run counter to their cherished conceptions. Religious conversion, which is followed by a radical change in life style, illustrates these processes. Preaching, accusation, and rhetoric are important in bringing about conversion; but it is essential

that people be put into situations in which they will feel guilt, feel and see their usual actions as strange, and be forced to review their past history and find themselves wanting.

Creation of a crisis provides the condition for changing the direction of the personal career, but in itself it is not enough. Crisis calls for self-appraisal and self-examination but does not automatically indicate direction. Some converts not only drop out or backslide, but move off in other directions—to alcohol, other social movements, or cynical manipulation of others. If the reformer is to make use of a crisis, he must help plot the course from there on in order to prepare the convert for difficulties and help the rationale of the course become part of her thinking. This is done in religious conversions by various devices, such as predicting the harshness of parents and relations when the convert tries to tell them about her revelations, and predicting that friends will abandon her because of the new beliefs. After the communist revolution in China, and intermittently since, so-called thought reform techniques were used all over China as part of a mass conversion of the citizenry. The explicit or implicit aims, according to Schein et al. (1961), were to create a new type of Chinese citizen, change attitudes, produce an obedient and energetic party worker, initiate into communist society those individuals who were not yet committed ideologically, and develop ideological unanimity throughout the land. *Thought reform* is essentially an attempt to break old loyalties, principally to family and social class, and to develop new loyalties to country and party. The tactics used on citizens varied considerably, depending both on those in charge of reform and on the status of those to be reformed. Some of the same tactics were also used on foreigners in China, and later on captured prisoners during the Korean War (Lifton, 1961, p. 25).

Hunter (1951, p. 25) has described the tactics used on students in the years immediately after the revolution. To begin with, propaganda and lectures unveiled a new terminology—that of the communists—that ran counter to familiar concepts in a great many ways. The meaning of the new terms could not be fully grasped at first, but they provided an initial vocabulary for the reinterpretation of events, persons, and groups. Students were sent to work in the fields so as to feel like the common people. They were sent to see village justice wreaked upon former landlords—often a harrowing experience for the onlooker, whose parents might also be landlords. Any who could not bear to watch were accused of sentimentality—a characteristic of the ruling class. A detailed biographical essay (called a "thought seduction essay") had to be written and turned in to the teacher, who criticized it as revealing "deep-set contradictions" in their lives. The point of this criticism was to force the students to reveal publicly their former beliefs and actions, especially when they themselves wanted to forget them because they were not in harmony with party teachings. Students were then induced or compelled to confess their sins in class, such as admitting that they had helped the Japanese, and so on. Criticism of each student by every other was encouraged, and those who held back were prodded by name-calling ("lagging-behind particle") and other punishments.

Presumably, some people were relieved by making their avowals and were supported by others' commentaries; but in general, public avowal and criticism are very destructive. Ordinarily, one is protected from certain kinds of adverse comment by the conspiracy of silence that governs polite intercourse. Selective inattention does not get much chance to operate effectively in such procedures as those we have described, because the individual's illusions about herself are challenged directly. This challenge was increased by the mutual hostility engendered during these sessions. The right to privacy was invaded; not only did current acts and thoughts come under scrutiny, but the intimate details of past history were examined. The student was asked to explain the "why" of her acts, and then alternative motivations were pressed upon her.

The turning point in the brainwashing process appears to have been the genuine public conession when the student got down to rock bottom and accused herself of having been a wastrel, an exploiter, a coward, and so forth. This amounted to a genuine public relinquishing of past identity. The anguish attending this process is suggested by the cutting off of contacts with parents, the renaming of one's family as "exploiters," and the sundering of relations with spouses. It was at this point that the more serious consequences of the new perspective began to come home to the convert; there was no turning back.

One of the final steps was the writing of a "thought conclusion essay," an autobiography written to show how far one had come in the desired direction and in what ways; it included a ruthless renunciation of the past. This essay had to be read aloud to the class and was subjected to public criticism. When the candidate was finished with this ordeal, she was compelled to rewrite the essay along more acceptable lines. Not everyone, of course, continued to the final steps in the process; some committed suicide, some ran away, and others were not deemed to require the full treatment. In 1956, the vigor of the criticism of Chinese intellectuals with regard to government action during the Hundred Flowers period apparently surprised even the high party officials. In 1967, it was apparent that large sections of the Chinese population were regarded by Mao Tse-tung as not entirely converted to the highest ideals of communist society.

There can be no doubt that thought reform is a technique of what one might call *forced conversion* or *coercive persuasion,* and that it sometimes brings about fundamental and permanent changes in outlook. In the testimony of Americans who have been temporarily subjected to the treatment, there is often a note of profound respect for its potency. Ardent anti-communists, who remain so after a period of communist indoctrination, often unwittingly use the communist vocabulary or accept some of its assumptions. This is true even of the Chinese who fled the country after being subjected to thought reform. As for those who remained, Lifton has suggested with some accuracy that even the intellectuals who recanted under pressure after their harsh criticism during the Hundred Flowers episode "may also have felt some genuine repentance, for thought reform had applied to them its special techniques for reclaiming backsliders." It may have persuaded them "that their critical views were out of step with the march of history, and that they had helped their country's enemies and harmed a noble cause." Lifton saw signs of this "reclaiming power" in many of the Chinese he interviewed intensively in Hong Kong during 1954 and 1955, "the guilty sense of having been a betrayer, along with a paralyzing fear of the communists, persisting long after the escape from communist control" (1961, p. 414).

Lifton's extensive interviews with foreigners who had lived in China and who had been subjected to thought reform also suggest some of the operative mechanisms and personal strategies that allowed some people to escape full conversion. Lifton notes that the "first form of resistance is the acquisition of a sense of understanding, a theory about what is going on, an awareness of being manipulated." This awareness and these theories give a partial sense of control over the situation and help "to dispel the fear of the unknown and the sense of complete helplessness." A second important tactic is the avoidance of emotional participation, the prisoner remaining "as much as possible outside the communication system of thought reform." This is done by refusing to learn Chinese if one does not know it, and by keeping contacts with Chinese prison-mates to a minimum. The agents of thought reform were somewhat kept off balance also by a show of stoicism and displays of humor. A final and most important "resistance technique" was that of "identity reinforcement." Thus a Catholic bishop kept reminding himself that the communist remolding was really a test of his Catholic steadfastness. "He sought always to maintain himself as a priest struggling against his selfishness, rather than a stubborn imperialist spy. To do this, he needed a continuous awareness of his own world of prayer, Catholic ritual, missionary experience, and Western cultural heritage." Since nothing in the prison reminded him of these anchors of identity, he had to find them within himself. One prisoner reminded himself by secretly drawing pictures of scenes from his boyhood. But Lifton notes that none of these tactics was entirely successful, for thought reform had some impact on all of the foreign prisoners whom he studied.

In short, brainwashing, conversion, and other socially or institutionally induced changes illustrate how the bases of an individual's self-control may shift without any genuine loss of self-control except that which he may wish to cede some group or organization. It would be erroneous to assume that in these induced processes individuals simply are coerced to change their belief and behavior. If coerced, they may leave the organization or commit suicide; they may act conformingly as if they believed, but in fact they are controlling their behavior so as to pass muster in what might otherwise be situations dangerous to life itself. In such situations, even coerced behavior may have privately derisive meanings. This is a phenomenon we all recognize, even when we do not recognize particular evidences of it; for instance, army privates who mock their officers with salutes that are executed just properly enough so that the implied disrespect is not recognized.

Demoralization

Brainwashing and thought reform are examples of situations where persons retain self-control, but change because of institutional forces. We will now consider a closely related form of institutionally induced changes in self-control—*demoralization*, which may occur within a military organization, a school system, or an urban neighborhood. After Shibutani (1978, pp. 5–6), we define demoralization as a condition which exists within an organized group when there is a breakdown of collective effort, an unwillingness on the part of persons to continue to perform tasks, and where there is bickering, factionalism, fights, arguments, and a general loss of morale. A demoralized group performs its functions in a desultory and sluggish manner; absenteeism may be high; members develop low self-esteem; there is no group pride. Members may pursue hedonistic activities or lose themselves in drugs and alcohol (Shibutani, 1978, p. 5). When confronted by adversity members may disintegrate and become preoccupied with self-preservation.

Consider the following example offered by Shibutani (1978, p. 1). It occurred at Fort Snelling, Minnesota on October 17, 1945. The participants were military trainees of Nisei, Americans of Japanese ancestry.

> The brawl started on a small streetcar—called the "dummy line"— . . . it was crowded with soldiers . . . in the pushing . . . one soldier, whose foot had been trampled, objected loudly and shoved the offender . . . as the protagonists faced one another, the irate man screamed, "You white! You t'eenk you better dan me! Look at me! Yellow! . . . The outnumbered men declined to fight . . . they were set upon by the gang. One man was beaten to the ground . . . he had been stabbed in the back."

This incident occurred with Company K, a Nisei unit characterized by high demoralization.

What causes demoralization? Shibutani enumerates a number of factors, including the following: First, if authority figures are disrespectful of a group, its goals, and its members, then the members may turn against the leader and act in a way which will undermine his authority. In this way, the group begins to work against any conditions that could create high morale or group satisfaction. Second, if authority figures become demoralized, a state of near anarchy may be created in a group (Shibutani, 1978, p. 425).

Members may then begin to fend only for themselves. Third, if violence breaks out, this contributes to more violence which may undermine group goals. Members may turn against one another. Fourth, as demoralization becomes established it sets in motion behaviors, emotions, and attitudes which assume a force of their own. That is, members, in a self-fulfilling fashion, create conditions which promote greater demoralization. The members cede self-control to a self-destructive process which is interactional in nature. In the case of demoralization, then, control goes over to a process that is both self-destructive and destructive of a social group.

Ceding Control as Status Passage: Biographical and Career Effects

Our discussion has placed the social effects that others may have on the self within a shifting context of self- and social control. The self and its variously implicated others are bound together in a variety of emergent and stabilized relationships which confer greater or lesser degrees of self-control. The effects of ceding control may be (1) positive, in the case of husbands and wives or members of communes; (2) neutral, as when a person submits to hypnotism; and (3) negative, as when a person is embarrassed, degraded, or formally excluded from a work organization.

If the temporal dimensions of the self-other relationship are considered, it can be seen that effects can be momentary and fleeting, or long term and heavily consequential for the given individual—the paranoid, for instance. Finally, if we consider the spatial aspects of ceding control, we can see that the commitment of oneself to another (or the control of oneself by another) can lead to upward, downward, or lateral social mobility. A person who becomes the protégé of a master cedes self-control or career control in return for the possibility of a high-status career. At the other extreme, we have individuals who—wittingly or unwittingly—give up self-control to others or have it taken away, and in the end find that they are doomed to failure and demotion. In the middle are those who incur few career costs when they contract for a lateral transfer from one department to another within the same work organization. So, the status passage process which accompanies the act of ceding self-control to another individual, a group, an organization, or a cause can result in movements "in" or "out" of an interactional network, or "up" and "down" within that same context.

These remarks suggest that the commitments an individual makes to others can carry significant biographical implications for her future career choices. For these and other reasons, people take some care over the choices they make. Furthermore, they are often led to develop and adopt a set of "self-protective" strategies that enhance their abilities to mold and direct their own lives. These strategies are often referred to as *coping devices*.

COPING MECHANISMS

It is commonly remarked how extraordinarily obtuse we are in situations in which our self-esteem is involved. People often embark upon and continue in relationships with other people without much insight into the character of the relationship. Such blindness, it is generally understood, is explicable in terms of one's self-conceptions. Psychiatrists who deal with gross and persistent errors of this kind speak of them in such terms as "defense mechanisms," "security operations," and the like, the central idea being that the person meets supposed threats to self-regard with characteristic modes of defense. Defense modes include, among others, selective inattention, anxiety reduction, evasion of responsibility, rationalization, pretense, and the disowning of undesirable qualities in oneself.

The techniques of self-defense, or coping, which psychiatrists have characteristically stressed and which have often been picked up uncritically by sociologists, are those that emphasize self-deception, avoidance, and reduction of information. Such classic forms of ego defense as repression, denial, reaction formation, isolation, and rationalization lean heavily upon minimizing the recognition of potentially traumatic aspects of experience, techniques characteristically used by those who go to psychiatrists. These coping devices are frequently pathological in nature in the sense that they may themselves create other problems for the person. There are, however, many other techniques of adjustment that are perhaps more successful, used by people who do not seek professional help. To indicate the existence of more normal techniques, we have called them *coping mechanisms* rather than defense mechanisms, and we shall include a discussion of some of them along with others of the better-known classical variety.

Common Defense Mechanisms

The theoretical treatment of anxiety by Sullivan (1953) points up some of these conceptions. Even in the earliest months, according to Sullivan's theory, children encounter situations that arouse their anxiety and they learn to grade them in terms of the anxiety they provoke and to stay away from those that are most severe. Unavoidable anxiety situations come to be handled by a variety of means designed to minimize anxiety and to maximize satisfaction. Sullivan states that "the self-system comes into being, because of, and can be said to have as its goal, the securing of necessary satisfaction without incurring much anxiety."

A fundamental conceptual device that children utilize, according to Sullivan, is to classify experiences as pertaining to the *good me*, the *bad me*, and the *not me*. The first category is for acts that are approved; the second, for acts that are disapproved, and hence induce some anxiety; and the third, for acts that are so anxiety-provoking that they are more or less disavowed or "dissociated." Sullivan notes that the *not me* is tied up with emotions of dread, horror, and loathing, and is expressed obliquely with a lack of awareness (for example, in nightmares).

The *self-system* arises from the child's attempt to avoid anxieties arising in interpersonal relations with significant others, especially with the mother. This system is not equivalent to an incorporation of the mother's perspective, but is based on the child's attempts to form a system of reaction that minimizes the anxiety that arises out of interactions with significant others (1953, pp. 159–61). Sullivan maintains that protection against the paralyzing effects of severe anxiety is a necessity, and that learning to protect oneself is part of one's educational experience.

The self-system tends to become stabilized in a generalized defense against anxiety. According to Sullivan, the person then becomes "selectively inattentive" to happenings that could change her, since change itself leads to anxiety. Hence, awareness of one's own acts is greatly restricted, as is the understanding of the acts of others. One need not assume with Sullivan that anxiety avoidance is the central feature of behavioral organization, but certainly ideas of self do interfere with what is noticed and what is learned. People do strive to maintain self-esteem, and they raise defenses against threats to it.

A person with the insight into his own deficiencies and weaknesses and the situations in which they become manifest to others may consciously maneuver to avoid competitive games, for example, and may choose as companions persons who will not shame him by their superior skills or attainments. Thus, the need to maintain self-regard often produces a vicious cycle; those very situations wherein a weakness could be overcome are avoided. A good part of social relations is unconsciously devoted to the search for companions and activities that allow weaknesses to remain hidden or relatively unnoticed while one's stronger points are exploited.

Characteristic defenses of self may occur without realization of their nature by the individual. Some of these have been given names. For instance, a person who has failed to reach certain goals may substitute less ambitious ones in a general lowering of his or her level of aspiration. Another well-known device is *rationalizing*, which we use in this context to mean explaining away or excusing one's failure. Another method characteristically used by some people is the shifting of one's own fault to another—*scapegoating*, or *displacement*. Persons aware of undesirable qualities in themselves may bolster their self-esteem by *projecting* the same qualities to others, as when a selfish person says that it is a selfish world (that is, that everyone else is selfish too). In handling personal relations, it is common for attack to be met by counterattack, whether verbal or physical. Among the more complex forms of defense is *identification* with an aggressor, which permits a vicarious sharing of some of his strength.

The cultural patterning of defense and coping mechanisms is reflected in the existence of the conventions of politeness, which function—at least in part—to shield sensitive egos and to allow delicate relationships to exist. As with other forms of behavior, different mechanisms are stressed in different groups, and the standards of politeness and rudeness vary accordingly.

There are also conventionally sanctioned tactics for defending the self that are constantly used in a conscious manner. These include both ordinary devices as physical withdrawal, changing the subject, doing favors for one's opponent or using flattery, creating diversions, sparring for time, and exploiting the vulnerable points of the attacker. Human interaction is such that one's status is often challenged, feelings hurt, and reputation impugned by the acts—intentional or not—of others. Anyone who does not learn to cope with these occurrences is in a peculiarly helpless and vulnerable position. Orrin E. Klapp (1949, pp. 159–61) has illustrated this point vividly in his discussion of fool-making situations. As he says:

Fool-making situations are so constantly presented to the average person that he may be unable to avoid occasionally falling into the role. Life is a continual process of fool-making . . . humor, derision, and belittlement are constantly assigning this role . . . social relations are continually rendered unstable by fool-making. . . . Among the major routes of escape from the fool role are the following: . . . Avoidance of the imputation by "taking" a joke and "laughing it off" implies that there has been no injury, that the jibe is ineffectual or inapplicable. . . . A counterjoke or effective repartee "turns the tables" and makes the other a fool; "having the last word" or getting the best of a contest of wits has, in fact, the effect of defining the winner as a clever hero. . . . A similar strategy involves acceptance of the fool role and its use as a "ruse" or "trap" for a clever victory. . . . [And] by suffering or showing "human" traits which arouse sympathy, a person can escape from the fool role. Excessive persecution, for example, "carrying a joke too far," tends to make a martyr out of the fool.

Psychiatrists have worked out elaborate terminologies and explanations of individual and unconsciously used defense mechanisms, for neurotic and psychotic patients are notable for lack of insight into their own behavior. We can accept many of the psychiatric descriptions of normal devices for self-defense without necessarily agreeing with the explanations of them. Psychiatrists tend to overstress the unconscious nature of these defense and coping processes, both because of the importance of the unconscious in their theoretical systems and because of their concern with patients in whom this aspect of behavior is exaggerated. The relatively stable and secure person may discover these processes or recognize them when they are pointed out. We need not be altogether skeptical about the role of rationality at this point; normal persons are able to assimilate a fair amount of criticism direct or implied, without series injury to self-esteem or reversion to self-delusion. Retrospective analysis of one's past actions cannot help giving one new perspectives and further insight into one's characteristic ways of handling personal reactions. Techniques used by the young child do not necessarily survive the maturing effects of broader experience.

Normal Coping Devices

Psychiatrists have systematically investigated how ordinary nondisturbed persons assimilate unfortunate, disastrous, or threatening experiences. One such study was concerned with parents whose children were discovered to have leukemia, an almost invariably fatal disease. The study included 26 mothers and 20 fathers from various socioeconomic levels, whose children were treated at the National Cancer Institute. The parents were systematically interviewed during the course of the illness, as well as after the deaths of their children (Friedman, et al., 1963).

The parents were initially stunned by the diagnosis and by the physicians' realistic explanation of the limitations of chemotherapy and the eventual outcome of the disease. A few parents who were psychologically unstable expressed hostile and aggressive reactions at the initial news, but most accepted it and expressed appreciation for having been told the worst so that they knew what to expect. At first, all the parents experienced guilt because they had not paid attention to the earliest symptoms of the disease. They were reassured when it was explained that this would have made no essential difference. Some parents assuaged their guilt feelings with respect to their earlier disciplining of their child by treating him or her overindulgently after the diagnosis.

Coping by Detachment

Transcendence of self is made possible by the fact that through using symbols and taking the roles of others, one may take the view of an outsider (observer) with regard to one's self and one's own actions. This may lead either to concern over self and reputation, or to *detachment*. Probably relatively few people achieve any large measure of disinterestedness in their view of themselves, but those who do are recognized and appreciated for it. It is one of the most effective ways of maintaining self-esteem.

One of the outstanding signs of the achievement of this detachment is a sense of humor—especially about one's own foibles, mistakes, and weaknesses. The person who can joke in the face of failure, danger, or death exhibits this detachment, as exemplified by the American officer in World War II who, in a critical phase of combat, asked his men: "What's the matter, do you want to live forever?" "Gallows humor"—like that of the conquered peoples of Europe who made bitter jokes at their own expense—is the expression of more than mere irony and resentment, since it indicates a realistic appreciation of an actual predicament. (See Chapter 4.)

Privacy and the Self

Privacy is also related to defense of self, as the expression "invasion of privacy" makes clear. All societies have unwritten rules that allow persons to withdraw from interaction in certain situations. The retreat to privacy may be used to escape from interaction that is troubling, embarrassing, or deflating; some people who cannot successfully cope with certain kinds of social relations make a virtual fetish of privacy.

Privacy has positive values as well. It is perhaps an absolute necessity to withdraw to repair one's energies, ruminate over the significance of past events, and plan. It is only in moments in which one is not reacting to other people that communication with self can be at its best. Periods of privacy designed for this very purpose are institutionlized in all societies; an obvious example is the prescription by various religions of periods of meditation, fasting, and prayer.

When others try to get at secret thoughts and intimate biographical details which the individual wishes to reveal to no one or only to very special persons, barriers are erected. Inopportune revelation of self leaves one at the mercy of others. Privacy may be conceptualized as a series of concentric circles: The inner circle is forbidden to all trespassers; one's trusted intimates may enter into the

second circle, and so on, as one moves to the outer circles that are accessible to all. This spatial symbolism is actually embodied in the architecture of dwellings, houses or worship, and public buildings, and in the rules permitting or forbidding entry into various rooms.

Allowing another person to enter into the ego's central core of privacy is a delicate process fraught with peril to both parties. It is attended by misgivings and release, and by hestitations and abrupt moments of confiding. Betrayal of this degree of confidence is destructive and corrosive; its effect is like being turned over to the enemy after seeking refuge in the house of a blood relation. The recipients of confidence are also in a delicate position, because they may unwittingly betray the confidence or it may put them in a moral dilemma. Impersonal, institutionalized places of confession (such as the church and the doctor's office) are designed to protect both parties.

Territoriality and the Self

The individual maintains the integrity of her self-conception through the use of an elaborate conception of *territoriality* and privacy. Lyman and Scott (1967. pp. 236–49) and Goffman (1971, pp. 28–61) have offered typologies which link the individual's conceptions of self and social space. There are *public territories* where people can come and go at will, and they are open to wide classes of the population. The sacred, private features of the self are likely to remain concealed in these settings. *Home territories* are those most sacred to the self, and they describe backstage regions for private, unobserved interaction. *Body territories* include the area immediately surrounding the physical body. More properly conceived as personal space, the individual is unlikely to permit other actors into that space.

Individuals develop territorial defenses that maintain the sanctity of those places most central to their self-conceptions. Through the use of markers, names, tags, labels, and addresses they communicate to outsiders what their spaces are, where those spaces end, and where the spaces of others take over. Spaces and their attached selves may be violated or challenged. Bodies may unexpectedly touch, glances may last too long, odors may be given off and communicate an untoward body state.

Individuals can challenge the credibility of their own self-conceptions by openly debasing themselves. Furthermore, they may befoul their own bodies, or in more drastic fashion they may expose the private parts of their bodies. In each of these self-acts they cease to make the self a private and hence sacred object; thereby letting down their defenses and permitting others openly to defy or denigrate them. Hence they place others in the uncomfortable position of having to process the behaviors of a derelict self. Failures to maintain self-privacy and keep up territorial defenses challenge the routine features of smooth, everyday interaction (Goffman, 1971, pp. 52–55).

Revelations and Self-Other Relations

It is interactionally useful to keep portions of oneself from others. In this sense an element of secrecy, as Simmel notes, surrounds each individual: His most private self-conceptions and fantasies may never be known by another individual (Simmel, 1950, pp. 330–33). A *pretense awareness context* exists in many relationships, even for those of the most intimate nature. The members agree not to challenge each other's moods and declarations, and they act as if they fully understand one another when, in fact, they are only "pretending." Thus, while they may suspect that the other is thinking something other than what he declares, they are tactful enough not to ask. But if the relationship is to take the turn toward deeper involvement, at some juncture they will be led to reveal the more private and hidden features of themselves. They move from the pretense and suspicion awareness context into the open context. This is not to say that their interactions will necessarily remain at the open level; a quasi-open context is more typical,

and in time the relationship may slip back into more elaborate modes of secrecy and self-concealment.

CONCLUSION

Individuals can voluntarily, involuntarily, or unexpectedly cede self-control to another individual, a group, an organization, or a cause. The loss of self-control under hypnosis indicates the extensive role of language mechanisms in voluntary behavior and suggests that the will should be conceived not as a psychic force or entity, but as a self-regulator by means of language cues. Behavior under hypnosis is a more extreme form of the type of influence constantly exerted by people over each other in ordinary social intercourse and designated by such terms as *suggestion* and *imitation*. Propaganda and media influences were compared to the *posthypnotic effects* hypnotists have on their subjects. Since social control also implies control of behavior by symbol manipulation, it is closely related to self-control. The behavior of the individual in the group situation illustrates the manner in which persons seem to lose self-control under the influences of social pressures. In certain institutionalized situations, such as when a person is hospitalized, it is expected that others will take over the control of some or much of her activities. The processes of *brainwashing* and other kinds of *coercive persuasion* may be considered as other instances of the partial loss of personal autonomy to outside forces, persons, or groups, as is the case for *embarrassment* and *degradation ceremonies*. Ceding control to others was compared to the phenomena of status passages. The *coping devices* persons use to salvage self-esteem were explored. Finally, it was noted that the privacy of the self is central to the maintenance of self-control.

SELECTED READINGS

EYSENCK, H. J. (1964). *Sense and nonsense in psychology.* Baltimore: Penguin Books. A critical and skeptical review of the research on hypnosis.

GOFFMAN, E. (1971). *Relations in public.* New York: Basic Books. A probing and sensitive analysis of the rituals of face-to-face interaction that persons use to shield themselves from one another.

HEILMAN, S. C. (1976). *Synagogue life: A study in symbolic interaction.* Chicago: University of Chicago Press. A rich analysis of life in a Modern Orthodox congregation where self-control and social control work off of one another.

LIFTON, R. J. (1961). *Thought reform and the psychology of totalism.* New York: W. W. Norton & Co., Inc. A valuable account of persons who experienced *thought reform* and *brainwashing.* Indicates how individuals attempt to shield themselves from others when self-control over their own behavior is virtually denied.

SHIBUTANI, T. (1978). *The derelicts of company K: A sociological study of demoralization.* Berkeley: University of California Press.

CHAPTER TWELVE
Selves, Careers, and Social Worlds

We have continually emphasized that the individual's self-conception arises out of his or her interpersonal relationships. In that regard, we will discuss the individual's moral careers in relation to membership in social worlds. We begin with a treatment of the concept of *career,* focusing on the varieties of careers (work, friendship, leisure, political, religious, intimate) that any given person has; then we move to the related concept of *social world,* indicating how individuals move in and out of small-scale careers into more complex worlds of discourse. We conclude with a discussion of *alienation* and an analysis of how individuals mutually affect and alter one another's careers.

CAREERS

To say that an individual has a career involves three interrelated notions (Becker, 1973; Goffman, 1961; Stebblins, 1970). The concept designates objective movements that he may make through a social structure. Here we refer to status passages: movements in and out of the labor market, educational settings, marriages, friendships, or groups. *Objective careers*—these movements through statuses and positions—produce a counterpart, termed the *subjective career*. In this category are the subtle and sometimes manifest changes in self-conception that accompany positional relocations. As Hughes (1937, 1958) noted, alterations in the objective career lead to changes in self-identity. The objective and subjective components of the career are especially important, since they set the stage for the larger redefinitions of self. Goffman (1961, pp. 127–28) has conveniently summarized the threefold nature (objective, subjective, self) of career:

Traditionally the term *career* has been reserved for those who expect to enjoy the rises laid out within a respectable profession. The term is coming to be used, however, in a broadened sense to refer to any social strand of any person's course through life. . . . One value of the concept of career is its two-sidedness. One side is linked to internal matters held dearly and closely . . . the other side concerns public position, jural relations, and style of life. . . . The concept of career, then, allows one to move back and forth between the personal and the public, between the self and its significant society. . . . The main concern will be with the moral aspects of career—that is, the regular sequence of changes that career entails in the person's self and in his framework of imagery for judging himself and others.

The sacredness of the self-conception, as noted by Goffman, must be emphasized. He has written that it is important to see that (1956, p. 497): "The self is in part a ceremonial thing, a sacred object which must be treated with proper ritual care and in turn must be presented in a proper light to others . . . practices must be institutionalized so that the individual will be able to project a viable, sacred self." Any alteration in an individual's moral worth, then, alters her standing in a network of others. Goffman's remarks suggest that individuals go out of their way to protect one another's self-conceptions; In this sense each individual is the guardian of others' *moral careers* as well as of his or her own. It may be, as Goffman argues, that (1956, p. 499):

This secular world is not so irreligious as we might think. Many gods have been done away with, but the individual himself stubbornly remains a deity of considerable importance. He walks with some dignity, and is the recipient of many little offerings. He is jealous of the worship due him, yet, approached in the right spirit, he is ready to forgive those who may have offended him. . . . Perhaps the individual is so viable a god because he can actually understand the ceremonial significance of the way he is treated, and quite on his own can respond dramatically to what is pro-offered him. In contracts between such deities there is no need for middlemen; each of these gods is able to serve as his own priest.

Aspects of Moral Careers

Any moral career is a temporal process that flows through the strands of the individual's life. Individuals have multiple careers, each linked into distinct universes of discourse; that is, into unique social worlds. In this sense individuals have careers with all of their interactive fellows. Some of these careers are short-term, as in a fleeting friendship. Some are long-term—marriage, or the work career of the individual who retires from the same university that hired her forty years earlier. Some careers have zigzag contours; a heroin user may, for instance, periodically "kick" the habit or move off hard drugs to soft drugs, and an alcoholic may move in and out of the drinking world. Careers have peak points of involvement, during which times the individual fully embraces the moral and subjective consequences of that involvement; at other times the involvement recedes into the background and may carry little, if any, implications for his other career commitments.

Careers are situated productions as well—that is, they are located in specific social situations. Careers are also "peopled productions": they involve interactions with other individuals. These other persons, in turn, influence the directions that the individual's career will take in the future. Thus, careers are joint productions that are temporarily and situationally specific to each person. David L. Westby's study (1960) of the career experiences of the symphony musician illustrates this point. He notes that images of conductors can significantly influence the career decisions of the musician. One violin player stated (Westby, 1960, p. 224): "As far as symphonies are concerned I'm better off here. I could have gone to (name of a somewhat more prestigious orchestra) last year on viola. The salary is better there, but I couldn't stomach the conductor."

Other people, then, positively and negatively influence the person's moral career. This is especially so for those careers which have an organizational locus (Blankenship, 1973; Faulkner, 1973). To have a career is to be involved in a set of commitments with other persons. Accordingly, it can be seen that trust and its imputation are central to the stability and shape of any career. An in-

dividual may overestimate or misrepresent, through selective inattention, the trustworthiness of another person. Or, that person may misrepresent herself to the person. Such misreadings, deliberate or accidental, often result in betrayals and blocked or negative careers. Thus many persons find themselves in mental hospitals or jails, and only later learn that their spouses were responsible for their commitment. A career is accomplished in the company of a set of *career others*—those individuals whose presence, commitment, and trust the individual comes to depend on.

As individuals move through any specific career—say, the academic or work world—their set of career others will change as they move from one position to another. That is, as the career takes on new forms or leads the individual into new areas, he finds himself in the presence of others who at an earlier time would not have been available to him. An individual has as many career others as he has ongoing careers; it should be clear, however, that these others may no longer be living, or they may have moved out of the person's immediate interactional world. Still, they continue to exert a symbolic influence over his behavior, and their imagined reactions may be assessed as the individual makes new decisions.

The multiple careers of any individual may be in harmony or in conflict with one another. Involvement in one social world—work, leisure, politics—may intrude into others—family, friends. As Simmel noted (1953), the person is led to develop a set of strategies which keep these competing career demands in some kind of balance. In the company of one set of others, she simply does not talk about or act on the perspectives of other competing worlds. Spouses may leave the work at the office; and children may not talk about their school experiences.

Career Visibility. While at any moment in time any individual is involved in multiple careers, some are more visible than others. The work career, for example, is highly prominent and visible and may go on display five or more days a week. Some careers are less visible: a person's interests in stamp collecting, or in a particular musician or artist, may never be known or may be made public only to a small set of others. A related characteristic is that some careers are over and done once traversed. Thus, when medical students complete their residency, their formal relationships with the medical establishment may be terminated. Similarly, many persons terminate careers (divorce) or have them terminated (death, demotion). Terminated careers are less visible than those that are ongoing, unless of course the previous career left the person with a set of markings that reveal his past. Abominations of the body—stigmata, like concentration camp markings, which are still visible—give away past involvements. Some careers, however, are simply buried; failures, broken love affairs, past criminal offenses may be kept secret or may be known only to a few people. All of us, then, give off clues to our career involvements through our verbal or nonverbal gestures. Our clothing and other personal possessions may be the basic conveyors of information about what these commitments are.

Career Entrance and Access. Careers may be entered voluntarily (the dating market), involuntarily (the military), or by recruitment (medical schools). Depending on the mode of entry and on how the individual defines other career involvements, she may show great attachment, detachment, or simple neutrality. Thus, someone just beginning to date may literally throw himself into the pursuit of a partner. In general, if the entry into the career has been voluntary, then perhaps the individual is more likely to commit and attach himself to the identifications that follow from his location in that social world.

The topic of career entrance raises the related matter of career access. Some careers are closed off to many groups of individuals, while others are open for the taking. Becker and Strauss (1956, pp. 255–56) observe:

There are problems attending the systematic restriction of recruiting. Some kinds of persons for occupationally irrelevant reasons (formally, anyway), may not be considered for some positions at all. Medical schools restrict recruiting in this way: openly, on grounds of "personality assessments," and covertly on ethnicity. Italians, Jews, and Negroes who do become doctors face differential recruitment into the formal and informal hierarchies of influence, power, and prestige in the medical world. Similar mechanisms operate at the top and the bottom of industrial organizations.

Career Control. Career access suggests that people can have differing degrees of control over their own and others' careers. While ostensibly a person should have the greatest control over her own life chances, that may not be the case—as small children, the elderly, the stigmatized, and the impoverished know. Power and its influence, whether legitimate or illegitimate, are central to the shaping and molding of all careers. However, any assessment of power and its application must do more than assert that organizations or societies make certain classes of individuals act in certain ways. Power and influence are always filtered through interpersonal relationships, and in the final analysis involve one individual exerting his authority (however legitimate) over another. Thus negative power—the threat to kill or to punish, for example—often leads persons to act in ways they find repulsive and repugnant. But the main point is that since careers involve others, power, influence, and controlling strategies are intrinsic to careers.

Encounters, sometimes called *turning points* (Strauss, 1969), describe those moments when individuals have a new and often drastically different set of self-identities thrust upon them. Mental patients who undergo mortification rites (where their identities may be challenged), military inductees who have their identity signs (like clothing) removed, and brides who walk down the aisle find that after the encounter they cannot return to the past in an unaltered form. In this sense, we can see that the career is continually being affected by matters not entirely under the control of the person.

Career Phases. In general, careers can be plotted in terms of a set of phases or substages. Thus the medical career may have at least four stages: (1) wishing to become a doctor; (2) gaining admission into medical school; (3) acquiring a clientele after graduation; (4) developing a set of informal relationships with medical colleagues. Each of these stages could be broken into subphases: making it through the first, second, third, and fourth years; securing a place to practice; and so on. Many careers have institutional markers that go with them. Thus Goffman observed (1961) that the mental patient's career fell into three phases: prepatient, inpatient, and postpatient. Location in or out of the institution that controls the activities associated with the control will place the person in or out of career. In this way, all persons who have not yet been—but will be—hospitalized for mental illness are prepatients. It would be misleading to assume that all careers are neatly patterned or phased; it is difficult, for example, to plot the marriage career accurately. In this sense many careers are open-ended.

Career Flow. As these remarks on career phases suggest, careers are temporal processes that flow through ongoing elements of social organization (Glaser & Strauss, 1967, 1971). Some carry the individual (the mental patient) into unwanted interactions. Others are more directly controlled by the person (marriage). The temporal elements of the career can be charted—each has a unique trajectory. Some trajectories are lingering; they speed up at certain points and then bog down, so to speak. Many deaths are like this (Strauss & Glaser, 1970). Some trajectories are rapid—a person dies soon after an automobile accident. And then, some careers move along at an even, predictable rate; a college student, for example, may move smoothly through freshman year to graduation three years later (Becker, Geer, & Hughes, 1968). In general, the flow—temporal shape—of a career will reflect its organizational embeddedness, which

in turn is influenced by the person's ability to control time's passage—that is, a person can find that other persons or organizations structure how she utilizes time; persons vary in the degrees of control they exercise over their own timetables. Organizational careers are more fixed and closed than are careers through marriages or friendships. Thus the more open-ended the career, the more likely it is that its temporal trajectory will be uneven, lingering, and emergent.

Moral Careers and Biographies

Whether or not they want to, all individuals have a personal moral career that encompasses all of their experiences, actions, and commitments up to and including the present moment. Thus, while many careers are optional, the personal moral career is not. Every individual, accordingly, has a set of accounts or stories which explain and justify the current status of his personal moral career. Sad tales are told by those who feel that their careers have gone astray; happy tales are told by those who are relatively pleased with the progress of their lives (Goffman, 1961, pp. 150–54). In practice, most accounts fall somewhere between sad and happy; this is because a person's multiple identities are never at the same stage of completion, fulfillment, or accomplishment. So she will most likely develop a story which is specific to each ongoing career, as well as a master story which accounts for all of them.

The presumed existence of a personal career leads others to make biographical assumptions about us. If others have only a minimum amount of information about our age, status, education, or family, they will almost necessarily impute a set of biographical details to us. They will assume that we have a work history or a mental history. Thus, the possession of a personal moral career makes everyone vulnerable to attack; we are accountable for our own career, and occasionally may be called upon to elaborate just who we are and why we are as we are (Denzin, 1971). We turn to the ways in which careers are linked with membership in social worlds.

The Moral Career of the Ex-Nun

Ebaugh (1984) has analyzed the career and self-experiences of women who leave the Catholic Church. Drawing on her own experiences as an ex-nun and upon interviews with sixty women who left different orders, she analyzed the six stages involved in the exit process. In each stage, various different career others, different self-conceptions, and different interactional and organizational forces influenced and shaped the women's experiences.

In stage 1, the nun began to doubt the Church and her place in it. A series of historical events created doubt for many nuns; after Vatican II many Catholic orders were radically transformed. While the three vows of poverty, chastity, and obedience remained fixed, nuns began to doubt whether the Church was still serving their needs, and whether they could meet the Church's needs. Group discussions were formed within the Church as nuns thrashed out what it meant to be a nun during this historic moment. For the first time in years, nuns began to interact with laypersons, coming into contact with changing social conceptions of men, women, marriage, God, and the Church in American society.

In stage 2, the nun realized that she had the freedom to decide to stay or leave. Rome was granting dispensations from final vows on a regular basis, and it became well known that one could leave the Church if one so desired. Ebaugh calls stage 3 "Trying Out Options." Nuns who were thinking of leaving engaged in imaginary role- and self-playing. They tried out new social identities they might enact if they were to leave the Church. They talked to nuns who had left the Church and visited friends who lived in apartments. They learned how to dress as laypersons, and how date, and how to establish a family life (Ebaugh, 1984, p. 166).

Ebaugh calls stage 4 the "vacuum." Nuns learned that if they left the Church the decision was nonretractable, because the orders were reluctant to readmit ex-members, and this caused anxiety and fear. The nuns compared the security of the order to the fear of leaving. For those nuns who wished to marry and have children, leaving had to be now or never. The fear of leaving kept many nuns in a state of nonbeing; they felt that they were both nuns and ex-nuns at the same time. Stage 5, the "Turning Point," came when the nun actually crystallized the decision to leave. Many different events created this turning point: If a nun had been assigned a job she did not like this helped her make the decision; if the nuns felt that their orders were not making the changes they desired, this also made the decision to leave easier. Many nuns saw final vows (the end of six years) as the time to leave.

Stage 6 is "Creating the Ex-Role," or the ex-nun self. Ebaugh sees this as involving three problem areas: (1) intimacies, friendship, and sexuality; (2) presentation of self—including dress, makeup, and style; (3) adjusting to and negotiating other people's reactions to the new identity as ex-nun (Ebaugh, 1984, p. 171). Each nun that Ebaugh interviewed resolved these problems differently. What each shared, however, was the fact they had to create a new moral career for themselves. They had to do this in the company of new career others, and they no longer had the institutional force of the Church behind them. In a basic sense, each ex-nun created a new social self with new identities and did this under uncertain social conditions (Kotarba, 1984, p. 230).

IDENTITY TRANSFORMATIONS

Travisano (1981) has offered an analysis of "alternation" and "conversion" as two different kinds of personal transformation. Alternations in identity refer to changes, transformations, and transitions to identities which are "prescribed or at least permitted within the person's established universes of discourse" (Travisano, 1981, p. 244). Conversions are transitions to identities which are proscribed (prohibited) within the person's social world; they negate prior identities. In conversion, the person experiences intense inner struggle, great trauma, anxiety, and often fear. Travisano suggests that a typical conversion would be the case where a person embraces a completely negative identity—for example, a Jew becoming a fundamental Christian. On the other hand, a person who shifts from being a Methodist to a Lutheran, or from being engaged to being married, experiences an alternation in identity.

Conversions in identity involve often radical changes in self-attitude, in career others, in interpersonal relationships, and in the basic languages one applies to oneself. Alternations in identity are less radical and sweeping in influence, changing from being a father to a grandfather, for example, is much less drastic than changing from being married to being widowed or divorced.

Identity changes, whether of the conversion or alternation kind, inform and change one's other identities; they also change one's interactional world. Converts, like ex-nuns, make their new identity central to almost all interactions (Travisano, 1981, p. 247). When identities change, social worlds change. Travisano suggests that ours is an age of alternation, but not of conversion: we pursue leisure, leave work at the office, and insist on self- and personal fulfillment. This may be changing, however; we noted in Chapter 1 for example, that more and more people in our society are experiencing problems with drugs and alcohol. To the degree that the social worlds of recovery from alcohol and drug addiction continue to expand and grow, the identities of recovering alcoholic and drug addict may become more and more common. Such identities are only accomplished through radical self changes of the type Travisano calls conversion.

Membership in Social Worlds

When discussing symbolic environments in Chapter 2, we touched on the concept of *social worlds*—groupings of individuals bound together by networks of communication or universes of discourse. Whether the members are geographically proximate or not, they share important symbolizations, and hence also share perspectives on "reality." It is significant that the term *social world* is commonly used to refer to such abstract collectivities as the worlds of theater, skiing, stamp collecting, and birdwatching, and to occupational groupings like those of medicine and science. The concept, however, is equally applicable to almost any collectivity—including families, perhaps—if we emphasize communication and membership; for membership is not merely a matter of physical or official belonging but also of shared symbolization, experiences, and interests. To emphasize this, there even exists a book about divorced people titled *The World of the Formerly Married* (Hunt, 1966).

The idea of the social world implies that members may be scattered in space. A family does not disintegrate merely because the members no longer live together (Hess & Handel, 1959); people who play chess and follow the competitions live all over the world; these players can talk about and play chess with anyone, no matter where they may travel. Stamp collectors also belong to an immensely scattered world; they can visit virtually any sizable city in the world and find a store that deals in stamps, where they can find other collectors with whom they can swap stamps and stories. Some social worlds, of course, are less than international in scope, and may even be quite localized, but the symbolic character of their membership is no less true.

These examples imply that the members can come from diverse backgrounds. Baseball fans discourse enthusiastically and heatedly across the boundaries of social class, region, or age. A cousin of one of the authors is the president of a large corporation and also an avid collector of Australian two-pence stamps. Once, when traveling on business, he arranged to meet another collector; after two hours of conversation about stamps, he discovered that the other collector was also a corporation official. Some social worlds, however, do not draw members from such a diversity of backgrounds; they are more closely linked with class, sex, occupation, and economic level. The world of labor union officials is closely linked with socioeconomic background; conversely, polo fans or collectors of antique Chinese porcelain generally are not "working class." Fishing enthusiasts seem to be mostly men, while mostly women are involved with the world of fashion.

Communication and Activity

Two key features of all these social worlds are *communication* and *activity*. Considering communication first, we note that all our examples involve conversation or some other form of communication. Typically, when people of a world come together, sooner or later they talk about things of mutual interest that pertain to their shared world. For instance, golfers talk about their recent games, their greatest victories and worst shots, the fine points of technique; and, of course, they swap golf jokes, some of which are about recognizable "social types" like duffers and experts. Any social world is likely to develop legends and myths which are told and retold; it will also develop some special language, or lingo, for referring to events, objects, and activities that "matter." Many worlds also develop channels of written communication; sailing, for instance, has many magazines, some of them quite specialized to correspond to the different subworlds. At any rate, at the heart of interaction "within" any world is communication—written or spoken—when its members are scattered. Then its media, supplemented by correspondence and by members who travel and speak, are vital to its existence and its membership.

Aside from communicative ability, the members also feel that they belong because they act in reference to these worlds. The members go places and do things: they buy skiing equipment; they ski; and they may "follow" actively the skiing activities of experts either by watching television or by actually going to meets. Even those who do not actually play a game but act the "passive spectator"—to use a term coined by critics of that kind of spectatorship—can be actively and even passionately involved in watching the sport. This is as true of elderly women watching boxing as of earnest young men mooning over female stars of the theater. We shall say more about the careers and identities of members of these worlds; but we must note that some members may be more "professionally" or commercially involved in the world's activities than are others. In evolving worlds, as in scuba diving during its early years, enthusiastic participants began to develop technology and later began to market scuba boards or other equipment. (Similar processes were prevalent in the "surfing" world.) (Irwin, 1977) In more developed worlds, there is an elaborate division of labor with built-in careers for many people, who profit either commercially or psychologically from their activities.

Subworlds

The more developed the world, the more *subcommunities* (or *segments* or *specialties*) it will have. This makes conceptualization—for the social psychologist—more difficult, since the more developed are these subcommunities the more differential perspectives are there likely to be toward the same broad spectrum of the "world" events. Surgeons, for instance, do not necessarily see eye to eye with internists on the question of what to do about ulcers, or a number of other potentially operable symptoms, which suggests what Bucher and Strauss (1961) have noted—namely, that between the members of related subworlds there may be great antagonism. At the very least, as their activities and interests take them further from each other, some subcommunities tend to be indifferent to each other. A good example is that of young painters who may first react with great antagonism to an older style of painting and then acquire their own audience, so that they are in social and work contact only with that audience and with other painters like themselves.

Central and Peripheral Members

One more feature of social worlds is worth mentioning, since it is related both to the kinds of participation engaged in by members and the kinds of self-conception which they have. This feature is that these collectivities have members who are more *central,* as well as those who are more *peripheral,* to the world's functioning. Said another way, some persons invest more of their time, energy, money, and themselves into activities associated with the world. These latter include not only the spectators and the amateurs, but a large percentage of the "pros"— whether they be managers, stars, sales personnel, or manufacturers. One need not argue whether, in the days of Hollywood's glory, the enthusiastic persons who ran the fan clubs were as central to Hollywood's success as the major investors in the industry; in any event, both were more involved in the movie world, albeit participating in it differently, than were the occasional movie-goers (Klapp, 1965). We shall turn to this aspect of social worlds when discussing what centrality and periphery mean to the participants themselves.

IDEOLOGIES AND SOCIAL WORLDS

To "belong" to a social world means to be affected, to a greater or lesser degree, by its *symbolic coordinates.* A technical term which is applicable to that phenomenon is *ideology* (Mannheim, 1936). Social scientists use the term to refer to any body of systematically

related and significant or basic beliefs held by a group. The term was invented during the 18th century and used within a political context by opponents who discredited each other's beliefs by finding their sources in selfish or class interests. However, *ideology* no longer conveys simply connotations of falseness and illusion. We shall discuss political and occupational ideologies as instances of how people's beliefs can be affected and sustained by participation in the communication networks of certain worlds.

Political Ideology

Citizens of modern nations, when they consider matters pertaining to their governments and how they impinge on things important to them, tend to join conflicting ideological camps. These political ideologies are linked with—but also cut across— regional, religious, occupational, class, racial, and other worlds. The ideology is sustained by organizations of committed professionals who mobilize and direct various channels of communication; they produce their own literature, hold meetings, raise money, and compete with other similarly organized groups for access to the mass media. When one ideological camp takes control of the government, it may block or restrict the attempts of others to disseminate their ideologies through the media.

In newly formed nations, ideological cleavages are readily apparent, often sharp and bitter, and may eventuate in violence. Even the minimum consensus necessary to form a nation does not exclude the resort to force or possibly civil war. In established, stable nations with long histories, sharp and bitter ideological divisions may exist for many decades. In 1954 a group of scholars (Hoffman, 1963) assessed the economic and political situation in France. They agreed that France was deeply divided along several ideological lines—class, regional, and religious especially—represented by a series of parties, organizations, newspapers, and other media. They pointed to this situation as the cause of France's inability to meet its grave economic, social, and international problems. The gravity of this political impasse in France eventually created a partial consensus among some of the more powerful groups who produced and supported the de Gaulle regime. Some of the old cleavages are undoubtedly still there behind the public scene.

The grass-roots basis of political ideology can be thought of as existing in the simplest forms of interaction between people. Individuals tend to have as their friends other people who have the same beliefs (Lazarsfeld, Berelson, & Gaudet, 1948). They exchange information and views and consequently validate and revalidate the interpretations they already hold, which are disseminated from power centers. Even in the case of the mass media, information and interpretation appear to exert their influence indirectly through the channels of personal communication between opinion leaders and the persons with whom the leaders talk. This latter phenomenon has been formally described in what has been called "the two-step theory of information flow" (Katz, 1966).

Selection pertains not only to choice of friends, but also to choice of newspapers, journals, and television and radio programs, all of which feed selective facts and interpretations to their audiences. If individuals are not "plugged in" to opposing channels of communication, there are no countering facts and interpretations. Hence, those who judge election results by polling their friends and associates are sometimes very surprised by the actual election results. Even when persons of a given political view receive the messages that circulate in other channels, they tend to perceive them selectively and fit them into their own conceptual frameworks.

It is sometimes said that people adopt a political position in terms of self-interest—their own interest or that of their family, class, occupation, or religion. This idea is erroneous, however, because it does not take into account that people interpret their own interests in different ways and are often uncertain of what their interests are. In the face of conflicting interpretations that are offered, they can be very confused about what their objectives are and end up by voting against themselves.

Like other ideas, political ideas and convictions are formed not on the basis of the way the world really is or on actual self-interest, but rather on the world as it is interpreted, and on what people are persuaded to believe to be their interests. The influence of the mass media is obviously great; but its effectiveness is limited by the influence of the smaller communication networks in which people are always involved. Interaction among friends, family members, and associates in work and recreational worlds provides a fund of detailed reports and interpretation of events directly observed or experienced. Such information is generally more persuasive than the more abstract, impersonal products of the mass media. It is perhaps for this reason that a unified propaganda "line," promulgated in nations in which only one official ideology is expressed in the mass media, is often far less effective than is popularly supposed (Klapper, 1966). This is pointed up by a joke reported from behind the iron curtain:

Question: What is the difference between capitalism and communism?

Answer: In capitalism man exploits man; in communism it's just the opposite.

Media Selves

David Altheide (1984) has suggested that in the modern world, the mass media plays an important part in determining how persons define themselves. He points to a decade of research on mass media aspects of political decision making, professional sports, television, radio, and newspaper journalism to support the conclusion that we live in a media age which significantly defines who we are, who our idols are, and what our ideal self-images are. The media serves to make the self problematic in ways that it would not be otherwise. The media offers models, images of far-off places, pictures of other cultures, scenarios of power and acclaim, biographies of astronauts, and stories of fallen presidents. These images and pictures offer formats or ways of structuring reality. They induce expectations of the self and lead to the cultivation of a media self. Famous persons hire press agents to help them cultivate certain self-appearances—for example, the "Miami Vice" look—and so on.

More and more, one's identity is "tied to products and styles" (Altheide, 1984, p. 178). These styles and identities constitute fads and fashions within the American scene. They offer new ways of thinking and being, open avenues for new social worlds, and introduce conflicts in interpersonal relationships. The media commodifies the self and promotes a public self and style that did not exist in the pre-mass television age.

Racial Ideology

Similar processes operate in the area of race and ethnic relations. The ideologies that groups develop to justify the discrimination process are often based on "definitions of the situation" that bear little relationship to "objective" social facts. Thus one team of researchers (Solaun & Kronus, 1973) noted that discrimination in Latin America, which is often based on the lightness of a person's skin, with a corresponding racial nomenclature to describe variations in skin color, commonly reflects a group's view of itself within the overall class structure. In Cartagena, Colombia, the team observed that when respondents were asked to place photographed Colombians in one of several racial groupings (based on skin color) (Solaun & Kronus, 1973):

The elites showed a tendency to darken people; the middle class tended to darken blancos but to lighten the overall population; the working and lower classes lightened the population, particu-

larly persons with high status, and were relatively imprecise in their definitions.

In this sense a person's definition of self as a member of a particular racial grouping, or category, is based on how far up the class ladder she has progressed. The Colombian elites and middle-class members were much more willing to discriminate against all other persons than were the working- and lower-class respondents.

Occupational Ideology

In Western nations, a chief source of ideology—for males at least—is their work. Hughes has asserted that (1958, p. 94): "In our particular society, work organization looms so large as a separate and specialized system of things, and work experience is so fateful a part of every man's life, that we cannot make much headway as students of society and of social psychology without using work as one of our main laboratories." Work today rarely stands alone, for relatively little of it is done outside of organizational structures. Even professionals who have private practices are increasingly abandoning their offices for work within professional organizations, and private entrepreneurs belong increasingly to trade associations. Hence, when we talk about work as a source of ideology, it is necessary to think not only about the nature of a person's work, but his occupation and position within a work organization. In general, the more rigorous the training demanded for a line of work, the more commitment an individual has to the work; the more social activity is structured around friends drawn from the work world, the more the larger symbolic world is likely to be affected by work.

Countless studies have demonstrated that occupational affiliation or position in work organization or work world profoundly affect people's views as well as their actual behavior. Thus, attitudes and behavior toward clients depend on the nature of the occupation. Undertakers, as Habenstein (1962, pp.

242–44) observes, handle their client's family with suave control. Physicians typically handle their clients with firm authority. Janitors ordinarily can do neither, because they stand in a different relation to their clients. One study shows how their management is a compound of open respect and concealed disrespect (Gold, 1952). Of course, not all people of the same occupation do the same types of work or meet others in the same types of relationships. Thus, some musicians play in large dance bands for affluent dancers, while other musicians play for intently listening audiences who would sooner be caught dead than dancing (Becker, 1973). Differential positions within work organizations and in different types of work organizations afford differential experiences with consequent impact on perspectives taken toward issues and audiences that may be far removed from the work itself. As Janowitz (1962) suggests in his study of the American military, there are striking differences between officers who have come up through administrative routes and those who are experienced in front-line battle; likewise, there are considerable differences between officers who work in the three armed services. All these constitute work worlds.

Work, occupation, and organizational position can contribute to the formation of a person's occupational ideology in quite complex ways. We will illustrate this from a study of Chicago psychiatrists (Strauss, et al., 1964). In the United States, there are two dominant ideologies held by psychiatrists; one gives priority to biological etiology and physical treatment, and the other gives priority to psychic processes and psychotherapeutic treatment. The first one, somatic ideology, receives continued support from the advances of biological science and from the biological orientation of most physicians. Nevertheless, the psychotherapeutic ideology has become more influential since the 1950s.

In general, these two groups of psychiatrists live in entirely separate professional worlds. They may know some of the other variety, providing they use the same hospital, but they tend to belong to quite different sociability and communication networks. They go to different professional meetings, or if they go to national ones, they move in different circles when there. They read a rather different array of journals. In a large city like Chicago, they may have only the foggiest notions of psychiatrists of other ideological positions and what these individuals think of them. When interviewed about the nature of Chicago psychiatry, the psychiatrists who tended toward either ideological position differed a great deal in their conceptions of what psychiatry consisted of in their city. Some psychiatrists and some institutions were visible to some respondents, but they were invisible to other respondents. The psychotherapists all knew, and many were affiliated with, the local psychoanalytic institute, but were vague about other psychiatric institutions (Strauss, et al., 1964, p. 42):

Well, there are those people who identify—I'll start from what is most familiar to me—identify themselves as analysts . . . in terms of their training and the professional activity in which they engage. Then we go to the other end which is furthest away from that—something which I'm not particularly familiar with at first hand, I don't have contact with these people. These are people who do predominantly somatic-type therapy, coupled with some kind of psychotherapeutic orientation on the part of those who are not analysts. . . . My God, what do people do who have not had analytic training or at least analytically based training. . . . I mean what do those people do who purport to do psychotherapy?

The somatic psychiatrists were even more vague about local institutions, because in general there was less communication among them than among the psychotherapists, who had the institute as a central training, educational, and sociability locale.

An occupational ideology is sustained through both formal and informal channels of communication. Once absorbed, it significantly influences how people regard and carry out their work, and how they form relationships to clients, assistants, and colleagues. It profoundly affects their perception so that they see symptoms selectively and interpretively. They diagnose and treat them accordingly. Their occupational convictions also deeply affect their self-conceptions; insofar as they regard certain kinds of work worth doing well, they also evaluate their own performances according to that standard. Thus, psychotherapists do not judge themselves in terms of pharmacological skills but in terms of success and failure with psychotherapeutic methods. Since their occupational convictions greatly affect the colleagues they see at work or socially, their self-conceptions are further affected.

In these respects, modern urban life can be viewed as a complex intermeshing of occupational, racial, political, and even residential ideologies. These ideologies come together inside the social worlds that urban inhabitants construct and destroy (Suttles, 1972, 1968).

REFERENCE GROUPS

There is a body of literature—now over forty years old—which relates to the concept of *reference group*. Although this concept was not developed in terms of social worlds except by Shibutani, it is useful to think of it that way (Shibutani, 1955, 1962). First, however, we shall present some standard materials bearing on this concept.

Reference group (Hyman & Singer, 1968; Hyman, 1960; Kemper, 1968; Kuhn, 1964a; Schmitt, 1972) is generally thought of as pertaining to the fact that people evaluate themselves and orient their behavior by reference to (1) the groups in which they hold official membership; (2) others to which they aspire or to which they hope to belong in the future; and (3) others which they reject and definitely do not wish to belong to. A reference group is thus any group with which people psychologically identify themselves, or in relation to which they think of themselves. Implicit in this idea is that their exist-

ing group memberships may be relatively meaningless to persons whose primary "ego anchorages" are established with reference to groups with which they are not formally or objectively linked. This type of anticipatory allegiance is especially noticeable in a mobile society in which the ambition to raise one's status is characteristically encouraged (Sherif, 1953; Sherif, White, & Hood, 1954).

Reference groups are thus said to establish the individual's organizing conceptions or frames of reference for ordering experiences, perceptions, and ideas of self. Sherif has stated the matter as follows (Sherif, 1953, p. 214):

The individual's directive attitudes, namely, ego-attitudes, which define and regulate his behavior to other persons, other groups, and to an important extent even to himself, are formed in relation to values and norms of his reference groups. They constitute an important basis of his self-identity, of his sense of belongingness, of the core of his social ties.

Hyman (1942, 1960) is credited with the first use of the term *reference group*, analyzing the influence of such groups on college students' conceptions of their status. He found that they compared themselves with others in the following respects, listed in order of frequency: (1) economic, (2) intellectual, (3) social, (4) looks, (5) culture, (6) athletics, (7) prestige, (8) general, (9) character, (10) politics, (11) sexual qualities, (12) religion, and (13) esteem. Among the matters mentioned by students in connection with the ratings they gave themselves were family background, membership in special groups, breeding, people known, money, dates, ability to get along with the other sex, degrees, achievement, race, formal education, reasoning ability, intelligence, appreciation of the arts, reading, worldly experience, and academic background of the family. Hyman noted that the groups referred to in making comparisons differed among the subjects and were of crucial importance in self-conception. Thus, one subject whose income was $336 per year gave $900 per year as an amount that would make her "joyous," whereas another subject with an income of $4,000 per year said he would be content with no less than $25,000. Hyman found that in general, small intimate groups were more important for reference in estimates of oneself than was the general population. Individuals chose the points on which they compared themselves with others so as to achieve the most satisfactory position possible.

Festinger's (1947) experiments with voting behavior in relation to religious affiliation also shed light on the way in which reference groups influence behavior. Festinger compared the voting of Catholic and Jewish girls in several types of situations. In one, the girls knew nothing of each other's or the candidates' religious affiliations; in another, they knew the affiliation of the candidates but not each other's; and in the third situation, they knew each other's affiliations as well as those of the candidates. These experiments showed that the Catholic girls tended to vote for Catholic candidates when their own affiliation was known to the other voters, and that the Jewish girls voted for Jewish candidates mainly when their religious affiliations were not so known. Festinger supposed that Jewish girls felt free to vote as Jews when they were anonymous, whereas Catholic girls felt compelled to vote as Catholics only when they were openly identified as such.

Early studies like Hyman's and Festinger's were done by psychologists, but for sociologists. Merton and Kitt (1950) made the concept better known when they reinterpreted findings reported in *The American Soldier* in the light of the reference group concept. They showed, for example, how inexperienced troops were influenced by association with soldiers who had combat experience. Inexperienced troops, desiring to affiliate themselves with those who had experience in battle, tended to take over the latter's norms and values and evaluate themselves by reference to them.

Positive, Negative, and Multiple Reference Groups

Newcomb (1950) extended this concept in a study of the relationship of the attitudes of Bennington College students to the attitudes of *positive* and *negative reference groups*—the former being those in which one desires to be accepted and treated as a member, and the latter those to which one is opposed and in which one does not desire membership.

The idea of the negative reference group emphasizes that when one commits oneself to the viewpoint of values of one group, this fact automatically places one in a potentially hostile or competitive position with respect to other groups. Thus, for a Democrat the Republican party is a negative reference group, particularly at election time, while the Democratic party performs this function for Republicans. This illustration points to a pervasive aspect of human social relationships, namely, that some degree of conflict, hostility, avoidance, or antagonism is generally apparent or implicit in them, and these negative features constitute essential aspects of social structure. The two dominant political parties in the United States are in conflict, but they also depend upon each other and upon the conflict between them for their continued existence. To be *for* something implies being *against* something else. If one associates with certain people and groups, one must to some extent avoid other people and groups. There are satisfactions in opposing or fighting against something. The views of the atheist and the communist-hater are examples of the influence of negative reference groups, because they are distinguished by what they are against rather than by what they are for. Some persons find particular satisfaction in such hostile relationships; they may be said to be predominately influenced by their negative, rather than their positive, reference groups.

The concept of the reference group has also been elaborated in an effort to make it square with the complexity of identifications involving *multiple group memberships*, positive and negative relationships to the same group, multiple positive and negative group influences in the same situation, and shifting loyalties and relationships. The problem of what constitutes group membership is none too easy except when one deals with formal membership (the tokens of which are payment of dues, membership, and active participation), and these memberships are often of little or no significance for the person's behavior. Membership in a social class, for example, involves none of these. Does this mean that a person's class membership is to be judged by her way of life and by how she thinks, regardless of occupation and income? If we ask whether the undercover FBI agent in the communist party is really a member of the party, some of the problems of determining membership in groups are obvious. Most people would probably say that in this case, even though the FBI man pays dues to the communist party and carries a membership card, he is not really a member because he does not identify himself with the party, nor does he adopt its position. The party is not a reference group for him, although it might be called a negative reference group.

Comparative and Normative Reference Groups

Besides the ideas of positive, negative, and multiple reference groups, an early distinction was drawn, initially by Harold Kelley, between comparative and normative reference groups (1952, 1963). *Comparative reference groups,* in the same sense as used in Hyman's study, pertained to the groups with which an individual compared herself. *Normative reference groups* were those which were the sources of the individual's values. All these distinctions—not all of which are used or agreed upon by everyone who uses the term—have recently led Margaret Williams, a sympathetic critic, to remark that the term is "still not conceptually clarified. . . ." She also warned that "reference group theory is fair prey to falling into the mold of extreme group determinism. . . . 'Reference groups determine behavior'" (Williams, 1970, pp. 550–52). Berhard Cohen has ironically phrased the same criticism this way: "Your reference group is a group that you behave like and you behave like them because they're your reference group" (1962, p. 104).

Other Ideas about Reference Groups

Considerations like these led Manford Kuhn, a leading symbolic interactionist, to comment that the concept of reference group "represents a vast simplification of the idea of the other" (1964; p. 13). He attributed the concept's quick rise in popularity to that simplification, and went on to criticize the questionnaire studies done by reference group researchers: "There is always some mental relief associated with the implication in any operation that a broad and elliptical idea is 'nothing but' these marks on these pieces of paper" (Kuhn, 1964, p. 11). He suggested (1964, p. 15) the complexity of who those others might be by noting "elementary distinctions" such as those based on time, continuity, physical and social space: "We can differentiate present others from absent others; proximal others from distal others; contemporary others from past others; continuous others from intermittent others; in-category others from out-category others; immediate, impulsive, passing others from considerable others." Kuhn then coined a term, *orientational other,* which refers to others to whom people are most fully committed, who have given them their most crucial concepts and categories, who have provided and continue to provide them with their categories of self and other and with meaningful roles to which such assignments refer, and to others with whom their self-conception is basically sustained or changed (Denzin, 1966).

Shibutani (1955, 1962) has suggested a redefinition of the reference group concept in terms of a conception of social worlds that squares with ours. Noting the salient characteristics of mass societies in which people frequently internalize discordant values of different groups, Shibutani suggested that "much of the interest in reference groups arises out of concern with situations in which a person is confronted with the necessity of acting on the basis of alternative definitions, where he must make a choice between two or more organized perspectives." The key problem "in the study of reference groups . . . is that of ascertaining whose confirming responses are needed in order to sustain a given point of view." This leads to a consideration of which audiences—actual, imagined, or potential—the person is acting toward and with chief reference to. Shibutani, in a paper on reference groups (1962), goes on to relate these diverse audiences to diverse social worlds. In each world, "there develops a universe of discourse. Pertinent experiences are categorized in particular ways, and a special set of symbols is used to refer to them. . . . Each world is a universe of regularized mutual response, an arena in which there is some kind of organization that facilitates anticipating the behavior of others." In short, the emphasis is on interacting members of social worlds, where "membership" is linked with participation in communication networks, or in Shibutani's phrasing, within social worlds whose boundaries "are set neither by territory nor formal group membership, but by the limits of effective communication" (Shibutani, 1962, p. 137).

Used in this way, the concept of the reference group can do more than merely point to audiences otherwise unsuspected by the observer; in its present state the concept is chiefly useful for focusing attention on the more subtle nuances of identification and loyalty. The problem of accounting for individual behavior in terms of reference groups, therefore, centers around discovering which communication networks are operating, what information is being channeled to the person, and toward which audiences he addresses himself and orients his behavior. The investigator's problem is thus complicated because he cannot rely on fixed external criteria like status, office, age, sex, or social class, but must seek out a more subtle range of symbolic involvements in a multiplicity of social worlds.

Indeed, Raymond L. Schmitt (1972), in the most extensive review of the reference group literature to date, concluded that there does not yet exist a viable or complete theory of the reference group. In his synthesis of this body of research, he argues that the concept refers to three interrelated notions: the reference other, the relationships between the individual and the reference other, and the individual in question. The reference other orientation, he proposes, must be placed more squarely within the symbolic interactionist framework. The present discussion of social worlds represents one way to make conceptual sense out of this tremendously vague and ill-defined concept.

CHANGING WORLDS: DANGER AND CHALLENGE

In modern societies, many social worlds are characterized by considerable rates of change, while others are even more highly volatile and unstable. If one thinks of activities like skiing, horse racing, or jogging, one can see that over the past 30 years the associated worlds have expanded amazingly both in number of participants and in audience size (Scott, 1968). Tennis, once the preserve of the American elite, is now a mass sport—complete with a vast increase in the manufacture and sales of equipment, new kinds of celebrities and competitive matches, and an explosion of media reporting. Into many worlds there is built an inner dynamism—especially those worlds that are expanding—that is reflected in a kind of "budding" process, whereby "the" world becomes differentiated and, as already mentioned, subcommunities of interested persons begin to talk about and do different things. Thus, while there is a general world of scuba divers, some members are interested exclusively in underwater photography, others are interested in exploration. In mountain climbing, some individuals are expert at climbing steep but not inordinately high ice mountains, while others organize expeditions to scale the Himalayas. Worlds and subworlds can also decline in popularity and size, and over time may even disappear. This phenomenon is associated sometimes with generational differences: for instance, the younger generations of mountain climbers use instruments that allow them to cling to the surface of mountains which they climb vertically; the generation that invented this mode of climbing looked with scorn upon the older climbers who scaled mountains by foot, regarding this merely as a species of hiking.

Whether the worlds are expanding or contracting, if they are changing at all they represent danger to some people and challenge to others. An older tennis player can be overwhelmed not only by the sheer number of newcomers, but by improvements in techniques, new jargon, and new perspectives toward the sport itself, for a mass sport cannot be a "gentleman's sport." Imagine what would happen if every talented ghetto youngster were given a tennis racket, training, and a chance to play freely at the most exclusive tennis clubs. We know how awkward it was for the first black tennis players when they were introduced into predominantly white, affluent American tennis competition—let alone the clubs. People can be wounded deeply—their self-conceptions battered, trampled on, wrenched —when their worlds are invaded by newcomers and leadership taken away. Politics is replete with stories of old leaders and elites who, when overwhelmed although not utterly vanquished by newcomers, mourned not merely the sharing of power, but felt bitterly the ignominy of their loss: their world of political and governmental elitism was no longer only theirs. On the other hand, changes in social worlds can also represent great opportunity to those who stand to, or can manage to, profit from the changes. This point is more

obvious for expanding worlds than for contracting ones, but even in the face of marked decline, some people are able to find satisfying substitute activities and careers. On the other hand, many social worlds trap their participants and limit their future career changes (Wiley, 1967; Irwin, 1977).

The Collapse of Social Worlds

The collapse or complete disappearance of a world, of course, seems more obviously to represent a threat. Its members may stand not only to lose fun or money, but self-esteem. An especially poignant instance of a collectively shared collapse of a world is when a nation is conquered or experiences a radical social revolution. Gedye, an English journalist who was in Austria when the Nazis took over that country, conveys some sense of what this was like. As in other countries, mass suicides were one response to the collapse of the normal world. Gedye wrote about the reaction of the Jews (Gedye, 1939, p. 305):

It is quite impossible to convey to anyone outside Austria in how matter-of-fact a way that Jews of Austria today refer to this way out of their agony . . . Jewish friends spoke to one of their intention to commit suicide with no more emotion than they had formerly talked of making an hour's journey by train. . . . It is impossible . . . to imagine what it means for one-sixth of the population of Vienna to be made pariahs overnight, deprived of all civil rights, including the right to retain property large or small, the right to be employed or to give employment, to exercise a profession, to enter restaurants, cafes, bathing beaches, baths or public parks, to be faced daily and hourly, without hope of relief, with the foulest insults which ingenious and vicious minds can devise, to be liable always to be turned overnight out of house and home, and at any hour of every day and every night to arrest without the pretense of a charge or hope of a definite sentence, however heavy—and with all this to find every country in the world selfishly closing its frontiers to you when, after being plundered of your last farthing, you seek to escape. For most of the non-Jewish victims of the Nazis, many of whom are now sharing the punishment of the Jews, there is a hope that one day the nightmare may pass. For the Jews there is none while the Nazis rule.

At the close of World War II, the counterpart of this phenomenon occurred as the Nazi leaders, in their turn, saw their world falling about them. Durkheim (1897) has described this type of suicide as *anomic suicide.* He contrasted it with another type of suicide, which he called *altruistic.* Rather than representing despair and reflecting group disorganization, this *altruistic* kind of self-destruction indicates a high degree of social integration.

Suicides also accompany social revolution and other major social catastrophes. Obviously, this is not the only response that people can make; sometimes they are able to emigrate to other countries, where they attempt to reconstruct something of their old social worlds. Societies of aristocratic Russian émigrés in Paris, and settlements of German emigrants who fled the Nazis and settled in American cities are notable for their communal adaptation to new circumstances. The adaptation is only partial, however, for the host country's ways are never thoroughly embraced, nor are those of the old country abandoned. After the Russian Revolution and between the two world wars, Russian restaurants abounded in Paris, as the émigrés made the most of their heritage. The restaurants provided them with financial support and symbolic reinforcement. When whole communities suffer the loss of position and homeland, they are able to confront their common loss together and create a new life. Inevitably, some of these individuals leave their huddled world and strike out into the larger society with various results. The children of immigrants face an entirely different set of problems, and their behaviors and solutions must also be different.

We might make one final comment to indicate how the variable solutions to collective loss of world are linked with structural conditions. When the Chinese communists successfully took over China, many emigrants fled to Hong Kong and Taiwan. Many of them have been successful in making an adaptation and not giving in to the collapse of their worlds. Hong Kong was—and is—thoroughly Chinese in character, and while many individuals have doubtless been permanently demoralized by migration, the immigrants as a whole seem to have made a successful adaptation. The merchants have been so successful that they are probably more affluent than they would be in China. In Taiwan, a different set of circumstances existed; the deposed Chinese government quite literally conquered the people of Taiwan, who had previously lived under Japanese control. The immigrants could not so easily reconstitute their worlds, because they were accustomed to ruling over a huge country. Although they rule over a considerable population, the island is tiny when compared with China; across a narrow body of water their successors rule without any apparent danger of being ousted. Any visitor to Taiwan who talks with the "mainland" Chinese soon becomes aware of some patterned forms of their discontent.

ALIENATION AND MODERN SOCIETY

A popular view of life in modern mass societies and the impersonal environment of urban centers stress alienation, frustration, and the sense of meaninglessness that contemporary mass societies sometimes or overwhelmingly generate. Mass media writers and social scientists use terms like "our sick society" and think of industrialized nations as consisting of large undifferentiated masses of robotlike individuals, regimented in their daily activities and their leisure time pursuits. Some views of alienation include management and manipulation by powerful conspiratorial elites who possess the major share of the nation's wealth and who control its mass media. From this point of view, the average citizen is seen as a victim or dupe of social forces and pressures that she does not understand and is powerless to control. A specific version of this set of beliefs surfaced during the 1960s, when the universities, so swollen in size, were criticized and reacted to in terms of their impersonality and bureaucratization. In general, it is argued that in the "advanced" institutionalized nations, the old values once represented by the family, the neighborhood, the church, and the small community have disintegrated, leaving people unattached, rootless, and disenchanted.

While this view of modern life no doubt seems overdrawn to most, and while it often reflects the personal backgrounds and experiences of those who hold it, it does focus attention upon some conspicuous features and trends in contemporary nations. It is true, as the literature on anomie emphasizes, that people are encouraged to strive for goals while simultaneously denied access to the means of attaining them; that there are many persons who fall by the wayside or stand on the sidelines; and that there are marginal persons who belong to few groups, remain uncommitted, and are not caught up in significant and meaningful social enterprises. There are others who actively revolt against what they perceive as the emptiness and meaninglessness of their lives by joining with other like-minded persons to promote causes, change the society, or find means of escaping from its demands.

In contrast to those who deal with their marginality problems collectively, there are individual isolates who float about from one job to another, and who manage to find only peripheral and often fleeting positions on the edges of group structures. These persons are often troubled, dissatisfied, unattached to work or the opposite sex, and generally unanchored in the web of relationships from which most people derive their satisfactions and their sense of identity and personal worth. Some of these unattached persons end up in mental hospitals, some spend time in jail or prison, but others stay out of "trouble." They join organizations, tending to drift through them, but rarely get committed in any deep sense to anything or anybody.

These people are not just at odds with the government, the middle class, or some other feature of the nation; they are truly alienated. Yet they are not simply alienated from some vague entity known as "society"; rather they have no genuine commitments to or identifications with any "meaningful" social world. Nor is it true that they never had such attachments—sometimes the worlds important to them have collapsed or disappeared or changed beyond endurance, but they have not had the flexibility or vitality to find others that "matter."

THE ARTICULATION OF IMPLICATED SELVES

The collapse of a world is the ultimate danger for the selves of those persons who are most deeply implicated in the realities of that world. Accordingly, one major aspect of self pertains to the matter of loyalty to one's social worlds. After participating in a social world, one develops deep obligations to what it stands for, as well as to fellow participants. To leave it, or to have it collapse, means more than a readjustment of one's activities; it means a foreclosing of obligations and perhaps even a smashing betrayal of the others' expectations. A classic instance is the upwardly mobile person who finds the requirements and satisfactions of her world of origin increasingly in conflict with the world of her aspirations. The sociological, as well as the fictional and biographical literature, reflect the various outcomes of this conflict. If roots in the old world are strong enough, mobility may be abandoned. The opposite can occur when roots are not deep or the mobile aspirant can find no ready compromise with family and friends; then all ties with the old world are cut. Among the most drastic examples of such severance is the abandonment of spouse and children; another is passing into a white, gentile, or bohemian world. A type of modified passing, wherein the person occasionally returns home or keeps former connections surreptitiously, illustrates the range of possibilities open to those who experience this conflict between staying back home and moving out.

However, such terrible strains can be engendered by balancing allegiance and aspiration that when attempts at articulation finally fail, a person opts for one or another competing path. A vivid instance of actual and symbolic leaving home for a successful career is described by Moss Hart (1959), who immediately after a big celebration following the initial performance of his first Broadway hit took a taxi to his home in Brooklyn. His family was asleep. He stood looking at the shabby apartment—he had for years hated his poverty—the "dust of countless black-hearted days clung to every crevice of the squalid ugly furniture" which he had known since childhood. "To walk out of it forever—not piecemeal, but completely—would give meaning to the wonder of what had happened to me, make success tangible, decisive. . . ." He woke his family, who in "stunned silence" listened while he told them they were all going to leave immediately for a hotel, without packing a thing. "We're walking out of here and starting fresh . . . with just what clothes you put on and tomorrow we'll get rid of those, too." An hour later, as they were leaving in a blinding rainstorm, Hart dashed back and threw the windows wide open so that the rain "whipped in through the windows like a broadside of artillery fire," flooding the furniture. He looked around "with satisfaction, feeling neither guilty nor foolish. . . . It was the hallmark, the final signature of defiance and liberation. Short of arson, I could do no more. I slammed the door behind me without looking back." As in many success stories, although the hero had cut his ties with a despised lower-class world, he had taken his family upwards with him.

Another aspect of the involved self pertains to "commitments"—that is, the resources, time, energy, money, emotions, which one has invested in certain activities and relationships. Entrance into any world involves increasing commitment, for not only do other persons' demands on the self increase, but the person makes certain demands upon himself as when he expends resources (Schwartz, 1967).

In extreme cases, when drawn almost totally into a new world, individuals may drop their commitments to old ones; thus, converts to a religious sect may be required to quit their jobs, take up residence in a communal setting, and devote themselves wholly to sectarian activities. They must end all or most of their previous relationships, including leaving their spouses or converting them. Most of us do not face that kind of black-and-white situation, but do juggle commitments to the multiple worlds in which we participate. Moreover, our commitments are not static, for we are likely simultaneously to be loosening some and tightening others.

This articulation of activities and resources can be a complex matter. Sometimes the requirements of worlds mesh pretty well, so that, for instance, a husband can devote evenings and weekends to his family but daytime hours to his work world. Or a businesswoman may get interested in the world of art and begin to collect paintings. Ordinarily she can, without undue strain, juggle the competing requirements of time, energy, and finances so that her avocational and vocational careers do not run grievously afoul of one another. However, those concerns not only may become slightly and occasionally competitive, but the collector's instinct may begin to run riot and use up time, effort, and money previously allocated to the business and family side of her life. Some collectors have solved this conflict by leaving their jobs and work careers to become owners of art galleries, immersing themselves thoroughly in the world of art. They continue to collect and yet stay comfortably and sometimes very profitably "in business." On the other hand, commitments to work and family may result in someone's sharply ending her participation in some other world; a friend of ours, for instance, eventually ended his commitment to the world of chess, because his wife's complaints about his neglect of her began to affect their relationship.

Dropping out of worlds, with accompanying end of commitment, may also occur under less conflicting circumstances. In fact, probably most dropping out is more of a "dropping away." People's interests change over the life cycle, so that they are no longer so concerned with doing well or properly with regard to participation in certain worlds, whether they be vocational, familiar, avocational. Also, as noted earlier, most worlds are continually changing, so that people may no longer find themselves comfortable in a particular world or may simply be less interested in its affairs. So they drift out of it, cutting down on their associated activities, modifying the nature of their associated careers, loosening their ties with those with whom they have been more or less deeply involved, and resisting efforts to draw them back. The "subjective" side of this withdrawal is that they have begun to think differently about "things" than the world's members, including their former self. Much later they may even be unable to recapture or recall the former perspectives which, at the very least, no longer make much sense to them. To grasp this point, the reader has only to watch adolescents who take up and drop various activities—stamp collecting, bird watching, basketball. Years later they either cannot recollect what it was like to do those things or even remember that they did them.

We must assume that the end of the commitment means simply a cessation of the activities that normally accompany membership in that world. At the very least, a small "portion" of the self is no longer involved in those activities and in the associated relationships with other persons. At the other extreme—as represented by major conversions—the very nature of reality is changed. This means that the symbolic coordinates, as well as the accompanying social relationships which are closely associated with them, of a person's life get drastically changed. Most of us, most of the time, stand somewhere be-

tween those two extremes. Characteristically, we are engaged in a continuous process of allowing ourselves to be involved, while also seeking to extricate ourselves from involvement in one or another social world. The articulation of those involvements is surely a central practical problem for the citizens of modern nations, just as it is a central theoretical problem for social scientists who wish to understand life in those complex "societies."

CONCLUSION

An individual's every action is potentially fateful or consequential. This is reflected in the fact that persons have moral careers which reflect their connections and commitments to other individuals. Persons are differentially able to control their own careers, but many times, when social worlds collapse, or when large-scale social disruptions occur, they find that their fates are determined by others or by events beyond their control. Any mass society can be studied from the standpoint of the social worlds that it encompasses. Some of these worlds are tight-knit; others are scattered over large social spaces. Some demand a great deal from their members; others demand little. The concept of reference group points up the fact that individuals relate themselves in various ways to different groups and that their group affiliations and commitments virtually shape their self-evaluation. We have argued also that when persons report feelings of alienation from their society, they are in fact expressing alienation from specific social worlds. Social life is an inherently moral concern, involving an articulation of actions that variously tie involved selves to one another.

SELECTED READINGS

BECKER, H. S. (1973). *Outsiders: studies in the sociology of deviance* (rev. ed.). New York: Free Press. A highly influential presentation of the related notions of careers and selves. It elaborates the symbolic interactionist view of deviance and deviant behavior and should be examined in the context of Chapter 14 of our book.

BECKER, H. S. (1982). *Art Worlds.* Berkeley: University of California Press. An in-depth, social organizational analysis of art worlds and the selves of artists.

DOUGLAS, J. D. & JOHNSON, J. (Eds.) (1977). *Existential sociology.* New York: Cambridge. An outstanding set of essays on the existential approach to understanding modern societies.

HUGHES, E. C. (1958). *Men and their work.* New York: Free Press. Presents the main threads of Hughes' work and observations on careers, selves, and work.

KOTARBA, J. A., & FONTANA, A. (Eds.) (1984). *The existential self in society.* Chicago: University of Chicago Press. Rich sociological essays on organizational selves, sociological theories of the self, self well-being, battered women, blood donors, ex-nuns, the media self, the homosexual self, wheelchair runners, and the existential self in society.

KUHN, M. H. (1964). "The reference group reconsidered." *Sociological Quarterly,* 5, 5–21. A major critique of the reference group concept and the concept of *other* within the symbolic interactionist tradition.

SCHMITT, R. L. (1972). *The reference other orientation: An extension of the reference group concept.* Carbondale, Ill.: Southern Illinois Press. Offers the most extensive and thorough review of the theoretical and research literature on the reference group concept.

STONE, GREGORY P., & FABERMAN, H. P. (Eds.) (1970). *Social psychology through symbolic interaction.* Waltham, Mass.: Blaisdell Publishing Company. Contains a thorough and systematic collection of essays and articles articulating the interrelationship between selves, others, and social situations.

CHAPTER THIRTEEN
Sexual Activity
and Sexual Identification

Sexual motivations are often regarded as biological in origin. The fact that erotic activity involves specialized organs and is so obviously linked with biological maturation makes this seem self-evident to many scientists as well as laypersons. A closer examination indicates, however, how inadequate this conception is. Sexual activity, like virtually all other complex human behavior, is of primarily symbolic and interactional—rather than biological—significance (Kuhn, 1954). The symbolic entanglements surrounding human sexual behavior make it extremely hazardous to apply to human beings the findings obtained from the study of lower animals. In this chapter we attempt to show concretely the great complexity of sexual activity and the enormous variety of modes of sexual expression. We will discuss the social, symbolic, and interactional foundations of sexual conduct.

THE EVOLUTIONARY PICTURE

The general picture of subhuman sex behavior is described in terms appropriate to our purposes by Beach (1947, 1965), a psychologist who has surveyed the available literature and carried out extensive investigations of the sex behavior of the lower animals. We can summarize his conclusions as follows: (1) mating behavior in lower animal forms is controlled primarily by inherited mechanisms; specifically, by hormonal secretions and by the strength and aggressiveness of the animal; (2) the central nervous system plays a relatively minor part in the control of sex behavior in the simpler animal forms, its regulatory significance increasing as one ascends the evolutionary scale; (3) past experience, as opposed to hereditary mechanisms, increases in importance as one proceeds from the simpler forms, such as the rat and guinea pig, to the more complex apes and humans. A significant part of the sex behavior of male chimpanzees, for example, is learned.

In support of these general statements,

we briefly note certain facts. In most lower forms, receptivity of the female to sexual advances is determined by hormone balance and other accompanying physiological changes occurring during the period of heat or estrus. With some exceptions, the female animal is receptive only when she is in heat. This, of course, is not true of the human female, who may actively desire or entirely reject sexual relations at any time during the menstrual cycle.

Removal or atrophy of the primary sex glands—the testes and the ovaries—produces relatively uniform results in the lower animals and highly variable, uncertain ones in human beings. Adult men who have been castrated, women who have had ovaries and uterus removed by surgery, and old people whose sex glands have ceased to function— all may and do continue to desire and enjoy coitus. Men who find themselves impotent sometimes have their potency restored either (1) by injection of an actual hormone; (2) by the injection of any substance which they believe to be a hormone; or (3) by psychiatric treatment.

The characteristic and differentiating features of human sex behavior can be traced to the fact that humans talk about sex and other animals do not. The possibility of engaging in any sex behavior is, of course, contained in the biological structure of the individual. The intensity of "the sex drive" and certain other general characteristics may be conditioned by biological factors. Isolated elements of the total pattern of sex activity are not learned; they are derived directly from man's biological structure. The orgasm, ejaculation, and nocturnal emission of men are examples. These relatively mechanical, nonvoluntary parts of sex behavior are natural biological acts.

Although we can designate various individual aspects of sex behavior as natural, unlearned, or inherited, the total organization and overall functioning of these aspects in given social situations cannot be so designated. The general pattern that an individual adopts cannot be explained biologically; it must be accounted for in terms of the standards or attitudes which individuals internalize toward themselves and their sexual activities. Social influences and expressions often shape sex behavior along lines that are contrary to what would be called "natural," or conventional, in the biological and social senses. Furthermore, social influences may lead to the complete elimination of some kinds of natural biological behavior.

HORMONES, HOMOSEXUALITY, AND INVERSION

A chief obstacle to proper understanding of the nature of human sex behavior is the assumption that hormones account for the vagaries of sexual behavior. According to this view, heterosexuality is the consequence of a hormone balance, which in the male is weighted on the side of androgens and in the female on the side of estrogens. (The *androgens* are the male hormones; the *estrogens,* the female hormones—both are found to some extent in both sexes.) The close connection between these hormones and the secondary sexual body characteristics has been scientifically demonstrated. Hence, many people think that when female hormones are relatively prevalent in a male or male hormones relatively prevalent in a female, the result is an effeminate male and a masculine female, respectively—that is, homosexuals. We shall indicate in the succeeding paragraphs that this conception is incorrect in almost every detail (Corey, 1951; Garfinkel, 1967; Freud, 1933; Boswell, 1980; Stoller, 1979).

It is necessary to distinguish among various aspects of sexual behavior and sexual characteristics, and to note the difference between homosexuality and inversion. *Inversion* refers to the assumption of a female role or identity by a male and conversely, of a male role or identity by a female. Inversion is a term descriptive of people, not of the sex act. Indeed, it is quite possible—though improbable—for an inverted male and female

to engage in heterosexual relations. *Homosexuality,* on the other hand, means sexual or love relationships between members of the same sex. Since male and female counter-roles are usually involved in the sex act, even homosexual partners often play opposite sex roles. Hence, in homosexual intercourse one partner can be characterized as inverted and the other cannot.

We must also bear in mind the distinctions between male and female secondary sexual characteristics: voice differences, distribution of hair, and so on. Moreover, the presence in a male of relatively female secondary physical characteristics does not imply either inversion or homosexuality. The distinction between homosexual and heterosexual behavior is based on the sex of the preferred partner. In short, the terms *homosexual, heterosexual,* and *inversion* refer to *behavior,* whereas *secondary sex traits* are structural, biological features of the organism—not forms of behavior.

In the light of these distinctions, we can make several observations. (1) Inversion and homosexuality are not identical terms. (2) In experiments on animals, through the injection of hormones of the opposite sex, secondary physical traits of the opposite sex and partial inversion have both been produced, but homosexuality in the human sense of the term has not been brought about. (3) The injection of hormones in humans neither produces nor cures homosexuality, its main effect being to stimulate sex activity without influencing the choice of partners. (4) Homosexuality usually occurs along with heterosexuality in a mixed form; many persons are bisexual. (5) Many male homosexuals are not effeminate, and many female homosexuals are not masculine. (6) Probably most effeminate men and masculine women engage in exclusively heterosexual relations. (7) Many forms of human sexual behavior, including homosexuality, have no parallel among the lower animals. If we account for it in terms of hormones, then we must ask what possible hormonal basis is involved when humans derive their sexual gratification from intercourse with lower animals and in many other ways, some of which are alluded to in the next section.

The crucial point in connection with the inversion of gender identities in humans is that a male or female identifies with the opposite sex. Thus, a female invert may assert that she is a man, wear masculine clothes, act like a man, assume much of the masculine role in sexual relations, adopt a masculine name, and perhaps even apply the male terminology to her sexual organs, calling the clitoris a "penis" and the ovaries the "testes." This type of inversion is no doubt brought about by the fact that adult sexual patterns are conceptually organized and to a pervasive degree regulated by social definitions of one's behavior and sexual identity as well as shaped by personal experiences.

These factors point to the learned and socially defined nature of gender identities. At birth, children do not identify themselves with either sex, for they do not know that the sexes exist. They gradually learn this identification and acquire the behavior deemed appropriate in their society (Isaacs, 1933; Klein, 1932). For example, the type of partner the male child will learn to prefer—blondes or brunettes, women or men, white, black, or brown—is not determined by human biological structure any more than religious, political, or ethical preferences are so determined. (Broderick, 1965; Hill & Aldous, 1969). Moreover, various deflections in this learning process may occur. Later we will give examples of how this might come about through parental desire that a child be of a given gender, through anatomical peculiarities, and through mistakes in identifying the child's gender at birth.

Newborn children respond positively to pleasant stimuli, regardless of the source; they do not classify or discriminate among sources. The male child is as likely to have an erection when handled by his father as when handled by his mother. As the child matures and learns ways of classifying stimuli and responding to them, his patterns of sexual expression gradually crystallize and become channelized. As Sullivan has observed (see Chapter 8), the patterning of sexual activity into a fixed set of identities occurs over a several-year period in the life cycle. The detailed description of this learning process and of the disorders that may occur is still a problem for the combined efforts of social scientists.

The Meanings of Homosexuality

We must remember that the word "homosexual" carries at least two levels of meaning. Objectively, "homosexuality refers to wanting or having sexual relations with members of the same sex" (Messinger & Warren, 1984, p. 197). Subjectively, "homosexuality refers to a belief that one is the sort of person who has those wants and experiences" (Messinger & Warren, 1984, p. 197). Too frequently, scientists try to explain homosexuality by theorizing about the sources of homosexual wants and desires. They often assume that homosexuality is a sexual deviance (Foucault, 1980) and characteristic of underlying personality disorders; hence, they bring a normative stigma to the phenomenon. Seldom do such theorists inquire into the subjective meanings homosexuality holds for the person. They seldom "carefully explore whether someone labeled 'homosexual' by others or by the self wants sexual contact with the same-sex others, has it, or believes that it is wanted" (Messinger & Warren, 1984, p. 197). They seldom examine how the label "homosexual" works and functions for the person who uses it (see Humphreys, 1972; Warren, 1974; Ponse, 1978; Krieger, 1983; Messinger & Warren, 1984).

Following Messinger and Warren (1984, p. 205), we should see that the "label" homosexual is vague, and like the "labels" of alcoholism or mental illness, does not refer to specific experiences, "but to frameworks for interpreting experiences" (Messinger & Warren, 1984, p. 205). The label *homosexual* is a normative label; it provides a general frame of reference which must be learned and fitted to actual personal and interactional experiences. The label serves to explain conduct and feelings, and distributes responsibility for the person. For example, persons might employ the Freudian theory of homosexuality to their personal experiences—in which case they might blame their father or mother for their homosexuality. When using terms like homosexuality, we must grasp the meanings these words have for the person, and connect these words and their meanings to the self-conceptions and interactional experiences of the people who use them.

The "Polymorphous Perverse" and Patterns of Sexuality

Research findings concerning the biology of sexual differentiation and early sexual behavior suggest that the human organism at birth probably should be viewed as essentially indeterminate sexually, with the potential of adopting one or several of a large number of modes of expression. In the early stages, the fetus is not sexually differentiated, but it becomes so before birth. The mechanisms that determine whether the child is to be a boy or a girl are not exactly understood. What the path of sexual development will be, presumably, is determined by early learning processes that are difficult to assess and have not been isolated. Freud's term *the polymorphous perverse* designates the child's potentiality for moving in any one of a number of directions. The term implies that knowledge of biological structures does not enable us to predict reliably how the individual will make use of these structures when she becomes an adult.

The modes of sexual expression engaged in by adults seem to present a picture of almost unlimited variability. In addition to the wide variety of relatively common heterosexual and homosexual patterns, there are many others. Thus, some persons obtain gratification not from engaging in the sex act, but by watching it performed by others (voyeurs), by peeping activities, by looking at pictures, or by reading pornographic material. "Masochists" obtain gratification from

being whipped or being made to suffer pain, while "sadists" enjoy inflicting pain or injury on others. "Pyromanics" find sexual pleasure in setting and watching fires. Another form of sexual expression is "fetishism," sexual interests being focused on objects that are endowed with erotic significance, such as shoes or undergarments. Sexual interests may be directed toward almost any part or function of the body. Gratification may be achieved via different sense modalities—vision, sound, touch, smell, and taste.

"Transvestism," or dressing up as a member of the opposite sex, is commonly misunderstood to be an aspect of homosexuality (Newton, 1972); however, most transvestites are heterosexuals. An interesting example is provided by the Institute for Sexual Research, established by Alfred C. Kinsey: A middle-aged man, happily married for many years, makes it a practice to serve his wife breakfast in bed. Before doing so, he slips on a feminine wig and carefully attires himself in a feminine costume from a special wardrobe reserved for the purpose. His wife usually compliments him on his appearance, and does not reproach or harass him. One fear does trouble him—that some outsider may appear at an inopportune time and thus create gossip or a scandal. To the outside world, he appears simply as an older married man.

The unusual patterns of erotic expression to which we allude do not constitute an exhaustive description of the full range of human sexual possibilities. There are many others—including that of sexual acts with lower animals—which sometimes are forbidden in the criminal code. Considering the immense variety of human sexual patterns—patterns that probably have no counterparts among lower animals—it is difficult to imagine that any purely biological or hormonal explanation could possibly account for them. The common assumption that heterosexuality is simply "natural" or "instinctive" is naïve and grossly inadequate. Actually, there are a multiplicity of competing theories which try to explain one or more of these nonheterosexual patterns.

Apart from the unresolved etiological battle, social psychologists need to be concerned with the social contexts within which the sexual patterns occur, and the social consequences of the behaviors. Much useless theorizing goes on about why men frequent prostitutes, why they have mistresses while happily married, why they engage in "wife-swapping," why men and women engage in group intercourse or allow themselves to be observed while "loving" their boyfriends or girlfriends. They even theorize about how it is possible that married couples in their late eighties are still lustily engaging in sex (Turner, 1984; Stoller, 1979). In Nabokov's consummately funny novel *Lolita,* the author wisely eschews any explanations of why his hero is so enduringly attracted to young girls, but merely tells us what happens because of that compulsion. His book suggests the further point that whatever the ingenious social psychologist can possibly imagine in the way of sexual relations—heterosexual or otherwise—in terms of object, place, time, or manner, one can be certain that it has been tried, found satisfying, and is practiced somewhere by some persons.

Some individuals, viewed as sexual deviants, have organized themselves to protest public and legal discrimination. Homosexuals have had such organizations for some time, and in recent years an aggressive "Gay Liberation Front" has attracted considerable public attention because of its attempts to reform the criminal code as that code affects homosexuals, and by its efforts to educate or inform the public and to bring the homosexuality issue into the open (Humphreys, 1972). Transvestites also have organizations, and extremely interesting accounts have been published of transvestite conferences and gatherings. There are also various informal types of "swinger" groups that engage in unconventional sexual activity, including group sex among outwardly conventional couples. A variety of publications serve these groups (Walshok, 1971).

Transvestism suggests a number of points of special interest to social psychologists. For example, a male transvestite might appear sexually attractive to a heterosexual male who mistakes him for a woman; one may ask whether such an attraction should be characterized as homosexual or heterosexual. Or suppose that two transvestites of opposite sex mistake each other's sexual identity and become erotically interested in each other: Would this be a heterosexual or a homosexual relationship? In view of these considerations, should not the usual definitions be revised to take account of the fact that a sexual attraction between two persons might be essentially homosexual for one of the pair and heterosexual for the other? The crucial elements appear to be beliefs that each holds concerning the sexual identity of the other, and that one or both members of a pair may hold erroneous beliefs—especially when assisted by attire and cosmetics.

An extraordinary example of the complexity introduced by these considerations is the case of a male homosexual invert who had his male genitalia removed by surgery and an artificial vagina installed. Subsequently this person married a male member of the armed forces and lived with him as his wife. When the soldier was transferred to Europe and separated from his "wife," they exchanged love letters of the standard type that any newly married couple might write. We might add that the army authorities and the church got involved in this marriage, debating whether or not it could be legal or otherwise recognized as an actual union. In such matters, the judgment of the "outside world" may or may not be crucial; thus a British male, after a similar transforming operation, married an American male. English people back home simply could not believe this person was no longer what he had been (an unmarried male), but his American acquaintances only knew him for what he now was (a married woman). On the other hand, after such operations, these persons often keep their biographies secret from everyone except spouses and very close friends (Garfinkel, 1967, pp. 116–85).

The sexual identity of practically all people in any society is made obvious by a variety of external signs such as hairstyle, dress, and demeanor. It is of theoretical interest to a social psychologist to imagine how sexual patterns and interrelationships might be altered if, instead of advertising sexual identity, every effort and artifice were utilized to make the sexes look exactly alike. Under such circumstances, budding romances might often come to an end with the discovery that the potential sweetheart was of the wrong sex. In such societies as postrevolutionary Russia and China—or in certain social circles where signs of sexual identity are muted in favor of other characteristics and are unclear—men and women nevertheless ordinarily do not make mistakes in their identification of each other.

Agnes: An Intersexed Person

Garfinkel (1967, pp. 116–85) and Stoller (1967, pp. 285–88) have provided an illustrative analysis of the management of sexuality that occurs in an intersexed person. At the time of Garfinkel and Stoller's study, Agnes presented herself as a 19-year-old girl raised as a boy. Her female measurements were 38-25-38 and were accompanied by a fully developed penis and scrotum. Garfinkel studied how Agnes achieved her right to live the gender identity of female, and used the term "passing" to refer to how she accomplished this feat.

Agnes was born a boy with normal-appearing male genitals, and was raised as a boy. Yet when she presented herself to medical officials at UCLA in 1958, her appearance was convincingly female. Not considered a transexual because (1) she denied taking estrogens and (2) there was no evidence that she had in fact taken estrogens, she was given a surgical operation to remove her penis and testes and construct an artificial vagina from the skin of the penis (Stoller, 1967, p. 286). She subsequently married and lived a full life as a woman. Five years later she returned, expressing doubts about the size and normality of her vagina.

Assured by a urologist that her genitalia were beyond suspicion, she revealed to Stoller that she actually had never had a biological defect that had feminized her—that she had been taking estrogen since age 12.

How did Agnes manage to pass as (1) a girl who had been born a boy and (2) as a person who had not taken estrogen? The answer to the second question is easily settled: Stoller had discounted her taking the drug because he felt she did not have the necessary knowledge to do so. Yet Agnes, at age 12, discovered that her voice was getting lower and she was growing pubic hair. She immediately started taking Stilbestrol—a drug her mother had been given following a pan-hysterectomy—and stole money from her mother to have the prescription filled. She continued to take this drug until she was 15, at which time she became "a lovely looking young 'woman,' though with a normal-sized penis" (Stoller, 1967, p. 288).

The answer to the first question: How did Agnes "pass" as a girl? is answered by Garfinkel in the following fashion. She created a "feminine" self. She fashioned a female history for herself; she learned how to cook, how to be a "lady." how to talk and cry like a woman. In short, she talked and acted herself into the identity of a woman. Lester (1984, p. 51) terms this "doing gender."

Agnes learned how to dress for the local Santa Monica beach (she wore tight-fitting underpants and a bathing suit with a skirt), and she avoided public bathrooms. When required to take a urine test, she persuaded her roommate to give her a sample of urine. She explained the scar on her stomach by saying there had been complications during an appendicitis operation. She refused intercourse with her boyfriend by saying that she required an operation.

Persons make gender happen by learning the cultural practices associated with the male and female gender identities our culture subscribes to. In short, gender identities are socially produced. They are not biologically determined, as Agnes' case convincingly demonstrates.

THE GENDER STRATIFICATION SYSTEM

The discussion of "doing gender" brings us to the topic of the gender stratification system in American society. Gender inequality, grounded in the social institution of gender, exists in the United States. We noted this in Chapter 2 when we discussed income differentials for males and females in the labor force. The social institution of gender refers to the interactions and identities that exist in our society between males and females, females and females, and males and males. There are two distinct gender cultures in America: male and female. Distinctly different modes of interaction exist within these two cultures and are based not on biological factors, but the gender belief system.

The Gender Belief System

Lengermann and Wallace (1985, pp. 19–58) have examined the gender belief system in the United States in terms of six components. These components are: (1) the belief that there are natural differences between the sexes based on biology; (2) the belief in male authority or male patriarchy; (3) the belief that the home is the woman's place and work is the man's place; (4) the belief that men and women do *different* kinds of work; (5) the belief that "love," sensual pleasure and erotic experiences only occur within the heterosexual marriage; (6) the belief that women should make themselves sexually and erotically attractive to males (Lengerman & Wallace, 1985, p. 51).

These six belief components are changing as radical, convervative, liberal, and traditional men and women in our society confront one another's beliefs about gender, sexuality, work, family, children, and marriage. The politics of gender shape and constrain how gender identities are formed and experienced in our society.

SEXUAL IDENTITY AND SELF-ESTEEM

Adolescence

While childhood experiences may be greatly significant in later sexual development (as we indicated in Chapter 9), establishing adult-type relationships—sexual and otherwise—with the opposite sex ordinarily begins after puberty (Schwartz & Merten, 1967; Sullivan, 1953). There is considerable anxiety and uncertainty in the minds of young people as to how they appear to the opposite sex and as to whether they will be able to function as "real" men and women. In initial intersexual relationships, there is often a period of testing and self-exploration in which the primary focus may be on self-assertion and validation. The young man venturing into the sexual world for the first time may be less interested intrinsically in his partner than in asserting and establishing his own identity and masculinity. The young woman during this period is similarly concerned with proving to herself and her peers that she is attractive to the opposite sex. Sullivan has indicated that this is a phase of early adolescence (1953).

In late adolescence, once this period of concern with self is presumably resolved and maturing adolescents have acquired greater confidence in their own essential masculinity or femininity, they are ready for more serious and enduring sexual relations than the "puppy love" of early adolescence. They are now on the verge of maturity, which Sullivan describes as the capability of becoming as concerned (or more concerned) over the well-being of another as over one's own. In Freudian terms, they have passed from the phallic to the genital stages of development (Freud, 1933). However, there are many points at which this developmental schedule on the way to heterosexual maturity can be deflected. When it is, the consequences, for obvious reasons, are often serious both for the person's self-esteem and for his subsequent sexual career. We turn to a more detailed statement about the development of sexual self-conceptions.

The Sexual Self-Conception

Through the socialization process, everyone comes to acquire a distinct set of self-conceptions, or identities, specific to sexual conduct and activity. These *personifications,* or images of self as a male or female, cluster into three categories: (1) the "good" sexual me, (2) the "bad" sexual me, and (3) the "not" sexual me. The "good" sexual me refers to those identifications and actions that bring the individual pleasure, pride, and positive self-identification. The "bad" sexual me describes those mis-identifications which challenge the individual's credibility and moral worth. Furthermore, the "bad" sexual me touches on those actions in the sexual arena which arouse guilt and anxiety on the part of the individual. The "not" sexual me refers to a small number of sexual acts and identifications the individual would never see himself engaging in, or which—like erotic dreams and nocturnal emissions—are automatic. These often relate to sexual taboos, and taking part in them produces shame and self-mortification. Women who have been raped, for example, disclaim any part in the sexual act and often view themselves afterward in tainted, morally repugnant terms.

Dimensions of the Sexual Self-Conception

Like the individual's other identities, or personifications, the sexual self-conception involves a number of interrelated dimensions. Three components of that identity have been noted—the "good," the "bad," and the "not" me. In addition, we draw attention to: (1) the individual's sexual appetite, (2) her sexual prowess, (3) her knowledge about sexual activity, (4) her conception of self as an experienced or inexperienced sexual actor. These latter aspects suggest that people view themselves as having particular levels of sexual desire—high, low, non-

existent. Furthermore, depending on their knowledge of sexual behaviors and the amount of their actual or fantasied sexual experience, they will see themselves as adept or inadept, powerful or impotent, interested or disinterested in sexual acts. The defined effect and outcome of first sexual experiences (whether autophilic, isophilic, or heterophilic) will shape the individual's conception of self as a sexual being. *Autophilic,* or masturbation, experiences may become the dominant focus of the individual's sexual behavior. *Isophilic,* or homosexual, experiences may predominate, and in this case the individual does not transfer his sexual appetite and self-conceptions to behaviors which lead to intercourse with members of the opposite sex, as in the case for *heterophilic* actors (Sullivan, 1953, p. 292).

Individuals may move through all three sexual cycles, alternating between autophilic and heterophilic acts, or their identity may focus solely on one of these three modes of sexual expression. Sometimes without observing behavior itself, it is not easy to know which mode is dominant. In any case, the identity is potentially modified in each sexual encounter. Like their other identities, individuals' sexual self-conceptions are open to change.

Sexual self-conceptions are also differently salient or prominent in the behavior repertoires of individuals. While Freud and the neo-Freudians made the sexual drive the predominant force in human behavior, the view presented in this chapter suggests that an individual may (1) never act out or act on the sexual identity—for example, priests who have taken the vows of celibacy; (2) engage in sexual behaviors only occasionally and then only on a fixed schedule—some Victorians; (3) frequently act in a sexual fashion—married partners in the honeymoon phase of the marriage. Thus, individuals can be studied in terms of the frequency with which they engage in sexual expression. The failure to act overtly does not suggest that the individual may not be privately and covertly daydreaming about sexual matters.

In general, it can be argued—following Sullivan (1953)—that the sexual identity is most important within the confines of intimate relationships. It is there that intimacy and sexuality blend together in the tightly knit worlds of love and emotional attachment. Sexual identity finds its peak expression in those relationships. Accordingly, sexuality more or less lies dormant, or at best is less prominent, in the person's other interactive relationships. This is not to say that traces of flirtation and coquetry are not ubiquitous features of many other face-to-face encounters between the sexes; it simply suggests that sexual identity arises in predictable situations and circumstances within which it also finds its fullest expression. Sexual identity is molded and built up out of experiences with a relatively small number of individuals. Indeed, many people may have sexual experiences with only one other individual besides themselves.

Sources of the Sexual Identity

The identity of male or female, and the sexual connotations that surround "maleness" or "femaleness," arise out of the individual's network of interpersonal relationships. Grounded in the intimate circles of the primary group, these identifications involve such matters as adornment and dress and the development of a set of covert, nonverbal gestures of a coquettish nature. The child learns to attach meanings to its sexual organs and learns "rules of privacy" concerning how these regions are clothed and shielded from the eyes of others (Conn & Kanner, 1947). The child's caretakers also instruct her in the ritual sacredness of certain behavior settings. Bathrooms and parental bedrooms take on moral significance in the daily domestic rhythms, and the child is taught to respect the rights of others when they occupy these settings. Body maintenance activities such as bathing, washing, and dressing also expand the child's awareness of its own and others' bodies. Sexuality is based on the body, and the body is displayed in concrete situations. In the moment of body display, the child

communicates (often unwittingly) a sexual sense of self.

The most direct source of sexual identity lies in the conversations and experiences the individual has with herself and with others. Indirect sources, however, play a large role in the elaboration of one's sexual self-conception. Fantasies, reveries, and daydreams, often sparked by erotic or semierotic novels, paintings, movies, or magazines, also contribute to the individual's view of self as a sexual actor. Thus, with some certainty we can assume that by the middle years of childhood and early adulthood, all individuals will have developed—however unelaborated—a set of conceptions surrounding the sexual self. Research indicates that by age 17, most males and females have had at least one sexual experience leading to coitus. Luckey and Nass' data from 2,230 male and female college students in the United States, Canada, England, Germany, and Norway revealed that the mean age of first coitus for males and females was as follows: United States 17.9, 18.7; Canada 18.5, 19.4; England 17.5, 17.5; Germany 19.0, 19.5; Norway 18.4, 18.8 (Luckey & Nass, 1969, p. 375).

The Sexual Drama

Gagnon and Simon (1970, p. 20) have remarked:

In general, the sexual dimension in our society comprises a limited biological capacity that is harnessed and amplified by varied social uses. . . . We have emphasized that the expression of the sexual component is the celebration of a social and psychological drama rather than a natural response. We have suggested that there may be substantial change in the social drama. In the past the drama has been a silent charade. Now we appear to be giving the drama a sound track and inviting the audience to participate.

As our society loosens the taboos surrounding the sexual act and as sexual identity becomes a more discussed topic, we may witness a greater openness concerning its various components. In the past—and we suspect the pattern will largely hold for the future—individuals have seldom "openly" talked about their sexual appetites, or their conceptions of sexual prowess; nor have they taken their partners fully into confidence concerning their sexual fantasies. As a consequence, the sexual identity—one of the individual's most ubiquitous elements of self-identification—has remained one of the least discussed features of the self. Discussions either are confined to same-sex friendship and gossip circles, or are played out in the private imagination of the individual. Thus, like other taboos surrounding discourse concerning the biological functions of the physical organism, the sexual self is seldom brought into the open; it represents a private set of acts and activities.

One final topic, the locus of the sexual act, remains to be treated. More specifically, what sexual identities do individuals bring into the sexual arena when they engage in sexual intercourse? The foregoing suggests that sexual identity is a complex mixture of positively and negatively defined elements. Accordingly, it can be seen that one person's "good" sexual me may be another person's "bad" or "not" sexual me. Thus, any sexual encounter is likely to be a mixed and compromised expression of each individual's preferred and nonpreferred sexual desires. !f someone finds that a stable sexual partner fails to conform with, or support and reward a preferred "good" me, he may take his sexual behavior elsewhere, thereby separating the intimate behavior from the sexual behavior. Sexual partners are continually socializing one another, teaching one another new techniques and new modes of expression. The sexual identity is a dynamic, shifting set of self-indications that are grounded, as Gagnon and Simon argue, in the most intimate, yet biological circumstances—the human body and its meetings with the bodies of others.

FALLING IN AND OUT OF LOVE

Falling in love has been likened to getting hooked on drugs (see Chapter 5). The process commonly begins as a "weekend habit."

As it continues, it imperceptibly becomes continuous, more serious—often without the realization of the participants, who become progressively more psychologically dependent on each other as they learn more about each other and the relationship becomes more intimate and permeated by mutual trust. The lovers discover there is nobody else who gives them the same "high" that they have learned to enjoy and crave. Ultimately, they experience withdrawal distress when they are separated from each other. Despite difficulties and contrary arguments from parents and friends who urge them to break their compulsion, they tend to relapse repeatedly. Finally, there is nothing to be done but to accept the fact of their addiction to each other, and they either legalize it by marriage (methadone maintenance) or live together "in sin" (the illicit market).

Like heroin addicts, lovers—when asked why they love each other—give varied, contradictory, and generally unilluminating answers. Like heroin users who praise the drug in exaggerated terms, lovers often extol the virtues of their partners in extremely unrealistic terms. Both love and drug addiction have their honeymoon periods when the habits are new, before reality intrudes itself and brings the individual back to earth. Disillusionment sets in when the joys of the habits lose their novelty and when the persons discover that they have been trapped by delusions about themselves and the objects of their craving. Like addicts who end up with "monkeys on their backs," lovers end up with "hostages to fortune" and with legal and financial obligations. When divorce occurs, the partners commonly remarry (relapse), a tendency that has been described as "the triumph of hope over experience." When one has been hooked on either love or drugs, she learns something new about the body and its potential, and it is inappropriate and futile to believe that she will ever forget it or be "cured" of it.

Both worlds of sex and drugs have their illicit markets and pushers, and in both worlds there are ways of obtaining highs without getting hooked or committed. Persons may avoid sexual commitments and marriage by going to prostitutes or by having episodic, temporary affairs with others who also are seeking to avoid commitment. (Men and women recently divorced, wary of hasty remarriage, are prime examples of people who engage in friendly sex without emotional commitment.) (Murstein, 1971; Waller, 1930) In the same way, it is possible for the drug user to consume a variety of substances, switching from one to another to avoid becoming hooked on any of them.

As with drugs, young people learn about sex primarily from their peer groups which exert pressure upon them to experiment—or, in conservative groups, not to experiment because to do so is wrong, dangerous, or sinful. Young Americans have learned not to trust "anyone over thirty" on either drug or sexual questions. Parental influence is often blocked either by inhibitions which prevent free communication between parents and children, or by the dominance of peer group perspectives over those of an older generation. Todays parents, like those of past ages, are consequently being confronted by new sexual realities which they often have difficulty accepting. A whimsical example is provided by a loving mother of the authors' acquaintance who was concerned that her daughter was living with a man to whom she was not married. In response to the daughter's praise of her partner, the mother timidly suggested marriage. The daughter replied, "Oh, but mother, I don't know him nearly well enough for *that!*"

Falling in love may occur suddenly or gradually. Very little is known about why people fall in love with certain kinds of persons rather than others. It has been suggested that the falling in love process is something like the "imprinting" that has been observed in lower animals. It has also been suggested that it may actually be an instance of imprinting of early childhood experiences with members of the opposite sex, perhaps even with one's parents. One author (Murstein, 1971) has suggested that after puberty, boys and girls tend to fall in love with the first

potential love object that happens to come along at the critical period when the situation is right. It is also argued that one who becomes the first love object to the budding adolescent is usually a new person in town, someone not too familiar. However naïve, these remarks point to the relatively impoverished state of knowledge concerning the formation of close, intimate relationships.

Love as Process

These remarks suggest that the act of falling in love, or forming an intimate and close relationship, must be viewed processually and in dynamic terms. To love another individual, as Sullivan (1953) remarked, "involves a situation where the person cares as deeply about another individual's fate and circumstances as they care about their own." A number of theories have been set forth to account for the formation of the love relationship. Goode (1959) sets forth a structural theory of love which argues that societies control the origins and distribution of the love emotion. Arranged marriages, child marriages, chaperoned dates, sorority and fraternity dating systems, and long engagements—all display some attempt to regulate entry into the marriage market. Goode's argument rests on a simple assumption: "If societies did not control the marriage arrangement, their economic and prestige systems would collapse. Furthermore, their systems of social stratification would be thrown off balance." Goode's formulations are taken to a higher level by Reiss (1971), who argues for a "wheel theory" of love. His model proposes that persons with like interests are thrown together by the stratification systems of societies. These interests, in turn, are reflective of common needs. Mating follows a process whereby persons with common interests and needs meet one another, reveal their selves to one another, and in that process learn that they are capable of meeting one another's basic needs. Reiss's theory elaborates the earlier work of Robert Winch, who formulated the complementary theory of needs (1967).

We applaud Reiss's work on a processual model of relational formation. However, we reject the notion that societies somehow structure the love-making process so as to maintain their systems of wealth and prestige. People—not societies—fall in love and structure the formation of intimate relationships. Furthermore, we reject any theory which rests on some notion of needs, basic impulses, or drives. And many persons fall in love more than once. Indeed, families are held together, in part, because of the "love rhetoric." Of course, remarriages assume a repetition of the falling in love process. (Neubeck, 1969). And members of the upper class often marry "down."

There are very few studies or theories which adequately structure the process whereby intimate relationships are formed. We suggest that persons symbolically and behaviorally commit themselves to other individuals in intimate and deeply emotional ways. These commitments lead to an embracement of the totality of that other person's selves and identities. This *embracement*, in turn, leads to interactions which reaffirm that person's uniqueness and sacred qualities. The other person comes to live an independent life in the fantasies and daydreams of the other individual (Berger & Kellner, 1964). Their selves become *lodged* in one another.

Falling out of love (Waller, 1930) involves a breaking away process. Often deeply emotional and agonizing, when lovers and intimates part they leave a portion of themselves behind. In this sense they are publicly exposed, and they may severely damage their self-conceptions in the process. This falling out process sometimes involves name changes and entire changes in lifestyle. New social worlds are entered, as old worlds are left behind. Just as falling in love involves the construction of new social worlds (Waller, 1930), falling out of love involves the destruction of existing worlds, along with the attendant building, or attempted rebuilding, of new or modified worlds.

SEXUAL ACTIVITIES AND EROTIC IMAGERY

We turn to sexual activities per se. Sexual intercourse requires that the overt behavior of the human male be accompanied and facilitated by an internal symbolic process or flow of thought, which is often called *erotic imagery*. Such a flow of erotic mental images and ideas is ordinarily, although not always, necessary before a man can achieve and maintain an erection, and it is certainly a requisite element in the desire to engage in sexual relations. The same is generally true of the human female. To be sure, a woman may engage in sexual relations without having any genuine erotic interest in such relations; however, if we conceive of the sex act as a relationship which is pleasurable and desirable to both parties, or which culminates in simultaneous or nearly simultaneous orgasms, then we may say that erotic imagery is equally necessary for both sexes. Erotic imagery may provide a common symbolic basis for the sexual act, and partners may come to share the same imagery. Social worlds differ in their vocabularies, or repertoires, of erotic imagery. Depending upon where persons are in their own sexual careers, their imagery of sexual activity will vary.

The term *erotic imagery* refers to a general process which we have already discussed in other connections as internalized language behavior, though it is not language in the narrow sense of the word. Through this process, social influences and past experiences exercise their regulatory effects on human behavior in general, including sex behavior. Because they apply some voluntary control over this internal symbolic process, individuals are able, in varying degrees, to hasten, retard, or entirely inhibit their own sexual responses.

Sexual Excitement

Stoller (1979, pp. 27–30) has enumerated some fifteen different perspectives on sexual excitement (and erotic imagery) that might be investigated. We list these as follows:

1. *Pornography:* Materials that represent sexual objects and erotic situations, including writings, drawings, paintings, sculpture, ceramics, private performances—recorded or spoken, plays, dance, film, religious rites, and music.
2. *Adornments:* Cosmetics, clothing, jewelry, tattoos.
3. *Taboos to heighten excitement:* The use of danger in an erotic situation to increase excitement; violence, whips, chains, and so on.
4. *Body styles:* Ways of walking, running, dancing, sitting, standing, and lying.
5. *Physical attributes:* Aesthetic-erotic ideals, lust-provoking physical characteristics, secondary sex (gender) characteristics including breast size, height, weight, bulk, penis size, muscle, fat, hair distribution, skin color, bisexual, and unisex body styles.
6. *Language:* Erotic spoken and written language, language which stimulates sexual excitement in foreplay, during, and after intercourse, use of profanity, and so on.
7. *Daydreams:* Pornography as formalized sexual fantasy, the content of sexual daydreams, when they occur, with whom, how they are begun and ended.
8. *Masturbation:* The mechanism that puts daydreams to work (Stoller, 1979, p. 28). Techniques of masturbation that are allowed and forbidden.
9. *Subliminal communications:* Subtle, nonverbal erotic passage of information (Stoller, 1979, p. 29). This includes the expressing of emotions with the eyes and face, as well as the voice.
10. *Looking at and being looked at:* What body parts excite, and what techniques there are for exposing and hiding the body and its parts; voyeurism, exhibitionism.
11. *Eroticism of body parts:* "Which body parts can be stimulated to excitement? Which techniques of stimulating are most likely to excite?" (Stoller, 1979, p. 29).
12. *Boredom:* The opposite of sexual excitement; what creates sexual boredom?
13. *Other sexually related areas:* Disgust, rage, fear, pain, cruelty, pleasure in pain, anxiety, false pleasures, or faked orgasms in erotic situations.
14. *Expectations Regarding Excitement:* Gender, age, class and education and religious differences in expectations concerning excitement, including styles and frequency of foreplay, different intercourse positions, afterplay, repeated performances, sleeping after intercourse or getting up and leaving, different expectations with lovers, spouses, same and opposite-sex partners, extragenital intercourse and so on.
15. *Aberrations:* Violent sexuality, sex with animals, young children, differences by race, class, gender, culture, age, and so on.

Stoller (1979, p. 30) suggests that we know very little about any of these dimensions. It is clear that these processes, and others like them, enter into the organization, production, and consummation of the sexual act. They are part of "doing gendered sexuality" in our culture.

Sexual Thought

The individual, as Sullivan (1953) argues, may have experiences at the prototaxic, parataxic, and syntaxic levels. A good deal of experience, he suggests, is not syntaxic. Such is the case with sexual thought and behavior; the individual seldom dissects her sexual feelings, reactions, or fantasies in a fully rational and logical fashion. Rather, she experiences these thoughts and behaviors at the more primitive prototaxic and parataxic levels. This is not to say that syntaxic thought cannot be employed, for it often is—as the research of Masters and Johnson reveals (1968, 1966).

Most modern American books on sex techniques emphasize the failure of many middle- and upper-class women to achieve a climax with a sufficient degree of regularity. A great deal of advice is proffered as to techniques the man may use to delay his own orgasm while, at the same time, he attempts to hasten his partner's. These procedures represent attempts to teach self-control, and have to do with a question which apparently never arises in the rest of the animal world.

Masters and Johnson's study (1968, 1966) clearly demonstrates that this attitude toward male control is very much a middle-class one. Their conclusion is worth quoting, for it brings out nicely the class-linked differences in meaning of sexual activity; it also suggests the class-linked relationships in generalized social relationships between the sexes. They assert (1966, p. 202):

Problems of premature ejaculation . . . disturbed the younger members of the study-subject population. These fears . . . were directed toward the culturally imposed fear of inability to control the ejaculatory process to a degree sufficient to satisfy the female partner. These expressed fears of performance were confined primarily to those . . . who had attained college or postgraduate levels of formal education. Only 7 of the total of 51 men whose formal education did not include college matriculation expressed the slightest concern with responsibility for coital-partner satisfaction. These men felt that it was the female's privilege to achieve satisfaction during active coition if she could, but certainly it was not the responsibility and really not the concern of the male partner to concentrate on satisfying the woman's sexual demands. Out of a total of 261 study-subjects with college matriculation, 214 men expressed concern with coital-partner satisfaction. With these men ejaculatory control sufficient to accomplish partner satisfaction was considered a coital technique that must be acquired before the personal security of coital effectiveness could be established.

Masturbation

A number of interesting human problems about human sexual behavior arise in connection with the practice of *masturbation*. Masters and Johnson in the 1966 report (Masters & Johnson, 1966) note that Kinsey (Kinsey, et al., 1948) had calculated that 92 percent of males had "positive masturbatory" histories, and that this figure had since been supported in the United States and abroad by more recent reports. In the Masters-Johnson study, all the subjects of both sexes described a positive history of "masturbatory facility" (1966, pp. 197–98).

There are those, like Kinsey, who seek to discuss sexual behavior largely in terms of overt behavior, excluding the accompany-

ing internal symbolic processes. This approach leads to some curious contradictions. If we defined homosexual behavior in purely overt terms as a positive sexual response to stimuli proceeding from the same sex, masturbation could be subsumed as a special case of homosexuality. Kinsey, of course, did not do this; he classified masturbation as either heterosexual, homosexual, or mixed—distinguishing among them in terms of the types of fantasy involved. That is, he distinguished in terms of criteria which he initially ruled out.

In line with our previous discussion, internal symbolic processes serve as integrative and organizing phenomena in human behavior. That they are cortical in nature and difficult to study in no way justifies us in disregarding or dismissing them. As we have shown, it is through the mediation of such cortical or internal symbolic processes that the mores or ethical codes of a society exert their regulatory influences on human behavior.

The internal symbolic processes, or the erotic imagery usually accompanying the act of masturbation, do not differ in any essential detail from those attending the ordinary heterosexual act. Kinsey noted that before and during masturbation, erotic literature and pictures are occasionally used by Americans of the better-educated classes; and he adds that "nearly, but not quite, all males experience sexual fantasies during masturbation. . . . The fantasies are heterosexual when the primary interests of the individual are heterosexual, homosexual when the individual's overt experience or psychic reactions are homosexual." A person's experiences in a social milieu determine which specific excitatory ideas are likely to occur to that person in the course of the heterosexual act.

It is significant to note the change in attitude toward masturbation in our country. This practice used to be regarded as the cause of all sorts of harmful physical effects, including feeblemindedness and insanity, but research by competent investigators has failed to substantiate such a view. Today it is generally conceded that (1) masturbation is not known to have any necessarily deleterious physical consequences; and (2) the negative effects it does have are chiefly psychological in nature and arise from such feelings as guilt, fear, and shame, which are frequently associated with the practice. The effects of masturbation, in other words, are bound up with the way in which the act is defined within a given group or society.

Inhibiting and Facilitating Stimuli

People sometimes speak of human sexuality in animalistic terms, implying that human sex urges are aroused, repressed, and even expressed in ways essentially identical to those of other mammals. This view is incorrect, for human sexual responses are channeled in ways which have no parallel in the animal world.

Whole segments of a population may be ruled out as sexual or marital partners for social rather than biological reasons. This is true of the mutual exclusion of the white and black sections of the American population, the various castes of India, and the exogamous clans found among many preliterate peoples. Thus, if a native tribe is divided into four clans or subgroups, an unmarried male in one of them may be required to seek his sexual partners only among the women of one of the three other clans. In such cases, eligible and healthy persons of the opposite sex may not even be perceived as desirable sexual objects if they fall into forbidden categories. In our own society, such barriers as social class, age, religion, race, and marital status limit the choice of sexual partners.

Someone else's mother may become an exciting object, particularly if she is a widow and not too elderly; but sexual responses toward one's own mother are not permissible. Although a woman may be sexually attractive to her own male children, she is generally a sexual nonentity. This is but one instance of the operation of incest taboos. Human standards of incest vary considerably from society to society, applying sometimes only to the intimate family group and sometimes to a wide circle of persons, many of whom are biologically unrelated (Thomas, 1928). Incest taboos are found only among humans; they are social, not biological, phenomena.

We may cite other instances of classificatory elimination of sexual partners. Many white Americans find it difficult to be aroused by a dark-skinned black because of strong race prejudice against black people. Indeed, some who are attracted by white-appearing persons feel repelled when these turn out to be mulatto. Black men and women have sometimes been repelled by the "washed-out" appearance of whites. Similar barriers may be created by religion, nationality, age differences, and a host of other matters connected with the individual's standards of beauty, cleanliness, and the like.

The arousal of inappropriate imagery may prevent or interrupt sexual activity. For example, laughter, anger, irritation, disgust, and shock are deterrents to sexual excitation. Conditions preventing or interrupting sexual activity may have nothing to do with relationships between the partners; such external factors as noise, light, lack of privacy, and fear of possible interruption can interfere with intercourse. Internal factors having no direct connections with the overall relationship between the partners can also prove a hindrance—fear of pregnancy or disease, guilt feelings of any kind. As an example, one newly married couple was physically incapable of carrying out the sex act as long as they lived with the bridegroom's parents. Potency was restored when the couple moved to their own living quarters.

Impotence and Frigidity

These two terms are used in a number of ways that are not altogether consistent or logical. *Impotence* generally refers to the inability of a man to achieve and maintain an erection sufficient to engage in intercourse, whereas *frigidity* refers to a general lack of interest or enjoyment of the sex act on the part of a woman. Both terms are highly relative; every man would be impotent and every woman frigid in some conceivable type of situation. A woman who is exclusively homosexual would probably be frigid with respect to men, and an exclusively homosexual man might be incapable of performing the sexual act with a woman. This statement needs qualification to allow for the fact that in many sexual relations, one of the partners may be activated to positive response primarily by fantasies concerning someone other than the actual sexual partner. It is perhaps, through the control of the fantasy process that certain individuals have been able to be homosexuals but be happily married and the parents of children (Ross, 1971; Boswell, 1980, pp. 26–28).

Since the anatomical and physiological bases of sex behavior constitute necessary, but not determining, conditions for the development of sexuality, it follows that impotence and frigidity may be the consequence of either organic or psychological conditions—the latter being the more common. In terms of the usual conception of frigidity, for example, it appears that American women of the urban middle class are more likely to be sexually unresponsive than those of the lower classes. No biological explanation of these class differences is available, whereas divergent social backgrounds may sufficiently account for them (Blumstein & Schwartz, 1983).

Although a decline in sexual interest and activity during old age is related to organic changes (Hamilton, 1939; De Beauvoir, 1952; Hite, 1976), the connection is not sufficiently close to be called a causal one. Hamilton, for example, notes that many men who came to his office complaining of impotence were between the ages of 37 and 40. Their ages, in short, were much less than the age at which the cessation of sex activity could be expected on purely biological grounds. Hamilton points out that, as one might anticipate, cases of this type often

respond favorably to suggestions that there is nothing wrong with them. Seward (1946), after surveying the research literature, has concluded that "impotence in the aging, to a surprising extent, is the product of psychological attitude."

Masters and Johnson's intensive study of a sample of aging men and women gives strong evidence that despite organic changes, frequent sexual activity can be enjoyed well into old age. Decline of interest and gratification is related—unless there are organic reasons, including illness—to what Masters and Johnson term "psycho- and sociophysiological problems" attendant on the aging process. These include the widespread cultural attitudes toward aging as nonsexual or asexual, the monotony of monogamous relations, mental or physical fatigue, overindulgence in food and drink, and fear of performance failure in the male (1968, pp. 238–70).

Thus, impotence and frigidity occur in individuals who are biologically sound. Conversely, sexual activity is engaged in by persons who lack what are often regarded as indispensable biological prerequisites. Women may continue to enjoy intercourse after passing through the menopause, up to and beyond the ages of 60 and 70 years, and Kinsey (1948) cited the case of an 88-year-old man who enjoyed regular sex relations with his 90-year-old wife. Males who are castrated when mature, as a consequence of war injuries for example, often continue to desire and enjoy sexual relations. Seward (1946) cited the case of a 53-year-old man, castrated at the age of twenty-four, whose sexual activities increased markedly after the operation. Prior to it, he had practiced coitus about once a month. Afterward, he had intercourse several times a week with his wife and sometimes with other women as well. His increased potency lasted for 30 years.

Impotence and frigidity, when not organic in origin, can be regarded as the consequences of the ways in which individuals think about themselves and about sexual matters. In other words, they are learned ways of behaving. The central aspects of this problem have to do with the nature of the internal symbolic processes evoked by sexual stimulation. Thus, if a woman is so affected by her early training that sexual excitation sets up an internal symbolic response in terms of concepts like "evil," "danger," "fear," "dirty," "pain," and "immorality," then these ideas will prevent or inhibit the flow of facilitating and stimulating erotic imagery. Moreover, if the individual has been consistently brought up in the manner implied by these concepts, she is not likely to possess an adequate repertory of sexually stimulating ideas. This means that even if she overcomes the ideas of evil, immorality, nastiness, and the like, she still may not be able to respond fully during sexual intercourse.

A similar point is made by Masters and Johnson concerning the problems of the impotent man (1968). They remark that when an impotent husband goes to bed with his wife, there may be more than one spectator who watches the episode: the wife who is attempting to stimulate and arouse him also is observing her own and her husband's behavior. "If he obviously isn't responding, what could I be doing wrong?" In her role as spectator, she may so distract herself that when a sexual opportunity really presents itself, she may be, as the authors say, "psychologically caught in the corner observing the physical proceeding rather than physiologically tied to the bed totally involved with her own mating." Both partners thus may be so involved as observers and so worried about their own performances that sexual stimuli become relatively ineffective for both of them. Neither may realize that the other is detached from and not wholly involved in what's going on. These observations by Masters and Johnson point up a general aspect of human behavior that was noted earlier—namely, that human beings are simultaneously subjects and objects; that they listen to themselves talk and observe their own actions, continuously

monitoring both as interaction proceeds. We use this old and cynical proverb to make a related point: "When two divorced people marry, four people get into bed."

Impotence in the male also is closely bound up with the individual's conception of self and is often associated with increasing age. The middle-aged man becomes aware of his advancing age and sexual decline. Since many American men place a high value on potency as a test and proof of masculinity, many middle-aged and elderly men conceive of diminished potency as a reflection on themselves. Often they seek to restore their self-esteem by consulting physicians or taking hormone pills. Some try to reassure themselves by seeking sexual adventures with women other than their wives. A substantial percentage of the sexual offenses committed against young girls are the acts of older men seeking to bolster their masculine self-esteem.

SEXUAL POLITICS: MEANINGS OF THE SEX ACT

Younger Americans familiar with current mores and attitudes toward sex sometimes do not appreciate the degree to which women in the past and in other cultures have been—or are—exploited by men, nor the degree of sexual animosity associated with that exploitation (Bernard, 1971; Denzin, 1984, 1985). In an anthropological study of a Greek shepherd community (Saramkatsan), in which men almost completely dominate the women, some of the attitudes of men and women are described (Campbell, 1964). The women feel a strong sense of solidarity that is expressed among those related by kinship or marriage through frequent talk of how they are exploited. They have many jokes about the male genitalia and speak often of their dislike of sexual relations, saying they obtain no pleasure from them. When a bride is being prepared for the wedding, her attendants commonly sympathize with her, saying they will never leave their own homes for the sake of a strange man. The bride is likely to sympathize with their views and may say that she plans to take a knife with her into bed and castrate her husband when he tries to have intercourse with her. Women invariably wish they had been born men.

The men's attitudes are the counterparts of those of the women. Women, they say, need copulation and beating, but the men do not discuss the intimate details of their sexual lives with each other. When seduction occurs, the man always blames it on the woman. Sexual activity is viewed approximately as a necessary evil and as pollution for the person who engages in it. The division of physical labor is organized to assign certain hard labor to women and, in some instances, a man will not help a woman at her work even though she may be ill. Outside the family itself, the social relations between the sexes are extremely restricted. While women are viewed as cunning, men think of themselves as courageous, strong, and proud. It is the cunning of women which is thought to attract men and to corrupt them by causing them to desire sexual relations. Cunning is also attributed to the Devil, who is believed to have a special hold over women. While the men's views are in some respects the counterparts of feminine attitudes, many beliefs are shared by both sexes—such as the idea that sexual relations are inherently evil, something like "original sin." As Campbell describes the accepted view of sex: "Sexual intercourse, then, is not an unmixed good. It is something which is 'unseemly' or 'out of alignment'. . . . Sexual activity is necessary in that it produces children, who are God's children, but evil in that some sexuality is unavoidable." Campbell goes on to say that sexual intercourse among these people "must be performed in the utmost secrecy, without speech, and the woman must remain motionless and passive. It is thought shameful for a husband to gaze on his wife's body" (Campbell, 1964, pp. 276–78).

Views similar to these were common in past generations within our own country,

and are still found today. The concept of original sin is often taken to refer to sexual intercourse, and many regard sex as a "dirty" subject that should be talked about as little as possible, and certainly excluded from the school curriculum. Many difficulties that married couples experience in sexual adjustment are known to have their origins in the training of children which emphasizes this negative view.

Countless American women probably believe, like their Greek peasant counterparts, that men have stronger or at least less controllable sexual appetites themselves. In a study of adolescents in Chicago, two anthropologists (Schwartz & Merten, 1967) report the girls saying about dating that it is the girl's "responsibility both to satisfy part of this inborn male desire for continued sexual satisfaction and to help the situation from getting out of hand." Although they admit to having "strong sexual feelings," they also believe that "they and not the boys are capable of rational control." (The researchers contrast this view with its opposite: "The Ngulu, by way of contrast, are convinced that women are born sexually insatiable.") (Schwartz & Merten, 1967, p. 467)

These instances bring out that sexual intercourse, like any other activity or object, can be viewed from a great variety of different perspectives and can have varied meanings to the participants. It can be fun or work, duty or a gift, sinful or unconnected with ideas of sin and vice; it can be seen as the lowest of human acts or as one of the finest. A pair of lovers may be "dead serious" in one session of lovemaking, and at other times find it comic. The act may be performed routinely and almost mechanically, as well as passionately. It may be an act of aggression or of affection, forgiveness or the reverse, betrayal or reconciliation, cooperation or competition. *In this sense, sexual politics intermingle with the politics of interpersonal relationships* (Scanzoni, 1972). Dominant moods are likely to vary with different partners; and when both members of a monogamous pair are in different moods, the session may be unsatisfactory to one or both. If mismatching becomes chronic—the partners constantly on different wavelengths or "out of phase"—we can say that this form of marital communication has broken down. As Masters and Johnson remark, husbands and wives (we might add, unmarried lovers, too) are commonly reluctant to "talk out" problems of this kind, and "when there is no security or mutual representation in sexual exchange, there rarely is freedom of other forms of marital communication" (1968, p. 15). Lovers caught in this situation may relatively easily break their relationship, but obviously this is more difficult for wife and husband, especially when they have children.

Mismatching in the bedroom commonly leads to inadequate sexual performance by one or the other of the spouses. Masters and Johnson say, of inadequate performance (1968, p. 15), "The wife is afraid of embarrassing or angering her husband if she tries to discuss his sexually dysfunctional condition. The husband is concerned that his wife will dissolve in tears if he mentions her orgasmic inadequacy or asks for suggestions to improve his sexual approaches."

To return to the theme of differential meanings given to sexual activity: The important point is not merely the enormous range of these meanings, but that they are engendered, emphasized, and often become customary and expected in different social worlds (Seward, 1946). It is said, probably with some reason, that to become a star on Broadway or in Hollywood, a woman must "cooperate" with many a male sponsor as she struggles up the ladder. Some circles, social groups, and societies simply take extramarital affairs for granted (Neubeck, 1969); others insist that the wife remain virtuous but permit the husband to take a mistress. Many masculine social worlds—auto racing, for instance—have their special sexual codes, complete with special terms ("old ladies," "groupies") for their associated females. Then there is the phenomenon of circles of middle-class "swingers," with their explicit codes of exchange of couples and

their implicit expectations of such ordinarily taboo behavior as the playful stimulation of genitals by female couples and collectivities (Bartell, 1972; Wolshok, 1971). The changing meanings of sex for each successive "younger generation" is another instance of evolving and declining social worlds—some younger people still adhering, nonetheless, to the standards and perspectives of their parents.

ABORTION AND ITS SYMBOLISM

Being able to anticipate the future, we are able to both anticipate that the outcome of a given act of sexual activity might be a pregnancy, and evaluate that outcome, positively or negatively, in advance. Furthermore, the thoughts or fantasies that precede and are produced by a particular sexual encounter may engender feelings of guilt, shame, or exaltation. For centuries, methods of contraception have been practiced with greater or lesser success. During the last decade, at least in industrialized countries, contraceptive methods have become so effective and widely used that it is possible to separate sex almost completely from having children, just as the sex act can be separated from intimacy and love. That means not only effective family planning, but also a changing perspective about providing contraception for one's children at an appropriate age. ("Why not give them the pill?") And the implication of *that,* as well as the increasingly vocal and behavioral effectiveness of women's demands that they be given more to say about their own lives, has brought about a considerable debate about abortion.

Abortion is only one method of preventing the birth of unwanted children, but since it actually involves the destruction of a fetus, the definitional aspects of the public debate are particularly intriguing. At what point does the fetus acquire the status of "human being," with rights, privileges, and a soul? When does beginning human life become sacred? How does one accommodate the rights of the mother to those of the child she is carrying? It is around such issues that the current debate rages (Luker, 1984).

Conservative lawyers have argued that our constitution guarantees individuals the right to counsel even when they cannot speak for themselves. The unborn child, they say, needs a lawyer to speak up for it, to point out that the Bill of Rights should apply and that the unborn child should be granted the right to "life, liberty, and the pursuit of happiness" like other citizens. Deliberate abortion, therefore, is defined as criminal homicide or as murder. Others on the conservative side speak in religious terms of the sanctity of life, sometimes even arguing against all or most forms of birth control. Abortion, they say, besides being a crime, is also a mortal sin. The Catholic Church in particular has been a leading force on the conservative side of the issue, in the United States it has been far more effective in publicly opposing abortion than in preventing the use of contraceptives among lay Catholics. In accordance with religious doctrine, which holds that only the baptized can be saved, members of the clergy sometimes perform the baptismal rites in the delivery rooms of hospitals in the case of a difficult birth or when it is feared the infant will not survive.

On the other side of the debate, there are the practical, no-nonsense views of those who regard it as absurd to talk of souls and the sanctity of the life of an unborn child. The arguments on this side are of a secular, scientific, and rationalistic type, stressing the wishes and the welfare of the woman rather than those of her unborn child. (Although the latter's welfare can also be argued, if the mother does not really wish the child.) The law sometimes has declared abortion to be criminal even when performed to end a pregnancy resulting from rape or to avoid jeopardizing the health or life of the mother. From this standpoint, the fetus—by implication or explicit relation—may not be considered a full-fledged autonomous human individual.

The debate over abortion is acrimonious and divisive, based as it is on assumptions and values that often are basically irrational and very deeply rooted (Luker, 1975, 1984). The issues are not such that they can be readily resolved by the accumulation of scientific evidence, by rational argument, or even by legislative action or decisions of the United States Supreme Court. Thus, some nurses and doctors have rebelled against a recent court decision on the liberal side simply by refusing categorically to do what the decision permitted them to do. Indeed, some hospitals have officially announced their refusal to change their policies on abortion despite the new law created by court decision. Even in abortion clinics, staff members have sometimes evidenced overt bias against their clients, particularly when they are "repeaters." This is all the more striking, since it is becoming apparent that increasing numbers of women are using early abortions as just another method of preventive contraception.

The combination of taboos, beliefs, and actions of individuals themselves is often strange and inconsistent. Members of religious groups opposed to abortion may support their church's position in public, but find rationalizations for disregarding religious precepts in their private actions. It can also be observed that many abortions in the early stages of pregnancy are self-induced for varied private reasons. In the instance of medically performed abortions, most are—or were in the recent past—sought by married women: here reputation is not at stake.

Where powerful taboos and a variety of conflicting ideologies and political lobbies exist, social change comes about relatively slowly and only after great public debate and, in this instance, the emergence of new contraceptive techniques. Official policies ordinarily change only after a long preliminary period during which the actual practices of citizens depart further and further from the old standards and from the implications of old laws. Legislatures are extremely reluctant to introduce new legislation in such areas, lest they lose the votes of conservative minorities that may be offended and accuse them of being on the side of the Devil, sin, and immorality. Presumably, it is with some relief that both married and unmarried lovers can increasingly escape the abortion debate simply because devices like the pill may make abortion virtually unnecessary. Some years ago, one of the authors listened to a mother talking in a shocked voice about the number of teen-age abortions in her daughter's school; the author suggested that soon we would have an injection that would "freeze" a child at the age of puberty only to be unfrozen to have children when she got married. The mother was horrified. Probably she would no longer be, since that day seems to be rapidly approaching.

Luker (1984), in a widely acclaimed study of abortion and the politics of motherhood, argues that the future of abortion in America remains uncertain. It is possible that the pro-life movement will succeed in having abortion defined as morally wrong. The pro-choice movement will continue to maintain that the choice to have an abortion should be made by the woman herself (Luker, 1984, p. 244). If abortion is outlawed then perhaps the IUD, the pill, and treatment after rape will disappear from the American scene (Luker, 1984, p. 244).

How about the future? Luker predicts that if the American economy fails to return to the "good old days" of economic surplus, and as more and more women find that they have to work, then the supporters of exclusive motherhood may decline to a small minority. If technology continues to advance as it has since the 1960s, we may soon see the day when abortions can be performed at home. We may even see "the ability to transplant one woman's fertilized egg to another womb, and even artificial uteruses that can support an embryo outside the woman's body from the earliest days of pregnancy. These developments are all closer to reality than to science fiction" (Luker, 1984, p. 244).

This public discussion of abortion, colored as it is with moral judgments and high passions about what are normal and abnormal practices, leads naturally to the topic of the next chapter: deviance.

CONCLUSION

Despite a widespread belief that sexual behavior and motivation are biologically determined, human sexual adjustments are primarily symbolic in nature, and the patterning of human sexual responses is learned through social experience in group contexts. A comparison of human and subhuman sexual activities shows that hormonal control declines and is replaced by cortical control and learning mechanisms as one ascends the evolutionary scale from simpler mammalian forms to the great apes and then to man. The influence of symbolic processes and of learning in human beings is predominant; many forms of sexual behavior, such as homosexuality, fetishism, and inversion, are unique to the human species. There is an absence of evidence indicating that human sex preferences are determined by the sex hormones, and there is positive evidence that the masculine and feminine roles are, like other social roles, learned systems of behavior. The profound influence of symbolic processes on human sexual behavior is evident in masturbation, erotic imagery, the control or inhibition of the orgasm, and in different ways of defining or interpreting the significance of sexual activities. Sexual identities are conferred upon persons through the socialization process; sexual self-conceptions arise out of intimate relationships. Falling in and out of love must be viewed processually. An individual's standing in the sexual arena often reflects her location in a society's or a group's stratification system. The profound symbolism that surrounds the sexual act and its consequences are expressed in the controversy surrounding the abortion issue.

SUGGESTED READINGS

ABEL, E., & ABEL E. K. (Eds.). (1983). *The signs reader: Woman, gender and scholarship*. Chicago: University of Chicago Press. An important collection of essays on such topics as the female world of love and ritual, feminism and science, compulsive heterosexuality and lesbian existence, racism and sexism, father-daughter incest.

BOSWELL, J. (1980). *Christianity, social tolerance, and homosexuality: Gay people in western Europe from the beginning of the christian era to the fourteenth century*. Chicago: University of Chicago Press. A powerful historical and institutional analysis of homosexuality. A complement to Foucault's *History of Sexuality, Vol. One* (1980).

LENGERMANN, P. M., & WALLACE R. A. (1985). *Gender in America: Social control and social change*. Englewood Cliffs, NJ: Prentice-Hall. A valuable sociological accounting of the gender stratification system in the United States.

LUKER, K. (1984). *Abortion and the politics of motherhood*. Berkeley: University of California Press. A controversial study of the meanings of abortion, abortion reform, the right-to-life movement, motherhood, and morality in America.

STOLLER, R. J. (1979). *Sexual excitement: Dynamics of erotic life*. New York: Pantheon. A provocative theory of sexual arousal which deals with gender identity and erotic desire.

CHAPTER FOURTEEN
Deviance and
Deviant Worlds

Sociologists, social psychologists, psychiatrists, politicians, and everyday individuals hold widely differing conceptions concerning the nature and origin of what is commonly termed *deviant behavior.* Concepts such as *homosexual, prostitute, drug addict, paranoid, alcoholic, wife-beater, insane, politically or morally corrupt,* and *revolutionary* cover a wide range of behaviors which defy classification under a single concept. Obviously, these phenomena are not all of the same genre. All result, however, in negative actions from groups who define them as problems. Reaction may be spontaneous (as to a person with a stigma, perhaps a dwarf), or so highly institutionalized that an elaborate control apparatus is developed to contain it (as with crime). A group can react to one of these problems with irritation, or it can regard the problem as genuinely threatening to the group's existence.

In this chapter we shall attempt to place the study of deviance within an expanded symbolic interactionist conception of social relationships and social worlds. Individuals, we have suggested, occupy positions in interlocking and interconnected social worlds. These worlds commit them to certain lines of action and lead to the development of special self-conceptions; each can be viewed as a special universe of discourse and experience. They are uniquely bounded worlds of meaning and thought. Each world, from some perspective, can be seen as deviant. A variety of deviant social worlds will be discussed.

CONCEPTIONS OF DEVIANCE

Deviance and its definitions arise out of the interactions of individuals who hold different degrees of power and authority over one another. In an ultimate sense, the state, its government, and its laws possess the final power to define what is and is not deviant or criminal behavior. The application of a deviant or criminal label to one individual or a group of individuals involves the political application of power (Becker, 1973; Gusfield 1967; Horowitz

& Liebowitz, 1968; Cockerham, 1979; Gove, 1980; Kitsuse & Spector, 1975; Foucault, 1980). Deviance and its study directly lead the sociologist into a consideration of power and its distribution within social groups and societies generally. In any society, there are experts on conventional behavior, normal behavior, deviant behavior, and criminal behavior. In a complex society, some things are deviant in some circles but not in others. Further, there are certain behaviors that simply go unnoticed—or if noticed, are passed off as uninteresting or irrelevant. Whether one eats breakfast, has blue eyes, or has long hair is basically irrelevant for one's biography and one's relationships with others. Other behaviors, however, traditionally become so publicly real that professional interpreters of them emerge. Psychiatrists, sociologists, lawyers, educators, and physicians all account for deviant behaviors with differing theories, some of which attain the status of scientific theories. Psychoanalysis, structural functionalism, and symbolic interactionism are some theories which purport to account for such actions as murder, rape, drug addiction, divorce, homosexuality, and insanity. Over time, as new issues become controversial—for example, civil rights, feminism, gay liberation, and urban riots—new theories emerge, or old theories are revised to explain what is occurring, and inevitably clashes in perspective occur. Militant feminists reject Freudian explanations of their behavior; politicians find irrelevant the scientific utterances of social scientists, including political scientists. Deviance and its discovery involve inherently social processes, which at root rest on political debates over what will be termed conventional, acceptable behavior (Kitsuse & Spector, 1973).

THE NATURE OF DEVIANCE

A basic preliminary point is that actions in themselves are not moral or immoral, deviant or nondeviant. It is the judgment that is passed on the behavior by others, and not the behavior itself, that determines and defines deviance. As Kai Erikson (1965, p. 6) remarks, "Deviance is not a property *inherent* in any particular kind of behavior; it is a property *conferred upon* that behavior by the people who come into direct or indirect contact with it. The only way an observer can tell whether a given style of behavior is deviant . . . is to learn something about the standards of the audience which responds to it." It is difficult—perhaps impossible—to think of any type of behavior outlawed in America today that has not been acceptable somewhere at some time.

There is nothing about many specific kinds of activity that automatically causes them to be regarded in the wider community as dangerous, queer, or perverted. Certain acts are sanctioned in some communities and negatively evaluated in others; over time, definitions inevitably change as public orientation shifts. Addiction to opiates, for example, is regarded as a medical problem in most Western countries, and was so regarded in the United States until recent decades. Homosexuals are discriminated against in Western countries, but this particular bias is not universally shared even there. Indeed, when people meet homosexuals under predominantly normal conditions, as in some occupations, homosexuality is taken for granted and homosexuals are assumed to be like other human beings.

Historical changes in definitions of deviancy are striking, and many illustrations could be cited. Thus, the treatment of religious sects is a highly variable matter, and in a given period depends upon whether the sect espouses practices that seem shocking or dangerous to its neighbors. During one period of its history a sect may be viewed as a menace to public morals, and at another it may be viewed as merely odd or peculiar. When politics get mixed into sectarianism, the sect may be regarded, at least for a time, as unpatriotic or even subversive. Of course, a sect or any other group may engage in practices running counter to general moral standards and yet escape widespread attention; but if the glare of publicity falls upon

the group, influential groups of good citizens may demand that something be done about its degenerate or dangerous practices. When public furor dies down, the group may continue its traditional practices more or less unmolested; but it remains vulnerable as long as the practices themselves fall within the current definition of deviancy.

Deviance, which takes a number of forms, may be viewed at various levels. In *the group framework,* it involves the public violation of group norms and the application of specialized procedures and sanctions to handle the deviant and control the volume of deviance. When the formal agencies of control lack jurisdiction over the behavior, it is dealt with by using informal control mechanisms, such as gossip or avoidance. On *the personal level,* deviance may be seen as behavior that violates the person's internalized norms and is believed to be controlled by internal psychic mechanisms, such as conscience.

Deviance may have its sources in the social structure or may be generated by causes within the individual. These causes may be consciously recognized and reported upon by the persons involved, or they may exist below the level of awareness as unnamed, unconscious, or subliminal influences. Since we have already touched on deviance in terms of self, generalized other, and conscience, we shall be concerned here with deviance at the group and interactional level. An attempt to explain deviance must focus not on the act as such, but on the social evaluation of the act that causes it to be regarded as deviant (Kitsuse, 1962; Gibbs & Erickson, 1975).

Sources of Definitions of Deviance

The foregoing discussion can be summarized by noting that individuals may become tainted or "spoiled" interactants for any of the following four reasons. First, they may commit an illegal act and be apprehended, arrested, charged, and convicted; then they find that their biographies have been significantly altered, and may be unable to return to their "normal" worlds of social interaction.

Second, as Goffman (1963) argues, they may belong to a work, ethnic, religious, or racial group that is viewed as less than desirable by the broader social order. Jews have suffered and died simply for being members of such a group, as have nearly all other major religious and ethnic groups in the world's history. Blacks, Italians, Irish, Japanese, Chinese, Germans, and Russians have, at different points in their collective world histories, been defined as political, economic, and moral threats to other sectors of humanity (Kronus, 1971). Whether or not group, economic, or political membership is viewed in undesirable terms depends largely on a group's standing in the broader society. Those groups with power can legislate their own conceptions of moral desirability and acceptability; those groups which are viewed as moral or economic threats, or those individuals who perform a country's "dirty work," often find themselves outside the mainstream of political processes. As a consequence, they suffer economic and moral abuse from other citizens. This phenomenon often leads such individuals to band together by living in common residential areas, where they at least find some social support for their world views. Of course, processes of discrimination and segregation often make it impossible for these individuals to live their lives in morally, economically, and politically acceptable circumstances.

Third, individuals may be stigmatized because of physical deformity, because they have acquired some disease or illness, or because they have deteriorated mentally or are mentally retarded (Jacobs, 1969; Mercer, 1973; Bullock, 1987). Fellow interactants assume that those they confront on a daily basis will "appear to be normal"; they will walk normally, speak intelligently, not be sight or hearing impaired, have the usual level of physical stamina, and be able to follow the train of a normal conversation with relative ease. Any alteration in these attributes leads others to define these individuals in less than positive terms. They have not committed a deviant, or illegal act; they are spoiled, stigmatized actors by virtue of how they publicly present and display their bodies.

Fourth, persons can have character flaws, or stigmas, which, while not publicly visible, would if made known also brand that individual as stigmatized. Those who have been hospitalized for mental illness, homosexuals, the recently divorced, unmarried parents, or former embezzlers, all share one common characteristic: Their deviance is not publicly visible. For the deviance to have interactional effects, the individuals must make public these hidden facts in their biographies. Often it is to their advantage to do so, for a tainted past hovers over their life; if they refuse to tell, they may find that someone else will.

The Asymmetry of Social Reactions

An individual—especially those who belong to undesirable groups or have undesirable physical attributes—may be stigmatized without ever having committed a deviant or criminal act (Cahman, 1968). On the other hand, it is impossible for a person not to be stigmatized, if only for a short period of time, after she has broken a law or engaged in a deviant act that evokes public outrage. There is an asymmetric relationship between stigma and deviance, and this asymmetry shifts over time as individuals move into new and different phases of their moral careers. What was deviant at one point in time may later be viewed as an attribute of excellence, bravery, or forward thinking.

The Benefits of Deviance and Stigma

The theoretical and research literature often exhibits a rather grim, humorless view of the deviant (Mizruchi & Perrucci, 1962). It is assumed that those individuals who gain what are called "immoral" sexual pleasures, engage in illicit drug practices, or make money illegally do so without reward, benefit, personal fulfillment, or professional advance. The fact is, a good deal of what is stigmatized as deviant and illegal is pleasurable, profitable, and rewarding. This simple fact offers one explanation for why many individuals are drawn into those pursuits that "good" people find morally repugnant, deviant, and criminal.

Dimensions of the Deviant Act

Deviance and its attribution arise from the definitions that individuals attach to themselves and their own ongoing activity. In this section we wish to stress the following elements of deviant activity. First, how frequently do deviant acts occur in the individual's activity cycle? Some, for example a murder, may only occur once; others occur at a high frequency. Heroin users or prostitutes may engage in their particular forms of deviance on a daily basis. Other deviant acts may be more rigorously scheduled—for example, the weekend "chipping" of drugs.

Closely related to frequency is the dimension of biographical consequentiality. That is, how consequential for the individual is the deviant label? On the one hand, we have the convicted murderer who finds that his total life chances are drastically modified as a result of deviance. On the other extreme, individuals who privately engage in sexual fetishism may never be publicly labeled as deviant; the act itself does not influence the individual's other self-identities. The consequentiality issue touches on the matter of how "sticky" the deviant label is. In general, it can be predicted that those labels which have been applied by the social control agencies will be more sticky than those which arise out of friendship circles. The former produce files and dossiers on those individuals they have apprehended for purposes of curing, incarcerating, or reeducating; these records become a permanent part of the individual's public identity and may even leak into media accounts. A related element of consequen-

tiality describes the threat or harm component of the deviant act. Simply put: "How risky" is the act for the individual and for others? Some acts—murder, for example, or armed burglary—carry high elements of risk both for the person and her biography. Others carry low elements of risk, but may be more consequential for the individul's biography. What Edwin M. Schur has termed "crimes without victims" fall in this category. Homosexuality, recreational drug use, and abortion describe potential deviant acts where there is no clear-cut victim (Schur 1965); the individual willingly engages in the deviant act or goes to another individual for deviant, or illegal services.

A third feature of the deviant act refers to the circumstances under which it is performed. It may be done alone or in the company of a small group of others; embezzlers (Cressey, 1971; Benson, 1985) typically work alone, burglars and robbers do not (Einstadter, 1969; Shover, 1985). In general, the more complex the network of others who are necessary to produce the deviant act, the more likely it is that individuals in that network will be apprehended. There are also situations of *double deviance,* where one deviant turns against another or simply botches an otherwise successful illegal act.

The circumstances of the act suggest the voluntary, coercive dimension: some deviant acts are forced on the individual—rape and armed robbery are obvious examples. The voluntary dimension also indicates that one person's deviant act may make another individual deviant in the process. The woman who has been raped may view herself in morally tainted terms, even though she had no choice in the matter. On the other hand, deviance may not produce new deviants, but simply lead others to view the individual as a fool, a dupe, or an easy mark (Goffman, 1952; Klapp, 1962). A good deal of public sympathy is likely to surround the individual who has been coerced into a deviant act; those who submit or are party to a deviant act because of stupidity or oversight are more likely to be viewed with scorn and ridicule.

The fourth dimension pertains to the range of accounts that individuals offer for their deviance. Their "story" may stress the pleasurable effects of the act; it may stress its money-making features; or it may be grounded in highly emotional terms—perhaps matters of love, hate, extreme anger, or frustration. Finally, individuals may use a scientific theory to explain their deviance, or they may resort to some political or ideological cause or rhetoric. In any case, deviants are often asked to "account" for their deviance, and in this accounting process they are under pressure to explain why they went astray (Lofland, 1969; Matza, 1969).

Finally, it must be asked: "Who does the labeling?" Individuals may label themselves as deviant, or they may be labeled deviant by others. Furthermore, they may or may not accept the opinions of others. In any case, any analysis of the deviant act must record who the "labeler" of the act was.

Fads and Fashions in Deviance

What is deviant at one point in time may become normal acceptable behavior at another point in history. Thus, at one time it was considered deviant and immoral to drink alcoholic beverages, but such definitions have given way to a view of drinking behavior as fashionable (Gusfield, 1967; Beauchamp, 1980). These definitions, however, are changing once again as we enter an era where "alcoholism" and other drug addictions have become major objects of public concern. Similarly, the cocaine laws which are now under revision and modifications—moving toward greater harshness—reflect the fact that cocaine addiction is now regarded as a major social problem; indeed, some speak of the "cocaine epidemic" that is sweeping the country (Gold, 1984). The current cocaine "craze" is being compared with the earlier epidemic which ended well before the 1920s, when it was not illegal to possess cocaine—but it was illegal not to be registered as a distributor of the drug, or to use the drug

without a physician's prescription. The fact that cocaine is no longer regarded as a fashionable, recreational drug but as a drug which addicts, reveals how social, medical, and political definitions change and shift over time.

In the late 1800s and early 1900s cocaine was endorsed by physicians, heads of state, Pope Leo XII, Jules Verne, Auguste Rodin, Thomas Edison, and Sigmund Freud. The drug was used to prevent malaria and influenza and as a local anesthetic, and some physicians used cocaine in the treatment of morphine addiction. The popular drink Coca-Cola contained cocaine until 1905. In 1984, virtually every state had laws which prohibited trafficking in cocaine, with penalties for a first offense ranging up to 15 years.

As new issues come to the public's attention, public moral conscience is aroused and people become outraged over new forms of illegal or deviant behavior. In this sense, a nation's social control agencies continually produce new side-effects of marijuana, heroin, birth control pill, cocaine, and alcohol. Nations are continually having or experiencing new epidemics of deviance. This keeps the social control agencies in business; it also clarifies ambiguous group boundaries and ambiguous conceptions of what is deviant and what is acceptable, (Coser, 1962; Erikson, 1965). Furthermore, each new form of deviance lays the groundwork for new behaviors which may eventually become fashionable and morally acceptable. (Simmons, 1965).

A critical question concerning fads and fashions in deviance involves the original source or locus of the deviance. That is, from what sectors of society does it emanate, and who is defining it as deviant? It appears that unacceptable fashions that flow from those lacking political power will not become acceptable until more powerful and influential citizens take up that new activity. Thus, marijuana laws were not modified until middle- and upper-class youths were apprehended for using it, and their parents began experimenting with the drug. So today's deviance may become tomorrow's fashion, and similarly, what is fashionable today may become outmoded and deviant in the future.

Techniques of Neutralization

On the other hand, persons who violate norms that they themselves accept as valid and legitimate ordinarily feel guilty about their behavior. The term *techniques of neutralization* is a recently coined expression that refers to the symbolic devices used in this situation to permit the behavior to continue and to assuage pangs of conscience. Its meaning is closely akin to that of *rationalization*. We should note that deviants do not necessarily feel guilty; this is especially true when they deny the validity of the public definition, as is the case with many mairjuana smokers, political dissenters, homosexuals, and others. Sykes and Matza (1959) enumerate techniques of neutralization as follows:

1. *Denial of harm*—little or no real harm has been done.
2. *Denial of the victim*—the victim provoked the action and got what was coming to him.
3. *Attacking the accusers*—the police are corrupt, brutal, and unfair, and the laws are unjust.
4. *Invoking other and higher loyalties*—that of loyalty to one's fellow gang members, for example.

The sense of guilt and the ideology used to neutralize it are indications that deviants are committed to the values they violate. They explain and excuse their behavior by means of concepts and ideas that are made available by the broader society. Thus, drug addicts and alcoholics account for and sometimes excuse their addiction in terms of neutralizing "motives" or excuses. The user of illicit drugs, for example, may utilize any or all of the techniques of neutralization by arguing that (1) no harm was done, (2) the laws are unjust, and (3) one's friends also use the drug.

DEVIANT CAREERS AND SOCIAL WORLDS

Much of the literature in criminology and the sociology of deviance assumes a relatively static view of the labeling, or defining process. To be termed a drug addict, a juvenile delinquent, a divorcee, a homosexual, or a radical means different things for the individual at different points in his moral career. One is not just delinquent (Finestone, 1957) or addicted to a certain class of drugs, or mentally ill. Rather, one becomes delinquent, addicted, mentally ill, or senile over a period of time. In each phase of the deviant career, individuals see themselves differently (Becker, 1973). The meanings that labels have for them and their significant others and for the public at large will vary in terms of how they act. If they exacerbate their deviance, parade it, so to speak, then it may eventually become a permanent part of their identity kit, for they will now be viewed as homosexuals or drug addicts by their interactive fellows. On the other hand, they may choose to hide or conceal their deviance; then its relevance for their day-to-day interactions is minimal (Kando, 1972). Some individuals assume a dramatic and emotional response in the first phases of their deviant careers, and then with the passage of time normalize their deviant identification (Birenbaum, 1970).

As we will show, an actor's response to an ascription of deviance depends largely on the public receptivity to her altered condition. Some forms of deviance have strong and massive institutional support—for example, organized crime (Chambliss, 1972). Others emerge in the forms of social movements. Women's liberation and gay liberation are two examples of how individuals have banded together in an attempt to have themselves collectively redefined by the broader social order. Many deviants fall heir to incipient, less well-defined social worlds. As our discussion of homosexuals will show, many individuals who are so defined can enter special bars, housing complexes, and public recreational areas where they will find other individuals who share their views of sexual behavior. Some deviants keep their deviant identities hidden altogether, or share it with only a small number of other individuals. What can be called *relational deviance* falls into this category. Marital partners may have their own private versions of the sexual act, which if made public would brand them deviant; those who carry on affairs, embezzle, "shoot" drugs on the weekend, or keep hidden stocks of pornographic magazines also usually keep their deviances to themselves. Finally, there are those deviants, or "outsiders," who belong to no organized social world or social relationship, and who furtively and secretly practice their deviant acts; transvestites, "closet" homosexuals, and eccentrics fall into this category.

Depending on the individual's location in any of the above social worlds, her response to the label of deviant or criminal will vary. Consequently, any analysis of the deviant career must simultaneously assume a temporal and interactional, or organizational, stance (Davis & Stivers, 1975). Many students of deviance have ignored these temporal, moral, and interactional features of deviants and their careers. We turn now to the consideration of a variety of different deviant worlds.

DEVIANT WORLDS AND INDIVIDUALS

In presenting a general framework for understanding deviant behavior, we noted that some forms of deviance are highly organized. Some shade off gradually and merge imperceptibly with conduct that is disapproved of or viewed as peculiar, yet is permitted and even protected when necessary by agents of the law. We shall examine several instances of the more organized types of deviance and then some of the less organized or unorganized types. All persons who label, or are labeled as, deviant are members of social worlds that differentially endorse those designations. All forms of deviant behavior find their locus in some social world, no matter how loosely organized. We shall il-

lustrate this by discussing political corruption and individual deviance, forms of behavior that too often have gone unnoticed by sociological students of deviance (Chambliss, 1975; Traub & Little, 1980).

Deviant Groups and the Wider Society

All deviant groups are related to and arise from the structure of the wider society. Some quite clearly perform functions for accepted groups. Respectable men of all social worlds take advantage of the availability of prostitutes, and quasi-criminal or quasi-underworld organizations capitalize on this patronage. It is not these organizations but the persistent market for prostitution that makes it difficult to suppress. The market for the prostitute's services presumably reflects the inadequacies of those legitimate institutions that regulate sexual and affectional behavior (Davis, 1937; Roby, 1969; Heyl, 1979). Occasionally, zealous advocates of vice suppression may succeed in outlawing a particular form of activity, such as gambling, which happens to be an integral part of the way of life of some people. Illegal organization then flourishes around the otherwise unfulfilled demand for the banished activity or commodity (Polsky, 1966).

Some deviant groups may be said to constitute *deviant worlds* or *deviant communities* because, while they are located in space, they also tend to transcend particular locales. They are not tightly organized, but consist of loosely connected groups or circles of deviants, not all of which know or have direct communication with other circles. We shall discuss three of these worlds.

CRIMINAL WORLDS

As we have remarked, American emphasis on success, money, and competition, as well as the great proliferation of occupations and divisions of labor, have resulted in the development of illegal occupations that are integral parts of our commercial and occupational world. Students of criminology have classified crime and criminals in a great variety of ways. The criminal underworld is a complicated social structure with occupational diversity and status systems. For our purposes, we may classify criminals into three categories: (1) conventional criminals, (2) white-collar criminals, and (3) racketeers (Sutherland & Cressey, 1966).

The Criminal Occupations

The conventional criminals may be either *professionals* or *amateurs; occupational* and *non-occupational* would be equivalent terms. Most instances of murder, rape, and arson, for example, are not committed as occupational activities, and a great many persons from respectable society commit an occasional theft, murder, or other offense. The *conventional criminal occupations* probably number in the hundreds. An immense number of specific devices and skills may be employed, while new ones are constantly being invented and old ones improved. These skills may be roughly classified as (1) those involving violence or threats; (2) those involving manual or mechanical dexterity and skill (such as pocket picking, shoplifting, safe cracking, and automobile stealing and stripping); and (3) those involving verbal dexterity and histrionic ability, frequently called swindling, fraud, and confidence games. In the last type, some mechanical or manual skill may be called for, as in the "shell game" or in "three-card monte." The specific types of fraud are legion.

Each of the various criminal occupations has its own specific rules and norms to guide and control the behavior of its practitioners. Each has a hierarchy of status positions and possesses prestige relative to others, this prestige reflecting underworld public opinion. There are codes regulating standard performances: a "fingering job" ordinarily yields a regular 10 percent; "the nut" (expenses) is always subtracted from the money gained "at the top" (before dividing).

White-collar crime consists of offenses committed in legitimate occupations or business—for example, by corporations in the course of their regular business operations (Sutherland, 1949). It is perhaps unnecessary to note that there is considerable crime committed by politicians and public officials on behalf of the public interest. A businessman may break the law knowingly either for mercenary reasons or because he feels that he must because his competitors do likewise; sometimes he may break a law because the law itself is vague and the boundaries of legality are not clear. Sometimes corporations challenge the legality of a statute by deliberately flouting it to see if the court decision will uphold their action. There is no world of white-collar crime as such.

The third general type of crime is *racketeering*. We use the term here to designate underworld business activities. This means the provision of contraband goods or services for a market which usually includes clientele from the respectable world. Gambling, prostitution, and the bootlegging of liquor and drugs are examples. These businesses are organized like any other, with certain special features such as the prominence of bribery—involving collusion of public officials—and the inability of underworld businessmen to enforce contracts and settle disputes in the courts. As a substitute for court decision, racketeers have their own methods for settling disputes and enforcing the fulfillment of contractual obligations. Racketeers, like conventional criminals, are part of the general criminal milieu.

Criminals of the first and third types have identifications with a somewhat vague but nonetheless real criminal world, a world that is somewhat wider than particular occupations or rackets. This world, much like that of the artist or the professional athlete, is *not* sharply set off from other worlds, but does command a certain loyalty and allegiance from its members. Criminal argot reflects something of the unity of the world when it designates all outsiders as "squares" and all insiders as "right." Marginal persons—such as lawyers who engage in dubious or dishonest practices—are called "kinky" to designate their separate status (Sutherland, 1949, pp. 164–66):

The professional thief . . . has semilegitimate acquaintances among lawyers, fences, fixers, bondsmen, and politicians. These . . . are making money from the thief but are supposed to be members of legitimate society. He may call upon them, also, for assistance for the less legitimate purposes. . . . The thief is somewhat suspicious of all individuals in legitimate society other than those mentioned. He believes that whoever is not with him is against him. Any noncriminal individual not personally known . . . is a possible danger and, as an individual, is somewhat disliked on that account. This feeling is reinforced by occasional trouble which results from perfectly proper acquaintances. . . . [There is considerable] danger that the thief may run into if he tries to make legitimate contacts with strangers. Because of this, the professional thief lives largely in a world of his own and is rather completely isolated from general society. The majority of them do not care to contact society except professionally.

The fact that all insiders are on the shady side of the law lends symbolic cohesion. The intense hatred felt for informers is an index of this cohesion and of the need for secrecy in the face of the outside world. Of course, all groups—occupational or otherwise—require for their very functioning that certain secrets be withheld from nonmembers. This is of special importance for criminal groups for obvious reasons. An important ingredient in the ideologies of the underworld is the preservation of trade secrets and the maintenance of a closed mouth before outsiders. Even the excriminal who writes a book about his experiences may feel uneasy about revealing current techniques, and may therefore write mainly of past history and well-known crimes. The lines drawn between underworld and general society necessarily involve a certain suspicion and wariness (Sutherland, 1949, pp. 168–69):

One of the personal characteristics of the thief is extreme suspicion. This may be accounted for by the fact that he exists in a suspicious world. . . .

The first thing in his mind in every touch is whether he is under suspicion. . . . He must decide whether there is an ulterior motive in any word or act of a prospect. He must often be courteous, kindly, and solicitous, and, because he has to play this role, he is naturally very sensitive to these characteristics in anyone else. Therefore, if someone would do or offer to do something for him which is unusually kindly, he immediately becomes suspicious.

Lifestyles of Criminals. Although criminals of any country resemble the citizens of that country in many ways, cherishing and striving for many of the same ends, they also develop their own lifestyle. A professional thief cheerfully says that "the professional thief rejoices in the welfare of the public. He would like to see society enjoy continuous prosperity, for then his own touches will naturally be greater" (Sutherland, 1949, p. 172).

Somewhat different styles within the criminal world arise from the different occupations; but existence within the criminal milieu lends certain general features to them. The professional criminal usually operates in terms of short-range goals; he becomes a liberal and unconcerned spender of money and worries only about the immediate future. Probably this is true even for the racketeer groups whose conspicuous consumption is a matter of public comment. In recent years, racketeers have tended to move into middle-class suburban areas and to take over some middle-class manners and standards. High living with an emphasis on drinking, horse racing, and gambling is a feature of most criminal circles. *In fact, in an economic sense, many criminals partly live off other criminals;* the holdup man may spend his gains with a bookie or lose his money at gambling. There is a famous apocryphal story about a criminal who found himself in a strange town, and who then asked an associate where they could gamble. He was told that there was only one "joint" but that it was "crooked." This information only led him to exclaim, as he prepared to be fleeced, "What are we going to do, there isn't any other."

Criminals often do not marry (but men

may use the term "wife" to refer to the woman with whom they are currently living). Men associate with women of easy virtue who are part of, or marginal to, the criminal milieu. Professional criminals are aware of their somewhat different lifestyle and of the attitudes that respectable citizens have toward them; they often partly accept the values of respectable society toward crime, and hence show symptoms of uneasy conscience. They protect themselves against their conscience by rationalizations that are extremely varied and often ingenious; if they steal from someone rich, they argue that the rich are themselves usually dishonest, and if they steal from the poor, they argue that they spend it on drink anyway. The confidence man likes to point out that victims have to be willing to cheat someone else before they themselves can be fleeced. (Incidentally, criminals invariably object to calling the victim a victim; they much prefer to call him or her "mark" or "sucker." As one thief said, "That makes it sound bad to call them 'victims.'") Criminals also like to point out that many persons, such as the police, lawyers, prison staffs, and others from respectable society, make money from them or have jobs dependent upon the existence of crime; they point to the stimulating influence they have on the insurance business and the manufacture of safes, locks, keys, and burglar alarms.

Professional criminals often think of their activities as an occupation or a business, and may not consider themselves enemies of society. They do not usually hate the police, lawyers, judges, and others who play a role in sending them to prison, unless they violate what seem to them to be the rules of the game and the standards of sportsmanship. As a famous "madam" complained (Adler, 1953, p. 144):

I didn't resent the honest cop and I was able to stay in business because of the dishonest variety. But the members of the gendarmerie who really started my adrenalin flowing like wine were the boys who believed in playing it both ways, and who wouldn't have turned a hair if their own mother happened to be the one caught in the middle.

Recruitment. Many criminals talk about going "legit." That they consider leaving the criminal life indicates its tensions and hazards. Criminals often feel a certain envy for those of their number who have managed to go straight; there is indeed a kind of folklore among them concerning instances of this kind. Nevertheless it is not easy to leave the underworld once people have become rooted in it and have an investment and involvement in it. Their friends are in the underworld, they are accustomed to its routines, satisfactions, and excitements, and their loyalties tie them to it. When they try to abandon it they are not only drawn back, but are also pushed back because they are tagged by respectable society and cannot escape their past. When they try the good life, they often find it dull and frustrating, and may discover that they do not have the requisite skills and knowledge to give them the standard of living to which they are accustomed. Not much is known about the drift out of the criminal world, but there is some evidence of a shift with increasing age to marginal, semilegitimate occupations. Individuals who make this change do not altogether renounce underworld associations, but do manage to avoid the worst risks.

There is extensive literature on the causation of criminal behavior, and all sorts of theories from biological determinism to the strictly environmental have been proposed and defended. Two broad problems exist in this area. One is to account for the origin of criminal groups; this is a historical and sociological problem and does not deal with the behavior of individuals. The other is to explain how a given individual comes to join a criminal group and accept its way of life; this is of interest to the social psychologist.

The criminal underworld does not maintain itself biologically, for reproduction rates are low and criminals who do have children often try to keep them from following a life of crime. (This statement does not necessarily apply to other countries; in India, for example, criminal occupations, as well as prostitution and begging, have been matters of caste heritage and have been passed on from parents to children.) As a consequence, the criminal population is maintained by a process of recruitment about which relatively little is known. It is commonly assumed that adult criminals are recruited from juvenile delinquents, but this is only partly true and varies by types of crime. A substantial portion of adult offenders have no records of juvenile delinquency, and evidently embark on criminal careers relatively late in life. An autobiographical account by a convict doing a life term in the Iowa State Penitentiary indicates that this man's first venture into crime was as a bank robber during the Depression when he was in his early twenties (Runyon, 1953). Statistical evidence indicates that close to one-half of the apprehended criminals each year are officially first offenders.

Most juvenile delinquents come from the slums of large cities and are brought up in homes characterized by poverty and ignorance. Such juvenile criminals, tough as they may sometimes be, are automatically disqualified from certain types of criminal occupations (such as the confidence game) that require the manners, dress, and speech of the better-educated classes. Tough urban juvenile delinquents, if they become adult criminals, are thus likely to become thugs or to enter some part of the occupational hierarchy of crime that makes demands that their slum training enables them to meet. In the higher branches of villainy and the more refined types of fraud, superior intelligence, command of language, histrionic ability, stable nerves, and other such qualities are required. Neuroticism, psychosis, and other abnormalities of character and personality are just as much obstacles to success in crime as elsewhere. This is why criminologists are, or ought to be, exceedingly cautious about drawing conclusions about criminals from the study of persons in prison. The more capable and successful criminals are probably not sent to prison as often as the defectives, the abnormal, and the unintelligent.

Virtually all criminal occupations offering reasonable returns without unreasonable risks require a certain amount of training or tutelage. Safecrackers, it is said, are recruited from persons in the mechanical trades. Receivers of stolen goods often come from the business world. For some years, the top American racketeers have had "heist" (holdup) backgrounds and have usually been of Italian origin. Confidence men, according to one criminal, usually come from small towns or the country.

Perhaps no other institution contributes so much to criminal recruitment as the prison. In it persons of all degrees of sophistication are thrown together for long periods of time. The stigma of the prison sentence prevents the exconvict from getting into noncriminal occupations, and imprisonment has provided him with information concerning a wide variety of illegal ways of making a living. Prison associates become contacts the amateur may use if he wishes to turn professional.

The Aging Criminal

Horowitz (1982, 1982) and Shover (1985) have studied the adult delinquent gang member and the aging criminal. Horowitz's analysis of delinquent gangs in an inner-city Chicano community revealed that these gangs and membership in them continued well into early adulthood for the men she studied. She explains this perpetuation of youth gangs in terms of the marginal economic positions of the young men and in terms of their continued commitment to an honor-based subculture in which dependence and lack of domination are experienced as dishonor (Horowitz, 1982, p. 3). By remaining gang members, these young adults maintained respect in the eyes of others; they were seen as independent men of honor.

Shover's study of 50 men over age 40 who had been involved in ordinary property crimes earlier in their lives revealed three patterns of feeling concerning the past criminal life. All these men had served prison sentences. One group was described by Shover as despairing; they expressed severe regrets about their past exploits and present life. They felt that their life of crime had not paid off for them, and saw little hope of reversing these effects. One man stated (Shover, 1985, pp. 133–34):

What I regret is that I didn't get some kind of occupation, where I could have had some security when I got this old. Like, I have such a little work record, that I couldn't even collect Social Security. So what am I going to do? I don't have nothing to fall back on.

A second group of men studied by Shover expressed satisfaction about their past lives, about the time they spent in prison, and about their present situations. One man stated (Shover, 1985, p. 138):

Well see, the idea sticks out in my mind that it took what happened, it was necessary for what happened to me to get to where I am at now, you know. With the outlook I have. And so, if I regret that—what happened—you understand, then I regret being where I'm at. And that might be an academic thought, but I don't feel that it was a great loss, you know.

A third group of men expressed ambivalence about their past and present lives. A self-employed man with a steady income made the following statement which expresses this ambivalent theme (1985, p. 139):

I wonder at times what (my life) would have been like if I had never been in jail. And got a job and worked from the time I was younger—what my life would be like today. Where I would be. What position in life I'd have. Would I be better off than I am now or would I be worse off than I am now?

Aging criminals look back on their criminal careers with mixed emotions. The status passage into prison, the loss of self-control, and the subjective career effects on self and relations with others are felt for life. Yet a certain amount of irony toward and affection for the past is expressed. One ex-convict reflects on his relations with close friends from the criminal past (Shover, 1985, p. 149):

We talk to each other on the telephone from time to time, and really talk about, you know, we say "what the heck was wrong with us back then?" We just talk about it, you know. I don't understand. I never will be able to understand what was wrong with us. We sure lost a lot of time getting our act together.

Studies like these indicate the importance of studying the social psychological dimensions of criminal and deviant conduct. Honor, pride, group membership, self-esteem, friendship, subjective, objective, and moral careers all lie at the center of those experiences we term deviant.

We turn to another social world of deviance—the addict's world. After discussing the social world of addiction, we will address cocaine addiction, drawing on our discussion of addiction in Chapter 5.

THE ADDICT'S WORLD

The Addict's Social World

It is well known that drug addicts constitute a submerged social group—albeit a loosely organized one—in the United States. This is a far from universal phenomenon.

Before the attempt at suppression of the drug trade that began in 1915, American drug addicts were scattered throughout respectable society and did not form a deviant subsociety or social world. When addicts are treated as medical cases, as they are in England and in most European countries, they are deviants in the same way as are people who take sleeping pills or insulin shots. *The social world of the drug addict is not called into being by the direct effects of the drug habit, but rather by the attitudes and actions of nonaddicts.* For example, it was reported that during World War II the Japanese failed to supply a number of diabetics in Hong Kong with insulin. Consequently, a flourishing black market arose and the diabetics joined together in exchanging information and generally helping each other to maintain their supplies. If the situation had become permanent, there is no doubt that a diabetic subsociety would have been formed.

Similarly, American opiate addicts joined together in a loose group organization only when they were compelled to by the effects of antinarcotic legislation. When police enforcement of this legislation threatened to deprive addicts of their supplies, an informal organization arose to cope with the situation by furnishing smuggled drugs to the users. Marked as criminals and outcasts, addicts gravitated together for mutual protection, aid, and consolation. Addicts exchange information concerning matters vital to getting a steady drug supply; they discuss techniques of drug use and of avoiding the police, and generally talk about their common experiences (Agar, 1973; Rosenbaum, 1981).

No doubt some drug users in the United States are outside the addict's special world and have little or no contact with other users. Most addicts in this category are probably either members of the medical or allied professions, or are well-to-do persons with steady and relatively untreated sources of drug supply. Some of these persons are not known to be addicts by any but a few intimate associates; others may be known as addicts in their local communities, yet participate fully in community life.

The Addict's Argot. Out of the interaction within this subculture, a special language or argot has arisen that reflects the special concerns of the addict: for example, the peddler from whom she buys is a "connection"; a disruption of distribution channels by arrests is a "panic"; a person who is experimenting casually is a "joy popper" with an "ice cream habit"; full-fledged addicts have a "monkey on their back"; a person who goes off drugs suddenly without medication "kicks the habit cold turkey"; one who sniffs the drug is a "snorter"; and one

who uses it hypodermically "shoots it," and is either a "skin shooter" or a "main liner." It is a significant sociological fact that the American drug users early developed a rich and varied argot, whereas European addicts apparently did not until fairly recently. The American scene was especially favorable for the spawning of drug subcultures and cults which spread to other countries via the mass media or were carried by American visitors. British and Canadian observers, for example, sometimes comment on this cultural transmission.

The Underworld Addict

Underworld addicts are set apart by public definition, and develop a way of life that is centered upon drugs as their dominant concern. Their lives are organized around the endeavor to keep themselves adequately supplied. Unlike the addict with a legitimate supply, the underworld user must depend upon the illegal peddler and must pay fantastic black market prices. Patronage of the black market requires much time and effort and also usually leads to arrest and acquisition of a criminal record, making it difficult to hold a legitimate job. In any case, most legitimate jobs do not pay well enough to support a drug habit at black-market prices. All of this means that the American drug user must seek other, quicker means of making money. Theft, prostitution, and drug peddling are the most common means employed. The fact that addicts often act as peddlers, or "pushers," is of considerable significance in the recruitment of new users, since this means that the tremendous drive of the habit is harnessed to the perpetuation of the drug problem.

The underworld addict is unable to focus on long-range goals because he is constantly preoccupied with today's and tomorrow's supply. A pervasive feature of the life of this type of addict is the frantic need to keep one step ahead of a dwindling and constantly threatened supply—hence the argot term, "frantic junkie." The addict's time is broken up according to the demands of the habit, and days center on the times when he or she customarily "scores" with the "connection" or when she takes the shots. For the poorer addict, these "connections" are erratic and irregular due to either difficulties in raising the necessary money or locating the elusive and suspicious peddler. In addition to these hazards, the addict must constantly be on the alert to avoid the police and the addicted "stool pigeons" who work for them. He must be ready to move at any moment, travel light, and if picked up he must be careful to have no incriminating evidence on his person. Addicts become exceedingly ingenious in all of these respects, so much so that even relatively unintelligent persons seem to have their dull wits sharpened by the need for dope. The drug user spends a good deal of his life inventing new devices and tricks and scheming and maneuvering to raise money to keep underworld connections and to evade detection.

Addicts become addicted not only to drugs, but to a way of life. When they try to renounce their habits, they find themselves drawn back to their old haunts and associates. They also find it difficult to adjust themselves to the normal routines and values of the ordinary world and escape the stigma of their past. The failure of addicts to "kick the habit" permanently is doubtless tied up with their reluctance to abandon old associates and a familiar environment. The use of drugs is much more than a biological matter or a mere question of pharmacology.

Women on Heroin

Rosenbaum (1981) has analyzed the social worlds of women addicted to heroin. She analyzes how women get into the heroin addict career, the risks and dangers they encounter in this social world, its effects on their abilities to be wives and mothers, how they get treatment, and how they get out of the heroin world. Recruitment occurs through a variety of different avenues—including the "hippie trip," "dropping out" of high school, becoming a member of a male gang, entering the "fast life," and eventually moving into the pre-existing social world of drug use where use is first social, before it becomes addictive. One of Rosenbaum's respondents described becoming an addict (Rosenbaum, 1981, p. 32):

You don't wake up one morning and decide to be a drug addict. It takes at least three months' shooting twice a day to get any habit at all. . . . You become a narcotics addict because you do not have strong motivations in any other direction. Junk wins by default. I tried it as a matter of curiosity. I drifted along taking shots when I could score. I ended up hooked. . . . You don't decide to be an addict. One morning you wake up sick and you're an addict.

A key to becoming a heroin and opiate addict is learning that use of the drug will alleviate withdrawal distress. The repetition of this experience constitutes addiction. We discussed this process in some detail in Chapter 5.

Public Attitudes Toward Addiction

Drug addiction is generally regarded as a medical, moral, or criminal problem. In the United States prior to 1915, it was regarded mainly as a medical matter. After the drug-suppression program began, it came to be viewed and treated as a criminal matter. Special interest groups played a part in developing this definition; this was accomplished relatively easily, since there existed a general public disapproval of addiction and a sense of mystery concerning the strange power of the habit and the transformation of character that it brought about. This negative imagery has now been elaborated and become more lurid. Lurid paperback books tell of "gripping true adventures of a T-man's war against the dope menace" and portray heavy-lidded young women toying with hypodermic needles with the masculine hands of the law hovering in the background.

The prohibition method of dealing with vice is itself a peculiarly American method. Critics of the use of police suppression regard it as a manifestation of a Protestant "uplift" fervor. Whatever the explanation, in terms of its consequences police suppression has succeeded no better with addiction than it has with other forms of vice such as alcoholism, gambling, and prostitution.

The recruitment of new addicts seems to be closely tied up with the existence of illegal supply lines and with the underworld culture of the addict, which are direct consequences of prohibition methods of control. The effects produced by prohibition set up a vicious cycle leading to enhanced demands for more prohibitory legislation. Such legislation gets increasing support as public imagery of the addict assumes even more lurid and melodramatic aspects. An interesting peripheral question that is raised here concerns the limits of legal control of deviant behavior.

European observers have often commented upon what seems to be a peculiarly American legal philosophy, which places special emphasis upon the idea that the law should express the highest ideals and make no compromise with evil. European legal philosophy, in contrast, places relatively greater emphasis upon adapting laws to existing practices in order to avoid the consequences of driving underground certain types of behavior.

To maintain the illusion that vice is being eliminated and that virtue is protected, it is necessary that various myths and stereotypes be maintained. Ceremonial gestures are made from time to time to reassure the public; among these are publicized "drives" against vice, exposés, stories of "ring busting," the glorification of the police, and reports of police accomplishments (Becker, 1973; Lindesmith, 1968).

Complete cynicism concerning the motives of police and newspaper publishers and other interested parties who stage cleanup campaigns is unwarranted. Such drives do achieve temporary results, and are demanded and appreciated by the public. Basic reforms, however, usually come more slowly and in less spectacular ways. Most persons "in the know" recognize the ceremonial and strictly short-run significance of these spectacular battles with evil.

Cocaine Addiction

We noted earlier that the American public has recently become concerned with the phenomenon of cocaine addiction. It is clear that over the past decade a social world of cocaine use has come into existence in our society, and it exists on college campuses, in high schools, and in the social worlds of leisure and recreation that are frequented by affluent American adults. Persons who become addicted to cocaine come from a variety of occupational worlds—including business, higher education, entertainment, the law, medicine, and professional sports.

Cocaine is a stimulant, an alkaloid extracted from the leaf of the coca bush. Once extracted, the drug is sold in crystal form or chopped into a white odorless powder. Cocaine is taken in three basic ways. A "line" is snorted through a straw or a rolled-up dollar bill. A line is usually 25 to 30 milligrams of cocaine and is called a line because the "snorter literally sets up the white powder on a mirror or shiny surface in a straight line measuring about ⅛ inch by one inch long" (Gold, 1984, p. 5). A second way of taking the drug is by injecting it into a vein; a third way is smoking, sometimes called freebasing.

Gold (1984, pp. 4–5) describes this process. Ordinary street cocaine is separated from its adulterants by mixing it with water and ammonium hydroxide. This cocaine base is then separated from the water by using a fast-drying solvent such as ether. The base is then smoked in a specially designed water pipe. The free base (cocaine base) is placed on a top screen in the water pipe, melted into an oil, and then slowly heated while air is drawn through the stem into the mouth. The cocaine moves quickly to the brain with this fastest method of using the drug, and creates a swift rush of pleasure. However, because ether is so highly flammable, it catches fire easily, making this a hazardous method.

Depending on how the drug is taken, its effects may be felt within a few seconds when it is smoked, a half minute when it is injected, or up to three minutes when it is snorted. It appears that 9 out of 10 persons who become addicted to cocaine start out snorting and do this on a social, recreational basis. Within minutes of taking the drug, the user feels a sense of well-being, confidence, strength, and a loss of appetite. The effects of the drug last about fifteen to thirty minutes. At a street cost of $75 to $100 a gram, the cocaine high costs about $3.00 a minute.

For people who experiment with the drug and then become addicted, the high becomes an obsession. The user increases the frequency of use, as well as the dosage. The "crash" from cocaine includes a loss of euphoria replaced by fatigue, depression, irritability, mood swings, loss of interest in work, and weight loss. These effects increase as the length of time of using the drug increases. With increased use comes the denial that one has become addicted to the drug.

As with opiate and heroin addiction, cocaine addiction lies in the process of connecting the withdrawal distress with taking the drug. In order to remove the pain of the effects of "crashing," users take the drug again; this creates an immediate high which obliviates the depression and fatigue that come from the crash. Addicted users take the drug daily, averaging 6 or more grams a week. The major factor limiting their use is the cost of the drug. It appears that users deny the negative side-effects of cocaine use.

Cocaine addiction is evidenced when the person demonstrates loss of control—that is, becomes unable to turn down the drug when it is offered, and cannot control the amount they use when they take it. Addicted users become depressed when they cannot get the drug, and they experience withdrawal distress. Many addicted users binge for 24 hours or more, and seem unable to stop for as long as a month. They find that the most important thing in their life is cocaine and its use. Addicted users have been known to steal money from their employers, write bad

checks, sell valued personal possessions, and go into debt in order to keep using the drug. Many lose their spouses, lovers, friends, and jobs; many attempt suicide, and at the end of their using careers have moved from snorting to intravenous use and then to freebasing.

The average cocaine user is a man or woman, about 30 years old, white, middle-class occupation, college education or more, with an annual income of $25,000 or more. He or she is a sick individual who has become, according to Gold, a white-collar criminal in order to support the cocaine habit.

An expanding social world of cocaine addicts and recovering addicts is emerging in the United States. Cocaine Anonymous Groups, modeled after A.A., are appearing in American cities, as are treatment centers for cocaine addicts. Such persons are entering the social worlds of recovery from alcoholism and drug addiction (Denzin, 1986b). As they do so, they are learning the languages of recovery and are becoming members of social groups organized around abstinence from drugs and alcohol. A national hotline (800-COCAINE) now exists for people worried about their use of cocaine; in this service's first two years, 1,350,000 men and women called seeking information and/or help (Gold, 1984, p. ix).

Becoming an Alcoholic

We can continue our analysis concerning becoming a deviant or an addict by discussing the phases a person goes through in becoming an alcoholic. We will confine our meaning of the word *alcoholic* to the drinker who either (1) calls herself an alcoholic or (2) displays an inability to abstain from drinking for any continuous period of time and who, when drinking starts, is unable to control the amount that is consumed.

Jellinek (1962, pp. 359–66) outlines four phases in the alcoholic career. The first phase is the prealcoholic symptomatic phase, in which the drinker learns to experience rewarding relief from stress and anxiety in drinking situations; ascribing relief to the situation and not to alcohol. Such persons often seek out drinking situations so that they may engage in "happy hour" cocktails, and so on. Over the course of 6 months to 2 years, this person becomes an almost daily drinker, although she may seldom be overtly intoxicated. This phase has two stages: occasional and constant relief drinking.

The second phase is called the prodomal phase. The drinker begins to drink secretly and becomes preoccupied with alcohol. He may begin to feel guilty about drinking, which by now is heavy. Blackouts begin to appear. As he tries to cover up the amount of alcohol that is consumed, rationalizations and excuses (accounts) begin to appear. In the third phase, which is called crucial, any drinking of alcohol starts off a chain reaction which is felt as a physical demand for alcohol. This felt need for alcohol often produces a drinking bout which continues for hours until the person is intoxicated. The bout of drinking which sets off this chain reaction need not be caused by physical discomfort; any social situation can trigger the drinking chain that leads to intoxication. Critical in this phase is loss of control. Like the cocaine addict, the alcoholic seems unable to control the amount of alcohol consumed once the first drink is taken. It appears that the drinker has crossed a line which no longer makes control of drinking possible. However, his pride leads him to denial of loss of control—and back to drinking (Bateson, 1972).

With the loss of control comes denial and even stronger rationalization schemes which justify continued drinking. Heavy drinking continues; the person experiences a loss of self-esteem while at the same time grandiose behaviors begin to appear (i.e., extravagant expenditures and the like). Marked aggressive behavior may appear, along with changes in drinking patterns, drinking friends, changes in job, family, marked self-pity, and extraordinary efforts to protect one's alcohol supply. A neglect of nutrition may also occur, as well as sexual jealousy and morning drinking. At this point in her drink-

ing career the person may be drinking on a continual—rather than a continuous—basis. The first drink may occur upon rising in the morning, then at 10 or 11 A.M., then around 1 P.M., and then continuous drinking starts around 5 P.M. (Jellinek, 1962, p. 365).

In the fourth phase of alcoholism, the chronic phase, there are prolonged periods of intoxication, even in the daytime. The person may resort to drinking anything that has alcohol in it. A loss of alcohol tolerance occurs; the person gets drunk on half the amount it used to take. Thinking is impaired, and fears and tremors appear as well. Vague religious desires may be experienced. At the end of this phase the person, now truly alcoholic, may express a desire for treatment (see Denzin, 1986a, 1986b, 1986c).

In order for a person to become alcoholic, he must (1) learn how to drink, (2) learn to define the effects of alcohol in a positive fashion, and (3) come to see that these effects bring desired personal and social ends, that is, the relief from anxiety and tension, the creation of friendship and fellowship, and so on. Once these three processes are met, persons must (4) increase their alcohol intake to the point where increased tolerance is created and (5) a physical addiction for alcohol is produced. At this point, (6) withdrawal effects must be experienced and (7) they must be connected, by the person, to the absence of alcohol in their body. Finally, (8) they must see that by drinking they remove those effects which are defined in a negative manner. Once this has occurred, the person has established the conditions for becoming an alcoholic. Like the opiate, heroin, and cocaine addict, she has learned that the drug will alleviate withdrawal distress. The repetition of this experience constitutes addiction to alcohol.

FAMILY VIOLENCE

We noted that in the crucial phase of alcoholism, marked aggressive behavior may appear. This aggression is often associated with the violent mood swings the alcoholic experiences. Others have observed that opiate, heroin, and cocaine addicts also become aggressive in the later phases of their careers. There is a subtle and complex relationship between violence and the use of drugs like alcohol. We cannot go into the complexities of this literature except to note the following. Drinking and drug use often occurs in the presence of close friends and family members. Violence, including homocides, occur with high frequency (50 percent) in family settings. Hence the two phenomena—drug use and violence—occur in the same setting. Which causes which is not known; that is, we do not know if persons are violent and then drink or use drugs, or if they drink and use drugs and then become violent (see Denzin, 1986a).

We do know, however, that family violence occurs in perhaps one out of every three households in the United States at least once a year (Gelles & Cornell, 1985). We will briefly discuss the stages of violence a violent home goes through. We will focus primarily on spousal violence (and not deal with child abuse, sexual abuse, abuse of the elderly, or sibling violence).

The Stages of Family Violence

We begin with the assumption that family violence is an interactional process which gets out of control. To use Kadushin and Martin's (1981) phrase, it is an interactional event which takes on negative, destructive features. The family of violence becomes a small social group which threatens to tear itself apart through violent actions and emotions.

The root meanings of violence include to treat with force, to abuse, to attempt to regain something that has been lost. We shall define violence as the attempt to regain, through the use of emotional and physical force, something that has been lost (Denzin, 1984, p. 488). What has been lost can be traced back to the self of the violent person, who has lost or never had valued self-feelings. Through the use of violent force, the violent person attempts to regain a sense of self that is located in the family group. The violent person becomes locked in negative emotions which spill over into everyday family life, creating negative, hostile, fearful emotional experiences for every family member. They lose their statuses as just spouses, daughters, or sons; they become victims of family violence. The father, if he is the abuser, becomes a violent man who is feared by those who want to love him.

The structure of social relations in the family group is altered and transformed. Cliques and factions emerge; members turn against one another; secret communications appear; family members become afraid to be in the same room with one another. When the violent family member comes home, other members make excuses to leave, and the violent person begins to feel like a family isolate. What the violent person desires most—love and care—is denied because of his or her violence. The violent home becomes an empty emotional shell, and the violence that goes on behind the closed doors of the home stigmatizes every family member. Everyone loses self-esteem; false hopes and promises fuel family life, while members attempt to deny the fact that they live in a violent house.

The negative symbolic interaction that attaches to the family of violence moves through several stages. The first stage is the denial of violence. The second stage is pleasure derived from violence. The third stage is the building of mutual hostility between spouses and other family members. The fourth stage is the development of misunderstandings. The fifth stage is the appearance of sexual jealousies between spouses. The sixth stage is increased violence which, seventh, either destroys the family, or eighth, stabilizes itself into a state of recurring violence.

Before violence can be denied, it must first make its appearance. Dobash and Dobash (1979) show that when violence first appears in a marriage it is isolated, attached to an oversight on the wife's part and defined as insignificant. After the violence makes its appearance, the husband may take some pleasure from being violent. He feels that by being violent he not only gets his own way, but also achieves a measure of self-esteem by keeping his wife and children in place. Hostilities increase, however, as do misunderstandings. The husband continues to blame his wife, while she comes to see that it is not all her fault. Family members are placed in a double bind situation: If their father loves them, why is he violent? If he is violent, it must mean he doesn't love them; yet he says he loves them. Both messages can't be true. Hence the double bind, as Bateson calls it (1972). With double binds come misunderstandings and empty communications. One wife, a graduate student in psychology, reported:

I stopped talking with my husband . . . anything I said made him mad. We barely said hi or goodbye to each other. He just seemed to get mad when he saw me. Then he would lash out, cut me down any way he could. Then he'd say, "I was happy before I met you. Look what you've done to me." He'd slam the door and walk out, and then come back in, grab the paper out of my hand and maybe twist my wrist till it got red, or swear at me and say he'd be home when he felt like it. Once he let the air out of the tires on my car. Another time he hit me so hard I had a cracked rib (Denzin, 1984, p. 492).

Sexual jealousy appears in the next stage. Each spouse begins to suspect the other of sexual infidelities. The husband may be violent towards her when they have sexual intercourse. With sexual jealousies comes increased violence of an emotional and physical nature; not only does the violent offender become more violent, but other family members begin fighting with one another as well. Violence permeates the family. Pizzey (1974, pp. 26–27) provides an example. The husband, a successful businessman,

would arrive home in a very drunken state and complain bitterly about everything I did or said to him. He was frightening when in this sort of aggressive mood . . . on my son's fourth birthday he arrived home . . . and insisted that I get James out

of bed. . . . After refusing . . . he picked him up and brought him into the kitchen, where he was very insulting to me and called me a slut and a whore . . . my husband grabbed James and punched me behind the right ear . . . He picked up the bread-knife and threatened to put it through my throat.

Such violent outbursts either take the family to the brink of self-destruction, or drive the members to seek help. A spouse may call the police, leave home with her children, go to a shelter for battered women, file for divorce, or push her husband to seek help for himself. Families appear to go in one of two directions: they self-destruct or they get better. Whichever direction they take, the legacy of violence will be felt by all members, perhaps to be carried into the next generation of family life.

Patterns of Violence and Abuse: Franz Kafka

Noy and Sharron (1985, pp. 261–87) have analyzed the family history of the novelist Franz Kafka. A victim of child abuse, Kafka's life history is instructive. Kafka was born in Prague on July 3, 1883. His father Herrmann was a self-made businessman, and he and his wife were from families of Jewish scholars. Besides Franz, they had three daughters, and two younger sons who died in infancy. Herrmann was disappointed in his son, and the wife expressed a preference for her dead second son. Franz felt humiliated by his father (who despised his artistic tendencies), neglected by his mother, and betrayed by his favorite sister. In life later Kafka had few friends and was engaged three times, twice to the same woman. Like Gregor in his famous story *The Metamorphosis*, Kafka spent virtually all his life depending on his parents and living in their home (Noy & Sharron, 1985, p. 263).

In November 1919, Kafka wrote a letter to his father which gave a detailed account of his feelings toward his father, whose hostility had haunted him his entire life. He gave the letter to his mother, who read the letter and returned it to her son; his father never received it. In 1912 Kafka had written to his closest friend Max Brod: "I hate them all, every one of them. . . . But hatred . . . again gets directed against me" (Noy & Sharron, 1985, p. 263).

Noy and Sharron suggest—and there is considerable evidence to support their position—that Kafka's stories, especially *The Metamorphosis,* can be read as autobiographical accounts of the violence and abuse Kafka experienced in his family. They suggest that his father was the "active" abuser in the family, his mother the "passive" abuser, and his sister a "first-row bystander" who sided with his parents against him.

Their analysis of active and passive abuse is instructive. Active abuse involves battering, neglect, the use of threats, ridicule and scorn, isolation, sexual abuse, and exploitation. Kafka's father used all of these forms except for sexual abuse. Passive abuse involves over-fondling, over-pampering, the use of double binds, interfering with decisions and choices, discouraging independence, and insulating the person from the outside world. This appeared to be how Kafka's mother treated him; all the while she undermined his standing in the family and took her husband's side against him.

The Victim's World

Three emotions dominate the victim's world: shame, fear, and guilt. Kafka felt shame in the eyes of his father and himself; he felt that he had not lived up to his father's expectations. The active and passive abuse he experienced created more shame, for he felt that he deserved what he received, and this created the feeling that he was unworthy of love or care. He felt fear—partly from the active abuse he received, but also from the isolation he experienced. He feared himself, the outside world, and his family. He felt that he had lost the capacity to speak and experienced a desperate guilt. He felt that he deserved the punishment and beating that his

father directed toward him (Noy & Sharron, 1985, p. 281).

Kafka divided this emotionally torn world into three parts. There was the world of his family, which had laws that he could never conform to. There was a second world, more remote, governed by others, where orders were issued and one worked. There was a third world where everybody but Kafka lived happily and free (Noy & Sharron, 1985, p. 284; Kafka, 1954, p. 148).

The fact that Kafka created these three worlds suggests how destructive family violence can be. Kafka found no ideal world for himself; the violence he experienced made him an outsider to himself. Oddly enough, Noy and Sharron (1985, p. 285) note, Kafka's presence in the family as a scapegoat unified the other family members into a cohesive unity. They appeared to live "relatively" well-adjusted lives.

The study and analysis of family violence is of great interest to the social psychologist because childhood socialization occurs in families. If the home is violent, then the course of self-development will be drastically altered, as the case of Franz Kafka suggests.

If family significant others, including parents, are alcoholics or drug addicts, then their ability to function as socializing agents will be dramatically altered. They may well become active and passive abusers in the senses that Kafka's parents were. We must note, however, that active and passive abuse may occur in the absence of any drug. It does not appear, for example, that Kafka's parents abused drugs or alcohol.

THE HOMOSEXUAL

In Chapter 13 we discussed the origins of homosexual behavior. Current consensus is that homosexual behavior, like heterosexual behavior, is a learned form of behavior. Authorities do not agree, however, on just how such behaviors are learned. Presumably the basis for it is laid at an early age when children form conceptions and attitudes on sexual matters from their experiences in the family group, and from experiences with their own bodies. Here we are interested in the place accorded the homosexual in society (Humphreys, 1972; Warren, 1974; Barton, 1985).

Public Opinion of Homosexuals. Like drug addicts, homosexuals may be so scattered as to have relatively little contact with others like themselves. Public censure, however, tends to cause them to congregate in places where heterogeneity and size of the population makes for more anonymity and tolerance. There are laws that make homosexual behavior illegal and criminal. As noted in Chapter 5, the current AIDS controversy has heightened the fear of homosexuals in our society.

As with other forms of behavior that are defined as deviant, there is divided or ambiguous public opinion concerning homosexuality. In general, homosexuality is recognized and tolerated with amusement, sympathy, compassion, and only mild disapproval. It is often accepted as a matter of fact in many segments of our society, particularly among people who have had close contact with it. The ambiguity of public opinion is reflected by people's tendency to maintain a conspiracy of silence about known homosexuality until it comes to public attention. When this happens, all parties are embarrassed, but agree that something must be done to assuage that portion of the public that thinks of homosexuality as a dire evil to be sternly suppressed by police action. The police of large cities ordinarily tolerate or ignore homosexual activity as such, and only become concerned when it involves open scandal or is associated with other illegal activities.

Known male homosexuals are not allowed to hold certain types of positions, but may be tolerated or even expected in others, such as hairdressing, designing women's clothes, artistic pursuits, or ballet. It is an interesting question as to why concentration should occur in certain professions and populations. This may possibly be partly accounted for by a tendency of male inverts (effeminate males) to seek and prefer employment in activities generally regarded as somewhat feminine, and not quite appropriate for males. Concentration in an occupation also may be accounted for by the opportunities it provides for contacts of the desired kind with other males.

There are many misapprehensions about homosexuals and the lives they lead. It is sometimes thought that homosexuals are always effeminate (or masculine), detached, suicidal, or inclined to antisocial conduct stemming from their sexual deficiency. Actually, like other social deviants the homosexual shares most values dominant in her country, social class, and occupation. What homogeneity there is among these persons, apart from their sexual behavior, is largely brought about by the negative public evaluation of them (Corey, 1951, p. 97):

If there is any characteristic of homosexual life that has been instrumental in the development of homogeneous group traits, it is probably the pretense and the mask. Millions of people could not possibly live through each day of the year, concealing, pretending, deliberately lying, without reacting in similar manner.

Apart from the constant threat of blackmail and public disgrace, it may be embarrassing to the homosexual in relations with ordinary persons to have them know of his peculiarity. Hence he may become skillful at concealing the homosexual identity and at manipulating interaction to discover whether or not he may safely reveal that identity to a given individual. Many homosexuals become sensitized to the detection of homosexuality in others and develop techniques of communicating with each other. Occasionally the signals are misread (as is also true in heterosexual relations), and thus the homosexual leaves herself open to unpleasantness or even danger. Like the criminal, she is wary of associations with outsiders unless she knows what to expect. As with other "minority groups," outsiders sometimes form friendships with insiders and so function as connecting links between respectable and nonrespectable worlds.

The Homosexual Subculture. There is a loosely organized homosexual subculture, and typical forms of association exist within it. Corey (1951, pp. 114–15) has described the world of the homosexual in general terms that fit the world of the criminal or the prostitute:

One writer describes it as a *submerged world,* while another speaks of a *society on the fringe of society.* Both are correct, accurate, yet incomplete, for there is not one submerged world, one society on the fringe of society, but several, almost countless, different and disparate and dissimilar and almost disconnected, yet all having some relationship to one another, sometimes through an individual or two who travel in several of these submerged-island societies at once, or related on the other hand merely by the similarity of pursuits and personalities, or perhaps related primarily by the association that exists only in the imagination of the hostile world.

In this world homosexuals court, make love, have friends and acquaintances, engage in ordinary business with each other, and develop a common argot and a group philosophy. Warren (1974, p. 114) discusses the significance of argot in the homosexual community:

Everyone [and every kind of sexuality] [can] be accounted for by some linguistic category of the gay world. Words . . . function to separate outsiders from insiders, to account for ambiguous persons within . . . sexual interaction and to describe the . . . relationships of insiders with one another. In such a way is a world set apart from other worlds.

Since they are under censure, they develop protective and operational rationales. One rationale is that homosexuality is a biological disorder, and hence other people should adopt a live-and-let-live attitude and not cast blame. Another is that homosexuals are superior to others in intelligence and sensitivity (artistic and other accomplishments by homosexuals are pointed to in evidence). Some will even argue that their forms of lovemaking are superior, and note with pride the complex domestic relations that grow up among them. Celebrations of homosexual romance in literature are used as support. Further powerful ideological support is gained by denigrating the general public (which misunderstands or discriminates) and by exaggerating the prevalence of homosexual practices. Kinsey's claim that some 40 percent of all males have had some homosexual experience was probably greeted with considerable satisfaction by many exclusively homosexual individuals. The "straight" world is often satirized in phrases like "Can heterosexuality be cured?" or "Heterosexuality is a dread dysfunction . . . which infects a surprising percentage of American males" (Warren, 1974, p. 129).

In a study of male homosexuals in Montreal, sociologist Maurice Leznoff (1956) has indicated that the core of homosexual society consists of those homosexuals who are relatively unsecretive in their activities and inclinations. The danger of being exposed as deviants either is disregarded or does not exist for them. These overt homosexuals are the mainstay of the homosexual world. They are easily recognized by outsiders, and since they do not fear detection they congregate in fairly public places—certain bars, restaurants, and the like. Within the homosexual world studied by Warren, a variety of social types—"Nelly" queen, mother, auntie, sister, and fag hag, are recognized. These labels designate specific identities within the gay community. (Warren, 1974, pp. 101–102). More numerous are those who practice homosexuality secretly or covertly. Those known in the lingo as "butches" are usually indistinguishable from ordinary heterosexual males because concealment is deemed vital. They hesitate to risk exposure by being seen in the company of known homosexuals or by appearing at homosexual parties and hangouts. However, as the homosexual's friendships, even among overt homosexuals, are not necessarily or even generally sexual in nature, the covert homosexual often has to seek a sexual partner. This often brings him into direct and even public contact with the overt homosexual at well-known hangouts; he thus risks discovery. Apparently there is some antagonism between overt and covert homosexuals, at least in Montreal; the covert homosexual, who generally is better educated and of higher occupational status, looks down on the other and is perhaps even hostile toward him because his very visibility calls public attention to the fact of homosexuality.

Other homosexual types include those who go further in their attempts to maintain secrecy; they confine their expressions of sexual interest to a single other person and never mingle in groups of their own kind. Undoubtedly there are others who, although they recognize their own homosexual impulses, do not reveal them overtly to anyone else.

Recruitment. The process of recruitment into the homosexual world is tied up with the public sanction against homosexuality and the discovery by individual deviants that such a world exists. People may even reach middle age without recognizing their homosexual tendencies. Discovery of identity may come in various ways, including contact with other homosexuals who introduce them to the ways of "the gay society." The uninitiated may be inducted by chance contact or by being picked up. It is sometimes averred that hardened homosexuals pervert or seduce other persons; this is extremely doubtful. Whatever the cause of homosexuality may be, it is not so simple as this. An individual may ordinarily be seduced only if he cooperates and finds the experience to his taste.

The discovery by homosexual isolates of a "preformed" world is an event of great psychological importance known as "coming out." It shows them that they are not alone and provides them with a supporting milieu. Probably most pronounced or exclusive homosexuals recognize their deviance during adolescence, so that most movement into the homosexual world takes place during adolescence or early maturity. As she enters into homosexual associations, the novitiate acquires the knowledge essential to her participation in the deviant world. This includes knowledge of social skills, the signs of recognition and communication, and the more subtle modes of interacting with both homosexuals and normal people. The Montreal study suggests that initial sexual contacts often are accompanied by confusion and guilt, since the new activities run counter to general public sanction against such activities, a sanction previously internalized by the person himself. The initial affair with an experienced homosexual not only inducts the neophyte into the strange new world, but affords him the rationales necessary for making the transition from the outside to the inside.

Homosexual experience of the trauma of aging is apparently similar to the experience of heterosexuals in our society. The Montreal homosexual world values youth. The aging homosexual seeks to avoid loneliness and isolation by means of a permanent union, or homosexual marriage. But these unions, because they lack the institutional supports given the heterosexual variety (and for a variety of other reasons), are usually unstable and temporary. As a consequence, loneliness is a common fate for the aging homosexual who finds himself unable to compete with younger persons.

Although we hitherto have been discussing homosexuality as something sharply set off from heterosexuality, the dividing line is actually not a clear one. Persons who are exclusively homosexual are far outnumbered by those who are in varying degrees capable of both kinds of attachments. Such persons sometimes move in and out of homosexual circles, but do not form groups of their own organized around their own catholicity of response. The subsociety of the exclusive homosexual is loosely organized and is thus able to absorb part-time homosexuals, homosexual isolates, and covert homosexuals, as well as those whose tastes and attachments are exclusively and overtly homosexual.

Subsequent to Leznoff and Westley's report on Montreal homosexuals, Evelyn Hooker—as part of a long-range study of male homosexuals that has been underway since the 1960's—has described some of the salient aspects of homosexual life in Los Angeles. Her account generally confirms, parallels, and extends the Montreal study, but focuses on the "gay" or homosexual bar around which leisure time and recreational activities of many homosexuals are organized. These bars also serve to introduce newcomers into the homosexual world. Besides facilitating sexual contacts much as ordinary bars do, gay bars also function as communication centers that disseminate news and information that is of interest to the members of the subgroup. Like others who have studied homosexuals, Hooker (1967) indicates that it is undoubtedly only a small portion of the homosexual population that becomes publicly visible to the outsiders who visit "gay" bars or other gathering places frequented by homosexuals. The major portion of homosexual communities probably consist of a series of small, somewhat overlapping, and loosely interconnected cliques or friendship groups, the members of which may rarely or never show up at the public gathering places (Mileski & Black, 1972).

The *neutralization* of the stigma associated with the homosexual identity is complex (Warren, 1974, p. 141) and often involves a celebration of the ritual solidarity gained by participation in the gay world. The theories which are offered as explanations for homosexuality are inverted and turned against "straight" society as the gay individual elevates the world of homosexuality to that of an aristocratic, secret, and stigmatized group (Warren, 1974). In this instance, the stigma is denied by the members of this social world.

POLITICAL WORLDS AND POLITICAL DEVIANCY

Some years ago, sociologist John Landesco (1968) remarked during a study of organized crime in Illinois that there were intimate and necessary relationships between American criminals and politicians; by this he meant both that criminals often required the services of politicians (including politically appointed judges and prosecutors), while some politicians profited from illegal payoffs. Politicians are faced not only with that kind of temptation, but because of the very exigencies of their offices, they almost necessarily tread a fine line between legal activities and those that vary from just a little illegal to those which are downright criminal.

In the words of George Washington Plunkitt (Riordon, 1966), for many years a highly successful Tammany politician during the late 19th century, "Everybody's talkin' these days about Tammany men growin' rich on graft, but nobody thinks of drawin' the distinction between honest graft and dishonest graft. There's all the difference in the world between the two." Dishonest graft is "blackmailin', gamblers, saloonkeepers, disorderly people, etc." whereas honest graft, exemplified by his own career, he sums up "as I seen my opportunities and I took 'em." For example, his party is in power and is about to make many public improvements; he gets tipped off about a new park about to be laid out, so "I see my opportunity and I take it. I go to that place and I buy up all the land I can in the neighborhood." Only afterward is the park plan made public, so, when the others rush forward to buy it, he says: "Ain't it perfectly honest to charge a good price and make a profit on my investment and foresight?" (1966, p. 3) Another kind of honest graft was when Tammany raised many salaries, despite "an awful howl of the reformers," but Tammany garnered ten votes for every one it lost. And Plunkitt adds, criticizing Lincoln Steffens's famous muckraking book, *The Shame of the Cities*, that a reformer like Steffens cannot distinguish between the two kinds of graft and consequently "gets things mixed up." The politician is not a looter of the public treasury; rather, he looks after "his own interests, the organization's interests, and the city's interest at the same time."

Plunkitt added that he never "monkeyed" with the penal code. To do that would be corrupt, as some foolish or self-serving politicians occasionally are, he admits. Despite Plunkitt's distinction between honest and dishonest graft, some of a political machine's business—in the days when political machines more obviously ran our cities—involved frankly illegal operations or at least less than honest transactions in connection with perfectly legal political offices and legislative rulings (Merton, 1957). Honest graft lies somewhere toward the middle of the entire range of political transactions—running from fully legitimate to quite illegitimate actions—which supports the organization's existence. Thus, one of Plunkitt's superiors, Boss Tweed, was later exposed as fabulously corrupt. All of New York City's financial affairs had become lucrative sources of graft, and the state and city legislation that Tweed's men influenced brought them handsome kickbacks from the businessmen who profited from this legislation. A species of extortion was used too, as when certain kinds of legislation were threatened unless the victims paid up. And Tweed's machine found that the best way to protect itself against newspaper action was to distribute city advertising as a token of peace—hush money which bound the press to silence (Callow, 1970). Of course, that was not the only kind of bribery that such a machine engaged in. However, all these kickbacks, tradeoffs, payments, and other negotiated covert agreements are essential to the smooth running of political machines.

Today it is claimed that such urban machines have been replaced by more modern kinds of organizations; but we safely say that old or new, urban or small-town, the American political organization skirts close to and often goes over the boundaries to clear il-

legality. Yet, seen from the side of the politician rather than the reformer or the mere layperson, politics is a pragmatic matter—so much so that idealism is either a chimera or hard to maintain in the face of "genuine reality." It is commonly said that crime does not pay; the assertion is probably not applicable to politicians.

Reformers periodically make attempts to firm up that fine line between political criminality and political legitimacy. Reformers see themselves as the defenders of the general welfare, and speak of "cleaning up" and use other synonyms for civic purity and virtue, such as "public order," "getting things back to normal," and restoring statesmanship to what otherwise is mere dirty politics. Reform movements bubble up eternally, resulting in exposés, trials, incarcerations, and occasionally in reform governments. Once in office, reformers face many of the same pragmatic considerations as their predecessors and eventually get involved in compromises and tradeoffs, but, it is hoped, more legitimate and legal. Eventually reformer officials become either relatively indistinguishable from the people they ousted or are voted out of office in preference of more professional types.

Whatever innocent citizens may think, on the national and state levels there is also the same ambiguity about legal and illegal actions. Our newspapers almost increasingly report on the indictment—and sometimes the imprisonment—of state officials, and in Washington, some congressmen are known for having far more probity than others; while the president himself may owe his election and his effectiveness somewhat, at least, to agreements made between his staff and influential state or city politicians who have less than saintly reputations. As for the executive agencies or the White House staff itself, occasionally someone is exposed, her corrupt action leading to resignation, sometimes to imprisonment. More rarely there is a full-fledged scandal touching on or located in the White House, resulting in such newsworthy events as the Teapot Dome investigation of 1923–1924, or the Watergate scandal, which was brought to light in 1972.

Corruption aside, from the politician's viewpoint there is always important work to be done, and it can only be accomplished by effective political organization; this involves making deals and giving certain people "breaks," but the work does get done. Politicians should not be too greedy, of course, and certainly not merely self-serving. The point is made clearly and with considerable justice by another famous Tammany politician, Richard Croker, who many years ago said, with what he doubtless considered straightforward realism (Riordon, 1966, p. xix):

Think what New York is and what the people of New York are. One half, more than one half, are of foreign birth. . . . They do not speak our language, they do not know our laws, they are the raw material with which we have to build up the state. . . . There is no denying the service which Tammany has rendered to the Republic. There is no such organization for taking hold of the untrained, friendless man and converting him into a citizen. Who else would do it if we did not? . . . although you may not like our motives or our methods, what other agency is there by which so long a row could have been hoed so quickly or so well.

If one accepts the generalized American system, he can only argue with Croker in terms of alternative organizational forms and their comparative potentials for more or less corruption. Of course, if—like some religious sects or radical political groups—one renounces the political system and feels that the whole system is corrupt, then it can only be rectified by radical action, like a successful revolution, or perhaps by divine intervention.

In a more general sense, we can see that corruption and illegality are constant features of the world of politics for a variety of reasons. First, politicians occupy positions of power that other individuals are denied. This means that they have greater opportunities to stray from the boundaries of conformity. Second, access to situations of power and influence gives the politician resources ordinarily denied other in-

dividuals. These resources, in turn, open the avenues for exploitation, advantage, and self-enhancement. Third, those in political power are seldom scrutinized, policed, and openly evaluated by the regular members of the nation's agencies of social control. This lack of open policing increases the likelihood that deviant behavior on the part of the politician, if it is not too flagrant, will go unnoticed and unchecked. Fourth, politicians are granted a range of privileges and given a set of "status symbols," including chauffeured cars, free postal services, and unlimited resources to hire family members as aides, secretaries, and assistants. The sheer receipt of these status symbols sets the politician off from others and makes it possible for common citizens to feel a sense of alienation—if not disrespect—for those in power. Thus, the politician often finds herself defined by some people in deviant if not unacceptable terms. As Horowitz (1971) and Mills (1959) have observed, a kind of "blunted immorality" characterizes today's politician.

The politician's "accounts" of his deviances are likely to differ from those offered by homosexuals, drug addicts, or underworld criminals. Unlike those who can lay no claim to political power, the politician shrouds the deviant acts around the dominant political ideology of the nation-state and its regional branches. Thus spying, espionage, blackmailing, murder, invasions of privacy, threats to freedom of speech, and election tampering are justified through recourse to a higher good or set of ideals which supposedly underpin the very workings of government. Political scientists, too, have often agreed that corruption is a necessary evil to get "things done," and even that it is a necessary accompaniment to the development of industrialized nations.

The political deviant, then, utilizes the ideology of the state to justify illegal and corrupt acts. The ordinary deviant seldom utilizes accounts of this political nature. Instead, the homosexual, drug addict, or burglar is likely to develop a "sad tale" that explains her deviance through a complex process of unraveling past biography. Somewhere in the past the individual will identify those forces that led her astray. These forces may be those stressed by a currently popular theory of personality development: thus many homosexuals explain their homosexual activity by referring to Freud's theory of personality or to the presence of a weak father or mother in the family. Of course, the forces may be couched in other vocabularies: religious, environmental, or biological.

Yet, unlike other deviants (Hall, 1972), the politician can often control those forces that would define him as corrupt. Royko has observed the mayor of one large city (1971, pp. 209–10):

> The limousine came that morning to take him to City Hall, but he sent it away. Reporters were told that he would spend the day at home with family and a few friends. The traditional birthday party was canceled. On his sixty-fifth birthday, in the city he had ruled for so long, he couldn't go to his own office because there would be questions for which he had no ready answers. The timing of the report seemed like a cruel act of fate. But it wasn't. As with most things that happened in his city, the timing of the report had been arranged by him. It gave him an excuse to stay home that day, and nobody could say he was hiding. In his Chicago, even a man's birthday could be put to political use. "Chicago ain't ready for reform yet," Alderman Bauler said when Daley was elected in 1955. And in 1970, ready or not, it wasn't getting it.

We turn next to eccentric deviants, who provide a convenient contrast to the "corrupt" politician.

INDIVIDUAL DEVIANCE

By the term *individual deviance,* we refer to deviant behavior that does not have a cultural base—that is, it is not prescribed as customary by a deviant group or social world. Some forms of individual deviation are linked with biological causes, and others with what may be called personal, or personal social, causes. The interaction between such individual deviants and others who regard them as in some way odd, strange, peculiar, different, or abnormal is of interest to social psychology. Some of these forms of individual deviance are formally dealt with as crime; others are handled by specialized agencies and procedures; still others are more or less officially ignored. We turn to some of the conspicuous types of such behavior.

The Eccentric

In contrast to the amorphous and complex deviant worlds, there exist a variety of organized groups which, when they come to the attention of outsiders, are regarded as queer, odd, peculiar, crazy, or strange. *When all the patterned forms have been sorted out and named, there remains a residue of behavior that does not seem to fit well into the established categories. This kind of behavior may be called eccentric.* In the psychiatric vocabulary, persons who engage in such behavior may be called *psychopaths* or *sociopaths*—these words being used to indicate that while someone is not clearly or simply psychotic, neurotic, or criminal, there is nevertheless something out of the ordinary about her and her actions. The conduct so characterized is heterogeneous and extremely varied, ranging from that which might be called simply independent, unconventional, or original to that which is dangerously odd, menacing, or mysterious.

The following may be considered forms of eccentricity: a prisoner spends his spare time building a carefully constructed gallows on which he executes insects; an elderly woman with a large fortune in securities begs for alms on street corners and lives in a hovel; a gentle, elderly immigrant who has difficulty meeting his simple needs makes ends meet by passing occasional counterfeit dollar bills, crudely manufactured by himself for this purpose; a man who lives in seclusion in the wilderness shoots at airplanes with a high-powered rifle because they disturb his solitude; a woman insists on dressing herself exclusively in bath towels carefully draped and pinned about her; one elderly millionaire gives away dimes, and another leaves a large fortune to his favorite horse; other persons collect and hoard golf balls, ballpoint pens, and so on. We must not confuse personal eccentricities with cultural differences; for example, an old woman who wears old-fashioned hats, or an Indian woman who wears a sari in the United States, should not be called eccentric. A Westernized native who returns to his tribal home in Africa in European clothes should also not be included in this category. However, although the logical distinction involved here is clear, it is often easier to make in theory than in practice.

On the other hand, eccentric behavior within certain limits may also be valued positively by a society; for example, it may be regarded as colorful, humorous, enterprising, or exciting. Apart from furnishing entertainment and interest, eccentrics serve as innovators, producing new modes of behavior that may be taken up as fads or as permanent parts of the social heritage. In countries (including the United States) in which change and innovation are valued and in which individuality and independence are stressed, idiosyncratic behavior often attracts favorable publicity and attention. As is often observed, a broad tolerance of variability promotes a sense of freedom and facilitates social change. This is quite evident in the areas of popular art, music, and current clothing fashion. The eccentric designer Coco Chanel, for example, left an indelible worldwide stamp on women's clothing styles.

The innovative function of eccentricity and its potential for arousing hostility or antagonism have been well brought out by Tumin (1950) in an interesting study of a small Guatemalan community, where he describes two of the principal deviants in the village. One was a hero and a successful curer of disease in a community where there is much anxiety over sickness. To his fellow Indian youth who are being alienated from traditional ways, his behavior represented "one of the few imaginable future alternatives" (1950, p. 206). On the other hand,

the second eccentric was wholly negativistic; he offered no alternatives for the norms that he violated; he was a scapegoat, disliked intensely, and viewed as a threat. Tumin (1950, p. 210) notes that "in each case the deviant behavior appears to have its genesis in relatively unique and idiosyncratic facts of the individual life histories. Their deviations . . . are not understandable as *products* of the culture pattern in any determinate sense."

The Lone Criminal

While some criminal activity is a group phenomenon, some of it, in all areas, is committed by persons who are not members of criminal groups. Even in those areas in which the influence of deviant subcultures is most pronounced, there are violators who act as individuals and who do not belong to the groups or do not even know of their existence. Although certain crimes are characteristically the work of what may be called "criminal isolates," there may be exceptional instances in which the offense in question is a group phenomenon. Most criminal homicide, for example, is committed on an individualistic basis by people who do not belong to any group advocating or condoning murder (Wolfgang, 1957). However, some groups promote aggressive and militant policies or lesser forms of violence that may lead to murder; some are explicitly committed to assassination and murder. As an example, we may refer to the hired killers of the organized, large-scale mobs referred to as the Syndicate, the Mafia, or in recent years, the Cosa Nostra. In the political area, assassination has frequently been used by dissident and militant revolutionary groups.

We have elsewhere discussed the professional thieves who make theft a means of livelihood, and there are many such occupations, including those of pickpocketing and shoplifting. While relatively little picking of pockets is done by amateurs from outside the criminal world, there is a great deal of shoplifting by such persons. It is well known that large department stores, self-service stores, and all sorts of industrial and commercial enterprises expect to lose annually a certain percentage of their supplies or products to thieves. The latter, as a rule, are not professionals, but are either employees or ordinary "noncriminal" customers. Shoplifters in grocery chains usually are housewives who are thrifty shoppers attempting to combat the high cost of living (Cameron, 1964). Embezzlers and white-collar criminals are generally also individualistic offenders. These offenses present quite different theoretical and practical problems from those posed by the crimes committed by members of criminal groups. The reaction of the offender to apprehension and punishment, his rationalizations and ways of reducing guilt feelings, the effectiveness of control measures, and the sources or causes of the behavior are markedly different (Cressey, 1971; Benson, 1985).

Because they are not members of a criminal organization or group, criminal isolates—prior to their apprehension—have a position or status in the legitimate world. When they are processed by the apparatus of the criminal law, this legitimate status is placed in jeopardy and is often lost or greatly reduced. If they are imprisoned, these offenders find themselves among a variety of persons who have little in common except that they are all prisoners or convicts; upon release, many of them will become exconvicts and share their recollections of having been "inside." This shared experience with the labeling, defining, and degrading ceremonies of the criminal law sometimes frightens the lone deviant and prevents her from repeating the offensive behavior. At other times, it may cause her to try to work her way into the social structure of the criminal world (Shover, 1985).

Because lone criminals stand to lose whatever status they have in respectable society by being tagged criminals, the trauma of formal punishment for them is likely to be roughly proportional to their status. While a short jail sentence may mean relatively little to casual workers and even less to professional criminals, it may represent a major personal tragedy to a corporation executive. Although the courts that impose punishment measure its severity in terms of time in prison and amount of fine, they cannot control loss of status.

Lacking the protective practical and symbolic devices the criminal societies invent to reduce the hazards of their activities and to assuage their consciences, and having no status in a criminal society, the lone or individualistic criminal is especially vulnerable to apprehension and punishment, as well as psychological trauma. In dealing with the latter, he must—if he does not move into a criminal society—rely on personal resources or on those provided by officials for the rehabilitation of offenders. For reasons of this nature, formal punishment is probably most effective for the individualistic criminal, and least effective for professional or subgroup crime.

CONCLUSION

Behavior and people are inherently neither deviant nor nondeviant, but come to be labeled one way or another by virtue of the reactions of others. These reactions range from strong approval to violent disapproval. Negative reactions to disliked persons and acts may, on the one hand, result in the application of formal control measures such as prosecution and imprisonment or, on the other, be expressed informally through gossip, rebukes, or simple avoidance. Persons may be stigmatized as deviants because of what they do, or they may be pushed into deviant social activities because of their appearance. They may drift into deviance, choose it, or become trapped in it through accident, ignorance, or unfortunate circumstances. Social psychologists have studied the ways in which behavior comes to be labeled as deviant, the effects that this has on the deviants and their groups, and the symbolic devices used to counteract or neutralize it. Measures designed to reduce or control deviance sometimes have the opposite effect. Deviance is a complex and pervasive phenomenon and occurs throughout the whole range of human relationships. It is found, for example, in the various agencies that are supposed to enforce the rules, and also in deviant groups in which members violate the deviant norms.

Some forms of deviant behavior are governed by norms and values of subgroups within the broader society—for example, political deviance. Other forms do not have direct group support, but are engaged in by persons as individuals rather than as group members. Criminals, drug addicts, and homosexuals form subsocieties within our culture, but by no means do all criminals, addicts, or homosexuals join these deviant social worlds. The lone deviant and the eccentric person present practical and theoretical problems that are very different from those posed by deviant groups.

SELECTED READINGS

BECKER, H. S. (1973). *Outsiders: Studies in the sociology of deviance.* New York: Free Press. Chapter 10, "Labelling Theory Revisited," summarizes and criticizes the responses to the interactionist view of deviance set forth by Becker in 1963.

LEMERT, E. (1972). *Human Deviance, Social Problems and Social Control.* (2nd ed.). Englewood Cliffs, NJ: Prentice-Hall. An important set of essays by a theorist who anticipated the theories of deviance that emerged in the 1960s.

ROSENBAUM, M. (1981). *Women on heroin.* New Brunswick, NJ: Rutgers University Press. A provocative theoretical and ethnographic analysis of the female heroin addict. Utilizing a social worlds perspective like the one developed in this text, the author shows how the worlds of heroin use differ for women as opposed to men.

SHOVER, N. (1985). *Aging criminals.* Beverly Hills, CA: Sage Publications. A valuable study of what happens to criminals as they age and attempt to live "straight" lives.

CHAPTER FIFTEEN
Illness, Aging,
and Dying

Illness, aging, and death, along with the rituals that surround their social organization, constitute social and biological facts that affect every human society. *Illness,* whether painful, chronic, transitory, or terminal, dislodges persons from their ordinary rounds of activity. *Aging,* often associated with entry into the social worlds of the elderly, the retired, and the chronically ill, signals the movement into the final stage of the life cycle. *Death* disrupts and alters ongoing social relationships. All social groups and societies develop procedures, routines, rituals, institutions, and classes of experts to manage the disorganizing and disruptive effects of these three interrelated phenomena. They are of interest to the social psychologist for a number of reasons.

First, illness is painful and pain is rooted in the body. Like dying, illness and pain are not merely biological events; they involve the subjective interpretation of physiologically based events. Groups and social worlds develop their own vocabularies for interpreting pain, illness, and illness-related processes. These vocabularies transform purely physiological and biological events into socially defined events that can be consensually understood and, hence, acted on. They connect the internal environment of the person with the socially based "naming process" (see Chapter 5).

Second, the definitions that surround the aging experience and the social worlds of the elderly constitute realities that bring new transformations to the self and its social relationships. These transformations deserve study in their own right, for they mark significant developmental changes in the life cycle.

Third, dying is not a biological process that stands independent of social interpretation or social interaction. A death must be socially produced. The person must be defined as "dead," an increasingly problematic definition to make. Social arrangements must be made for disposing of the dead; these involve rituals which signify the "passing on" of the dead (Sudnow, 1967), and may include the scheduling of funeral and inter-

ment services (Salomone, 1973). Periods of mourning and grief may be observed. Ties to the dead must be severed at least partially, and the commitment of the living to their ongoing social life among the living must be reestablished.

Fourth, the reality of death must somehow be conceptualized within any society, such that its existence does not overly disrupt ongoing social interactions. Death must be assigned some "meaning" which minimizes its effect upon the living. Societies and groups vary in the definitions which they bring to this experience; indeed, it can be said that in many societies persons die socially before they die biologically. It may take such rituals as the funeral to affirm the finality of a physiological death (Riley, 1983, pp. 191–216).

CHRONIC ILLNESS, PAIN, AND MEDICAL TECHNOLOGY

In Chapter 5, we discussed pain in terms of location in the body, its frequency of appearance, duration, and intensity. We examined how pain is defined in terms of personal and medical labels. Here, we wish to go a bit deeper into issues related to pain, including chronic illness and medical technology. We will first discuss pain-entered emotions.

The Linguistic Foundations of Pain-Centered Emotions

What arouses the emotional expression of pain is determined by social situations rather than by physiological processes. The physiology of a painful experience does not determine how it will be emotionally expressed. The arousal and expression of a pain-centered emotion may be analyzed in terms of three phases:

1. A stimulus or situation that is defined or interpreted in certain ways; for instance, a contraction during childbirth.
2. An internal response to the defined situation, involving both physiological and symbolic pro-

Act	Situation	Definition	Resulting Emotion
Contraction of stomach muscles	During childbirth	Allowable pain	Pleasure that it's starting; frustration
Contraction of stomach muscles	Onset of menstruation	Normal, to be expected	Irritation
Contraction of stomach muscles	A boxing match	"He got me!"	Anger; chagrin
Contraction of stomach muscles	Suffering from the flu	"Why me?"	"When will it end?"; show of pain and discomfort

cesses. Here, the source of the pain must be located; its frequency of occurrence, duration, and intensity may also be noted.

3. An outward, conventionalized expression (by means of words, gestures, and facial expressions) that serves to indicate and hence convey the emotion and pain to others.

A given external situation or act does not call forth a pain-centered emotion until it has been interpreted in a certain way. The emotion is a response not to a raw stimulus as such, but to a defined, classified, and interpreted stimulus, to signs with meanings that vary according to situation, as shown in the accompanying table. The physiological aspects of emotional response (such as a rise in blood pressure, a changed heartbeat, and increased activity of the ductless glands) are not learned forms of behavior. On the other hand, the symbolic processes involved in emotion are learned. The third phase of emotional behavior sometimes has been called the *mimicry* of emotion because persons may voluntarily utilize the conventional means of emotional expression without actually experiencing the genuine emotion. The actor does this constantly, but mimicry is commonly used in ordinary life as people strive to conform to the polite usages of social intercourse and to evoke on the part of others their own felt sense of pain and discomfort.

People may pretend to be in pain when they are not, and others may suspect that they are pretending. In certain circum-stances, it is clear to all parties that excruciating pain is being experienced; no pretense is necessary when a young child suffers a broken finger as the result of a slammed car door.

The Taboo of Pain

In Western societies, there is a social taboo against the excessive *experiencing* of pain, just as there are taboos against the excessive or overly dramatic *expression* of pain. While ill persons are expected to experience and express pain, the experiencing of pain is regarded as evidence of medical neglect, just as the repeated assertion that one is suffering from unbearable pain is taken as evidence that the person is not being properly treated. Properly ill persons do feel pain, but their pain and their expression of pain should fall within socially prescribed dimensions. Modern health care systems, for example, are organized to minimize the importance of pain during one's stay in the hospital. Those who challenge social understandings about pain and its expression make medical nuisances of themselves.

People who claim intense and worsening pain often find that the medical staff begins to ignore them. Strauss and Glaser (1970, p. 109) report one such instance:

Since Mrs. Abel . . . complained loudly for all to hear, the nursing staff found her an increasingly difficult cross to bear. . . . They reacted not only by spending less and less time within beckoning distance of the patient but by disengaging each other from her room when stuck there. They carefully arranged staff rotation, so that nobody would have to spend much time with her.

If it is illegitimate or deviant to express excessive pain, it is also inappropriate to acknowledge the fact that certain persons, especially those who have just died, may have actually died in pain. Death, in contemporary Western cultures (Aries, 1974), is expected to be a peaceful event into which one slides without pain or discomfort. Sudnow (1964, p. 146) observes:

The concern over whether or not the deceased experienced any pain before his death is typically voiced by the relative, who asks . . . "Did he have much pain before he died, Doctor?" . . . Universally, it seems, the doctor answers, "No," when asked if pain was experienced and in most instances provides a form of "elaboration" which the following recorded comment typified: "He was under heavy sedation right until the end and I can assure you that he experienced no discomfort at all."

Chronic Illness and Pain

Chronic illness, in contrast to acute illnesses and diseases—such as an appendicitis attack or a sudden heart attack—is characterized by recurring, chronic pain. It is estimated that over 20 million Americans constantly seek medical care for chronic pain (Kotarba, 1977, p. 257; 1983). The chronic pain experience often leads to a dependency on pain-killing drugs and to their abuse; indeed, persons suffering from chronic pain may become drug addicts. Such persons also seek out medical doctors and acupuncturists for treatment.

According to Kotarba (1977, p. 260), sufferers of chronic pain develop a certain level of secrecy about their feelings and suffering. We quote one of Kotarba's respondents, a 60-year-old widow who injured her arm in a fall (Kotarba, 1977, p. 261):

I don't complain to anyone about my arm. In the first place it's nobody's business. People call you a

hypochondriac if you complain all the time. . . . It's better just to keep it to yourself and your doctor. . . . My sister complains all the time and everybody makes fun of her.

People who suffer from chronic pain learn how to manage it. They may treat themselves with heating pads and aspirin. Not accustomed to being in pain, the person who suffers chronic pain soon comes to believe that the pain cannot be relieved. Being in pain becomes part of how the person defines herself. Some patients undergo operations in the hopes that their pain can be removed. As the pain lingers, and if operations are not successful, chronic pain sufferers learn to alter their daily routines so as to lessen the pain they experience. They may alter their patterns of lovemaking; they may change jobs and drop certain hobbies. They may "spend all leisure time on sedentary activities such as watching television" (Kotarba, 1977, p. 269).

Age significantly influences how chronic pain is defined and experienced. Middle-aged persons may accept chronic pain as part of growing old. Young persons may face a crisis of self because of the pain (Kotarba, 1977, p. 270).

Self-Pity and the Chronically Ill

Self-pity is a common emotion for those who suffer chronic illness and chronic pain. Charmaz (1980, pp. 123–45) has studied the social construction of self-pity in the chronically ill. By self-pity, she refers to a label which includes the tendency to "overindulge" in self, to have grief and regret about one's situation, and to feel sadness, a sense of loss, a feeling of victimization, misfortune, helplessness, and injustice about one's plight. Persons feeling self-pity often ask, "Why me?" and develop resentments toward others who do not suffer from the chronic illness they are inflicted with.

Three factors seem to shape how self-pity is defined. These are the self-concept of the ill person, lifelong patterns of self-concern, and the nature of one's relationships with others. Individuals may not express self-pity to close family members because they want to maintain a self-image of not being sufferers or complainers. Such individuals may express their self-pity to others, including nurses, social workers, and physicians. The development of self-pity, according to Charmaz (1980, pp. 129–35), occurs under socially structured conditions. These conditions are (1) when the illness is discovered or defined as being progressive; (2) when ill persons have been defined as socially discredited because of the illness and because of their past responses to it; and (3) when the ill person comes to see herself as a burden to others. Charmaz (1980, p. 133) quotes one woman:

All I can do is dissolve in tears—there's nothing I can do. I just get *immobilized*—you sort of reach a point, you can't improve, can't remedy the situation, and you're told you aren't in the right category for getting the services you need and can't get for yourself. It makes me madder and madder at myself for being in the situation in the first place.

Self-pity may be transitory, or it may totally engulf a person's life. Charmaz (1980, p. 142) quotes a woman who went through both phases of feeling self-pity:

I was sick of their pitying looks and concerned voices. I didn't want their pity—I would just stay away if they felt like that. So I withdrew. But after a time I realized I pitied myself more than anyone else pitied me. So then and there I decided, I wouldn't let this keep me down; I was going to do something with the rest of my life.

Chronic Illness Trajectories

People have careers with chronic illness and pain. We have seen how people who experience self-pity move from intense involvement in pity to a position where they get past feeling sorry for themselves. Strauss, Fagerhaugh, Suczek, and Wiener (1985) have examined illness trajectories of the chronically ill; they have also examined the medical technology and medical work that go into the treatment of chronic illness. We shall summarize part of their findings.

By illness trajectory, they refer to "not only the physiological unfolding of a patient's disease but to the total *organization of work* done over that course, plus the *impact* on those involved with that work and its organization" (Strauss et al., 1985, p. 8). For different chronic illnesses. the trajectory will be different and will involve different medical personnel, different treatments, different life experiences, and so on.

Trajectories can be routine or problematic, lingering or fast, and they can occur in multiples involving several different treatments at the same time, or in sequence. A heart patient, for example, may require immediate acute care and then be shifted to long-term care where physical therapy and the like are required. Strauss et al. (1985, pp. 15–16) offer the example of a patient who had been hospitalized for the fourth time. She had been diagnosed as having lupus erythematosus. As a result of her lupus she now had (1) pericarditis, (2) pleuritis, (3) cerebritis, (4) chronic obstructive lung disease caused by her lupus and heavy smoking, and (5) as a result of the steroid treatments she was receiving she had gastric ulcers and (6) cushingoid syndrome.

This patient required several different types of treatment. She had a trajectory that was regarded by everyone (physicians, nurses, and herself) as problematic. She had several different medical and illness trajectories going on at the same time. She had multiple treatment managers who often became confused over their areas of responsibility. Several different medical and technical departments had to be used. It was difficult to predict treatment outcomes given the several different medical interventions that were going on simultaneously.

This case illustrates how multiple forms of chronic illness in the same patient create interactional and social organizational problems for both patient and staff. It suggests that control and contingencies, unforeseen events, scheduling problems, diagnostic projections, and therapeutic action all have to come together if treatment is to be accomplished. The chronically ill face special problems, not the least of which is understanding what all the treatments they receive mean.

A key problem for the chronically ill, especially those who are required to be treated by modern medical technology, is coordinating their illnesses and their bodies to machines.

Medical Technology

Strauss and his associates have analyzed the machine work that goes on in hospitals. As any visitor to a modern hospital will quickly notice, machines are everywhere: X-ray and EKG machines; respiratory machines; TV screens monitoring the operations of machines; computers monitoring other machines. These machines present several problems, two of which are tending and monitoring; a third is teaching patients how to be compliant so that the machines can do their work on them.

Hospital staff are now trained to tend, monitor, and maintain machines. When machines break down, they have to be repaired; the safety of machines has to be monitored, and the accuracy of the machines must be maintained.

Every machine used with patients requires connection to the patient's body. These connections differ from machine to machine. The problems with machine connection vary by the trajectory phase of the patient and the condition of the receiving part of the body. Strauss and associates (1985, pp. 55–56) note that some machines go inside the body, and others attach to the outside of the body; some must be connected for long periods of time, and others are temporary; some machines cause pain and discomfort, and some are dangerous to use.

These problems affect medical work, the treatment process, and the patient; there is always the danger that a patient will die while on a machine (Strauss, et al. 1985, p. 58).

Chronic Illness, Technology, and Hospital Organization as Sources of Hazard

Many chronic illnesses, of course, are life-threatening. When the illness is coupled with the technology required to treat it, two sources of hazard are combined. For example, a person suffering from cancer is threatened both by the illness and by the old and new chemotherapeutic drugs used to control the disease (Strauss et al., 1985, p. 70). Similar processes are at work with open-heart or brain surgery, where surgical procedures and machines can cause life-threatening problems.

The organization of hospitals also creates problems concerning medical treatment of the chronically ill. Hospitals are generally quite decentralized in terms of ward functioning and work; this decentralization affects the safety of patients. Each ward is responsible for the functioning of its own machines; if there are safety departments, they often lack force to have their guidelines carried out. This means that there are often only a few safety guidelines that are monitored. Strauss et al. (1985, p. 72) offer an example of this problem. The researcher had been discussing a recent electrical blowout in the hospital with an environmental safety person:

He had been discussing, with the dialysis staff, emergency plans for evacuating patients in case of disaster. When he found out it takes an hour to unhook the patients, he hit the ceiling. He kept mentioning during the interview twenty minutes for evacuation, like it was a magic number—the usual time required to get people out. He had been pushing the physician, he said, to come up with a plan so that patients can be unhooked as quickly as possible without endangering them.

This same person, when pushed by the researcher, revealed that he had no safety plans for unhooking patients from machines in the critical care areas of the hospital. Chronically ill people often appear to be in a situation where they may die from their illness, or from the technology created to treat the illness.

Sentimental Work

An essential feature of chronic illness is that it impinges on the emotional life of the person. Crippling, deforming, and stigmatizing symptoms are sources of self-pity for patients. Accordingly, a great deal of medical work involves dealing with these negative emotional experiences. Strauss et al. (1985, pp. 129–50) call this sentimental work. There are several different types of sentiment work; Strauss and associates discuss the following: (1) interactional work, (2) trust work, (3) composure work, (4) biographical work, (5) identity work, (6) awareness context work, and (7) rectification work. We will briefly discuss each.

Interactional work involves organizing treatment so that the patient is not treated just like an inanimate object. Often patients are not treated as moral, individual beings. For example:

When my daughter-in-law had that burned retina, they had a parade of thirty doctors come through, and all that they told her was that, "You're going to be presented in rounds." . . . So there was this army that walked through, but nobody looked at anything but the eye in the dark (Strauss, et al., 1985, p. 133).

Trust work is when staff build a relationship with the patient that is caring and creates, for the patient, a belief that staff can be trusted. *Composure work* is when staff help patients maintain poise and self-control. This often involves getting to know the patient and his biography. This kind of *biographical work* blurs with *identity work*, where medical staff make an effort to understand a patient's personal identity. Such understandings also involve considerations of *awareness context work*—asking what the patient knows about her situation at any given moment in time. *Rectification work* occurs when patients become upset about the treatment they are receiving; here, staff attempt to rectify errors and soothe a patient's feelings.

Chronic illness creates special problems for patients and medical personnel. The preceding discussion indicates how the social psychologist studies and analyzes just a few of these problems.

THE SOCIAL WORLDS OF THE DYING CHILD

Myra Bluebond-Langner (1978) has studied the private yet social worlds of the dying child. Her subjects were young children, ages 3 to 9, who were dying from leukemia. She examined how the children came to know they were dying, how and why they attempted to conceal this information from their parents and medical staff, and how these adults attempted to conceal from the children their awareness of the child's impending death.

She learned that young children learn to confront the death taboo in our society, the idea that one does not discuss impending death. She found that the dying children directly confronted their own and other children's death; they became preoccupied with death and disease imagery in play, art, and literature. They often sought out adults to discuss their own death, avoided talking about the future, and became concerned with getting things done immediately. She found that the children, contrary to many theories of child development, took an active hand in the organization of their own lives. They were able to conceptualize death and its meanings. They were able to move from the world of living to the world of death with some ease. The stages of dying that Elizabeth Kübler-Ross (1969) has identified—denial, anger, bargaining, depression, and acceptance—were all confronted and dealt with by these young children; often they did a better job than their parents.

Awareness of Death

Bluebond-Langner utilized Glaser and Strauss's (1965) concept of awareness context as it relates to the dying trajectory (see

Chapter 10). The awareness context refers to what a person in a situation knows about his own and the other's status in the context of their shared interaction. Glaser and Strauss identified four types of awareness contexts: closed, suspected, mutual pretense, and open awareness. In the closed context, related to the dying trajectory, the patient does not know of her impending death, even though everyone else does. In the suspected context, the patient suspects what the others know and tries to confirm or invalidate that suspicion. In the mutual pretense context, both parties (patient and family or staff) define the patient as dying but agree to act as if she were going to live. In the open awareness context, everyone is aware that the patient is going to die and they act on this awareness relatively openly.

The awareness context affects the interaction that goes on between the patient, staff, and family. For the children that Bluebond-Langner studied, the mutual pretense context was the dominant mode of interaction. Even when children tried to open up interactions and directly confront their death, their parents did not cooperate.

Stages of Dying Awareness

The leukemic children acquired factual information about themselves and their disease in five stages. Following the diagnosis of leukemia, these stages were: (1) learning that this was a serious disease; (2) learning the names of drugs and their side-effects; (3) learning the purposes of treatment procedures; (4) experiencing the disease as a series of relapses and remissions minus death; (5) experiencing the disease as a series of relapses and remissions that would lead to the child's death (Bluebond-Langner, 1978, p. 166).

Each of these stages was marked by more disease-related information. What was learned in one stage was necessary for moving to the next stage; however, in order to move from one stage to the next, the child needed specific disease experiences like nosebleeds and bone

pain to gather disease-related information. As children moved through these stages, they related the information they had acquired to their specific experiences in the clinic, with various medications, and so on.

Changes in Self-Concept

As they moved through the five stages of acquisition of information, they also passed through five different definitions of themselves (Bluebond-Langner, 1978, p. 169). These different self-conceptions are labeled (1) well (prior to diagnosis); (2) seriously ill (after diagnosis); (3) seriously ill and getting better; (4) always ill and will never get better; (5) dying (terminally ill).

The following dialog reveals how these children moved from stage 4 to 5, both in terms of information and self-conception (Bluebond-Langner, 1978, p. 183).

Tom: Jennifer died last night. I have the same thing. Don't I?

Nurse: But they are going to give you different medicines.

Tom: What happens if they run out?

Other children made statements like: "You see, I'm dying"; "I'm not going to be here for your birthday"; "I'm not going back to school" (Bluebond-Langner, 1978, p. 184).

We will take up the topic of dying and death in greater detail next: We introduced this discussion of the private worlds of dying children at this point to indicate how children, as competent interactants, structure and give meaning to the pain and illnesses they experience when they are about to die.

THE SOCIAL WORLDS OF THE OLD

Aging is a social process that is subject to different definitions. The age 65 as a significant milestone in the aging process is supported by biological criteria, for the average life-expectancy for man in thirteen European countries of Western culture is 65 years

(Havinhurst, 1956; Cowgill, 1980). For women, the age is slightly higher. Chronological age is somewhat arbitrary, however, and some have proposed a social definition that stresses reductions in social competence (Havinhurst, 1956). Nonetheless, the age 65 is commonly utilized when enumerating the proportion of a population that is old or aging. Most Western societies, in fact, employ this definition, as evidenced in their pension, health care, and social security programs (Schultz, et al. 1974), although some countries may vary from the standard of 65 years by a few years either way. By using the definition of aging as 65 years or older, we discover that approximately 10 percent of the total population of Americans is in the aging category. Western societies, for various reasons, vary in the proportion of their population which is age 65 or older. In Denmark, 12 percent of the population falls in this category; in Finland, 8 percent; in the German Democratic Republic, 15 percent; in Sweden, 13 percent; and in the U.S.S.R., 7 percent. These figures suggest that the social worlds of the old and the aging are sizable. In addition, we can expect these worlds to increase. When the post-World War II "baby boom" population becomes 65 and over, there will be a significant increase in the proportion of "aged" to "nonaged" people in American society. By the year 2030, the ratio of the retired population (over 65) to working population (20–64) in the United States will change from 18 to 26 percent.

Attributes and Images of the Old

It has been suggested that an old age "subculture" is emerging in the United States (Hochschild, 1973, pp. 24–25). This subculture, in part a reaction to the increasing stratification of American society along age-specific, work-related, and kinship lines, stresses a return to the values and ideologies of rural America at the turn of the century. The values of the small town, of an ethnically divided nation, and a fond memory of earlier historic times and customs are seen as characteristic of this "subculture" (Hochschild, 1973, pp. 7–9). The old have formed this social world perspective in response to (1) pressures to retire by age 65; (2) increased leisure time as a result of early retirement or loss of family roles; and (3) a weakening of the family's functions as social welfare and educational agencies take over the family's responsibilities in the areas of health care, child supervision, and extended family support in the forms of financial, moral, and social assistance.

The elderly, it is argued (Cumming & Henry, 1961, pp. 14–23; Cumming, Henry, & Damianopoulos, 1961, pp. 210–218), have been cut off from the mainstream of modern industrialized society. They may become social and psychological isolates who have *disengaged* themselves from society. Freed (or cut off) from the interactions and demands of family and work, the old are thrown together and often forced to live in age-segregated residences, which may range from retirement villages to care-centers, from run-down hotels to the back wards of mental hospitals for the senile. This isolation from the "youthful" and gainfully employed sectors of society reinforces the construction of an age-based subculture or social world and further isolates the elderly from their familiar worlds of discourse, thought, and remembrance.

Disengagement Theory

A popular theory of aging has been set forth by Cumming and Henry (1961). Termed *disengagement theory,* it contains the following postulates:

1. Although individuals differ, the expectation of death is universal. . . . Therefore a mutual severing of ties will take place between the individual and those others in his society who belong to his social groups.

2. Disengagement becomes a self-perpetuating process, for once bonds have been cut, the

freedom from other bonds is thereby increased.

3. Because males occupy instrumental roles in American society and females occupy affective roles, the process of disengagement will differ accordingly.

4. Disengagement may be initiated by the individual or by society, as when a male fails to adequately perform on the job.

5. When both the individual and society are ready for disengagement to occur, complete disengagement results. When society is ready and the individual is not, the result is usually disengagement.

6. Because disengagement results in the loss of central roles, personal crises will be produced for the individual if he cannot find new roles to fill.

7. Persons can ready themselves for disengagement if they perceive that death is near.

These postulates and a number of additional correlates suggest that elderly and aging individuals in American society often die socially before they die biologically.

Disengagement theory assumes that the growing isolation of the elderly person is a natural process, in part a consequence of the increasing "depersonalization" and industrialization of American society. Furthermore, it assumes that kinship ties cease to function as symbolic and moral links to the common worlds of family life. The theory does not account for the "nondisengaging" behaviors of certain groups and of certain individuals. Elderly rural Americans, for example, are still commonly absorbed into the fabric of the extended family; those persons who do not leave the labor market at age 65 often have been observed to lead healthy, involved, and politically influential lives into their late 80s. Both Charles de Gaulle and Winston Churchill were in their mid-80s when they died; Pablo Casals was 93, and Picasso was 86.

Disengagement theory, then, may apply only to special sectors or populations of the aged. In addition, it may apply only under specific social circumstances.

The Functions of Disengagement

We must recognize, however, that the disengagement of the aged in modern society, as Blauner (1968, p. 352) observes, enhances "the continuous functioning of social institutions." It permits the changeover of personnel in an orderly manner, without the disruption that would occur if positions were filled only after persons worked to the end and died on the job. Blauner remarks on the chaos that followed the Kennedy assassination and suggests that most bureaucracies could not tolerate or function in the face of high mortality in the middle years of the adult work-cycle.

Consistent with our social psychological perspective, we are inclined to argue that persons' attitudes toward aging will directly reflect the definitions they hold toward themselves as aging individuals. A theory of aging which ignores personal and social identities will be devoid of insights into the subjective elements of the aging process. As presently stated, disengagement theory tends to neglect the *interpersonal context* in which aging occurs. There is also an assumption that death represents an ugly and undesirable end to the life cycle. This view is contradicted by the beliefs of many individuals and social groups (Aries, 1974, p. 32).

If the interpersonal context of aging is considered, we would assume that like-situated persons who share similar world views and experiences would develop, over the course of time, a set of friendly, if not intimate, primary group relationships that would integrate each of them into a common community of discourse and interaction. If a newcomer finds herself fitting into such a structure of social relationships, and if others accept that person, a niche for her will be found, if not created. If the identities, social relationships, and images of self offered to individuals fit their ongoing conceptions of themselves, then they will not experience isolation, or negative disengagement. In short, as Rosow and Hochschild (1967; 1973) have suggested, old people living in a community of peers are much less likely to disengage, to isolate or cut themselves off from society, or to feel that they have been so cut off.

We turn to a study of a community of the aged which was conducted by Hochschild among the residents of Merrill Court, a small apartment building for the elderly and the retired in the San Francisco Bay area.

An Unexpected Community

The residents of Merrill Court were mostly rural-born, white, working class, Anglo-Saxon Protestant, widowed females in their sixties. Only five were men, three of whom were widowed. The widows' husbands had been carpenters, construction workers, farmers, grocery clerks, and salesmen. Three-fourths of them had come to California in the early 1940s. These residents of Merrill Court had developed their own community, based on close, almost "sisterly" bonds. The widows of Merrill Court exchanged cups of coffee, lunches, potted plants, kitchen utensils, and baked goods. They watched after one another's apartments, and they took phone calls for each other. They shared in common conversations, and their topics ranged over problems which confronted all of them: would Medicare pay for chiropractors, what were the visiting hours at various hospitals, which kinds of dentures were best, how much were TV repairs, and what was the latest development in daytime TV soap operas.

Merrill Court, Hochschild (1973, p. 38) reports, "was a beehive of activity." There were weekly meetings of the Service Club, bowling schedules to be met, Bible study classes to be attended, birthdays to organize for, crafts to be made out of discarded household items, and Christmas cards to be cut out for the Hillcrest Junior Women's Club.

The social arrangements of Merrill Court took on a life of their own. "They were designed, as if on purpose, to assure an *on-going* community" (Hochschild, 1973, p. 47). The residents of Merrill Court felt that they were valued members of the local community. Della, a club president who like past presidents had come from a small town, expressed this sense of belonging as follows:

Since I've been president here, I feel we are part of [the town] just like the VFW and the Eagles. "Why do they come to us [referring to other organizations]?" some of the women ask. They come and say they want 50 favors to be made for the Mayor's conference. They come to us because they think we can do the job; they wouldn't come to us if they didn't think that. It's an honor (Hochschild, 1973, p. 56).

The residents of Merrill Court had disengaged themselves from their earlier social worlds and social relationships. Within their own group, however, they produced an *unexpected community,* a social world unique in its customs, rituals, and routines. Hochschild's research provides an empirical challenge to disengagement theory and suggests that more ethnographies of the social worlds of the elderly are needed.

What, for example, do the aging worlds of the racial and ethnic minorities in the United States look like? How do American Indians, Japanese-Americans, Spanish-Americans, Greeks, and Hungarians age and grow old in large metropolitan locales? How do the ill and poor age and carve out lives in diners, parks, rundown apartment houses, and cheap hotels? Recent research suggests that the average income of couples over age 65 is on or near the poverty level. The mental and physiological deteriorations of the body, which accompany aging, must be coupled in future ethnographies with studies of the elderly urban and rural poor. Such persons often lack access to proper medical care, thereby increasing the negative effects of aging.

Hochschild discovered a community of elderly people who were not isolated. It remains for future investigators to probe the worlds of such persons as the following elderly male (Hochschild, 1973, pp. 137–38):

He lingers at the counter making talk with the waitress.

"What'll it be today?"

"Well, what do you have for me? You got some of that homemade potato soup? That's a good soup. We used to have that at home. Back in Michigan."

"Anything else today?"

"Coffee. My usual coffee. My mother won a prize at the county fair with her potato soup. She had a secret recipe."

"And what else? Some dessert?"

At a quarter of five, he is slowly eating his potato soup, his pie, and sipping his cup of coffee. He remarks:

"I used to be a very busy person. I used to have plenty of friends." He lives at the Executive Hotel at $2.00 a day. He plays solitaire in his room and watches television in the downstairs lobby.

"The Executive's alright," he says. "Now I just came here four years ago; but there are some older folks who *live* here."

Social Involvement in the Social Worlds of the Elderly

David R. Unruh (1980, 1983) has criticized disengagement theory for its failure to consider a social worlds perspective in the study of the lives of older people. He notes (1980, pp. 159–65) that a variety of social worlds and subworlds of involvement exist for the elderly, and these are often ignored. The following are examples of what he has in mind: (1) the subworld of senior gleaners; (2) the California Old Folks bicycling club; (3) the worlds of ballroom dancing and bingo; (4) the social world of antique selling and gathering.

Each of these social worlds draws elderly persons into networks of communication and interaction. They provide the opportunity for trying on new and multiple social and personal identities. Various types and levels of involvement in these worlds can be identified. Senior centers, for example, allow strangers to get involved in new social worlds like art, dance, and music. Some elderly people act like tourists and become involved in new worlds out of curiosity and make few, if any long-term commitments. Others become regulars and insiders to new worlds of involvement. Unruh quotes a 78-year-old bicyclist (1980, p. 164):

I've brought a lot of guys into cycling, ya know. When they see the publicity I get, they say, "By gosh, I'm going to do that too! If that guy can do it, so can I." There are a lot of good racers out there who are twenty or thirty years younger than I who have seen me and got started in cycling. Some of them turned into very good racers and that makes me feel good.

This man is a regular and an insider in the world of cycling. The social worlds perspective that Unruh develops suggests that students of aging examine the social, organizational, and interactional structures that bring the elderly together. A social world perspective alerts us to the multiple strands and lines of action that unite older people with others, including their age peers and others who share similar interests with them (Unruh, 1980, p. 165).

Living and Dying Behind Closed Walls

Fontana (1977) and Gubrium (1975) have studied the social lives of elderly persons who live in nursing homes. We shall review some of their research.

Fontana employed a dramaturgical framework in his study of Sunny Hill Convalescent Center. The stage where this drama of life occurred consisted of a building with two wards, situated one below the other. The center was located on a six-acre site in the middle of a small town. Rooms with two beds were located on both sides of the corridors with adjoining toilets between two rooms. Each ward had a large recreational lounge furnished with sofas, armchairs, chairs, and a television set. Each also had a nursing station. At the end of each corridor was a large bathroom where aides washed patients. The lower ward had a small waiting hall for visitors.

The actors in this setting were the staff—consisting of an administrator, a bookkeeper, two janitors, a laundry person, the kitchen staff, and the nursing staff and aides. The rest of the cast consisted of the patients. Staff classified patients into two categories: those who were "up and about," and those "in chairs," meaning those in wheelchairs. Another classification consisted of "feeders" and "nonfeeders." "Nonfeeders" were patients who could feed themselves; "feeders" had to be fed by staff.

The interaction that occurred in the center could be divided between staff-to-patient, patient-to-staff, staff-to-staff, and patient-to-patient. The Cheshire Cat, from *Alice In Wonderland,* might have been a resident at Sunny Hill for she captures, in the following lines, the approach to patients at this facility (Fontana, 1980, pp. 486–87):

"But I don't want to go among mad people," Alice remarked. "Oh, you can't help that," said the Cat: "We're all mad here. I'm mad, you're mad." "How do you know I'm mad?" said Alice. "You must be," said the Cat, "or you wouldn't have come here."

Staff-to-patient interaction is characterized by Fontana, following Strauss and Glaser (1970), as "work-time." "Work-time" at the center was organized in terms of shift-time. The day shift had the responsibility of getting patients up for breakfast, changing their bed linens, feeding them, bathing them, and taking them to lunch and back to their rooms after lunch. In addition, medications had to be given. There was never enough time to treat patients as human beings; they were treated as work objects. This meant that patients competed with one another for staff time. Patients existed on another time schedule, their own, and in that schedule they often tried to get personal attention from the staff; they would wave their hands or call to aides.

Many of the patients felt that they were prisoners. Fontana (1980, pp. 492–93) describes one patient as follows:

Mr. Anderson used to live in a boarding house. One day the people who managed the house told him that he had to go to the doctor for a check-up. He was taken to the center and has been there ever since. He feels that this is illegal, and that the doctor signed his release to the center because he is a good patient, ambulatory and quiet, and they wanted his money. He has written to his daughter about it but has received no reply. Mr. Anderson . . . feels as if he were in a prison.

In many cases the patients Fontana studied felt that the only person they had to interact with was themself.

Living and Dying at Murray Manor

Jaber F. Gubrium (1975) studied a nursing home he called Murrary Manor. Part of his research involved examining how the clients in the nursing home spent their time. He identified a number of major time categories, including: (1) passing time, (2) sitting around, (3) keeping track of time, (4) eating, (5) walking, (6) sleeping, (7) watching, (8) talking, (9) ceremonials (eg. church services), (10) therapy.

A great deal of time at Murray Manor was involved in what Gubrium called body-work. By this he refers to bathing, eating, walking, taking medications, sleeping, and bowel movements. A great deal of staff and patient talk concerned talk about bowels. Many patients were either constipated or had diarrhea, or were incontinent; some had to have daily enemas. Complaints about the disgusting habits of certain patients were common—those who piddled on the floor, "crapped in others' rooms," or just couldn't keep clean (Gubrium, 1975, p. 186). One patient described this concern for bowels in the following words (Gubrium, 1975, p. 186):

I know it's funny sometimes when you think about all the talk that goes on here about it (bowels). But ya talk and ache about your bowels all the time. I don't know why an eighty-two-year-old woman has to be bothered with bowels. I'm so packed, if I don't have a movement, I'll blow up. I sit down and hit my stomach and it's hard. Ever since I came here, it's been bowel problems all the time—all that rice and noodles that we eat.

Dying and Death at Murray Manor

According to Gubrium (1975, p. 197), there were three worlds of dying and death at Murray Manor: the worlds adhered to by top staff, floor staff, and clientele. These worlds often clashed. Top staff (administrators) viewed death and dying as part of the routine work of floor personnel; they treated it like an administrative problem. Floor staff felt that the administrators treated the dying of clients like "funeral men."

All patients and residents defined their futures in terms of death (Gubrium, 1975, p. 198). The problem, for them, was when they would die. They all had "dying" self-conceptions, to use Bluebond-Langner's term. One resident speaks about his death (Gubrium, 1975, p. 198):

All I can think about is that God will call me someday. They'll take me out and bury me. I don't think nothin'. I take it day by day. I don't plan anything, because generally when you plan somethin', it never turns out that way anyway. So I don't try to think or make any plans whatsoever. I take it day by day and leave the rest in God's hands.

When patients and residents died, staff had to prepare them for removal from the center. This meant they had to be bathed and dressed. Gubrium (1975, p. 213) describes this process:

Aides washed the body of the deceased, as if they were performing the usual bed-and-body work on living bedfast patients. For example, when an "alert" roommate is present on the other side of a pulled curtain, aides preparing the body refrain from talking about it in a depersonalized fashion, since this would signify to the roommate that it is lifeless. The dead patient is adjusted (face and body posture) to make him appear to be sleeping. His eyes are closed, his mouth shut, and his head turned to one side. The appearance of the "sleeping" dead and the sleeping living are strikingly similar.

Old age is a stage in the life cycle that nearly every individual enters (Quadagno, 1980). The social worlds of the old are diverse; they cross-cut income, racial, ethnic, religious, sexual, occupational, and kinship boundaries. Entry into this world signals a confrontation with dying and death, which we discuss next.

DYING AND DEATH

Every social structure must confront the biological and social realities that surround the eventual death of its members. Whether expected or accidental, whether involuntary or deliberate, death is a "biological and existential fact of life that effects every human society." Death, an approaching reality for the elderly, is an obdurate factor of everyone's reality, however frequently dismissed. Death produces serious organizational, moral, occupational, political, religious, and kinship problems for all human societies. The statuses held and the functions previously performed by the dead person must be filled and carried on. Orderly transitions of power and leadership from the dead to the living must be organized. Affective obligations and duties, previously met by the dead person, must be transferred to other members of the community. The symbolic and sacred moral worth of the dead person must be established and either affirmed or denied. The bonds that tie the dead individual to the living, whether these be relatives, citizens of a nation, or coworkers and friends from the past, must also be symbolically signified. In short, all social structures organize ritual acts which recognize and take note of death and of the dead.

In recognizing the "passing on" of the dead (Sudnow, 1967), societies and social groups establish a moral and symbolic distance between the living and the dead. As Blauner (1968, p. 357) suggests:

The social distance between the living and the dead must be increased after death, so that the group first, and the most affected grievers later, can reestablish their normal activity without a paralyzing attachment to the corpse.

There are, however, efforts to maintain a symbolic link or social and historical relationship with the deceased person. Funerals and interment ceremonies, while formerly disposing of the deceased body, symbolically announce that the living have properly cared for the body, the self, and the reputation of the person who has died. Grave markers, flowers placed on graves, photographs of the deceased, printed announcements in newspapers commemorating the death of a father or mother, memorabilia such as treasured rings, watches, quilts, smoking pipes, books, coin collections, and other valued objects (often passed from generation to generation) all serve to record the fact that the dead person still occupies a place in the social worlds of the living.

But before links to the dead can be established, their death must be a confirmed fact. A death, as was noted at the beginning of this chapter, must be socially produced.

Dying

David Sudnow (1967) investigated the place and production of death and dying in the social organization of hospitals. Such an investigation was warranted on at least two grounds. First, hospitals are the major setting for dying in our society, and second, little sociological attention has been given to the care and definition of the "terminally ill" or dying patient.

Sudnow's concern was with an identification of the events, cues, and symptoms physicians utilize when they define a patient as "terminal." His interest was processual, for persons must first be defined as dying before their deaths can be certified. He notes that (1967, p. 65)

In certain medical circles there is considerable disagreement over the precise biological meaning of death; some argue that the cessation of cellular activity constitutes death, and others insist upon a more specific attention to properties of cellular multiplication. . . . Some persons argue that "dying" is a thing which becomes recognized once a deadly disease is located, i.e., that "dying" is a state wherein a person suffers from a disease which is nonreversible and is known to "produce death."

The location of a "death-causing disease" will not explain those deaths where no disease is discovered; for example, death from a gunshot wound. The cessation of cellular activity also will not explain the cause of death, for it is only a "sign" at best, an operational definition of the fact that a "death" is in process.

These remarks suggest that disease categories and measures of cellular multiplication are not, in and of themselves, causes of death in any biological sense. They are social categories, or linguistic labels, which members of the medical community utilize when they formulate a diagnosis and prognosis of a patient who appears to be "dying." Such categories are predictive indicators that serve to make the *dying trajectory* of the terminally ill patient understandable (in medical and lay terms) and, hence, controllable.

Social Death, Clinical Death, and Biological Death

Considerations of this order led Sudnow (1967, p. 62) to propose that deaths occur within a social order that links the person not only to the medical order of the hospital, but also to the social worlds of kinship, work, aging, and illness. "Dying" provides a set of definitions that permit not only the patient but also the patient's kin and the hospital personnel to orient their actions to the future; that is, they can prepare for death's actual occurrence. By placing persons in the "dying" category, hospital personnel establish a way of attending to them (1967, p. 75).

It places an interpretative frame around the experiences of dying persons such that these experiences can be processed within the medical order of the hospital.

In County Hospital—one of two medical settings Sudnow studied—patients who were considered "dying" or "terminally ill" had their names posted on the "critical patients list." Morgue attendants would regularly consult this list so that they could make an estimate of the work load for the coming week. Physicians who were in need of special organs for research projects were alerted to upcoming deaths, and nurses were encouraged to speak with members of the patient's family concerning the chances of getting permission to relinquish the patient's eyes, liver, or other organs for research.

At County Hospital, the Catholic chaplain would regularly check the critical patients list to determine which patients should be administered their last rites. Many "posted patients" did not die, even after they had received their last rites. The priest reported that "such cleansing [was] not permanent . . . and that upon readmission to the hospital one must, before he dies, receive last rites again; the first administration is [was] no longer operative" (1967, p. 73).

In these senses, seriously ill "posted patients" can be regarded as candidates for an autopsy *before* their death; that is, their medical death actually precedes their biological death.

It is now possible to distinguish three categories of death: *clinical death,* which signals the appearance of "death signs" upon physical examination; *biological death,* which is marked by the cessation of cellular activity; and *social death,* which occurs at that time when the patient is "treated essentially as a corpse, though perhaps still 'clinically' and 'biologically' alive" (1967, p. 74). Socially dead persons are, for all practical, moral, and symbolic purposes, treated "as if" they are dead. Once persons have socially died, they can be treated as absent others whose affairs now become the sole concern of others. Their personal effects can be disposed of; funeral ceremonies can be scheduled; caskets can be picked out; and the final costs of a burial plot can be paid for. Insurance policies can be cashed, and retirement benefits can be applied for.

Sudnow (1967, p. 77) gives a typical instance of a "social death." A male patient was admitted to the emergency unit with a perforated duodenal ulcer. He was in critical condition for six days following his operation, and his wife was informed that his chances of survival were slim. She stopped visiting the hospital upon receipt of this information. The patient, however, began to show marked improvement and was released from the hospital after two weeks. He was readmitted the next day and died shortly thereafter of a severe coronary attack. Before he died, he told the following story concerning his experiences upon returning home. His wife had removed all his clothing and his personal effects, and had made arrangements for his burial. He found his wife with another man, and she was not wearing her wedding ring. The patient reported that he left his house, began to drink heavily, and suddenly suffered a heart attack.

If the *dying trajectory* of the terminally ill person were to be charted, it would appear that clinical death precedes (though not always) social death, followed then by actual biological death. However, a person may be defined as socially dead even before a clinical diagnosis is performed. Indeed, there are certain benefits to narrowing the temporal gap between clinical, social, and biological death, not the least of which involve the fact that an inevitable process is brought to rapid conclusion, thereby lessening social and psychological grief. A rapid death reduces the ambiguities—interactional and personal—that surround the relationships between the living and the dead, and it permits the living to return to the routine demands of their everyday worlds. (Morticians, furthermore, find that their best results are obtained "if the subject is embalmed before life is completely extinct—that is, before cellular death has occurred" (Mitford, 1963, p. 70). In the average case this would mean within one hour after the heart ceased beating. Such haste raises fears of live burial, fears which are allayed by embalming itself. The removal of blood from the body, which "prevents" infection and discoloration, "has made the chances of a live burial quite remote" (Mitford, 1963, p. 70).

Dying Trajectories

The dying career of a terminally ill person has a variable temporal shape (Glaser & Strauss, 1965, p. 23). It may be short-term, or long and lingering, or it may vacillate between periods of recovery and periods of "near" death. The social, clinical, and biological definitions that surround one's dying career also shift and take on new meaning over time. If patients' biological death lingers, their social death may be hastened. On the other hand, if their biological death is unexpected and perhaps instant (as in an accident), it may take days or weeks before their social death is actually realized.

A patient's dying career appears to involve a series of "critical junctures" (Glaser & Strauss, 1965, p. 13). First, the patient is defined as dying. Second, staff and family make preparations for the death. Third, death is defined as inevitable. The fourth juncture is the final descent into death, which ends in the fifth (the last hours), the sixth (the death watch), and the seventh (the death itself). At some point in this career, announcements may be made that the patient is dying, or that he is leaving one phase and entering another. After death, legal pronouncements must be made, and then the death is made public.

The Awareness of Dying

As the patient moves through the dying trajectory, the awareness or knowledge of the impending death becomes problematic. Members of the medical staff may withhold critical knowledge about a patient's state of "dying" from kin as well as from the patient. Physicians may not inform members of the nursing staff that a patient is about to die. The information each person in the dying situation has about the identity of the other and her own identity in the eyes of the other refers, as we noted earlier, to the *total awareness context of a social situation* (Glaser & Strauss, 1965, p. 10). In the dying situation (as in all situations), four contexts of awareness can be identified. An *open* awareness context exists when each interactant is aware of the other's true identity; in this case, a patient and her family would both know that the patient is terminally ill and that death is near. A *closed* awareness context exists when neither party to the interaction knows the other's identities or intentions. In many dying situations, patients may not know that they are about to die, and they are thus unaware that their family is making plans for their death. A *suspicion* awareness context prevails when at least one party to the interaction suspects the true identity of the other. A wife may suspect that her husband is dying, yet neither the husband nor the hospital staff have informed her of his condition. A *pretense* awareness context is produced when both parties are fully aware of one another's identities, but act as if they are not. In many situations, for example, a husband and a wife will deny the fact that the husband is dying.

THE SOCIAL CONSEQUENCES OF DEATH: MOURNING

Death sets in motion a series of processes that serve to distinguish the living from the dead and thereby establish a continuity in the life cycle. Perhaps its major consequence is to disrupt the relational worlds of the living, in particular those intimates who mourn the passing of the deceased (Gorer, 1965, p. 112).

On the basis of extensive research in Great Britain, Gorer (1965, p. 11) proposed that most adult mourners pass through three stages: a short period of shock, which usually lasts between the occurrence of the death and the disposal of the body; a period of intense mourning accompanied by withdrawal from the external world, often linked with weight loss and lack of rest; and a final period of readjustment in which mourners return to their normal rounds of activity. Gorer (1965, p. 112) observes that

The first period of shock is . . . generally given social recognition. Kinsfolk gather around the mourners for the family gatherings, religious ceremonies and, often, ritual meals. . . . Once the funeral, and possibly the post-funeral meal, are finished, the ritual which might give support to the bereaved is finished too, and they are left to face the period of intense mourning without either support or guidance. . . . The customs of Britain . . . prescribe usually in great detail the costume and behavior appropriate to mourners in the period of intense mourning after the funeral; they also typically impose an etiquette on all those who come in contact with the mourners; and usually designate the number of days, weeks, months or years that this behavior should be followed.

Mourning, while a social process and one which reflects each mourner's relationship to the deceased, is concomitantly a ritual act that is imposed upon the person by the social group. On this, Durkheim (1947, p. 397) has argued:

. . . mourning is not the spontaneous expression of individual emotions . . . mourning is not a natural movement of private feelings wounded by cruel loss; it is a duty imposed by the group. One weeps, not simply because he is sad, but because he is forced to weep. It is a ritual attitude which he is forced to adopt . . . but which is, in a large measure, independent of his affective state.

Among mourners in contemporary American society, the mourning debt is repaid, in part, through purchasing floral arrangements, visiting the funeral home, and assisting the preparation of post-funeral meals for the members of the immediate family. One's relationship to the deceased, and to the living members of the deceased's

family, stands suspended until one or more of these ritual acts have been completed, or at least attempted. For the immediate family, the purchase of the casket (Salomone, 1973) takes on some significance; not only must a casket (or some suitable substitute) be purchased, but its cost will define the moral worth of the deceased person (and perhaps of her remaining family). If a casket cannot be purchased, the funeral ceremony cannot be completed, and the mourners find themselves in the uneasy situation of still having to grieve. A 1979 strike involving four major vault manufacturers and Teamsters Union Local 786 in Cook County, Illinois (O'Connor, 1977) placed some 1500 families in a situation where their funerals could not be promptly completed because of the unavailability of caskets. One woman remarked (O'Connor, 1977, p. 5):

It is hard enough to lose your mother, but this kind of thing just leaves you hanging—knowing the funeral is not completed. . . . Now we'll have to go through all of that grief again when we bury her. . . . At the time of the funeral, you are surrounded by relatives and friends. Now when we go out there [to the cemetery], it will just be us.

The obligatory character of mourning is well displayed in the death practices of the Kiowa Apache, reported on by Opler and Bittle (Opler & Bittle, 1967, p. 473):

Among the Kiowa Apache the reaction to a death was immediate and violent. Close relatives wailed, tore their clothes, and exposed their bodies without shame; some shaved the head, lacerated the body, and cut off a finger joint. . . . A widower went to great lengths to show his grief. Sometimes he requested relatives of his wife to gash his forehead or to cut off all his hair, and gave presents to the one who performed the service.

The Social Shaping of Grief

Lofland (1985, pp. 171–90) has examined the proposition that grief is a universal feature of human nature. She defines grief (1985, p. 172) as "a response to the involuntary loss through death of a human being who is viewed as significant by the actor of reference." She argues that the data which would test the universality of the grief emotion are not available; this makes the universalistic hypothesis suspect. She further suggests that grief is shaped by social factors including (1) the level of significance of the one who dies; (2) the definition of the situation surrounding the death; (3) the character of the self experiencing the death; and (4) the interactional setting in which the prior three features occur.

Lofland (1985, p. 176) offers the following example to make her point. She quotes from Volkart's discussion of an anthropologist's (M. W. Spiro) analysis of the Ifaluk people.

In his study of the Ifaluk people, Spiro was puzzled by some features of bereavement behavior there. When a family member dies, the immediate survivors displayed considerable pain and distress, which behavior was in accordance with local custom. However, as soon as the funeral was over, the bereaved were able to laugh, smile and behave in general as if they had suffered no loss or injury at all.

Grief, then, is an emotion which follows death; but its shape, its meaning, the length of time it is expressed, and how it is expressed vary from one cultural and historical group to another. The character of grief, like that of mourning, is variable. The conditions that appear to produce grief are these: (1) the person is connected to a small number of highly significant others; (2) death is defined as personal annihilation and as unusual and tragic except among the aged (Lofland, 1985, p. 181); (3) persons take their emotionally states seriously; and (4) there are interactional settings which provide the opportunity to contemplate and express the loss (Lofland, 1985, p. 181).

THE MEANINGS OF DEATH

As an event which disrupts social structures, death represents an elaborate ritual occurrence that forces the living to define and re-

establish their own relational ties to one another. The paradoxical consequence of death, then, is that the movement of a member out of a social group becomes the occasion for affirming the group's very foundation and basis of existence. For without acknowledging—however ritualistically—the "passing on" of one of its members, the group as a collectivity runs the risk of having no one recognize its collective or individual death. The rituals of death, from this point of view, function in a self-serving manner for the group.

Death and its rituals reaffirm the social order. As a social process, death and dying represent the interplay, at the group level, of biological and social events. For as we have shown, a biological death cannot occur until the occurrence of "social death" has been established. That social death often precedes biological death is a measure of humans' control over the termination of the life cycle of themselves and their fellows. Peter Freuchen's discussion of the problem of the aged in Eskimo society makes this point rather forcefully. He describes the social and then biological death of an elderly woman named Naterk (Freuchen, 1967, p. 178–81):

[Old Naterk called her son Mala]. "I am tired and I am old. You must build me a snow house because I shall go on a very long journey all alone." . . . Thus Mala built a house . . . . Then she crawled into the house built for her and quietly stretched out on the old skin. Soon Mala came. . . . He now took his knife, cut a block of snow and walled up the entrance with it. . . . There, then, the old woman reposed, waiting for death. . . . How hard it was to play dead. But Old Naterk was no longer to be reckoned among the living. To the others she had passed on; she was gone. . . . Life, surely, was much more wearisome than death. But the most wearisome thing of all was this slow transition from life to death.

CONCLUSION

Illness, aging, dying, and *death* represent social and biological processes that find their meanings and interpretations both in the human body and in the human social group.

They are of concern to the social psychologist because they are recurring events that all social structures and all groups must confront. Their meanings are often lodged in disparate social groups, so that illness, aging, and dying vary from group to group. The social worlds of the elderly have assumed a subcultural flavor which emphasizes solidarity and mutual support of others. Death, whether clinical, biological, or social, is surrounded by a complex network of ritual acts that serve to establish the relationships between the living and the deceased.

SELECTED READINGS

BLUEBOND-LANGNER, M. (1978). *The private worlds of dying children.* Princeton, NJ: Princeton University Press. A troubling and powerful study of the way young children confront and experience death.

GUBRIUM, J. F. (1975). *Living and dying in Murray Manor.* New York: St. Martin's Press. A useful ethnographic depiction of life in a nursing home.

SUDNOW, D. (1967). *Passing on: The social organization of dying.* Englewood Cliffs, NJ: Prentice-Hall. An outstanding account of death and dying in the modern hospital.

Epilogue:
Science as Symbolic Activity

Social psychology, like other social sciences, aspires to be scientific; but like them, its status as a genuine science is disputed and often denied. Certainly none of the social sciences can be said to have produced an organized, precise, structured body of reliable knowledge that compares with those of the advanced natural sciences. There are many who believe, indeed, that this is not possible, that there is a basic indeterminacy or unpredictability in human behavior—perhaps even "free will"—which makes the search for a science of human behavior futile.

SCIENCE AS SYMBOLIC ACTIVITY

We have noted that the symbolizing capacities of humans mean that they live in symbolic environments. The world out there is not reacted to directly, but through the mediation of symbols. So even if different groups live on the same physical terrain and under the same sky, it is not necessarily the same terrain or the same sky for all of them. The sky, for instance, can be the abode of a family of gods, the container for a hierarchy of seven ascending heavens, or the small segment of an expanding universe that is available to the naked eye from one small body called Earth. This idea of symbolic environments is also pertinent to changing conceptions and emergent communities; the same terrain and sky—say, in and over the high Sierras—are, or were, symbolized and reacted to differently by painters, mountain climbers, environmental geologists, and by the explorers and travelers of a century ago.

These examples purposely include the idea of science because science, too, gives new and ever-changing conceptions of the physical universe. As one historian of science, Thomas Kuhn, has asserted (correctly, we believe) in writing about scientific paradigms (or conceptual frameworks) (1970, p. 110):

Examining the record of past research from the vantage point of contemporary historiography, the historian of science may be tempted to exclaim

that when paradigms change, the world itself changes with them . . . Of course, nothing of quite that sort does occur: there is no geographical transplantation; outside the laboratory everyday affairs usually continue as before. Nevertheless, paradigm changes do cause scientists to see the world of their research-engagement differently.

Of course, the scientists in any given field have complex versions of the reality which they thus seek to conceptualize. In the following pages, science will be discussed with primary emphasis on two matters: its relation to changing symbolic environments, and its aspects as a conceptualizing activity.

THE HISTORY OF SCIENCE

The Emergence of Modern Science

Modern science, as a specialized institution and form of human symbolic activity, appeared on the historical scene in approximately 1600 and is associated particularly with the famous investigations of Galileo. Its emergence is often referred to as the "Galilean revolution" because it signaled the rejection of an old tradition dominated in Europe by religious philosophers and theologians, and by the doctrines of Aristotle that had long been imbedded in the teachings of the Church. Prior to this approximate date, what we now call scientific thinking was not sharply differentiated from other types of intellectual activity, and there was no separate and distinct literature, logic, method, point of view, or tradition that characterized what we, in retrospect, regard as significant contributions to the early development of the scientific view. Modern science, with its own methods and its own logic, developed rapidly in Europe during the 1600s with the organization of the first scientific associations, stimulated by the accomplishments of a long list of famous scientific giants: Galileo, Harvey, Descartes, Newton, and others. Since that time, science has become a basic social institution that has revolutionized social life and thought throughout most of the world. Modern science did not come into being suddenly in one fell swoop, but was preceded by a long earlier evolution that made it possible. The writings of the ancient Greeks are prime examples.

The Classical Greeks

While the ancient Greeks are credited with many important prescientific and scientific ideas, Greek science did not become science in the modern sense, although one may say that it was a near miss. The Greeks are said to have invented logic, and from them we inherited the phonetic alphabet, which revolutionized communication and made Greece perhaps the first significantly literate society. The Greeks glorified "Logos," the intellectual processes, and they glorified logical discourse, but they never hit upon the idea of an expanding system of knowledge and theory geared to direct observation, with experiment as its test. They also never succeeded in using their knowledge to harness nature as we have done through the creation of an elaborate technology. Prestige was associated primarily with the skillful and persuasive use of words and mathematical symbols, rather than with the direct, systematic confrontation with evidence. This may have been connected with the existence of slavery, which led the Greek intellectual aristocrats to think of the hard, messy labor involved in much research as something beneath them, something for slaves to do.

The Arabian Period

The answer to the our query is that, apart from the Greek influence that was preserved and perpetuated by the Church—especially by the incorporation of Aristotelianism into Christian dogma—Greek learning was kept alive and added to by the Arabs, who translated many of the Greek documents into Arabic. During the period from about A.D. 900 to 1200 there was especially intense intellectual activity within the Arabic world, and a number of cities within the Arab empire became famous centers of learning, where scholars met and had access to the best libraries then in existence. When, after several centuries, European interest in the East was stimulated (as, for example, by the Crusades), European scholars began to use more frequently materials and ideas made accessible to them through Arabic sources. This process added greatly to the ferment of ideas in Europe which was the basis and source of the emergence there of modern science.

Preconditions of Science

To appreciate more fully that modern science is a social institution deeply rooted in society and dependent and responsive to developments within it, we should note some of the earliest social developments prior to the flowering of ancient Greek civilization. Over a period of several thousand years, the human populations had greatly increased; and when the first great civilizations came into being, people began to live together in relatively large numbers in cities. The prior development of agricultural arts and technologies, such as the cultivation of grain and the domestication of animals, made a settled agricultural life possible, and also—by making the production of food easier and more efficient—created the possibility of social classes, including a leisure class that devoted itself to intellectual, religious, and artistic pursuits.

Commerce and trade developed between the peoples and empires of the ancient world, promoting the collection, recording, and transmission of information and ideas from one place to another. Numerical and writing systems were invented and improved as the centuries passed. Observations were made concerning all sorts of natural phenomena—for example, the apparent movement of the stars, planets, and the sun and moon. A remarkably accurate calendar was devised by the ancient Babylonians. The art of shaping metals for use in warfare and in other pursuits was gradually improved. As various empires, city-states, and kingdoms evolved during this period, they found that trade was absolutely vital to them, for example, as a means of producing the metals needed to forge effective weapons for warding off invaders and political enemies. Transportation of materials and of people by land and sea promoted exploration, fostered the exchange of ideas and the spread of inventions, and stimulated the curiosity of those with intellectual natures. Of particular importance was the gradual perfection of written languages and numerical systems, which made it possible to record observations and happenings and laid the foundations for the beginnings of mathematical reasoning and logic.

The classical civilization of Greece thus did not burst into bloom in a vacuum, but was instead the product of a long historical evolution, dating from the time that our human ancestors ceased to be hunters and nomads and adopted a settled, agricultural lifestyle. The Greeks, like all civilizations before and after, depended upon prior cultural, political, and technological accomplishments and built upon them.

A SCIENTIFIC MODEL: THE CAUSE OF MALARIA

As a model of the successful solution of a scientific problem, we take an example from the biological sciences—the discovery of the cause of malaria. This model is widely known and relatively simple, and is from a natural science field that is not so advanced and far removed from the social sciences as nuclear physics is, for example. (We mention physics because social scientists often draw their models from it.) The model proposed here has additional advantages in that it suggests modes of analysis and problem solving that seem applicable to human behavior.

We will describe how the explanation of malaria was discovered, and then indicate some of the implications that this example has concerning various aspects of scientific method. We will confine ourselves strictly to points that are either implicitly or explicitly involved in our example. John Dewey, incidentally, used the same example to illustrate the nature of scientific logic (1938, pp. 433–36).

The literal meaning of the word *malaria* is "bad air," and it reflects early theories which attributed this disease and others to polluted atmosphere, putrid miasmas, exhalations from swamps and stagnant waters, or simply night air. Malaria was a serious scourge in ancient times and was described by Hippocrates in the 5th century B.C., as well as by early Chinese, Arabic, and Roman writers. Before the time of Christ, the connection between the disease and stagnant water was noted, and drainage was utilized as one preventive measure along with a host of others. It was also suggested that mosquitoes might have something to do with spreading the disease, but many other theories were also proposed, and malaria was often confused with a number of other diseases. Long before the cause of malaria was discovered in the late 19th century, the disease was treated with the bark of a tree that contained quinine.

The cause of malaria today seems to many to be such a simple, taken-for-granted fact that it should be observed that About 20 years of research by many scientists in various nations were involved in the discovery of malaria's cause. About 200 years earlier, a pioneer in microscopic observation—van Leeuwenhoek—observed and described bacteria, but little attention was given to his observations until the second half of the 19th century, when the sciences of bacteriology and immunology were established by Pasteur, Koch, and Lister. At this time, the microorganisms involved in a number of plant and animal diseases were identified and studied, and the role of insects in transmitting diseases became known. The guilt of the mosquito with respect to disease other than malaria was established before the crucial research on malaria was done.

The discovery of the cause of malaria began in 1880, when a French physician described a malarial parasite obtained from the blood of one of his patients. Italian investigators later demonstrated that the disease could be transmitted from human to human by infected blood, and in the 1890s British and Italian scientists suggested the mosquito (anopheles) as the transmitter of the disease. By 1900, it had been established that this theory was correct, by demonstrating that the disease was acquired only from the bite of an infected mosquito, and that persons protected from this mosquito did not contract the disease even in regions where malaria was rife. The biological cycles of the parasite had been traced out in sufficient detail to explain why quinine was an effective remedy, why the bite of an infected anopheles mosquito did not transmit the disease until days after the mosquito had become infected, and why other kinds of mosquitoes than the anopheles did not transmit the disease.

There are four subtypes of the malarial parasite, which is known as plasmodium—each of which has its own characteristic pattern of biological changes as it passes from its primary host (the mosquito) to its secondary host (the human). In the mosquito, the parasite undergoes sexual reproduction in the mosquito's stomach and, after a variable period of days, spores or seeds produced in the walls of the mosquito's stomach enter its salivary glands and thereafter are injected, along with saliva, into the bodies of future victims. It is only when this occurs that the insect becomes capable of spreading the disease.

When injected into the human skin by the mosquito, the "sporozoites" migrate to the liver, where they grow and multiply asexually. Again, after a period of time, they begin to release, periodically, broods of new parasites called merozoites, which enter the blood stream and invade the red blood corpuscles. Inside these corpuscles they multiply until the corpuscle ruptures and releases a cluster of new parasites that invade other corpuscles to repeat the cycle.

When an anopheles mosquito draws some of the blood of a malarial victim into its stomach along with parasites, a small percentage of the parasites (known as gametocytes) are not digested and it is these that reproduce sexually inside the mosquito's stomach. There are about 200 kinds of anopheles mosquitoes, some 60 or so of which transmit malaria. Other kinds of mosquitoes do not transmit the disease because when they ingest the parasites, they digest all of them.

Repeated attacks of malaria may confer immunity of varying degrees, but this immunity is specific, not only with respect to the four species of plasmodium, but also with respect to the numerous strains within each. A person immune to one strain may be reinfected by another. In addition to humans, monkeys, birds, reptiles, and some other mammals are susceptible to malaria.

Malaria is not ordinarily fatal, but it tends to recur because some of the parasites are able to hibernate in the liver for as long as 20 to 30 years. In some instances, persons may have in their blood malarial gametocytes which die if they are not sucked up by a mosquito, but which do not attack the red corpuscles or produce the disease. Such persons can transmit malaria even though they themselves do not have it. Death from malaria may result from anemia produced by destruction of red corpuscles, from excessive fever, or from clogging of blood vessels in vital bodily parts.

The story of the cycles of biological change that the malarial parasite goes through in its two hosts has only been sketched here in incomplete form. It has been noted that the parasite moves from stomach, to salivary glands, to skin, to liver, to blood stream, changing in size, appearance, and form as it does so. We have also noted that the symptoms of the disease vary greatly from case to case, depending on a wide variety of factors such as the individual's condition, the species or strain of the parasite, degrees of immunity, and others. The onset of malaria still sometimes is not recognized at once, but may be definitely established by microscopic examination of a blood sample. Counting the number of parasites in a given unit of blood provides a rough indication of the severity of the attack.

SCIENTIFIC LOGIC

The Nature of Causal Processes

Using our example as a point of departure, we can note that the theory of the cause of malaria that was demonstrated to be correct at the end of the 19th century is now accepted as an established fact. Ordinary laypersons speak of malaria as a disease with a known cause, and while it may be affected by a wide variety of factors in its severity and incidence, it is ordinarily said to have only one cause—there is only one way in which the typical pattern of symptoms is produced. There are many other diseases that have been similarly analyzed and explained; there are others, like cancer, that are not understood and whose causes are unknown. While it is said today that there are about 30 substances that produce or cause cancer in humans or in lower animals, the term "cause" is used in a popular and statistical sense only—not in the same sense in which this term has been traditionally used in modern science. Thus, while there may be some 30 substances that sometimes cause cancer in a loose sense, it is only too obvious that cancer is not understood today, and that its cause has not been established with a certainty at all comparable to that of malaria. Unlike the cancer situation, the cause of malaria is always present when the disease exists, and the disease cannot occur when it is absent. Moreover, in the case of malaria, in addition to the *invariability* of the relation between cause and effect, there is the element of *uniqueness* of the relationship. The cause of malaria produces malaria only; it does not produce any other disease.

To make sense of this, it is necessary to conceive of cause as a process—not as a thing, factor, event, or variable. Only if this is done does it make sense to say that any disease has a single cause. If one chooses to designate as "causes" all of the things, events, factors, and variables that are involved in a disease, the situation becomes hopelessly complex. For example, if one considered the vast numbers of such items in the causation of malaria—there are so many of them at the submolecular level alone, and so many of them are not understood—it would be necessary to say that the cause of malaria was unknown and could only be known when the science of biology had reached perfection and there was nothing more to be learned.

The idea that cause must be conceived as a process is not exclusively ours, nor is it confined to biological sciences. John Dewey, after using malaria as an example just as we have, remarked of scientific induction generally: "The integral role of determination of modes of interaction in scientific method involves processes to which the name causation is given" (Dewey, 1938, p. 440). Even more explicitly, the authors of a contemporary textbook on diseases and disease processes caution the student reader (Snively & Beshear, 1972, p. 248):

> The key word is *process*. In the Introduction . . . disease was described as dysfunction. Going one step further, it becomes evident that *dysfunction* is also a *process*. In his study of pathophysiology the student should keep in mind the question, What process or processes within the body have resulted in the expression of clinical disease? By always posing this question, the student may always avoid developing shallow, mechanical notions about the nature of illness.

Almost an identical caution is applicable in our field. Margenau, a professor of physics and natural philosophy at Yale, concludes concerning causes: "A partial cause may be a thing or an event, whereas a total cause is always a stage in a process" (Margenau, 1950, p. 425).

Following the leads suggested by Dewey and Margenau, we may describe a cause as a two-stage process in which the first stage is called *cause* and the second *effect*, and in which the first stage leads to or produces the second in a series of interconnected and complex occurrences. A causal explanation of a phenomenon—be it a form of behavior, a disease, or a physical event—involves two problems. The first of these is the discovery or identification of the cause or causal process; the second is the description and explanation, insofar as this is possible, of precisely how the alleged cause operates to produce the effect. The discovery of a presently unknown causal process is not easy because of the fact that science concerns itself largely with causal processes that are not directly and easily observable. In the case of malaria, the parasite that is instrumental in producing the disease is invisible to the naked eye— its identification and the tracing of its role in the disease required the prior invention of the microscope and the systematic investigation of microbes. On the other hand, there has never been any kind of scientific mystery involved in identifying the causal agent involved when a person is poisoned by the bite of a deadly snake, since the snake is highly visible and the effects of its venom appear quickly. In the case of other kinds of phenomena—such as physical phenomena—the identification of causal processes may require a restructuring of reality and the invention of new concepts, as exemplified by modern studies of motion and gravitational fields. At other times, causal processes are difficult to access because they occur either in the interior of an organism or at a subatomic, submolecular, or even a submicroscopic level.

The second phase of causal explanation is also difficult in many instances, for much the same reasons as those cited previously. A causal process like that involved in disease may consist of a series of interrelated events, or what might be called a complex causal chain operating over a fairly extended period of time. A person infected with malaria may exhibit no symptoms for a substantial period of time. The difficulties involved in providing a full explanation and description of exactly what goes on during this period of incubation are demonstrated by the fact that there is considerable research on malaria still going on today, more than 70 years after the cause of the disease was discovered.

If one thinks of cause and effect as a continuous process, it is interesting to note that an effective means of interrupting this process in the case of malaria was known in Europe about 250 years before the disease itself was understood. By using the drug quinine, extracted from the South American quinchona tree, Europeans were able to interrupt the disease process, either in its initial or its later stage. In the former case, one speaks of preventing the disease; in the latter, of curing it. Public interest in the search for presently unknown causes of disease rests upon the realization that when the cause of a disease is known, the possibilities of successful intervention to prevent or cure it are likely to be greatly increased.

Scientific Generalization

The causal generalization in our example was of the following form: "If A, then and then only, B," where A is the causal process and B is the malaria that it produces—the effect. This type of generalization is called a *universal* because it says something about all the members of a class—that is, all instances of malaria. A contrasting type of proposition is one that applies only to some of the instances as, for example, when we say that malaria is *sometimes* fatal. The latter are called *particular* propositions. We have indicated that there is no single item, condition, factor, or influence which by itself produces malaria, but that there is one single unitary causal process that does. It is quite complex, involving many factors, items, and conditions in a series of interactions.

There is much variability in the world—so much, indeed, that one may say that no two things are ever exactly alike, whether they be physical objects, organisms, or persons. In the social sciences, this point is often emphasized by the assertion that individuals are unique, and the claim that this variability fatally handicaps the search for generalizations. If we turn to the case of malaria, we note great variability, some of which falls into types that are easily accounted for (for example, by species and strains of the causal agent); some of it, however, is a relatively simple expression of what one may perhaps describe as the natural tendency of things to vary. It is safe to say that no two cases of malaria are ever exactly the same. How, then, has it been possible to attribute malaria to a single causal process present in every case?

Generalization is possible because, while things differ and vary, there are also similarities among them. The generalization about the cause of malaria, which began as a theory and is now an accepted fact, deals with features of the disease which are recurrent and common, but does not deny the existence of differences. It is necessary to distinguish between what may be called the *essential similarities* upon which scientific definitions and theories focus, and the *nonessential differences* between instances which are always there. A similar consideration applies to the various factors and conditions that influence this disease. Some are necessary; others may be present or absent when the disease occurs. A cause, or causal process, in contrast is both *necessary* and *sufficient* in that it is always present and guarantees the effect. A necessary condition only makes it possible. Thus to get malaria, one must be a creature of a certain type, but most of these creatures do not contract the disease. Similarly, the parasite is necessary, but not in itself sufficient to produce the disease.

An interesting logical problem raised by our example is that of accounting for our confidence that all of the countless instances of malaria that must have existed prior to the discovery of the cause of the disease were caused in the same way as at present. After all, none of these instances was ever examined to determine whether or not such an assumption was valid. And how can we be confident that this is the way malaria will be produced in the future?

The fact that a scientific generalization is often stated in the form of a universal does not mean that it claims to be an absolute truth. The term merely describes the form of the assertion. If we say that all dogs have three legs, this is a universal, even though it is patently false. If we say some dogs are brown, this is true but is not a universal, simply because it applies only to some dogs—not all of them.

The role of universals in scientific generalization is closely linked to their logical form, for by making the claim of being applicable to all instances, they focus scientific attention on possible exceptions. When unambiguous exceptions to such a generalization are bound, they discredit the theory which they contradict, and stimulate the search for a better one. The exceptional instance, in short, is the growing point of science. Theories of nonuniversal, "particular," or statistical nature do not serve this function. For example, if it had been proposed in the early 19th century that poverty was the cause of malaria since most of its victims were poor this latter statement would have been true but of little significance, for everyone knew that rich persons also sometimes contracted the disease. A theory of this sort admits the exceptions in advance, and deprives them of the crucial importance that they ordinarily have in scientific work. A false universal is thus of greater importance than a valid proposition that is nonuniversal, simply because the search for exceptions that it invites stimulates attempts to improve or replace it with a better one.

The progress of science is based on ways of conceptualizing reality that foster problems connected with achieving logical consistency within the structure of current theory, and on attempts to invent improved theories that take full account of accumulating evidence. The resolution of a given difficulty tends to generate new ones, and the real world always seems to be less tidy and more complex than the theories designed to explain it.

Conceptions and Definitions of Reality

Up to this point, we have dealt primarily with modes of causal analysis and generalization and types of theories that have been proposed concerning phenomena in the natural world. We need to turn our attention to the fact that successful scientific analysis ordinarily presupposes and requires new ways of viewing—new ways of classifying and defining—the objects of inquiry. Just as scientific findings produce new views of the world, so also do new ideas of the nature of the world precede scientific developments.

As an example, we remind the reader that Hippocrates, who wrote about and practiced medicine in the fourth century B.C., is still honored and remembered today for his contributions to medical science. Why, then, did Greek medicine not continue to evolve and improve in the centuries that followed? Part of the answer is found in the Greek conceptions of health and the nature of the human body that prevailed at the time. Health was thought to involve a proper balance between the four elements (earth, air, fire, and water) and their main properties, which were said to be hot, cold, dry, and moist. Corresponding to these were the four bodily "humors": blood, phlegm, yellow bile, and black bile. The four humors, the theory held, were stirred and kept at the correct mixture by something called the "pneuma," or vital heat operating in the heart. It was unknown that blood circulates in the body, and there was only the vaguest idea of bodily structures and organs and their functions. Moreover, diseases were not sharply differentiated, since all supposedly arose from an improper mixture of the humors. Scientific research and progress obviously required the abandonment of these concepts. Later, during the Christian era, these concepts were commonly discarded in favor of the theory that disease was either an expression of the wrath of God or the malice of the Devil, to be cured by worship and prayer or by pilgrimages to shrines and holy places in order to seek miracle cures.

When events and their elements are not correctly explained and the causes of phenomena are unknown, we are uncertain or ignorant of what they are and how they should be classified. Thus, before the cause of malaria was known, malaria was commonly confused with other diseases like yellow fever; indeed, fever itself was regarded as a disease and attributed to many causes.

For the social scientist, the definitional process is especially important because many current concepts are vaguely defined, and sociological concepts often lump together obviously dissimilar forms of behavior or distribute essentially similar forms in different categories. The sociologist's problem is something like that of the biologist's in studying disease. Forms and instances of behavior that display essential, sociologically relevant similarities need to be isolated, unambiguously defined, and related to the causal processes—usually learning processes—that produce them. The prefabricated definitions that are provided us by our society and by commonsense are not likely to serve the purpose, since they are loaded with logical inconsistencies and disparities. Commonsense definitions serve practical rather than intellectual purposes, although they are commonly the starting points of systematic inquiry.

Definitions are of various types; the most obvious are those that specify types of objects or forms of simple overt behavior so as to distinguish them from other similar types. Definitions may be arbitrary, as when one wishes to talk about heavy men as opposed to men who are not heavy, distinguish between hot and cool weather, or distinguish between persons who are rich and those who are not.

Because scientists are concerned with a twofold problem of (1) generalizing about phenomena, and (2) defining and classifying phenomena in such a manner as to make generalization possible, they must be continuously alert to the possibility that failure to generalize may be the consequence of faulty definitions or classifications, or misconceptions of reality. In the process of scientific advance, the scientist's point of departure is the commonsense view, but as scientific knowledge increases, the gap between the two tends to increase, and it becomes more and more difficult for the layperson to understand scientific language and concepts.

Unintelligibility of discourse is not, however, a criterion of scientific achievement, since scientists write mainly for each other and not for the general public. Commonsense itself may not be grasped by the layperson if it is expressed in jargon or "gobbledygook."

INVENTING AND TESTING THEORY

Our model suggests that the explanation of phenomena that are presently not understood requires the search for processes that are presently unknown and unidentified. The examination of instances of the problematic situation does not automatically make the causal process evident, no matter how many instances may be observed. It is not a question of determining which one of a multiplicity of already identified influences is the crucial one, but of discovering something new, a process not previously noticed. Causal processes are not simply lying around waiting for someone to link them with their effects; they must be uncovered and are usually subsurface.

There are no established rules as to how new theories are invented. Great scientists have sometimes described the situations in which they hit upon new ideas, but little can be said of these except that they are varied. One theorist has said that his best ideas came to him as he walked up a gentle slope; another was inspired as he watched the flames in a fireplace; Newton is reported to have been struck with the idea of gravitation as he watched an apple fall to the ground. Sometimes the new insight came in a sudden and totally unexpected flash of intuition. In all these cases, the persons who made the new discovery had been deeply preoccupied with a problem. Brilliant scientific advances are not made by ignorant or idle people, but by those who are immersed in the scientific tradition and acquainted with existing knowledge. (Students interested in pursuing this line should examine books like *The Double Helix* by James Watson (1968), a fascinating description of the way in which Watson and Crick succeeded in discovering the structure of the genetic molecule, an achievement that earned them the Nobel Prize.)

Theories, once proposed, are tested in two general ways. First, they must account for the specific problem with which they are concerned. The theory of malaria, for example, had to apply to that disease and account for its symptoms; it was, of course, further corroborated in a practical way—by the reduction of the incidence of the disease through mosquito control and other measures that it suggested.

The second method of testing a theory involves how the theory relates logically to other theories and to existing knowledge. An isolated or ad hoc theory, invented to explain only a specific phenomenon, is not counted as scientific because it does not fit into a general structure. Also, no theory in any field can be accepted if it contradicts established truths or laws in other disciplines.

In the advanced sciences, theories are ordered roughly in hierarchic structures ranging from the highly general and abstract to those which are specific and concrete. Ideally, this structure should be such that all of its parts are logically interrelated and internally consistent with each other. No such perfect structure exists, but some disciplines come closer to it than others. Change in these structures is generated by cognitive dissonance which occurs when the exploration of specific theories of low generality generate embarrassing evidence that conflicts with traditional ways of thinking. This cognitive dissonance may tend to spread into the higher levels, and cast doubt on the adequacy of more general and fundamental principles which may then be revised.

Quantification

We note that neither malaria nor its cause was described quantitatively. It is often said that quantification is the essence of science, and that scientific theories must be mathematical rather than merely verbal. Apart from the fact that mathematical theories—like all others—are verbal in that they consist of written or spoken propositions, it appears that the insistence on quantification has been overstated. There are many diseases with known causes, and none has been described or explained either statistically or quantitatively. There is presently an intensive search underway for the cause or causes of cancer, and various types of theories have been proposed—none of them mathematical. However, these assertions in no way deny the enormous importance and advantages of quantitative methods and measurement when these are appropriate to the nature of the data under consideration.

In view of the emphasis upon statistical methods in the social sciences, it should be noted that while modern Western science is said to have originated in about 1600, statistical science matured about 300 years later. Galileo, for example, was definitely a mathematician, but he was not and could not have been a statistician. Statistics is actually one of many branches of mathematics, and hence, while statistics is mathematics, the latter covers much more than statistics.

In the study of diseases like malaria, the main application of statistical methods is probably the study of epidemiology or disease rates. The case against cigarettes, for example, was made in statistical form by demonstrating that the probability of lung cancer is increased by smoking. It should be observed that cigarette smoking is not called the cause of lung cancer, a valid point emphasized by the tobacco lobby. While some statisticians currently use the word *cause*, they use it in the diluted sense in which one may say that cigarette smoking causes cancer, but not in the way in which one describes the "cause" of malaria. The epidemiological study of malaria shows that malaria rates are highly correlated with poverty; and poverty, from a commonsense viewpoint, might be called one of its causes. This use of the term is radically different from the way it is used in our example and employed in the scientific tradition.

Statistical methods, it is argued, entered into the natural sciences such as physics when the particles the physicist studied became too minute to be observed directly and had to be dealt with indirectly or in the aggregate (Einstein & Infeld, 1961). In the biological sciences, statistical methods were sometimes adopted because many processes of living tissues and organisms could not be directly observed. From this point of view, statistical method is regarded as a set of techniques for describing, and analyzing, the numerical attributes of aggregates and their interrelationships. The series is the unit of analysis, not the individual. The logic involved is that of statistical probability, not that of causal analysis as illustrated in the study of malaria.

When, as in physical science, it is possible to describe causal processes and the objects of investigation in precise numerical terms, an enormous advantage is attained. Small discrepancies between predicted numerical consequences of a theory and the actual ones have, for example, often contributed to the formulation of important new ideas, as with Einstein's statement of relativity theory. However, in the behavioral and biological fields, such precise measurements of phenomena and causal processes are usually not possible. Quantification is commonly achieved by the resort to statistical description of aggregates, which necessarily involves abandoning the search for causal processes of the type exemplified by the processes that produce diseases. Considering the vital role that the latter type of analysis plays in the advanced sciences, this is an unacceptable price to pay, and most biologists—indeed, most scientists—have not done so.

Techniques of Investigation and Sources of Data

The social psychologist who is concerned with the causal analysis of complex social behavior and interactional processes must recognize that internal cortical activities or thinking processes must be considered as vital parts of the problem. This is less true of statistical studies in which the focus is on aggregates rather than on individuals, but even in this case investigators commonly feel constrained to explain their numerical findings by referring to theories about the behavior of individuals. Internal symbolic processes are obviously both complex and relatively inaccessible to close observation, a fact which poses a central issue for investigators. How are they to gain reliable information concerning these processes? The position sometimes taken—that these processes are subjective—is erroneous and unacceptable, and amounts to giving up without trying.

An obvious principle that guides all scientific inquiry is that no relevant data of any kind with a possible bearing on one's problem should be set aside or ignored. Another principle is that investigators must immerse themselves in their problem, familiarizing themselves in all possible ways with the objects of study, getting as close to them as they can so that they may observe directly whenever that is possible. Another principle is that of limited inquiry. No one, in a single inquiry, can hope to deal intensively and adequately with many theoretical issues at the same time; he must therefore deal with only one or, at most, a few issues at a time. This point is especially important in the study of human behavior, where little scientific consensus exists concerning the fundamentals and where most basic issues remain unresolved.

In the more advanced sciences, what we refer to as the principle of limited inquiry is commonly discussed in terms of the concept of a "closed system." A closed system may be regarded as the body of evidence, influences, and facts that may be relevant to a particular problem. What the nature of the facts, influences, and problems is depends upon the particular scientific field in which they are formulated. Biologists, for example, deal with biological problems and facts, not with those of other disciplines. Systems may be closed either empirically (as in a controlled laboratory experiment) or by logical devices that focus attention upon a specific issue, ruling out matters that are logically peripheral or irrelevant. Thus, in the search for the cause of malaria, investigators ignored a great deal of interesting information about the approximately 2500 existing species of mosquitoes. Had they attempted to present all such data, they probably never would have gotten around to doing anything else. Instead, they operated within a closed system, the boundaries of which were defined by the problem they were trying to solve. The same type of consideration applies to behavioral research; it is nonsense to ask investigators to tell us everything about their subjects.

From these considerations, an obvious source of information about what goes on in people's minds is what they say about it. The French scientist Fournié said, "Speech is the only window through which the scientist can view the cerebral life." And the psychologist Lashley observed that "the problems raised by the organization of language seem . . . to be characteristic of almost all other cerebral activity." (Laver, 1972, p. 61). What people report on this matter, however, cannot be simply accepted as true, since people report in different ways to different people in different situations; they may also lie or systematically distort for a wide variety of reasons and motivations. When asked why they do the specific things that one is investigating, they commonly do not know, and the answers that they give—while they may be honest and sincere—fall far short of meeting scientific requirements and standards. All of this means not that one should refrain from talking with the subjects, but rather that one should talk a great deal with them and their associates in order to ferret out inconsistencies, distortions, gaps in knowledge, and the like. What one subject says may then be compared with what others say; what they say may be compared with what they do and, in general, related systematically to any other relevant evidence in a search for recurring patterns and common features that may suggest possible modes of explanation. Once a possible theory or hypothesis is tentatively formulated, the nature of the inquiry is likely to changes its focus. Investigators, for example, may find that the implications of their hypotheses suggest new questions to ask, new distinctions or concepts that need to be formulated, and new places to look for evidence. In particular, conscientious inquiry dictates that there should be search for evidence that may not fit the hypothesis from those sources or subjects that are most likely to provide such embarrassing data should the hypothesis be false.

In addition, we should observe that once a tentative theory is under consideration, it will suggest relationships between the specific subject matter and other similar subject matters. A theory concerning some aspect of homosexual behavior and how it is acquired, for example, should bear some relationship to what is known about how heterosexual behavior is established. All of this, we repeat, implies that a great deal of talking must be done with the subjects, and even that one may need to return to them again and again with new queries.

The novelist and the dramatist commonly assume that they must familiarize themselves thoroughly with the personages and aspects of life they seek to portray; they must try to understand motivations, perspectives, ways of life. Often, the presentation in a novel or on the stage has its roots in the biography of the writer or is a portrayal of her own experiences or recollections. This brings out a point that is equally applicable to the social psychologist—namely, that self-observation is a vital aspect of understanding other people. This kind of understanding needs to be sharply differentiated from the kind that follows from scientific explanation, but in the study of human behavior it is an indispensable preliminary to the latter. Social psychologists studying people must first become thoroughly acquainted with them, perhaps by the technique known as *participant observation*, before they turn to the task of theorizing about them (Denzin, 1988). They must, in short, note what others say and do and what they themselves say, do, and think, and they should seek to work themselves into the perspective or viewpoints of those whom they study. The symbolic interactionist, in so-

ciology, has especially emphasized this approach.

We are not arguing that this is the only way to conduct a fruitful study of human interaction; only that it is one important means that is often neglected. As we have said, no source of data and no technique of inquiry should be excluded. However, we do regard as suspect those attempts to theorize about what makes human beings do and say what they do, that are not derived from direct observation and experience with the subjects. For example, we doubt if a valid theory of criminality in individuals of a given type is ever likely to be formulated by a person who has never encountered or talked with a criminal. Similarly, one may question whether the investigator whose object of study is really numbers, or "social indicators," rather than the behavior indicated by the numbers, can be expected to discover causal processes involved in the latter. Similarly, the researcher-bureaucrat who directs a large-scale study of something with the actual research being done by low-echelon employees, is too far removed from the empirical world being investigated to contribute vital new insights into it, although he may add low-level descriptions to the literature.

Another vital methodological point is that techniques of inquiry should be adapted to problems and data, not the reverse. In other words, researchers should not permit their preference for a given method—say, the statistical method—to dictate the exclusion of data not readily handled statistically, and they should not ignore important questions or problems that are not amenable to statistical formulation. At another level, no research should assume that the techniques used by those who are currently seeking to unravel the complex mechanisms, processes, and interconnections that occur in different parts of the brain are the only ways to study human intelligence and mental activity. At the same time, social psychologists can ill afford to neglect either statistical or neurological studies when the findings of these studies are relevant to their interests.

Experimentation with human beings is

sharply limited both by ethical considerations and, more basically, by the inherent incapability of controlling influences that exist within the subjects. Experimenters, of course, can readily control the external laboratory situation in which they place their subjects, but it is extremely difficult to control or even find out what the subjects may be thinking about as they answer questions or apparently follow the instructions given them. In the natural sciences, a distinction is commonly made between experiments as such and *crucial experiments*, which are definitive tests of one theory against another or others. It is the latter that are of decisive importance in the acceptance or rejection of theories. The state of theory in social psychology, coupled with the difficulties of controlled experimentation, has contributed to the remarkable scarcity of crucial experiments in this field.

On the other hand, social psychologists have access to some kinds of information that natural scientists do not. We have already emphasized one of these—talk; another such unique source is history. In the present state of our knowledge, information of an historical nature is vital for the understanding of both individuals and societies; scientific generalizations in the natural sciences are ordinarily ahistorical. Perhaps, if our knowledge of human beings were better than it is, we might be able to decide whether or not we want to associate with particular persons without reference to their biographies. As things are, it is of great relevance to know biographical data. Knowledge of the past is available in books and libraries, where one can listen to the talk of people of past ages so that one may even be able to project oneself into their perspectives and social worlds. As has been observed, most of the people who have ever lived are presently dead and therefore cannot be interviewed; books enable us to establish a kind of one-way contact with some of these people.

Scholars rely heavily on libraries, and there are many kinds of scholarly activities in the area of human behavior that are appropriately carried out in them. However, if the object of study is one that implies naturalistic observation of human animals in their native habitat, the library may be a hazard (Glaser & Strauss, 1967). The air-conditioned comfort of a convenient library may seduce ambitious scholars into skipping the arduous, time-consuming business of going out into the field to observe directly the phenomena they propose to write about. After all, the books not only describe the phenomenon, but present a variety of theories concerning it. Why then venture out to repeat observations that capable observers have already made? Why try to invent a new theory when there already are a dozen or two that seem plausible?

The fallacy in this procedure is that the world of books is different from the real world. Nothing in the library can substitute for firsthand experience with an object of study, especially when this object consists of human behavior; a balance therefore needs to be struck between the library and the field. Firsthand contact with the real world can provide us with a standard of judgment when we move into a library, and may immunize us against overly hasty commitment to prestigious theories handed down by great thinkers. (Glaser & Strauss, 1967). It can also help us to realize that an oft-repeated statement in the literature may not reflect an important truth, but may be a simple consequence of the fact that many scholars of the past have copied from the same source.

Apropos of a tendency to speak somewhat contemptuously of mere library research, we should keep in mind that all research of any kind, if it is to have significance, must be reported, recorded, and stored—usually in libraries. The hard-nosed empiricist who disparages those who spend more time with books than she thinks they should sometimes seems to imply that when her own investigations are completed, written up, and deposited in libraries, no one ought to read them. Of course, library research is an indispensable and vital source of data in the scientific enterprise. Social psychologists who propose what they regard as an important new idea or theory solely on the basis of their own research or observations, without consulting the library, have neglected an important part of their duties. When they do go to the library, they may find that their new idea is an old one that has been explored and debated for decades—perhaps one first suggested by Aristotle. Wirth has quipped that what is commonly taken for originality is usually simple ignorance of the contents of libraries. On the other hand, someone who is struggling to explore the implications of an idea that is really new is likely to find the library a gold mine of additional information that he could not possibly have collected independently. In any genuinely scientific tradition, investigators can scarcely begin their research without first acquainting themselves with the state of knowledge in the area they have chosen to explore. When they report on their own findings, by the same token, they are expected to relate them to the previous findings of others. All of this implies library research.

We return to the problem of understanding the seemingly inaccessible internal psychological or symbolic activities which play a central role in the determination of behavior. This type of problem is not actually a new one for scientists, but is as old as science itself. When events of importance are known to occur beyond the range of observation, scientists have always tried to comprehend them intellectually by inference. Sometimes it has turned out that new technologies have brought things within the orbit of direct observation which were once thought to be beyond its range. For millennia, humans have looked at the moon from a distance of more than 200,000 miles and have drawn inferences about it which turned out to be astonishingly accurate when a human actually set foot on the moon. Similar things have happened in the study of the human body, of microorganisms, and of the minute invisible particles that occupy the attention of nuclear physicists. As Einstein and Infeld observe in *The Evolution of Physics* (1961, p. 31):

In our endeavor to understand reality we are somewhat like a man trying to understand the mechanisms of a closed watch. He sees the face and the moving hands, even hears its ticking, but he has no way of opening the case. If he is ingenious he may form some picture of a mechanism which could be responsible for all the things he observes, but he may never be quite sure his picture is the only one which could explain his observations. He will never be able to compare his picture with the real mechanism and he cannot imagine the possibility or the meaning of such a comparison.

The inferential process through which one tries to get at and comprehend inaccessible things or events has been designated as *triangulation* (Denzin, 1988, pp. 16–17). What this means, in the natural sciences, is that various lines of evidence are taken into account in the inferential process. When these diverse types of data all seem to point to the same conclusion, it is often possible to form reasonably clear, plausible, or even precise conceptions of the inaccessible objects or processes.

Applying the triangulation idea to the study of human mental processes, one may get various kinds of evidence concerning them. For example, one source is what people report and what they do; other sources are the manner in which people report in different contexts and the signs that they give off unwittingly which may tell more than the words they use. Another source is the life history of the person, both as seen by her and by others; another source is the observations made of the person by her associates. As we have indicated, people's overt actions occur in a context of meanings within which mental processes also occur—a point that emphasizes the necessity of relating them to external events and which also brings the observers themselves into the formula. This has been expressed by Sullivan in a discussion of the psychiatrist as participant observer (1954, p. 19):

The fact is that we cannot make any sense of, for example, the motor movements of another person except on the basis of behavior that is meaningful to us—that is, on the basis of what we have experienced, done ourselves, or seen done under circumstances in which its purpose, its motivation, or at least the intentions behind it were communicated to us. Without this past background, the observer cannot deduce, by sheer intellectual operations, the meaning of the staggering array of human acts.

When evidence from these various lines seems to converge and be mutually reinforcing and consistent, then observers who are properly qualified by their own experience and knowledge of themselves may be able to make shrewd inferences about what kinds of processes are actually going on in another person's mind. In fact, while the inferential approach is less secure than that of direct observation, it also has its triumphs—as when an observant outsider informs a person of things going on inside his head of which he was totally unaware until they were called to his attention.

Another possibility that social psychologists should remember is that apart from the kind of research that they and their colleagues do, there are many other disciplines with interests that overlap their own from which enlightenment may come. Unfortunately, there is a tendency—created by the organizational structures of universities—for scholars not to keep up on the literature in other fields; indeed, it is difficult for them to do so. The triangulation process also applies at the interdisciplinary level, with special force. In writing this book, for example, we have been impressed by findings reported by biologists studying the human brain, as well as anthropologists, linguists, philosophers, and psychologists.

A final point is that those aspects of human experience which are genuinely subjective do not come within scientific jurisdiction at all. This is because, by a proper definition of this much abused term, subjective aspects of experience remain the private possessions of unique individuals and are incommunicable. Scientific knowledge is always in the form of propositions derived from communication and consensus within a scientific community. Knowledge, in short, is consensually validated experience; subjective experience is something else. The scientific mode of discourse is a public process from which purely personal or idiosyncratic aspects are systematically excluded because they interfere with objectivity and hence distort inquiry. In the study of social interaction, this poses a particularly difficult and important problem because the investigators are themselves social beings, part and parcel of what they are studying. The detachment that is indispensable in objective inquiry is achieved only by much greater effort than that needed to achieve a similarly objective stance with respect to the phenomena of astronomy or physics, for example.

SUGGESTED READINGS

Couch, C. (1984). *Constructing Civilizations.* Greenwich, CT: JAI Press. An interactionist interpretation of time, calendars, counting, social structure, science, and the rise of civilizations.

Denzin, N. K. (1987). *Interpretive interactionism.* Beverly Hills, CA.: Sage Publications. Presents an interpretive account of the newer hermeneutic approach to the study and analysis of social process.

Glaser, B. G. & Strauss, A. L. (1967). *The discovery of grounded theory.* Chicago: Aldine. A classic statement of the interactionist approach to discovering and writing theory in the social sciences.

Pickering, A. (1984). *Constructing quarks: A sociological history of particle physics.* Chicago: University of Chicago Press. A history of modern physics and the discovery of quarks; examines the research practices that brought quarks into "scientific" existence.

Glossary

Addict: A person addicted to a drug and to a way of life.

Alcoholic: (1) A person who calls herself an alcoholic, often (2) displaying an inability to abstain from alcohol for any continuous period of time and who, once drinking starts, is unable to control the amount that is consumed.

Amnesia: An inability to remember past experiences. One form, *childhood amnesia*, refers to the dearth of recollections of childhood experiences.

Anthropomorphism: The projection of human traits upon things not human, like lower animals.

Aphasia: The loss of the power or ability to use language; types include verbal, nominal, syntactic, and semantic. Recent research classifies aphasia in terms of *expressive* disorders (problems understanding and producing written and spoken speech), and *receptive* disorders (problems producing speech which is understandable to others).

Artificial Intelligence Theory: A cognitive social psychology that models human thinking after the inner workings and problem-solving activities of computers.

Atomism: The error of reducing a whole to the sum of its parts.

Attachment: An affectional bond that ties one person to another over an extended period of time.

Awareness Context: The total combination of what each interactant in a situation knows about the identity of the other and his own identity in the eyes of the other. Types are: *open, closed, pretense, suspicion.*

Base: Marxist term referring to the underlying material, economic basis of social structure.

Career: Involves three interrelated notions: (1) *objective*—a person's objective movement from one position to another through a social structure; (2) *subjective*—changes in self-conception that accompany these movements; and (3) *moral*—moral meanings of self that follow these objective and subjective changes.

Categorical Attitude: Consists of the following: (1) things can be named; (2) things can be grouped and classified; (3) by naming and classifying we create new possibilities of behavior.

Cause: (1) *Scientific*—antecedent processes which precede events and influence their occurrence. *Commonsense*—Reasons every-day interactants give for their actions, also called accounts.

Childhood Socialization: Those interactional experiences that build human nature into the child.

Chronic Illness (or pain): An illness or pain that often has no cure, and hence is lifelong.

Chronological Age: The actual age of a person.

Code: How a message or spoken utterance is organized—in terms of a formal logic, a computer program, a commonsense framework, and so on.

Cognitive Social Psychology: A point of view which stresses rational, thinking processes, and often tends to be experimental and statistical. Examples include AI theories, role-identity theories, exchange theory, and dramaturgical formulations.

Collective Behavior: Emergent, extra-institutional forms of behavior—including crowds, rumor, gossip, panic, fashion, fads, and collective protest.

Componential Analysis: Studying and classifying the meanings, terms, cognitions, and perceptions utilized by a cultural group.

Conventional Sign: A term that derives its meaning from social consensus, for example, the American flag. *First-order sign:* A sign which operates for lower animals like a bell. *Second-order sign:* A sign which operates for humans which is applied to visual and auditory data, often called a conventional sign.

Coping Mechanism: A technique of self-defense, may include selective perception, the use of accounts, disclaimers, scapegoating, rationalizing, projection, denial, detachment, and the use of privacy.

Criminal World: The social worlds of crime and criminals in a society, usually divided into three categories: (1) conventional criminals, (2) white-collar criminals, (3) racketeers. May also be classified in terms of amateurs and professionals.

Death: Three meanings in modern Western societies—(1) *clinical*, (2) *biological*, (3) *social*. Death is organized in terms of a dying trajectory which moves persons through these three categories. *Stages of acceptance* are denial, anger, bargaining, depression, acceptance.

Demoralization: A breakdown in group morale and collective group effort, and the appearance of bickering, fighting, and factionalism.

Deviance: A definition conferred on behavior by others, often including a conception of behavior which departs from the "normal."

Disclaimer: A verbal device people use when they wish to ward off criticisms of something they are about to do or say.

Discourse: Extended speech or language behavior in any context; includes conversations between speakers and a writer's printed text.

Disengagement Theory: A popular theory of aging which assumes that as people age, they disengage from their normal social obligations and relationships.

Dream Work: Transforming the latent content of a dream into manifest meanings; also called secondary elaboration.

Dualistic Error I: Believing that the mind and the body are separate entities.

Dualistic Error II: To conceptualize thinking as independent of the more overt forms of language behavior, including speech.

Egocentric Utterance: Self-centered speech; contrasted with sociocentric speech, which merges speech with the perspective of others.

Emotional Associate: Persons who, directly or indirectly, share in an emotional experience.

Emotionality: The process of being emotional; consists of self-feelings. There are four forms of emotional experience—*sensible feelings*, or sensations like pain; *feelings of the lived body*, like sorrow; *intentional value-feelings*, as when we feel anger at a mistake we have made; and *feelings of the self*, like self-loathing or self-pride.

Emotional Situations: Situations where emotions are recognized, defined, shared, and experienced.

Emotional Understanding: Knowing, comprehending, and interpreting through emotional means—including sympathy and imagination—the intentions, feelings, and thoughts of another.

Energy Principle: Freudian concept referring to the argument that energy can be neither destroyed nor created.

Erotic Imagery: The internal flow of thought that accompanies sexual experience.

Ethnomethodology: The study of how individuals create taken-for-granted meanings and understandings in social situations.

Family Violence: An interactional process that is self-destructive, involving physical and emotional abuse of family members.

Fixation Process: Addiction to a drug occurring when a person uses the drug to alleviate withdrawal distress. The person uses "fixes," or injections of the drug to alleviate the withdrawal distress.

Functional Autonomy of Motives: A behavior first performed as a means to an end becomes an end in itself when the original purpose has disappeared.

Gender: The cultural patterning of maleness and femaleness.

Gender Belief System: A society's beliefs about gender. In Western society, it has six components—(1) belief in the natural differences between the sexes based on biology; (2) belief that the home is the woman's place; (3) belief in male patriarchy; (4) belief that men's and women's work are different; (5) belief that married heterosexual love is the only natural love; (6) belief that women should be sexually and erotically attractive to men.

Gender Code: How gender is coded—or worked into selfhood—involving the learning of masculine and feminine identities in childhood.

Gender Stratification System: how men and women are located within the economic and prestige systems of a society.

Generalized Other: Mead's term referring to the organized community of attitudes to which the person responds in a social situation. Also called by Mead the third stage of self-development.

Genetic Fallacy: Confusing the last event in a chronological series with the first event in the sequence; common in some versions of Freudian theory.

Homosexuality: (1) *scientific*—wanting or having sexual relations with members of the same sex; (2) *commonsense*—holding the belief that one is the sort of person who has, or wants, those experiences.

Icon: A sign which represents something else—for example, the cross in Christianity.

Ideolect: The speech or language of a specific linguistic community or particular speaker.

Identity: How one is situated by others in a social situation in terms of social categories which are meaningful—father, husband, student, daughter, Mrs. Jones, etc.

Identity Transformation: The changes and transformations of self that can occur during a person's lifetime. One type, alternation, refers to changes within the prescribed boundaries of one's social group—for example, movement from identification as a Methodist to a Lutheran. The other type, conversion, describes identity changes that embrace negative self-identities—for example, a Jew becoming a fundamentalist Christian.

Individual Deviance: Deviance that does not have a cultural base; often called eccentric behavior.

Inner Speech: Inner thought.

Interactional Age: The amount of time a person spends interacting with a particular form of experience, like a game or television.

Interactional Loss: Self-control is ceded to an interactional situation.

Interactional Repertoire: Characteristic lines of action associated with a particular self or person.

Internal Environment: The world of the body and its feelings and sensations, as contrasted to the external environment of the physical world. Both environments are mediated by the symbolic environment, which is based on language.

Interpersonal Theory of Psychiatry: Sullivan's theory, which is at odds with orthodox Freudian accounts of the self and development, draws heavily on symbolic interactionist concepts. It has seven stages of development—infancy, childhood, juvenile era, preadolescence, adolescence, late adolescence, and adulthood.

Interpretive Social Psychology: A point of view which stresses the emotional, interpretive, emergent, historical, and personal dimensions of human experience; symbolic interactionism is an example.

Inversion: The assumption of a female gender identity by a man, or a male gender identity by a woman.

Kinesics: The study of nonverbal behavior, including body gestures—which range from batons, to ideographs, deictic, spatial, and rhythmic movements, kinetographs, and pictographs.

Language: A system of signs or words—organized by a set of rules called syntax—given meaning through semantics, and including speech behavior itself and the institution of speaking, thinking, and using words within a society, group, or culture. Language's key properties are (1) duality, (2) productivity, (3) arbitrariness, (4) interchangeability, (5) specialization, (6) displacement, (7) cultural transmission.

Linguistic Emotional Ritual: Words, gestures, and phrases which acknowledge respect of others; includes words like "please" and "thank you"; important in the socializing of emotions in childhood.

Linguistic Experience: Sullivan asserts there are three modes of linguistic experience, which refer to the manner in which experience is registered and to the degree that inner elaboration is produced. These modes are (1) *prototaxic,* where there is a minimum of inner elaboration; (2) *syntaxic,* where there is maximum inner elaboration and where this can be communicated to others (unlike the prototaxic); and (3) *parataxic,* where experience is partially organized, but there are elements of which the person is unaware.

Looking-Glass Self: The imagination of our appearance to others, the imagination of their judgment of our appearance, and some sort of self-feeling based on that judgment; Cooley's concept.

Love: Caring as much about another person's life as one cares about one's own life.

Media Self: (1) images of self and identity offered through the mass media, and (2) the selves attached to celebrities in our culture who become "media" personalities.

Mesostructure: Interactional processes that mediate between the world of immediate social interaction and larger institutional and organizational structures—for example, the war game played in the American military.

Metaphor: Speaking of something as if it were something else—for example, describing a helicopter as if it were a hovering insect.

Metonymy: The name of one thing is given to another thing related to it—for example, giving the name of the French town Bordeaux to the wine produced there.

Mirror Phase: In Lacan's theory, a phase of self-development in which the infant first sees an image of herself in the eyes and words of the other.

Motive: The explanation a person gives for his actions. Includes various styles (intimate, causal, consultative, formal, frozen) and types (in-order-to and because). The disclaimer is an example.

Myth: Text from everyday life which hides or veils meaning; based on everyday phenomenon (ex: advertisements for fast food chains).

Natural Language: The language of everyday speakers, as compared to a *formal language* (machine language) like FORTRAN or PASCAL, which is based on a symbol token system and utilized in computer programming.

Natural sign: a term and what it relates to occur together, for example, the sound of a siren and the passing of a fire engine.

Neologism: New, made-up words used by young children; can be used in a *declarative* or *manipulative* manner—that is, for drawing attention to an object or for putting an object to work for the child through the assistance of an adult.

Orientational Other: Those significant others the person is most fully committed to, who have given persons their most crucial concepts and categories of self.

Perception: How organisms respond to the stimuli picked up by their sense organs; it is selective, and organized by schemata.

Power: Force applied to others, making them comply with one's will; often involves violence and death.

Pseudo-Communication: When speakers use the same words in different ways, and are unaware of it.

Psychosocial Crisis: Key concept in Erikson's theory of development; involves interpersonal crises concerning trust and mistrust, autonomy and doubt, intimacy and confusion, integrity and despair.

Rationalization: (1) *Freudian*—Repression of painful experiences; (2) *Sociological*—The interpretations persons give of their behaviors in problematic situations.

Reductionism: Analyzing human social behavior in terms of biological, neurological, or genetic processes.

Reference Group: Any group the person psychologically identifies with; types include positive, negative, comparative, and normative.

Remembering: The response and interpretation of signs which relate to past experience, based on memory; it is a symbolic process.

Role (Self) Distance: Placing a distance between one's situated identity and one's expressed feelings in the situation.

Schemata: Abstractions which organize information processing, based on group languages.

Selective Inattention: Ignoring or misperceiving things that would be damaging to the self or ego.

Self: Set of interpretations on a conceptual level that exercise a regulatory function over other responses and interpretations of the same organism at lower levels; also refers to how the person sees herself as a subject and object in a social situation. The self is an organization of behavior imposed on the person by themselves and by others. It is an elusive process that haunts and is always in front of the person.

Self-Awareness: Being aware of who we are in a social situation.

Self-Control: How persons guide, direct, and interpret their own lines of behavior.

Self-Fulfilling Prediction: Acting in a way to make a belief come true. Also called self-fulfilling prophecy.

Selfhood: Becoming reflectively self-aware. Involves three stages: play, game, generalized other (also termed preparatory, interactional, and participatory stages).

Self-Negating Prediction: Acting in a way to disprove a prediction.

Self-System: The system or structure of defenses and reactions the person constructs to avoid anxieties. Consists of three components: (1) *good me*—self-acts one approves of; (2) *bad me*—self-acts one disapproves of and which produce anxiety; and (3) *not me*—acts which provoke deep anxiety and are disavowed and dissociated.

Semiology: The science that studies the life of signs within a society.

Sensorimotor Intelligence: Piaget's term referring to the forms of intelligence displayed by young children prior to acquisition of language; this is displayed through touch, sight, and movement.

Sentimental Work: The organization of work in a hospital which is directed to the emotional life of the patient.

Sexual Identity: Self-identifications involving sexuality and gender, involving three types of self-identities specific to gender and sexual conduct: (1) good sexual me, (2) bad sexual me, (3) not sexual me.

Sign: A term (word) that is unmotivated and exact. A sign has two components: the *signifier*, or sound-image that is heard when a word is spoken; and the *signified*, or the concept that is seen as lying behind the sound-image, that is, our image of ox.

Significant Other: A person who exerts influence over a person's thoughts, emotions, actions, and languages of self.

Signification: The process of using signs; also called *signifying acts*.

Sign System: The organization of signs for any society or given group; organized in terms of *myths*. Examples include sign systems for food, the garment industry, or higher education.

Small Social Group: A network of one-, two-, and three-person social relationships organized around a framework of shared emotional and interactional experiences.

Social Control: How society—in the form of other individuals, language, and cultural and moral feelings—enters into the organization of individual conduct.

Social Psychological Imagination: A perspective which attempts to grasp the larger historical context that shapes lives and group experience.

Social Psychology: The study of the interplay between lives and social structure, or biography and society.

Social Relationship: An ongoing interaction between two or more people based on shared understandings, languages, and activities. Types include (1) *interpersonal*—entered by the exchange of personal names; (2) *structural*—entered by the exchange of titles and the movement into an already existing position in a social structure, like an office; (3) *human*—those relations based on shared, universal human characteristics like age, sex, race, and ethnicity; (4) *larger public*—relations entered anonymously, as in the public.

Social World: Groups of individuals bound together through networks of shared communication, common meanings, and shared experiences and activities—for example, the social world of the elderly.

Sociobiology: A branch of evolutionary biology which studies the biological bases of all social behavior.

Sociolinguistics: The study of the social organization of language behavior in social situations; includes *discourse* and *conversational analysis.*

Speech Act: The production of a verbal utterance that is understandable to at least one other person.

Specious Present: Mead's term for merger of the past and the future in the present.

Status Passage: The movement of persons in and out of positions in a social structure.

Superstructure: Mental products in society formed and shaped by the base; includes ideology, consciousness, self, motive, and emotion.

Symbol: The ability of a sign to stand for something else; implies a relationship between thing and sign that is indirect. For example, the American flag means more than the United States.

Symbolic Environment: The world of reality, based on language, which mediates between humans and the direct physical environment.

Symbolic Interactionism: The social psychological point of view which studies the underlying symbolic, linguistic foundations of human interactional experience.

Technique of Neutralization: Symbolic devices (motives and accounts) used by persons so that they can continue a line of action that would otherwise cause guilt. Forms include (1) denial of harm, (2) denial of the victim, (3) attacking the accuser, and (4) invoking higher authorities.

Trance Logic: The ability of hypnotized subjects to tolerate and act on logical incongruities.

Universal Singular: Each person's life has universal themes which are unique to her experiences.

Violence: The attempt to regain, through the use of force, something that has been lost by the self.

Voluntary Behavior: A type of activity involving the internalization of language.

W. I. Thomas's Dictum: "If human beings define situations as real, they are real in their consequences."

Zoomorphism: Explaining human behavior in terms of principles derived from the study of lower animals.

Bibliography

ABERLE, D. F. (1966). *The peyote religion among the Navaho.* Viking Fund Publications in Anthropology, no. 42. New York: Wenner-Gren Foundation for Anthropological Research.

ADLER, P. (1953). *House is not a home.* New York: Holt, Rinehart & Winston.

AD HOC DAY CARE COALITION. (1985). *The crisis in infant and toddler child care.* Washington D.C.

AGAR, M. (1973). *Ripping and running: A formal ethnography of urban heroin addicts.* New York: Seminar.

AGAR, M. H., & HOBBS, J. R. (1985). How to grow schemata out of interviews. In J. W. D. Dougherty (Ed.), *New directions in cognitive anthropology* (pp. 413–431). Urbana IL: University of Illinois Press.

AINSWORTH, M. D. S. (1973). The development of infant-mother attachment. In B. M. Caldwell & H. N. Riciuti (Eds.), *Child development and social policy: Review of child development research,* vol. 3. Chicago: University of Chicago Press.

ALEXANDER, C. N. AND WILEY, M. G. (1981). Situated activity and identity formation, in M. Rosenberg and R. H. Turner (Eds.), *Social psychology: sociological perspectives,* (pp. 269–289). New York: Basic Books.

ALEXANDER, F., AND ROSS, H. (eds.) (1952). Development of the fundamental concepts of psychoanalysis. In *Dynamic Psychiatry,* pp. 30–68. Chicago: University of Chicago Press.

ALLEE, W. (1931a). *Animal aggregations: A study in general sociology.* Chicago: University of Chicago Press.

ALLEE, W. (1931b). *Cooperation among animals* (rev. ed.). New York: Abelard-Schuman.

ALLPORT, G. W. (1961). *Pattern and growth in personality.* New York: Holt, Rinehart & Winston.

ALLPORT, G. W. (1937). *Personality.* New York: Holt, Rinehart & Winston.

ALLPORT, G., & POSTMAN, L. (1947). The basic psychology of rumor. In T. Newcomb & E. L. Hartley (Eds.), *Readings in social psychology* (pp. 547–558). New York: Holt, Rinehart & Winston.

ALTHEIDE, D. (1984). The Media Self. In J. A. Kotarba & A. Fontana (Eds.), *The existential self in society* (pp. 177–195). Chicago: University of Chicago Press.

ALTHEIDE, D. (1985). *Media power.* Beverly Hills, CA: Sage Publications, Inc.

ALTHUSSER, L. (1969). *For Marx.* Harmondsworth, England: Penguin.

AMES, L. (1948). The development of a sense of time in the young child. *Journal of Genetic Psychology, 68,* 97–125.

ANDERSON, J. R. (1984). The development of self-recognition: A review. *Developmental Psychobiology, 35–49.*

ANDERSON, P. (1984). *In the tracks of historical materialism.* Chicago: University of Chicago Press.

ARGYLE, M. (1969). *Social interactions.* Chicago: Aldine.

ARIES, P. (1962). *Centuries of childhood.* New York: Random House.

ARIES, P. (1974). *Western attitudes toward death: From the middle ages to the present.* Baltimore: Johns Hopkins University Press.

ASCH, S. E. (1962). *Social psychology.* Englewood Cliffs, NJ: Prentice-Hall.

ASQUITH, P. J. (1984). The inevitability and utility of anthropomorphism in description of primate behavior. In R. Harré & V. Reynolds (Eds.), *The meaning of primate signals* (pp. 30–61). Cambridge: Cambridge University Press.

ATKINSON, J. M. & HERITAGE, J. (Eds.). (1984). *Structures of social action: Studies in conversation analysis.* Cambridge: Cambridge University Press.

ATTWELL, P. (Summer 1974). Ethnomethodology since Garfinkel, *Theory and Society, 2,* 179–210.

BAIN, R. (May 1936). The Self- and Other Words of a Child, *American Journal of Sociology, 41,* 767–775.

BALDWIN, J. M. (1987). *Social and ethical interpretations in mental development.* New York: Macmillan.

BARBER, T. X. (September 1961). Antisocial and criminal acts induced by "Hyponosis." *Archives of General Psychiatry, 5,* 301–12.

BARBER, T. X. (1969). *Hypnosis: a scientific approach.* New York: Van Nostrand Reinhold.

BAR-HILLEL, Y. (1960). *The present status of automatic translation of languages.* In F. L. Alt (Ed.), *Advances in computers,* (vol. 1) (pp. 140–175). New York: Academic Press.

BARTELL, G. (1972). *Group sex: A scientist's eyewitness report on the way of swinging.* New York: Peter Wyden.

BARTHES, R. (1967/1964). *Elements of semiology.* New York: Hill & Wang.

BARTHES, R. (1973/1957). *Mythologies.* New York: Hill & Wang.

BARTLETT, F. C. (1932). *Remembering.* New York: Cambridge University Press.

BARTON, R. W. (1985a). Signs, contexts, and the narrative structure of social practice. In N. K. Denzin (Ed.), *Studies in symbolic interaction,* (vol. 6), pp. 113–147.

BARTON, R. W. (1985b). *Language and theorizing about the sexual subject.* In N. K. Denzin (Ed.), *Studies in symbolic interaction,* (vol. 6) pp. 351–375.

BATESON, G. (1972). *Steps to an ecology of mind.* San Francisco: Chandler.

BATESON, G. (1979). *Mind and nature.* New York: Dutton.

BAUDRILLARD, J. (1981/1972). *For a critique of the political economy of the sign.* St. Louis: Telos Press.

BAUDRILLARD, J. (1983). *Simulations.* New York: Semiotext(e), Foreign Agent Press.

BEACH, F. A. (1947). Evolutionary changes in the physiological control of mating behavior in mammals. *Psychological Review, 54,* 297–315.

BEACH, F. A. (Ed.). (1965). *Sex and behavior:* New York: Wiley.

BEACH, H. D. (1957). Morphine Addiction in Rats. *Canadian Journal of Psychology, 11,* 104–111.

BEAUCHAMP, D. E. (1980). *Beyond alcoholism: Alcohol and public health policy.* Philadelphia: Temple University Press.

BECKER, H. S. (1982). *Art Worlds.* Berkeley: University of California Press.

BECKER, H. S. (1953). Becoming a marijuana user. *American Journal of Sociology, 59* 235–252.

BECKER, H. S. (1964). *The other side: Perspectives on deviance.* New York: Free Press.

BECKER, H. S. (September 1967). History, culture, and subjective experience: An exploration of the social bases of drug-induced experiences. *Journal of Health and Social Behavior, 8,* 163–176.

BECKER, H. S., ed. (1973). *Outsiders: Studies in the sociology of deviance* (rev. ed. with new Chap. 10). New York: Free Press.

BECKER, H. S., GEER, B., & HUGHES, E. (1968). *Making the grade: The academic side of college life.* New York: Wiley.

BECKER, H. S., & STRAUSS, A. L. (November 1956). Careers, personality and adult socialization. *American Journal of Sociology, 62,* 253–263.

Behavior Today: The Newsletter of Mental Health and Social Work Professionals. (1985). Infants at physical/psychological risk in day care. vol. 16 (15).

BELLUGI, U., & R. BROWN (Eds.). (1964). The acquisition of language: Report of the fourth conference sponsored by the Committee on Intellective Processes Research of the Social Science Research Council. *Society for Research in Child Development, 29,* no. 1, Chicago: University of Chicago Press.

BENEDEK, T. (1952). Personality Development. In F. Alexander & H. Ross (Eds.), *Dynamic psychiatry.* Chicago: University of Chicago Press.

BENEDEK, T. (1946). *The chrysanthemum and the sword.* Boston: Houghton Mifflin.

BENEDICT, R. (1959). *Patterns of culture.* Boston: Houghton Mifflin.

BENJAMIN, J. (1981). The Oedipal riddle: Authority, autonomy and the new narcissism. In J. P. Diggins & M. E. Kann (Eds.), *The problem of authority in America* (pp. 195–224). Philadelphia: Temple University Press.

BENSON, M. (1985). The fall from grace: White collar criminality. *Criminology 17,* 456–470.

BERGER, J. & ZELDITCH, M. (Eds.). (1985). *Status, rewards, and influence.* San Francisco: Jossey-Bass.

BERGER, P., & KELLNER, H. (1964). Marriage and the

construction of reality: An exercise in the micro-sociology of knowledge. *Diogenes, 46,* 1–23.

BERGER, P., & LUCKMANN, T. (1967). *The social construction of reality.* Garden City, NY: Doubleday.

BERINGER, R. E., HATTAWAY, H., JONES, A., & STILL, W. N. JR. (1985). *Why the South lost the Civil War.* Athens: University of Georgia Press.

BERKOWITZ, L. (Ed.). (1964). *Advances in experimental psychology,* (vol. 1). New York: Academic Press.

BERNARD, J. (1971). *Women and the public interest.* Chicago: Aldine.

BERNSTEIN, B. (1958). Some sociological determinants of perception. *British Journal of Sociology, 9,* 150–158.

BERNSTEIN, B. (1964). Elaborated and restricted codes: Their social origins and some consequences. In J. Gumperz & D. Hymes (Eds.), The ethnography of communication. *American Anthropologist, 66,* no. 2, 55–69.

BERNSTEIN, B. (1973). *Class, codes and control,* (vol. 1). London: Routledge & Kegan Paul.

BERTAUX, D. (Ed.). (1981). *Biography and society: The life history approach in the social sciences.* Beverly Hills, CA: Sage Publications, Inc.

BIERENS DE HAAN, J. (1929). *Animal psychology for biologists.* London: Hutchinson Publishing Group.

BIRDWHISTLE, R. (1966). Some relations between American kinesics and spoken American English. In A. G. Smith (Ed.), *Communication and culture* (pp. 182–189). New York: Holt, Rinehart & Winston.

BIRDWHISTLE, R. (1970). *Kinesics and context.* Philadelphia: University of Pennsylvania Press.

BIRENBAUM, A. (September 1970). On managing a courtesy stigma. *Journal of Health and Social Behavior, 11,* 196–206.

BLANKENSHIP, R. L. (Winter 1973). Organizational careers: An interactionist perspective. *Sociological Quarterly, 14,* 88–98.

BLAU, P. (1964). *Exchange and power in social life.* New York: John Wiley.

BLAUNER, R. (1968). Death and Social Structure. In Marcello Truzzi (Ed.). *Sociology and everyday life* (pp. 346–367). Englewood Cliffs, NJ: Prentice-Hall.

BLEIER, R. (1984). *Science and gender: A critique of biology and its theories in women.* New York: Pergamon Press.

BLONDEL, C. (1928a). *Introduction à la psychologie collective.* Paris: Librarie Armand, Colin.

BLONDEL, C. (1928b). *La conscience morbide.* Paris: Librairie Félix Alcan.

BLONDEL, C. (1939). Les Volitions. In G. Dumas (Ed.), *Nouveau traité de psychologie.* Paris: Librairie Félix Alcan.

BLUEBOND-LANGNER, M. (1978). *The private worlds of dying children.* Princeton, NJ: Princeton University Press.

BLUM, A., AND McHUGH, P. (1971). The social ascription of motives, *American Sociological Review,* vol. 36, pp. 98–109.

BLUM, G. S. (1984). Hypnosis as a research tool. In Raymond J. Corsini (Ed.), *Encyclopedia of psychology,* Vol. 2 (pp. 174–175). New York: John Wiley.

BLUM, R., & BLUM, E. (1965). *Health and healing in rural Greece.* Stanford, CA: Stanford University Press.

BLUMER, H. (1962). Society as symbolic interaction. In A. Rose (Ed.). *Human behavior and social processes* (pp. 179–192). Boston: Houghton Mifflin.

BLUMER, H. (1969). *Symbolic interactionism.* Englewood Cliffs, NJ: Prentice-Hall.

BLUMER, H. (1971). Social problems as collective behavior. *Social Problems, 18,* 298–306.

BLUMER, H. (1978). Social unrest and collective protest. In Norman K. Denzin (Ed.), *Studies in symbolic interaction,* (vol. 1) (pp. 1–54). Greenwich, CN: JAI Press.

BLUMSTEIN, P., & SCHWARTZ, P. (1983). *American couples.* New York: Basic Books.

BOSSARD, J. H. S., & BOLL, E. S. (1960). *The sociology of child development* (3rd ed.). New York: Harper & Row, Pub.

BOSTER, J. S. (1985). Requiem for the omniscient informant: There's life in the old girl yet. In J. W. E. Doughtery (Ed.), *New directions in cognitive anthropology* (pp. 177–197). Urbana, IL: University of Illinois Press.

BOSWELL, J. (1980). *Christianity, social tolerance, and homosexuality: Gay people in Western Europe from the beginning of the Christian era to the fourteenth century.* Chicago: University of Chicago Press.

BOUTAN, L. (1913). Le pseudo-language: observations effectuées sur un anthropoide: le gibbon, *Actes de la société linné de bordeaux,* vol. 16, pp. 5–77.

BOWLBY, J. (1953). *Child care and the growth of love.* Baltimore: Penguin Books.

BRECHER, E. I. (1969). *The sex researchers.* Boston: Little, Brown.

BREHM, J. W. (1966). *A theory of psychological reactance.* New York: Academic Press.

BREHM, J. & COHEN, A. (1962). *Explorations in cognitive dissonance.* New York: John Wiley.

BRIDGES, K. (1931). *The social and emotional level of the preschool child.* London: Routledge & Kegan Paul.

BRODERICK, C. B. (1965). Social heterosexual relationships among urban Negroes and whites. *Journal of Marriage and the Family, 28,* 200–203.

BROOKS-GUNN, J., & LEWIS, M. (1982). Affective exchanges between normal and handicapped infants and their mothers. In T. Field & A. Fogel (Eds.), *Emotions and early interactions* (pp. 178–191). Hillsdale, NJ: Erlbaum.

BROWN, R. (1956). Language and categories. In J.

Bruner, (Ed.), *A study of thinking*. New York: John Wiley.

BROWN, R. (1958). *Words and Things*. New York: Free Press.

BROWN, R. (1965). *Social psychology*. New York: Free Press.

BROWN, R. (1970). *Psycholinguistics*. New York: Free Press.

BROWN, R., & LENNEBERG, E. (1954). A study in language and cognition. *Journal of Abnormal and Social Psychology, 49* 454–462.

BROWNLEE, S. (October 1985). A riddle wrapped in a mystery. *Discover*, pp. 85–93.

BRUNER, J., & OLIVER, R. (1963). The development of equivalence transformations in children. In J. Wright & J. Kagan (Eds.), Basic cognitive processes in children. *Society for research in child development*, (vol. 28). Chicago: University of Chicago Press.

BRUNER, J. S., & TAGIURI, R. (1954). The perception of people. In G. Lindsey (Ed.), *Handbook of social psychology*, (vol. 2). Cambridge, MA: Addison-Wesley.

BRYNNER, W. (1929). *The Jade Mountain*. New York: Knopf.

BUCHER, R., & STRAUSS, A. L. (January 1961). Professions in process. *American Journal of Sociology, 66*, 325–334.

BULLOCK, C. C. (1987). Interpretive lines of action of mentally retarded children in mainstreamed play settings. In N. K. Denzin (Ed.), *Studies in Symbolic Interaction* (vol. 9). Greenwich, Conn.: JAI Press.

BURGESS, E. W. (Ed.). (1960). *Aging in Western societies*. Chicago: University of Chicago Press.

BURKE, K. (1936). *Performance and change*. New York: New Republic Press.

BURKE, K. (1936). *Permanence and Change*. New York: New Republic Press.

BURR, A. R. (1934). *Alice James: Her brothers—her journal*. Cornwall, NY: Dodd, Mead.

CAHMAN, W. J. (1968). The stigma of obesity. *Sociological Quarterly, 9*, 283–299.

CALDWELL, B., & FEYER, M. (1982). Day care and early education. In B. Spokek (Ed.), *Handbook of research in early education* (pp. 96–130). New York: Free Press.

CALKINS, K. (1970). Time: Perspectives, marking and styles of usage. *Social Problems, 17*, 487–501.

CALLAHAN, D. (1970). *Abortion: Law, choice and morality*. New York: Macmillan.

CALLOW, A. B., JR. (1970). *The tweed ring*. New York: Oxford University Press.

CAMERON, M. O. (1964). *The booster and the snitch*. New York: Free Press.

CAMERON, N., & MAGARET, A. (1951). *Behavioral pathology*. Boston: Houghton-Mifflin.

CAMPBELL, D. T. (1975). On the conflicts between biological and social evolution and between psychology and moral tradition. *American Psychologist, 30*, 1103–1126.

CAMPBELL, J. K. (1964). *Honour, family and patronage*. New York: Oxford University Press.

CARMICHAEL, L., HOGAN, H. P., & WALTER, A. A. (1932). An experimental study of the effect of language on the reproduction of visually perceived form. *Journal of Experimental Psychology, 15*, 78–86.

CARSTAIRS, G. M. (1954). Daru and Bhang. *Quarterly Journal of Studies in Alcohol, 15*, 220–237.

CARVER, R. (1983). *What we talk about when we talk about love*. New York: Vintage.

CASSIRER, E. (1944). *An essay on man*. New Haven: Yale University Press.

CASSIRER, E. (1953–57). *The Philosophy of Symbolic Forms*. (3 vols). New Haven, CT: Yale University Press.

CASSON, R. W. (1983). Schemata in cognitive anthropology. In B. J. Siegel, A. R. Beals, & S. A. Tyler (Eds.), *Annual Review of Anthropology*, vol. 12 (pp. 429–462). Palo Alto, CA: Annual Reviews Inc.

CHAMBLISS, W. J. (1972). *BOX MAN: A professional thief's journal by Harry King* as told to and ed. by W. J. Chambliss. New York: Harper & Row.

CHAMBLISS, W. J. (1975). Toward a political economy of crime. *Theory and Society, 2*, 149–170.

CHAPANIS, N. P., & CHAPANIS, A. (1964). Cognitive dissonance: Five years later. *Psychological Bulletin, 61*, 1–22.

CHARMAZ, K. (1980). The social construction of self-pity in the chronically ill. In N. K. Denzin (Ed.), *Studies in symbolic interaction*, (Vol. 3) (pp. 123–145).

CHASE, S. (1938). *The tyranny of words*. New York: Harcourt Brace Jovanovich, Inc.

CHEAL, D. J. (1984). Transactions and transformational models. In N. K. Denzin (Ed.), *Studies in symbolic interaction*, Vol. 5 (pp. 141–151). Greenwich, CN: JAI Press.

CHENEY, D. L. (1984). Category formation in varet monkeys. In R. Harrè & V. Reynolds (Eds.), *The meaning of primate signals* (pp. 127–140). Cambridge: Cambridge University Press.

CHERRY, C. (1957). *On human communication*. New York: John Wiley.

CHOMSKY, N. (1965). *Aspects of the theory of syntax*. Cambridge, MA: MIT Press.

CHURCH, J. (1961). *Language and the discovery of reality*. New York: Random House.

CICOUREL, A. (1974). *Cognitive sociology*. New York: Free Press.

CLARKE-STEWART, A. (1982). *Day care*. Cambridge, MA: Harvard University Press.

COCKERHAM, W. (1978). *Medical sociology.* Englewood Cliffs, N.J.: Prentice-Hall.

COHEN, B. (1962). The process of choosing a reference group. In J. Criswell, H. Solomon, & P. Suppes (Eds.). *Mathematical methods in small group processes* (pp. 101–118). Stanford, CA: Stanford University Press.

COLEMAN, J. S. (1973). Loss of power. *American Sociological Review, 38,* 1–17.

COLES, R. (1972). *Erik H. Erikson.* Boston: Little, Brown.

COLLINS, R. (1975). *Conflict sociology.* New York: Academic Press.

COLLINS, R. (1981). *Sociology since midcentury: Essays in theory cumulation.* New York: Academic Press.

COLLINS, R. (1986). Is 1980s sociology in the doldrums? *American Journal of Sociology 91,* no. 6, 1336–1355.

CONN, J. H., & KANNER, L. (1947). Children's awareness of sex differences. *Journal of Child Psychiatry, 1* 3–57.

COOK-GUMPERZ, J. (1975). The child as practical reasoner. In M. Sanches and B. G. Blount (Eds.), *Sociocultural dimensions of language use* (pp. 45–67). New York: Academic Press.

COOLEY, C. H. (1902). *Human nature and social order.* New York: Scribner's.

COOLEY, C. H. (1930). A study of the early use of self-words by a child. In *Sociological theory and social research.* New York: Holt, Rinehart & Winston.

COREY, D. W. (1951). *The homosexual in America.* Philadelphia: Chilton.

CORSARO, W. A. (1981). Friendship in the nursery school: school organization in a peer environment. In S. R. Asher and J. M. Gottman (Eds.), *The development of children's friendships.* Cambridge and New York: Cambridge University Press, pp. 207–241.

COSER, L. A. (1975). Presidential address: Two methods in search of a substance. *American Sociological Review, 40,* 691–700.

COTTRELL, L., & GALLAGHER, R. (1941). Developments in social psychology, 1930–1940. In *Sociometry Monographs,* no. 1. Beacon, NY: Beacon House.

COUCH, C. J. (1984a). Symbolic interactionism and generic sociological principles. *Symbolic Interaction, 7,* 1–13.

COUCH, C. J. (1984b). *Constructing civilizations.* Greennwich, CT: JAI Press.

COUCH, C. J., SAXTON, S. L., & KATOVICH, M. A. (Eds.). (1986). *Studies in symbolic interaction: The Iowa school.* Greenwich, CT: JAI Press.

COWARD, R., & ELLIS, J. (1977). *Language and materialism: developments in semiology and the theory of the subject.* London: Routledge & Kegan Paul.

COWGILL, D. O. (1980). The aging of populations and societies. In J. S. Quadagno (Ed.), *Aging, the individual and society: readings in social gerontology,* pp. 15–33. New York: St. Martin's Press.

CRESSEY, D. (1932). *The taxi-dance girl changes her name.* Chicago: University of Chicago Press.

CRESSEY, D. (1953). *Other people's money.* New York: Free Press. (reissued 1971; Belmont, Calif.: Wadsworth).

CRESSEY, D. (Ed.). (1961). *The prison: Studies in institutional organization and change.* New York: Holt, Rinehart & Winston.

CRISWELL, J., SOLOMON, H., & SUPPES, P. (1962). *Mathematical methods in small group processes.* Stanford, CA.: Stanford University Press.

CUMMING, E., & HENRY, W. E. (1961). *Growing old: The process of disengagement.* New York: Basic Books.

CUMMING, E., HENRY, W. E., & DAMIANOPOULOS, E. (1961). A formal statement of disengagement theory. In E. Cumming & W. E. Henry (Eds.), *Growing old: The process of disengagement* (pp. 210–227). New York: Basic Books.

DALE, E. (1954). *Audio visual methods in teaching* (rev. ed.). New York: Holt, Rinehart & Winston.

DAMON, W. (1977). *The social world of the child.* San Francisco: Jossey-Bass.

DANCE, F. E. X. (1967). Speech communication theory and Pavlov's second signal system. *Journal of Communication, 17,* 13–24.

DAVIS, F. (1963). *Passage through crisis.* Indianapolis: Bobbs-Merrill.

DAVIS, F. (Ed.). (1966). *The nursing profession.* New York: John Wiley.

DAVIS, F. (1972). *Illness, interaction and the self.* Belmont, CA: Wadsworth.

DAVIS, F. J., & STIVERS, R. (Eds.). (1975). *The collective definition of deviance.* New York: Free Press.

DAVIS, J., & BOULDING, K. (1961). Two critiques of Homans' *social behavior. American Journal of Sociology, 67* 454–461.

DAVIS, K. (1937). The sociology of prostitution. *American Sociological Review, 2,* 744–755.

DAVIS, N. J. (1972). Labelling theory in deviance research. *Sociological Quarterly, 13,* 447–474.

DE BEAUVOIR, S. (1952). *The second sex.* New York: Knopf.

DE CERTEAU, M. (1984). *The practice of everyday life.* Berkeley: University of California Press.

DEGLER, C. N. (1980). *At odds: Women and the family in America from the revolution to the present.* New York: Oxford University Press.

DE LAGUNA, G. M. (1927). *Speech: Its functions and development.* New Haven: Yale University Press.

DENZIN, N. K. (1966). The significant others of a college population. *Sociological Quarterly, 7,* 298–310.

DENZIN, N. K. (1971). Children and their caretakers. *Transaction, 8,* 62–72.

DENZIN, N. K. (1972). The genesis of self in early childhood. *Sociological Quarterly, 13* 291–314.

DENZIN, N. K. (1977). *Childhood socialization.* San Francisco: Jossey-Bass.

DENZIN, N. K. (1979). Toward a social psychology of childhood socialization. *Contemporary Sociology 8,* no. 4, 550–556.

DENZIN, N. K. (1982). The significant others of young children: Notes toward a phenomenology of childhood. In K. M. Borman (Ed.), *The social life of children in a changing society* (pp. 29–46). Hillsdale, NJ: Erlbaum.

DENZIN, N. K. (1982). A note on emotionality, self and interaction. *American Journal of Sociology* 89, no. 2.

DENZIN, N. K. (1984a). *On understanding emotion.* San Francisco: Jossey-Bass.

DENZIN, N. K. (1984b). Retrieving the small social group. In N. K. Denzin (Ed.), *Studies in interaction,* Vol. 5 (pp. 35–48). Greenwich, CN: JAI Press.

DENZIN, N. K. (1984c). Toward a phenomenology of domestic, family violence. *American Journal of Sociology, 3,* 483–513.

DENZIN, N. K. (1985a). Emotion as lived experience. *Symbolic Interaction, 8,* no. 2, 223–240.

DENZIN, N. K. (1985b). On the phenomenology of sexuality, desire and violence. *Current Perspectives in Social Theory, 6* (pp. 39–56).

DENZIN, N. K. (1986a). *The alcoholic self.* Beverly Hills, CA: Sage Publications, Inc.

DENZIN, N. K. (1986b). *The recovering alcoholic.* Beverly Hills, CA: Sage Publications, Inc.

DENZIN, N. K. (1986c). *Treating Alcoholism.* Beverly Hills, CA: Sage Publications.

DENZIN, N. K. (1988). *The Research Act* (3rd ed.). Englewood Cliffs: Prentice-Hall.

DERRIDA, J. (1976). *Of Grammatology.* Baltimore: Johns Hopkins University Press.

DEVILLIERS, P., & DEVILLIERS, J. G. (1979). *Early language,* Cambridge: Harvard University Press.

DEVINE-HAWKINS, P. (1981). *Family day care in the United States: Executive summary.* Final Report of the National Day Care Home Study. Washington, D.C.: Department of Health and Human Services.

DEWEY, J. (1922). *Human nature and conduct.* New York: Holt, Rinehart & Winston.

DEWEY, J. (1925). *Experience and nature.* La Salle, IL: Open Court Publishing Company.

DEWEY, J. (1934). *Art as experience.* New York: Minton, Balch and Company.

DEWEY, J. (1938). *Logic: The theory of inquiry.* New York: Holt, Rinehart & Winston.

DEWEY, J., & BENTLEY, A. F. (1949). *Knowing and the known.* Beacon, NY: Beacon House.

DIAMOND, A. C. (1959). *The history and origin of language.* New York: Philosophical Library.

DIRENZO, G. (1971). [Review of H. Taylor, Balance in small groups]. *American Sociological Review, 36* 134–135.

DOBASH, R. E., & DOBASH, R. P. (1979). *Violence against wives.* New York: Free Press.

DOUGHERTY, J. W. D. (Ed.). (1985). *Directions in cognitive anthropology.* Urbana, IL: University of Illinois Press.

DOUGHERTY, J. W. D., & KELLER, C. M. (1985). Taskonomy: A practical approach to knowledge structures. In J. W. D. Dougherty (Ed.). *Directions in cognitive anthropology* (161–174). University of Illinois Press.

DOUGLAS, J. D. (Ed.). (1970). *Understanding everyday life.* Chicago: Aldine.

DOUGLAS, J. D., & JOHNSON, J. M. (Eds.), (1977). *Existential sociology.* New York: Cambridge University Press.

DOUGLAS, J. D., ADLER, P. A., ADLER, P., FONTANA, A., FREEMAN, C. R., & KOTARBA, J. A. (1980). *Introduction to the sociologies of everyday life.* Boston: Allyn & Bacon.

DURKHEIM, E. (1897). *Le suicide.* Paris: Librairie Félix Alcan.

DURKHEIM, E. (1947). *Elementary forms of religious life.* New York: Free Press.

EBAUGH, H. R. F. (1984). Leaving the convent: The experience of role exit and self-transformation. In J. A. Kotarba & A. Fontana (Eds.), *The existential self in society* (pp. 156–176). Chicago: University of Chicago Press.

EBIN, D. (Ed.). (1961). *The drug experience.* New York: The Orion Press.

ECO, U. (1976). *The theory of semiotics.* Bloomington, IN: Indiana University Press.

EDEL, L. (1964). *The diary of Alice James.* New York: Dodd, Mead.

EDGERTON, R. B. (1964). Pokot intersexuality: An East African example of the resolution of sexual incongruity. *American Anthropologist, 66,* pp. 1288–1299.

EDMONSTON, W. E. JR. (1984). Hypnotic age regression. In R. J. Corsini (Ed.), *Encyclopedia of psychology,* (vol. 2) (pp. 177–178). New York: John Wiley.

EHRMEN, L., & PARSONS, P. A. (1976). *The genetics of behaviour.* Sunderland, MS: Sinauer Associates.

EIBL-EIBESFELDT, I. (1970). *Ethology.* New York: Holt, Rinehart & Winston.

EINSTEIN, A., & INFELD, L. (1961). *The evolution of physics.* New York: Simon & Schuster. (First published, 1938).

EINSTADTER, W. (1969). The social organization of armed robbery. *Social Problems, 17,* 64–82.

EKMAN, P. (1970). Universal facial expressions of emotion. *California Mental Health Research Digest, 8,* 151–158.

EKMAN, P. (1972). Universals and cultural differences in facial expression of emotions. In J. R. Cole (Ed.), *Nebraska symposium on motivation* (pp. 100–130). Lincoln: University of Nebraska Press.

EKMAN, P. (1973). *Darwin and facial expression.* New York: Academic Press.

EKMAN, P. (1980). Biological and cultural contributions to body and facial movement in the expression of emotion. In A. Rorty (Ed.), *Explaining Emotions* (pp. 56–75). Berkeley: University of California Press.

EKMAN, P., & FRIESEN, W. (1972). Hand Movements. *Journal of Communication, 22,* 353–374.

ELKIND, D. (1981). *The hurried child.* Reading, PA: Addison-Wesley.

EMERSON, R. M. (1981). Social exchange theory. In M. Rosenberg and R. Turner (Eds.), *Social psychology: sociological perspectives,* pp. 30–65. New York: Basic Books.

EMERSON, R. M. (1976). Social exchange theory. In A. Inkles, J. Coleman, and N. Smelser (Eds.), *Annual Review of Sociology,* Vol. 2 (335–362). Palo Alto, Ca.: Annual Reviews.

EPSTEIN, C. F. (1971). *Woman's place.* Berkeley, CA: University of California Press.

ERICSSON, K., & SIMON, H. A. (1984). *Protocol analysis: Verbal reports as data.* Cambridge, MA: The MIT Press.

ERIKSON, E. H. (1950). *Childhood and society.* New York: W. W. Norton & Co., Inc.

ERIKSON, E. H. (1959). Identity and the life cycle. In G. S. Klein (Ed.), *Psychological issues.* New York: International Universities Press.

ERIKSON, E. H. (1962). *Young man Luther.* New York: W. W. Norton & Co., Inc.

ERIKSON, E. H. (Ed.). (1965). *The challenge of youth.* Garden City, NY: Doubleday.

ERIKSON, E. H. (1969). *Gandhi's truth.* New York: W. W. Norton & Co., Inc.

ERIKSON, K. (1965). *Wayward puritans.* New York: John Wiley.

EVANS, F. J. (1984). Hypnosis. In R. J. Corsini (Ed.), *Encyclopedia of psychology,* (vol. 2) (pp. 172–174). New York: John Wiley.

EYSENCK, H. J. (1964). *Sense and nonsense in psychology.* Baltimore: Penguin Books.

FARBERMAN, H. A. (1980). Fantasy in everyday life: Some aspects of the interaction between social psychology and political economy. *Symbolic Interaction, 3,* 29–22.

FARIS, R. E. L. (1952). *Social psychology.* New York: Ronald Press.

FAULKNER, R. R. (1973). Orchestra interaction: Some features of communication and authority in an artistic organization. *Sociological Quarterly, 14,* 147–157.

FELD, T. (1979). Differential behavioral and cardiac responses of 3-month-old infants to a mirror and peer. *Infant Behavior Development, 2,* 179–184.

FERGUSON, C. A. (December 1964). Baby talk in six languages. *American Anthropologist, 66,* part 2, 103–114.

FESTINGER, L. (1947). The role of group belongingness in a voting situation. *Human Relations, 2,* 154–180.

FESTINGER, L. (1957). *A theory of cognitive dissonance.* New York: Harper & Row, Pub.

FESTINGER, L. (1962). Cognitive dissonance. *Scientific American, 207,* 1–9.

FINE, G. A. (1984). Humorous interaction and the social construction of meaning: making sense in a jocular vein. In N. K. Denzin (Ed.), *Studies in Symbolic Interaction* 5: 71–82. Greenwich, Conn.: JAI Press.

FINESTONE, H. (1957). Cats, kicks, and color. *Social Problems, 5,* 3–13.

FINKELSTEIN, J. (1985). Dining out: The self in search of civility. In N. K. Denzin (Ed.). *Studies in symbolic interaction,* vol. 6 (pp. 183–212).

FISHBERG, M. (1911). *The Jews.* New York: Scribner's.

FISHMAN, J. (Ed.). (1968). *Readings in the sociology of language.* The Hague: Mouton.

FLAHERTY, M. G. (1984). A formal approach to the study of amusement in social interaction. In N. K. Denzin (Ed.), *Studies in Symbolic Interaction* 5: 49–67. Greenwich, Conn.: JAI Press.

FONTANA, A. (1977). *The last frontier.* Beverly Hills, CA: Sage Publications, Inc.

FONTANA, A. (1980). Growing old between walls. In J. S. Quadagno (Ed.), *The individual and society: Readings in social gerontology* (pp. 482–499). New York: St. Martin's Press.

FOUCAULT, M. (1980). *The history of sexuality: Vol. 1: An introduction.* New York: Pantheon.

FOUCAULT, M. (1980). *Power/knowledge: Selected interviews and other writings:* In C. Gordon (Ed.), C. Gordon, L. Marshall, J. Mepham, K. Soper, Trans. New York: Pantheon.

FRAKE, C. (1962). Cultural ecology and ethnology. *American Anthropologist, 64,* 53–59.

FRAKE, C. (1961). The diagnosis of disease among the Subanun of Mindanao. *American Anthropologist, 63,* 113–132.

FRANK, L. K. (1966). Tactile communication. In Alfred G. Smith (Ed.). *Communication and culture* pp. 199–208. New York: Holt, Rinehart & Winston.

FRANKLIN, J. H. (1956). *From slavery to freedom: A history of American Negroes.* (2d ed) New York: Knopf.

FRENCH, T. (1952). Dreams and rational behavior. In F. Alexander & H. Ross (Eds.), *Dynamic psychiatry* (pp. 35–39). Chicago: University of Chicago Press.

FREUCHEN, P. (1967). The problem of the aged in eskimo society. In R. C. Owen, J. F. Deetz, & A. D. Fisher (Eds.), *The North American indians: A sourcebook* (pp. 175–183). New York: Macmillan.

FREUD, S. (1933). *New introductory lectures on psychoanalysis.* W. W. Norton & Co., Inc.

FREUD, S. (1933). The psychology of women. In *New introductory lectures on psychoanalysis* (pp. 153–183). New York: W. W. Norton & Co., Inc.

FREUD, S. (1938). *The basic writings of Sigmund Freud,* trans. and ed. with an Introduction by A. A. Brill. New York: Random House.

FRIEDMAN, S. B., CHODOFF, P., MANN, J. W., & D. A. HAMBURG. (Oct. 1963). Behavioral observation on parents anticipating the death of a child. *Pediatrics, 20,* 610–624.

GAGNON, J. H., & W. SIMON (Eds.). (1967). *Sexual deviance.* New York: Harper & Row, Pub.

GAGNON, J. & SIMON, W. (1970). Perspectives on the sexual scene. In J. Gagnon & W. Simon (Eds.), *The sexual scene* (pp. 1–21). Chicago: Aldine.

GAMBLE, T., & E. ZIGLER. (1986). Effects of infant day care: Another look at the evidence. *American Journal of Orthopsychiatry, 56,* 26–42.

GARDINER, J. (1970). *The politics of corruption: Organized crime in an American city.* New York: Russel Sage Foundation.

GARDNER, B., & GARDNER, R. A. (1969). Teaching sign language to a chimpanzee. *Science, 165,* 664–672.

GARFINKEL, H. (1956). Conditions of successful degradation ceremonies. *American Journal of Sociology, 61,* 420–424.

GARFINKEL, H. (1967). Passing and the managed achievement of sex status in an intersexed person. part 1. In H. Garfinkel. *Studies in ethnomethodology* (pp. 116–185). Englewood Cliffs, NJ: Prentice-Hall.

GARFINKEL, H. (1967). *Studies in ethnomethodology.* Englewood Cliffs, NJ: Prentice-Hall.

GARFINKEL, H., LYNCH, M., & LIVINGSTON, E. (1981). The work of a discovering science construed with material from the optically discovered pulsar. *Philosophy of the Social Sciences, 11,* 131–158.

GARFINKEL, H., AND H. SACKS (1970). On formal structures of practical actions. In J. C. McKinney and E. A. Tiryakian (Eds.), *Theoretical sociology: perspectives and developments,* 119–151. New York: Appleton-Century-Crofts.

GEDYE, G. E. (1939). *Fallen Bastions.* London: Victor Gollancz.

GEERTZ, C. (1973). *The interpretation of cultures.* New York: Basic Books.

GEERTZ, C. (1983). *Local Knowledge.* New York: Basic Books.

GELLES, R. J., & CORNELL, C. P. (1985). *Intimate Violence in Families.* Beverly Hills, Ca.: Sage Publications.

GERGEN, K. J. (1973). Social psychology as history. *Journal of Personality and Social Psychology, 26,* 309–320.

GERGEN, K. J. (1982). *Toward transformation in social knowledge.* New York: Springer-Verlang.

GERGEN, K. J., & GERGEN, M. M. (Eds.). (1984). *Historical social psychology.* Hillsdale, NJ: Erlbaum.

GIBBS, J. P., & ERICKSON. M. L. (1975). Major developments in the sociological study of deviance. *Annual Review of Sociology, 1,* 21–42.

GIBSON, J. J. (1953). Social perceptions and perceptual learning. In M. Sherif & D. Wilson (eds.), *Group relations at the crossroads* (pp. 120–138). New York: Harper & Row, Pub.

GIDDENS, A. (1979). *Central problems in social theory.* Berkeley: University of California Press.

GIDDENS, A. (1981). *A contemporary critique of historical materialism, vol. 1, power, property and state.* Berkeley: University of California Press.

GIDDENS, A. (1984). *The constitution of society.* Berkeley: University of California Press.

GIGLIOLI, PIER P. (Ed.). (1972). *Language and social context: Selected readings.* Baltimore: Penguin Books.

GILLIGAN, C. (1982). *In a different voice: Psychological theory and women's development.* Cambridge, MA: Harvard University Press.

GLASER, B., & STRAUSS, A. L. (1964). Awareness contexts and interaction. *American Sociological Review, 29,* 669–679.

GLASER, B., & STRAUSS, A. L. (1965). *Awareness of dying.* Chicago: Aldine.

GLASER, B., & STRAUSS, A. L. (1967). *The discovery of grounded theory.* Chicago: Aldine.

GLASER, B., & STRAUSS, A. L. (1968). *Time for dying.* Chicago: Aldine.

GLASER, B., & STRAUSS, A. L. (1971). *Status passage.* Chicago: Aldine.

GOFFMAN, E. (1974). *Frame analysis.* New York: Harper & Row, Pub.

GOTTMAN, E. (November 1952). On cooling the mark out: Some aspects of failure. *Psychiatry, 15,* 451–463.

GOTTMAN, E. (1955). On face-work: An analysis of ritual elements in social interaction. *Psychiatry, 18,* 213–231.

GOTTMAN, E. (1956). The nature of deference and demeanor. *American Anthropologist 58,* 480–488.

GOTTMAN, E. (1959). *The presentation of self in everyday life.* Garden City, NY: Doubleday.

GOTTMAN, E. (1961). *Encounters.* Indianapolis: Bobbs-Merrill.

GOTTMAN, E. (1961). The moral career of the mental patient. In *Asylums: Essays on the social situation of mental patients and other inmates* (pp. 128–169). Garden City, NY: Doubleday.

GOTTMAN, E. (1963). *Stigma.* Englewood Cliffs, NJ: Prentice-Hall.

GOTTMAN, E. (1967). *Interaction ritual.* Chicago: Aldine.

GOTTMAN, E. (1969). *Strategic interaction.* Philadelphia: University of Pennsylvania Press.

GOTTMAN, E. (1971). *Relations in public.* New York: Basic Books.

GOTTMAN, E. (1981). *Forms of talk.* Philadelphia: University of Pennsylvania Press.

GOTTMAN, E. (1983). The interaction order. *American Sociological Review. 48,* 1–17.

GOLD, M. S. (1984). *800-COCAINE.* New York: Bantam Books.

GOLD, R. (1952). Janitors versus tenants: A status-income dilemma. *American Journal of Sociology, 57,* 486–493.

GOLDSTEIN, K. (1940). *Human nature in the light of psychopathology.* Cambridge, Mass.: Harvard University Press.

GOLDSTEIN, K., AND SCHEERER, M. (1941). Abstract and concrete behavior: an experimental study with special tests, *Psychological Monographs,* vol. 53, no. 2.

GOODE, W. (February 1959). The theoretical importance of love. *American Sociological Review, 24,* 37–48.

GOODMAN, M. E. (1970). *The culture of childhood.* New York: Teachers College Press, Columbia University.

GOODY, J., & WATT, I. (1972). The consequences of literacy. In Pier P. Giglioli (Ed.), *Language and social context* (pp. 311–357). Baltimore: Penguin Books.

GOODY, J. (1962). *Death, property and the ancestors.* Stanford, CA: Stanford University Press.

GORER, G. (1965). *Death, grief, and mourning in contemporary britain.* London: The Cressey Press.

GOULDNER, A. (1970). *The coming crisis of Western sociology.* New York: Basic Books.

GOVE, W. R. (Ed.). (1980). *The labelling of deviance* (2nd ed.). Englewood Cliffs: NJ: Prentice-Hall.

GRAY, D. (January 1972). Turning out: A study of teenage prostitution. *Urban Life and Culture, 1* 401–425.

GREEN, P. J., MORGAN, C. J., & BARASH, D. P. (1979). Sociobiology. In S. G. McNall (Ed.), *Theoretical perspectives in sociology* (pp. 414–430). New York: St. Martin's Press.

GREIMAS, A. J., & COURTES, J. (1982). *Semiotics and language: An analytical dictionary.* Bloomington, IN: Indiana University Press.

GRIFFIN, J. (1962). *Black like me.* New York: Signet Books.

GRIMSHAW, A. D. (1981). Talk and social control. In M. Rosenberg & R. H. Turner (Eds.), *Social psychology: Sociological perspectives* (pp. 235–268). New York: Basic Books.

GROSS, E., & STONE, G. P. (July 1964). Embarrassment and the analysis of role requirements. *American Journal of Sociology, 70,* 1–15.

GROSZ, G. (1946). *A little yes and a big no.* New York: The Dial Press.

GUBRIUM, J. F. (1975). *Living and dying at murray manor.* New York: St. Martin's Press.

GUBRIUM, J. F. (1986). The social preservation of mind: The Alzheimer's disease experience. *Symbolic Interaction, 9,* 37–51.

GUMPERZ, J. (1964). Linguistics and social interaction in two communities. *American Anthropologist, 66,* 137–154.

GUMPERZ, J., & HYMES, D. (Eds.). (1964). *The ethnography of communication. American Anthropologist, 66,* no. 2.

GUSFIELD, J. R. (Fall 1967). Moral passage: The symbolic process in public designations of deviance. *Social Problems, 15,* 175–188.

GUZE, H. (1951). Hypnosis as wish fulfillment: A projective approach. *British Journal of Medical Hypnotism, 2,* 6–10.

GUZE, H. (1953). Hypnosis as emotional response: A theoretical approach. *Journal of Psychology, 35,* 313–328.

HABENSTEIN, R. W. (1962). Sociology of occupations: The case of the American funeral director. In A. Rose (Ed.), *Human behavior and social processes* (pp. 225–246). Boston: Houghton Mifflin.

HALBWACHS, M. (1925). *Les cadres sociaux de la mémoire* Paris: Librairie Félix Alcan.

HALBWACHS, M. (1950). *La mémoire collective.* Paris: Presses Universitaires.

HALL, C. S. (1953). A cognitive theory of dream symbols. *Journal of General Psychology, 48,* 169–186.

HALL, E. (1969). *The hidden dimension.* Garden City, NY: Anchor Books.

HALL, P. M. (1972). A symbolic interactionist analysis of politics. *Sociological Inquiry, 42,* 35–75.

HALL, P. M. (Winter 1986). Interactionism and the study of social organization. *Sociological Quarterly, 26.*

HALL, S. (1980). Cultural studies and the centre: Some problematics and problems. In S. Hall, D. Hobson, A. Lowe, & P. Willis (Eds.), *Culture, media and language: Working papers in cultural studies, 1972–1979* (pp. 1–49). London: Hutchinson.

HAMBURG, D. A., HAMBURG, B., & DE GOZA, S. (February 1953). Adaptive problems and mechanisms in severely burned persons. *Psychiatry, 16,* no. 1, 1–20.

HAMILTON, G. (1939). Changes in personality and psychosexuality with age. In E. V. Cowdry (Ed.), *Problems of aging: Biological and medical aspects* (pp. 459–482). Baltimore: Williams and Wilkins.

HANDEL, G. (Ed.). (1985). *The psychosocial interior of the family,* (3rd ed.). New York: Aldine.

HARDIN, J. B., POWER, M. B., & SUGRUE, N. M. (1986). The progressive concretization of phenomenological sociology. In N. K. Denzin (Ed.), *Studies in symbolic interaction, Part A* (pp. 49–77). Greenwich, CT: JAI Press.

HARMAN, L. D. (Spring 1986). Sign, symbol and metalanguage: Against the integration of semiotics and symbolic interaction *Symbolic Interaction, 9,* 147–160.

HARRÉ, R. (1982). Psychological Dimensions. In P. F. Secord (Ed.), *Explaining human behavior: Consciousness, human action and social structure* (pp. 93–114). Beverly Hills, CA: Sage Publications, Inc.

HARRÉ, R. & V. REYNOLDS (Eds.), (1984) *The meaning of primate signals.* Cambridge: University Press.

HARRÉ, R., & SECORD, P. (1972). *The explanation of social behaviour.* London: Blackwell.

HART, M. (1959). *Act one.* New York: Knopf.

HARTLEY, E. M., ROSENBAUM, R., & SCHWARTZ, S. (1948). Children's perceptions of ethnic group membership, *Journal of Psychology* 26: 387–398.

HARTUP, W. W. (April 1959). The social worlds of childhood. *American Psychologist, 34,* 944–950.

HAUGELAND, J. (1985). *Artificial intelligence: The very idea.* Cambridge, MA: The MIT Press.

HAVIGHURST, R. (1956). *Psychological aspects of aging.* Washington, D.C.: American Psychological Association.

HAWKES, T. (1977). *Structuralism and Semiotics.* Berkeley, Los Angeles: University of California Press.

HAYES, C. (1926). *Essays on nationalism.* New York: Macmillan.

HAYES, C. (1951). *The ape in our house.* New York: Harper & Row, Pub.

HEAD, H. G. (1926). *Aphasia and kindred disorders of speech.* New York: Macmillan.

HEAP, J. L., & ROTH, P. (June 1973). On phenomenological sociology. *American Sociological Review, 38,* 354–367.

HEATH, A. (1971). Review Article: *Exchange Theory. British Journal of Political Science, 1,* 90–119.

HEIDEGGER, M. (1962/1927). *Being and time.* New York: Harper & Row, Pub.

HEIDEGGER, M. (1982). *Basic problems in phenomenology.* Bloomington, IN: Indiana University Press.

HEIDEGGER, M. (1977). *Basic writings from being and time (1927) to The task of thinking (1964).* New York: Harper & Row, Pub.

HEIDER, F. (1958). *The psychology of interpersonal relations.* New York: John Wiley.

HENRY, J. (1963). *Culture against man.* New York: Random House.

HENSLIN, J. (Ed.). (1971). *The sociology of sex.* New York: Appleton-Centry-Crofts.

HERITAGE, J. (1984). *Garfinkel and ethnomethodology.* Cambridge: Polity.

HERITAGE, J. & GREATBATCH, D. (July 1986). Generating applause: A study of rhetoric and response at party political conferences. *American Journal of Sociology, 92,* 110–157.

HERTZLER, J. O. (1961). *A sociology of language.* New York: Random House.

HESS, R. D. & HANDEL, G. (1959). *Family Worlds.* Chicago: University of Chicago Press.

HEWES, G. W. (Feb.–April 1973). Primate communication and the gestural origin of language. *Current Anthropology, 14,* nos. 1–2, 5–12.

HEWITT, J. P. (1984). *Self and society: A symbolic interactionist social psychology,* (3rd ed.). Boston: Allyn & Bacon.

HEWITT, J. P., & HALL, P. M. (June 1973). Social problems: Problematic situations and quasi-theories. *American Sociological Review, 38,* 367–374.

HEWITT, J. P., & STOKES, R. (Feb. 1975). Disclaimers. *American Sociological Review, 40,* 1–11.

HEYL, B. S. (1979). *The madam as entrepreneur: Career management in house prostitution.* New Brunswick, NJ: Transaction Books.

HILL, R., & ALDOUS, J. (1969). Socialization for marriage and parenthood. In D. Goslin (Ed.), *Handbook of socialization theory and research* (pp. 885–950). Chicago: McNally & Company.

HILLER, E. T. (1933). *Principles of sociology.* New York: Harper & Row, Pub.

HITE, S. (1976). *The Hite report: A nationwide study of female sexuality.* New York: Dell.

HOCHSCHILD, A. R. (1973). *The unexpected community.* Englewood Cliffs, NJ: Prentice-Hall.

HOCHSCHILD, A. R. (March 1979). Emotion work, feeling rules, and social structure. *American Journal of Sociology, 85,* 551–575.

HOCHSCHILD, A. R. (1983). *The managed heart.* Berkeley: University of California Press.

HOCKETT, C. F. (September 1960). The Origin of Speech. *Scientific American, 203,* pp. 88–96.

HOCKETT, C. F. (1965). *A course in modern linguistics.* New York: Macmillan.

HOFFMAN, H. (1963). Child rearing practices and moral development: Generalizations from empirical research. *Child Development, 34,* pp. 295–318.

HOFFMAN, S. (1963). et al. *In search of France,* Cambridge, MA: Harvard University Press.

HOMANS, G. C. (1961). *Social behavior: Its elementary forms.* New York: Harcourt Brace Jovanovich.

HONIGMANN, J. J. (1954). *Culture and personality.* New York: Harper & Row, Pub.

HOOKER, E. (1967). The homosexual community. In J. H. Gagnon & W. Simon (Eds.), *Sexual deviance* (pp. 157–184). New York: Harper & Row, Pub.

HOROWITZ, E. (1936). The development of attitudes toward the Negro. *Archives of Psychology, 2,* no. 194.

HOROWITZ, I. L. (September 1971). The Pentagon papers and social science. *Transaction. 8,* 37–46.

HOROWITZ, I. L., & LIEBOWITZ, M. (Winter 1968). Social deviance and political marginality. *Social Problems, 15,* 280–296.

HOROWITZ, R. (1943). A pictorial method for the study of self-identification in preschool children. *Journal of Genetic Psychology, 62,* 135–148.

HOROWITZ, R. (1936). Spatial localization of the self. *Journal of Social Psychology, 6,* 379–387.

HOROWITZ, R. S. (April 1982). Adult delinquent gangs in a chicano community. *Urban Life, 11,* 3–27.

HOUSE, J. (1977). The three faces of social psychology. *Sociometry, 40,* 161–177.

HUBER, J. (April 1973). Symbolic interaction as a pragmatic perspective: The bias of emergent theory. *American Sociological Review, 38,* 274–284.

HUDGINS, C. V. (1933). Conditioning and the voluntary control of the pupillary light reflex. *Journal of General Psychology, 8,* 3–51.

HUDSON, W. (1960). Pictorial depth perception in subcultural groups in Africa. *Journal of Social Psychology, 52,* 183–208.

HUGHES, E. C. (1937). Institutional office and the person. *American Journal of Sociology, 43,* 404–413.

HUGHES, E. C. (1958). *Men and their Work.* New York: Free Press.

HULETT, J. E., JR. (1964). Communication and social order: The search for a theory. *Audio-Visual Communication Review, 12,* 458–468.

HULL, C. L. (1933). *Hypnosis and suggestibility.* New York: Prentice-Hall.

HUMPHREYS, L. (1970). *Tearoom Trade,* Chicago: Aldine.

HUMPHREYS, L. (1972). *Out of the closets: The sociology of homosexual liberation.* Englewood Cliffs, NJ: Prentice-Hall.

HUNT, M. (1966). *The world of the formerly married.* New York: McGraw-Hill.

HUNTER, E. (1951). *Brainwashing in red China.* New York: Vanguard Press.

HURLOCK, E. B. (1950). *Child development.* New York: McGraw-Hill.

HYMAN, H. (1942). *The psychology of status. Archives of Psychology, 269,* 1–94.

HYMAN, H. (1960). Reflections on reference groups. *Public Opinion Quarterly, 24,* 303–396.

HYMAN, H., & SINGER, E. (Eds.). (1968). *Readings in reference group theory.* New York: Free Press.

HYMES, D. H., (Ed.). (1964). *Language in culture and society.* New York: Harper & Row, Pub.

HYMES, D. H., (1972). Toward ethnographics of communication: The analysis of communicative events. In P. P. Giglioli (Ed.), *Language and social context: Selected readings* (pp. 21–44). Baltimore: Penguin Books.

HYMES, D. H., & GUMPERZ, J. (1969). *Directions in sociolinguistics.* New York: Holt, Rinehart & Winston.

ICHHEISER, G. (Sept. 1949). Misunderstandings in human relations. *American Journal of Sociology, 55,* part 2, 1–70.

ICHHEISER, G. (1970). *Appearances and realities: Misunderstandings in human relations.* San Francisco: Jossey-Bass.

IRWIN, J. (1977). *Scenes.* Beverly Hills, CA: Sage Publications, Inc.

ISAACS, S. S. (1933). *Social development in young children.* London: Routledge & Kegan Paul.

ITTELSON, W., & CANTRIL, H. (1954). *Perception: A transactional approach.* Garden City, NY: Doubleday.

JACOBS, J. (1969). *The search for help: A study of the retarded child in the community.* New York: Brunner Mazel.

JAKOBSON, R. & MORRIS, H. (1956). Two aspects of language and two aspects of aphasic disturbances, *Fundamentals of Language,* pp. 69–96. The Hague: Mouton.

JAMES, H. (1913). *A small boy and others.* London: Macmillan and Company.

JAMES, W. (1950/1890). *The principles of psychology.* New York: Dover.

JANOWITZ, M. (1962). *The professional soldier.* New York: Free Press.

JASPEN, N., & BLACK, H. (1960). *The thief in the white collar.* Philadelphia: Lippincott.

JELLINEK, E. M. (1962). Phases of alcohol addiction. In D. J. Pittman & C. R. Snyder (Eds.), *Society, culture, and drinking patterns* (pp. 356–368). New York: John Wiley.

JENNINGS, H. S. (1942). The transition from the individual to the social level. In J. Cattell (Ed.), *Biological symposia, 8,* 105–119.

JERSILD, A. (1947). *Child Psychology* (3rd ed.). Englewood Cliffs, NJ: Prentice-Hall.

JOFFE, C. (Aug. 1971). Sex role socialization and the nursery school: As the twig is bent. *Journal of Marriage and the Family, 33,* 467–475.

JOHNSON, J. M., & FERRARO, K. J. (1984). The victimized self: The case of battered women. In J. A. Kotarba & A. Fontana (Eds.), *The existential self in society* (pp. 119–130). Chicago: University of Chicago Press.

JORDAN, W. (1968). *White over black.* Chapel Hill, NC: University of North Carolina Press.

JUDD, C. H. (1926). *The psychology of social institutions.* New York: Macmillan.

JUDD, C. H. (1939). *Educational psychology.* Boston: Houghton Mifflin.

KADUSHIN, A., & MARTIN, J. A. (1981). *Child abuse: An interactional event.* New York: Columbia University Press.

KAHA, C. (1987). Wittgenstein, Merleau-Ponty and the

poetic gestalt. forthcoming in N. K. Denzin (Ed.), *Studies in symbolic interaction,* (vol. 9). Greenwich, CT: JAI Press.

KANDO, T. J. (Fall 1972). Passing and stigma management: The case of the transsexual. *Sociological Quarterly, 13,* 475–483.

KAPLAN, B. unpublished study, Clark University.

KANTER, R. (1972). *Communities and commitment.* Cambridge, MA: Harvard University Press.

KATZ, E. (1966). Communications research and the image of society: Convergence of two traditions. In A. G. Smith (Ed.), *Communication and culture.* New York: Holt, Rinehart & Winston.

KAZIN, A. (1951). *A walker in the city.* New York: Harcourt Brace Jovanovich.

KEIR, J. (1945). An experiment in mental testing under hypnosis. *Journal of Mental Science, 91,* 346–352.

KELLEY, H. (1952). Two functions of reference groups. In G. Swanson, T. Newcomb, E. Hartley (Eds.), *Readings in social psychology* (pp. 410–414). New York: Holt, Rinehart & Winston.

KELLOGG, W. N. (1961). *Porpoises and sonar.* Chicago: University of Chicago Press.

KELLOGG, W. N. & KELLOGG, L. A. (1933). *The ape and the child.* New York: McGraw-Hill.

KELLY, G. A. (1963). *A theory of personality: The psychology of personal constructs.* New York: W. W. Norton, & Co., Inc.

KEMPER, T. D. (Feb. 1968). Reference groups: Socialization and achievement. *American Sociological Review, 33,* 31–45.

KEMPER, T. D. (1978). *A social interactional theory of emotions.* New York: John Wiley.

KINSEY, A. C., et al. (1948). *Sexual Behavior in the Human Male.* Philadelphia: W. B. Saunders.

KINSEY, A. C., et al. (1954). *Sexual behavior in the human female.* Philadelphia: W. B. Saunders.

KITSUSE, J. K. (1962). Societal reaction to deviant behavior: Problems of theory and method. *Social Problems, 9,* 247–257.

KITSUSE, J. K. (June 1975). Social problems and deviance: Some parallel issues. *Social Problems, 22,* 585–594.

KITSUSE, J. K., AND SPECTOR, M. (Spring 1973). Toward a sociology of social problems: Value-judgments, and social problems. *Social Problems, 20,* 407–419.

KLAPP, O. (1949). The fool as a social type. *American Journal of Sociology, 55,* 157–162.

KLAPP, O. (1962). *Heroes, Villains and Fools.* Englewood Cliffs, N.J.: Prentice-Hall.

KLAPP, O. (1965). *Symbolic Leaders.* Chicago: Aldine.

KLAPPER, J. (1966). What we know about the effects of mass communication: The brink of hope. In A. G. Smith (Ed.), *Communication and culture* (pp. 535–551). New York: Holt, Rinehart & Winston.

KLAUS, MARSHALL H., & KENNELL, J. H. (1982). Parent-to-infant bonding. In Jay Belsky (Ed.), *The beginning: Readings on infancy.* New York: Columbia University Press.

KLEIN, M. (1932). *The psychoanalysis of children.* London: Hogarth Press.

KLEIN, M., GUZE, H., & HAGGERTY, A. (1954). *An experimental study of the nature of hypnotic deafness. Journal of Clinical and Experimental Hypnosis, 2,* 145–156.

KLINEBERG, O. (1940). *Social psychology.* New York: Holt, Rinehart & Winston.

KLINEBERG, O. (1954). *Social psychology* (rev. ed.) New York: Holt, Rinehart & Winston.

KLUCKHOHN, C. (1961). Notes on some anthropological aspects of communication. *American Anthropologist, 639,* 895–910.

KLUCKHOHN, C., & LEIGHTON, D. (1946). *The Navaho.* Cambridge, MA: Harvard University Press.

KLUCKHOHN, C., & MURRAY, H. A. (Eds.). (1948). *Personality in nature, society, and culture.* New York: Knopf.

KLUEGEL, J. R., & SMITH, E. R. (1986). *Beliefs about inequality: American's views of what is and what ought to be.* New York: Aldine De Gruyter.

KOCH, H. L. (1954). Child Psychology. *Annual Review of Psychology, 5,* 1–26.

KOHLBERG, L. (1963a). The development of children's orientations toward a moral order: A sequence in the development of moral thought. *Vita Humana, 6,* 11–33.

KOHLBERG, L. (1963b). Moral development and identification. In *National Society for the Study of Education* (62nd Yearbook). Chicago: University of Chicago Press.

KOHLBERG, L. (1966). Cognitive stages and preschool education. *Human Development, 9* 5–7.

KOHLBERG, L. (1969). Stage and sequence: The cognitive-developmental approach to socialization. In D. Goslin (Ed.), *Handbook of socialization theory and research* (pp. 180–213). Chicago: Rand McNally.

KOHLBERG, L. (1971). From is to ought: How to commit the naturalistic fallacy and get away with it in the study of moral development. In T. Mischel, (Ed.), *Cognitive Development and Epistemology* (pp. 79–83). New York: Academic Press.

KOHLBERG, L. (1976). The Study of Moral Development. In T. Lickona (Ed.), *Moral development and behavior* (pp. 102–136). New York: Holt, Rinehart & Winston.

KOHLBERG, L. (1981). *The philosophy of moral development.* San Francisco: Harper and Row.

KÖHLER, W. (1926). *The mentality of apes.* New York: Harcourt Brace Jovanovich.

KOHUT, H. (1977). *The Restoration of Self.* New York: International Universities Press.

KOLERS, P. A. (1983). Perception and representation. In R. Rosenzweig & L. W. Porter (Eds.), *Annual review of psychology*, vol. 34 (pp. 129–166). Palo Alto: CA: Annual Reviews Inc.

KOSHTOYANTS, K. S. (Ed.). (1955). *I. P. Pavlov: Selected works.* Moscow: Foreign Language Publications.

KOTARBA, J. A. (1977). The chronic pain experience. In J. D. Douglas & J. M. Johnson (Eds.), *Existential Sociology*, 257–272. New York: Cambridge University Press.

KOTARBA, J. A. (1984). A synthesis: The existential self in society. In J. A. Kotarba & A. Fontana (Eds.), *The existential self in society* (pp. 222–239). Chicago: University of Chicago Press.

KOTARBA, J. A., & FONTANA, A. (Eds.). (1984). *The existential self in society,* Chicago: University of Chicago Press.

KRAUSE EHEART, B., & LEAVITT, R. L. (1986). Training day care home providers: Implications for policy research. *Early Childhood Quarterly, 1,* 119–132.

KRIEGER, S. (1983). *The mirror dance.* Philadelphia: Temple University Press.

KRONUS, S. J. (1971). *The black middle class.* Columbus, OH: Charles E. Merrill.

KÜBLER-ROSS, E. (1969). *On death and dying.* New York: Macmillan.

KUHN, M. H. (1960). Self-attitudes by age, sex, and professional training. *Sociological Quarterly, 1,* 39–55.

KUHN, M. H. (1954a). Kinsey's view of human behavior. *Social Problems, 4,* 119–125.

KUHN, M. H. (1954b). Factors in personality: Socio-cultural determinants as seen through the Amish. In F. L. K. Hsu (Ed.), *Aspects of culture and personality* (pp. 43–60). New York: Abelard-Schuman.

KUHN, M. H. (Spring 1964a). The reference group reconsidered. *Sociological Quarterly, 5,* 5–24.

KUHN, M. H. (Spring 1964b). Major trends in symbolic interaction theory in the past twenty-five years. *Sociological Quarterly, 5,* 61–84.

KUHN, T. S. (1970). *The structure of scientific revolutions.* Chicago: University of Chicago Press.

LABOV, W. et al. (1968). *A study of the non-standard English of Negro and Puerto Rican speakers in New York City.* Washington, D.C.: Office of Education.

LACAN, J. A. (1977). *Ecrits: A selection.* New York: W. W. Norton, & Co., Inc.

LACLAU, E., & MOUFFE, C. (1985). *Hegemony and socialist strategy: Towards a radical democratic politics.* London: Verso.

LANDESCO, J. (1968). *Organized crime in Chicago: Part 3 of the Illinois crime survey, 1929.* Chicago: University of Chicago Press.

LANG, K., & LANG, G. (1961). *Collective dynamics.* New York: Macmillan.

LANGER, S. K. (1948). *Philosophy in a new key.* Baltimore: Penguin Books.

LARGEY, G., & WATSON, D. (1972). The sociology of odors. *American Journal of Sociology, 77,* 1021–1034.

LAVER, J. (1972). The production of speech. In J. Lyons (Ed.), *New horizons in linguistics* (pp. 53–75). Baltimore: Penguin Books.

LAZARSFELD, P. F. (1972). *Qualitative analysis: Historical and critical essays.* Boston: Allyn and Bacon.

LAZARSFELD, P. F., BERELSON, B., & GAUDET, H. (1948). *The people's choice.* New York: Columbia University Press.

LE BON, G. (1916). *The crowd.* London: Ernest Benn.

LEE, D. (1954). Symbolization and value. In L. Byson, et al. (Eds.), *Symbols and values: An initial study* (pp. 73–85). New York: Harper & Row, Pub.

LEE, M., & OFSHE, R. (Jan. 1981). The impact of behavioral style and status characteristics on social influence: A test of two competing theories. *Social Psychology Quarterly, 44,* 73–82.

LEFEBVRE, H. (1984/1971). *Everyday life in the modern world.* New Brunswick, NJ: Transaction Books.

LEMERT, E. M. (1957). *Social pathology.* New York: McGraw-Hill.

LEMERT, E. M. (1958). The behavior of the systematic check forger. *Social Problems, 6,* 141–149.

LEMERT, E. M. (March 1962). Paranoia and the dynamics of exclusion. *Sociometry, 25,* 2–20.

LEMERT, E. M. (1971). *Human deviance, social problems and social control* (2nd ed.). Englewood Cliffs, NJ: Prentice-Hall.

LENGERMANN, P. M., & WALLACE, R. A. (1985). *Gender in America: social control and social change.* Englewood Cliffs, NJ: Prentice-Hall.

LERNER, E. (1937). The problem of perspective in moral reasoning. *American Journal of Sociology, 30,* 249–269.

LESTER, M. (1984). Self: Sociological portraits. In J. A. Kotarba & A. Fontana (Eds.), *The existential self in society* (pp. 18–68). Chicago: University of Chicago Press.

LEVER, J. (1976). Sex differences in the games children play," *Social Problems, 23,* 478–487.

LEVER, J. (1978). Sex differences in the complexity of children's play and games. *American Sociological Review, 43,* 471–483.

LEWIS, J. N., & SARBIN, T. R. (1943). Studies in psychosomatics: The influence of hypnotic stimulation on gastric hunger contractions. *Psychosomatic Medicine, 5* 125–131.

LEWIS, M., MICHALSON, L. (1983). *Children's emotions and moods.* New York: Plenum Press.

LEWIS, M. M. (1936). *Infant speech.* New York: Harcourt Brace Jovanovich.

LEWIS, M. M. (1948). *Language in society.* New York: Social Science Research Council.

LEWIS, M. M. (1959). *How children learn to speak.* New York: Basic Books.

LEWONTIN, R. C., ROSE, S., & KAMIN, L. J. (1984). *Not in our genes: Biology, ideology, and human nature.* New York: Pantheon.

LEZNOFF, M. & WESTLEY, W. A. (1956). The homosexual community. *Social Problems, 3,* 257–263.

LIEBAN, R. W. (1966). Sorcery, illness, and social control in a Philippine municipality. In W. R. Scott & E. H. Volkart (Eds.), *Medical care: Readings in the sociology of medical institutions* (pp. 222–32). New York: John Wiley.

LIFTON, R. J. (1961). *Thought reform and the psychology of totalism.* New York: W. W. Norton & Co., Inc.

LILLY, J. C. (1961). *Man and dolphin.* Garden City, NY: Doubleday.

LINDESMITH, A. R. (1946). Can chimpanzees become morphine addicts? *Journal of Comparative Psychology, 39,* 109–117.

LINDESMITH, A. R. (1947). *Opiate addiction.* Bloomington IN: Principia Press.

LINDESMITH, A. R. (1965). *The addict and the law.* Bloomington, IN: Indiana University Press.

LINDESMITH, A. R. (1965). Basic problems in the social psychology of addiction a theory. In J. A. O'Donnell & J. C. Ball (Eds.), *Narcotic addiction* (pp. 91–109). New York: Harper & Row, Pub.

LINDESMITH, A. R. (1968). *Addiction and opiates.* Chicago: Aldine.

LINDESMITH, A. R. (1975). A reply to McAuliffe and Gordon's "test of Lindesmith's theory of addiction," *American Journal of Sociology,* 81 (July), 147–153.

LINTON, R. (1942). Age and sex categories. *American Sociological Review, 7,* 589–603.

LIPPMANN, W. (1922). *Public opinion.* New York: Harcourt Brace Jovanovich.

LISKA, A. E. (1977). The dissipation of sociological social psychology. *American Sociologist, 12,* 2–8.

LOFLAND, J. (1966). *Doomsday Cult.* Englewood Cliffs, NJ: Prentice-Hall.

LOFLAND, J. (1969). (with the assistance of L. H. Lofland), *Deviance and identity.* Englewood Cliffs, NJ: Prentice-Hall.

LOFLAND, J. (1981). Collective behavior: The elementary forms. In M. Rosenberg & R. Turner, (Eds.), *Social psychology: Sociological perspectives* (pp. 411–446). New York: Basic Books.

LOFLAND, J. & STARK, R. (1965). Conversion to a deviant perspective. *American Sociological Review, 30,* 862–875.

LOFLAND, L. H. (1985). The social shaping of emotion: The case of grief. *Symbolic Interaction, 8,* 171–190.

LORIMER, F. (1929). *The growth of reason.* New York: Harcourt Brace Jovanovich.

LOWRY, M. (1947). *Under the volcano.* London: Jonathan Cape.

LUCKEY, E. B., & NASS, G. D. (1969). A comparison of sexual attitudes and behavior in an international sample. *Journal of Marriage and the Family, 17,* 364–379.

LUGO, J. O., & HERSEY, G. L. (1974). *Human development.* New York: Macmillan.

LUKER, K. (1975). *Taking chances: Abortion and the decision not to contracept.* Berkeley: CA: University of California Press.

LUKER, K. (1984). *Abortion and the politics of motherhood.* Berkeley, CA: University of California Press.

LURIA, A. R. (1928). The problem of the cultural behavior of the child. *Journal of Genetic Psychology, 35,* 493–504.

LURIA, A. R. (1959). The directive function of speech in development and dissolution. *Word, 15,* 341–365.

LURIA, A. R. (1960). *The nature of human conflicts: An objective study of disorganization and control of human behavior.* New York: Grove Press.

LURIA, A. R. (1966). *Higher cortical functions in man.* (trans. by B. Haigh). New York: Basic Books.

LURIA, A. R. (1972). *The man with a shattered world: The history of a brain wound.* New York: Basic Books.

LURIA, A. R. (1976). *Cognitive development: Its cultural and social foundations* (trans. by Marin Lopez-Morillas and Lynn Solotaroff, ed. by Michael Cole). Cambridge, MA: Harvard University Press.

LURIA, A. R., & YUDOVICH, F. (1959). *Speech and the development of mental process in the child: An experimental investigation.* London: Staples Press.

LYMAN, S., & SCOTT, M. (1967). Territoriality: A neglected social dimension. *Social Problems, 15,* 236–249.

LYNCH, R. (1982). Play, creativity and emotion. In N. K. Denzin (Ed.), *Studies in Symbolic Interaction,* Vol. 4: 45–62. Greenwich, Conn.: JAI Press.

MCAULIFFE, W. E. AND GORDON, R. A. (1974). A test of Lindesmith's theory of addiction: the frequency of euphoria among long-term addicts. *American Journal of Sociology, 77,* 795–840.

MCCALL, G. J., & SIMMONS, J. L. (1966, 2nd ed. 1978). *Identities and interactions.* New York: Free Press.

MCCALL, G. J., & SIMMONS, J. L. (1981). *Social psychology.* New York: Free Press.

MCNEILL, D. (1966). The creation of language. *Discovery, 27,* 34–38.

MCPHAIL, C. & MILLER, D. (1973). The assembling process: A theoretical and empirical examination. *American Sociological Review, 38,* 721–735.

MCPHAIL, C., & WOHLSTEIN, R. T. (1986). Collective locomotion or collective behavior. *American Sociological Review 51,* 447–464.

MACAULAY, E., & WATKINS, S. (1926). An investigation into the moral conceptions of children. *Educational Forum. 4,* 13–33, 92–108.

MACCANNEL, D. (1976). The past and future of symbolic interaction. *Semiotica 16,* 99–114.

MacCannel, D. (1986). Keeping symbolic interaction safe from semiotics: A response to Harmon. *Symbolic Interaction, 9,* 161–168.

MacCannel, D. & MacCannell, J. F. (1982). *The time of the sign.* Bloomington, IN: Indiana University Press.

MacIver, R. (1942). *Social causation.* Boston: Ginn.

MacRae, E. R. (1954). A test of Piaget's theories of moral development. *Journal of Abnormal and Social Psychology, 49,* 14–18.

Maines, D. R. (1977). Social organization and social structure in symbolic interactionist thought. *Annual Review of Sociology, 3,* 235–259.

Maines, D. R. (1978). Bodies and selves. Notes on a fundamental dilemma in demography. *Studies in Symbolic Interaction,* vol. 1, *1,* 241–266.

Maines, D. R. (1979). Mesostructure and social process. *Contemporary Sociology, 8,* 524–527.

Maines, D. R. (1982). In search of mesostructure: Studies in the negotiated order. *Urban Life, 11,* 267–279.

Maines D. & Charlton, J. (1985). The negotiated order approach to analysis of social organization. In H. A. Farberman and R. S. Perinbanayagam (Eds.) *Foundations of interpretive sociology.* Greenwich, CT: JAI Press.

Maines D., Sugrue, N. M. & Katovich, M. A. (1983). The sociological import of G. H. Mead's theory of the past. *American Sociological Review 48,* 161–173.

Mannheim, K. (1936). *Ideology and utopia.* New York: Harcourt Brace Jovanovich.

Manning, P. K. (1987). Structuralism and social psychology. In N. K. Denzin (Ed.), *Studies in symbolic interaction,* (vol. 8). Greenwich CT: JAI Press.

Manning, P. K., & Fabrega, H. Jr. (1973). The experience of self and body: Health and illness in the Chiapas highlands. In G. Psathas, (Ed.), *Phenomenological sociology.* New York: John Wiley.

Margenau, H. (1950). *The nature of physical reality: A philosophy of modern physics.* New York: McGraw-Hill.

Markey, J. F. (1928). *The symbolic process and its integration in children.* New York: Harcourt Brace Jovanovich.

Markey, J. F. (1928). *The symbolic process and its integration in children: A study in social psychology.* New York: Harcourt, Brace, Jovanovich. Reissued, 1978, Chicago: University of Chicago Press.

Martin, G. B., & Clark, R. D. (1982). Distress crying in neonates: Species and peer specificity. *Developmental Psychology, 11,* 571–578.

Marx, K. (1983/1844). From the Eighteenth Brumaire of Louis Bonaparte. in E. Kamenda (Ed.), *The portable Karl Marx.* New York: Penguin Books.

Masters, W., & Johnson, E. (1966). *Human sexual response.* Boston: Little, Brown.

Masters, W., & Johnson, E. (1968). *Human sexual inadequacy.* Boston: Little, Brown.

Matza, D. (1964). *Delinquency and drift.* New York: John Wiley.

Matza, D. (1969). *Becoming deviant.* Englewood Cliffs, NJ: Prentice-Hall.

Maurer, D. (1940). *The big con.* Indianapolis: Bobbs-Merrill.

Maxwell, M. A. (1984). *The alcoholic experience: A close-up view for professionals.* New York: McGraw-Hill.

Mayrl, W. (1973). Ethomethodology: Sociology without society. *Catalyst, 7,* 15–29.

Mead, G. H. (1929). The nature of the past. In John Coss (Ed.), *Essays in honor of John Dewey.* New York: Henry Holt.

Mead, G. H. (1932). *The philosophy of the present.* LaSalle, IL: Open Court.

Mead, G. H. (1934). *Mind, self and society.* Chicago: University of Chicago Press.

Mead, G. H. (1936). *Movements of thought in the nineteenth century,* Chicago: University of Chicago Press.

Mead, G. H. (1938). *The philosophy of the act,* Chicago: University of Chicago Press.

Mead, M. (1955). Children and ritual in bali. In M. Mead & M. Wolfenstein (Eds.), *Childhood in contemporary cultures.* Chicago: University of Chicago Press.

Mead, M. & Wolfenstein M. (Eds.). (1955). *Childhood in Contemporary Cultures.* Chicago: University of Chicago Press.

Meeker, B. (1981). Expectation states and interpersonal behavior. In M. Rosenberg and R. Turner (Eds.), *Social psychology* (pp. 290–319). NY: Basic Books.

Mehan, H. (1975). *The reality of ethnomethodology.* New York: John Wiley.

Mehan, H., & Wood, H. (Feb. 1976). De-Secting Ethnomethodology. *American Sociologist, 11,* 13–21.

Meltzer, B. N. (1972). Mead's social psychology. In J. G. Manis and B. N. Meltzer (Eds.), *Symbolic interaction: A reader in social psychology* (2nd ed.) pp. 4–22. Boston: Allyn & Bacon.

Mercer, J. R. (1973). *Labelling the mentally retarded.* Berkeley, CA: University of California Press.

Merleau-Ponty, M. (1973). *Consciousness and the acquisition of language.* Evanston, IL: Northwestern University Press.

Merleau-Ponty, M. (1962). *The phenomenology of perception.* London: Routledge & Kegan Paul.

Merleau-Ponty, M. (1963). *The structure of behavior.* Boston: Beacon Press.

Merleau-Ponty, M. (1964). *The primacy of perception.* Evanston, IL: Northwestern University Press.

Merleau-Ponty, M. (1968). *The visible and the invisible.* Evanston, IL: Northwestern University Press.

Merton, R. K. (1957). *Social theory and social structure* (rev. ed.). New York: Free Press.

Merton, R. K. & Kitt, A. S. (1950). Contributions to

the theory of reference group behavior. In R. K. Merton & P. F. Lazersfeld (Eds.), *Studies in the scope and method of "The American Soldier"* (pp. 70–105). New York: Free Press.

MERTON, R. K., & NISBET, R. A. (Eds.). (1966). *Contemporary social problems* (rev. ed.). New York: Harcourt Brace Jovanovich.

MESSINGER, S. L., & WARREN, C. A. B. (1984). The homosexual self and the organization of experience: The case of Kate White. In Joseph A. Kotarba and A. Fontana (Eds.), *The existential self in society* (pp. 196–206). Chicago: University of Chicago Press.

MESSNER, S. F. (1986). Television violence and violent crime: An aggregate analysis. *Social Problems, 33*, 218–235.

METZ, C. (1982). *The imaginary signifier: Psychoanalysis and the cinema.* Bloomington, IN: Indiana University Press.

MILESKI, M., & BLACK, D. J. (1972). The social organization of homosexuality. *Urban Life and Culture, 1*, 187–202.

MILFORD, J. (1963). *The American way of death.* New York: Simon & Schuster.

MILLER, D. (1985). *Collective behavior.* Dubuque, IA: Brown.

MILLER, D. E. (1986). Hypnosis as Asymmetric Interaction. In C. J. Couch, S. L. Saxton, and M. A. Katovich (Eds.), *Studies in Symbolic Interaction: A Research Annual. Supplement Two, The Iowa School. Part A,* pp. 167–194. Greenwich, Conn.: JAI Press, 1986.

MILLER, J. C. (1942). *Unconsciousness.* New York: John Wiley.

MILLER, N. E., & DOLLARD, J. (1941). *Social learning and imitation.* New Haven: Yale University Press.

MILLS, C. W. (1939). Language, logic, and culture. *American Sociological Review, 4*, 670–675.

MILLS, C. W. (1940). Situated actions and culture. *American Sociological Review, 5*, 904–913.

MILLS, C. W. (1958). *The power elite.* New York: Oxford University Press.

MILLS, C. W. (1959). *The sociological imagination.* New York: Oxford University Press.

MILLS, T. M. (1959). Equilibrium and the processes of deviance and control. *American Sociological Review, 24*, 671–679.

MITCHELL, J. (1983). Introduction—I. In J. Mitchell & J. Rose (Eds.), *Feminine sexuality: Jacques Lacan and the Ecole Freudienne.* New York: Pantheon Books.

MIYAMOTO, F. (1970). Self, motivation, and symbolic interactionist theory. In T. Shibutani (Ed.), *Human nature and collective behavior.* Englewood Cliffs, NJ: Prentice-Hall.

MIZRUCHI, E. M., & PERRUCCI, R. (1962). Norm qualities and differential effects of deviant behavior. *American Sociological Review, 27*, 391–399.

MOLSEED, M. J., & MAINES, D. R. (1987). Sources of

imprecision and irrationality in expectation states theory. In N. K. Denzin (Ed.), *Studies in symbolic interaction,* (vol. 8). Greenwich, CT: JAI Press.

MORENO, J. (1934). *Who shall survive?* Washington, D.C.: Nervous and Mental Disease Publishing Company.

MORGAN, L. (1894). *Introduction to comparative psychology.* New York: Young Scott Books.

MORRIS, C. (1946). *Signs, language, and behavior.* Englewood Cliffs, NJ: Prentice Hall.

MULLAHY, P. (Ed.). (1952). *The contributions of H. S. Sullivan: A symposium.* New York: Hermitage House.

MULLINS, N. (1973). *Theories and theory groups in contemporary American sociology.* New York: Harper & Row, Pub.

MURPHY, G., MURPHY, L. & NEWCOMB, T. (1937). *Experimental social psychology.* New York: Harper & Row, Pub.

MURSTEIN, B. (Ed.). (1971). *Theories of attraction and love.* Berlin: Springer-Verlag.

NASH, J. (1985). *Social psychology: Self and society.* St. Paul, MN: West Publishing Company.

NEUBECK, G. (Ed.). (1969). *Extramarital relations.* Englewood Cliffs, NJ: Prentice-Hall.

NEWCOMB, T. (1950). *Social psychology.* New York: Holt, Rinehart & Winston.

NEWCOMB, T. TURNER, R., & CONVERSE, P. (1965). *Social psychology.* New York: Holt, Rinehart & Winston.

NEWTON, E. (1972). *Mother camp: Female impersonators in America.* Englewood Cliffs, NJ: Prentice-Hall.

New York Times. (February 9, 1948). (pp. 1, 3).

NICHOLS, J. R. (1965). How opiates change behavior. *Scientific American, 212,* 80–88.

NICHOLS, J. P., HEADLEE, C. P., & COPPOCK, H. W. (Dec. 1956). Drug addiction I: Addiction by escape training. *Journal of the American Pharmaceutical Association, 45,* no. 12, 788–791.

NICHOLS, J. R., & DAVIS, W. M. (May 1959). Drug addiction II: Variations of addiction. *Journal of the American Pharmaceutical Association, 48,* no. 5, 259–262.

NOY, R. S., & SHARRON, A. (1985). The indiscretion of Franz Kafka: The artist as a victim of child abuse. *Studies in Symbolic Interaction, 6,* 261–287.

NURGE, E. (1961). Etiology of illness in Guinhangdan. *American Anthropologist, 63,* 113–132.

O'CONNOR, P. J. (July 23–24, 1977). Burial vault strike: A double dose of grief. *Chicago Daily News,* (p. 5).

O'NEILL, J. (1985). *Five bodies: The human shape of modern society.* Ithaca, NY: Cornell University Press.

OPIE, I., & OPIE, P. (1969). *Children's games in street and playground.* New York: Oxford University Press.

OPLER, M. E., & BITTLE, W. E. (1967). The death practices of the Kiowa Apache. In R. C. Owen, J. J. F. Deetz, & A. D. Fisher (Eds.), *The North American Indi-*

ans: *A sourcebook* (pp. 472–482). New York: Macmillan.

ORNE, M. T. (1970). Hypnosis, motivation and the ecological validity of the psychological experiment. In W. J. Arnold & M. M. Page (Eds.), *Nebraska Symposium on Motivation* (pp. 23–46). Lincoln, NB: University of Nebraska Press.

ORNE, M. T. (1979). On the simulating subject as a quasi-control group in hypnosis research: What, why and how. In E. Fromm & R. E. Shor (Eds.), *Hypnosis developments in research and new perspectives* (pp. 102–143). Chicago: Aldine.

OSGOOD, C. E., & TANNENBAUM, P. H. (1955). The principle of congruity in the prediction of attitude change. *Psychological Review, 62,* 42–55.

PACKARD, V. (1983). *Our endangered children.* Boston: Little, Brown.

PANNABECKER, B. J., EMDE, R. N., JOHNSON, W., STENBERG, C., & DAVIS, M. (1980). Maternal perceptions of infant emotions from birth to eighteen months: A preliminary report. Paper presented at the International Conference of Infant Studies, New Haven, CT.

PARSONS, T. (1951). *The social system.* New York: Free Press.

PARSONS, T. (1954). Psychology and sociology. In J. Gillin (Ed.), *For a science and social man* (pp. 67–101). New York: Macmillan.

PARSONS, T., & PLATT, G. M. (1970). Age, social structure and socialization in higher education. *Sociology of Education, 43,* 1–37.

PARTEN, M. B. (1932). Social participation among preschool children. *Journal of Abnormal and Social Psychology, 27,* 263–269.

PATTEE, F. (1935). A report of attempts to produce uniocular blindness by hypnotic suggestion. *British Journal of Medicine and Psychology, 15,* 230–241.

PATTEE, F. (1940). The genuineness of unilateral deafness produced by hypnosis. *American Journal of Psychology, 63,* 84–86.

PATTERSON, N. (1985). Kolko. *National Geographic 95,* 400–409.

PAVLOV, I. P. (1929). *Conditioned reflexes.* New York: Oxford University Press.

PAVLOV, I. P. (1960). *Conditioned reflexes: An investigation of the physiological activity of the cerebral cortex.* New York: Dover Press.

PEIRCE, C. (1960). Elements of logic. In C. Hartshorne & P. Weiss (Eds.), *Collected papers of Charles Sanders Peirce,* Vol. 2. Cambridge: Harvard University Press.

PERINBANAYAGAM, R. S. (1985). *Signifying acts.* Carbondale: Southern Illinois University Press.

PERINBANAYAGAM, R. S. (1986). The meaning of uncertainty and the uncertainty of meaning. *Symbolic Interaction 9,* 105–126.

PHILLIPS, D. (1986). The federal model child care standards act of 1985: Steps in the right direction or hollow gesture. *American Journal of Orthopsychiatry, 56,* 54–56.

PIAGET, J. (1937). Principal factors determining intellectual evolution from childhood to adult life. In *Factors determining human behavior.* Cambridge, MA: Harvard University Press.

PIAGET, J. (1948). *The moral judgment of the child.* New York: Free Press.

PIAGET, J. (1950a). *The psychology of intelligence.* London: Routledge & Kegan Paul.

PIAGET, J. (1951a). *Play, dreams, and imitation in childhood.* New York: W. W. Norton & Co., Inc.

PIAGET, J. (1951b). *Play, dreams, and imitation in childhood.* London: William Heinemann.

PIAGET, J. (1951c). *The child's conception of the world.* New York: Humanities Press.

PIAGET, J. (1952a). *The child's conception of number,* New York: Humanities Press.

PIAGET, J. (1952b). *The origins of intelligence in children.* New York: International Universities Press.

PIAGET, J. (1952c). *Judgment and reasoning in the child.* New York: Humanities Press.

PIAGET, J. (1954). *The construction of reality in the child.* New York: Basic Books.

PIAGET, J. (1959). *The language and thought of the child.* New York: Humanities Press.

PIAGET, J. (1960). *The child's conception of physical causality.* Paterson, NJ: Littlefield, Adams.

PIAGET, J. (1967). *The child's conception of the world.* Totowa, NJ: Littfield, Adams. (first published 1929)

PIAGET, J. (1970). *Structuralism.* New York: Basic Books.

PIAGET, J. (1983). *Intelligence and affectivity: their relationship during child development.* Palo Alto, CA: Annual Reviews, Inc.

PIAGET, J., & INHELDER, B. (1969). *The psychology of the child.* New York: Basic Books.

PITTINGER, R. E., & SMITH, H. L. (1967). A basis for some contributions of linguistics to psychiatry. *Psychiatry, 20,* 61–78.

PIZZEY, E. (1974). *Scream quietly or the neighbors will hear.* Baltimore: Penguin.

POLSKY, N. (1966). *Hustlers, beats, and others.* Chicago: Aldine.

PONSE, B. R. (1978). *Identities in the lesbian world,* New York: Greenwood Press.

POSTMAN, N. (1982). *The disappearance of childhood,* New York: Laurel Book.

POWELL, J. H. (1965). *Bring out your dead: The great plague of yellow fever in Philadelphia in 1793.* New York: Time-Life Books.

POWER, M. B. (1985). The ritualization of emotional

conduct in early childhood. *Studies in Symbolic Interaction, 6,* 213–227.

PREMACK, A. J., & PREMACK, D. (1972). Teaching language to an ape. *Scientific American, 227,* 92–99.

QUADAGNO, J. S. (Ed.) (1980). *Aging, the individual and society: readings in social gerontology.* New York: St. Martin's Press.

QUIATT, D. (1984). Devious intentions of monkeys and apes. In R. Harré & V. Reynolds (Eds.), *The meaning of primate signals.* Cambridge: Cambridge University Press.

QUINT, J. (1963). The impact of mastectomy. *American Journal of Nursing, 63,* 88–92.

RAGLAND-SULLIVAN, E. (1986). *Jacques Lacan and the philosophy of psychoanalysis.* Urbana, IL: University of Illinois Press.

RAINWATER, L. (1970). *Behind ghetto walls.* Chicago: Aldine.

REISS, I. L. (1971). *The family system in America.* New York: Holt, Rinehart & Winston.

RESKIN, B. F. (1984). *Sex segregation in the workplace.* Washington, D.C.: Women's Research and Education Institute.

REYNOLDS, V. (1984). Introductory comments. In R. Harré & V. Reynolds (Eds.), *The meaning of primate signals.* Cambridge: Cambridge University Press.

RICHARDSON, S. A. (1969). The effect of physical disability on the socialization of the child. In D. A. Goslin (Ed.), *Handbook of socialization theory and research* (pp. 1047–1064). Skokie, IL: Rand McNally.

RICOEUR, P. (1981). *Hermeneutics and the human sciences.* Cambridge: Cambridge University Press.

RIEZLER, K. (1950). *Man: Mutable and immutable.* Chicago: Henry Regnery.

RILEY, J. W. JR. (1983). Dying and the meanings of death: Sociological inquiries. *Annual Review of Sociology, 9,* 191–216.

RIORDON, W. (1966). *Plunkitt of tammany hall.* New York: Dutton.

ROBSON, R. (1968). The present state of theory in sociology. In I. Lakatos & A. Musgrove (Eds.), *Problems in the philosophy of science.* Amsterdam: North-Holland.

ROBY, P. (1969). Politics and criminal law: Revision of the New York State penal law on prostitution. *Social Problems, 17,* 83–109.

ROCK, P. (1979). *The making of symbolic interactionism,* Totowa, NJ: Rowman & Littlefield.

ROONEY, E. & GIBBONS, D. C. (1965). Social reactions to "crimes without victims." *Social Problems, 13,* 400–410.

ROPERS, R. (1973). Mead, Marx and social psychology. *Catalyst, 7,* 42–61.

ROSE, J. (1983). Introduction—II. In J. Mitchell and J.

Rose (Eds.), *Feminine sexuality: Jacques Lacan and the Ećole Freudienne.* New York: Pantheon Books.

ROSENBAUM, M. (1981). *Women on heroin.* New Brunswick, NJ: Rutgers University Press.

ROSENBLUETH, A. (1970). *Mind and brain: A philosophy of science.* Cambridge, MA: M.I.T. Press.

ROSENTHAL, R. (1966). *Experimental effects in behavioral research.* New York: Appleton-Century-Crofts.

ROSOW, I. (1967). *Social integration of the aged.* New York: Free Press.

ROSS, H. L. (1971). Modes of adjustment of married homosexuals. *Social Problems, 18,* 385–393.

ROSSI, A. S. (1965). Naming children in middle class families. *American Sociological Review, 30,* 499–513.

ROSSI, A. S. (1984). Gender and parenthood. *American Sociological Review, 49,* 1–19.

ROYKO, M. (1971). *Boss: Richard J. Daley of Chicago.* New York: Dutton.

RUDE, G. (1964). *The crowd in history.* New York: John Wiley.

RUNYON, T. (1953). *In for life.* New York: W. W. Norton & Co., Inc.

RUSSELL, W. R., & ESPIR, L. E. (1961). *Traumatic aphasia: A study of aphasia in war wounds of the brain.* New York: Oxford University Press.

SACKS, O. (1985). *The man who mistook his wife for a hat and other clinical tales.* New York: Harper.

SAFILIOS-ROTHCHILD, C. (ed.) (1972). *Toward a sociology of women.* Lexington, MA: Xerox College Publishing.

SALOMONE, J. J. (1973). An empirical report on some controversial American funeral practices. *Sociological Symposium, 1,* 47–66.

SAMSON, W. (1956). *A contest of ladies.* London: Hogarth.

SANDBURG, C. (1936). Elephants are different to different people. In L. Untermeyer (Ed.), *A critical anthology: Modern American poetry* (p. 249). New York: Harcourt Brace Jovanovich.

SAPIR, E. (1942). Communication. In *Encyclopedia of the Social Sciences* (vol. 2). (pp. 78–81).

SAPIR, E. (1949a). The status of linguistics as a science. In D. G. Mandelbaum (Ed.), *Selected writings in language, culture, and personality.* Berkeley: University of California Press.

SAPIR, E. (1949b). Time perspective in aboriginal American culture: A study in method. In D. G. Mandelbaum (Ed.), *Selected writings in language, culture and personality.* Berkeley: University of California Press.

SARBIN, T. R. (1950). Contributions to role-taking theory, I: Hypnotic behavior. *Psychological Review, 57,* 255–270.

SARBIN, T. R. (1950). Mental changes in experimental regression. *Journal of Personality, 19,* 221–228.

SARTRE, J.-P. (1956/1943). *Being and nothingness*, New York: Philosophical Library.

SARTRE, J.-P. (1960/1976). *The critique of dialectical reason*. London: NLP.

SARTRE, J.-P. (1981). *The family idiot: Gustave Flaubert. Vol. 1: 1821–1857.* Chicago: University of Chicago Press.

SAUSSURE, F. DE. (1959). *Course in general linguistics.* New York: McGraw-Hill.

SAXTON, S. L. JR. AND HALL, P. M. (1987). Two social psychologies: New grounds for discussion. In N. K. Denzin (ed.), *Studies in symbolic interaction*, (vol. 8). Greenwich, CT: JAI Press.

SCANZONI, J. (1972). *Sexual bargaining: Power politics in the American marriage.* Englewood Cliffs, NJ: Prentice-Hall.

SCHACHTEL, E. (1947). On memory and childhood amnesia. *Psychiatry, 10,* 1–26.

SCHACHTER, S., & SINGER, J. E. (1962). Cognitive, social, and physiological determinants of emotional states. *Psychological Review, 69,* 379–399.

SCHAFFER, H. R. (1971). *The growth of sociability.* Baltimore: Penguin Books.

SCHATZMAN, L., & STRAUSS, A. (1955). Social class and modes of communication. *American Journal of Sociology, 60,* 329–338.

SCHEERER, M. (1967). Cognitive theory. In G. Lindzey (Ed.), *Handbook of social psychology.* Reading, MA: Addison-Wesley.

SCHEFFLER, I. (1967). *Science and subjectivity.* Indianapolis: Bobbs-Merrill.

SCHEIN, E. I., SCHUCIER, & BARKER, J. (1961). *Coercive persuasion.* New York: W. W. Norton & Co., Inc.

SCHMITT, R. L. (1972). *The reference other orientation: An extension of the reference group concept.* Carbondale, IL: Southern Illinois University Press.

SCHNEIRLA, T. (1946). Problems in the biopsychology of social organization. *Journal of Abnormal and Social Psychology, 41,* 390–398.

SCHNEIRLA, T. (1949). Levels in the psychological capacities of animals. In R. Sellars (Ed.), *Philosophy for the future.* New York: Macmillan.

SCHNEIRLA, T. (1953). Animal behavior and human relations. In M. Sherif & C. Sherif (Eds.) *Groups in harmony and tension.* New York: Harper & Row, Pub.

SCHNEIRLA, T. (1953). The concept of levels in the study of social phenomena. In M. Sherif & C. Sherif (Eds.), *Groups in harmony and tension* (pp. 54–75). New York: Harper & Row, Pub.

SCHEFF, T. J. (1979). *Catharsis in healing, ritual, and drama.* Berkeley: University of California Press.

SCHRIER, A. M., HARLOW, H. H., AND STOLLNITZ, F. (Eds.). (1965). *Behavior of nonhuman primates.* New York: Academic Press.

SCHULTZ, J. CARRIN, G., KRUPP, H., PEOCHKE, M., SCLAR, E., & VAN STEENBERGE, J. (1974). *Providing adequate retirement income.* Hanover, N.H.: Brandeis University Press.

SCHUR, E. M., (1965). *Crimes without Victims: Deviant Behavior and Public Policy.* Englewood Cliffs, NJ: Prentice-Hall.

SCHUR, E. M. (1971). *Labelling deviant behavior.* New York: Harper & Row, Pub.

SCHUTZ, A. (1962). *Collected papers vol. 1: The problem of social reality.* The Hague: Martinus Nijhoff.

SCHUTZ, A. (1964). *Collected papers, vol. 2. Studies in social theory.* The Hague: Martinus Nijhoff.

SCHUTZ, A. & LUCKMANN, T. (1973). *The structures of the life world,* Evanston, IL: Northwestern University Press.

SCHWARTZ, B. (1967). The social psychology of the gift. *American Journal of Sociology, 73,* 1–11.

SCHWARTZ, GREEN, C., & K. M. J. (1973). *Conflict and contradiction in psychiatry: The evolution of a professional sub-speciality.* Mimeographed.

SCHWARTZ, D., & MERTEN, G. (1967). The language of adolescence. *American Journal of Sociology, 72,* 453–468.

SCHWARTZ, D., & MERTEN, G. (1971). Participant observation and the discovery of meaning. *Philosophy of Social Science, 1,* 290–295.

SCOTT, M. (1968). *The racing game.* Chicago: Aldine.

SCOTT, M. B., & LYMAN, S. M. (Dec. 1968). Accounts. *American Sociological Review, 33,* 46–62.

SCOTT, M. B., & STANFORD, M. L. (1969). *The socialization of blind children.* In D. A. Goslin (Ed.), *Handbook of socialization theory and research* (pp. 1025–1045). Skokie, IL: Rand McNally.

SCOTT, M. & LYMAN, S. (1970). *A sociology of the absurd.* New York: Appleton-Century-Crofts.

SCOTT, M. B., & LYMAN, S. M. (1970). Paranoia, homosexuality, and game theory. In S. M. Lyman & M. B. Scott, *A sociology of the absurd* (pp. 71–88). New York: Appleton-Century-Crofts.

SEARLE, J. R. (1970). *Speech acts.* New York: Cambridge University Press.

SECORD, P. F. (Ed.) (1982). *Explaining human behavior: consciousness, human action and social structure.* Beverly Hills, Ca.: Sage Publications.

SECORD, P. F., & BACKMAN, C. W. (1964). *Social psychology.* New York: McGraw-Hill.

SEGALL, CAMPBELL, M. D., & HERSKOVITZ, M. J. (1964). *The influence of culture on visual perception.* Indianapolis: Bobbs-Merrill.

SELMAN, R. L. (1981). The child as a friendship philosopher. In S. R. Asher & J. M. Gottman (Eds.), *The development of children's friendships* (pp. 242–272). New York: Cambridge University Press.

SEWARD, G. H. (1946). *Sex and the social order.* New York: McGraw-Hill.

SEYFARTH, R. (1984). What the vocalization of monkeys means to humans and what they mean to the monkeys themselves. In R. Harrè & V. Reynolds (Eds.), *The meaning of primate signals.* Cambridge University Press.

SHERIF, M. (1948). *An outline of social psychology.* New York: Harper & Row, Pub.

SHERIF, M. (1953). *Group relations at the crossroads.* New York: Harper & Row, Pub.

SHERIF, M., & CANTRIL, H. (1947). *The psychology of ego-involvement.* New York: John Wiley.

SHERIF, M., HARVEY, J. O., WHITE, B. J., & HOOD, R. (1954). *Theoretical and experimental studies in interpersonal and group relations.* Norman, OK: University of Oklahoma Press.

SHIBUTANI, T. (1955). Reference groups as perspectives. *American Journal of Sociology, 60* 562–569.

SHIBUTANI, T. (1961). *Society and personality: An interactionist approach to social psychology.* Englewood Cliffs, NJ: Prentice-Hall.

SHIBUTANI, T. (1962). Reference groups and social control. In Arnold Rose (Ed.), *Human behavior and social process.* Boston: Houghton Mifflin.

SHIBUTANI, T. (1966). *Improvised news: A sociological study of rumor.* Indianapolis: Bobbs-Merrill.

SHIBUTANI, T. (1978). *The derelicts of company K: A sociological study of demoralization.* Berkeley: University of California Press.

SHINN, M. W. (1891). Notes on the development of a child. *Education, 1,* 140–145.

SHOVER, N. (1973). The social organization of burglary. *Social Problems, 20,* 499–514.

SHOVER, N. (1985). *Aging criminals.* Beverly Hills, CA: Sage Publications, Inc.

SHWEDER, R. A., & LEVINE, R. A. (Eds.). (1984). *Culture theory: Essays on mind, self and emotion.* London: Cambridge University Press.

SIMMEL, G. (1950). *The sociology of Georg Simmel,* trans. by Kurt Wolff. New York: Free Press.

SIMMEL, G. (1953). *Conflict and the web of group affiliations,* ed. and trans. by R. Bendix & E. C. Hughes. New York: Free Press.

SINGELMANN, P. (1972). Exchange as symbolic interaction: Convergence between two theoretical perspectives. *American Sociological Review, 37,* 414–424.

SINGER, C. (1959). *The history of scientific ideas to 1900.* New York: Oxford University Press.

SINGER, J. L. (1975). *The inner world of daydreaming.* New York: Harper & Row, Pub.

SKOLNICK, A. S., & SKOLNICK, J. H. (Eds.). (1977). *Family in transition.* Boston: Little, Brown.

SMELSER, N. (1963). *Theory of collective behavior.* New York: Free Press.

SNIVELY, W. D. JR., & BESHEAR, D. R. (1972). *Textbook of pathophysiology.* Philadelphia: Lippincott.

SOLAUN, M., & KRONUS, S. (1973). *Discrimination without violence: miscegenation and racial conflict in Latin America.* New York: John Wiley.

SOLOMON, D. (1964). LSD: *The consciousness-expanding drug.* New York: Putnam's.

SOLOMON, D. (Ed.). (1966). *The marijuana papers.* Indianapolis: Bobbs-Merrill.

STEBBINS, R. A. (1970). Career: The subjective approach. *Sociological Quarterly, 11,* 32–49.

STENDLER, C. (1949). *Children of brasstown.* Urbana, IL: University of Illinois Press.

STOLLER, R. S. (1967). Appendix to chapter five. In H. Garfinkel, *Studies in ethnomethodology.* Englewood Cliffs, NJ: Prentice-Hall.

STOLLER, R. S. (1979). *Sexual excitement: Dynamics of erotic life.* New York: Pantheon.

STONE, B. (1982). Saussure, Schutz and symbolic interactionism on the constitution and interpretation of signitive behavior. In N. K. Denzin (Ed.), *Studies in symbolic interaction,* (vol. 4). (pp. 91–106). Greenwich, CT: JAI Press.

STONE, G. P. (1962). Appearance and the self. In A. M. Rose (Ed.), *Human behavior and social process* (pp. 86–118). Boston: Houghton Mifflin.

STONE, G. P. (1981). Appearance and the self: A slightly revised version. In G. P. Stone & H. A. Faberman (Eds.), *Social psychology through symbolic interaction* (2nd ed.) (pp. 187–202). New York: John Wiley.

STONE, G. P. (1985). Conceptual problems in small group research. In N. K. Denzin (Ed.), *Studies in symbolic interaction,* (vol. 5), pp. 3–21. Greenwich, CN: JAI Press.

STRAUSS, A. (1952). The development and transformation of monetary meanings in the child. *American Sociological Review, 17,* 275–286.

STRAUSS, A. (1954). The development of conceptions of rules in children. *Child Development, 23,* 193–208.

STRAUSS, A. (Ed.). (1964). *George Herbert Mead on social psychology.* Chicago: University of Chicago Press.

STRAUSS, A. (1969). *Mirrors and masks.* San Francisco: Sociology Press.

STRAUSS, A. (1971). *The contexts of social mobility.* Chicago: Aldine.

STRAUSS, A. (1977). Sociological theories of personality. In R. J. Corsini, (Ed.), *Current personality theories,* 277–302. Itasca, IL.: F. E. Peacock.

STRAUSS, A. (1978). *Negotiations: Varieties, contexts, processes, and social order,* San Francisco: Jossey-Bass.

STRAUSS, A., FAGERHAUGH, S., SUCZEK, B., & WIENER, C. (1985). *The social organization of medical work.* Chicago: University of Chicago Press.

STRAUSS, A., & GLASER, B. G. (1970). *Anguish: A case history of a dying trajectory.* San Francisco: Sociology Press.

STRAUSS, A., SCHATZMAN, L., BUCKER, R., EHRLICH, D., & SABSHIN, M. (1964). *Psychiatric ideologies, and institutions.* New York: Free Press.

STRAUSS, A. S., ET AL. (1963). The hospital and its negotiated order. In E. Freidson (Ed.), *The hospital in modern society* (pp. 142–169). New York: Free Press.

STRYKER, S. (1977). Developments in "two social psychologies": toward an appreciation of mutual relevance. *Sociometry 40,* 145–160.

STRYKER, S. (1981). Symbolic interactionism: Themes and variations. In M. Rosenberg & R. K. Turner (Eds.), *Social psychology: Sociological perspectives* (pp. 3–29). New York: Basic Books.

STRYKER, S. (1985). Symbolic interaction and role theory. In G. Lindzey & E. Aronson (Eds.), *The handbook of social psychology.* (3rd ed.) (pp. 311–378). New York: Random House.

SUDNOW, D. (1967). *Passing on: The social organization of dying.* Englewood Cliffs, NJ: Prentice-Hall.

SUDNOW, D. (Ed.). (1972). *Studies in social interaction.* New York: Free Press.

SUDNOW, D. (1978). *Ways of the hand.* New York: Knopf.

SUDNOW, D. (1979). *Talk's body.* New York: Knopf.

SULLIVAN, H. S. (1953). *The interpersonal theory of psychiatry.* New York: W. W. Norton & Co., Inc.

SULLIVAN, H. S. (1954). *The psychiatric interview.* New York: W. W. Norton & Co., Inc.

SURANSKY, V. P. (1982). *The erosion of childhood.* Chicago: University of Chicago Press.

SUTHERLAND, E. H. (1937). *The professional thief.* Chicago: University of Chicago Press.

SUTHERLAND, E. H. (1949). *White-collar crime.* New York: Holt, Rinehart & Winston.

SUTHERLAND, E. H., & CRESSEY, D. (1966). *Principals of criminology.* (7th ed.). Philadelphia: Lippincott.

SUTTER, A. G. (1969). Worlds of drug use on the street scene. In D. Cressey & D. A. Ward (Eds.), *Delinquency, crime and social process.* New York: Harper & Row, Pub.

SUTTER, A. G. (1972). Playing a cold game: Phases of a ghetto career. *Urban Life and Culture, 1,* 77–91.

SUTTLES, G. D. (1968). *The social order of the slum.* Chicago: University of Chicago Press.

SUTTLES, G. D. (1972). *The social construction of communities.* Chicago: University of Chicago Press.

SYKES, G. M. (1958). *The society of captives.* Princeton, NJ: Princeton University Press.

SYKES, G. M., & MATZA, D. (1959). Techniques of neutralization: A theory of delinquency. *American Sociological Review, 22,* 664–670.

TAINE, H. (1877). Note on the acquisition of language by children and in the human species. *Mind, 2,* 251–253.

TAJFEL, H. (1969). Social and cultural factors in perception. In G. Lindzey & E. Aronson (Eds.), *The handbook of social psychology, vol. 3: The individual in a social context,* (2nd ed.). (pp. 315–394). Reading, MA: Addison-Wesley.

TANNENBAUM, F. (1938). *Crime and the community.* Boston: Ginn and Co.

TAYLOR, C. (1982). Consciousness. In P. F. Secord (Ed.), *Explaining human behavior: Consciousness, human action and social structure* (pp. 38–51). Beverly Hills, CA: Sage Publications, Inc.

TAYLOR, C. (1985). *Human agency and language: Philosophical papers.* Cambridge, Cambridge University Press.

TAYLOR, H. (1970). *Balance in small groups.* New York: Van Nostrand Reinhold.

TERRANCE, H. S. (1984). Language in apes. In R. Harré & V. Reynolds, *The meaning of primate signals* (pp. 130–155). Cambridge: Cambridge University Press.

THOMAS, D. S. (1928). *The child in America.* New York: Knopf.

THOMAS, W. I. (1936). *Primitive behavior.* New York: McGraw-Hill.

THORNE, B., & LURIA, Z. (Feb. 1986). Sexuality and gender in children's daily worlds. *Social Problems, 33,* 176–190.

TONER, M. (1986). The talking chimp. *National Wildlife 30,* 22–26.

TRAUB, S. H., & LITTLE, C. B. (EDS.). (1980). *Theories of deviance* (2nd ed.). Itasca, IL: F. E. Peacock.

TRAVISANO, R. (1981). Alternation and conversion as qualitatively different transformations. In G. P. Stone & H. A. Farberman (Eds.), *Social psychology through symbolic interaction* (pp. 237–248). (2nd. ed.). New York: John Wiley.

TRIANDIS, H. C. (1964). Cultural influences upon cognitive processes. In L. Berkowitz (Ed.), *Advance in experimental social psychology,* (vol. 1). New York: Academic Press.

TRIVERS, R. (1971). The evolution of reciprocal altruism. *Quarterly Review of Biology, 46,* 35–57.

TUMIN, M. M. (1950). The hero and the scapegoat in a peasant community. *Journal of Personality, 10,* 197–211.

TURIEL, E. (1975). The development of social concepts. In D. DePalma & J. Foley, (Eds.), *Moral development* (pp. 150–176). Hillsdale, NJ: Erlbaum.

TURNER, B. (1984). *The body & society: Explorations in social theory.* Oxford: Basil Blackwell.

TURNER, R. H. (1954). Self and others in moral judgment. *American Sociological Review, 19,* 254–258.

TURNER, R. H. (1956). Role-taking, role standpoint and reference groups. *American Journal of Sociology, 69,* 316–328.

TURNER, R. H. (1962). Role-taking: Process versus conformity. In A. Rose (Ed.), *Human behavior and social processes* (pp. 20–40). Boston: Houghton Mifflin.

TURNER, R. H. (1968). Role: *Sociological aspects*. In D. Sills (Ed.), *International Encyclopedia of the Social Sciences*, (vol. 13). New York: Free Press.

TURNER, R. H. (1968). The self-conception in social interaction. In C. Gordon & K. J. Gergen (Eds.), *The self in social interaction* (pp. 93–106). New York: John Wiley.

TURNER, R. (1969). The public perception of protest. *American Sociological Review, 34,* 815–831.

TURNER, R. (1972). Deviance disavowal as neutralization of a commitment. *Social Problems, 19,* 308–321.

TURNER, R. & KILLIAN, L. (1957). *Collective behavior.* Englewood Cliffs, NJ: Prentice-Hall.

TWAIN, M. (1976). *The portable Mark Twain,* Bernard DeVoto, (ed.). New York: Penguin Books.

UNRUH, D. R. (1980). The social organization of older people: A social world perspective. *Studies in Symbolic Interaction, 3,* 147–170.

UNRUH, D. R. (1983). *Invisible lives.* Beverly Hills, CA: Sage Publications, Inc.

VAIHINGER, H. (1924). *The philosophy of "as if."* London: Routledge & Kegan Paul Ltd.

VAN GENNEP, A. (1960). *The rites of passage.* Trans. by M. B. Visedom & G. L. Caffee. Chicago: University of Chicago Press.

VENDRYES, J. (1925). *Language.* New York: Knopf.

VINACKE, W. E. (1953). *The psychology of thinking.* New York: McGraw-Hill.

VYGOTSKY, L. (1939). Thought and speech. *Psychiatry, 2,* 29–52.

VYGOTSKY, L. (1962). *Thought and Language.* Ed. and trans. by E. Haufmann & G. Vakar. Cambridge, MA: M.I.T. Press.

VYGOTSKY, L. & LURIA, A. R. (1930). The fate and function of egocentric speech. *Proceedings and Papers,* Ninth International Congress of Psychology. Princeton, NJ: Princeton University Press.

WALLACE, P. M. (1984). Aphasia. In R. J. Corsini (Ed.), *Encyclopedia of psychology. vol. 1.* (p. 80). New York: John Wiley.

WALLACE, R. A., & WOLF, A. (1986). *Contemporary sociological theory: Continuing the classical tradition* (2nd ed.). Englewood Cliffs: NJ: Prentice-Hall.

WALLACE, S. E. (1965). *Skid row as a way of life.* New York: Bedminister Press.

WALLER, W. (1930). *The old love and the new: divorce and readjustment.* New York: Liveright.

WALSHOK, M. (1971). The emergence of middle-class deviant subcultures: The case of swingers. *Social Problems, 18,* 488–495.

WARNER, W. L. (1953). *American life: Dream and reality.* Chicago: University of Chicago Press.

WARNER, W. L. (1959). *The living and the dead.* New Haven: Yale University Press.

WARREN, C. A. B. (1974). *Identity and community in the gay world.* New York: John Wiley.

WATKINS, J. G. (1947). Antisocial compulsions induced under hypnotic trance. *Journal of Abnormal and Social Psychology, 42,* 256–259.

WATKINS, J. G. (1984). Hypnotherapy. In R. J. Corsini (Ed.), *Encyclopedia of psychology,* (vol. 2) (pp. 175–177). New York: John Wiley.

WATSON, J. D. (1968). *The double helix: A personal account of the discovery of the structure of DNA.* New York: Atheneum.

WEBER, M. (1946). *From Max Weber: essays in sociology.* (H. Gerth and C. W. Mills, eds.) New York: Oxford University Press.

WEBER, M. (1936). Paraphrased by K. Mannheim in *Ideology and utopia.* New York: Harcourt Brace Jovanovich.

WEINSTEIN, E., & DEUTSCHBERGER, P. (1963). Some dimensions of altercasting. *Sociometry, 26,* 454–466.

WEITZENHOFFER, A. M. (1953). *Hypnotism: An objective study in suggestibility.* New York: John Wiley.

WERKMEISTER, W. H. (1940). *A philosophy of science.* New York: Harper & Row, Pub.

WERNER, H., & KAPLAN, B. (1963). *Symbol formation: An organismic-developmental approach to language and expression of thought.* New York: John Wiley.

WEST, C. (1984). *Routine complications: Troubles with talk between doctors and patients.* Bloomington, IN: Indiana University Press.

WESTBY, D. L. (1960). The career experience of the symphony musician. *Social Forces, 38,* 223–230.

WESTOFF, MOORE, C. E., & RYDER, N. (1969). The structure of attitudes toward abortion. *Millbank Memorial Fund Quarterly, 47,* 11–37.

WHITE, R. W. (1941). A preface to the theory of hypnosis. *Journal of Abnormal and Social Psychology, 36,* 503–506.

WHITING, B. B. (Ed.). (1963). *Six cultures: Studies of child rearing.* New York: John Wiley.

WHORF, B. L. (1956). *Language, thought, and reality.* Ed. by J. B. Carroll. Cambridge, MA: M.I.T. Press.

WILEY, N. (Fall 1967). The ethnic mobility trap and stratification theory. *Social Problems, 15,* 147–159.

WILEY, N. (1979). Notes on self genesis: From me to we to I. In N. K. Denzin (Ed.), *Studies in symbolic interaction,* (vol. 2) (pp. 87–107). Greenwich, CT: JAI Press.

WILLIAMS, M. (1970). Reference groups: A review and commentary. *Sociological Quarterly, 11,* 545–554.

WILSON, E. O. (1975). *Sociobiology: The new synthesis.* Cambridge, MA: Belknap Press of Harvard University Press.

WINCH, R. (1967). *Mate-selection: A study of complementary needs.* New York: Harper & Row, Pub.

WINN, M. (1983). *Children without childhood.* New York: Pantheon.

WITHERS, C. (May 1946). The folklore of a small town. *Transactions of the New York Academy of Sciences, 8,* 234–251.

WITTENGENSTEIN, L. (1953). *Philosophical investigations.* Oxford: Basil Blackwell.

WOLBERG, L. (1947). Hypnotic experiments in psychosomatic Medicine. *Psychosomatic Medicine, 9,* 337–342.

WOLFENSTEIN, M. (1954). *Children's humor.* Glencoe, IL: Free Press.

WOLFENSTEIN, M. (1955). French parents take their children to the park. In M. Mead & M. Wolfenstein (Eds.), *Childhood in contemporary cultures* (pp. 99–117). Chicago: University of Chicago Press.

WOLFGANG, M. E. (1957). *Patterns in criminal homicide.* Philadelphia: University of Pennsylvania Press.

WRIGHT, R. (1945). *Black boy.* New York: Harper & Row, Pub.

WRIGHTSMAN, L. S. (1972). *Social psychology in the seventies.* Monterey, CA: Brook/Cole.

WYLIE, L. (1973). (As reported in an interview). *The San Francisco Chronicle,* July 8. p. 2.

YERKES, R. M., & YERKES, A. W. (1945). *The great apes: A study of anthropoid life.* New Haven: Yale University Press.

YOUNG, K. T., & ZIGLER, E. (1986). Infant and toddler day care: Regulations and policy implication. *American Journal of Orthopsychiatry, 56,* 43–55.

YOUNG, M. & WILLMOTT, P. (1957). *Family and kinship in east London.* London: Routledge & Kegan Paul.

YOUNG, P. C. (1940). Hypnotic regression: Fact or artefact? *Journal of Abnormal and Social Psychology, 35,* 273–278.

ZAJONC, R. (1960). The concepts of balance, congruity, and dissonance. *Public Opinion Quarterly, 24,* 280–296.

ZELIZER, V. A. (1985). *Pricing the priceless child: The changing social value of children.* New York: Basic Books.

ZIGLER, E. F., & HARTER, S. (1969). The socialization of the mentally retarded. In D. A. Goslin (Ed.), *Handbook of socialization theory and research* (pp. 1065–1102). Skokie, IL: Rand McNally.

ZIMMERMAN, D. H. (Feb. 1976). A reply to professor coser. *American Sociologist, 11,* 4–13.

ZIMMERMAN, D. & WIEDER, L. (1970). Comment on Denzin. In J. D. Douglas (Ed.), *Understanding everyday life,* pp. 275–290. Chicago: Aldine.

ZURCHER, L. A. (Fall 1985). The war game: Organizational scripting and the expression of emotion. *Symbolic Interaction, 8,* 191–207.

ZURCHER, L. A., & SNOW, D. A. (1981). Collective behavior and social movements. In M. Rosenberg & R. H. Turner (Eds.), *Social psychology: Sociological perspectives* (pp. 447–483). New York: Basic Books.

ZURIFF, G. E. (1985). *Behaviorism: A conceptual reconstruction.* New York: Columbia University Press.

Index

Henry, W. E., 350
Heritage
  collective, 133
  social. *See* Culture
Heritage, J., 14
Heroin, 115–16
  women on, 325
Hess, R. D., 272
Heterophilic experiences, 296
Hewes, G. W., 38
Hewitt, J. P., 145, 146
Heyl, B. S., 318
Hilgard, E. R., 190
Hill, R., 291
Hitler, E. T., 71, 72, 80, 81
Historical communication, 133–34
Historical epochs, theory of, 143
Historical social psychology, 13–14
Hite, S., 304
Hobbs, J. R., 125
Hochschild, A. R., 96, 98, 212, 350–53
Hockett, C. F., 40, 61
Hoffman, S., 274
Homans, G. C., 18, 21
Homecoming celebrations, 234
Home territories, 263
Homosexuality, 195, 293, 296, 331–35
  meanings of, 291–92
  public opinion of, 332–33
  subculture of, 333–35
Hood, R., 278
Hooker, E., 335
Hormones, 290–91
Horowitz, I. L., 162, 312, 337
Horowitz, R. S., 162, 178, 322
Hospital
  dying in, 230–31
  organization, 347
House, J., 9
Huber, J., 7
Hudgins, C. V., 241–42
Hughes, E. C., 134, 267, 270, 276
Hulett, J. E., Jr., 162
Hull, C. L., 241, 242, 251, 252
Humor, 82–84
Humphreys, L., 291, 293, 332
Hunt, M., 272
Hunter, E., 256
Husserl, E., 4
Hyman, H., 278–79
Hymes, D. H., 3
Hypnosis, 241, 249–54
  conceptual control under, 251–52
  moral behavior under, 250–51
  speech mechanisms and, 253–54
  theories of, 252–54
Hypochondriac, 123
Hysteria, 113

Ichheiser, G., 229
Iconomic memory, 122
Icons, 43, 53, 58
Ideas, 43. *See also* Concept(s)
Identification, 261
Identity(ies), 226
  conceptions of, 208–9
  crisis, 188
  interaction and, 5–6
  sexual, 295–98
    sources of, 297
  theories of, 20–21

transofrmations, 271–74
  work, 348
  See also Self, the
Ideology
  Marxist sense of, 142
  occupational, 276–78
  political, 274–75
  psychotherapeutic, 277
  racial, 276
  social worlds and, 274–78
  somatic, 277
Idiographic approach to behavior, 138
Idiolect, 51, 70
Ifaluk people, 360
Illness
  chronic, 343–48
    self-pity and, 345–46
    sentimental work and, 348
    trajectories, 346–47
  terminal, 356
    dying trajectory of, 357
Illusions, optical, 124
Illustrators, 64–65
Imagery, erotic, 300–301
Images of the social, 10–11
Imagination
  situations and, 223
  social psychological, 4
I-me exchange of children, 177
Implied objective past, 132
Impotence, 303–5
Impression management, 228
Impulses, instinctive, 88
Inattention, selective, 124, 141, 191
Incest taboos, 303
Indexes, 43, 53, 58
Indians, American, 133
Indissociation, 174
Individual, the
  deviance of, 338–40
  opposition between society and, 180
Individuality, 243
  social character of self and, 177–81
Induction, scientific, 367
Infant(s), 192
  gestures of, 154
  selfhood of, 182–83
  See also Children
Infeld, L., 372, 376
Inferential approach, 376–77
Information flow, two step theory of, 275
Inhibitions, 254
In jokes, 83
Inquiry, limited, 373
Instinct, 88, 196
Instrumental behavior, 241
Intellectual orientation of students, 208
Intelligence
  artificial, 22–25
  sensorimotor, 165–66
Intentional value-feelings, 100
Interaction(s), 6, 82–84, 221–38
  approaches to, 222–26
  dramaturgical theory of, 21
  face-to-face, 171, 233
  identity and, 5–6
  loss of self-control during, 245–49
  mesostructures and, 234–37
  presenting and assessing in, 227–31
  rituals, 232–24
  self and, 171–73

413

Interaction(s) (*cont.*)

in small groups, 231–34
spurious, 248
status passage and, 226–27
See also Behavior; Culture; Social worlds; Society
Ineractional age, 205
Interactional experience, 6
Interactional order, 232–34
Interactional repertoires, 222–23
Interactional rituals, 6
Interactional stage of selfhood, 181–82
Interactional stream of experience, 223–24
Interactional work, 348
Interactionism, symbolic. *See* Symbolic interactionism
Interchangeability as property of language, 61
Interment ceremonies, 356
Interpersonal context of aging, 351–52
Interpersonal relationships, 225–26
Interpersonal theory of psychiatry, 191
Interpretation, 143–44
of experience, 123
perception vs., 122
Interpretive social psychologies, 12–17
Intersexed person, 294
Intersubjectivity, 7
Interview, prolonged, 138
Intimacy, need for, 194–95
Intimate style, 144
Inversion, sexual, 294
Investigation, techniques of, 372–77
Irwin, J., 273, 282
Isaacs, S. S., 218, 291
Isophilic (homosexual) experiences, 296

Jacobs, J., 314
Jakobson, R., 91–92, 105
James, A., 131
James, H., 131, 132
James, R., 132
James, W., 4, 7, 135
Janowitz, M., 277
Jealousy, sexual, 330
Jefferson, G., 79
Jellinek, E. M., 327, 328
Jennings, H. S., 29
Jersild, A., 166
Jivaro, 125–26
Joffe, C., 164, 217
Johnson, E., 301–2, 305, 307
Johnson, J. M., 13
Johnson, W., 212
Jokes, 82–83
Jones, A., 133
Jones, E., 252
Jordan, W., 133
Judd, C. H., 71, 129
Jung, C., 52
Justifications, 144
Juvenile delinquents, 322
Juvenile era, 192

Kadushin, A., 329
Kafka, F., 330–31
Kahne, M. J., 189
Kamin, L. J., 33
Kando, T. J., 317
Kanner, L., 215, 216, 219, 297
Kant, I., 4
Kanter, R., 243, 244
Kaplan, B., 68, 78

Katovich, M. A., 13, 132–33
Katz, E., 275
Kazin, A., 72
Keller, C. M., 123
Kelley, H., 19, 280
Kellner, H., 300
Kellogg, L. A., 37
Kellogg, W. N., 37, 41
Kemper, T. D., 96, 278
Kennell, J. H., 171
Keynes, J. M., 91
Kinesics, 61–65
Kinesthetic mass, 102
Kin selection, 32
Kinsey, A. C., 217, 292, 302, 304
Kinship systems, 78
Kiowa Apache, 359
Kitsuse, J. K., 312, 313
Kitt, A. S., 279
Klapp, O. E., 261, 274, 315
Klapper, J., 275
Klaus, M. H., 171
Klein, M., 218–19, 291
Klineberg, O., 72, 96
Kluckhohn, C., 77, 178
Kluegel, J. R., 48, 49
Knowledge structures, power and, 237
Koch, H. L., 186
Kohlberg, L., 32, 182, 210–11
Kohler, W., 35, 36, 38
Kohut, H., 182
Kolers, P. A., 122
Kotarba, J. A., 13, 271, 345
Krieger, S., 291
Kronus, S. J., 276, 314
Krupp, H., 350
Kübler-Ross, E., 348
Kuhn, M. H., 10, 172, 204, 278, 280, 289
Kuhn, T. S., 208, 363

LaBarre, 63
Labor, division of, 4
schemata and, 126
Labov, W., 155
Lacan, J. A., 137, 164, 181, 187–89
Laclau, E., 143
Lakatos, 22
Landesco, J., 335
Langer, S. K., 57, 87, 90–91, 142
Language, 3–4, 50–92
absence among lower animals of, 37–41
acquisition of, 152–69
according to Chomsky, 160–62
"constructionist" view of, 160–61
declarative and manipulative functions, 157–60
instrumental use of gestures and, 154–55
self and, 153
use and comprehension of symbols and, 155–57
AI theory of, 25
aphasia and impairment of, 109–10
associative dimension of, 92
attitude (categorical attitude), 54–57
baby talk, 71, 156–57
body, 62–64
as conversation of gestures, 154
experience and, 2
gender stratification and, 3–4
group basis of, 70–73
group experiences and, 72–73
as humankind's "fundamental institution," 71

Prospective social acts, 146
Protective devices, 155
Protests, 236, 237
Prototaxic experience, 102–3, 191–92
Proust, M., 131
Pseudo-communication, 81–82
Pseudo-language, 39–40
Psychiatry, interpersonal theory of, 191
Psychological social psychology, 9
Psychological sociology, 9
Psychopaths, 338
Psychosexual developmentalists, 183
Psychosocial developmentalists, 183
Psychotherapeutic ideology, 277
Psychotics, 85, 101–2
Public place others, 204
Public territories, 263
Puns, 83
Purpose, 145, 146–47. *See also* Motive(s)
Pyromaniacs, 292

Quadagno, J. S., 355
Quantification, 371–72
Quiatt, D., 36

Race, 47–48
Racial ideology, 276
Racism, 49
Racketeering, 319
Ragland-Sullivan, E., 137, 187
Rationalization, 143–44, 193, 261, 317
    alcoholism and, 328
    Freudian sense of, 142
Rational thought, 201–2
Reactions, social, asymmetry of, 314
Reading, 65–66
Reality
    conceptions and definitions of, 369–71
    experience and, 2
    play, 84
    principle, 184
Reasoning, child development and, 165–68
Reconstructive memory, 145
Recruitment
    into criminal world, 321–22
    into homosexual world, 334–35
    of new addicts, 326
Rectification work, 348
Reductionism, 12
Reference, direct and symbolic, 107–8
Reference groups, 278–81
Reflective self-consciousness (self-reflectiveness), 6, 45
Regression, 88
Regulations, social, 233
Reid, 20
Reiss, I. L., 299
Relational deviance, 318
Relationships, social, 225–26
Religious affiliation, voting behavior and, 279
Religious groups, drug-based, 103
Remembering, 128
    categorization and, 129–30
    as symbolic process, 129–34
    See also Memory(ies)
Repertoires, interactional, 222–23
Repression, 140–41, 185
Research, library, 375–76
Reskin, B. F., 48
Response, delayed, 135
Revelations, self-other relations and, 264
Reveries, 87, 194
Reynolds, V., 30, 32, 36

Richardson, S. A., 171
Riley, J. W., Jr., 343
Riordon, W., 335, 337
Ritual(s), 87
    apology, 214
    of death, 359–60
    group, 231–32
    interaction, 6, 232–34
    linguistic emotional, 214
    social, 81
    temporal, 214
Robson, R., 18
Roby, P., 318
Rock, P., 5
Role(s), 222–26
    conceptions of children, 205–12
    distance, 244
    playing of, 223
        by children, 205
Role-identity theory, 20–21
Role theory of hypnosis, 252–53
Ropers, R., 9
Rose, J., 183
Rose, S., 33
Rosenbaum, M., 324, 325
Rosenbaum, R., 207
Rosow, I., 351–52
Ross, H. L., 138, 143, 304
Rossi, A. S., 29, 32, 175
Roth, P., 14
Rowland, 250
Royko, M., 338
Rude, G., 249
Rules, 222–26
    feeling, 212
Rumors, 129
Runyon, T., 322
Russell, W. R., 109
Russian émigrés, 283

Sabshin, M., 277
Sacks, H., 40, 79
Sacks, O., 82, 104
Sacredness of self-conception, 267
Sadists, 292
Salomone, J. J., 343, 359
Samson, W., 225
Sandburg, C., 125
Sapir, E., 71, 76, 78
Saramkatsan shepherd community, 305–6
Sarbin, T. R., 250, 253
Sartre, J. P., 4–7, 14, 224, 236
Satiation-deprivation proposition, 18
Saussure, F. De., 3, 5, 25, 52, 92
Saxton, S. L., Jr., 9, 13, 14
Scanzoni, J., 306
Scapegoating, 261
Schachtel, E., 130
Schachter, S., 98
Schaffer, H. R., 174
Scheff, T. J., 96
Schein, E. I., 256
Scheler, 4
Schemata, 125–26, 133
Schilder, P., 252
Schizophrenia, 102
Schlegoff, E., 79
Schmitt, R. L., 278, 281
Schneirla, T., 29, 31, 33
Schucier, 256
Schultz, J., 350